TM 55-1520-210-10

UH-1 IROQUOIS
Pilot's Flight
Operating Instructions

ARMY MODEL
UH-1H/V HELICOPTERS

©2011 Periscope Film LLC
All Rights Reserved
ISBN #978-1-935700-65-4
www.PeriscopeFilm.com

by HEADQUARTERS, DEPARTMENT OF THE ARMY

15 FEBRUARY 1988

NOTICE:

This manual is sold for historic research purposes only, as an entertainment. It is not intended to be used as part of an actual flight training program. No book can substitute for flight training by an authorized instructor. The licensing of pilots is overseen by organizations and authorities such as the FAA and CAA. Operating an aircraft without the proper license is a federal crime.

TM 55-1520-210-10

OPERATOR'S MANUAL

ARMY MODEL

UH-1H/V HELICOPTERS

This manual supersedes TM 55-1520-210-10 dated 1 December 1986, including all changes.

HEADQUARTERS, DEPARTMENT OF THE ARMY

15 FEBRUARY 1988

TM 58-1520-210-10
C 18

CHANGE

No. 18

HEADQUARTERS
DEPARTMENT OF THE ARMY
WASHINGTON, D.C., 8 October 1999

OPERATOR'S MANUAL

ARMY MODEL

UH-1 H/V HELICOPTER

DISTRIBUTION STATEMENT A: Approved for public release; distribution is unlimited

TM 55-1520-210-10, 15 February 1988, is changed as follows:

1. Remove and insert pages as indicated below. New or changed text material is indicated by a vertical bar in the margin. An illustration change is indicated by a miniature pointing hand. An illustration revision is indicated by a change bar.

Remove pages	**Insert pages**
----------	A and B
i through ii	i through ii
iii through iv	iii through iv
1-1 and 1-2	1-1 and 1-2
2-23 and 2-24	2-23 and 2-24
2-29 and 2-30	2-29 and 2-30
2-33 and 2-34	2-33 and 2-34
3-21 and 3-22	3-21 and 3-22
----------	3-22.1 through 3-22.28
3-31 and 3-32	3-31 and 3-32
----------	3-32.1 through 3-32.24
index 1 through index 4	index 1 through Index 4

2. Retain this sheet in front of manual for reference purposes.

By Order of the Secretary of the Army:

ERIC K. SHINSEKI
General, United States Army
Chief of Staff

Official:

JOEL B. HUDSON
Administrative Assistant to the
Secretary of the Army
9927804

DISTRIBUTION:
TO be distributed in accordance with initial Distribution Number (IDN) 310275, requirements for TM 55-1520-210-10

TM 55-1520-210-10
C17

CHANGE

NO 17

HEADQUARTERS
DEPARTMENT OF THE ARMY
WASHINGTION, D.C., 13 February 1997

Operator's Manual
ARMY MODEL
UH- IH/V HELICOPTERS

TM 55-1520-210-10, 15 February 1988, is changed as follows:

1. Remove and insert pages as indicated below. New or changed text material is indicated by a vertical bar in the margin. An illustration change is indicated by a miniature pointing hand.

2. Pages 2-23 and 2-24 may have been omitted in some copies of Urgent Change 16. Therefore, these pages have been included as part of this Change 17. Note, however, that these pages will retain their Change 16 designation.

Remove pages	Insert pages
i and ii	i and ii
2-1 through 24	2-1 through 2-4
24.1/(2.4.2 blank)	2-4.1/(24.2 blank)
2-5 through 2-8	2-5 through 2-8
.----.-.-.--	2-8.1/(2-8.2 blank)
2-9 through 2-12	2-9 through 2-12
.-.-.-.-.--	2-12.1/(2-12.2 blank)
2-13 through 2-16	2-13 through 2-16
.-.-.-.-.--	2-16.1/(2-16.2 blank)
2-17 through 2-24	2-17 through 2-24
2-35 and 2-36	2-35 and 2-36
3-11 and 3-12	3-11 and 3-12
3-12.1 and 3-12.2	3-12.1 and 3-12.2
3-27 through 3-32	3-27 through 3-32
3-37 and 3-38	3-37 and 3-38
3-41 and 3-42	3-41 and 3-42
4-5/(4-6 blank)	4-5/(4-6 blank)
(4-7 blank)/4-8	(4-7 blank)/4-8
4-9 and 4-10	4-9 and 4-10
5-1 through 5-4	5-1 through 5-4
6-1 through 6-4	6-1 through 64
7-3 and 74	7-3 and 74
---------	7-4.1/(74.2 blank)
7-5 and 76	7-5 and 7-6
7-47 and 748	747 and 748
7.1-3 and 7.14	7.1-3 and 7.14
------------	7.1-4.1/(7.14.2 blank)
7.1-5 and 7.1-6	7.1-5 and 7.16

TM 55-1520-210-10
C17

Remove pages	Insert pages
7.1-45 and 7.1-46	7.1-45 and 7.1-46
8-1 and 8-2	8-1 and 8-2
8-5 through 8-10	8-5 through 8-10
8-10.1 and 8-10.2	8-10.1/(8-10.2 blank)
8-11 through 8-16	8-11 through 8-16
9-3 through 9-8	9-3 through 9-8
9-8.1/(9-8.2 blank)	9-8.1/(9-8.2 blank)
A-I/(A-2 blank)	A-I/(A-2 blank)
B-3 and B-4	B-3 and B-4
C-1 through C-4	C-i through C4
C-5/(C-6 blank)	

3. Retain this sheet in front of manual for reference purposes.

By Order of the Secretary of the Army:

DENNIS J. REIMER
General, United States Army
Chief of Staff

Official

JOEL B. HUDSON
Administrative Assistant to the
Secretary of the Army
03259

DISTRIBUTION:

To be distributed in accordance with DA Form 12-31-E block No. 0275, requirements for TM 55-1520210-10.

URGENT

CHANGE

NO 16

TM 55-1520-210-10
C16
HEADQUARTERS
DEPARTMENT OF THE ARMY
WASHINGTON, D.C., 13 August 1996

Operator's Manual
ARMY MODEL
UH-1HN HELICOPTERS

DISTRIBUTION STATEMENT A: Approved for public release; distribution is unlimited

TM 55-1520-210-10, 15 February 1988, Is changed as follows.

1. Remove and insert pages as indicated below New or changed text material is indicated by a vertical bar in the margin. An illustration change Is indicated by a miniature pointing hand.

Remove pages	Insert pages
iii through v/(vi blank)	iii through v/(vi blank)
2-23 and 2-24	2-23 and 2-24
2-29 and 2-30	2-29 and 2-30
3-67 and 3-68	3-67 and 3-68
--------------	3-68.1 through 3-68.3/(3-68.4 blank)
8-3 and 8-4	8-3 and 8-4
9-3 and 9-4	9-3 and 9-4
Index 1 and Index 2	Index 1 and Index 2

2. Retain this sheet in front of manual for reference purposes.

By Order of the Secretary of the Army:

DENNIS J. REIMER
General, United States Army
Chief of Staff

Official

JOEL B HUDSON
Administrative Assistant to the
Secretary of the Army
02158

DISTRIBUTION:

To be distributed in accordance with DA Form 12-31-E, block no. 0275, requirements for TM 55-1520-210-10.

TM 55-1520-210-10
C15

URGENT

CHANGE

NO. 15

HEADQUARTERS
DEPARTMENT OF THE ARMY
WASHINGTON, D.C., 14 February 1996

Operator's Manual

ARMY MODEL

UH-1H/V HELICOPTERS

DISTRIBUTION STATEMENT A: Approved for public release; distribution is unlimited.

TM 55-1520-210-10, 15 February 1988, is changed as follows:

1. Remove and insert pages as indicated below. New or changed text material is indicated by a vertical bar in the margin. An illustration change is indicated by a miniature pointing hand.

Remove pages	Insert pages
2-4.1/(2-4.2 blank)	2-4.1/(2-4.2 blank)
2-5 and 2-6	2-5 and 2-6
2-9 and 2-10	2-9 and 2-10
2-19 and 2-20	2-19 and 2-20
5-3 through 5-6	5-3 through 5-6
9-1 through 9-4	9-1 through 9-4
Index 3 and Index 4	Index 3 and Index 4

2. Retain this sheet in front of manual for reference purposes.

By Order of the Secretary of the Army:

DENNIS J. REIMER
General, United States Army
Chief of Staff

Official:

YVONNE M. HARRISON
Administrative Assistant to the
Secretary of the Army
01309

DISTRIBUTION:
To be distributed in accordance with DA Form 12-31-E, block no. 0275, requirements for TM 55-1520-210-10.

URGENT

NOTICE: THIS CHANGE HAS BEEN PRINTED AND DISTRIBUTED OUT OF SEQUENCE. IT SHOULD BE INSERTED IN THE MANUAL AND USED. UPON RECEIPT OF THE EARLIER SEQUENCED CHANGE ENSURE A MORE CURRENT CHANGE PAGE IS NOT REPLACED WITH A LESS CURRENT PAGE.

TM 55-1520-210-10
C 14

CHANGE

NO. 14

HEADQUARTERS
DEPARTMENT OF THE ARMY
WASHINGTON, D.C., 9 MARCH 1994

Operator's Manual

ARMY MODEL

UH-1H/V HELICOPTERS

DISTRIBUTION STATEMENT A: Approved for public release; distribution is unlimited.

TM 55-1520-210-10, 15 February 1988, is changed as follows:

1. Remove and insert pages as indicated below. New or changed text material is indicated by a vertical bar in the margin. An illustration change is indicated by a miniature pointing hand.

Remove pages	Insert pages
4-5 and 4-6	4-5/(4-6 blank)
4-6.1/(4-6.2 blank)	----
4-7 through 4-10	4-8 through 4-10
4-15 and 4-16	4-15 and 4-16
6-11 through 6-14	6-11 through 6-14

2. Retain this sheet in front of manual for reference purposes.

By Order of the Secretary of the Army:

GORDON R. SULLIVAN
General, United States Army
Chief of Staff

Official:

MILTON H. HAMILTON
Administrative Assistant to the
Secretary of the Army
06202

DISTRIBUTION:
To be distributed in accordance with DA Form 12-31-E, block no. 0275, requirements for TM 55-1520-210-10.

URGENT

NOTICE: THIS CHANGE HAS BEEN PRINTED AND DISTRIBUTED OUT OF SEQUENCE. IT SHOULD BE INSERTED IN THE MANUAL AND USED. UPON RECEIPT OF THE EARLIER SEQUENCED CHANGE ENSURE A MORE CURRENT CHANGE PAGE IS NOT REPLACED WITH A LESS CURRENT PAGE.

TM 55-1520-210-10
C 13

CHANGE

NO. 13

HEADQUARTERS
DEPARTMENT OF THE ARMY
WASHINGTON, D.C., 30 NOVEMBER 1993

Operator's Manual

ARMY MODEL

UH-1H/V HELICOPTERS

DISTRIBUTION STATEMENT A: Approved for public release; distribution is unlimited.

TM 55-1520-210-10, 15 February 1988, is changed as follows:

1. Remove and insert pages as indicated below. New or changed text material is indicated by a vertical bar in the margin. An illustration change is indicated by a miniature pointing hand.

Remove pages	Insert pages
9-3 through 9-8	9-3 through 9-8

2. Retain this sheet in front of manual for reference purposes.

By Order of the Secretary of the Army:

GORDON R. SULLIVAN
General, United States Army
Chief of Staff

Official:

MILTON H. HAMILTON
Administrative Assistant to the
Secretary of the Army
05801

DISTRIBUTION:
To be distributed in accordance with DA Form 12-31-E, block no. 0275, requirements for TM 55-1520-210-10.

URGENT

NOTICE: THIS CHANGE HAS BEEN PRINTED AND DISTRIBUTED OUT OF SEQUENCE. IT SHOULD BE INSERTED IN THE MANUAL AND USED. UPON RECEIPT OF THE EARLIER SEQUENCED CHANGE, ENSURE A MORE CURRENT CHANGE PAGE IS NOT REPLACED WITH A LESS CURRENT PAGE.

TM 55-1520-210-10
C 12

CHANGE

NO. 12

HEADQUARTERS
DEPARTMENT OF THE ARMY
WASHINGTON, D.C., 23 July 1993

Operator's Manual

ARMY MODEL

UH-1H/V HELICOPTERS

DISTRIBUTION STATEMENT A: Approved for public release; distribution is unlimited.

TM 55-1520-210-10, 15 February 1988, is changed as follows:

1. Remove and insert pages as indicated below. New or changed text material is indicated by a vertical bar in the margin. An illustration change is indicated by a miniature pointing hand.

Remove pages	Insert pages
i and ii	i and ii
1-1 and 1-2	1-1 and 1-2
2-7 and 2-8	2-7 and 2-8
6-11 and 6-12	6-11 and 6-12

2. Retain this sheet in front of manual for reference purposes.

By Order of the Secretary of the Army:

GORDON R. SULLIVAN
General, United States Army
Chief of Staff

Official:

MILTON H. HAMILTON
Administrative Assistant to the
Secretary of the Army
03923

DISTRIBUTION:

To be distributed in accordance with DA Form 12-31-E, block no. 0275, requirements for TM 55-1520-210-10.

TM 55-1520-210-10
C11

CHANGE

NO. 11

HEADQUARTERS
DEPARTMENT OF THE ARMY
WASHINGTON, D.C., 1 July 1993

OPERATOR'S MANUAL

FOR

ARMY MODEL
UH-1H/V HELICOPTERS

DISTRIBUTION STATEMENT A: Approved for public release; distribution is unlimited

TM 55-1520-210-10, 15 February 1988, is changed as follows:

1. Remove and insert pages as indicated below. New or changed text material is indicated by a vertical bar in the margin. An illustration change is indicated by a miniature pointing hand.

Remove pages	Insert pages
7.1-3 and 7.1-4	7.1-3 and 7.1-4
7.1-7 and 7.1-8	7.1-7 and 7.1-8
9-1 thru 9-4	9-1 thru 9-4

2. Retain this sheet in front of manual for reference purposes.

By Order of the Secretary of the Army:

GORDON R. SULLIVAN
General, United States Army
Chief of Staff

Official:

MILTON H. HAMILTON
Administrative Assistant to the
Secretary of the Army
07502

DISTRIBUTION:
To be distributed in accordance with DA Form 12-31-E, block no. 0275, requirements for TM 55-1520-210-10.

URGENT

TM 55-1520-210-10
C 10

CHANGE

NO. 10

HEADQUARTERS
DEPARTMENT OF THE ARMY
WASHINGTON, D.C., 18 April 1991

Operator's Manual

ARMY MODEL

UH-1H/V HELICOPTERS

TM 55-1520-210-10, 15 February 1988, is changed as follows:

1. Remove and insert pages as indicated below. New or changed text material is indicated by a vertical bar in the margin. An illustration change is indicated by a miniature pointing hand.

Remove pages	Insert pages
9-1 and 9-2	9-1 and 9-2

2. Retain this sheet in front of manual for reference purposes.

By Order of the Secretary of the Army:

CARL E. VUONO
General, United States Army
Chief of Staff

Official:

THOMAS F. SIKORA
Brigadier General, United States Army
The Adjutant General

DISTRIBUTION:
To be distributed in accordance with DA Form 12-31-E, block no. 0275, -10 & CL maintenance requirements for TM 55-1520-210-10.

URGENT

URGENT

TM 55--1520-210-10
C 9

CHANGE

NO. 9

HEADQUARTERS
DEPARTMENT OF THE ARMY
WASHINGTON, D.C., 5 March 1991

Operator's Manual

ARMY MODEL
UH-1H/V HELICOPTERS

TM 55-1520-210-10, 15 February 1988, is changed as follows:

1. Remove and insert pages as indicated below. New or changed text material is indicated by a vertical bar in the margin. An illustration change is indicated by a miniature pointing hand.

Remove pages	Insert pages
9-1 and 9-2	9-1 and 9-2

2. Retain this sheet in front of manual for reference purposes.

By Order of the Secretary of the Army:

CARL E. VUONO
General, United States Army
Chief of Staff

Official:

THOMAS F. SIKORA
Brigadier General, United States Army
The Adjutant General

DISTRIBUTION:
To be distributed in accordance with DA Form 12-31-E, block no. 0275, -10 & CL maintenance requirements for TM 55-1520-210-10.

URGENT

URGENT

TM 55-1520-210-10
C 8

CHANGE

NO. 8

HEADQUARTERS
DEPARTMENT OF THE ARMY
WASHINGTON, D.C., 27 December 1990

Operator's Manual

ARMY MODEL
UH-1H/V HELICOPTERS

TM 55-1520-210-10, 15 February 1988, is changed as follows:

1. Remove and insert pages as indicated below. New or changed text material is indicated by a vertical bar in the margin. An illustration change is indicated by a miniature pointing hand.

Remove pages	Insert pages
i and ii	i and ii
- - - -	ii.1/ii/2
iii and iv	iii and iv
- - - -	v/vi blank
1-1 and 1-2	1-1 and 1-2
2-7 through 2-10	2-7 through 2-10
5-1 through 5-4	5-1 through 5-4
5-7/5-8	5-7 and 5-8
7-1 and 7-2	7-1 and 7-2
- - - -	7.1-1 through 7.1-53/7.1-54
8-10.1/8-10.2	8-10.1/8-10.2
9-1 through 9-4	9-1 through 9-4
9-7 and 9-8	9-7 and 9-8
9-8.1/9-8.2	9-8.1/9-8.2
9-9 through 9-12	9-9 through 9-12
- - - -	9-13 and 9-14
Index 1 through Index 4	Index 1 through Index 4

2. Retain this sheet in front of manual for reference purposes.

By Order of the Secretary of the Army:

CARL E. VUONO
General, United States Army
Chief of Staff

Official:

THOMAS F. SIKORA
Brigadier General, United States Army
The Adjutant General

DISTRIBUTION:
To be distributed in accordance with DA Form 12-31, -10 & CL Maintenance requirements for UH-1H and UH-1V Helicopter, Utility.

URGENT

URGENT

TM 55-1520-210-10
C 7

CHANGE

NO. 7

HEADQUARTERS
DEPARTMENT OF THE ARMY
WASHINGTON, D.C., 17 December 1990

Operator's Manual

Army Model
UH-1H/V Helicopters

TM 55-1520-210-10, 15 February 1988, is changed as follows:

1. Remove and insert pages as indicated below. New or changed text material is indicated by a vertical bar in the margin. An illustration change is indicated by a miniature pointing hand.

```
        Remove Pages              Insert pages

        iii and iv                iii and iv
        2-23 and 2-24             2-23 and 2-24
        - - - -                   2-26.1/2-26.2
        2-27 through 2-30         2-27 through 2-30
        3-1 through 3-12          3-1 through 2-12
        - - - -                   3-12.1 and 3-12.2
        3-13 and 3-14             3-13 and 3-14
        3-14.1/3-14.2             - - - -
        3-15 through 3-46         3-15 through 3-46
        - - - -                   3-47 through 3-90
        A-1/A-2                   A-1/A-2
        Index 1 through Index 4   Index 1 through Index 4
```

2. Retain this sheet in front of manual for reference purposes.

By Order of the Secretary of the Army:

CARL E. VUONO
General, United States Army
Chief of Staff

Official:

THOMAS F. SIKORA
Brigadier General, United States Army
The Adjutant General

DISTRIBUTION:
To be distributed in accordance with DA Form 12-31, -10 & CL Maintenance requirements for UH-1H and UH-1V Helicopter, Utility.

URGENT

URGENT

TM 55-1520-210-10
C 6

CHANGE
NO. 6

HEADQUARTERS
DEPARTMENT OF THE ARMY
WASHINGTON, D.C., 2 April 1990

Operator's Manual

ARMY MODEL
UH-1H/V HELICOPTERS

TM 55-1520-210-10, 15 February 1988, is changed as follows:

1. Pages 4-17 and 4-18 were erroneously depicted as pages being inserted in change 5, please disregard.

2. Remove and insert pages as indicated below. New or changed text material is indicated by a vertical bar in the margin. An illustration change is indicated by a miniature pointing hand.

Remove pages	Insert pages
2-33 and 2-34	2-33 and 2-34
- - - -	8-10.1/8-10.2
9-1 through 9-6	9-1 through 9-6
- - - -	9-8.1/9-8.2
9-9 and 9-10	9-9 and 9-10

3. Retain this sheet in front of manual for reference purposes.

By Order of the Secretary of the Army:

CARL E. VUONO
General, United States Army
Chief of Staff

Official:

WILLIAM J. MEEHAN II
Brigadier General, United States Army
The Adjutant General

DISTRIBUTION:
To be distributed in accordance with DA Form 12-31, -10 & CL Maintenance requirements for UH-1H and UH-1V Helicopter, Utility.

URGENT

TM 55-1520-210-10
C 5

CHANGE
NO. 5

HEADQUARTERS
DEPARTMENT OF THE ARMY
WASHINGTON, D.C., 11 December 1990

Operator's Manual

ARMY MODEL
UH-1H/V HELICOPTERS

TM 55-1520-210-10, 15 February 1988, is changed as follows:

1. Remove and insert pages as indicated below. New or changed text material is indicated by a vertical bar in the margin. An illustration change is indicated by a miniature pointing hand.

Remove pages	Insert pages
i through iv	i through iv
2-13 through 2-20	2-13 through 2-20
2-23 and 2-24	2-23 and 2-24
2-27 and 2-28	2-27 and 2-28
2-33 and 2-34	2-33 and 2-34
2-37/2-38	2-37/2-38
3-5 and 3-6	3-5 and 3-6
3-9 through 3-14	3-9 through 3-14
-----	3-14.1/3-14.2
3-15 and 3-16	3-15 and 3-16
3-25 and 3-26	3-25 and 3-26
3-43 and 3-44	3-43 and 3-44
-----	3-45 and 3-46
4-5 and 4-6	4-5 and 4-6
-----	4-6.1/4-6.2
4-7 through 4-12	4-7 through 4-12
-----	4-17 and 4-18
5-1 through 5-7/5-8	5-1 through 5-7/5-8
6-1 through 6-6	6-1 through 6-6
6-11 and 6-12	6-11 and 6-12
7-1 through 7-4	7-1 through 7-4
7-13 through 7-16	7-13 through 7-16
8-1 through 8-12	8-1 through 8-12
9-1 through 9-10	9-1 through 9-10
C-1 and C-2	C-1 and C-2
-----	C-3 and C-4
Index 1 and Index 2	Index 1 and Index 2
2028's and Envelopes	2028's and Envelopes

2. Retain this sheet in front of manual for reference purposes.

By Order of the Secretary of the Army:

CARL E. VUONO
General, United States Army
Chief of Staff

Official:

WILLIAM J. MEEHAN II
Brigadier General, United States Army
The Adjutant General

DISTRIBUTION:
To be distributed in accordance with DA Form 12-31, -10 & CL Maintenance requirements for UH-1H and UH-1V Helicopter, Utility.

URGENT

TM 55-1520-210-10
C 4

CHANGE

NO. 4

HEADQUARTERS
DEPARTMENT OF THE ARMY
WASHINGTON, D.C., 15 March 1989

ARMY MODEL

UH-1H/V HELICOPTERS

TM 55-1520-210-10, 15 February 1988, is changed as follows:

1. Remove and insert pages as indicated below. New or changed text material is indicated by a vertical bar in the margin. An illustration change is indicated by a miniature pointing hand.

Remove pages	Insert pages
9-3 and 9-4	9-3 and 9-4

2. Retain this sheet in front of manual for reference purposes.

By Order of the Secretary of the Army:

CARL E. VUONO
General, United States Army
Chief of Staff

Official:

WILLIAM J. MEEHAN II
Brigadier General, United States Army
The Adjutant General

DISTRIBUTION:

To be distributed in accordance with DA Form 12-31, -10 & CL Maintenance requirements for UH-1H and UH-1V Helicopter, Utility.

URGENT

URGENT

CHANGE

NO. 3

TM 55-1520-210-10
C 3
HEADQUARTERS
DEPARTMENT OF THE ARMY
WASHINGTON, D.C., 15 May 1989

OPERATOR'S MANUAL

ARMY MODEL

UH-1H/V HELICOPTERS

TM 55-1520-210-10, 15 February 1988 is changed as follows:

1. Remove and insert pages as indicated below. New or changed text material is indicated by a vertical bar in the margin. An illustration change is indicated by a miniature pointing hand.

Remove pages	Insert pages
2-9 and 2-10	2-9 and 2-10
8-9 and 8-10	8-9 and 8-10
	8-10.1/8-10.2

2. Retain this sheet in front of manual for reference purposes.

By Order of the Secretary of the Army:

CARL E. VUONO
General, United States Army
Chief of staff

Official:

WILLIAM J. MEEHAN II
Brigadier General, United States Army
The Adjutant General

DISTRIBUTION:
To be distributed in accordance with DA Form 12-31, -10 & CL Maintenance requirements for UH-1H and UH-1V Helicopter, Utility.

URGENT

URGENT

TM 55-1520-210-10
C 2

CHANGE

No. 2

HEADQUARTERS
DEPARTMENT OF THE ARMY
WASHINGTON, D.C., 17 October 1988

ARMY MODEL

UH-1H/V HELICOPTERS

TM 55-1520-210-10, 15 February 1988, is changed as follows:

1. Pages listed below which are preceded by an asterisk (*) are being provided for reprint only.

2. Remove and insert pages as indicated below. New or changed text material is indicated by a vertical bar in the margin. An illustration change is indicated by a miniature pointing hand.

Remove pages	Insert pages
2-3 and 2-4	2-3 through 2-4.1/2-4.2
2-9 and 2-10	2-9 and 2-10
*6-19 and 6-20	* 6-19 and 6-20
7-7 and 7-8	7-7 and 7-8
* 7-15 through 7-18	* 7-15 through 7-18
* 7-29 through 7-48	* 7-29 through 7-48
7-51 and 7-52	7-51/7-52
9-11 and 9-12	9-11 and 9-12

3. Retain this sheet in front of manual for reference purposes.

By Order of the Secretary of the Army:

CARL E. VUONO
General, United States Army
Chief of Staff

Official:

R. L. DILWORTH
Brigadier General, United States Army
The Adjutant General

DISTRIBUTION:
 To be distributed in accordance with DA Form 12-31, -10 & CL Maintenance requirements for UH-1H and UH-1V Helicopter, Utility.

URGENT

URGENT

TM 55-1520-210-10
C 1

CHANGE

NO. 1

HEADQUARTERS
DEPARTMENT OF THE ARMY
WASHINGTON, D.C., 28 July 1988

ARMY MODEL

UH-1H/V HELICOPTERS

TM 55-1520-210-10, 15 February 1988 is changed as follows:

1. Remove and insert pages as indicated below. New or changed text material is indicated by a vertical bar in the margin. An illustration change is indicated by a miniature pointing hand.

Remove pages	Insert pages
2-9 and 2-10	2-9 and 2-10
9-7 and 9-8	9-7 and 9-8
- - -	9-8.1/9-8.2
9-9 and 9-10	9-9 and 9-10

2. Retain this sheet in front of manual for reference purposes.

By Order of the Secretary of the Army:

CARL E. VUONO,
General, United States Army
Chief of Staff

Official:

R. L. DILWORTH
Brigadier General, United States Army
The Adjutant General

DISTRIBUTION:
To be distributed in accordance with DA Form 12-31, -10 & CL Maintenance requirements for UH-1H Helicopter, Utility and UH-1V Helicopter, Utility.

URGENT

TM 55-1520-210-10

LIST OF EFFECTIVE PAGES

insert latest changed pages. Dispose of superseded pages in accordance with regulations.

NOTE: On a changed page, the portion of text affected by the latest change is indicated by a vertical line in the outer margin of the page. Changes to illustrations are indicated by a miniature pointing hand.

DATES OF ISSUE FOR ORIGINAL AND CHANGED PAGES ARE:

Original ....0...........	15 February 1988	
Change.......... 1............	28 July 1988	
Change.......... 2............	17 October 1988	
Change.......... 3............	09 December 1988	
Change..........4............	15 March 1989	
Change.......... 5............	11 December 1989	
Change.......... 6............	02 April 1990	
Change .... 7............	17 December 1990	
Change.......... 8............	27 December 1990	
Change .... 9............	05 March 1991	

Change .... 10............	18 April 1991
Change 11	01 July 1993
Change .... 12............	23 July 1993
Change 13	30 November 1993
Change .... 14............	09 March 1994
Change .... 15............	14 February 1996
Change .... 16............	13 August 1996
Change ....17............	13 February 1997
Change .... 18..	08 October 1999

TOTAL NUMBER OF PAGES IN THIS PUBLICATION IS 254, CONSISTING OF THE FOLLOWING:

Page Number	*Change Number
Cover 0
A - B 18
i 16
ii - ii.1 8
ii.2 blank 8
iii - iv 18
v 16
vi blank .... .16
1-1 18
1-2 8
2-1 0
2-2 - 2-4.1 17
2-4.2 blank 17
2-5 - 2-8.1 17
2-8.2 blank 17
2-9 -2-12.1 17
2-12.2 blank 17
2-13 - 2-16.1 17
2-16.2 blank .... .17
2-17-2-22 17
2-23 - 2-24 18
2-25 - 2-26 0
2-26.1 7
2-26.2 blank 7
2-27 7
2-28 0
2-29 18
2-30 - 2-33 0

Page Number	*Change Number
2-34 18
2-35 17
2-36 0
2-37 5
2-38 blank 5
3-1 0
3-2 - 3-11 7
3-12 - 3-12.2 17
3-13 - 3-21 7
3-22 - 3-22.28 18
3-23 - 3-27 7
3-28 - 3-30 17
3-31 7
3-32 - 3-32.24 18
3-33 - 3-36 7
3-37 - 3-38 17
3-39 - 3-40 7
3-41 - 3-42 17
3-43 - 3-87 7
3-68 - 3-68.3 16
3-68.4 blank 16
3-69 - 3-90 7
4-1 - 4-4 0
4-5 17
4-6 blank 17
4-7 blank 17
4-8-4-10 17
4-11 - 4-12 5

Change 18 A

TM 55-1520-210-10

Page Number	*Change Number	Page Number	*Change Number
4-13 - 4-14	0	7.1-4.2 blank	17
4-15	14	7.1-5 - 7.1-6	17
4-16	0	7.1-7	11
5-1 - 5-3	17	7.1-8 - 7.1-45	8
5-4	0	7.1-46	
5-5	15	7.1-47 - 7.1-53	5
5-6	0	7.1-54 blank	8
5-7 - 5-8	8	8-1 - 8-2	17
6-1 - 6-4	17	8-3 - 8-4	16
6-5	0	8-5	
6-6	5	8-6 - 8-10.1	17
6-7 - 6-10	0	8-10.2 blank	17
6-11 - 6-14	14	8-11 - 8-15	17
6-15 - 6-20	0	8-16	0
7-1	6	9-1	15
7-2	5	9-2	11
7-3 - 7-4.1	17	9-3	5
7-4.2 blank	17	9-4 - 9-6.1	17
7-5 - 7-6	17	9-8.2 blank	17
7-7	2	9-9	8
7-8 - 7-13	0	9-10	0
7-14 - 7-15	5	9-11 - 9-14	8
7-16 - 7-47	0	A-1	17
7-48	17	A-2 blank	17
7-49 - 7-50	0	B-1 - B-2	0
7-51	2	B-3 - B-4	17
7-52 blank	2	C-1 - C-5	17
7.1-1 - 7.1-2	6	C-6 blank	17
7.1-3 - 7.1-4.1	17	Index 1 - Index 4	18

*A zero in this column indicates an original page.

B Change 18

TM 55-1520-210-10

TECHNICAL MANUAL

HEADQUARTERS
DEPARTMENT OF THE ARMY
WASHINGTON D.C., 15 February 1988

OPERATOR'S MANUAL

ARMY MODEL
UH-1 H/V HELICOPTER

REPORTING ERRORS AND RECOMMENDING IMPROVEMENTS

You can help improve this publication. if you find any mistakes, or if you know of a way to improve the procedures, please let us know. Mail your letter, DA Form 2028 (Recommended Changes to Publications and Blank Forms), or DA Form 2028-2 located in the back of this manual direct to: Commander, U. S. Army Aviation and Missile Command, ATTN: AMSAM-MMC-LS-LP, Redstone Arsenal, AL 35898-5239. A reply will be furnished to you. You may also send in your comments electronically to our e-mail address: ls-lp@redstone.army.mil or fax 256-642-6546/DSN 788-6546. Instructions for sending an electronic 2028 may be found at the back of this manual immediately preceding the hard copy 2026.

Distribution Statement A. Approved for public release; distribution is unlimited.

TABLE OF CONTENTS

			Page
CHAPTER 1		INTRODUCTION	1-1
CHAPTER 2		HELICOPTER AND SYSTEMS DESCRIPTION AND OPERATION	2-1
	Section I	Helicopter	2-1
	ii	Emergency Equipment	2-3
	iII	Engine and Related Systems	2-3
	IV	Helicopter Fuel System	2-6
	V	Flight Control System	2-7
	VI	Hydraulic System	2-6
	VII	Power Train System	2-9
	VIII	Rotors	2-10
	IX	Utility Systems	2-10
	X	Heating and Ventilation	2-11
	Xi	Electrical Power Supply and Distribution System	2-12
	XII	Lighting	2-13
	xiii	Flight instruments	2-17
	xiv	Servicing Parking and Mooring	2-19
CHAPTER 3		AVIONICS	3-1
	Section I	General	3-1
	II	Communication	3-1
	III	Navigation	3-22
	IV	Transponder and Radar	3-32.24
CHAPTER 4		MISSION EQUIPMENT	4-1
	Section I	Armament	4-1
	II	Mission Avionics	4-5
	III	Cargo Handling	4-5

Change 18

TM 55-1520-210-10

TABLE OF CONTENTS (CONT)

			Page
CHAPTER 5		OPERATING LIMITS AND RESTRICTIONS	5-1
Section	I	General	5-1
	II	System Limits	5-1
	III	Power Limits	5-1
	IV	Loading Limits	5-2
	V	Airspeed Limits	5-2
	VI	Maneuvering Limits	5-2
	VII	Environmental Restrictions	5-3
	VIII	Height Velocity	5-3
	XI	Internal Rescue Hoist (Breeze Only)	5-3
	X	Other Limitations	5-3
CHAPTER 6		WEIGHT/BALANCE AND LOADING	
Section	I	General	6-1
	II	Weight and Balance	6-1
	III	Fuel/Oil	6-2
	IV	Personnel	6-2
	V	Mission Equipment	6-2
	VI	Cargo Loading	6-3
	VII	Center of Gravity Limits	6-4
CHAPTER 7		PERFORMANCE DATA	
Section	I	Introduction	7-1
	II	Torque Available	7-3
	III	Hover	7-4
	IV	Takeoff	7-4
	V	Cruise	7-5
	VI	Drag	7-6
	VII	Climb-Descent	7-6
	VIII	Fuel Flow	7-7
CHAPTER 7.1		PERFORMANCE DATA	
Section	I	introduction	7.1-1
	II	Torque Available	7.1-3
	III	Hover	7.1-4
	IV	Takeoff	7.1-4
	V	Cruise	7.1-5
	VI	Drag	7.1-6
	VII	Climb-Descent	7.1-6
	VIII	Fuel Flow	7.1-7
CHAPTER 8		NORMAL PROCEDURES	
Section	I	Mission Planning	8-1
	II	Crew Duties	8-1
	III	Operating Procedures and Maneuvers	8-1
	IV	Instrument Flight	8-9
	V	Flight Characteristics	8-9
	VI	Adverse Environmental Conditions	8-11
CHAPTER 9		EMERGENCY PROCEDURES	
Section	I	Helicopter Systems	9-1

TABLE OF CONTENTS (CONT)

APPENDIX	A	REFERENCES A-1
	B	ABBREVIATIONS AND TERMS B-1
	C	TABULAR PERFORMANCE DATA C-1
INDEX		.... Index 1

TM 55-1520-210-10

LIST OF ILLUSTRATIONS

FIGURE	TITLE	PAGE
2-1	General Arrangement Diagram	2-23
2-2	Principal Dimensions Diagram - Typical	2-25
2-3	Pilot/Copilot Seats - Typical	2-26
2-4	Instrument Panel - Typical	2-26.1
2-5	Crew Compartment - Typical	2-28
2-6	Engine/Miscellaneous Control Panel Typical	2-31
2-7	Heating and Defrosting System	2-32
2-8	Electrical System Typical	2-34
2-9	Caution Panel - Typical	2-35
2-10	Servicing Diagram - Typical	2-36
3-1	Signal Distribution Panel SB-329/AR	3-2
3-2	Signal Distribution Panel C-1611/A/C	3-3
3-3	Signal Distribution Panel C6533/ARC	3-4
3-4	UHF Control Panel C6287/ARC-51BX	3-6
3-5	UHF Control Panel C-4677/ARC-51X	3-7
3-6	UHF Control Panel C-1827/ARC-55B	3-8
3-7	Control Panel AN/ARC-115	3-10
3-6	VHF Control Panel C-7197/ARC-134	3-11
3-9	VHF Control Panel 614U-6/ARC-73	3-13
3-10	Control Panel AN/ARC-114 and AN/ARC-114A	3-14
3-11	FM Radio Set Control Panel AN/ARC-131	3-15
3-12	FM Radio Set Control Panel C-3835/ARC-54	3-16
3-13	FM Control Panel and Switch Assembly AN/ARC-44	3-17
3-14	Voice Security Equipment	3-18
3-14.1	HF Radio Set AN/ARC-220 Control Panel C12436/URC	3-22.2
3-14.2	Remote Control Unit (TSEC/KY-100)	3-22.17
3-14.3	Processor (TSEC/KY-100)	3-22.21
3-15	HF Radio Control Panel	3-23
3-16	Direction Finder Control Panel ARN-83	3-24
3-17	ADF Control Panel ARN-59	3-26
3-18	Navigation Control Panel ARN-82	3-27
3-19	VHF Navigation Receiver Control Panel ARN-30E	3-27
3-20	Course Deviation Indicator ID-43/ARN-30 and ID-1347/ARN-82	3-28
3-21	Gyromagnetic Compass Indicator (RMI)	3-30
3-22	Marker Beacon Controls	3-31
3-22.1	Receiver/Display Unit	3-32.2
3-22.2	Instrument Panel - AN/ASN-175 System Components	3-32.7
3-23	DME indicator ID-2192/ARN-124	3-33
3-24	Transponder Set AN/APX-72	3-34
3-25	Transponder Set (AN/APX-100) Control Panel	3-35
3-26	AAU-32/A Altitude Encode/Pneumatic Altimeter	3-39
3-27	AN/APN-209 Radar Altimeter	3-39
3-28	Proximity Warning Panel	3-40
3-29	Radar Warning System	3-43
3-29.1	Receiver-Transmitter Radio RT-1167/ARC-164(V)	3-44
3-29.2	Control-Display Panel Layout	3-52
3-29.3	HF Volume Control	3-55
3-29.4	Channel Selection	3-56
3-29.5	Channel Stewing	3-57
3-29.6	Numbered Keys	3-57
3-29.7	Frequency Select	3-57
3-29.8	Frequency Slewing (RX only)	3-58
3-29.9	Power Level Select	3-59
3-29.10	Modulation Mode Source	3-59
3-29.11	Modulation Mode	3-60
3-29.12	Store	3-60

Change 18   iii

TM 55-1520-210-10

LIST OF ILLUSTRATIONS (CONT)

FIGURE	TITLE	PAGE
3-29.13	Selective Receive Address	3-60
3-29.14	Selective Transmit Address	3-61
3-29.15	Seladr ON/OFF	3-61
3-29.16	Test Mode Display	3-62
3-29.17	Failed Test Display	3-62
3-29.18	Passed Test Display	3-63
3-29.19	Tune Mode Single Channel	3-63
3-29.20	Tune Mode - All Channels	3-63
3-29.21	Scan Mode	3-63
3-29.22	Executing Scan	3-64
3-29.23	HF Volume Control	3-65
3-29.24	LF/ADF Control Panel C-7932/ARN-89	3-66
3-29.24.1	ADF Control Panel C-12192/ARN-149(V)	3-68.1
3-29.25	Radio Receiving Set AN/ARN-123(V)	3-69
3-29.26	Doppler Navigation Set AN/ASN-128	3-72
3-29.27	Doppler Lamp Test Mode Display	3-75
3-29.28	Horizontal Situation Indicator Control (C-11740/A)	3-84
3-29.29	Horizontal Situation Indicator (ID-2103/A)	3-85
3-29.30	Voice Security System Equipment	3-87
3-30	AN/ASC-15A(V) 1,2,3 and 4 Equipment Configuration	3-88
4-1	Mine Dispenser Control Panel - Typical	4-13
4-2	Hoist Installation - Typical	4-14
4-3	Pendant Control - Rescue Hoist	4-15
4-4	Hoist Cable Cutter Switch . Pilot - Typical	4-15
4-5	Hoist Cable Cut Switch - Hoist Operator - Typical	4-15
4-6	Control Pendant Assembly	4-16
4-7	AN/ASC-11 5A(V) 1, 2, 3 and 4 Equipment Configuration	4-17
5-1	Instrument Markings	5-4
5-2	**MB** Airspeed Operating Limits Chart	5-7
5-2.1	**CB** Airspeed Operating Limits Chart	5-8
6-1	Helicopter Station Diagram	6-5
6-2	Fuel Loading	6-6
6-3	Personnel Loading	6-8
6-4	Hoist Loading Limitations (Lateral CG)	6-9
6-5	Hoist Loading Limitations (Longitudinal CG)	6-10
6-6	System Weight and Balance Data Sheet	6-11
6-7	Hoist Installation Positions	6-14
6-8	Cargo Compartment	6-15
6-9	Cargo Tiedown Fitting Data	6-16
6-10	Internal Cargo Weight and Moment	6-17
6-11	External Cargo Weight and Moment	6-18
6-12	Center of Gravity Limits	6-19

TM 55-1520-210-10

LIST OF ILLUSTRATIONS (CONT)

FIGURE		TITLE	PAGE
7-1	MB	Temperature Conversion Chart	7-12
7-2	MB	Maximum Torque Available (30 Minute Operation) Chart	7-13
7-3	MB	Hover (Power Required) Chart	7-14
7-4	MB	Control Margin	7-16
7-5	MB	Takeoff Chart	7-18
7-6	MB	Cruise Chart	7-21
7-7	MB	Drag Chart	7-48
7-8	MB	Climb-Descent Chart	7-50
7-9	MB	Idle Fuel Flow Chart	7-51
7-1.1	CB	Temperature Conversion Chart	7.1-8
7-1.2	CB	Maximum Torque Available (30 Minute Operation) Chart	7.1-9
7-1.3	CB	HoverChart	7.1-11
7-1.4	CB	Control Margin Chart	7.1-15
7-1.5	CB	Takeoff Chart	7.1-17
7-1.6	CB	Cruise Chart	7.1-20
7-1.7	CB	Drag Chart	7.1-46
7-1.8	CB	Climb Chart	7.1-50
7-1.9	CB	Fuel Flow Chart	1-52
8-1		Danger Area	8-15
8-2		Extenor Check Diagram	8-16
9-1		Emergency Exits and Equipment	9-10
9-2	MB	Autorotational Glide Charactenstr-s Chart	9-11
9-2.1	CB	Autorotational Glide Characteristics Chart	9-12
9-3	MB	Height Velocity Diagram	9-13
9-3.1	CB	Height Velocity Diagram	9-14

Change 16   v/(vi blank)

TM 55-1520-210-10

Operator's Manual for

UH-1H/V Helicopters

Placement of tables, figures, and appendixes. Full page tables, figures, and appendixes (in that order) included in this UPDATE printing are located following the chapters in which they were referenced.

User Information. The proponent agency of this manual is the US Army Aviation and Missile Command (AMCOM). Submit changes for improving this publication on DA Form 2028 (Recommended Changes to Publications and Blank Forms) to: Commander, U.S. Army Aviation and Missile Command ATTN: AMSAM-MMC-LS-LP, Redstone Arsenal, AL 35898-5230.

Types of comments that should be avoided on DA Form 2028 are those that: (1) Ask a question instead of giving an answer; (2) Are based on minor differences of opinion or wording; (3) Point out obvious editorial errors, mispellings, or errors in punctuation, unless the errors change the intended meaning. (Reference AR 25-30, Chapter 2).

Distribution. Special distribution of this issue has been made in accordance with DA Form 12-31-R Requirements For Technical Manuals. The number of copies requested in Block 275 and 668 of the subscribers DA Form 12-31-R.

Resupply. Limited copies of this publication are available from the St. Louis Publications Center for emergency requirements. Users should take action to insure they are receiving the correct number by updating their DA 12-Series Forms.

Explanation of Change Symbols. Changes in text material and tables will be shown by a bar in the left margin. Correction of minor inaccuracies such as spelling, punctuations, relocation of material, etc. will not be shown unless such corrections changes the meaning of instructive information and procedures.

Change 18 1-1

Chapter 1

Introduction

1-1. General These instructions are for use by the operator(s). They apply to UH-1H/V helicopter.

1-2. Warnings, Cautions, and Notes Warnings, Cautions, and Notes are used to emphasize important and critical instructions and are used for the following conditions.

WARNING

An operating procedure, practice, etc., which if not correctly followed, could result in personal injury or loss of life.

Caution

An operating procedure, practice, etc., which if not strictly observed, could result in damage to or destruction of equipment.

NOTE

An operating procedure, condition, etc., which it is essential to highlight.

1-3. Description This manual contains the best operating instructions and procedures for the UH-1H/V helicopter under most circumstances. The observance of limitations, performance and weight balance data provided is mandatory. The observance of procedure is mandatory except when modification is required because of multiple emergencies, adverse weather, terrain, etc. Your flying experience is recognized, and therefore, basic flight principles are not included. THIS MANUAL SHALL BE CARRIED IN THE HELICOPTER AT ALL TIMES.

1-4. Appendix A, References Appendix A is a listing of official publications cited within this manual applicable to and available for flight crews.

1-5. Appendix B, Abbreviations and Terms Definitions of all abbreviations and terms used throughout the manual are included in appendix B.

1-6. Index The index lists every titled paragraph contained in this manual. Chapter 7 performance data has an additional index within the chapter.

1-7. Army Aviation Safety Program Reports necessary to comply with the safety program are prescribed in AR 385-40.

1-8. Destruction of Army Materiel to Prevent Enemy Use For information concerning destruction of Army materiel to prevent enemy use, refer to TM 750-244-1-5.

1-9. Forms and Records Army aviators flight records and helicopter maintenance records which are to be used by the operators and crew members are prescribed in DA PAM 738-751 and TM 55-1500-342-23

1-10. Designator Symbols Designator Symbols H UH-1H and V UH-1V are used in conjunction with text contents, text headings and illustration titles to show limited effectivity of the material. One or more designator symbols may follow a text heading or illustration title to indicate proper effectivity, unless the material applies to all models and configurations within the manual. If the material applies to all models and configurations, no designator symbols will be used. The Designator Symbols used for the Composite Main Rotor Blade is CB and the Metal Main Rotor Blade is MB

1-11. Use of Words Shall, Should, and May Within this technical manual, the word "shall" is used to indicate a mandatory requirement. The word "should" is used to indicate a non-mandatory but preferred method of accomplishment. The word "may" is used to indicate an acceptable method of accomplishment.

Chapter 2

Helicopter and Systems Description and Operation

Section 1. HELICOPTER

2-1. General Description The UH-1H/N helicopters are thirteen-place single engine helicopters. The maximum gross weight is 9500 pounds.

2-2. General Arrangement Figure 2-1 depicts the general arrangement. Indexed items include access openings and most of the items referred to in the exterior check paragraph in section III of chapter 8.

2-3. Principal Dimensions Figure 2-2 depicts the principal dimensions.

2-4. Turning Radius Turning radius is about 35 feet when pivoted around the mast.

2-5. Fuselage The fuselage is the forward section of the airframe extending from the nose to the forward end of the tailboom. The fuselage consists primarily of two longitudinal beams with transverse bulkheads and metal covering. The main beams are the supporting structure for the cabin, landing gear, fuel tanks, transmission, engine, and tailboom. The external cargo suspension unit is attached to the main beams near the center of gravity of the helicopter.

2-6. Tailboom The tailboom section is bolted to the aft end of the fuselage and extends to the aft end of the helicopter. It is a tapered, semi-monocoque structure comprised of skins, longerons, and stringers. The tailboom supports the tail rotor, vertical fin, and synchronized elevator. It houses the tail rotor driveshaft and some electronic equipment.

2-7. Landing Gear System

  a. Main Landing Gear. The main landing gear consists of two aluminum arched crosstubes mounted laterally on the fuselage with two longitudinal skid tubes attached to the crosstubes. The skid tubes are made of aluminum and have steel skid shoes attached to the bottom to minimize skid wear.

  b. Tail Skid. A tubular steel tail skid is installed on the aft end of the tailboom. It acts as a warning to the pilot upon an inadvertent tail-low landing and aids in protecting the tail rotor from damage.

2-8. Crew Compartment Diagram The crew compartment is depicted in figure 2-5.

2-9. Cockpit and Cabin Doors

  a. Cockpit Doors. The cockpit doors are formed aluminum frames with transparent plastic windows in the upper section (fig 2-1). Ventilation is supplied by the sliding panels in the windows. Cam-type door latches are used and doors are equipped with jettisonable door releases.

  b. Cabin Doors. The two cabin doors are formed aluminum frames with transparent plastic windows in the upper section (fig 2-1). These doors are on rollers and slide aft to the open position allowing full access to the cargo area. Hinged doorpost panels are forward of the cabin doors. They provide a larger entrance to the cargo area. An open door lock is provided to hold the door in the aft position to prevent door separation in flight.

2-10. Pilot/Copilot Seats The pilot and copilot seats may be conventional seats or armored seats (fig 2-3). The armored seats have a release to recline the seats to aid in removal of injured personnel. The conventional seats do not have the reclining feature.

  a. Pilot and Copilot Seats (Conventional). The pilot and copilot seats are vertical and fore-aft adjustable and the nonreclining type. The vertical height adjustment handle is under the right side of the seat. The fore and aft adjustment is under the left side of the seat. Webbing on the back of the seat can be removed to accept use of a back-pack parachute. The seats are equipped with lap safety belts and inertia reel shoulder harness.

b. Plot and Copilot Seats (Armored). Armored seats can be installed m the helicopter for the pilot and copilot. They are equipped with lap safety belt and inertia-reel shoulder harness They are adjustable fore and aft and vertically. The vertical adjustment handle Is under the right side of the seat and the fore and aft handle on the left. The seats are equipped with a quick release, on each side at the back of the seat, for reclining the seat. The seat back, bottom, and sides are protected by ceramic and aluminum armor plate. Hip and shoulder areas are protected by ceramic type armor.

c. Inertia Reel Shoulder Harness. An inertia reel and shoulder harness is incorporated in the pilot and copilot seats with manual lock-unlock handle (fig 2-3). On the conventional seat, the control handles are located on the left front of the seat. On the armored seat, the control handles are located on the night front of the seat. With the control in the unlocked position (aft) and the shoulder straps properly adjusted, the reel strap will extend to allow the occupant to lean forward; however, the reel automatically locks when the helicopter encounters an impact force of 2 to 3 'G' deceleration. The reel can be locked (handle forward) from any position and will take up slack in the harness. To release the lock, it is necessary to lean back slightly to release tension on the lock and move the control handle to the unlock position. It is possible to have pressure against the seat back whereby no additional movement is possible and the lock cannot be released. If this condition occurs. It will be necessary to loosen the harness. The reel should be manually locked for emergency landing. Straps must be adjusted to fully retract within the inertia reels to prevent rebound overshoot in the event of impact. Seat belt must be securely fastened and firmly tightened prior to adjustment of shoulder harness to prevent submanning in event of Impact.

2-11. Personnel Seats. Various arrangements of personnel seats can be installed to accommodate from one to eleven personnel besides the pilot and copilot. The seats are constructed of tubular steel and reinforced canvas. Each seat is equipped with a lap safety belt. For additional information on the personnel seats, refer to chapter 6. Patients will be secured to litters utilizing the approved patient securing straps when the helicopter is used for medical evacuation missions. Instruments and Controls.

2-12 Instruments and Controls

a. Instrument Panel. The location of all the controls, indicators, instruments, and data placards installed on the instrument panel is depicted m figure 24 V Some instruments may be relocated.

b. Pedestal Panel. The panels and controls installed in the pedestal are depicted in figure 2-5.

c. Overhead Console. The location of the controls and circuit breakers installed in the overhead console is depicted in figure 2-5.

d. External Stores Jettison Handle. The external stores Jettison handle Is located to the left of the pilot collective when installed. Pulling up on the handle will Jettison external stores through mechanical linkage.

e. Other Instruments and Controls. Instruments, controls, or indicators not shown in figure 2-5 or figure 2-6 are shown in the chapter/section which describes their related systems.

2-12.1 Wire Strike Protection System (WSPS).

The WSPS provides protection for 90 % of the frontal area against impacts with horizontally strung mechanical and power transmission cables. The basic system consists of an upper cutter/deflector, a windshield protector/deflector/cutter, a lower cutter/deflector and a pair of windshield wiper deflectors (fig 2-1). The lower cutter assembly features a 'Breakaway Tip' designed to shear when relatively large ground contact forces are experienced and before helicopter structural damage is incurred. However, the tip shear rivets are designed to withstand the smaller forces experienced during wire strikes and the tip will still effectively deflect wires/cables into the cutter blades.

Section II. EMERGENCY EQUIPMENT

2-13. Emergency Equipment. The emergency equipment location, illustration, and emergency procedures are covered in chapter 9.

2-14. Portable Fire Extinguisher. A portable hand-operated fire extinguisher is carried in a bracket located aft of the pedestal, or to the right of the pilot seat.

2-15. First Aid Kits. Four general purpose type first aid kits have been provided in the cabin area (fig 9-1) Two kits are secured to the night center doorpost. The other two kits are secured to the left doorpost. First aid kits can be easily removed for immediate use.

Section III. ENGINE AND RELATED SYSTEMS

2-16. Engine. The UH-IH/ are equipped with a T53-L-13 engine.

2-17. Engine Compartment Cooling. The engine compartment is cooled by natural convection through engine compartment screens.

2-18. Air Induction System. Three different air induction systems are used on these helicopters. They are discussed m the following paragraphs:

a Non-Self Purging Particle Separator. The non-self-purging particle separator is an inertial type. A lip extending into the airstream deflects the particle-laden air into a large chamber. Large particles in the air settle in the chamber; fine particles are removed as the air is drawn through a filter assembly. Removed particles are held m porous foam box assembles. The box assemblies can be removed and cleaned. Other components used with the particle separator are: ENG AIR FILTER CONT circuit breaker on the overhead console, an engine air differential pressure switch on the firewall, and an cateye type on the instrument panel or of the segment type on the caution panel.

b. Self-Purging Particle Separator. Helicopters serial No. 68-15779 and subsequent are equipped with a self-purging particle separator. This is an inertial-type separator. Particle-laden air is directed through a large annular chamber and through an air cleaner. A constant supply of bleed air from the engine flows through the venture-type ejector and carries particles overboard through airframe plumbing. Some self-purging particle separator systems have operational ENGINE INLET AIR caution panel segment lights.

c Foreign Object Damage Screen Foreign Object Damage (FOD) screen prevents large particles from entering the engine inlet.

NOTE
The ice detector system is not applicable on helicopters equipped with the self-purging particle separator.

d. DE-ICE. Engine de-ice is a bleed air system activated by the DE-ICE switch on the ENGINE panel (fig 2-6). In the ON position bleed air is directed through the engine inlet to provide the protection. Power losses caused when the system is on are shown m chapter 7. In the event of dc electrical failure or when the DE-ICE ENG circuit breaker is out de-ice is automatically on. System power is provided by the dc essential bus and protected by the ANTI-ICE ENG circuit breaker.

e. Improved Particle Separator Some UH.-I's may be equipped with an improved particle separator. This unit has a number of vortex tubes which ar-highly effective in removing sand and dust from the engine inlet air. The sand and dust are dumped overboard through outlets on each side of the Separator.

2-19. Engine Fuel Control System.

a Engine Mounted Components. The fuel control assembly is mounted on the engine. It consists of a metering section a computer section and an overspeed governor.

(1) The metering section is driven at a speed proportional to N1 speed. It pumps fuel to the engine through the main metering valve or if the main system falls through the emergency metering valve which is positioned directly by the twist grip throttle.

(2) The computer section determines the rate of main fuel delivery by biasing main metering valve opening for N I speed, inlet air temperature and pressure, and throttle position. It also controls the operation of the compressor air bleed and operation of the variable inlet guide vanes.

(3) The overspeed governor is driven at a speed proportional to N2 speed. It biases the main metering valve opening to maintain a constant selected N2 rpm.

b. Starting Fuel Flow. During engine start, energizing the start fuel switch opens the fuel solenoid valve, allowing fuel from the fuel regulator to flow through the starting fuel manifold and into the combustion chamber. When N1 reaches sufficient speed, the start switch is de-energized, causing the solenoid valve to close and stop-starting fuel flow. Starting fuel nozzles are purged by air from the combustion chamber through a check filter valve. Engine starting fuel solenoid valve is controlled by the engine starter switch on helicopters which do not have a starting fuel switch. The engine solenoid valve (engine starting fuel solenoid valve) cannot be individually controlled during engine starts.

c. Power Controls (Throttles). Rotating the pilot or copilot twist grip-type throttle (fig 2-5) to the full open position allows the overspeed governor to maintain a constant rpm. Rotating the throttle toward the closed position will cause the rpm to be manually selected instead of automatically selected by the overspeed governor. Rotating the throttle to the fully closed position shuts off the fuel. An idle stop is incorporated in the throttle to prevent inadvertent throttle closure. To bypass the idle detent press the IDLE REL switch and close the throttle. The IDLE REL switch is a momentary on, solenoid-operated switch. The IDLE REL switch is located on the pilot collective stick switch box. IDLE REL switch receives power from the 28 Vdc bus and is protected by a circuit breaker marked IDLE STOP REL. Friction can be induced in both throttles by rotating the pilot throttle function ring counterclockwise (fig 2-5). The ring is located on the upper end of the pilot throttle.

d. Governor switch. The GOV switch is located on the ENGINE control panel (fig 2-6). AUTO position permits the overspeed governor to automatically control the engine rpm with the throttle in the full open position. The EMER position permits the pilot or copilot to manually control the rpm. Because automatic acceleration, deceleration, and overspeed control are not provided with the GOV switch in the EMER position, control movements must be smooth to prevent compressor stall, overspeed, over-temperature, or engine failure. The governor circuit receives power from the 28 Vdc essential bus and is protected by the GOV CONT circuit breaker.

2-20. Engine Oil Supply System.

a. Description. The dry sump pressure type oil system is entirely automatic in its operation. The system consists of an engine oil tank with de-aeration provisions, thermostatically controlled oil cooler with by-pass valve, pressure transmitter and pressure indicator, low pressure warning switch and indicator, sight gages, and oil supply return vent, and breather lines. Drain valves have been provided for draining the oil tank and cooler. Pressure for engine lubrication and scavenging of return oil are provided by the engine-mounted and engine-driver oil pump. On helicopters equipped with Oil Debris Detection System (ODDS), and external oil separator, with integral chip detector, and a 3-micron filter are installed down stream of the sump. Oil specification and grade are specified in the Servicing Table 2-1

b. Oil Cooler. Engine oil cooling Is accomplished by an oil cooler. The cooler is housed within the fuselage area under the engine deck (fig 2-1). Air circulation for oil cooling is supplied by a turbine fan which operates from turbine bleed air. The fan is powered at all times when the engine is operating and no control is required except the bleed air limiting office.

2-21. Ignition Starter System. The starter ignition switch is mounted on the underside of the pilot collective pitch control lever switch box. An additional switch may be installed on the copilot stick. The switch is a trigger switch, spring-loaded to the off position (fig 2-5). The starter and ignition unit circuits are both connected to the trigger switches. The circuits receive power from the 28 Vdc essential bus and are protected by circuit breakers marked STARTER RELAY and IGNITION SYSTEM IGNITER SOL. The starter circuit is energized when the STARTERJGEN switch is in the START position and the trigger switch is pulled (fig 2-5).

The ignition circuit is energized when the FUEL MAIN ON/OFF switch on the engine control panel is m the ON position and the trigger switch is pulled. The ignition keylock is located by the AC circuit breaker panel. The OFF position deactivates the igniters and start fuel to prevent engine starting. The ON position allows engine starting.

2-21.1. Infrared (IR) Scoup Suppressor. Aircraft equipped with the IR Scoup Suppressor System will have an upturned insulated exhaust duct assembly, an exhaust extension, and a forward duct assembly mounted at the tailpipe. The IR Scoup Suppressor System reduces the IR signature of the aircraft by directing engine exhaust into the rotor blades for dispersion.

2-22. Governor RPM Switch. The pilot and copilot GOV RPM INCR/DECR switches are mounted on a switch box attached to the end of the collective pitch control lever (fig 2-5). The switches are a three-position momentary type and are held in INCR (up) position to increase the power turbine (N2) speed or DECR (down) position to decrease the power turbine (N2) speed. Electrical power for the circuit is supplied from the 28 Vdc essential bus and is protected by a circuit breaker marked GOV CONT.

2-23. Droop Compensator. A droop compensator maintains engine rpm (N2) as power demand is increased by the pilot. The compensator is a direct mechanical linkage between the collective stick and the speed selector lever on the N2 governor. No crew controls are provided or required. The compensator will hold N2 rpm to j40 rpm when properly rigged. Droop is defined as the speed change in engine rpm (N2) as power is increased from a no-load condition. It is an inherent characteristic designed into the governor system. Without this characteristic instability would develop as engine output is increased resulting in N l speed overshooting or hunting the value necessary to satisfy the new power condition. If N2 power were allowed droop other than momentarily the reduction in rotor speed could become critical.

2-24. Engine Instrument and Indicators. All engine instruments and indicators are mounted in the instrument panel and the pedestal (figs 24 and 2-5).

  a. Torquemeter Indicator. The torquemeter indicator is located in the center area of the instrument panel and is marked TORQUE PRESS (fig 24). The indicator is connected to a transmitter which is part of the engine oil system. The torquemeter indicates torque in pounds per square inch (psi) of torque imposed upon the engine output shaft. The torquemeter receives power from the 28 Vac bus and is protected by a circuit breaker marked TORQUE in the ac circuit breaker panel b. Exhaust Gas Temperature Indicator. The exhaust gas temperature indicator is located in the center area of the instrument panel and is marked EXH TEMP (fig 24).
The indicator receives temperature indications from the thermocouple probes mounted in the engine exhaust diffuser section. The temperature indications are in degrees celsius. The system is electrically self-generating.

  c. Dual Tachometer. The dual tachometer is located in the center area of the instrument panel and indicates both the engine and main rotor rpm (fig 2 4). The tachometer inner scale is marked ROTOR and the outer scale is marked ENGINE. Synchronization of the ENGINE and ROTOR needles indicates normal operation of helicopter. The indicator receives power from the tachometer generators mounted on the engine and transmission. Connection to the helicopter electrical system is not required.

  d. Gas Producer Tachometer. The gas producer indicator is located in the right center area of the instrument panel and is marked PERCENT (fig 24). The indicator displays the rpm of the gas producer turbine speed in percent. This system receives power from a tachometer generator which is geared to the engine compressor. A connection to the helicopter electrical system is not required.

  e. Oil Temperature Indicator. The engine oil temperature indicator is located in the center area of the instrument panel and is marked OIL 'C (fig 24). The indicator is connected to an electrical resistance-type thermocouple. The temperature of the engine oil at the engine oil inlet is indicated in degrees celsius. Power to operate the circuit is supplied from the 28 Vdc essential bus. Circuit protection is provided by the TEMP IND ENG & XMSN circuit breaker.

  f. Oil Pressure Indicator The engine oil pressure indicator is located in the center area of the instrument panel and is marked OIL PRESS (fig 2-4). The indicator receives pressure indications from the engine oil pressure transmitter and provides readings in pounds per square inch (psi). The circuit receives electrical power from the 28 VAC bus and circuit protection Is provided by the ENG circuit breaker in the ac circuit breaker panel.

  g. Oil Pressure Caution Light The ENGINE OIL PRESS caution light Is located in the pedestal mounted CAUTION panel. The light is connected to a low pressure switch. When pressure drops below approximately 25 psi the switch closes an electrical circuit causing the caution light to illuminate. The circuit receives power from the 28 Vdc essential bus and is protected by the circuit breaker marked CAUTION LIGHTS.

  h. Engine Chip Detector Caution Light. A magnetic plug is installed in the engine. When sufficient metal particles accumulate on the magnetic plug to complete the circuit the ENGINE CHIP DET segment illuminates. The circuit receives power from the 28 Vdc essential bus and is protected by the circuit breaker marked CAUTION LIGHTS. On Helicopters equipped with ODDS, the chip detector which is connected to the caution light is part of the external oil separator.

i. Engine Ice Detector. The ice detector system (ENGINE ICE DET caution light) is not connected.

j. Engine Icing Caution Light The ENGINE ICING segment of the caution panel is not connected.

NOTE
Engine inlet air filter clogged/caution lights are not utilized for aircraft with the improved particle separator. However, some self-purging particle separators have operational ENGINE INLET AIR segment lights.

k Engine Inlet Air Filter Clogged Warning Light On helicopters pnor to Serial No. 68-16066 the ENGINE INLET FILTER CLOGGED warning light is mounted on the upper area of the instrument panel (fig 2-4). When the inlet air filter becomes clogged, a differential pressure switch senses the condition and closes contacts to energize the filter caution light. Power is supplied from the 28 Vdc bus and circuit protection is provided by the CAUTION LIGHTS circuit breaker.

i Engine Inlet Air Caution Light The ENGINE INLET AIR segment of the caution panel will illuminate when the inlet air filter becomes clogged. Power is supplied from the 28 Vdc bus and protection is provided by the CAUTION LIGHT circuit breaker.

m. Failure of either fuel pump element will close an electrical circuit illuminating the caution light. The system receives power from the 28 Vdc essential bus and is protected by a circuit breaker marked CAUTION LIGHTS. One type of switch used on some aircraft will illuminate the caution light until normal operating pressure is reached. This momentary lighting does not indicate a pump element failure.

n. Emergency Fuel Control Caution Light The emergency fuel control caution light is located m the pedestal-mounted caution panel. The Illumination of the worded segment GOV EMER Is a remainder to the pilot that the GOV switch is in the EMER position. Electrical power for the circuit is supplied from the 28 Vdc bus and is protected by a circuit breaker marked CAUTION LIGHTS.

o. Fuel Filter Caution Light The FUEL FILTER caution light Is located in the pedestal-mounted caution panel or a press to test light is located on the instrument panel. A differential pressure switch is mounted m the fuel line across the filter. When the filter becomes clogged, the pressure switch senses this and closes contacts to energize the caution light circuit. If clogging continues, the fuel bypass opens to allow fuel to flow around the filter. The circuit receives power from the 28 Vdc essential bus and Is protected by a circuit breaker marked CAUTION LIGHTS.

Section IV. HELICOPTER FUEL SYSTEM

2-25. Fuel Supply System.

a. Fuel System The fuel system consists of five interconnected cells all filled from a single fitting on the right side of the helicopter. The two forward cells each contain a submerged boost pump. The boost pumps provide fuel pressure to prime the fuel line to the engine driven fuel pump. Each forward fuel cell is divided into two compartments by a lateral baffle fitted with a flapper valve to allow fuel flow from front to rear. The submerged boost pump is mounted on a sump assembly near the aft end of each forward cell and is connected by a hose to the pressure line outlet to the engine. Part of the pump output is diverted forward through a flow switch and hose to an ejector pump at front of cell. Induced flow of the ejector pump sends fuel through a hose over the baffle into the rear part of the cell, so that no slgnmficant quantity of fuel will be unusable in any flight attitude. The crashworthy system is designed to contain fuel during a severe, but survivable, crash Impact to reduce the possibility of fire. Frangible fittings used to secure the fuel cells m the airframe are designed to fuel and permit relative movement of the cells, without rupture, in event of a crash; self-sealing break-away valves are installed in the fuel lines at the fuel cell outlets and certain other locations. The break-away valves are designed to permit complete separation of components without loss of fuel. Rollover vent valves are installed on the aft fuel cells to provide protection m the event of a helicopter rollover during a crash. The system has 50 caliber ballistic protection in the lower two-thirds of the cell.

b. Closed Circuit Refueling System Helicopter serial number 69-15292 and subsequent and modified helicopters provide a closed circuit refueling system when used with the mating nozzle. This system is capable of automatic shut-off of fuel flow when full.

c Gravity Refueling. If helicopter is equipped with closed circuit refueling system and fuel servicing vehicle is not equipped with related nozzle for closed circuit refueling, a gravity system may be used.

2-26. Controls and Indicators.

a Fuel Switches. The fuel system switches consist of a main fuel switch, start fuel switch, and fuel transfer switches (fig 2-6). The FUEL START switch is not applicable on helicopters Serial No. 66-8574 through 66-8577, 66-16034 and subsequent, and earlier models so modified.

(1) Main Fuel Switch The FUEL MAIN ON/OFF switch is located on the pedestal-mounted ENGINE panel (fig 2-6). The switch is protected from accidental operation by a spring-loaded toggle head that must be pulled up before switch movement can be accomplished. When the switch is in the ON position, the fuel valve opens, the electric boost pump(s) are energized and fuel flows to the engine. When the switch is in the OFF position the fuel valve closes and the electric boost pump(s) are de-energized. Electrical power for circuit operation is supplied by the 28 Vdc essential bus and is protected by circuit breakers FUEL VALVES, LH BOOST PUMP and RH ROOST PUMP.

(2) Fuel Start Switch. The FUEL START ON/OFF switch is located on the ENGINE panel. In the ON position the starting fuel solenoid valve is energized when the starter-ignition switch is pulled. When the START FUEL switch is in the OFF position the igniter solenoid valve is de-energized. Electrical power for the circuit is supplied by the 28 Vdc essential bus and is protected by circuit breaker IGNMTION SYSTEM IGNITER SOL.

(3) Fuel Control. Fuel flow and mode of operation is controlled by switches on the pedestal-mounted engine control panel (fig 26). The panel contains the MAIN FUEL ON/OFF or FUEL ON/OFF switch, START FUEL ON/OFF switch, two INT FUEL TRANS PUMP or INT AUX FUEL switches, and GOV AUTO/EMER switch. The switch over to emergency mode is accomplished by retarding the throttle to idle or off position and positioning the GOV AUTO/EMER switch to the EMER position. In the EMER position fuel is manually metered to the engine, with no automatic control features, by rotating the throttle twist grip.

b. Fuel Quantity Indicator. The fuel quantity indicator is located in the upper center area of the instrument panel (fig 2-4). This instrument is a transistorized electrical receiver which continuously indicates the quantity of fuel m pounds. The indicator is connected to three fuel transmitters mounted m the fuel cells. Two are mounted in the night forward cell and one in the center aft cell. Indicator readings shall be multiplied by 100 to obtain fuel quantity m pounds. Electrical power for operation is supplied from the 115 Vac system and is protected by circuit breaker FUEL QTY in the ac circuit breaker panel.

c Fuel Gage Test Switch The FUEL GAGE TEST switch is used to test the fuel quantity indicator operation (fig 2-4).Pressing the switch will cause the indicator pointer to move from the actual reading to a lesser reading. Releasing the switch will cause the pointer to return to the actual reading. The circuit receives power from the 115 Vac system and is protected by a circuit breaker marked FUEL QTY m the ac circuit breaker panel.

d Fuel Pressure Indicator The fuel pressure indicator displays the psi pressure of the fuel being delivered by the boost pumps from the fuel cells to the engine (fig 2-4). The circuit receives power from the 28 Vac bus and is protected by the FUEL PRESSURE circuit breaker in the ac circuit breaker panel.

e. Fuel Quantity Low Caution Light The 20 MINUTE FUEL caution light will illuminate when there is approximately 170 pounds remaining. The illumination of this light does not mean a fixed time period remains before fuel exhaustion, but is an medication that a low fuel condition exists. Electrical power is supplied from the 28 Vdc essential bus. The caution lights circuit breaker protects the circuit.

NOTE
Low fuel caution systems alert the pilot that the fuel level in the tank has reached a specified level (capacity). Differences in fuel densities due to temperature and fuel type will vary the weight of the fuel remaining and the actual time the aircraft engine may operate. Differences in fuel consumption rates, aircraft attitude and operational condition of the fuel subsystem will also affect actual time the aircraft engine may operate.

f Fuel Boost Pump Caution Lights. The LEFT FUEL BOOST and RIGHT FUEL BOOST caution Lights will illuminate when the left/right fuel boost pumps fail to pump fuel. The circuits receive power from the 28 Vdc essential bus. Circuit protection is provided by the CAUTION LIGHTS, RH FUEL BOOST PUMP and LH FUEL BOOST PUMP circuit breakers. On helicopters prior to Serial No. 69-15292 a FUEL TANK SUMP PUMP circuit breaker is used instead of RH and LH BOOST PUMP circuit breakers.

2-27. Auxiliary Fuel System.

Complete provisions have been made for installing an auxiliary fuel equipment kit in the helicopter cargo passenger compartment. Two crashworthy bladder type tanks can be installed on the aft bulkhead and transmission support structure. This allows the helicopter to be serviced with an additional 300 U.S. gallons of fuel (table 2-1).

 a. Internal Fuel Transfer Switches. Two switches marked INT AUX FUEL LEFT/RIGHT are mounted in the ENGINE control panel (fig 2-6). Placing the switches to the forward position energizes the auxiliary fuel system. Fuel is transferred to the main fuel cells. An overfill limity switch Is installed in the main fuel tank to prevent the auxiliary fuel pumps from overfilling the main fuel cells. Power is supplied by the dc essential bus and protected by the FUEL TRANS PUMP circuit breaker.

 b. Auxiliary Fuel Low Caution Light. An AUX FUEL LOW caution light Is provided to indicate when the auxiliary fuel tanks are empty. The light will Illuminate only when the fuel transfer switches are in the forward position, and the auxiliary tanks are empty. The circuit receives power from the 28 Vdc essential bus and is protected by the CAUTION LIGHTS circuit breaker.

Section V. FLIGHT CONTROL SYSTEM

2-28. Description. The flight control system is a hydraulic assisted positive mechanical type, actuated by conventional helicopter controls. Complete controls are provided for both pilot and copilot. The system includes a cyclic system, collective control system, tail rotor system, force the system, synchronized elevator, and a stabilizer bar.

2-29. Cyclic Control System. The system is operated by the cyclic stick movement (fig 2-5). Moving the stick in any direction will produce a corresponding movement of the helicopter which Is a result of a change in the plane of rotation of the main rotor. The pilot cyclic contains the cargo release switch, radio ICS switch, armament fire control switch, hoist switch and force the switch. Desired operating friction can be induced into the control stick by hand tightening the friction adjuster.

 a. Synchronized Elevator. The synchronized elevator (fig 2-1) is located on the tailbroom. It is connected by control tubes and mechanical linkage to the fore and-aft cyclic system. Fore and aft movement of the cyclic control stick will produce a change in the synchronized elevator attitude. This improves controllability within the cg range.

 b. Stabilizer Bar. The stabilizer bar is mounted on the main rotor hub trunnion assembly in a parallel plane, above and at 90 degrees to the main rotor blades. The gyroscopic and inertial effect of the stabilizer bar will produce a damping force in the rotor rotating control system and thus the rotor. When an angular displacement of the helicopter/mast occurs the bar tends to remain in its trim plane. The rate at which the bar rotational plane tends to return to a position perpendicular to the mast Is controlled by the hydraulic dampers. By adjusting the dampers, positive dynamic stability can be achieved, and still allow the pilot complete responsive control of the helicopter.

2-30. Collective Control System. The collective pitch control lever controls vertical flight (fig 2-5). When the lever is in full down position, the main rotor is at minimum pitch. When the lever is in the full up position, the main rotor Is at maximum pitch. The amount of lever movement determines the angle of attack and lift developed by the main rotor, and results in ascent or descent of the helicopter. Desired operating friction tan be induced into the control lever by hand-tightening the friction adjuster (fig 2-5). A grip-type throttle and a switch box assembly are located on the upper end of the collective pitch control lever. The pilot switch box contains the starter switch, governor rpm switch, engine idle stop release switch, and landing light/searchlight switches. A collective lever down lock is located on the floor below the collective lever. The copilot collective lever contains only the grip-type throttle, governor rpm switch, and starter switch when installed. The collective pitch control system has built-in breakaway (friction) force to move the stick up from the neutral (center of travel) position of eight to ten pounds with hydraulic boost ON.

2-31. Tail Rotor Control System. The system is operated by pilot/copilot anti-torque pedals (fig 2-5). Pushing a pedal will change the pitch of the tail rotor blades resulting in directional control. Pedal adjusters are provided to adjust the pedal distance for individual comfort. A force the system is connected to the directional controls.

2-32. Force Trim System. Force centering devices are incorporated in the cyclic controls and directional pedal controls. These devices are installed between the cyclic stick and the hydraulic servo cylinders, and between the anti-torque pedals and the hydraulic servo cylinder. The devices furnish a force gradient or "feel' to the cyclic control stick and anti-torque pedals. A FORCE TRIM ON/OFF switch is installed on the miscellaneous control panel to turn the system on or off (Fig 2-6). These forces can be reduced to zero by pressing and holding the force trim push-button switch on the cyclic stick grip or moving the force trim switch to OFF.

Section VL HYDRAULIC SYSTEM

2-33. Description. The hydraulic system is used to minimize the force required by the pilot to move the cyclic, collective and pedal controls. A hydraulic pump, mounted on and driven by the transmission supplies pressure to the hydraulic servos. The hydraulic servos are connected into the mechanical linkage of the helicopter flight control system. Movement of the controls in any direction causes a valve, in the appropriate system, to open and admit hydraulic pressure which actuates the cylinder, thereby reducing the force-load required for control movement. Irreversible valves are installed on the cyclic and collective hydraulic servo cylinders to prevent main rotor feedback to the cyclic and collective in the event of hydraulic system malfunction.

2-34. Control Switch. The hydraulic control switch is located on the miscellaneous panel (Fig 2-6). The switch is a two-position toggle type labeled HYD CONTROL ON/OFF. When the switch is in the ON position, pressure is supplied to the servo system. When switch is in the OFF position the solenoid valve is closed and no pressure is supplied to the system. The switch is a fail-safe type. Electrical power is required to turn the switch off.

2-35. Reservoir and Sight Glass. The hydraulic reservoir is a gravity feed type and is located at the right aft edge of the cabin roof (fig 2-10). The reservoir and sight gage are visible for inspection through a plastic window in the transmission fairing.

2-36. Hydraulic Filter. A line filter is installed on helicopters prior to Serial No. 68-16050. Thus filter has no indicator. Helicopters Serial No 63-16050 and subsequent, or those modified by MWO have an improved filter system. When the filter is clogged it will give a visual warning by raising a red indicator button. The red button pops out when a set differential pressure across the element is exceeded. Once actuated, the indicator will remain extended until reset manually When the indicator TM 55-1520-210-10 is in reset position, it will be hidden from view. An inspection window may be provided to permit ready visual access to the filter indicator. The transparent window is located on forward face of the transmission bulkhead.

2-37. Hydraulic Pressure Caution Light. Low hydraulic system pressure will be indicated by the illumination of HYD PRESSURE segment on the CAUTION panel. Moderate feedback forces will be noticed in the controls when moved.

2-38. Electrical Circuit Electrical power for hydraulic system control is supplied by the 28 Vdc essential bus. The circuit Is protected by the HYD CONT circuit breaker.

Section VII. POWER TRAIN SYSTEM

2-39. Transmission. The transmission is mounted forward of the engine and coupled to the power turbine shaft at the cool end of the engine by the main dnveshaft. The transmission is basically a reduction gearbox, used to transmit engine power at a reduced rpm to the rotor system. A freewheeling unit is incorporated m the transmission to provide a quick-disconnect from the engine if a power failure occurs. This permits the main rotor and tail rotor to rotate m order to accomplish a safe auto-rotational landing. The tail rotor drive is on the lower aft section of the transmission. Power is transmitted to the tail rotor through a series of driveshafts and gearboxes. The rotor tachometer generator, hydraulic pump, and main dc generator are mounted on and driven by the transmission. A self-contained pressure oil system is incorporated in the transmission. The oil is cooled by an oil cooler and turbine fan. The engine and transmission oil coolers use the same fan. The oil system has a thermal bypass capability An oil level sight glass, filler cap. and magnetic chip detector are provided. A transmission oil filter is mounted in a pocket in the upper right aft corner of sump case, with inlet and outlet ports through internal passages. The filter incorporates a bypass valve for continued oil flow if screens become clogged. The transmission external oil filter is located in the cargo-sling compartment on right side wall, and is connected into the external oil line. On Helicopters equipped with ODDS, a full flow debris monitor with integral chip detector replaces the integral oil filter. A bypass valve is incorporated, set to open at a set differential pressure to assure oil flow if filter element should become clogged.

A bypass condition will be indicated by extension of a red indicator on the filter head. On Helicopters equipped with ODDS, the external oil filter is rated to 3 microns.

2-40. Gearboxes.

 a Intermediate Gearbox 42 Degree. The 42 degree gearbox is located at the base of the vertical fin. It provides 42 degree change of direction of the tail rotor dnveshaft The gearbox has a self-contained wet sump oil system. An oil level sight glass, filler cap, vent (fig 2-10) and magnetic chip detector are provided.

 b. Tail Rotor Gearbox 90 Degree. The 90 degree gearbox is located at the top of the vertical fin. It provides a 90 degree change of direction and gear reduction of the tail rotor driveshaft. The gearbox has a self-contained wet sump oil system. An oil level sight glass, vented filler cap (fig 2-10) and magnetic chip detector are provided.

2-41. Driveshafts.

 A Main Dnveshaft The main dnveshaft connects the engine output shaft to the transmission input drive quill.

 b. Tall Rotor Driveshaft The tail rotor dnveshaft consists of six dnveshaft and four hanger bearing assemblies. The assemblies and the 42 degree and 90 degree gearboxes connect the transmission tail rotor drive quill to the tail rotor.

2-42. Indicators and Caution Lights.

a. **Transmission Oil Pressure Indicator.** The TRANS OIL pressure indicator is located in the center area of the instrument panel (fig 24). It displays the transmission oil pressure in psi. Electrical power for the circuit is supplied from the 28 Vac bus and is protected by the XMSN circuit breaker in the ac circuit breaker panel.

b. **Transmission Oil Pressure Low Caution Light.** The XMSN OIL PRESS segment in the CAUTION panel will illuminate when the transmission oil pressure drops below about 30 psi. The circuit receives power from the essential bus. Circuit protection is supplied by the CAUTION LIGHTS circuit breaker.

c. **Transmission Oil Temperature Indicator.** The transmission oil temperature indicator is located in the center area of the instrument panel (Fig 24). The indicator displays the temperature of the transmission oil in degrees Celsius. The electrical circuit receives power from the essential bus and is protected by the TEMP IND ENG XMSN circuit breaker in the dc breaker panel. This is a wet bulb system dependent on fluid for valid indication.

d. **Transmission Oil Hot Caution Light.** The XMSN OIL HOT segment in the CAUTION panel will illuminate when the transmission oil temperature is above 110°C (230°F). The circuit receives power from the essential bus and is protected by the CAUTION LIGHTS circuit breaker. This is a wet bulb system dependent on fluid for valid indication.

e. **Transmission and Gearbox Chip Detector**

(l) **Chip Detector Caution Light.** Magnetic inserts are installed in the drain plugs of the transmission sump, 42 degree gearbox and the 90 degree gearbox. On helicopters equipped with ODDS, the transmission chip gap is integral to a full-flow debris monitor. When sufficient metal particles collect on the plugs to close the electrical circuit the CHIP DETECTOR segment In the CAUTION panel will illuminate. A self-closing, spring-loaded valve in chip detectors permits the magnetic probes to be removed without the loss of oil The circuit is powered by essential bus and protected by the CAUTION LIGHTS circuit breaker.

(2) **Chip Detector Switch.** A CHIP DET switch (fig 2-6) is installed on a pedestal mounted panel. The switch is labeled BOTH, XMSN, and TAIL ROTOR and is spring-loaded to the BOTH position. When the CHIP DETECTOR segment in the CAUTION panel lights up position the switch to XMSN, then TAIL ROTOR to determine the trouble area. CHIP DET caution light will remain on when a contaminated component is selected. The light will go out if the noncontaminated component is selected.

Section VIII. ROTORS

243. Main Rotor.

a. **Description.** The main rotor is a two bladed senm-rigid, seesaw type. The two types of rotor blades are metal and composite material and must not be intermixed. The two blades are connected to a common yoke by blade grips and pitch change bearing with tension straps to carry centrifugal forces. The rotor assembly is connected to the mast with a nut. The nut has provisions for hoisting the helicopter. A stabilizer bar is mounted on the trunnion 90 degrees to the main rotor. Blade pitch change is accomplished by movements of the collective and cyclic controls. The main rotor is driven by the transmission through the mast. The mast is tilted 5 degrees forward.

al. **Hub Spring.** As an aid in controlling rotor flapping a hub spring kit has been installed in the rotor system for those helicopters modified by MWO 55-1520-242-50-1. Two nonlinear elastometric springs are attached to a support affixed to the mast. The hub springs 2-10 Change 17 provide an additional margin of safety in the event of on inadvertent excursion of the helicopter beyond the approved flight envelope.

b. **RPM Indictor.** The rpm indicator is part of the dual tachometer (fig 24). The tachometer inner scale displays the rotor rpm. The inner scale pointers is marked with an 'R'.

2-44. Tail Rotor.
The tall rotor is a two-bladed semi-rigid delta-hinge type. Each blade is connected to a common yoke by a grip and pitch change bearings. The hub and blade assembly is mounted on the tail rotor shaft with a delta-hinge trunnion and a static stop to minimize rotor flapping. Blade pitch change is accomplished by movement of the anti-torque pedals which are connected to a pitch control system through the tail rotor (90 degree) gearbox. Blade pitch change servos to offset torque and provide heading control.

Section DC UTILITY SYSTEMS

2-45. Pilot Heater. The piton tube is equipped with an electrical heater (Figure 2-1). The PITOT HTR switch is on the overhead console panel (Figure 2-5). ON position activates the heater in the tube and prevents ice from forming m the pilot tube. OFF position de-activates the heater. The electrical circuit for the system receives power from the essential bus and is protected by the PITOT TUBE HTR circuit breaker.

2-46. Heated Blanket Receptacles. Two or six electrical receptacles are provided to supply 28 Vdc for heated blankets. They are mounted on the inside cabin roof structure aligned with the forward edge of the transmission support structure. The electrical circuit for the receptacles receive power from the nonessential bus. Circuit protection is provided by the HEATED BLANKET circuit breakers.

2-47. Data Case. A data case for maps, flight reports, etc., has been provided and is located at the aft end of the pedestal (Figure 2-5).

2-48. Blackout Curtains. Provisions have been made for Installing blackout curtains behind pilot and copilot seats and between forward and aft cabin sections. Other blackout curtains may be installed over both cabin door windows and window in removable doorpost.

2-49. Blood Bottle Hangers. Provisions have been made for six blood bottle hangers on the inside of the cabin roof structure within easy reach of the medical attendant station, for administration of blood to litter patients in flight.

2-50. External Cargo Rear View Mirror. A mirror may be installed under the right lower nose window to give the pilot clear visibility of the external cargo. This mirror may be removed and stowed in the heater compartment when provisions are installed.

2-51. Windshield Wiper.

WARNING

Do not operate the wiper on a dry or dirty windshield.

a Two windshield wipers are provided, one for the right section of the windshield and one for the left section of the windshield.

b. The wipers are driven by electric motors with electric power supplied by the dc electrical system. Circuit protection is provided by WINDSHIELD WIPER PILOT and WINDSHIELD WIPER COPILOT circuit breakers on the dc circuit breaker panel.

c The windshield wiper switches on the overhead console mounted MISC panel (Figure 2-5) have five positions: HIGH, MED, LOW, OFF, and PARK.

d The panel also has a selector which permits the operation of windshield wiper for pilot, copilot or both as desire.

Section X. HEATING AND VENTILATION

2-52. Ventilating System.

a Description The ventilating system consists of four independently controlled exterior air scoop ventilators. Two single orifice air scoops are located on * top of the cabin section, and two double orifice air scoops are on top of cabin. The amount of air entering the cabin through the ventilators is regulated by the butterfly valve control.

b. Operation Rotate butterfly valve control to desired position to provide outside air for flight.

2-53. Heating and Defrosting System. Three different types of heating and defrosting systems may be used on these helicopters. They are the bleed air heater, combustion heater, and the auxiliary exhaust heat exchanger. Each system is described separately in the following paragraphs.

a Bleed Air Heating and Defrosting System There are some differences in the bleed air heating systems in use. These differences are shown in Figure 2-7 with the following exception: helicopters prior to Serial No. 5-9565 have under-seat heater outlets; subsequent helicopters have aft pedestal outlets instead of the under-seat outlets. Heat is supplied to all bleed air heaters by the compressor bleed air system. Electric power for operation of the controls Is supplied from the essential bus and is protected by the CABIN HEATER CONT circuit breaker. On helicopters Serial No. 66-16868 through 70-16518, temperature is controlled by a thermostat located on the right doorpost. Helicopters Serial No. 71-20000 and subsequent are protected by two circuit breakers marked CABIN HEATER OUTLET VALVE and CABIN HEATER AIR VALVE. Refer to Figure 2-7 for controls and their function.

b Combustion Heating and Defrosting System With the combustion heater installed, a combination of bleed air heat and combustion heat is available for heating, Bleed air may be used for defrosting and combustion heat for heating, or combustion heat may be used for defrosting only with bleed air heat off. The MAIN FUEL switch must be ON, actuating the right boost pump, before fuel is available for combustion heater operation (Figure 2-6). A purge switch keeps the blowers operating after shutdown to prevent residual heat buildup. If blower air pressure drops too low, the combustion heater will stop automatically. An overheat switch also automatically turns the heater off in the event of malfunction. The starting cycle has to be repeated to start the combustion heater. Electric power to operate the heater controls is supplied from the essential bus and is protected by the CABIN HEATER CONT circuit breaker. Refer to Figure 2-7 for controls and their function.

c Auxiliary Exhaust Heater System The auxiliary exhaust heater system consists of an exhaust gas exchanger, and a bleed air driven fan for circulating ambient air through the heat exchanger. A mixing valve controls air to maintain the desired outlet temperature. The exhaust heater system controls consist of the cabin heating panel (Figure 2-7), a thermostat dial on the right door post and the air directing lever on the pedestal.

Section XI. ELECTRICAL POWER SUPPLY AND DISTRIBUTION SYSTEM

2-54. DC and AC Power Distribution. Figure 2-8 depicts the general schematic of the dc and ac power distribution system. The dc power is supplied by the battery, main generator, standby starter-generator, or the external power receptacle. The 115 Vac power is supplied by the main or spare inverters. The 28 Vac power Is supplied by a transformer which is powered by the inverter.

2-55. DC Power Supply System. The dc power supply system is a single conductor system with the negative leads of the generator grounded in the helicopter fuselage structure. The main generator voltage will vary from 27 to 28.5 depending on the average ambient temperature. In the event of a generator failure-the nonessential bus is automatically de-energized. The pilot may override the automatic action by positioning the NON-ESS BUS switch on the DC POWER control panel to MANUAL ON.

2-56. External Power Receptacle. The external power receptacle (Figure 2-1) transmits the ground power unit 28 Vdc power to the power distribution system. A 7.5 KW GPU is recommended for external starts.

the event of main generator failure.

2-57. Battery.

| WARNING |

If battery overheats, do not open battery compartment. Battery fluid will cause burns. An overheated battery may cause thermal burns and may explode.

The battery supplies approximately 2-4Vdc power to the power distribution system when the generators and external power receptacle are not in operation (Figure 2-1).

2-58. Main and Standby Starter-Generator. The 30 volt 300 ampere main generator is mounted on and driven by the transmission. A standby starter-generator, rated at 300 amperes is mounted on the engine accessory drive section. The standby furnishes generator power in

2-59. DC Power Indicators and Controls.

a. Main Generator Switch The MAIN GEN switch (fig 2-5) is on the overhead console DC POWER panel. In the ON position the main generator supplies power to the distribution system. The RESET position is spring-loaded to the OFF position. Momentarily holding the switch to RESET position will reset the main generator. The OFF position isolates the generator from the system. The circuit is protected by the GEN & BUS RESET in the dc circuit breaker panel.

b. Battery Switch The BAT switch is located on the DC POWER control panel (fig 2-5). ON position permits the battery to supply power. ON position also permits the battery to be charged by the generator. The OFF position isolates the battery from the system.

c. Starter-Generator Switch The STARTER GEN switch is located on the DC POWER control panel (fig 2-5).The START position permits the starter-generator to function as a starter. The STBY GEN position permits the starter-generator to function as a generator.

d. Nonessential Bus Switch. The NON-ESS BUS switch is located on the DC POWER control panel (fig 2-5). The NORMAL ON position permits the nonessential bus to receive dc power from the main generator. The MANUAL ON position permits the nonessential bus to receive power from the standby generator when the main generator is off line.

e. DC Voltmeter Selector Switch The VM switch is located on the DC POWER control panel (fig 2-5). The switch permits monitoring of voltage being delivered from any of the following; BAT, MAIN GEN, STBY GEN, ESS BUS, and NON-ESS BUS.

f. DC Voltmeter. The dc voltmeter is located in the center area of the instrument panel and is labeled VOLT DC (fig 2-4). Direct current voltage is indicated on the voltmeter as selected by the VM switch in the overhead console.

g. DC Loadmeters-Main and Standby. Two direct current loadmeters are mounted in the lower center area of the instrument panel (fig 24). The MAIN GEN loadmeter indicates the percentage of main generator rated capacity being used. The STBY GEN loadmeter indicates the percentage of standby generator rated capacity being used. The loadmeters will not indicate percentage when the generators are not operating.

2-60. DC Circuit Breaker Panel. The dc circuit breaker panel Is located in the overhead console (fig 2-5). In the "pushed in" position the circuit breakers provide circuit protection for dc equipment. In the "pulled out' position the circuit breakers deenergize the circuit. In the event of an overload the circuit breaker protecting that circuit will "pop out". Each breaker is labeled for the particular circuit it protects. Each applicable breaker is listed m the paragraph descanting the equipment it protects.

2-61. AC Power Supply System. Alternating current is supplied by two inverters (fig 2-8). They receive power from the essential bus and are controlled from the AC POWER control panel (fig 2-5).

24-62. Inverters. Either the main or spare inverter (at the pilots option) will supply the necessary 115 Vac to the distribution system. The inverters also supply 115 Vac to I the 28 volt ac transformer which in turn supplies 28 Vac to the necessary equipment. Circuit protection for the inverters is provided by the MAIN [NVTR PWR and SPARE NVTR PWR circuit breakers.

2-63. AC Power Indicators and Controls.

 a Inverter Switch. The INVTR switch is located on the AC POWER control panel in the overhead console (fig 2-5). The switch is normally in the MAIN ON position, to energize the main inverter. In the event of a main inverter failure the switch can be positioned to SPARE ON to energize the spare inverter. Electrical power to the INVTR switch is supplied from the essential TM 55-1520-210-10 bus. Circuit protection is provided by the INVTR CONT circuit breaker.

 b. AC Failure Caution Light. The INST INVERTER caution light will illuminate when the inverter m use fails or when the INVTR switch is m the OFF position.

 c AC Voltmeter Selector Switch. The AC PHASE VM switch is located on the AC POWER control panel (fig 2-5). The switch is used to select any one of the three phases of the 115 Vac three-phase current for monitoring on the ac voltmeter. The three positions on the switch are: AB, AC, and BC. Each position indicates that respective phase of the 115 Vac on the ac voltmeter

 d. AC Voltmeter. The ac voltmeter Is mounted on center area of the instrument panel (fig 24). The ac voltage output from the inverter (main or spare) is indicated on this instrument. The voltage indicated on any of the three selected positions should be 1 12 to 1 18 Vac 2-64. AC Circuit Breaker Panel. The ac circuit breaker panel is located on the right side of the pedestal panel (fig 2-5). The circuit breakers in the "pushed m" position provide circuit protection for the equipment. The breakers m the "pulled out" position de-energize the circuit. The breakers will pop out automatically m the event of a circuit overload. Each breaker is labeled for the particular circuit it protects. Each applicable breaker Is listed in the paragraph describing the equipment it protects.

Section XII. LIGHTING

NOTE

Visible light means the light is visible to the unaided eye. NVG light means the light is visible only with the aid of the Night Vision Goggles.

2-65. Position Lights. The position lights consist of eight visible lights and five NVG lights (fig 2-1).

 a Visible Position Light Lights.

 (1) Configurations. Two red lights are mounted on the left side of the fuselage, one above and one below the cabin door. Two green lights are mounted on the right side of the fuselage, one above and one below the cabin door. Two white lights are mounted on top of the fuselage just inboard of the red and green lights. One white light is mounted on the bottom center of the fuselage, and one white light is mounted on the

tailboom vertical fin. Electric power to operate the lights is supplied from the essential bus. Circuit protection is provided by the NAV LIGHTS circuit breaker in the dc circuit breaker panel. Some position lights may be protected by the FUS LIGHTS circuit breakers.

(2) Operation of Visible Position Lights. The position lights are controlled by the POSITION switches on the EXT LTS panel on the overhead console (fig 2-5). A three-position switch permits selection of STEADY, OFF, or FLASH. Another two-position switch control brilliance and is marked DIM and BRIGHT. When the three-position switch is in STEADY position, all eight navigation lights are Ilumunated. In FLASH position, on helicopters prior to Serial No. 64-13901, the colored lights illuminate alternately with the white lights. On later models only the colored lights and the aft white light flash.

b. NVG Poisson Lights

(I) Configuration. These lights are invisible to the unaided eye They are designed to provide observed aircraft position, attitude, and distance during covert formation NVG flight and other covert multi-aircraft NVG operations. Lights are located on the top left and right side above the jump door of each side and one each under the pilot and copilot doors. The rear NVG position light is located on a mount under the visible position light.

(2) Operation of the NYG Position Lights. The control panel for the lights is located in the frontmost panel of the left overhead console (fig 2-5). Five intensity positions are provided on the control panel; OFF, 1, 2, 3, 4, and BRT (BRIGHT). The lights are invisible to the unaided eye and should be checked or otherwise viewed with AN/PVS-5 AN/AVS-6 or AN/PVS-7 NVG. The visible position EXT LTS must be in the off position when the NVG lights are used. The NVG lights should be in the off position when not being used with NVG. The NVG lights do not flash. Circuit protection is provided by the NAV lights circuit breaker.

2-66. Anti-Collision Light.

a General. The anti-collision light is located on the top aft fuselage area (fig 2-I). Electric power to operate the light is supplied from the essential bus. Circuit protection is provided by the ANTI COLL LIGHT circuit breaker.

b. Operation The ON position of the ANTI COLL light switch illuminates the anti-collision light and starts rotation of the light (fig 2-5). OFF position de-energizes the light.

NOTE
The IR Band-Pass Filter (I.R. COVER) is authorized to be installed on either the landing light or the searchlight or may be removed from the aircraft for unaided (NON-NVG) flights dependent on operational considerations or requirements. Both the landing light and searchlight operation with the band-pass filter installed is the same as normal landing light and searchlight operation, except that NVGS must be worn to use it. The band-pass filter (P/N EGD-0931 1) shall not be used with lamps exceeding 250 watts.

2-67. Landing Light.

a General The landing light is flush-mounted to the underside of the fuselage (fig 2-1). It may be extended or retracted to improve forward illumination. Electric power to operate the system is supplied from the essential bus. Circuit protection is provided by the LDG LIGHT PWR and LDG SEARCH LIGHT CONT circuit breakers.

b. Operation Landing light switches are on the pilot collective lever switch box (fig 2-5). The ON position of the LDG LT switch causes the landing light to illuminate; OFF turns the light off. The EXT position of the LDG LT EXT OFF RETR extend the landing light to the desired position; RETR position retracts the light. The OFF position stops the light during extension or retraction. The light automatically stops at the full extend/retract position.

2-68. Searchlight.

a. General The searchlight is flush-mounted to the underside of the fuselage (fig 2-1). The light can be extended and retracted for search illumination. At any desired position in the extend or retract arc, the light may be stopped and rotated to the left or right. Electric power to operate the light is supplied from the essential bus. Circuit protection is provided by the SEARCHLIGHT PWR and LDG & SEARCHLIGHT CONT circuit breakers.

b Operation. The pilot SL switch ON position illuminates the light (fig 2-5). The OFF position deactivates the light. The STOW position retracts the light into the fuselage well.

2-69. Dome Lights.

NOTE
Aircraft modified by MWO 55-1520-210-5012 the dome light switch, if installed, is not connected.

a General The dome lights provide overhead lighting for the cabin area The forward light is controlled by the FWD switch on the DOME LT panel when installed on the overhead console. When the DOME LT panel is not installed the FWD and AFT DOME LT are controlled by the aft switch in the roof. The aft dome lights are controlled by the switch on the AFT DOME LTS panel on the roof. Electric power to operate the dome light is supplied from the 28 Vdc essential bus. Circuit protection is provided by the DOME LIGHTS circuit breaker.

b. Operation To operate the FWD dome light position the FWD switch to WHITE for white light NVG for green light and OFF to turn light off. The aft dome lights panel has two switches. The WHITElOFF NVG switch functions are the same as the FWD Switch. Rotation of the rheostat marked OFF/MED/BRT increases or decreases the brightness of the aft dome lights.

2-70. Cockpit Map Lights.

a General. Two cockpit lights (NVG Green) are provided, one above the pilot and one above the copilot (fig 2-5). Each light is controlled individually The lights receive power from the essential bus and are protected by the COCKPIT LIGHTS circuit breaker.

b. Operation Rheostat switches are part of each light assembly. Brightness is increased by turning the rheostat clockwise or dimmed by turning counterclockwise. These lights are for NVG or unaided eye use.

2-71. Instrument Lights.
The instrument lights control panel is located in the overhead console (fig 2-5). The panel contains six switch/rheostats for activating and controlling the brightness of the various instrument lights. Each switch/rheostat functions the same. The OFF position de-energizes the circuit, clockwise rotation increases brightness of the lights and counterclockwise rotation decreases brightness. The lights of all instruments receive electric power from the 28 Vdc essential bus, except the pilot attitude indicator, the pilot RMI, and the turn and slip indicators which receives 5 Vdc from the essential bus through resistor R24. On UH-IH helicopters equipped I with radar altimeters, the pilot attitude indicator, lot's RMI, and the turn and slip indicators receive the 5 Vdc from the pilot solid state device for providing 5 Vdc from the 28 Vdc essential bus. On UHI H helicopters equipped with radar altimeters, instruments are illuminated by 28 Vdc from the 28 Vdc essential bus. On UHI H aircraft the instrument lighting is protected by CONSOLE PEDLIGHTS, INST PANEL LIGHTS, and INST SEC LIGHTS circuit breakers. On UHI H helicopters equipped I with radar altimeters, the measurements lights are protected by the same circuit breakers as the UHI H aircraft, except the PILOT 5 VOLT LIGHTS circuit breaker is included in the protection. On UH-IH helicopters equipped with radar altimeters, the "HI" and "LO" indicators and the digital readout illumination levels on the radar altimeter are controlled by the pilot's and co-pilot's lighting rheostats.

a. Pilot Instrument Lights The pilot instrument lights furnish illumination for the following instruments; gas producer tachometer, torquemeter, exhaust temperature indicator, dual tachometer, airspeed indicator, clock, vertical velocity indicator, turn and slip indicator, altimeter, attitude indicator, radio magnetic indicator, standby compass, pilot collective switch box and radar altimeter (if installed). These lights are all on one circuit and are controlled by the switch/rheostat marked PILOT on the INST LTG control panel. DIM switch controls 23, page 3-33. Circuit protection is provided by the INST PANEL LIGHTS and PILOT 5 VOLT LIGHT (UH-IV) circuit breakers.

b. On UH-IV aircraft when the radar altimeter, AN/APNV-209 is installed, turning the pilot rheostat to OFF I provides full illumination to the digital readout and HI-LO warning lights on the pilot and copilot height indicators. This feature enables the pilot and copilot to read the displays during daytime operations.

c Copilot Instrument Lights. The copilot instrument lights furnish illumination for the instruments on the copilot section of the instrument panel. These instruments consist of an airspeed indicator, attitude indicator, radar altimeter (if installed on UH-1V), altimeter, vertical velocity indicator and radio magnetic indicator. The copilot instrument lights are all on one circuit, and are controlled by the switch/rheostat marked COPILOT on the INST LTG control panel. Circuit protection is provided by INST PANEL LIGHTS circuit breaker. Circuit protection is provided by INST PANEL LIGHTS and COPILOTS 5 VOLT LIGHTS circuit breaker.

d. Engine Instrument Lights. The engine instrument lights furnish illumination for the following instruments: transmission oil temperature, fuel quantity, transmission oil pressure, engine oil pressure, loadmeters, ac voltmeter, fuel pressure indicator, engine oil temperature gage, and dc voltmeter Each instruments is individually illuminated and control is accomplished by the switch/rheostat marked ENGINE on the INST LTG control panel. Circuit protection is provided by the INST PANEL LIGHTS circuit breaker

e Secondary Instrument Lights.
pre-flight check to meet the operators needs.

(1) The four secondary instrument lights are (spaced across the top of the instrument panel shield (fig 24). These lights furnish secondary illumination for the instrument panel face. The lights are activated and controlled by the switch/rheostat marked SEC on the INST LTG control panel. Circuit protection is provided by the INST SEC LIGHTS circuit breaker.

(2) Pedestal Utility Light. The pedestal utility light is provided for general use but also provides illumination for radios which are not illuminated. The light is operated by an OFF and ON switch on the panel on which it is mounted. The intensity of the Light is controllable from full bright to dim by a rheostat on the some panel. The light Is protected by the COCKPIT LTS circuit breaker.

f Emergency Lighning. Master Caution Fire Warning and Low RPM Indicators. The Master Caution, Fire, and Low RPM Warning Indicators are equipped with flip filters for use during NVG operations. The indicators must be uncovered for unaided operations during daylight and night.

2-72. Overhead Console Panel Lights. The overhead console panel lights furnish illumination for all overhead panels (fig 2-5). Each panel Is individually illuminated and control is accomplished by the switch/rheostat, marked CONSOLE on the INST LTG control panel. Circuit protection is provided by the CONSOLE PED LIGHTS circuit breaker.

NOTE
All "press-to-test" and cateye indicators are dimming type NVG green. Differentiation as to which indicator is illuminated must be determined by location since color coding is not used. In addition, the operator must return all indicators to the full bright position to assure visibility. On applicable indicators, dimming may be accomplished during

2-73. Pedestal Lights. The pedestal lights provide illumination for the control panels on the pedestal (fig 2-5). Most panels are individually illuminated and intensity control is accomplished by the switch/rheostat marked PED on the INST LTG control panel overhead. On some panels, the internal lighting has been discontinued. These panels are illuminated by the goosenecked utility light mounted to the rear of the pedestal. The illumination can be placed on any area of the pedestal by adjusting the gooseneck position. The intensity and ON-OFF function is controlled by the switch/rheostat mounted on the panel with the utility light. Circuit protection for the pedestal lighting is provided by the CONSOLE PED LIGHTS circuit breaker.

2-74. Transmission Oil Level Light. A transmission oil level light is installed to provide illumination to check the transmission oil sight gage. The circuit is activated by TM 55-1520-210-10 a button-type switch marked XMSN OIL LEVEL LT SWITCH and is located on the right side of the transmission forward bulkhead. Electric power for the transmission oil level light circuit is supplied by the battery. Circuit protection is provided by the battery voltmeter circuit breaker located in the oil cooler compartment or forward radio compartment.

2-75. Spare Lamp Kit. The spare lamp kit is located on the left side of the overhead console. The kit contains spare light bulb for the segment panel lights, the instrument lights, pedestal and overhead console lights, master caution and segment caution lights, all press-to-test lights, the rpm and fire warning lights, and the dome lights. All bulbs except the dome light bulbs may be replaced without the use of tools.

Section XIIL FLIGHT INSTRUCTIONS

2-76. Airspeed Indicators. The pilot and copilot airspeed indicators display the helicopter indicated airspeed (IAS) in knots (fig 2-4). The IAS is obtained by measuring the difference between impact air pressure from the pitot tube and the static air pressure from the static ports (fig 2-1).

NOTE
Indicated airspeeds are unreliable below 20 knots due to rotor downwash.

2-77. Turn and Slip Indicator. The turn and slip indicator displays the helicopter slip condition, direction of turn and rate of turn (fig 2-4). The ball displays the slip condition. The pointer displays the direction and rate of the turn. The circuit receives power from the essential bus and is protected by the TURN & SLIP IND circuit breaker.

2-78. Vertical Velocity Indicator. The vertical velocity indicator displays the helicopter ascent and descenated by the rate of atmospheric pressure change.

2-79. Pressure Altimeter. The pressure altimeter (ALT) furnishes direct readings of height above sea level and is actuated by the pitot static system (fig 24). Two altimeters are provided, one for the pilot and one for the copilot. (Refer to chapter 3 for operation.)

2-80. Attitude Indicators.
a. Pilot Attitude Indicator. The pilot attitude indicator is located on the pilot section of the instrument panel (fig 24). The indicator displays the pitch and roll attitude of the helicopter. An OFF warning flag in the indicator is exposed when electrical power to the system is removed. However, the OFF flag will not indicate internal system failure. The attitude indicator has an electrical trim in the roll axis m addition to the standard pitch trim. The attitude indicator is operated by 115 Vac power, supplied by the inverter. Circuit protection is provided by the PILOT ATTD circuit breakers in the ac circuit breaker panel.

CAUTION
The copilot attitude indicator shall be caged only in a straight and level attitude. The caging knob shall never be pulled violently.

b. Copilot Attitude Indicator The copilot attitude indicator is located in the copilot section of the instrument panel (fig 2-4). It is operated by 115 Vac power supplied by the inverter. Circuit protection is provided by the COPILOT ATITD circuit breakers in the ac circuit breaker panel. In a climb or dive exceeding 27 degrees of pitch the horizontal bar will stop at the top or bottom of the case and the sphere then becomes the reference. The copilot attitude indicator may be caged manually by pulling the PULL TO CAGE knob smoothly away from the face of the instrument to the limit of Its travel and then releasing quickly.

2-81. Free-Air Temperature Indicator (FAT). The free-air temperature indicator is located at the top center area of the windshield (fig 2-5). The indicator displays the free air temperature m degrees Celsius.

2-82. Standby Compass. The standby (magnetic) compass is mounted in a bracket at the center right edge of the instrument panel (fig 24). A deviation m magnetic compass indications will occur when the landing light, searchlights, or pitot heat are turned on.

2-83. Fire Detector Warning System. A FIRE WARNING light is located in the upper nght section of the instrument panel (fig 24). The press to test (FIRE DETECTOR TEST) test switch is located to the left of the fire warning light. Excessive heat m the engine compartment causes the FIRE light to illuminate. Pressing the press-to-test switch also causes the light to Illuminate. Electric power for the circuit is supplied from the 28 Vdc essential bus and is protected by the FIRE DET circuit breaker.

2-84. Master Caution System.
NOTE
Aircraft are equipped with NVG compatibility devices, flip-filters for the "Master Caution," "Low RPM," and "Fire Warning" indicators. These filters must be flipped over away from the indicators during visual flight conditions. A slide drawer filter is also provided for the caution panel. This filter must be stowed in the pedestal stowing position when not being used for NVG flight. To stow, lift the front end of the filter to the vertical position and allow the filter to gently slide into the vertical cavity in the pedestal above the caution panel.

a NVG Flight Conditions.

(1) Follow all procedures used for visual flight conditions, except the "Master Caution," 'Low RPM," and 'Fire Warning flip-filters and "Caution Panel" slide drawer filter must be placed over the indicators.

(2) Flip instrument panel indicator filters over indicators and press lightly in place to avoid light leakage around edges.

(3) Gently pull the slide drawer filter up from stowed position until it is at the top vertical position and place it over the caution panel.

b. Master Caution Indicator The master caution indicator light on the instrument panel will Illuminate when fault conditions occur (figure 2-4). This illumination alerts the pilot and copilot to check the caution panel for the specific fault condition.

c. Caution Panel. The CAUTION panel is located on the pilot side of the pedestal (figure 2-9). Worded segments illuminate to identify specific fault conditions. The worded segments are readable only when the light illuminates. When a light illuminates, flickers or full illumination, it indicates a fault condition. Refer to figure 2-9 for explanation of the fault conditions.

(1) *Bright-Dim Switch* The BRIGHT-DIM switch on the CAUTION panel permits the pilot to manually select a bright or dimmed condition for all the individual worded segments and the master caution indicator. The dimming switch position will work only when the pilot instrument lights are on. The master caution system lights will be in bright illumination after each initial application of electrical power, when the pilot instrument lights are turned OFF, or a loss of power from the dc essential bus occurs.

(2) *Reset-Test Switch* The RESET-TEST switch on the CAUTION panel enables the pilot to manually reset and test the master caution system. Momentarily placing the switch in the RESET position, extinguishes and resets the master caution indicator light so it will again illuminate should another fault condition occur. Momentarily placing the switch in TEST position will

cause the illumination of all the individually worded segments and the master caution indicator. Only the lamp circuitry is tested; the condition circuitry is not. Testing of the system will not change any particular combination of fault indications which might exist prior to testing. The worded segments will remain illuminated as long as fault condition or conditions exist, unless the segment is rotated.

d. Electrical Power. Electric power for the master caution system is supplied from the essential bus. Circuit protection is provided by the CAUTION LIGHTS circuit breakers.

2-85. RPM High-Low Limit Warning System. The rpm high-low limit warning system provides the pilot with an immediate warning of high and low rotor or engine rpm. Main components of the system are a detector unit, warning light and audio signal circuit, low RPM AUDIO/OFF switch, and electrical wiring and connectors. The warning light and audio warning signal systems are activated when any one of the following rpm conditions exist:

a Warning light only:
(1) For rotor rpm of 329-339 (High Warning).

(2) For rotor rpm of 300-310 (Low Warning).

(3) For engine rpm of 6100-6300 (Low Warning).

(4) Loss of signal (circuit failure) from either rotor tachometer generator or power turbine tachometer generator.

b. Warning light and audio warning signal combination:

(1) For rotor rpm of 300-310 and engine rpm of 6100-6300 (Low Warning).

(2) Loss of signal (circuit failure) from both rotor tachometer generator and power turbine tachometer generator.

c *Rotor Tachometer Generator and Power Turbine* Tachometer Generator. The rotor tachometer generator and power turbine tachometer generator both send signals to the high-low rpm warning light and audio warning circuits. When the warning light only is energized determine the cause of indication by checking the torquemeter and cross referencing other engine instruments. A normal indication signifies that the engine is functioning properly and that there is a tachometer generator failure or an open circuit to the warning system rather than an actual engine failure. Electrical power for system operation is supplied by the 28 Vdc essential bus.

d. *Light - High Low Limit RPM Warning.* The high low warning light (fig 24) is located on the instrument panel. This light illuminates to provide a visual warning of low rotor rpm low engine rpm or high rotor rpm.

e. *Switch - LOW RPM A UDIO/OFF.* The LOW RPM AUDIO/OFF switch is on the engine control panel (fig 2-6). When in OFF position the switch prevents the audio warning signal from functioning during engine starting. Current production helicopters use a spring-loaded switch. When the switch has been manually turned off for engine starting It will automatically return to the AUDIO position when normal operating range is reached.

2-85.1. Oil Debris Detection System (ODDS).

ODDS improves oil filtration and reduces nuisance chip indications caused by normal wear particles on detector gaps. When a chip gap is bridged by conductive particles, a power module provides an electrical pulse which burns away normal wear particles.

a. *Powerplant ODDS Components.*

(1) Oil separator (Lubriclone) located in engine service compartment.

(2) Oil Filter, equipped with 3-micron filter element, located in engine service compartment.

(3) Chip detector located at bottom of oil separator. Detector is wired to Engine Chip Detector Caution Capsule.

b. *Drive System ODDS Components.*

(1) Full-Flow Debris Monitor in transmission sump replaces wafer disc filter.

(2) External Filter with 3-micron element located in Cargo Sling Compartment (hell hole). Filter replaces existing 25 micron external filter.

(3) Three chip detectors, one in debris monitor, and one each in 42 and 90 degree gearboxes. Detectors are wired to the Chip Detector Caution Capsule.

c. *Electrical System Component.* Power module located in overhead in cabin provides electrical power to pulse (burn) away ferrous (iron, steel) debris less than 0.005 inch in cross section. Larger debris will not pulse away, but bridges chip gap and closes the circuit to caution capsule.

Section XIV. SERVICUNG PARKING AND MOORING

2-86. Servicing

a. *Servicing Diagram* Refer to figure 2-10.

b. *Approved Military Fuels, Oils and Fluids.* Refer to table 2 -1.

c. *Fuel Sample.* Settling time for AVGAS is 15 minutes per foot of tank depth and one hour per foot depth for Jet (JP) fuels. Allow the fuel to settle for the prescribed period before any fuel samples are taken. Tank depth is about 29 inches.

2-87. Fuel System Servicing

Servicing personnel shall comply with all safety precautions and procedures specified in FM 1068 Aircraft Refueling Field Manual.

a. Refer to table 2-1 for fuel tank capacities.
b. Refer to table 2-1 for approved fuel.

c The helicopter is serviced as follows:

(1) Refer to figure 2-10 for fuel filler location.

(2) Assure that fire guard is in position with fire extinguisher

(3) Ground servicing unit to ground stake.

(4) Ground servicing unit to helicopter.

(5) Ground fuel nozzle to ground receptacle located adjacent to fuel receptacle on helicopter.

CAUTION

Ensure that servicing unit pressure is not above 125 psi while refueling.

(6) Closed circuit.

(a) Remove fuel filler cap and assure that refueling module is in locked position. Refer to figure 2-10.

(b) Remove nozzle cap and insert nozzle into fuel receptacle and lock into position.

(c) Activate flow control handle to ON or FLOW position. Fuel flow will automatically shut off when fuel cell is full. Just prior to normal shut off fuel flow may cycle several times as maximum fuel level is reached.

(d) Assure that flow control handle is in OFF or NO FLOW position and remove nozzle.

(7) Gravity or open port:

(a) Remove fuel filler cap.

(b) Using latch tool attached to filler cap cable open refueling module

(c) Remove nozzle cap and insert nozzle into fuel receptacle.

(d) Fill for specified level.

(e) Remove nozzle

(f) Close refueling module by pulling cable until latch Is in locked position. Refer to figure 2-10.

(8) Replace fuel nozzle cap.

(9) Replace fuel filler cap.

(10) Disconnect fuel nozzle ground.

(11) Disconnect ground from helicopter to servicing unit

(12) Disconnect servicing unit ground from ground stake.

(13) Return fire extinguisher to designated location.

d. Rapid (Hot) Refueling.

(1) Before rapid refueling.

(a) Throttle - idle.

(b) FORCE TRIM - ON or controls frictioned.

(c) Refuel as described in paragraph c. above.

(2) During rapid refueling. A crewmember should observe the refueling operation (performed by authorized refueling personnel) and stand fire guard as required. One crewmember shall remain in the helicopter to monitor controls. Only emergency radio transmission should be made during RAPID refueling.

(3) After rapid refueling, the pilot shall be advised by the refueling crew that fuel cap is secure and grounding cables have been removed.

2-88. Approved Commercial Fuel, Oils, and Fluids.

a. Fuels. Refer to table 2-1.
b. Oils. Refer to table 2-1.
c Fluids. Refer to table 2-1

2-89. Use of Fuels.

a There are no special limitations on the use of Army standard or alternate fuels but certain limitations are imposed when emergency fuels used. A fuel mixture which contains over 10 percent leaded gasoline shall be recorded as all leaded gasoline. The use of emergency fuels shall be recorded m the FAULT/REMARKS column of DA Form 2408- 13, Aircraft Maintenance and Inspection Record noting the type of fuel, additives, and duration of operation.

b. When mixing of fuel in helicopter tanks or changing from one type of authorized fuel to another, for example, JP-4 to JP-5, it is not necessary to drain the helicopter fuel system before adding the new fuel

Table 2-1
Servicing Table of Approved Fuels, Oils, and Fluids.

System	Specification
Fuel MIL-	T-5624 (JP4)a
Crashworthy System- Total: 208 5 U.S Gallons (789 2 liter). Usable: 206.5 U S gallons (781 6 liters) Internal Auxiliary Tanks- Usable 300 U S gallons (1135.5 liters)	
Oil:	
Engine	MIL-L-2369934
	*MIL-L-780824
Transmission	MIL-L-2369934
	DOD-L-8573434
	*MIL-L-7808 24
42' Gearbox	MIL-L-2369934
	DOD-L-8513424
	*MIL-L-780824
90' Gearbox	MIL-L-2369934
	DOD-L-8573424
	*MIL-L-780824
Hydraulic System	MIL-H- 560667
	*MIL-H-8328267
Main Rotor Grip	MILL-4615267
	MIL-L-2369934
	*MIL-L,780824
	MIL,L-210489
	MIL-L-461789
Pillow Block Oil	MIL-L2369934
	MIL-L7808 248
	*MIL-L,-210489
	MIL-L-4615289
	MIL-L-4616789

FOOTNOTES
Army Standard fuel is MIL-T-5624 (IP-4) NATO code is F-40
Alternate fuels are MILT-5624 (IP-5) (NATO F-44) and MIL-T-83133 (P-8) (NATO F-34). Emergency fuel is MIL-G-5572 (any AV gas) (NATO F-12, F-18, F-22). Refer to TM 55-9150-200-24.
The helicopter shall not be flown when emergency fuel has been used for a total cumulative time of 50 hours The engine manual also limits operation to 25 hours when TCP s m the fuel.

CAUTION

* Lubrication oil made to MIL-L-7808 by Shell Oil Company under their part number 307, qualification number 7D-1 shall not be used in the engine or aircraft systems. It contains additives which are harmful to seals in the system.

2*MIL-L-7808 NATO code is 0-148. For use in ambient temperatures below minus 32'C/25'F. May be l used when MIL-L-23699 or DOD-L-85734 oil is not available. Not for use m main rotor hub P/N 204-012-101-31

CAUTION

Under no circumstances shall MIL-L-23699 or DOD-L-85734 oil be used in ambient temperatures below minus 32°C/25'F.

3 MIL-L-23699 NATO code Is O-156 For use in ambient temperatures above minus 32' C/25'F. Not for use in main rotor hub P/N 204-012-101-31.

4 Do not mix MI-LL-2104, MI-L-46152, MI L-46167, MIL-L-23699, DOD-L-85734, and or MILL-7808 oils, except during an emergency. If the oils are mixed the system shall be flushed within six hours and filled with the proper oil. An entry on DA Form 2408-13 is required when the oils are mixed.

5 MILH-5606 NATO code is H-515. For use in ambient temperatures below minus 35'C/30'F (Refer to TB 55-1500-344-25)

6 For use In ambient temperatures above minus 35°C/30°F.

WARNING

Prolonged contact with hydraulic fluid or its mist can irritate eyes and skin. After any prolonged contact with skin, immediately wash contacted area with soap and water. If liquid contacts eyes, flush immediately with clear water. If liquid is swallowed, do not induce vomiting; get immediate medical attention. When fluid is decomposed by heating, toxic gases are released.

7 It is not advisable to mix MIL-H-5606 and MIL-83282 fluids, except during an emergency. An entry on DA Form 2408-13 is required when the fluids are mixed. When changing from MIL-H-5606 to MILH-83282, not more than two percent of MIL-H-5606 may be present in the system.

8 Refer to stencil on grip assembly to determine proper lubrication requirements.

9 MIL-2104, MIL-L-46152, and MILL-46167, must be used in hub P/N 204-012-101-31 as follows:

Average Temp Range	Specifications
+5°C and above	MILL-2104, Grade 40, NATO Code 0-230
-18°C to + 5°C	MIL2104, Grade 30, NATO Code 0-230 or MIL-L6152, Grade 30
-29°C to -18°C	MILL-2104, Grade 10, NATO Code 0-230 or MIL-L46152, Grade 10W30
-54'C to -20°C	MILL-46167, DEXRON II Aut6matlc transmission fluid.

Approved domestic commercial fuels (spec. ASTM- D-1655-70: Manufacturer's designation-

Jet B-JP4 Type	Jet A-JP5 Type	Jet A-1-JP8 Type
American JP4	American Type A	
AeroJet B	AeroJet A	AeroJet A-i
		Richfield A
B.P.A.T.G.		B.PA.T K
Caltex let B		Caltex Jet A-1
	CITGO A	
Conoco IJP-4	Conoco Jet-50	Conoco Jet-60
Gulf let B		Gulf let A Gulf Jet A-
EXXON Turbo Fuel B	EXXON A	EXXON A-I
Mobil Jet B	Mobil Jet A	Mobil Jet A-I
Philjet JP-4	PhilJet A-50	
Aeroshell JP4	Aeroshell 640	Aeroshell 650
	SuperJet A	Superjet A-1
	Jet A Kerosine	Jet A 1Kerosime
Chevron B	Chevron A-50	Chevron A-1
Texaco Avjet B	Avjet A	AvJet A-I
Union IP4	76 Turbine Fuel	

Change 17   2-21

Approved foreign commercial fuels:

Country	F40	F-44
Belgium	BA-PF-2B	
Canada	3GP-22F	3-6P-24e
Denmark	JP-4 MIL-T-5624	
France	Air 3407A	
Germany (West)	VTL-9130-006	UTL 9130-007/ UTL 9130-010
Greece	JP4 MIL-T-5624	
Italy	AA-M-C-1421	AMC-143
Netherlands	JP-4 MIL-T-5624	D. Eng Rd 2493
Norway	JP4 MIL-T-5624	
Portugal	JP-4 MILT-5624	
Turkey	YP4 MIL-T-5624	
Untied Kingdom (Britain)	D. Eng Rd 2454	E. Eng Rd 2498

NOTE: Anti-icing and Biocidal Additive for Commercial Turbine Engine Fuel - The fuel system icing inhibitor shall conform to MIL-I-27686 The additive provides anti-icing protection and also functions as a biocide to kill microbial growths in helicopter fuel systems. Icing microbial conforming to MIL-I-27686 shall be added to commercial fuel, not containing an Icing inhibitor, during refueling operations regardless of ambient temperatures. Refueling operations shall be accomplished m accordance with accepted commercial procedures. Commercial product 'PRIST' conforms to MIL-I-27686.

Approved domestic commercial oils for Mil-L-7808:
Manufacturers designation-PQ Turbine Oil 8365 ESSO/ENCO Turbo Oil 2389 RM- 184A/RM-201A151

CAUTION

Do not use Shell Oil Co, part No. 307, qualification No. 7D-1 oil (MIL-L-7808). It can be harmful to seals made of silicone.

Approved domestic commercial oils for MIL-L-23699:
Manufacturers designation-PQ Turbine Lubricant 5247/6423/6700/7731/8878/9595

Brayco 899/899-G/899-S
Castrol 205
Jet Engine Oil 5
STO-21919/STO-21919A/STD-6530
HATCOL 3211/3611
Turbo Oil 2380 (WS-6000)/2395 (W-6459)2392/2393
Mobil Jet II RM-139A/Mobil Jet II RM-147A/Avrex S
Turbo260/Avrex S
Turbo 265
Royco 899 (C-915)/899SC/Stauffer Jet II
Aeroshell Turbine Oil 500
Aeroshell Turbine Oil 550
Chevron Jet Engine Oil 5
Stauffer 6924/Jet I
SATO 7377n730,TL-8090

Approved domestic commercial fluids for MIL-H-5606:
Manufacturers designation-
"PO" 4226
Brayco 757B
Brayco 756C
Brayco 7561D
Hyspin A
Univis J41
Aero HFB
Petrofluid 5606B
Petrofluid 4607
Royco 756C/D
Royco 782
XSL 7828
PED 3565
PED 3337
TL-5874
Aero Hydroil 500
YT-283
FP-221

Approved domestic commercial fluids for MIL-H-83282:
Drayco Micronic 882
Hanover R-2
HF 832
XRM 230A
XRM 231A

TM 55-1520-210-10

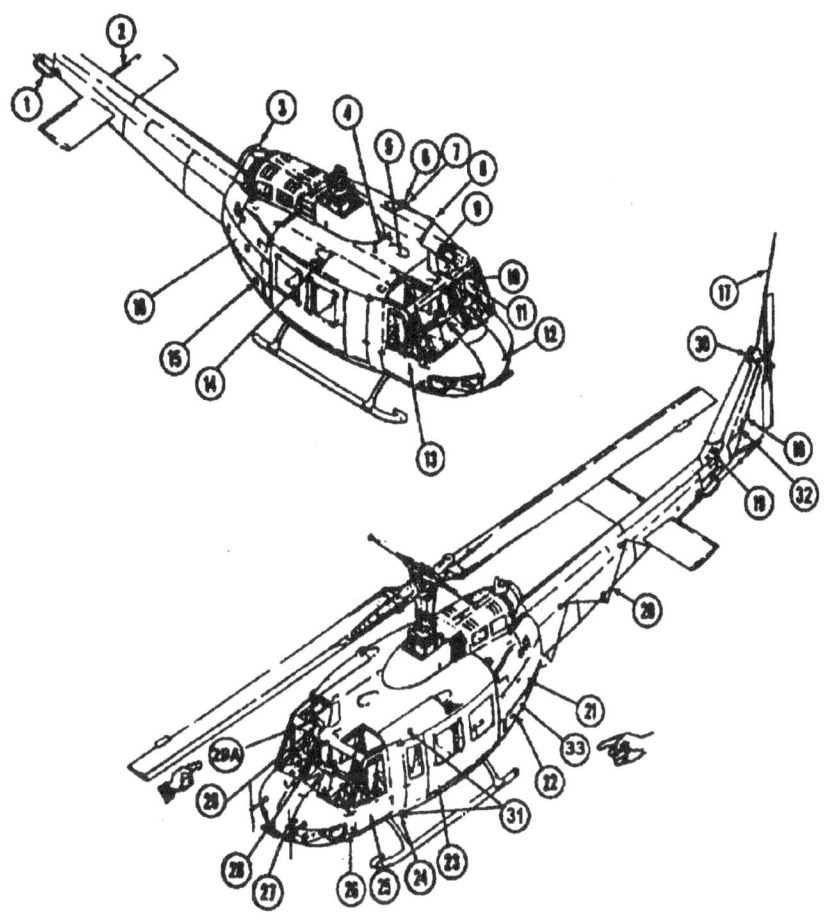

1	VHF navigation (Omni) antenna	18	Aft position light (White)
2	Synchronized elevator	19	42 degree gearbox
3	Anti-collision light	20	HF long wire antenna
4	FM homing antenna No.1	21	Electrical compartment access door
5	Loop (ADF) antenna (Removed W/MWO 1-1620-210-50-30)	22	Aft radio compartment access doors
6	Position light (White)	23	Cabin door
7	Position light (Red)	24	Position Light (Red)
8	FM communications antenna No.2	25	Copilot door
9	VHF/UHF antenna	26	Static port
10	Pitot tube	27	Pitot tube
11	WSPA Windshield Wiper Deflector	28	WSPS Windshield Deflector
12	Radio compartment and fwd battery location assess door	29	WSPS Upper Cutter
13	Pilot door	29A	AN/ASN-175 antenna
14	Position fights (Green upper and lower)	30	90 degree gearbox
15	Heater compartment access door	31	Position Light (NVG)
16	Oil cook fan access door	32	Aft position light (NVG)
17	FM communications antenna No. 1	33	KY - 100 Processor

Figure 2-1. General Arrangement Diagram - Typical (Sheet 1 of 2)

Change 18   2-23

TM 56-1520-210-10

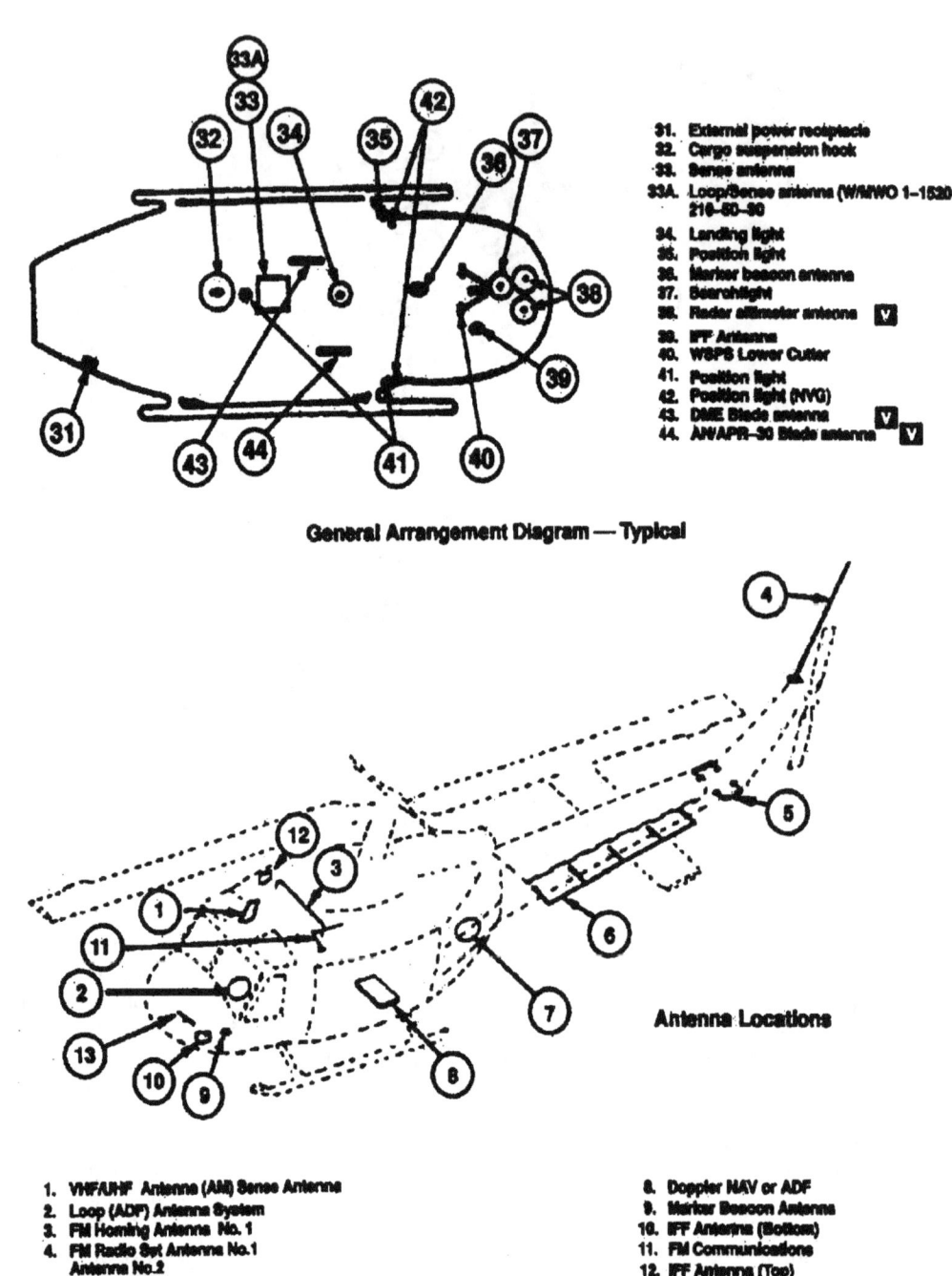

31. External power receptacle
32. Cargo suspension hook
33. Sense antenna
33A. Loop/Sense antenna (W/MWO 1-1520-210-50-30)
34. Landing light
35. Position light
36. Marker beacon antenna
37. Searchlight
38. Radar altimeter antenna [V]
39. IFF Antenna
40. WSPS Lower Cutter
41. Position light
42. Position light (NVG)
43. DME Blade antenna [V]
44. AN/APR-39 Blade antenna [V]

General Arrangement Diagram — Typical

Antenna Locations

1. VHF/UHF Antenna (AM) Sense Antenna
2. Loop (ADF) Antenna System
3. FM Homing Antenna No. 1
4. FM Radio Set Antenna No.1 Antenna No.2
5. VHF Navigation (Omni) Antenna System
6. HF Shorted Loop Antenna (MWO-1-1520-210-50-33)
7. Sense Antenna, ADF Sense, when Doppler NAV installed
8. Doppler NAV or ADF
9. Marker Beacon Antenna
10. IFF Antenna (Bottom)
11. FM Communications
12. IFF Antenna (Top)
13. Glideslope

Figure 2-1. General Arrangement Diagram Typical (Sheet 2 of 2)

TM 55-1520-210-10

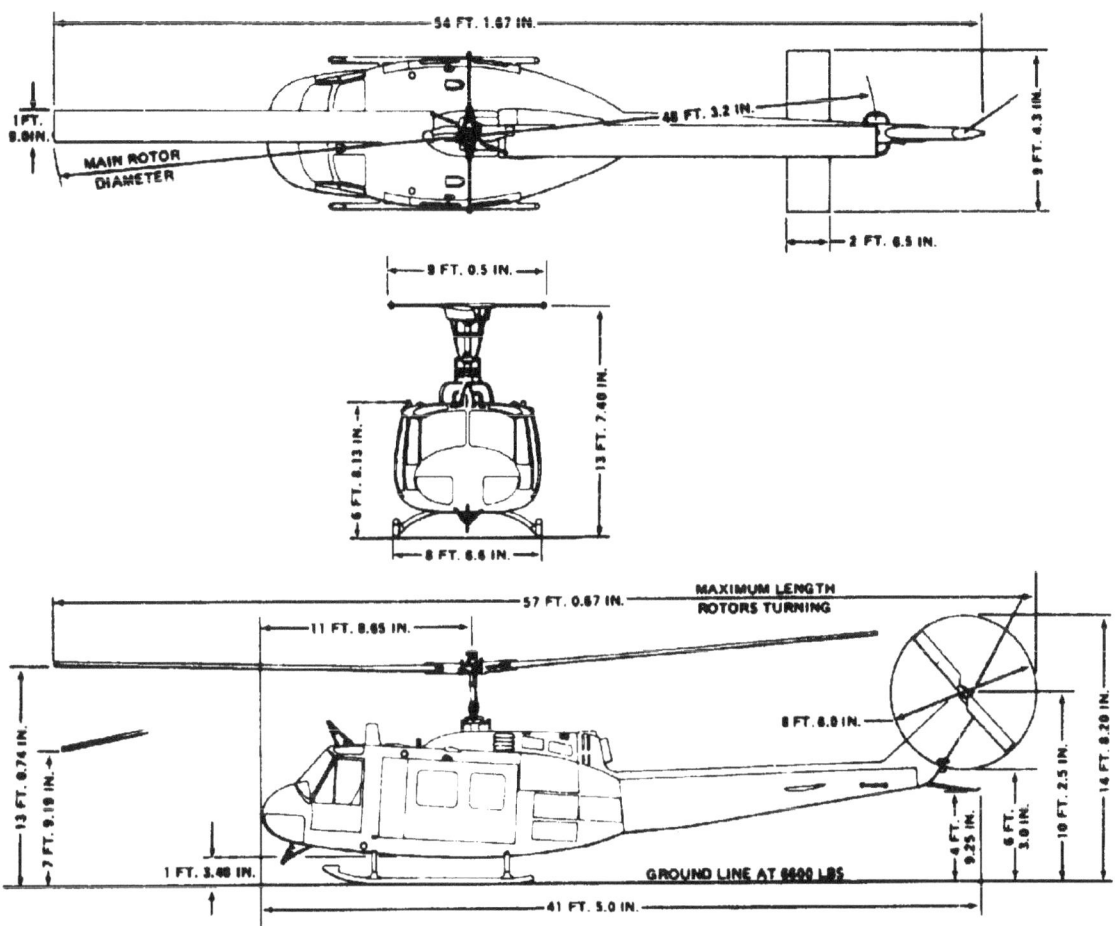

Figure 2-2. Principal Dimensions Diagram–Typical

TM 55-1520-210-10

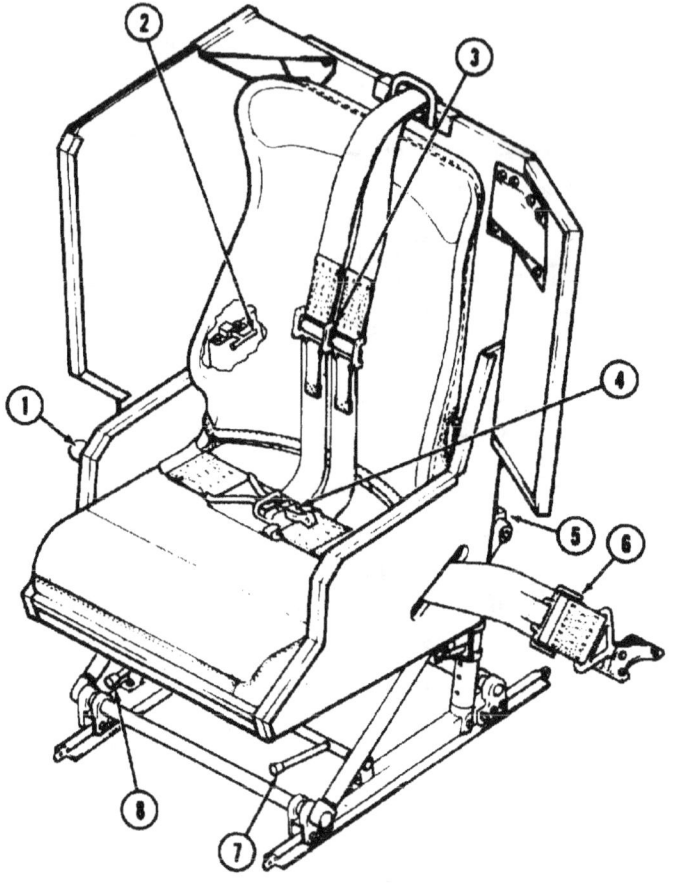

1. Shoulder harness lock - unlock control
2. Armor plate adjustment lock
3. Shoulder harness adjuster
4. Seat bolt latch
5. Quick release
6. Seat bolt adjuster
7. Seat adjustment fore and aft
8. Seat adjustment vertical

Figure 2-3. Pilot/Copilot Seat–Typical

2-26

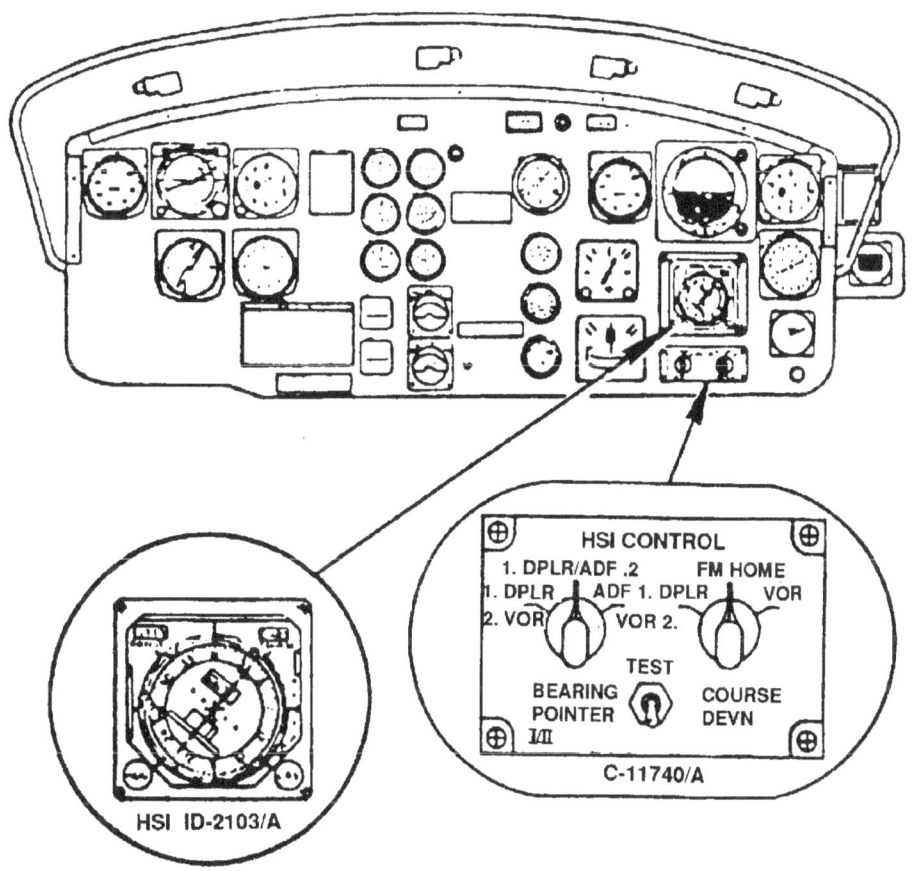

Figure 2-4. Instrument Panel (Typical)(Sheet 1 of 2)

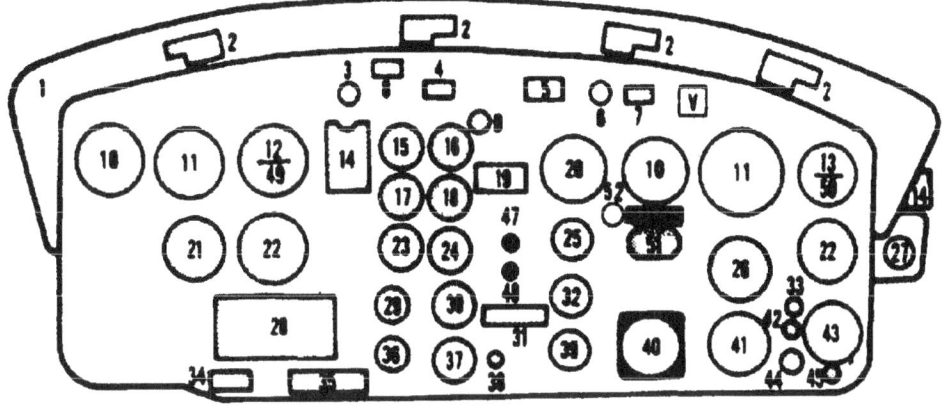

1. Glareshield
2. Secondary Lights
3. Engine INlet Filter Clogged Warning Light
4. Master Caution
5. RPM Warning Light
6. Fire Detector Test Switch
7. Fire Warning Indicator Light
8. Radio Call Designator
9. Fuel Gage Test Switch
10. Airspeed Indicator
11. Attitude Indicator
12. Altimeter Indicator (AAU-32/A)
13. Altimeter Indicator (AAU-31/A)
14. Compass Correction Card Holder
15. Fuel Pressure Indicator
16. Fuel Quantity Indicator
17. Engine Oil Pressure Indicator
18. Engine Oil Temperature Indicator
19. Cargo Caution Decal
20. Dual Tachometer
21. Radio Compass Indicator
22. Vertical Velocity Indicator
23. Transmission Oil Pressure Indicator
24. Transmission Oil Temperature Indicator
25. Torquemeter Indicator
26. Radio Compass Indicator
27. Magnetic Compass
28. Operating Limits Decal
29. Main Generator Loadmeter
30. DC Voltmeter
31. Engine Caution Decal
32. Gas Producer Tachometer Indicator
33. Marker Beacon Light
34. Engine Installation Decal
35. Transmitter Selector Decal
36. Standby Generator Loadmeter
37. AC Voltmeter
38. Compass Slaving Switch
39. Exhaust Gas Temperature Indicator
40. Turn and Slip Indicator
41. Course Deviation Indicator
42. Marker Beacon Sensing Switch
43. Clock
44. Marker Beacon Volume Control
45. Cargo Release Armed Light
47. IFF Code Hold Light
48. IFF Code Hold Switch
49. ⑦ Receiver-Transmitter, Height Indicator
50. ⑦ Height Indicator Remote
51. ⑦ DME Indicator
52. ⑦ DME Hold Light

Figure 2-4. Instrument Panel (Typical) (Sheet 2 of 2)

TM 55-1520-210-10

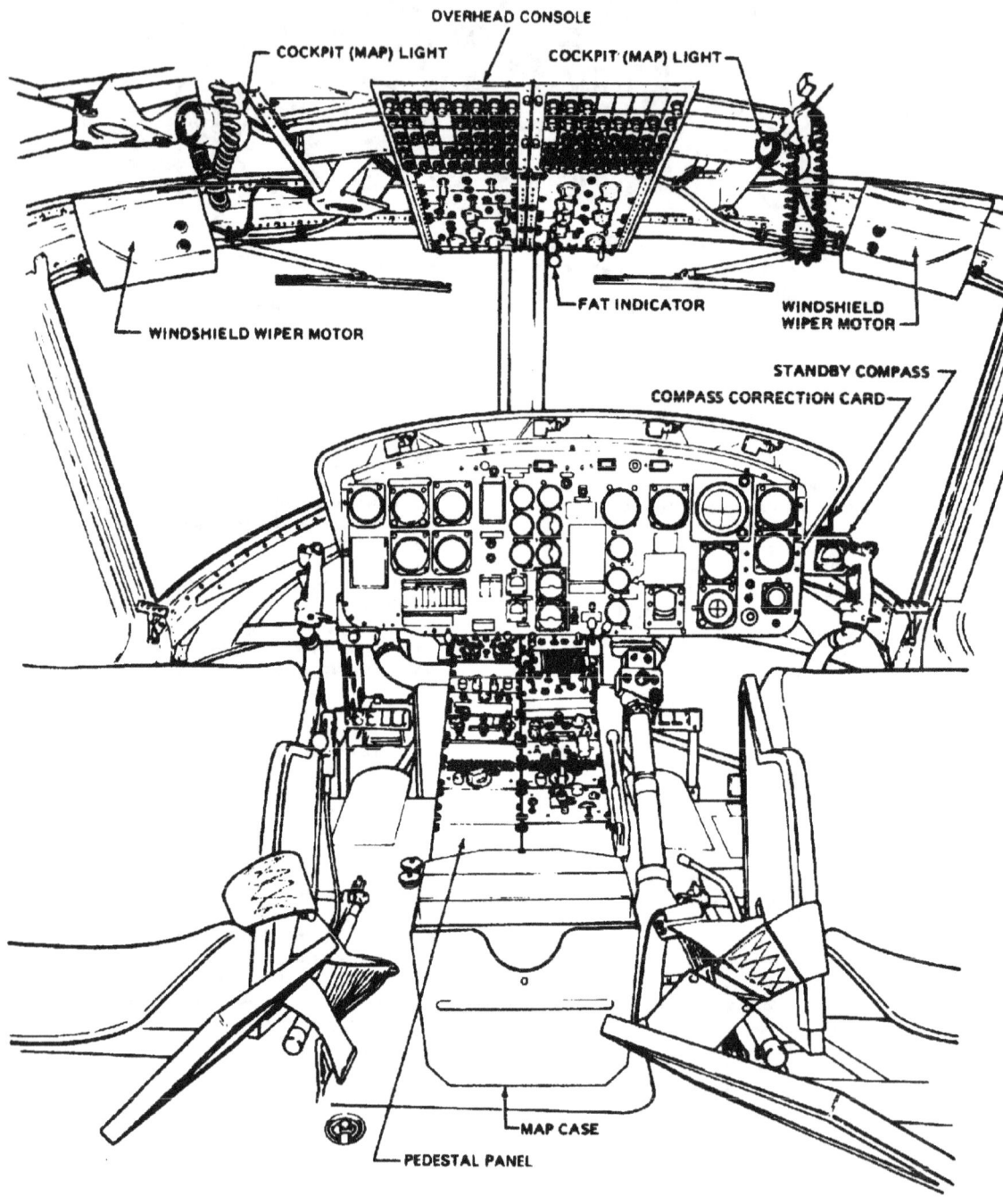

Figure 2-5. Crew Compartment-Typical (Sheet 1 of 3)

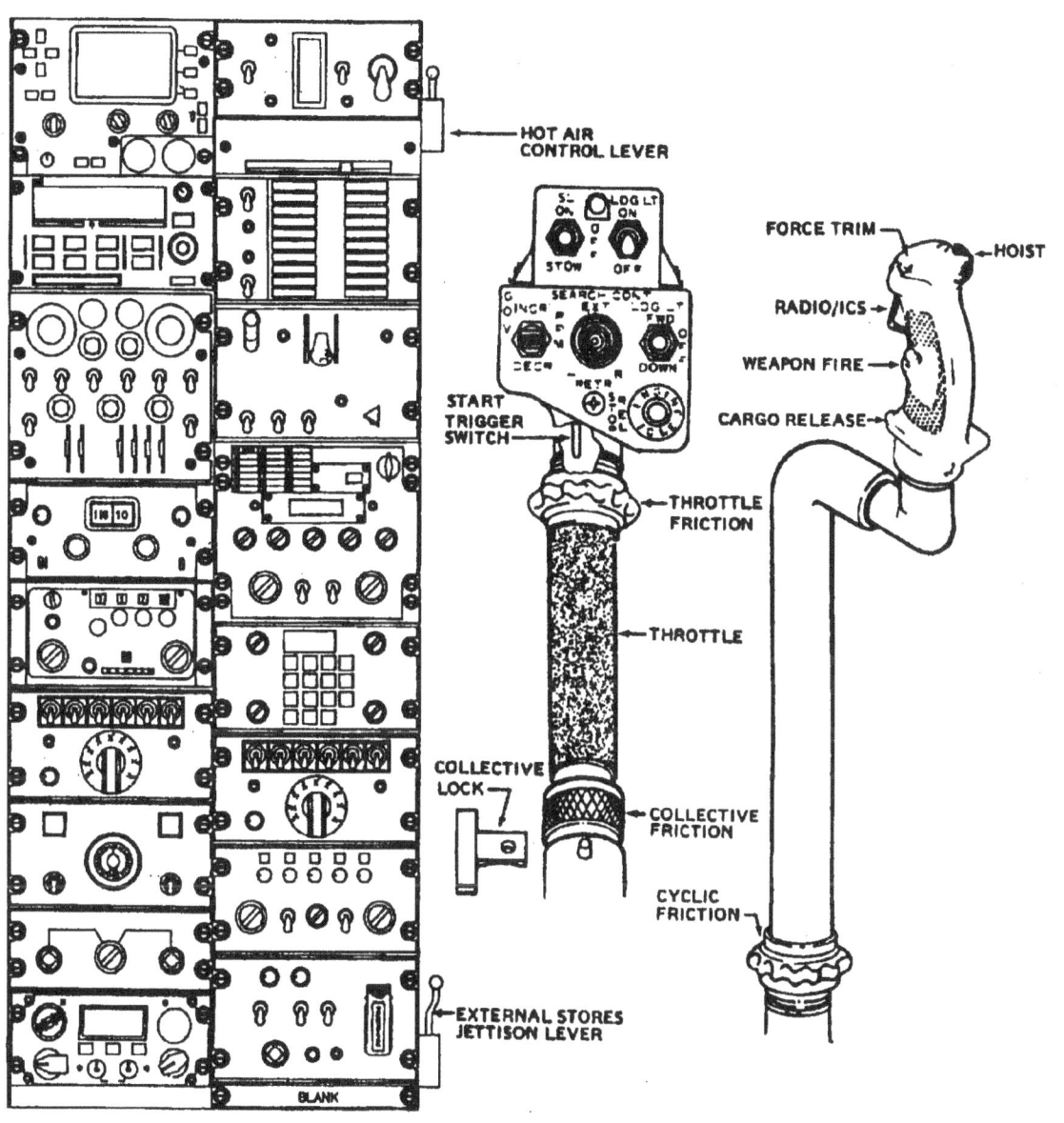

Figure 2-5. Crew Compartment - Typical (Sheet 2 of 3)

TM 55-1520-210-10

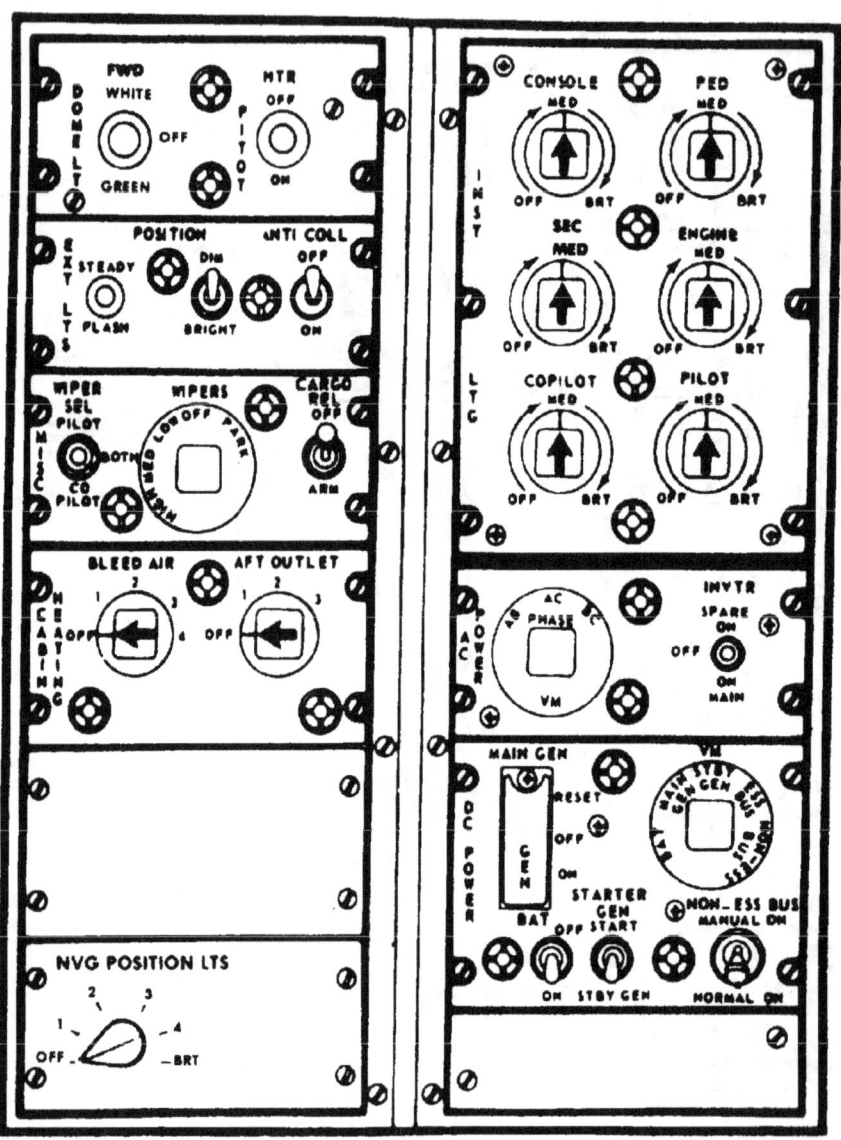

Figure 2-5. Overhead Console–Typical (Sheet 3 of 3)

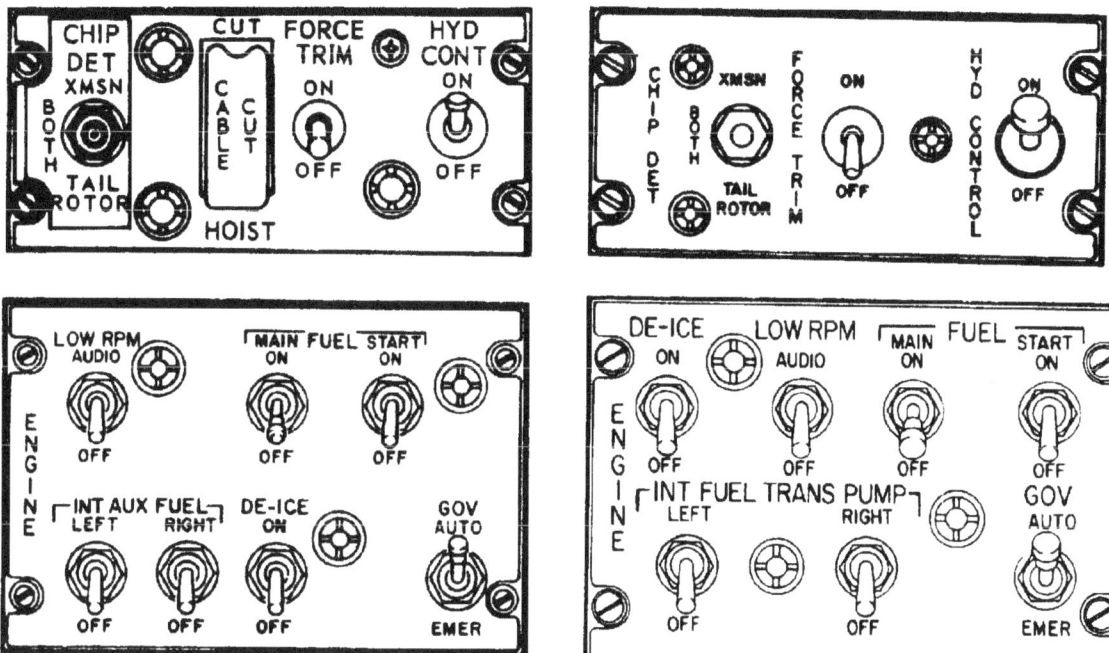
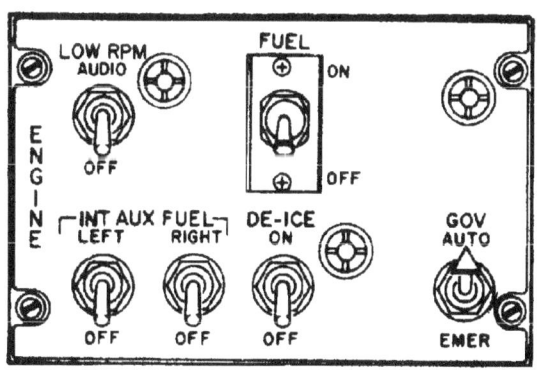

Figure 2-6. Engine and Miscellaneous Control Panel—Typical

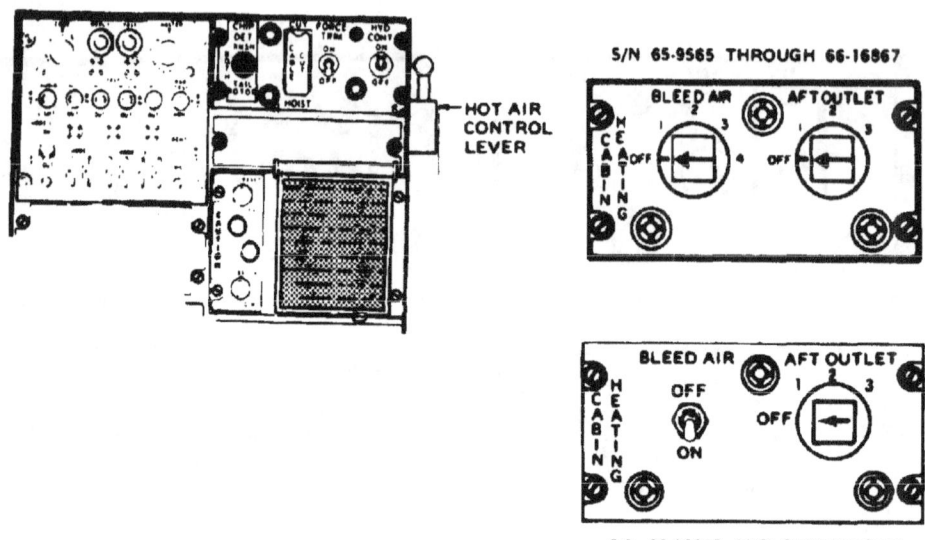

SWITCH/CONTROL	POSITION	FUNCTION
BLEED AIR (Rotary)	Clockwise Rotation	Increases amount of heated air.
	OFF	Turns bleed air off.
AFT OUTLET	Clockwise Rotation	Increases amount of air to doorpost outlets.
	OFF	Doorpost are closed, all air is direct to pedestal outlets.
Pedestal Lever	Full Forward	All heated air to defrost nozzles.
	Full Aft	All heated air to cockpit and cabin.
	Intermediate	Partial defrost and partial cockpit and cabin heat.
BLEED AIR (ON/OFF)	ON	Turns bleed air heat on.
	OFF	Turns bleed air heat off.

Figure 2-7. Heating and Defrosting System—Typical (Sheet 1 of 2)

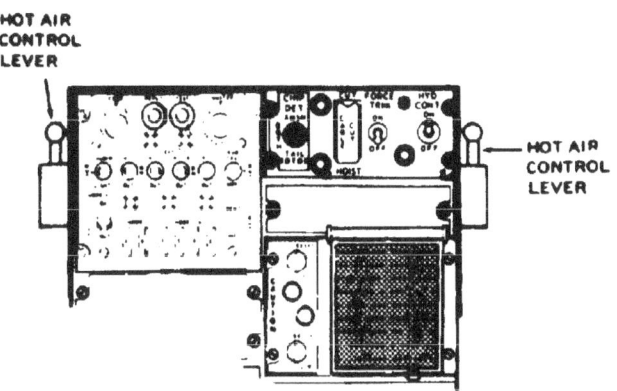 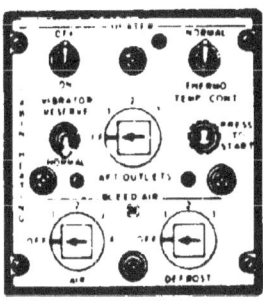

HEATER PANEL AND CONTROLS (PRIOR TO S/N 65-9565)

SWITCH/CONTROL	POSITION	FUNCTION
ON/OFF	ON	Energizes the blower.
	OFF	Stops combustion heater operation.
VIBRATOR	NORMAL	Builds up electrical charge for starting
	RESERVE	Builds up reserve charge, used only if combustion does not occur in NORMAL
	OFF	Turns vibrator off.
PRESS TO START	Press	Closes ignition circuit. VIBRATOR
NORMAL/THERMO	THERMO TEMP. CONT.	Actuates thermostatic control.
	NORMAL	Thermostat is not actuated. must be in NORMAL or RESERVE.
AFT OUTLETS	1 – 2 – 3	Clockwise rotation increases heat.
AIR	1 – 2 – 3 – 4	Clockwise rotation increases air volume.
DEFROST	OFF	100% of air to underseat outlets.
	1	33% defrost – 67% underseat outlets.
	2	67% defrost – 33% underseat outlets.
	3	100% of air to defrost nozzles
Pedestal Lever Right Inboard	AFT FORWARD	Actuates bleed air system. Shuts off bleed air.
Pedestal Levers Outboard	AFT FORWARD	Admits air to underseat outlets. Closes valve to underseat outlets.

Figure 2-7. Heating and Defrosting System–Typical (Sheet 2 of 2)

TM 55-1520-210-10

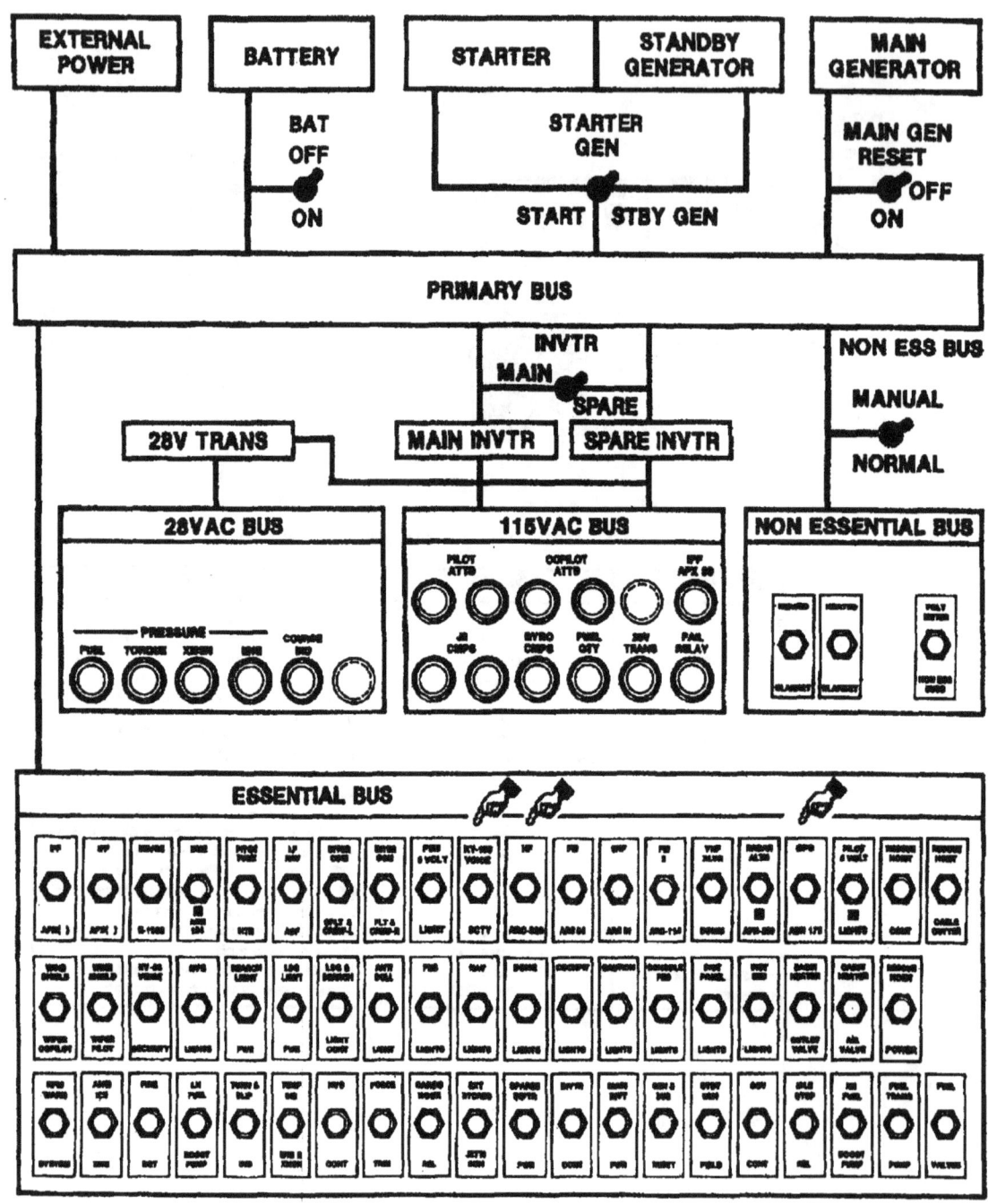

Figure 2-8 Electrical System (Typical)

TM 55-1520-210-10

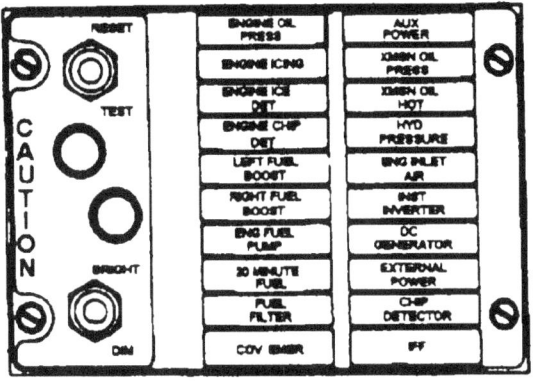

CAUTION PANEL

CAUTION PANEL WORDING	FAULT CONDITION
ENGINE OIL PRESS	Engine oil pressure below 25 psi
*ENGINE ICING	Engine Icing detected
*ENGINE ICE DET	Not connected
ENGINE CHIP DET	Metal particle in engine oil
LEFT FUEL BOOST	Left fuel boost pump inoperative
RIGHT FUEL BOOST	Right fuel boot pump inoperative
ENG FUEL PUMP	Engine fuel pump inoperative
20 MINUTE	Fuel quantity bout 170 lbs
FUEL FILTER	Fuel filter Impending bypass
*GOV EMER	Governor switch m emergency position
AUX FUEL LOW	Auxiliary fuel tank empty
XMSN OIL PRESS	Transmission oil pressure below 30 psi
XMSN OIL HOT	Transmission oil temperature above 110°C
HYD PRESSURE	Hydraulic pressure Low
*ENGINE INLET AIR	Engine air filter clogged
INST INVERTER	Failure of inverter
DC GENERATOR	DC Generator failure
EXTERNAL POWER	External power access door open
CHIP DETECTOR	Metal particles present in 42' or 90' gearbox or main- transmission
*IFF	IFF System inoperative
*May not be installed on all configuration	

Figure 2-9. Caution Panel - Typical

TM 55-1520-210-10

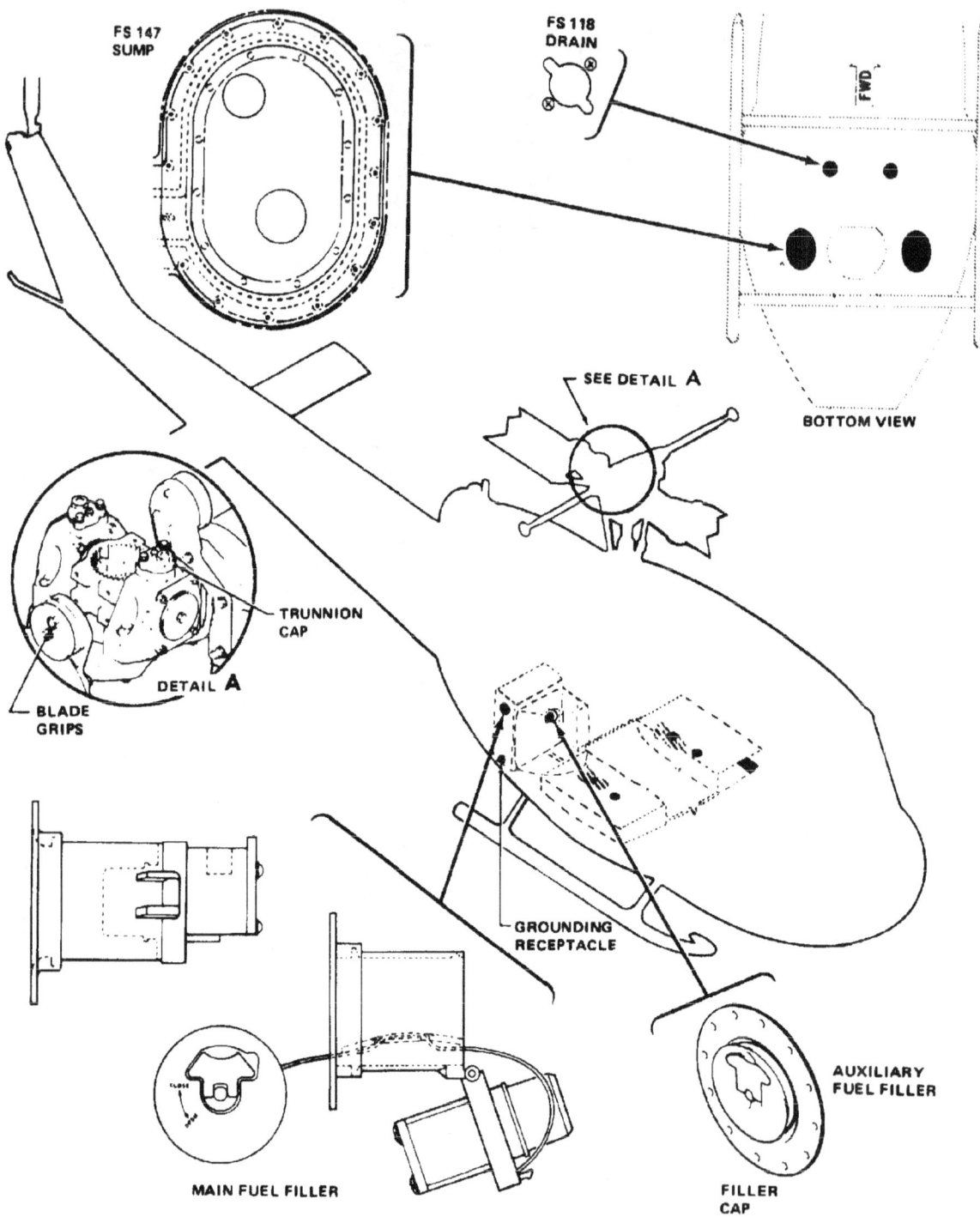

Figure 2-10. Servicing Diagram–Typical (Sheet 1 of 2)

2-36

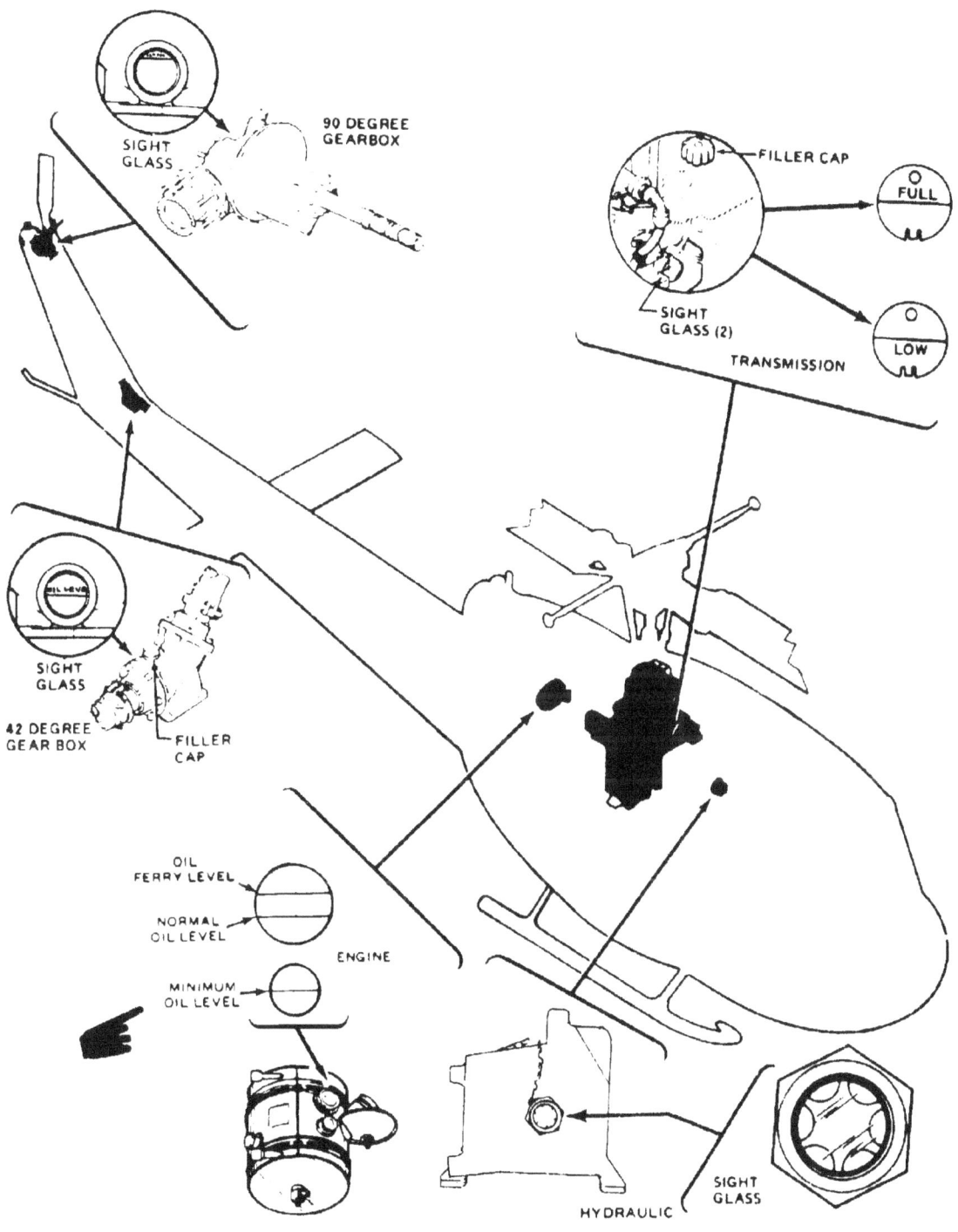

Figure 2-10. Servicing Diagram—Typical (Sheet 2 of 2)

Chapter 3

Avionics

Section I. GENERAL

3-1. General This chapter covers the avionics equipment configuration. It includes a brief description of the avionics equipment, its technical characteristics, capabilities, and location. The chapter also contains complete operating instructions for all avionics equipment installed. For mission avionics equipment, refer to chapter 4, Mission Equipment.

3-2. Avionics Equipment Configuration The configuration consists of the following:

a. *Headset Cordage.* The pilot and copilot cordage connectors are located at their respective sides near the aft portion of the overhead console. The crew cordage connectors are located near the overhead mounted signal distribution panel (figs 3-1, 3-2, and 3-3) at each crew station.

b. *Keying Switches.* A trigger type keying switch is located on each (pilot and copilot) cyclic control stick grip. The half depressed (first detent) position of the trigger switch is used for keying the interphone. The fully depressed (second detent) position of the trigger switch keys the radio selected with the transmit-interphone selector switch on the signal distribution panel. A foot-operated type keying switch (pilot and copilot) is located at each side of the center console, between the center console and cyclic control stick, and on the cabin floor at each crew station. The depressed position of the foot-operated switch keys the radio or interphone selected with the rotary selector switch at the appropriate signal distribution panel.

c. *Power Supply and Circuit Breakers.* Refer to figure 2-8.

d. *Operation.* The operation of the avionics equipment in this helicopter is dependent on the operation of the interphone system (figs 3-1, 3-2, and 3-3). Do not turn interphone system off until the end of flight day.

Section II. COMMUNICATIONS

3-3. Signal Distribution Panel-SB-329/AR

a. *Description.* The Signal Distribution Panel, located at each crewmember station, amplifies and controls the distribution of audio signals between each headset-microphone, to and from radio transmitters and receivers, and from navigation receivers. The system is used for intercommunications between crewmembers and for monitoring communication and navigation receivers singly or in combination.

b. *Controls and Functions.* Refer to figure 3-1.

c. *Operation.*

(1) FM Switch panel AN/ARC-44 number 31CS switch-up.

(2) RECEIVERS switches—As desired.

(3) TRANS selector switch—As desired.

(4) VOL control—Adjust.

3-4. Signal Distribution Panel C-1611/AIC

a. *Description.* The Signal Distribution Panel amplifies and controls the distribution of audio signals applied to or from each headset-microphone, to or from communication receivers and transmitters, from navigation receivers, intercommunication between crewmembers, and for monitoring the communication and navigation receivers singly or in combination. In addition the C-1611/AIC panel permits the operator to control four receiver-transmitters. A private interphone line is also provided.

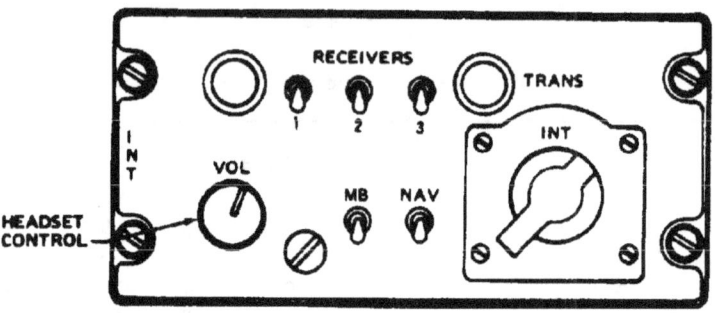

CONTROL/INDICATOR	FUNCTION
Receive switches	The switches marked 1, 2, 3 MB and NAV are for connecting or disconnecting receiver audio signals to the associated headset. The up position is on and connects the receiver. The down position is off and disconnects the receiver. The number 1 switch is for the FM receiver, number 2 switch is for the UHF receiver and switch number 3 is for the VHF receiver when installed. The switch marked MB connects audio from the marker beacon receiver, and the switch marked NAV connects audio from the ADF or VHF navigation receivers.
TRANS selector switch	This is a rotary type switch with indicator window at the top. The switch has four positions, INT, 1 (FM), 2 (UHF), and 3 (VHF). Positions 1, 2, and 3 select the receiver-transmitter to be used to receive or transmit regardless of the position of the RECEIVERS 1, 2, 3 switches. The INT position connects signal distribution panels for interphone operation. The operator will hear side tone when transmitting. The other crewmember will hear the interphone message regardless of the position of their TRANS selector switch.
VOL control	Adjusts the volume level of the audio applied to the headset associated with the INT signal distribution panel.

Figure 3-1. Signal Distribution Panel SB-329/AR

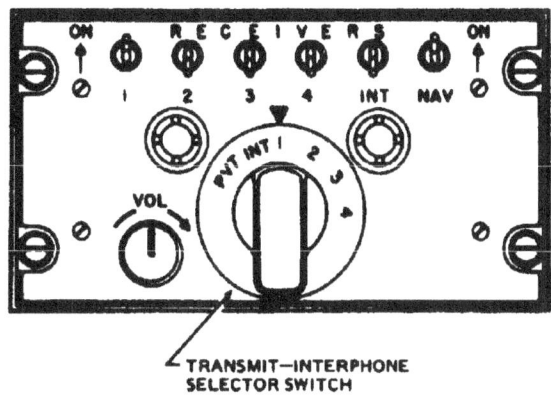

CONTROL	FUNCTION
RECEIVERS switches 1 (FM), 2 (UHF), 3 (VHF), and 4 (#2 FM/HF)	Turns audio from associated receiver ON or OFF.
INT switch	ON position enables operator to how audio from the interphone.
NAV switch	ON position enables operator to monitor audio from the navigation receiver.
VOL control	Adjusts audio on receivers except NAV receivers.
Transmit-interphone selector switch	Positions 1 (FM), 2 (UHF), 3 (VHF), 4 (#2 FM/HF) and INT permits INT or selected receiver-transmitter to transmit and receive. The cyclic stick switch or foot switch must be used to transmit. PVT position keys interphone for transmission.

Figure 3-2. Signal Distribution Panel C-1611/AIC

TM 55-1520-210-10

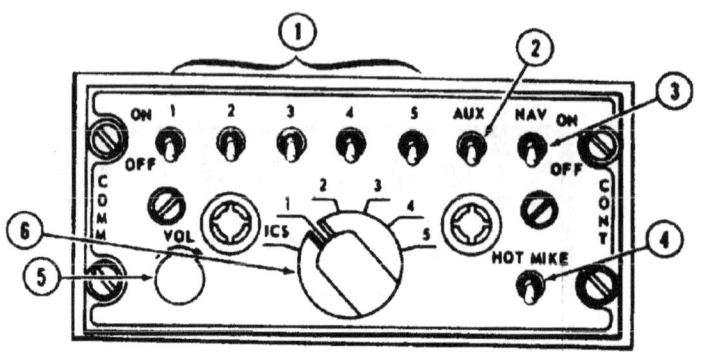

CONTROL/INDICATOR	FUNCTION
1. Receiver Switches	Connect (ON) or disconnect OFF) communications receivers from the headsets.
1 – FM No. 1 ARC-54 or ARC-131	
2 – UHF ARC-51BX	
3 – VHF ARC-115	
4 – HF ARC-102	
6 – FM No. 2 ARC-114	
2. AUX Receiver Switch	Connects (ON) or disconnects (OFF) VOR omni receiver ARN-82 from the headset.
3. NAV Receiver Switch	Connects (ON) or disconnects (OFF) ADF navigation receiver ARN-83 from the headset.
4. HOT MIKE Switch	Permits hand-free intercommunications with transmit-interphone selector in any position.
6. VOL Control	Adjusts volume from receivers. Adjusts intercommunications volume.
6. Transmit- Interphone Selector	Selects transmitter to be keyed and connects microphone to transmitters.
1 – FM No. 1 ARC-54 or ARC-131	
2 – UHF ARC-51BX	
3 – VHF ARC-115	
4 – HF ARC-102	
6 – FM No. 2 ARC-114	
ICS	Connects the microphone to the intercommunications system only, disconnecting microphone from transmitters.

Figure 3-3. Signal Distribution Control Panel (C-6533/ARC)

When the selector switch is in the PVT position it provides a hot line (no external switch is used) to any station in the helicopter which also has PVT selected. A HOT MIC switch is also provide on the C-1611/AIC control panel at the medical attendants station. Four C-1611/AIC units may be installed in serial no. 63-8739 and subsequent. One each of the units are installed for the pilot and copilot, and two are installed in the crew/passenger compartment of the crew. All four of the C-1611/AIC units are wired to provide interphone operations for the crew, and full transmit and receive facilities for all communication and navigation equipment.

b. *Controls and Functions*. Refer to figure 3-2.

c. *Operation*.

(1) Transmit interphone selector switch–As desired.

(2) RECEIVERS switches–As desired.

(3) Microphone switches–As desired.

(4) VOL control–Adjust.

3-5. Signal Distribution Panel C-6533/ARC

a. *Description*. Two panels are installed in the pedestal for the pilot and copilot and two panels are installed in the cabin roof aft of the overhead console for the right and left crewmembers. The system is used for intercommunications and radio control. The system has three modes of operation; two way radio communications, radio monitoring, and interphone.

b. *Controls and Functions*. Refer to figure 3-3.

c. *Operation*.

(1) NAV receiver switch–As desired.

(2) AUX receiver switch–As desired.

(3) Transmit-interphone selector switch–As desired.

(4) Receiver switches–As desired.

(5) HOT MIKE switch–As desired.

(6) VOL control–Adjust.

3-6. UHF Radio Set AN/ARC-51BX

a. *Description*. The Radio Set provides two way communications in the UHF (225.0 to 399.9 MHz) band. The set located at the left side of the pedestal, tunes in 0.05 MHz increments and provides 3500 channels. The set also permits 20 preset channels and monitoring of the guard channel. Transmission and reception are conducted on the same frequency.

b. *Controls and Functions*. Refer to figure 3-4.

c. *Operation*.

(1) UHF function select switch–T/R (T/R+G as desired)

(2) UHF mode selector switch–PRESET CHAN.

(3) RECEIVERS switch No. 2–ON

(4) Channel–Select.

NOTE

An 800-cps audio tone should be heard during channel changing cycle.

(5) SQ DISABLE switch–OFF.

(6) VOL–Adjust.

(7) Transmit-interphone selector switch–No. 2 position.

d. Emergency Operation.

(1) UHF mode switch–GD XMIT.

(2) UHF function switch–T/R+G.

3-7. UHF Radio Set AN/ARC-51X

a. *Description*. The radio set provides two way communications in the UHF (225.0 to 399.9 MHz) band. The set located at the left side of the pedestal, tunes in 0.1 MHz increments and provides 1750 channels. The set also permits monitoring of the guard channel. Transmission and reception are conducted on the same frequency.

b. *Controls and Functions*. Refer to figure 3-5.

c. *Operation*.

(1) UHF function selector switch–T/R (T/R+G as desired). Allow five minute warmup.

(2) Frequency–Select.

(3) RECEIVERS switch No. 2–ON.

(4) SENS and VOL controls–Adjust.

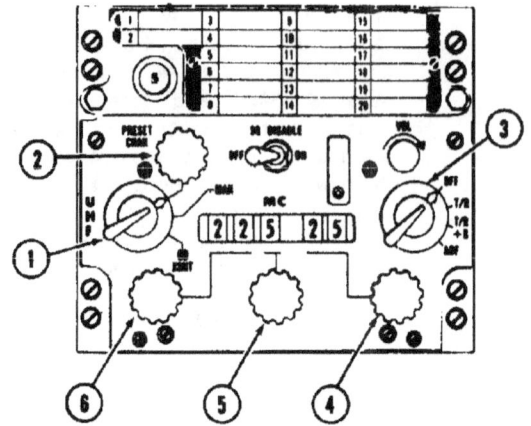

1. Mode selector
2. Preset channel control
3. Function select switch
4. 0.05 megahertz control
5. 1 megahertz control
6. 10 megahertz control

CONTROL/INDICATOR	FUNCTION
Function select switch	Applies power to radio set and selects type of operation as follows:
	OFF position — Removes operating power from the set.
	T/R position — Transmitter and main receiver ON.
	T/R + G position — Transmitter, main receiver and guard receiver ON.
	ADF position — Energizes, UHF-DF system when installed.
VOL control	Controls the receiver audio volume.
SQ DISABLE switch	In the ON position squelch is disabled. In the OFF position, the squelch is operative.
Mode Selector	Determines the manner in which the frequencies are selected as follows:
	PRESET CHAN position — Permits selection of one of 20 preset channels by means of preset channel control.
	MAN position — Permits frequency selection by means of megacycle controls.
	(GD XMIT position — Receiver-transmitter automatically tunes to guard channel frequency (243.00 MHz).
PRESET CHANnel	Permits selection of any one of 20 preset channels.
Preset channel indicator	Indicates the preset channel selected by the preset channel control.
Ten megahertz control	Selects the first two digits (or ten-megahertz number).
One megahertz control	Selects the third digit (or one-megahertz number).
Five-hundredths megahertz control	Selects the fourth and fifth digits (or 0.05 megahertz number).

Figure 3-4. UHF Control Panel C-6287/ARC-51BX

1. Frequency selector (first two digits)
2. Frequency selector (third digit)
3. Frequency selector (fourth digit)
4. Function selector switch

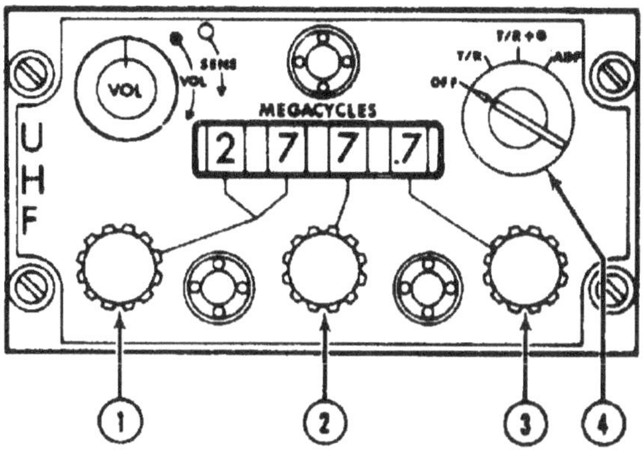

CONTROL/INDICATOR	FUNCTION
Function select switch	Applies power to the radio and selects type of operation as follows: OFF position – Removes operating power from radio set. T/R position – Applies power to the set and permits transmission and reception; guard receiver is not operative. T/R + G position – Permits transmission and reception; guard receiver is operative. ADF position – Not used.
VOL control	Controls the receiver audio volume.
SENS control	Adjusts main receiver sensitivity. When rotated fully clockwise the control disables the squelch.
Ten-megahertz control	Selects the first two digits (or ten-megahertz number).
One-megahertz control	selects the third digit (or one-megahertz number).
One-tenth megahertz control	Selects the fourth digit (or tenth-megahertz number).

Figure 3-5. UHF Control Panel C-4677/ARC-51X

TM 55-1520-210-10

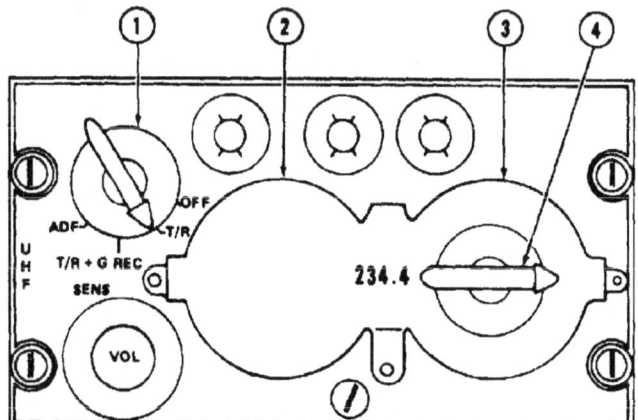

1. Function selector switch
2. Frequency selector (first two digits)
3. Frequency selector (third digit)
4. Frequency selector (fourth digit)

CONTROL/INDICATOR	FUNCTION
Selector switch	Applies power to the radio set and selects the mode of operation OFF position – turns off primary power. T/R position – transmitter and main receiver are on. T/R + G REC position – transmitter, main receiver and guard receiver are on. ADF position – not used.
Volume sensitivity control	This is a dual purpose rotary control. The larger or outer knob is marked SENS, and controls receiver sensitivity. The smaller or inner knob is marked VOL, and controls receiver volume.
Tuning controls	The tuning controls consist of two large control knobs, an inner control knob, and an indicator window. The large knob on the left side selects the first two digits (or ten megahertz number). The large knob on the right side selects the third digit (or one megahertz number). The inner knob selects the fractional (or tenth megahertz number).

Figure 3-6. UHF Control Panel C-1827/ARC-55B

(5) Transmit-interphone selector switch—No. 2 position.

d. Emergency Operation. Select guard frequency 243.0 MHz.

3-8. UHF Radio Set AN/ARC-55B

a. Description. The UHF command set provides two way, amplitude-modulated communications on any of 1750 channels within 225.0 to 399.9 MHz. Channel selection is manual and the guard channel may be monitored.

b. *Controls and Functions.* Refer to figure 3-6.

c. *Operation.*

(1) UHF function selector switch—As desired.

(2) Frequency—Select.

(3) RECEIVERS switch No. 2—ON.

(4) UHF VOL-SENS controls—Adjust.

(5) Transmit-interphone selector switch—No. 2 position.

d. Emergency Operation. Select guard frequency 243.0 MHz.

3-9. VHF Radio Set AN/ARC-115

a. Description. The VHF Radio Set provides amplitude-modulated, narrow band voice communications within the frequency range of 116.000 to 149.975 MHz on 1360 channels for a distance of approximately 50 miles line of sight. A guard receiver is incorporated and fixed tuned to 121.50 MHz. The panel is labeled VHF AM COMM and mounted on the left side of the pedestal.

b. *Controls and Functions.* Refer to figure 3-7.

c. *Operation.*

(1) Function selector—As desired.

(2) Frequency—Select.

(3) RCVR TEST—Press to test.

(4) AUDIO—Adjust.

(5) Transmit-interphone selector switch—No. 3 position.

(6) RADIO transmit switch—Press.

d. Emergency Operation. Select guard frequency 121.50 MHz.

3-10. VHF Radio Set-AN/ARC-134

a. Description. The set transmits and receives the same frequency. The panel (VHF COMM) is located on the left side of the pedestal. The set provides voice communications in the VHF range of 116.000 through 149.975 MHz on 1360 channels spaced 25 kHz apart.

b. Controls and Functions Refer to figure 3-8.

c. Operation.

(1) OFF/PWR switch—PWR. Allow set to warm up.

(2) Frequency—Select.

(3) RECEIVERS switch No. 3—ON.

(4) Volume—Adjust. If signal is not audible with VOL control fully clockwise, press COMM TEST switch to unsquelch circuits.

(5) Transmit-interphone selector switch—No. 3 position.

(6) OFF/PWR switch—OFF.

d. Emergency Operation. Select guard frequency 121.500 MHz.

3-11. VHF Radio Set-AN/ARC-73

a. Description. The VHF Command Set is an alternate set for the UHF radio. The set provides transmission and reception of AM radio signals in the VHF range. The receiver may be tuned within its frequency range of 116.00 to 151.95 MHz in 50 kHz increments to any of the 720 available channels. The transmitter may be tuned within its frequency range of 116.00 to 149.95 MHz in 50 kHz increments to any one of its 680 available channels. The distance range is limited to line of sight or a distance of approximately 50 miles.

b. Controls and Functions. Refer to figure 3-9.

c. *Operation.*

(1) POWER switch—ON.

(2) Frequency—Select.

(3) RECEIVERS switch No. 3—ON.

TM 55-1520-210-10

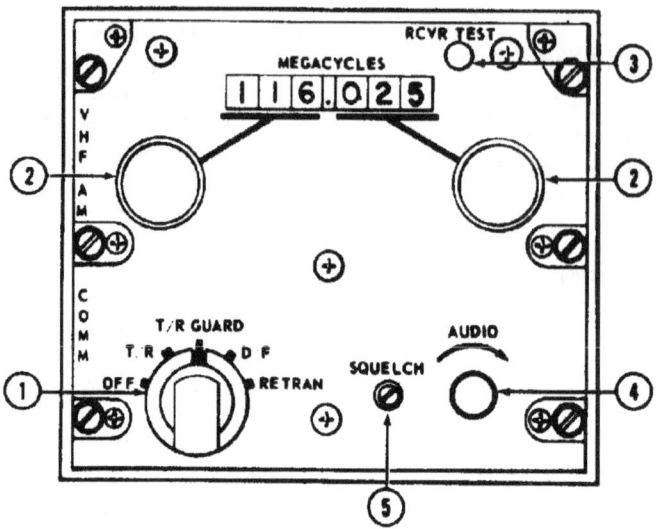

CONTROL/INDICATOR	FUNCTION
1. Function Selector	
OFF	Power off.
T/R	Receiver — On; Transmitter — Standby.
T/R GUARD	Receiver — On; Transmittal — Standby; Guard Receiver — On.
	NOTE
	Reception on guard frequency is unaffected by frequencies selected for normal communications.
D/F	Not used.
RETRAN	Not used.
2. Frequency Selectors	
Left	Selects first three digits of desired frequency.
Right	Selects fourth, fifth and sixth digits of desired frequency.
3. RCVR TEST switch	When pressed, audible signal indicates proper receiver performance.
4. AUDIO control	Adjusts receiver volume.
5. SQUELCH control	Squelch control adjusted by maintenance personnel only.

Figure 3-7. Control Panel AN/ARC-115

1. Frequency indicator
2. Communication test switch
3. Volume control
4. Kilohertz selector
5. Off/power switch
6. Megahertz selector

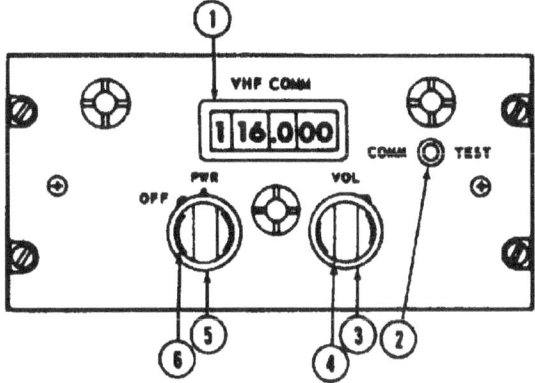

CONTROL/INDICATOR	FUNCTION
OFF-PWR switch	Turns power to the set ON-OFF.
VOL control	Controls the receiver audio volume.
COMM-TEST switch	Turns squelch on or off.
Megahertz control	Selects whole number part of operating frequency.
Kilohertz control	Selects the decimal number part of the operating frequency

Figure 3-8. VHF Control Panel C-7197/ARC-134

(4) SQ and VOL controls - Adjust.
(5) Transmit interphone selector switch - No. 3 position.
   d. Emergency Operation Select guard frequency 121.500 MHz.

3-12. FM Radio Set - AN/ARC-114 and -114A.

a Description The FM Radio Set provides two way frequency modulated (FM) narrow band voice communications and homing capability within the frequency range of 30.00 to 75.95 MHz on 920 channels for a distance range limited to line of sight. A guard receiver is incorporated in the set and is fixed tuned to 40.50 MHz. It has the additional capability -for retransmission of voice, or X-mode communications in conjunction with radio set AN/ARC-131. The radio set is marked VHF FM COMM and is mounted on the center console, on helicopter serial Nos. 71-20000 and subsequent.

b. Controls and Functions. Refer to figure 3-10.

c. Operation.
   (1) Two Way Voice Communication.
      (a) Function selector - As desired.
      (b) Frequency - Select.
      (c) RCVR TEST - Press to test.
      (d) AUDIO - Adjust.
      (e) Transmit interphone selector - No. 5 position.
   (2) Retransmission.

NOTE

For transmission both FM circuit breakers must be in.

      (a) Frequencies - Select (both FM sets). -
      (b) Communications - Establish with each facility by selecting number I position and then number 5 position on the transmit-interphone selector.
      (c) Function selectors - RETRAN (both FM sets).
      (d) Receivers switches - Number I and number 5 positions as desired for monitoring.

d. Emergency Operation. Select guard frequency 40.50 MHz.

3-13. FM Radio Set - AN/ARC-131.

   a. Description The FM Radio Set consists of a receiver-transmitter, remote control panel unit; communication antenna and a homing antenna The radio set provides 920 channels spaced 50 kHz apart within the frequency range of 30.00 to 75.95 MHz. Circuits are included to provide transmission sidetone monitoring. The control panel is located on the pedestal. Homing data is displayed by the course indicator (fig 3-20) on the instrument panel. A channel changing tone should be heard in the headset while radio set is tuning. When the tone stops, the radio set is tuned. Operation in DIS position is possible; however flags on course deviation indicator will be inoperative. When the first FM radio set is m the homing mode, the homing indicator may deflect left or right of on course indication while the second FM radio set Is keyed.

   b. Controls and Functions. Refer to figure 3-1 1.

   c. Operation Depending on the settings of the control panel controls, the radio set can be used for the following types of operation: Two way voice communication and homing (fig 3-12).

   (1) Two Way Voice Communication.
      (a) Mode control switch - T/R (allow two minute warm up).
      (b) Frequency - Select.
      (c) RECEIVERS No. I switch - ON.
      (d) VOL control - Adjust.
      (e) SQUELCH control - Set for desired squelch mode.
      (f) TRANS selector switch - No. I.

   (2) Homing Operation.
      (a) Mode control switch - HOME.
      (b) Frequency - Adjust to frequency of selected homing station
      (c) SQUELCH control may be set to CARR or TONE, however, the carrier squelch is automatically selected by an internal contact arrangement on HOME position.
      (d) Fly helicopter toward the homing station by heading in direction that causes homing course deviation indicator right-left vertical pointer to position itself m the center of indicator scale. To ensure that helicopter is not heading away from the homing station, change the heading slightly and note that the course deviation indicator vertical pointer deflects in direction opposite that of the turn.

(3) Retransmit Operation. Start the equipment and proceed as follows for retransmit operation:

(a) Mode controls (both control units) - RETRAN.

(b) SQUELCH controls (both control units) - Set as required. Do not attempt retransmit operation with SQUELCH controls set to DIS. Both controls must be set to CARR or TONE. To operate satisfactorily the two radio sets must be tuned to frequencies at least 3 MHz apart.

(c) Frequency adjust (both control units) for the desired operation.

(4) Stopping Procedure. Mode control switch - OFF.

3-14. FM Radio Set AN/ARC-54.

a. Description The FM Radio Set provides two-way communications within the frequency range of 30.00 to 69.95 MHz. Voice communication permits selective calling (TONE) and when used with the homing antenna and course indicator the pilot is provided with a homing facility. A channel changing tone should be heard in the headset while radio set is tuning. When the tone stops the radio set is tuned. Voice reception is possible m HOME position. With two or more FM radio sets installed and the first FM radio set is in the homing mode, the homing indicator may deflect left or right of on-course indication while the second FM radio set is keyed.

b. Controls and Functions. Refer to figure 3-12.

C Operation.

(1) Two Way Voice.

(a) FM mode selector switch - PTT (allow three minute warm-up).

(b) Frequency - Select.

(c) FM VOL control - Adjust.

(d) FM SQUELCH control - CARR (or as desired).

(e) RECEIVERS switch No. 1 -- ON.

(f) TRANS selector switch - No. 1.

(g) Microphone switch - Press.

(2) Homing Operation. FM mode selector switch - HOME.

(3) Retransmit Operation. Start the equipment and perform the following for retransmit operation.

(a) Mode controls (both control units) - RETRAN.

(b) SQUELCH controls (both control units) - Set as desired.

NOTE

Do not attempt retransmit operation with the SQUELCH controls set to DIS. Both controls must be set to CARR or TONE.

(c) Adjust frequency (both control units) desired operation. To operate satisfactorily the two radio sets must be tuned to frequencies at least 5 MHz apart.

(4) Stopping Procedure. FM mode selector switch -OFF.

3-15. FM Radio Set AN/ARC-44

a. Description. The FM Radio Set provides two way communications within the frequency range of 24.0 to 51.9 MHz on 280 preset channels. Signal distribution panel SB-329 and control panel assembly 204-075-219 (FM switch assembly), to provide squelch control and power to the antenna group are used in conjunction with the FM Liaison Radio Set (fig 3-2 and fig 3-14). The set provides a homing facility on signals between 24.0 and 49.0 MHz. Cycling may take place in the receiver transmitter. This will be indicated by a 400-cycle-per-second signal heard in the headset

b. Controls end Functions. Refer to figure 3-13.

c. Operation

(1) Preliminary Setup.

(a) FM power switch - ON.

(b) FM home switch - Down.

(c) TRANS selector switch -   No. 1 position.

(d) REM-LOCAL switch -   LOCAL.

(e) Frequency - Select.

(2) Standing Procedures.

(a) BAT switch - ON (OFF for APU).

(b) INT and FM circuit breakers - In.

TM 55-1520-210-10

(c) ICS switch - Up (allow three minute warm up).
   (3) Interphone Operation.
      (a) Microphone switch - Press.
      (b) Speak into the microphone - Adjust interphone volume.
   (4) FM Receive-Transmit Operation.
      (a) ICS switch - Up.
      (b) FM ON-OFF power switch - ON.
      (c) FM VOL control - As desired.
      (d) TRANS selector switch - No. I position.
      (e) Microphone switch - Press to transmit.
   (5) FM Home Operation. FM HOME switch - Up.
   (6 Stopping Procedures.
      (a) FM HOME switch - Down.
      (b) FM POWER switch - OFF.
      (c) ICS Switch - Down.

3-16. Voice Security Equipment - TSEC/ KY-28.
   a. Description. The Voice Security Equipment is used with the FM Command Radio to provide secure two way communication (figs 3-11 through 3-14). The equipment is controlled by the control-indicator mounted in the pilot right console. The POWER switch must be in the ON position regardless of the mode of operation whenever the equipment is installed.
   b. Control and Functions. Refer to figure 3-14.
   c. Operation. Normal operation will exist without its encoder/decoder and control indication being installed in the helicopter. However two operation modes are available when they are installed. PLAIN mode for enciphered radio transmission or reception and CIPHER mode for ciphered radio transmission or reception. Both modes may be operated with or without retransmission nits.

(1) Preliminary
   (a) Set the control indicator POWER switch to ON.
   (b) Apply power to FM radio set.
   (c) When power is initially applied an automatic alarm procedure is initiated.
      1. A constant tone is heard in the headset and after approximately two seconds the constant tone will change to an interrupted tone.
      2. To clear the interrupted tone press and release the press to talk switch the interrupted tone will no longer be heard and the circuit will be in a standby condition ready for either transmission or reception. No traffic will be passed if the interrupted tone is still heard after pressing and releasing the press to talk switch. (d) Set control unit function switch for desired type of operation (2 and 3 below).
(2) Plain Mode.
(a) Set the control indicator POWER switch to ON.
   (b) Set the PLAIN-CIPHER switch to PLAIN (indicated by red light).
   (c) Set the RE-X-REG switch to REG; except when operating with retransmission units, at which time-switch will be placed in the RE-X position.
   (d) Press the press to talk switch and speak into the microphone to transmit. Release the press to talk switch for reception.
   (3) Cipher Mode.
      (a) Set the PLAIN-CIPHER switch to CIPHER (indicated by a green light).
      (b) Place the RE-X-REG switch to REG except when operating with retransmission units at which time the switch will be placed in RE-X position. (c) To transmit press the press to talk switch. DO NOT TALK; in approximately one-half second a be will be heard. This indicates the receiving station is now capable of receiving your message. Transmission can now commence. Only one voice security system can transmit on a given frequency. Always listen before attempting to transmit to assure that no one else is transmitting.

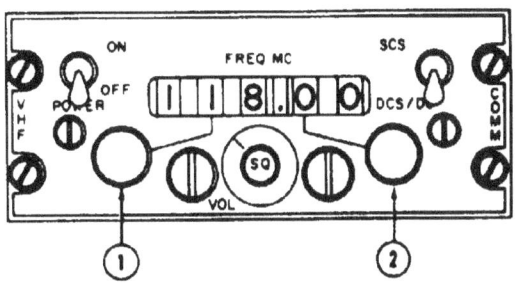

1. Megahertz control knob
2. Kilohertz control knob

CONTROL/INDICATOR	FUNCTION
POWER switch	Turns primary power to the radio set ON or OFF
VOL control knob	Controls the *receiver* audio volume.
SQ control knob	Adjusts the squelch threshold level of the receiver output.
Megahertz control knob	Selects receiver and transmitter frequency in 1 - mhz steps.
Kilohertz control knob	Selects receiver and transmitter frequency in 50-khz steps
FREQ MC indicator window	Indicates receiver and transmitter frequency selected.
SCS-DCS/DCD switch	Not used.

Figure 3-9. VHF Control Panel 614U-6/ARC-73

TM 55-1520-210-10

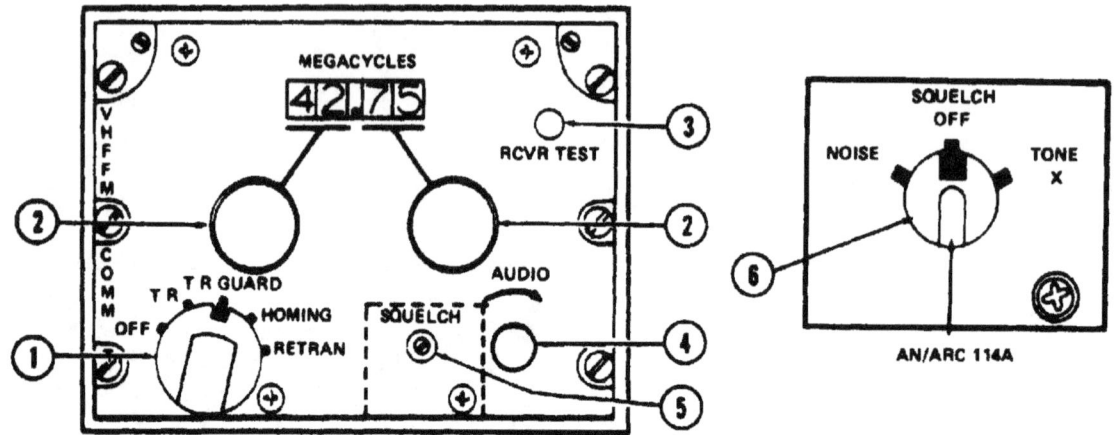

CONTROL/INDICATOR	FUNCTION
1. Function Selector	
OFF	Power Off
T/R	Receiver – On; Transmitter – Standby.
T/R GUARD	Receiver – On; Transmitter – Standby; Guard Receiver – On.
	NOTE
	Reception on guard frequency is unaffected by frequencies selected for normal communications.
HOMING	Not Used.
RETRAN	Activates the Retransmission Mode in Conjunction with Radio Set ARC-54 or ARC-131.
2. Frequency selectors	
Left Selector	Selects first two digits of desired frequency
Right Selector	Selects third and fourth digits of desired frequency.
3. RCVR TEST	When pressed audible signal indicates proper receiver performance.
4. AUDIO	Adjusts receiver volume.
5. SQUELCH (ARC 114)	Squelch control adjusted by maintenance personnel only.
6. SQUELCH (ARC 114A)	
OFF	Disables squelch.
NOISE	Enables noise squelch.
TONE X	Enables tone squelch and Secure Voice operation.

Figure 3-10. Control Panel AN/ARC-114 and AN/ARC-114A

3-14 Change 7

1. Tens megahertz digit frequency selector
2. Frequency indicators
3. Units megahertz digit frequency selector
4. Tenths magahertz digit frequency selector
5. Frequency indicators
6. Hundredths megahertz digit frequency selector
7. Mode control switch

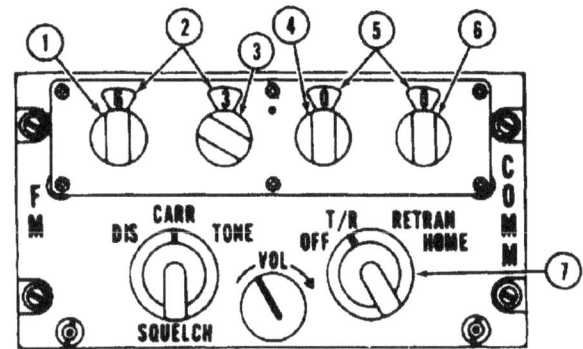

CONTROL/INDICATOR	FUNCTION
Mode control switch (four-position switch)	
OFF	Turns off primary power.
T/R (transmit/receive)	Radio set operates in normal communication mode (reception). (Aircraft transmit switch must be depressed to transmit.)
RETRAN (retransmit)	Radio set operates as a two-way relay station. (Two radio sets are required set at least 3 MHz apart.)
HOME	Radio set operates as a homing facility. (Requires a homing antenna and indicator.)
VOL control	Adjusts the audio output level of the radio set.
SQUELCH switch (three-position rotary switch)	
DIS (disable)	Squelch circuits are disabled.
CARR (carrier)	Squelch circuits operate normally in presence of any carrier.
TONE	Squelch opens (unsquelches) only on selected signals (signals containing a 150-cps tone modulation).
Frequency indicator	
Tens megahertz frequency selector	Selects the tens megahertz digit of the operating frequency.
Units megahertz frequency selector	Selects the units megahertz digit of the operating frequency.
Tenths megahertz frequency selector	Selects the tenths megahertz digit of the operating frequency.
Hundredths megahertz frequency selector	Selects the hundredths megahertz digit of the operating frequency.
Frequency indicator	Displays the operating frequency of the radio set.

Figure 3-11. FM Radio Set Control Panel AN/ARC-131

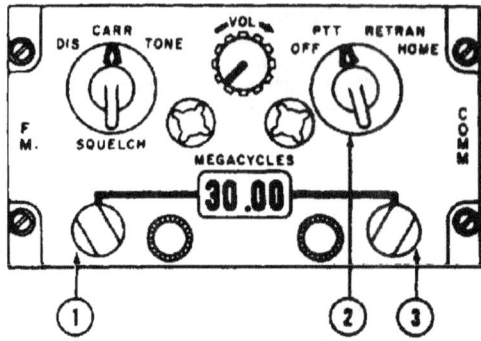

1. Frequency control whole – megahertz
2. Mode selector switch
3. Frequency control decimal – megahertz

CONTROL/INDICATOR	FUNCTION
Mode selector switch	Applies power to the set and selects the mode of operation. OFF position – Turns off primary power. PTT (push-to-talk) applies power. Radio set operates in normal communication mode. (Radio cyclic stick switch or foot switch must be pressed to transmit.) RETRAN (retransmit) – Applies power. Radio set operates as a two-way relay station. (Two radio sets are required set at least 5 MHz apart) HOME position – Applies power and radio set operates with 637A-2. Homing Antenna and Course Indicator as a homing facility. Voice capability is provided in all three operating positions.
VOL control	Controls the receiver audio volume.
SQUELCH control	Selects one of three squelch modes as follows: DIS (disable) position – Squelch circuits are disabled. CAR (carrier) position – Squelch circuits operate normally. TONE position – Squelch opens (unsquelches) only on signals containing a 150-cps tone modulation.
Frequency control whole-megahertz digit	Selects the whole megahertz digits
Frequency control decimal-megahertz digit	Selects the decimal-megahertz digits.
Megahertz display window	Displays the selected operating frequency.

Figure 3-12. FM Radio Set Control Panel C-3835/ARC-54

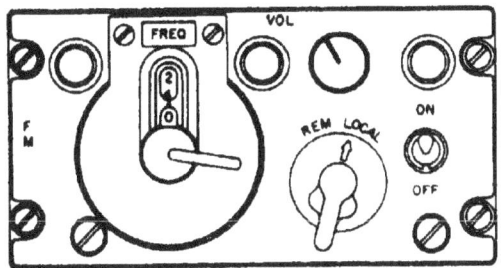
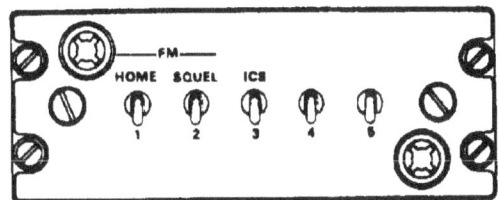

CONTROL/INDICATOR	FUNCTION
ON-OFF switch	Applies and removes power.
REM LOCAL switch	Always use LOCAL. REMote is used only with two or more panels.
FREQ control	Outside knob selects whole megahertz. Inside knob selects tenth megahertz.
VOL control	Adjusts FM receiver audio.
FM/HOME-1 switch	Up position energizes homing circuit Down position disables homing circuit.
FM/SQUEL-2 switch	Up position squelches FM receiver output. Down position opens the squelch and background noise can be heard.
ICS-3 switch	Up position energizes ICS circuits. Down position disables ICS.
4 switch	Up position energizes the auxiliary FM receiver. Down position disables the auxiliary.
5 switch	Not used.

Figure 3-13. FM Control Panel and Switch Assembly AN/ARC-44

TM 55-1520-210-10

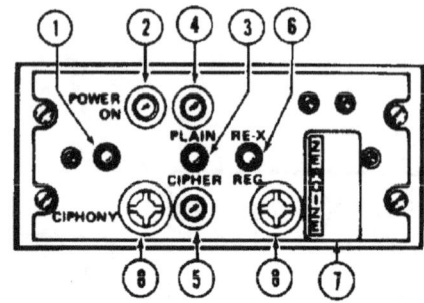

CONTROL/INDICATOR	FUNCTION
1. POWER ON Switch (Two-Position Circuit Breaker)	Connects power to the associated TSEC/KY-28 cipher equipment in the ON (forward) position, and disconnects power from the equipment in the OFF (aft) position. NOTE Switch must be in the ON (forward) position for operation in the PLAIN or CIPHER mode.
2. POWER ON (Amber) Indicator (with Dimmer Switch)	Lights when the associated POWER ON switch is placed in the ON (forward) position.
3. PLAIN CIPHER Switch (Two-Position Locking Toggle)	In the PLAIN position, permits normal (unciphered) communications on the associated FM radio set. In the CIPHER position, permits ciphered communications on the associated radio set.
4. PLAIN (Red) Indicator (with Dimmer Switch)	Lights when the associated PLAIN-CIPHER switch is in the PLAIN position.
5. CIPHER (Green) Indicator (with Dimmer Switch)	Lights when the associated PLAIN-CIPHER switch is in the CIPHER position.
6. RE-X-REG Switch (Two-Position Locking Toggle)	In the RE-X position, permits ciphered communications through a retransmission unit (at a distant location). In the REG position, permits normal ciphered communications or clear text.
7. ZEROIZE Switch (Two-Position Locking Toggle, Under Spring-Loaded Cover)	CAUTION Do not place the ZEROIZE switch in the ON (forward) position unless a crash or capture is imminent. Normally in OFF (aft) position. Placed in ON (forward) position during emergency situations to neutralize and make inoperative the associated TSEC/KY-28 cipher equipment.
8. Panel Lights	Illuminate the control-indicator (controlled by aircraft panel lights).

TSEC/KY-28

Figure 3-14. Voice Security Equipment (Sheet 1 of 2)

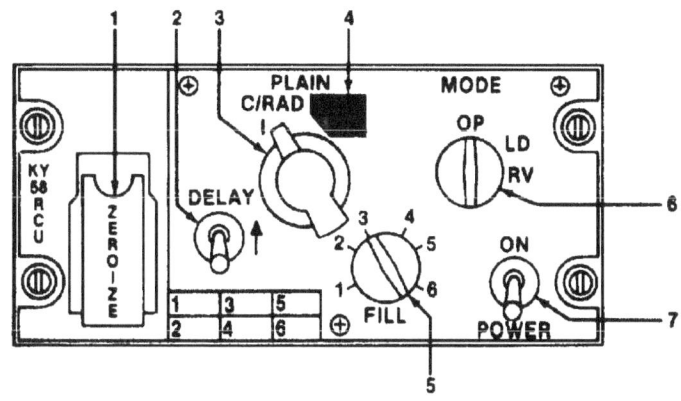

CONTROL/INDICATOR	FUNCTION
1. ZEROIZE switch (two-position momentary toggle, under spring loaded cover)	Zeroizes the KY-58; clears any encoding in the system
2. DELAY switch 2 position toggle	Used when signal is to be retransmitted.
3. PLAIN-C/RAD Switch rotary 2 position selector switch	In the PLAIN position, permits normal (unciphered) communications on the associated FM radio set. In the C/RAD position, permits ciphered communications on the associated radio set.
4. C/RAD2 Switch stop	Location of stop for C/RAD2 on front panel
5. FILL switch 6 position rotary switch	Permits pilot to select one of 6 storage registers for filling.
6. MODE Switch three position rotary	In the OP position KY-58 normal operating. In the LD position for filling. In the RV position KY-58 in Receive-Variable. Filled from another external source.
7. POWER ON switch two position toggle	Connects power to the associated TSEC/KY-58 cipher equipment in the ON (forward) position, and disconnects power from the equipment in the OFF (aft) position. Turns on power to TSEC/KY-58.

T/SEC KY-58

Figure 3-14 Voice Security Equipment (Sheet 2 of 2)

(d) When transmission is completed, release the press to talk switch. This will return equipment to the standby condition.

(e) To receive, it is necessary for another station to send you a signal first. Upon receipt of a signal the cipher equipment will be switched automatically to the receive condition, which will be indicated by a short beep heard in the headset. Reception will then be possible. Upon loss of the signal, the cipher equipment will be automatically returned to the standby condition.

3-16.1 Voice Security Equipment TSEC/KY-58

a. Description. The voice security equipment is used with the FM Command Radio to provide secure two way communication. The equipment is controlled by the control-indicator (Z-AHP) mounted in the right pedestal panel. The POWER switch must be in the ON position, regardless of the mode of operation, whenever the equipment is installed.

b. Controls and Functions. Refer to Figure 3-14.

c. Operating Procedures.

(1) Operating procedures for secure voice.

NOTE

To talk in secure voice, the KY-58 must be "Loading" with any number of desired variables.

(a) Set to MODE switch to OP.

(b) Set the FILL switch to the storage register which contains the crypto-net variable (CNV) you desire.

(c) Set the POWER switch to ON.

(d) Set the PLAIN C/RAD switch to C/RAD.

(e) If the signal is to be retransmitted, set the DELAY switch to (ON).

(f) At this time a crypto alarm, and background noise, in the aircraft audio intercom system should be heard. To clear this alarm, press and release PTT in the aircraft audio/intercom system. Secure voice communication is now possible.

NOTE

When operating in either secure or clear (plain) voice operations the VOLUME must be adjusted on the aircraft radio and intercom equipment to a comfortable operating level.

(2) Clear Voice Procedures:

(a) To operate in clear voice (plain text) simply:

1 Set the Z-AHP(RCU) PLAIN-C/RAD switch to PLAIN.

2 Operate the equipment

(3) Zeroing Procedures

NOTE

Instructions should originate from the Net Controller or Commander as to when to zeroize the equipment

(a) To zeroize the KY-58: (Power must be on).

1 Lift the red ZEROIZE switch cover on the RCU.

2 Lift the spring-loaded ZEROIZE switch. This will zeroize positions 1-6.

3 Close the red cover.

The equipment is now zeroized and secure voice communications are no longer possible.

(4) Automatic Remote Keying Procedures

NOTE

Automatic Remote Keying (AK) causes an "old" crypto-net variable (CNV) to be replaced by a "new" CNV. Net Controller simply transmits the "new" CNV to your KY-58.

(a) The Net Controller will use a secure voice channel, with directions to stand by for an AK transmission. Calls should not be made during this standby action.

(b) Several beeps should now be heard in your headset. This means that the "old" CNV is being replaced by a "new" CNV.

(c) Using this "new" CNV, the Net Controller will ask you for a "radio check."

(d) After the "radio check" is completed, the Net Controller instructions will be to resume normal communications. No action should be taken until the net controller requests a "radio check."

(5) Manual Remote Keying Procedures.

(a) The Net Controller will make contact on a secure voice channel with instructions to stand by for a new crypto-net variable (CNV) by a Manual Remote Keying (MK) action. Upon instructions from the Net Controller:

1 Set the Z-AHP FILL switch to position 6. Notify the Net Controller by radio, and stand by.

2 When notified by the Net Controller, set the Z-AHP MODE switch to RV (receive variable). Notify the Net Controller, and stand by.

3 When notified by the Net Controller, set the Z-AHP FILL switch to any storage position selected to receive the new CNV (May be unused or may contain the variable being replaced). Notify the Net Controller, and stand by.

NOTE

When performing Step 3, the storage position (1 through 6) selected to receive the new CNV may be unused, or it may contain the variable which is being replaced.

(b) Upon instructions from the Net Controller:

1 Listen for a beep on your headset.

2 Wait two seconds

3 Set the the RCU MDOE switch to OP

4 Confirm

(c) If the MK operation was successful, the Net Controller will now contact you via the new CNV.

(d) If the MK operation was not successful, the Net Controller will contact you via clear voice (plain) transmission; with instructions to set your Z-AHP FILL selector switch to position 6, and stand by while the MK operation is repeated.

(6) It is important to be familiar with certain KY-58 audio tones. Some tones indicate normal operation, while other indicate equipment malfunction. These tones are:

(a) Continuous beeping, with background noise, is cryptoalarm. This occurs when power is first applied to the KY-58, or when the KY-58 is zeroized. This beeping is part of normal KY-58 operation. To clear this tone, press and release the PTT button on the Z-AHQ (after the Z-AHQ LOCAL switch has been pressed. Also the PTT can be pressed in the cockpit.

(b) Background noise indicates that the KY-58 is working properly. This noise should occur at TURN ON of the KY-58, and also when the KY-58 is generating a cryptovariable. If the background noise is not heard at TURN ON, the equipment must be checked out by maintenance personnel,

(c) Continuous tone, could indicate a "parity alarm." This will occur whenever an empty storage register is selected while holding the PTT button in. This tone can mean any of three conditions:

1 Selection of any empty storage register.

2 A "bad" cryptovariable is present.

3 Equipment failure has occurred. To clear this tone, follow the "Loading Procedures" in TM 11-5810-262-OP. If this tone continues, have the equipment checked out by maintenance personnel.

(d) Continuous tone could also indicate a cryptoalarm. If this tone occurs at any time other than in (c) above, equipment failure may have occurred. To clear this tone, repeat the "Loading Procedures" in TM 11-5810-262-OP. If this tone continues, have the equipment checked out by maintenance personnel.

(e) Single beep, when RCU is not in TD (Time Delay), can indicate any of three normal conditions:

1 Each time the PTT button is pressed when the KY-58 is in C (cipher) and a filled storage register is selected, this tone will be heard. Normal use (speaking) of the KY-58 is possible.

2 When the KY-58 has successfully received a cryptovariable, this tone indicates that a "good" cryptovariable is present in the selected register.

3 When you begin to receive a ciphered message, this tone indicates that the cryptovariable has

passed the "parity" check, and that it is a good variable.

(f) A single beep, when the RCU is in TD (Time Delay) occurring after the "preamble" is sent, indicates that you may begin speaking.

(g) A single beep, followed by a burst of noise after which exists a seemingly "dead" condition indicates that your receiver is on a different variable than the distant transmitter. if this tone occurs when in cipher text mode: Turn RCU FILL switch to the CNV and contact the transmitter in PLAIN text and agree to meet on a particular variable.

3-17. HF Radio Set AN/ARC-102

a. Description. HF AM/SSB Radio Set AN/ARC-102 is a long range, high frequency (hf), single side band (ssb), transceiver that transmits and receives in the 2.0 to 30.0 MHz range. The control panel is located on the right side of the pedestal and tunes in one kHz stops to any of 28,000 manually selected frequencies. The primary mode of operation is ssb. However, it can also transmit end receive compatible amplitude modulated (am) signals.

b. Controls and Functions. Refer to figure 3-15.

c. Operation.

WARNING

When ground testing ARC-102 equipment, be sure that personnel are clear of antenna. Serious bums can result if body contact is made with the antenna during ground testing.

(1) Function selector switch - As desired.

(2) Frequency controls - Desired frequency. if the function selector is moved from the OFF position to an operating mode and the desired operating frequency is already sat up on the control panel, rotate the first selector knob one digit off frequency and then back to the operating frequency. This will allow the system to return to the frequency.

(3) RF-SENS-Adjust.

(4) intercommunications HF switch-As desired.

d. Emergency Operation. The AN/ARC-102 HF radio has two built-in protective devices that could cause the set to stop operating. The condition and corrective steps are as follows:

(1) A protective circuit is designed to turn the receiver-transmitter off, when a short exists in the output circuit. To restore the receiver-transmitter to operation, move the function selector to OFF position and then back to the desired operating mode:

(2) When the associated antenna coupler is required to complete several consecutive tuning cycles it may become overheated. In this event a thermal relay in the coupler unit is designed to turn off the receiver-transmitter. If the receiver-transmitter stops operating after a series of tuning cycles, position the function selector switch to OFF position, allow the thermal relay to cool for two minutes and return the function selector to the desired operating mode.

(3) if the above procedure does not return the HF radio set to normal operation, place the frequency selector to 29.000 MHz and function selector in the "OFF" position. Report the failure to the maintenance personnel.

3-17.1 HF Radio Set AN/ARC-220 (MWO 1-1520-210-50-33)

WARNING

Make sure that no personnel are within 3 feet of the HF antenna when transmitting, performing radio checks or when in ALE mode. Do not touch the RF output terminal on the antenna coupler, the antenna lead-in wire, the Insulated feed trough, or the antenna itself while the microphone is keyed (after the tuning cycle is complete) or while the system is in transmit self-test. Serious RF burns can result from direct contact with the above criteria.

WARNING

Tow aircraft outside of hanger or metal-covered building before performing power-on checks.

 a. *Description.* The AN/ARC-220 is a high frequency, single-side band radio set. It receives and transmits on any one of 280,000 manually-selected frequency channels spaced at 100-Hz increments in the HF band (2.0 to 29.9999 MHz). Preset channels can be manually programmed by an operator or preprogrammed as part of the communications mission load information. The AN/ARC-220 provides secure and nonsecure voice and data communications. Voice communications are possible using either simplex or half-duplex operation in the upper sideband (USB), lower sideband (LSB), amplitude modulation equivalent (AME), and continuous wave (CW) modes. Data may be transmitted or received in USB or LSB modes. In addition to conventional HF communication, the AN/ARC-220 provides automatic link establishment (ALE) and two types of electronic counter countermeasures (ECCM) communications. The ALE simplifies HF radio operation by automatically establishing a 2-way link on the best available frequency.

The two types of ECCM communications (MIL-STD-188-141A ECCM and Army enhanced ECCM) provide a frequency hopping technique that combats the effects of communications jammer and direction finding attempts. Although two different types of ECCM are available, system operation is the same regardless of the type used.

The AN/ARC-220 also supports both standard and advanced narrow-band digital voice terminal (ANDVT). Digital data interfaces compatible with MIL-STD-188-114A allow transmission and reception of data from improved data modem (IDM) and data secured by the AIRTERM (TSEC/KY-100). In addition, the AN/ARC-220 includes a MIL-STD-110A data modem which may, in noisy environments, allow data to be received when voice communications cannot. Power to operate the AN/ARC-220 is supplied from the 28 vdc essential bus through the HF ARC-220 circuit breaker on the pilot overhead circuit breaker panel. A shorted loop antenna is located on the rear left side of the aircraft (figure 2-1. The length of the antenna is approximately 12.6 feet in length.

 b. *Controls and Functions.* Refer to figure 3-14.1 and the following table.

TM 55-1520-210-10

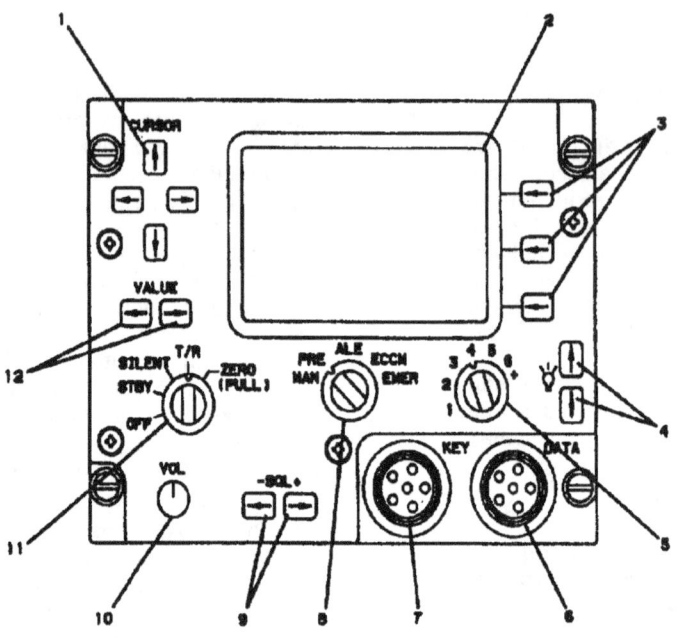

Figure 3-14.1. HF Radio Set AN/ARC-220 Control Panel C-12436/URC

Controls and Functions of Control Panel C-124361URC

CONTROL /INDICATOR	FUNCTION
1. Cursor switches	Four pushbutton switches that position cursor vertically or horizontally on display (2).
2. Display	Liquid crystal display (LCD), consisting of six display lines, for displaying advisory information. Depending on operation, information that may be displayed on each line is as follows:
Line 1	Alpha-numeric display of 15 characters maximum containing channel title (call sign). Default value is Mode: channel #.
Line 2 ALE Address	Alpha-numeric display of 15 characters maximum containing Call To (ADRS: xxx) or Self (SELF: xxx)Address. (ADRS:) and (SELF:) labels are removed for addresses greater than 10 characters in length.
Noise Reduction	Character display (ON, OFF) having display format of NOISE REDUCE: xxx. Default value is ON.

3-22.2 Change 18

Controls and Functions of Control Panel C-12436/URC (Cont)

CONTROL /INDICATOR	FUNCTION
Fill Type	Character display (KEY, DATA) having display format of TYPE: xxxx x. Default is DATA.
Contention Control	Character display (ON, OFF) having display format of LBC: xxx. Default is OFF.
Line 3 Receive Frequency	Numeric display (2.0 to 29-9999 MHz) with display format of RCV: xx.xxxxxxxx.
ECCM Station Type	Character display (MEMBER, ALTERNATE, MASTER, NET ENTRY, ALT NET ENT). Default is MEMBER.
Lines 3,4	Character display of emission mode (USB, LSB, AME, CW) one space to right of frequency. Default is USB.
Line 4 Transmit Frequency	Numeric display (2.0 to 29.9999 MHz) with display format of XMT: xx.xxxxxxxx.
Time	Numeric display (00:00:00 to 23:59:59) with display format of Hour:Minute:Second.
Line 5 Link Protection	Character display (OFF, ON) with display format of LINK PROT: xxx, Default is ON (OFF if no link protection datafill).
Date	Alphanumeric display (01 JAN 00 to 31 DEC 99) with display format of dd MM yy.
Antenna Type	Character display (T/R, RCV) with display format of ANT: xxx. Default is T/R.
Line 8 Power Level	Character display (LOW, MED, HIGH) with display format of PWR: xxxx. Default is HIGH.
Squelch	Alpha-numeric display (TONE, 0 to 5) with display format of - SQ: xxx.
Volume	Numeric display (1 to 8) with display format of VOL:x.
Listen Before Talk	Character display (ON, OFF) with display format of LBT: xxx.. Default value is OFF.

Controls and Functions of Control Panel C-12436/URC (Cont)

	CONTROL/INDICATOR	FUNCTION
3.	Line-select switches	Three pushbutton switches that select options displayed to left of each switch.
4.	Brightness switches	Two pushbutton switches that varies display screen brightness.
5.	Channel/Net selector switch	Seven-position rotary switch that selects programmed operating channels or nets, depending on operating mode. The + position of switch allows additional channel/net selections using VALUE switches (12).
6.	Data connector	Interfaces AN/ARC-220 system to data transfer device for datafill.
7.	Key connector	Interfaces AN/ARC-220 system to data transfer device for keyfill.
8.	Mode switch	Five-position rotary switch that selects following modes of operation:
	MAN	Permits single channel selection of operating frequency and emission mode for conventional HF communications.
	PRE	Permits preprogrammed preset channel operation for conventional HF communications.
	ALE	Selects automatic link establishment mode of operation.
	ECCM	Selects electronic counter-countermeasure mode of operation.
	EMER	Used during emergency situations to place a distress call. The mode (manual, preset, ALE, or ECCM), frequency, net, etc., is determined by the datafill.
9.	-SQL + switches	Two pushbutton switches (left arrow) and (right arrow) that control radio squelch and audio muting.
10.	VOL switch	Eight position rotary switch that varies receive audio output level.

Controls and Functions of Control Panel C-12436/URC (Cont)

CONTROL /INDICATOR	FUNCTION
11. Function switch	Five-position rotary switch that selects system operation as follows:
OFF	Turns AN/ARC-220 system off.
STBY	Turns AN/ARC-220 system on and places system in-standby. In standby, built-in-test (BIT), setup, or fill operations can be performed to ready system for operation.
SILENT	Used in ALE or ALE-ECCM mode to preventAN/ARC-220 system from automatically responding to incoming calls,
T/R	Allows AN/ARC-220 system to transmit and receive in selected mode of operation.
ZERO (PULL)	Erases ail data (including datafill and keyfill) that has been loaded into system. Switch must be pulled before setting it to this position.
12. Value	Two pushbutton switches that increment field value or single character value, depending on cursor position.

c. *Operating Modes/Functions.*

(1) Power ON/OFF. On Function Switch.

(2) System Turn-On. Turning Function Switch clockwise from OFF to STBY turns system on and selects standby function. SYSTEM TESTING is displayed while power-up BIT (P-BIT) is in process. SYSTEM-GO will be displayed if all tests pass or SYSTEM-NO-GO if not.

(3) CRT Brightness. Two pushbutton switches used to vary brightness. The ↑ (up arrow) increases intensity while the ↓ (down arrow) decreases intensity.

(4) Audio Volume. Eight-position rotary switch used to vary audio output level. Setting is displayed on line 6 (bottom) of display for 5 seconds when system is first turned on or when VOL setting is changed. Display levels are 1 through 8.

(5) Channel Selection. Channel number may be changed using seven-position rotary channel/net selector switch. The + position of switch allows channels 7 or greater to be selected using VALUE switches.

(6) Modulation Mode. Four modes are available: USB, LSB, AME, and CW. The modulation mode is determined by the data fill except for the manual mode. Modulation mode can be changed on manual channels

(7) Receive/Transmit Frequency. 2.0 to 29.9999 MHz, programmable in 100 Hz steps. To change frequencies, depress EDIT line select switch. While in Edit screen, use CURSOR to position cursor under appropriate frequency. Use VALUE switches to change frequency. (Note: XMT frequency will automatically change with RCV frequency, but the reverse is not true).

(8) Squelch Level/Audio Muting (-SQL +). Two pushbutton switches ← (left arrow) and → (right arrow), when pressed, displays squelch status on line 6 of display for 5 seconds. Settings are TONE and 0 through 5. TONE provides no muting and no squelch. Position 0 provides muting but no squelch. Positions 1 through 5 provide muting and increasing levels of squelch. Muting is normally enabled during ALE operation.

(9) Output Power Level. Three output levels are selectable for display screen by using EDIT line-select switch, which brings up edit mode, moving cursor under power character field and using VALUE switches to change field. Depress RTN line-select switch which stores the change and returns to normal operating mode.

(10) Test. There are two Built-in-Test (BIT) features which concerns the operator, P-BIT and C-BIT. The Power-Up Bit (P-Bit) tests the ARC-220 when initially turned on. P-Bit exercises basic radio control functions which must be operational prior to entering system operational mode. A GO/NO-GO status appears on display and defaults to stand-by mode upon completion. When NO-GO status appears, depressing INOP line-select switch displays INOP MODES so an operator can see if limited capability exists. Continuous Bit (C-BIT) is automatically performed during system operation without any operator intervention. Critical system functions are monitored. Any failures cause a NO-GO advisory, accompanied by portion of system which failed, to appear on line 5 of display. C-Bit failures are stored in nonvolatile memory.

(11) Store. RTN line-select key, used to terminate edit mode, automatically stores any change(s) made.

(12) Data Fill. Contains preset frequencies, scan lists, addresses, data messages and ALE and/or ECCM parameters. With system in STBY, press FILL line-select switch. From the FILL screen, use the line select switch to select DATA. Connect data transfer device (DTD) of DATA connector on radio set control front panel and initiate fill from DTD. LOADING is displayed during data-fill From the DATAFILL screen, use the line select switch to select LOAD. FILL ENABLED is displayed during datafill. The AN/CYZ-10 DTD will indicate when the datafiil is completed. Use the line-select switch to select RTN after the DTD indicated datafill completed. The display will return to the screen showing DATAFILL VERSION. The approporated Datafill Version is displayed for a successful fill. A copy of loaded datafill can be sent to DTD by pressing COPY line-select switch. COPYING is displayed during operation, COPY COMPLETE is displayed if successful, COPY FAIL if copy cannot be completed.

Press RTN line-select switch to return to STBY screen when datafill is complete. Disconnect DTD.

(13) Key Fill. Loads secure keys. From the FILL screen, use the line-select switch to select KEY. Connect DTD to KEY connector on radio set control front panel. From the KEYFILL screen, use the line-select switch to select LOAD. Fill enabled IS DISPLAYED DURING KEYFILL. Initiate keyfill from DTD. The AN/CYZ-10 DTD will indicate when the keyfill is completed. Use the line-select switch to select RTN after the DTD indicates keyfill is completed. The display will return to the screen showing ECCM KEY and LP KEY. The appropriate keys are displayed for a successful fill. To erase selected loaded keys, press ZERO line-select switch. A ZEROIZE screen appears. Press YES or NO line-select switch. If YES is pressed, a ZEROIZED advisory is displayed, then fill screen reappears. If NO is pressed, fill screen reappears. Press RTN line select switch to return to STBY screen when all keys are loaded.

d. *Operation.*

(1) Starting Procedure.

(a) Function switch - STBY. SYSTEM TESTING is displayed while power up built in test (PBIT is in process. SYSTEM - GO will be displayed upon successful completion of PBIT.

(b) FILL line select key - Press. Status of PRE, ALE, ECCM, and EMER modes will be displayed.

(2) Load Presets. Datafill contains preset frequencies, scan lists, addresses, data messages, and non secure information needed for ALE/ECCM operation. If the DTD is configured to receive data, it may be copied from the radio to the DID by pressing COPY line select key on the DATA FILL page.

(a) Initialize the data transfer device (DTD). Connect the DTD to the DATA connector.

(b) With the FILL page selected, DATA line select key - Press.

NOTE

Pressing RTN line select key on DATA FILL page stops the fill process.

(c) On the DATA FILL page, FILL line select key - Press. FILL ENABLED screen will appear.

(d) Start data fill on DTD. Monitor DTD to see when data transfer is complete.

(3) Load Secure Keys. Key fill contains secure information needed for ALE link protection and ECCM operation.

(a) Initialize the DTD. Connect the DTD to the KEY connector.

(b) With the FILL page selected, KEY line select key - Press.

NOTE

Pressing RTN line select key on KEY FILL page stops the fill process.

(c) On the KEY FILL page, LOAD line select key - Press. FILL ENABLED message will appear.

(d) Start keyfill on DTD. Monitor DTD to see when data transfer is complete.

(4) Zero Secure Keys.

(a) Access KEY FILL page. From FILL screen, KEY fixed function key - Press. Select key to zero with VALUE keys.

(b) ZERO line select key - Press.

NOTE

If you do not want to zero the key, press NO. The FILL screen will then appear.

(c) Confirm zero by pressing YES line select key. ZEROIZE advisory message will appear, followed by the FILL screen.

(5) Emergency (EMER) Operation. The mode, frequency, and net to be used in the EMER position is determined by the datafill. To use the emergency mode, do the following:

    (a) Function switch - T/R.

    (b) Mode switch - EMER

    (c) ICS Transmitter selector - Position 4.

    (d) Radio push-to-talk switch - Press to talk; release to listen.

(6) Shut Down

    (a) Function switch - OFF.

    (b) To erase all preprogrammed information, Function switch - Pull and turn to ZERO (PULL).

(7) Messages. The following table lists display advisory messages that may appear during operation of the radio:

AN/ARC-220 Messages

ADVISORY	MEANING	ACTION
ALE - NO DATA	ALE mission data not loaded.	Load mission data.
ALE - NO KEYS	ALE link protection keys not loaded.	Load keys.
CALL FAIL	Radio failed to complete an outgoing call.	
CALLING	Radio is placing an ALE - call to another address.	
CHANNEL BUSY	ALE or ECCM net is in use.	Walt or try another net
CHANNEL INOP	ALE or ECCM keys are not loaded, or not correct.	
CHECK MSG	A data message has been received.	
COPY COMPLETE	Copying process finished successfully.	
COPY FAIL	Copying process was unsuccessful.	
COPYING DATA	The radio is copying datafill contents from DTS.	
ECCM - NO DATA	ECCM data not installed.	Load mission data.
ECCM - NO KEYS	ECCM keys not Installed.	Load keys.
EMER	Mode or net selected for emergency communication Is inoperative.	
EMERG - NO KEYS	No keys available for net selected for emergency communication.	Load keys.
EOM	End of message.	
EXT FAIL	Radio failed due to external device, such as antenna.	

TM 55-1520-210-10

AN/ARC-220 Messages (Cont)

ADVISORY	MEANING	ACTION
GO DATA	Link quality analysis values too low for reliable voice communication; data transmissions recommended.	
HELD	ALE call being held in specific frequency by operator.	
INCOMING CALL	Another radio is establishing an ALE link.	
INOP MODES EXIST	Warning to expect inoperative modes.	
LINKED	An ALE link is established.	
LOAD COMPLETE	Keys and data successfully loaded into radio.	
LOAD FAIL	Keys and data not successfully loaded into radio.	
LOADING DATA	Radio currently loading data.	
LOADING KEYS	Radio currently loading keys.	
MSG ABORT	Radio discontinuing sending of current message.	
NET INOP	Selected net contains no data, corrupted data, or hardware cannot support the selected mode of operation.	
NO AUTO XMT	Radio has been instructed not to make any automatic transmissions.	
NO DATA	Database is not filled with necessary data to perform requested operations.	
NO KEYS LOADED	Keys are not loaded for current selected mode or net.	

3-22.10 Change 18

TM 55-1520-210-10

AN/ARC-220 Messages (Cont)

ADVISORY	MEANING	ACTION
NO RCVD MSGS	No messages have been received.	
PAC FAIL	Failure of radio in PA coupler.	
PRE - NO DATA	Preset data not loaded.	
PTT FOR XMIT BIT	Instruction to press microphone PTT switch to enable transmission BIT.	
RCV BIT - GO	Receiver BIT functions completed without failure.	
RCV READY	Ready to receive ECCM transmissions.	
RCVG PREAMBLE	ECCM preamble being received.	
RCVG DATA	Radio currently receiving data.	
RT FAIL	Receiver Transmitter inoperative.	
RX - TX DEGRADED	Receive and transmit capabilities are degraded.	
RX - TX FAIL	Radio cannot receive or transmit.	
SENDING DATA	Radio currently sending data.	
SOUND	Radio sending an ALE sound.	
SYNCING	Time synchronization being performed.	
TESTING	BIT in progress.	
TIME SYNC FAIL	Radio failed in attempt to synchronize.	
TRANSEC FAIL	BIT detected a failure that will not allow ECCM operation.	

Change 18   3-22.11

AN/ARC-220 Messages (Cont)

ADVISORY	MEANING	ACTION
TUNE XX %	Indicates percentage of ECCM frequencies tuned for current net.	
TUNING	Radio is currently tuning itself.	
TX DEGRADED	BIT detected a failure that is causing transmission capability to be degraded.	
TX FAIL	Radio cannot transmit.	
UNSYNC	ECCM is not synchronized.	
UNTUNED	An ECCM hop set is not tuned.	
XMT READY	Radio is ready to transmit in ECCM mode.	
ZEROIZED	All mission datafill and keys have been erased.	

e. *Modes of Operation.*

(1) Manual (MAN) Mode. Use manual mode to change transmit and receive frequencies, sidebands and transmit power, and operate the radio manually.

(a) To change radio settings:

1. Mode switch - MAN.

2. Function switch - T/R.

2. Select the desired net (l through 20), net selector switch - 1 through +. Use VALUE keys to select 7 through 20.

2. EDIT line select key - Press.

NOTE

Changing the receive frequency and mode will also change the transmission frequency and mode the same values. Changing the transmission frequency and mode will not change the receive frequency and mode.

5. Edit frequency, emission mode and transmit power by placing the cursor under field to be edited with CURSOR key, and change field value with VALUE keys.

6. To end edit and store changed data, RTN line select key - Press.

(b) To operate in manual mode:

1. Function switch - T/R.

2. Mode switch - MAN

3. -SQL+ switch - Set squelch to 0.

4. VOL switch - Adjust for comfortable listening level.

NOTE

If the radio breaks in and out of squelch, Increase setting as required.

5. -SQL+ switch - Set squelch to 1.

6. Select the desired net (1 through 20) net selector switch -1 through +. Use VALUE keys to select 7 through 20.

7. ICS Transmitter selector - Position 4.

8. Radio push-to-talk switch - Press to talk; release to listen.

(2) Preset (PRE) Mode. Preset mode stores preprogrammed frequencies and emission modes that cannot be changed by the operator. To use the radio in preset mode, do the following:

(a) Function switch - T/R

(b) Mode switch - PRE.

(c) -SQL+ switch - Set squelch to 0.

(d) VOL switch - Adjust for comfortable listening level.

NOTE

If the radio breaks in and out of squelch, increase setting as required.

(e) -SQL+ switch - Set squelch to 1.

(f) Select the desired net (1 through 20), net selector switch - 1 through +. Use VALUE keys to select 7 through 20.

(g) ICS Transmitter selector - Position 4.

NOTE

If tune tone is heard, wait until it stops before talking. When radio push-to-talk switch is pressed, XMT frequency is displayed. Display returns to preset display when switch is released.

(h) Radio push-to-talk switch - Press to talk; release to listen.

(3) Automatic Link Establishment (ALE) Mode.

WARNING

When In ALE mode, the radio transmits Interrogating signals (sounds) and replies to ALE calls automaticalty without operator action. To avoid personnel Injury, ensure the function switch Is not set to ALE when personnel are working near the helicopter, during refueling or loading ordinance.

NOTE

Self address must be selected before using, ALE.

ALE mode may be used for communications, either normal or link protected, or position reporting.

(a) To set up the radio for ALE communications, do the following:

1. Function switch - T/R.

2. Mode switch - ALE.

3. Select the desired net (1 through 20), net selector switch - 1 through +. Use VALUE keys to select 7 through 20.

4. -SQL+ switch - Set squelch to TONE.

5. VOL switch - Adjust for comfortable listening level.

NOTE

Earphone audio is muted until a link is established. If the link is noisy, set squelch to 1. Higher squelch settings are not recommended in this mode.

6. SQL+ switch - Set squelch to 0.

7. To synchronize time in a link protected channel, SYNC soft key - Press.

8. To broadcast AN/ARC-220 system time as net control, EDIT, then TXTIM soft keys - Press. Time will be transmitted, and radio will return to scan mode.

(b) To receive a ALE call:

1. INCOMNG CALL is displayed, followed by the caller's ALE address. A short tone sounds, and LINKED is displayed.

2. Transmitter selector - Position 4.

NOTE

Wait for the calling station to make the first transmission.

3. Radio push-to-talk switch - Press to talk; release to listen.

(c) To place a ALE call:

1. Select ALE address:

a. Select the desired net (1 through 20), net selector switch - 1 through +. Use VALUE keys to select 7 through 20. Net name and address will be displayed.

b. VALUE switch - Press, to scroll through address list.

c. EDIT soft key - Press. Enter address one character at a time with CURSOR and VALUE switches. To accept the edit and return to ALE screen, RTN soft key - Press.

2. ICS Transmitter selector - Position 4.

NOTE

Press ABORT to stop the calling process.

3. Radio push-to-talk switch - Press. CALLING, then LINKED is displayed with a short gong tone in headphone.

NOTE

ALE will cancel the link, and return to scan mode if there is no activity on a link for 60 seconds. To maintain a link, press HOLD soft key. When communications are complete, or to return to scan mode, press SCAN soft key.

(d) Radio push-to-talk switch - Press to talk; release to listen.

(e) When communication is complete, to return to scanning mode, HOLD, then SCAN soft key - Press.

(4) Electronic Counter Countermeasures (ECCM) Mode. The radio changes frequency in a sequence determined by the ECCM key. Datafill and keyfill must be loaded prior to using ECCM mode, and system time must be synchronized between stations. Frequencies used in hop sets are pretuned in the radio, as ECCM requires frequencies to be changed many times per second. Frequency hopping is performed in both standard ECCM and ALE modes of operation. To use this mode, do the following:

(a) Initialize the net

1. Function switch - T/R.

2. Mode switch - ECCM.

NOTE

If the selected net is an ALE ECCM, the address of the station being called is also displayed.

2. Select the desired net (1 through 12), net selector switch - 1 through +. Use VALUE keys to select 7 through 12.

3. To change values on screen, EDIT soft key - Press. Use CURSOR to position cursor under area to change, and VALUE to change the field to desired value.

5. To save changes and return to top level screen, RTN soft key - Press.

6. Push-to-talk switch - Press, to tune and time synchronize the radio.

(b) To communicate in ECCM only mode, do the following:

1. -,SQL+ switch - Set squelch to TONE.

2. VOL switch - Adjust for comfortable listening level.

NOTE

If the frequency is noisy, set squelch to 1. Higher squelch settings are not recommended in this mode.

3. -SQL + switch - Set squelch to 0.

4. Press and hold the push-to-talk switch until XMT READY is displayed. Wait for preamble tones to stop.

5. Talk. Release switch to listen.

(c) To communicate in ALE ECCM mode, do the following:

1. -SQL+ switch - Set squelch to TONE.

2. VOL switch - Adjust for comfortable listening level.

3. Select the ALE address, as required with VALUE switches, or use EDIT soft key, then CURSOR and VALUE switches to manually select an address.

4. When an incoming call is being received, INCOMING CALL, then LINKED is displayed. RCV READY is displayed while the ECCM information is being received, and disappears when receive sequence is completed.

5. To place a call, press the push-to-talk switch. CALLING, then LINKED is displayed. Press and hold the push-to-talk switch, and wait for the ECCM preamble tone to stop. When XMT READY is displayed, begin talking. When the transmission is completed, release the switch. XMT READY disappears when the ECCM postamble is sent.

(5) Message Mode. The radio can store up to 10 transmit data and 10 received data messages. Each message may be 500 characters long. Messages are numbered from 1 to 10. Message 10 is the oldest, and will be deleted if a new message is received. Messages may be composed using the AN/ARC-220 CDU dictionary or with a custom dictionary listing locally generated words, which may be loaded with datafill.

(a) To view a received message:

1. MSG soft key - Press.

2. Use CURSOR keys to scroll left or right, or up and down in a message.

3. Use VALUE keys to page up and down in a message.

4. To view additional messages, position cursor under message number with CURSOR keys. Use VALUE keys to scroll to the next message number.

5. To retain received messages, RTN soft key - Press.

6. To delete received messages, position the cursor under the message number and DEL soft key - Press, until messages are deleted. To return to top screen, RTN soft key -Press.

(b) To edit or compose a message:

1. MSG soft key - Press.

2. From MESSAGE screen, PGRM soft key - Press.

3. Select message to be edited by placing cursor under the message number with CURSOR keys, and change number with VALUE keys.

4. Edit message by placing cursor under area to be changed. Use VALUE keys to change one character at a time. Press DEL to delete one character at a time.

2. To insert a word from the dictionary in a message do the following:

a. Position cursor where the word is to be inserted.

b. WORD soft key - Press.

c. Select the word with VALUE keys,

d. To insert word with blank in message, SELECT soft key - Press. If desired, return to message without inserting a word by pressing CANCL.

6. To load edited message in R/T memory and return to top level screen, RTN soft key - Press.

(c). To send a message:

1. Access PRGM MSG screen by pressing MSG, then PRGM soft keys.

2. Select message to send as desired by placing cursor under message number, and pressing VALUE keys until desired message is displayed.

NOTE

Message will be sent to currently selected address (ALE modes) or transmitted on the currently selected frequency and mode (MAN, PRE, or ECCM).

3. SEND soft key - Press.

3-17.2. Voice Security Equipment TSEC/KY-100.

a. *Description.* The Voice security equipment TSEC/KY-100 provides two-way clear or secure half-duplex voice or data communication for HF Radio Set AN/ARC-220. Power to operate the TSEC/KY-100 is supplied from the dc essential bus through the KY-100 VOICE SCTY circuit breaker located on the pilot overhead circuit breaker panel.

b. Controls and Functions for Remote Control Unit (RCU). Refer to figure 3-14.2.

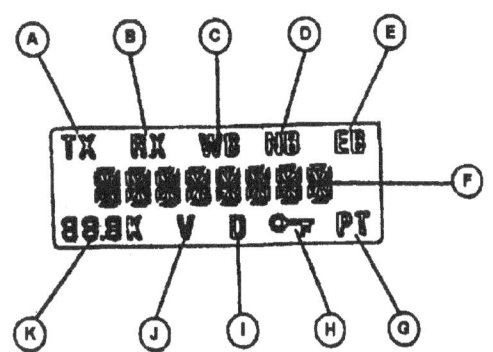
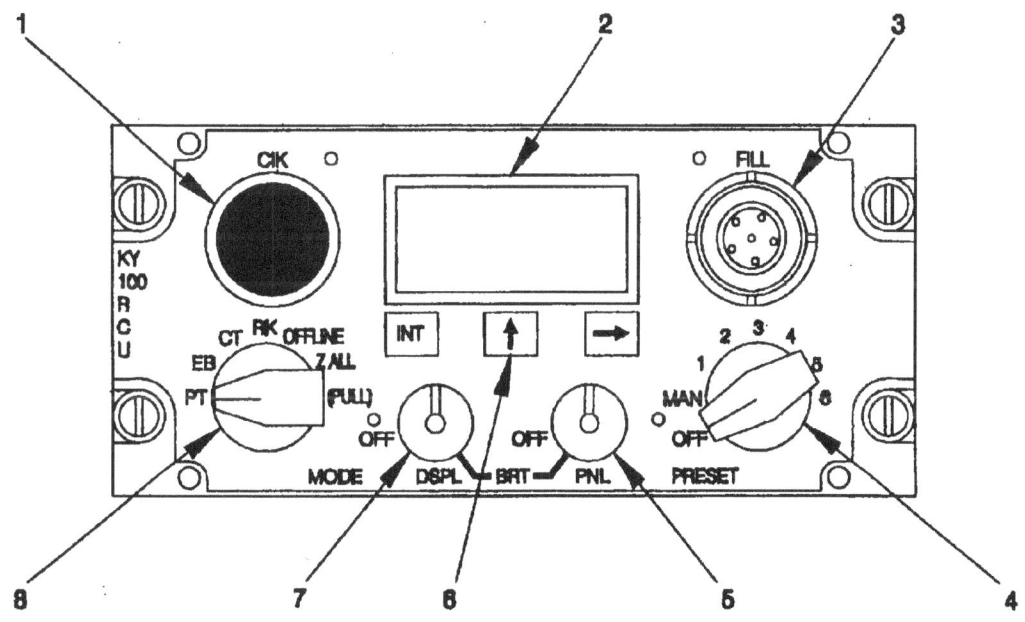

Figure 3-14.2. Remote Control Unit (TSEC/KY-100)

Controls and Functions of Remote Control Unit TSEC/KY-100

CONTROL /INDICATOR	FUNCTION
1. CIK Receptacle	Interfaces with 'C" Ignition 'K" which enables all secure voice and data communications. This function is currently disabled.
2. Display	Liquid crystal display (LCD) that displays operational status, operator prompts and messages as follows:
A. TX Annunciator	Displayed when KY-100 is transmitting.
B. RX Annunciator	Displayed when KY-100 is receiving.
C. WB Annunciator	Displayed when KY-100 is in wideband (VINSON) configuration.
D. NB Annunciator	Displayed when KY-100 is in narrowband (ANDVT) configuration.
E. EB Annunciator	Displayed when MODE switch is in emergency backup (EB) position.
F. Alphanumeric Display	Displays prompts, messages, and operating modes.
G. PT Annunciator	Displayed when KY-100 is processing plain text voice.
H. Key Symbol	Displayed when menu system is locked.
I. D Annunciator	Displayed when in data mode.
J. V annunciator	Displayed when in voice mode.
K. Bate Display	Displays voice or data rate.
3. FILL Connector	Used to load cryptographic keys through use of common fill device such as KYK-13/TSEC Electronic Transfer Device, KYX-15/TSEC Net Control Device, AN/CYZ-10 Data Transfer Device (DTD), or KOI-18/TSEC General Purpose Tape Reader.

Controls and Functions of Remote Control Unit TSEC/KY-100 (Cont)

CONTROL /INDICATOR	FUNCTION
4. PRESET Switch	Eight position rotary switch that controls unit operating power and settings stored in memory as follows:.
OFF	Removes power from KY 100.
MAN	Manual position which allows operating modes to be selected using both OFFLINE and on-line menu system.
1 thru 6	Six separate preset modes which can only be set up in OFFLINE mode.
5. PNL/OFF BRT Control	Two-function rotary switch that controls on/off status and backlight intensity of LCD display.
6. Three Button Keypad Switches	Three momentary pushbutton switches that are active in both OFFLINE and on-line modes. They are used to enter and exit submenus, activate selected mode, select fields, and to scroll through menus and options as follows:
INIT Switch	In OFFLINE mode, activates displayed menu mode and provides entry into submenus. In on-line modes (CT, RK, EB, PT), selects display field to be changed.
Up Arrow (?) Switch	In OFFLINE mode, scrolls through menus from top to bottom. In online modes (CT, RK, EB, PT), scrolls through available options for display field being changed. When used simultaneously with right arrow (4 switch, exits submenu.
Right Arrow (4 Switch	In OFFLINE mode, scrolls through menus from bottom to top. In on-line modes (CT, RK, EB, PT), selects display field to be changed. When used simultaneously with up arrow (↑) switch, exits submenu.
7. DSPL/OFF BRT Control	Two-function rotary switch that controls on/off status and backlight intensity for front panel.

Controls and Functions of Remote Control Unit TSEC/KY-100 (Cont)

CONTROL /INDICATOR	FUNCTION
8. Mode switch	Six-position rotary switch that selects the following modes of operation:
PT	Plaintext mode to allow reception or transmission of unencrypted analog voice.
EB	Emergency Back-up mode to use emergency back-up key to encrypt voice for transmission or reception.
CT	Ciphertext mode to allows transmission of encrypted voice or data and reception of encrypted or unencrypted voice or data, and non-cooperative terminal re-keying.
RK	Remote keying mode to allow KY-100 to perform automatic and manual rekey operations.
OFFLINE	Disables communications and accesses system menus to allow mode selection, self-test operation, and data fills with cryptovariables.
Z ALL (PULL)	Zeroize mode to erase all cryptographic data stored in KY-100 except emergency back-up key. Switch must be pulled before setting it to this position,

c. Controls and Functions for Processor.
Refer to figure 3-14.3 and the following table:

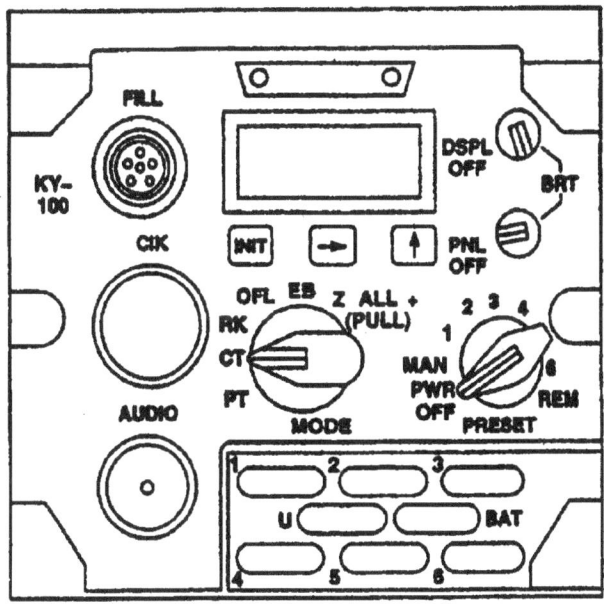

Figure 3-14.3 Processor (TSEC/KY - 100)

Controls and Functions of Processor TSEC/KY-100

CONTROL/INDICATOR	FUNCTION
Audio	Speaker for audio tones.
CIK	Cryptographic ignition key. Not used in this installation.
FILL connector	Used to connect external fill device to KY-100.
INT. → and ↑	Function keys used to access and 'navigate in software menus.
DSPL OFF	Varies light intensity of display. Display turned off in OFF position.

Change 18   3-22.21

Controls and Functions of Processor TSEC/KY-100 (cont)

CONTROL/INDICATOR	FUNCTION
PNL OFF	Varies light intensity of backlit display panel. Display turned off in OFF position.
PRESET switch	Controls power to set, and which key is active.
PWR OFF	Removes power from set.
MAN	Manual rekeying enabled.
1, 2, 3, 4, 5, 6	Selects preset settings for use.
REM	Allows control of KY-100 from a remote control unit (RCU).
MODE switch	
PT	Sets KY-100 to plaintext mode.
CT	Sets KY-100 to ciphertext mode.
RK	Allows cooperative terminal rekeying in receive mode.
OFL	Sets KY-100 to off line mode. Disables communications and accesses screens to select mode settings, test and fill screens.
EB	Select emergency back up key.
Z ALL + (PULL)	Erases all cryptographic data (keys) except the emergency back up key.

c. *Operation.*

NOTE

During all operation procedures the KY-100 processor MODE switch is set to CT and PRESET switch to REM.

(1) Turn-On Procedures.

NOTE

When KY-100 is turned on, tests are automatically performed to determine equipment's operating status. The results of these tests will be presented on display. Also, CLd START message will be displayed.

(a) Cold start turn-on.

1. Turn on KY-100 by setting PRESET switch to MAN position.

2. The KY-100 will initiate self-test. The display reads CLd STRT and then PSH INT.

3. Connect fill device to KY-100 fill connector using fill cable. Select fill position containing valid key and turn it on.

4. Press INIT pushbutton switch.

5. The KY-100 displays KEY 1 O1, PASS.

NOTE

If fill device is not connected to KY-100 when INIT pushbutton is pressed, dEV ERR (Device Error) message will be displayed and an error tone will be heard in the headset. When this occurs, the only available communication mode will be PT (Plaintext).

6. If FAIL message is displayed, notify the next level of maintenance.

7. To load additional keys (up to a total of 6), proceed to Key Loading Section.

(b) Normal Turn-On.

1. Set MODE switch to OFL position.

2. Rotate DSPL and PNL switches clockwise, out of OFF detent positions and adjust display and panel lighting for comfortable viewing.

3. Set PRESET switch to MAN (manual) position to apply power to KY-100. Power-on tests will automatically be run when primary power is applied.

4. Upon successful completion of power-on tests, test results should appear on display. If PASS is displayed, continue with turn-on procedures. However, if FAIL message appears on display, notify next level of maintenance. If PUSH INIT is displayed, perform cold start procedures as described above in paragraph (a).

(2) Key Loading Procedure.

NOTE

Key loading may be accomplished using AN/CYZ-10, KYK-15, KYK-13 or KOI-18. One Key Encryption Key (KEK), up to six Traffic Encryption Keys (TEKs), and one Emergency Backup (EB) key can be loaded in KY-100. A Fill Cable (ON190191) is required when using one of these devices. Proceed with the following generic Key Loading procedures:

(a) Set MODE switch to OFFLINE position.

(b) If KY-100 is not on, turn PRESET switch to MAN position.

(c) Connect fill device to KY-100 fill connector

(d) Press up arrow or right arrow pushbutton switch until KEY OPS is displayed.

(e) Press INIT pushbutton switch. LOAD KEY will be displayed.

(f) Press INIT pushbutton switch. LOAD n with flashing n will be displayed. The flashing n indicates currently selected key location.

(g) Press up arrow or right arrow push-button switch until required location (1, 2, 3, 4, 5, 6, or U) is #splayed.

(h) Press INIT pushbutton switch. The entire LOAD n message will now be flashing.

(i) Turn on fill device and select key to be loaded.

NOTE

Do not press INIT pushbutton switch (or pull tape through tape reader) on fill device.

(j) Press INIT pushbutton switch. (When using KOI-18 pull tape through tape reader at steady rate after terminal INIT pushbutton switch is pressed). Upon completion of successful load, pass tone will be heard and display will momentarily indicate KEY n, where n is key location loaded.

(k) The display will again show LOAD n with n flashing. To load additional keys, repeat steps (g) through (j) until all desired key locations have been loaded.

(l) Turn off and disconnect fill device from KY-100.

(m) Rotate MODE switch out of OFFLINE to exit Key Load.

(3) Zeroize Procedures.

(a) Zeroize All Keys.

NOTE

This procedure is active even if primary power is removed from KY-100. All key locations within KY-100 will be zeroized. Once zeroized, only PT voice communications are possible until new Traffic Encryption Key (TEK) is loaded.

1. Pull MODE switch and rotate it to Z ALL position. All keys stored in locations 1-6 and U will be erased.

2. If KY-100 is on when this procedure is performed, ZEROED will be displayed, and tone will be heard.

3. If KY-100 power is on when MODE switch is rotated out of Z ALL position, PUSH. INIT will be displayed

(b) Zeroize Specific Key Locations.

1. Set MODE switch to OFFLINE position.

2. If KY-100 is not on, set PRESET switch to MAN position.

3. Press up arrow or right arrow push-button switch until KEY OPS is displayed.

4. Press INIT pushbutton switch. LOAD KEY will be displayed.

5. Press up arrow or right arrow push-button switch until ZERO is displayed.

6. Press INIT pushbutton switch. ZERO n with flashing n will be displayed. The flashing n indicates currently selected key location to be zeroized.

7. Press up arrow or right arrow push-button switch until required location (1, 2, 3, 4, 5, 6, or U) is displayed.

8. Press INIT pushbutton switch. The entire ZERO n message will now be flashing.

9. Press INIT pushbutton switch. The display will go blank while key zeroize process is being performed. Upon completion of successful key zeroizing, pass tone will be heard and display will briefly indicate ZEROED n, where n is key location.

10. To zeroize additional keys, wait until display indicates ZERO n (with n flashing), then repeat steps 7 through 9.

11. Rotate MODE switch out of OFFLINE position to exit key load.

TM 55-1520-210-10

(4) Online Mode Selection Menu Procedure

NOTE

This procedure is used to modify Online Mode configuration.

(a) Set MODE switch to CT position.

(b) Set PRESET switch to MAN position. If PRESET switch is in position 1, 2, 3, 4, 5, or 6, mode selections cannot be modified. Refer to section on changing preset settings to modify preset configuration.

(c) Press INIT pushbutton switch. The WB (wideband) or NB (narrowband) enunciator, as applicable, will begin flashing.

NOTE

The KY-100 will be operated in narrowband mode only with ARC-220 Radio Set.

(d) Press up arrow pushbutton switch until desired enunciator (WB or NB) is flashing.

(e) Press right arrow pushbutton switch. The mode field will be flashing.

(f) Press up arrow pushbutton switch until desired mode setting (NT or PP) is flashing.

(g) Press right arrow pushbutton switch. The modem field will be flashing.

(h) Press up arrow pushbutton switch until desired modem setting (HF, LS, or BD) is flashing.

(i) Press right arrow pushbutton switch. The key field will be flashing.

(j) Press up arrow pushbutton switch until desired key location (1, 2, 3, 4, 5, or 6) is flashing.

(k) Press right arrow pushbutton switch. The data rate field will be flashing.

(l) Press up arrow pushbutton switch until desired data rate (300, 600, 1.2K, or 2.4K) is flashing.

(m) After all fields have been set properly, press INIT pushbutton switch to save settings and return to standard operation procedures.

(5) Cipher/Plain Text Volume Level Modification Procedure.

NOTE

The following procedure are used to modify Receive Cipher Text Volume Level, Receive Plain Text Volume Level, and CT/PT or Cipher Text Only menus.

(a) Set MODE switch to CT position.

(b) Set PRESET switch to MAN position.

NOTE

To modify Receive Ciphertext Volume, proceed to step (c). To modify CT/PT or Ciphertext Only setting, proceed to step (h). To modify Receive Plaintext Volume, proceed to step (m).

(c) Press up arrow or right arrow pushbutton switch until RXCTV n (where n represents current receive level) is displayed.

(d) Press INIT pushbutton switch. The n in RXCTV n will begin to flash.

(e) Press up arrow or right arrow pushbutton switch until desired receive level is displayed.

(f) Press INIT pushbutton switch. The n in RXCTV n will stop flashing.

(g) Press up arrow or right arrow pushbutton switch until operating mode is displayed. This completes Receive Ciphertext Volume adjustment.

(h) Press up arrow or right arrow pushbutton switch until CT or CT ONLY is displayed.

(i) Press INIT pushbutton switch. The CT or CT ONLY will begin to flash.

Change 18   3-22.25

(j) Press up arrow or right arrow pushbutton switch until CT (Ciphertext and Plaintext operation) or CT ONLY (Ciphertext only operation) is displayed.

(k) Press INIT pushbutton switch. The CT or CT ONLY will stop flashing.

(l) Press up arrow or right arrow pushbutton switch until operating mode is displayed. This completes CT/PT or CT ONLY setting.

(m) Press up arrow or right arrow pushbutton switch until RXPTV n (where n represents current receive level) is displayed.

(n) Press INIT pushbutton switch. The n in RXPTV n will begin to flash.

(o) Press up arrow or right arrow pushbutton switch until desired receive level is displayed.

(p) Press INIT pushbutton switch The n in RXPTV n will stop flashing.

(q) Press up arrow or right arrow pushbutton switch until operating mode is displayed. This completes Receive Plaintext Volume adjustment.

(6) Normal Operating Procedures.

NOTE

These procedures describe normal transmit/receive operation for ciphertext and plaintext voice messages.

(a) Set PRESET switch to MAN (for manual selection) or desired preset position,

(b) For ciphertext operation, set MODE switch to CT position. Ciphertext messages can now be transmitted or received. If CT, CT ONLY menu is set for CT, plaintext messages can also be received. When transmitting in ciphertext, TX and V enunciators will be lit. When receiving ciphertext message, RX and V enunciators will be lit. When receiving plaintext message, PT enunciator will be lit.

(c) For plaintext operation, set MODE switch to PT position. The CT, CT ONLY menu must be set for CT to be able to transmit or receive plaintext messages. When transmitting in plaintext, TX enunciator will be lit. When receiving plaintext message, RX and PT enunciators will be lit. Refer to the following for Setting Summaries:

TESC/KY-100 Setting Summary

PRESETS
Narrow Band,
HF
VC
NT,
TEK I,
Rate 24,
BD.

AUDIO-DATA INTERFACE

Menu Item	Setting	Default
GUARD	GRD OFF	YES
MIC	MIC UNBAL	YES
BALANCE	RX UNBAL	YES
IMPED	150 OHMS	NO
DAT SENS	MARK +	YES
RX COUP	RX AC	YES
TX COUP	TX AC	YES
TX CLK	J2-V	YES

RADIO INTERFACE

NOTE
You must go through the Narrow Bend selection to get to the following menus.

Menu Item	Setting	Default
TX CLKS	EXT CLK	NO
TRN SEQ	6	YES
TX DELAY	135 ms	YES
PREAM	ENHAN	NO
DAT SENS	MARK -	YES
CTS-BD/BDL	188	NO
CTS-HF/PT	188	NO
CTS-LOS	188	NO
MILSTAR	OFF	YES
TX LVL	0	YES
IMPED	150 OHMS	NO
RTS/PTT-BD/BDL	RTS	NO
RTS/PTT-HF	PTT	NO
RTS/PTT-LOS	PTT	NO
RTS/PTT-PT	PTT	NO

(7) Operating Tests

(a) Fail Message Test

NOTE

Follow these procedures if KY-100 displays FAIL message during equipment configuration or normal operation.

1. Set PRESET switch to PWR OFF position.

2. Set MODE switch to OFL position.

3. Set PRESET switch to MAN.

4. If KY-100 does not display FAIL message after self test, return to normal operation.

5. If KY-100 does display FAIL message after self test, set PRESET switch to PWR OFF position.

6. Pull MODE switch and rotate it to Z ALL position.

7. Perform Cold Start procedures.

8. If KY-100 does not display FAIL message after self test, return to normal operation.

9. If KY-100 does display FAIL message after self test, notify next level of maintenance.

(b) Off-Line Test.

NOTE

The off line TEST menu consists of automatic (AUTO) tests, user-selectable (USER) tests and software version (VERSION) checking procedures.

1. Preliminary.

a. Set MODE switch to OFL position.

b. The display will indicate TEST which is the first OFFLINE menu.

c. Press INIT pushbutton switch to access TEST submenus.

d. Press up arrow or right arrow pushbutton switch until desired sub-menu option (AUTO or USER) is displayed.

e. Proceed to paragraph 2, 3, or 4, as applicable.

2. Automatic (AUTO) Tests.

a. With AUTO displayed, press INIT pushbutton switch to start automatic tests.

b. At conclusion of automatic tests, test results will be displayed.

c. If automatic tests are successful, PASS will be displayed end pass tone will be heard. Next, display will indicate USER which is next sub-menu. To perform USER tests, proceed to paragraph 3. To exit, rotate MODE switch out of OFFLINE position.

d. If failure is detected during automatic tests, FAIL message will be displayed.

3. User Test.

a. With USER displayed, press INIT pushbutton switch to start user tests.

b. PT LOOP will be momentarily displayed to indicate that plaintext loopback test will be performed. Next, PTT prompt is displayed.

c. Depress and hold PTT switch and, with TALK prompt displayed, speak into microphone. Looped back plaintext voice will be heard in handset receiver.

d. Release PTT switch.

e. CT LOOP will be momentarily displayed indicating that KY-100 is In cipher text loopback mode. Next, PTT operator prompt is displayed.

f. Press end hold PTT switch and, with TALK prompt displayed, speak into microphone until TALK prompt disappears (approximately 15 seconds).

Change 18   3-22.27

g. Release PTT switch. The LISTEN prompt is displayed. Listen to synthesized speech at receiver. Upon completion of speech loopback, observe that PANEL is displayed.

NOTE

To exit end skip remaining USER tests, press up arrow or right arrow pushbutton switch within 5 seconds.

h. Within 5 seconds after completion of CT loopback test, observe that all LCD segments are on. At completion of display test, momentary MT operator prompt is displayed indicating start of front panel switch test.

NOTE

Failure to perform any of the front panel pushbutton and switch prompts within 30 seconds will result in fail tone and FAIL FP (Front Panel) display.

i. Press INIT pushbutton switch. A right arrow is displayed.

j. Press right arrow pushbutton switch. An up arrow is displayed.

k. Press up arrow pushbutton switch. PT is displayed.

l. Set MODE switch to PT. CT is displayed.

m. Set MODE switch to CT. RK is displayed.

n. Set MODE switch to RK. OFL is displayed.

o. Set MODE switch to OFFLINE. Eb is displayed.

p. Set MODE switch to EB. PRESET will be momentarily displayed, followed by MAN.

q. Set PRESET switch to MAN. A '1' is displayed.

r. Set PRESET switch to 1. A '2' is displayed.

s. Set PRESET switch to 2. A '3' is displayed.

t. Set PRESET switch to 3. A '4' is displayed.

u. Set PRESET switch to 4. A '5' is displayed.

v. Set PRESET switch to 5. A '6' is displayed.

w. Set PRESET switch to 6. A pass tone will be heard indicating that front panel test was completed successfully.

x. Upon completion of USER tests, menu will sequence to VERSION. Exit user test mode at this time by rotating MODE switch out of OFFLINE position.

Section III NAVIGATION

3-18. ADF Set AN/ARN-83

a. *Description.* The Automatic Direction Finder set provides radio aid to navigation, on helicopter serial Nos. 66-746 and subsequent, within 190 to 1750 kHZ frequency range. In automatic operation, the set presents continuous bearing information to any selected radio station end simultaneously provides aural reception of the stations transmission. In manual operation, the operator determines the bearing to any selected radio station by controlling the aural null of the directional antenna. The set may also be operated as a receiver.

b. *Controls and Functions.* Refer to figure 3-16

c. *Operation.*

(1) Automatic Operation.

(a) RECEIVERS NAV switch - ON

(b) Mode selector switch - ADF

(c) Frequency - Select

(d) Volume - Adjust

TM 55-1520-210-10

1. Frequency selector (first two digits)
2. Frequency selector (fifth digit)
3. Frequency selector (fourth digit)
4. Frequency selector (third digit)
5. Function selector switch

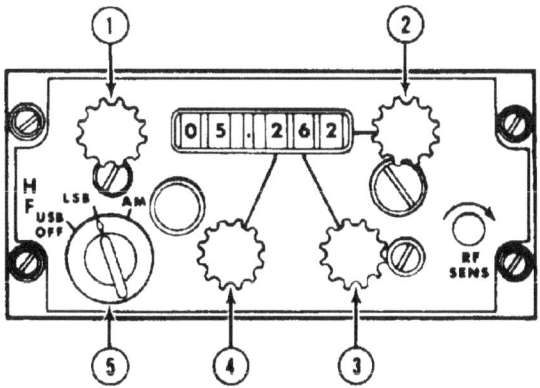

CONTROL/INDICATOR	FUNCTION
Function selector switch (4-position rotary switch)	OFF position — Turns off primary power to the radio set. USB position — Energizes radio set for upper sideband mode of operation. LSB position — Energizes radio set for lower sideband mode of operation. AM position — Energizes radio set for amplitude modulation mode of operation.
Megahertz select knobs	Four knobs used to select the desired frequency as follows: Upper left knob selects the first two digits of the desired frequency. Left center knob selects the third digit. Right center knob selects the fourth digit. Upper right knob selects the last digit of the operating frequency.
RF SENS knob	Controls the receiver audio volume.

Figure 3-15. HF Radio Control Panel

TM 55-1520-210-10

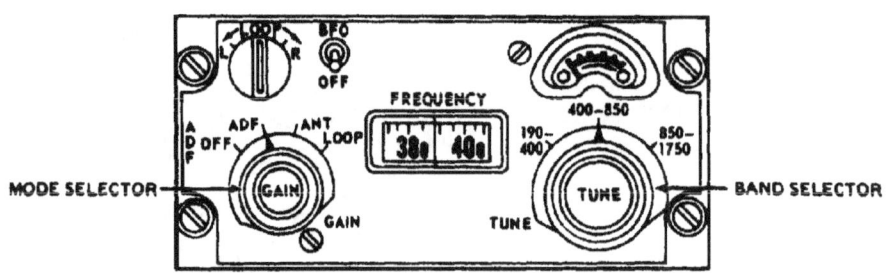

CONTROL/INDICATOR	FUNCTION
Band selector switch	Selects the desired frequency band.
TUNE control	Selects the desired frequency.
Tuning meter	Facilitates accurate tuning of the receiver.
GAIN control	Controls receiver audio volume.
Mode selector switch	Turns set OFF and selects ADF, ANT and LOOP modes of operation.
LOOP L-R switch	Controls rotation of loop left or right.
BFO switch	Turns BFO, on or off.

Figure 3-16. Direction Finder Control Panel ARN-83

(2) *Manual Operation.*

(a) Mode selector switch—LOOP.

(b) BFO switch-ON.

(c) LOOP L/R switch—Press right or left and rotate loop for null.

3-19. ADF Set AN/ARN-59

a. Description. The Direction Finder Set is a radio compass system to provide continuous automatic visual indication of the direction from which an incoming selected radio signal is received. It may also be used for homing and position fixing, or as a manually operated direction finder. The control panel, located in the pedestal, provides control for aural reception of AM signals in the 190 to 1750 kHz range.

b. Controls and Functions. Refer to figure 3-17.

c. Operation.

(1) *Automatic Operation.*

(a) ADF VOL control—ON.

(b) RECEIVERS NAV switch—ON.

(c) Frequency-Select.

(d) Function switch-COMP.

(2) *Manual Operation.*

(a) Function switch—LOOP.

(b) BFO switch-ON.

(c) LOOP switch-Press right or left and rotate loop for null.

3-20. VHF Navigation Set AN/ARN-82

a. Description. The Navigation Receiver set provides reception on 200 channels, with 50 kHz spacing between 108.0 and 126.95 MHz. This permits reception of the VHF omnidirectional range (VOR) between 108.0 and 117.95 MHz. The Vocalizers are received on odd-tenth MHz, between 108.0 and 112.0 MHz and energized as selected. Both VOR and localizer are received aurally through the interphone system. The VOR is presented visually by the course indicator and the number 2 pointer on the bearing indicator and the localizer is presented visually by the vertical needle on the course deviation indicator (CDI) (fig 3-20). When the R-1963/ARN Glideslope/Marker Beacon Receiver is installed, the glideslope frequency is selected by tuning an associated localizer frequency on the control panel.

b. Controls and Functions. Refer to figure 3-18.

c. *Operation.*

(1) Function switch—PWR.

(2) RECEIVERS NAV switch—ON.

(3) Frequency—Select.

(4) VOL—Adjust.

3-21. VHF Navigation Set-AN/ARN-30E

a. Description. The VHF Navigation Receiver Set provides reception of 190 channels at 0.1 MHz intervals between 108.0 and 126.95 MHz. The VOR ILS control panel is located on the pedestal and permits reception and interpretation of VHF omnidirectional range and localizer signals broadcast by ground stations. Line of sight operation varies from 12 nautical miles at 100 feet altitude to 160 nautical miles at 20,000 feet altitude.

b. Controls and Functions. Refer to figure 3-19.

c. Operation.

(1) VOL-OFF switch—On and adjust.

(2) SQUELCH control—Counterclockwise.

(3) Frequency selectors—Select.

The warning flag for the vertical pointer is an indication of signal strength and reliability. Under no circumstances should navigation be attempted if the flag is visible. If the TO-FROM indicator remains blank, do not attempt VOR navigation.

(4) Vertical pointer and TO-FROM indicators (fig 3-20)—Masked.

(5) SQUELCH control—Adjust.

3-22. Course Deviation Indicators ID-453 and ID-1347/

a. Description. The Course Deviation Indicator, used with the VHF Navigation Receiver system, is installed in the instrument panel (figs 3-18 and 3-19). The purpose of the indicator is to depict bearing and deviation of the helicopter from the selected station. Also, information is presented from the FM Receiver when the mode selector switch is in HOME position (figs 3-10, 3-11, 3-12, and 3-13). When the R-1963/ARN Marker Beacon/Glideslope

TM 55-1520-210-10

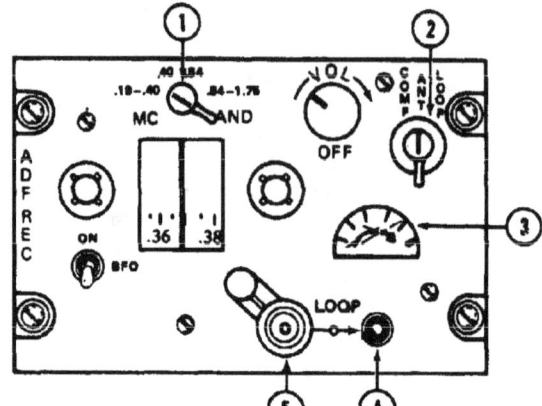

1. Band switch
2. Function switch
3. Tuning meter
4. Loop switch
5. Tuning crank

CONTROL/INDICATOR	FUNCTION
MC BAND switch	Selects the desired frequency band.
VOL-OFF control	Turns direction finder set on or off and adjusts receiver audio volume.
Function switch	COMP position — Receiver operates on combined loop and sense antennas as a radio compass.
	ANT position — receiver operates with sense antenna. Loop position — receiver operates with loop antenna.
LOOP switch	Positions the loop antenna when the function switch is in either COMP or LOOP position.
Tuning crank	Tunes the receiver to the frequency of the received signal.
Tuning meter	Facilitates accurate tuning of the receiver.
BFO switch	Turns BFO ON or OFF.

Figure 3-17. ADF Control Panel ARN-59

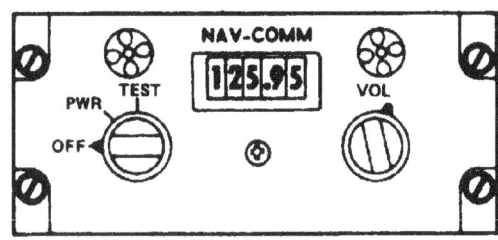

CONTROL/INDICATOR	FUNCTION
VOL control	Controls receiver audio volume.
Power switch	Turns primary power to the radio set and to the R-1963/ARN Marker Beacon/Glideslope Receiver ON or OFF. Allows for accuracy of Course Deviation Indicators and Marker Beacon indicator lamp in the TEST position.
Whole megahertz channel selector knob	This is the control knob on the left side. It is used to select the whole megahertz number of the desired frequency.
Fractional megahertz channel selector knob	This is the control knob on the right side. It is used to select the fractional megahertz number of the desired frequency.

Figure 3-18. Navigation Control Panel ARN-82

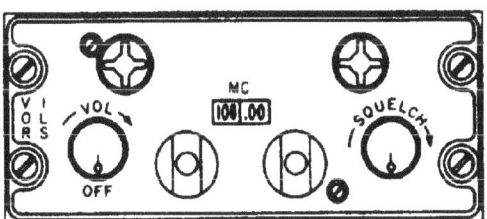

CONTROL/INDICATOR	FUNCTION
VOL-OFF switch	Turns primary power to the radio set ON or OFF and controls the receiver audio volume.
SQUELCH control	Controls receiver squelch circuit.
Whole megahertz control	Selects receiver and transmitter frequency in 1 MHz steps
Fractional megahertz control	Selects receiver and transmitter frequency in 0.1 MHz steps

Figure 3-19. VHF Navigation Receiver Control Panel ARN-30E

TM 55-1520-210-10

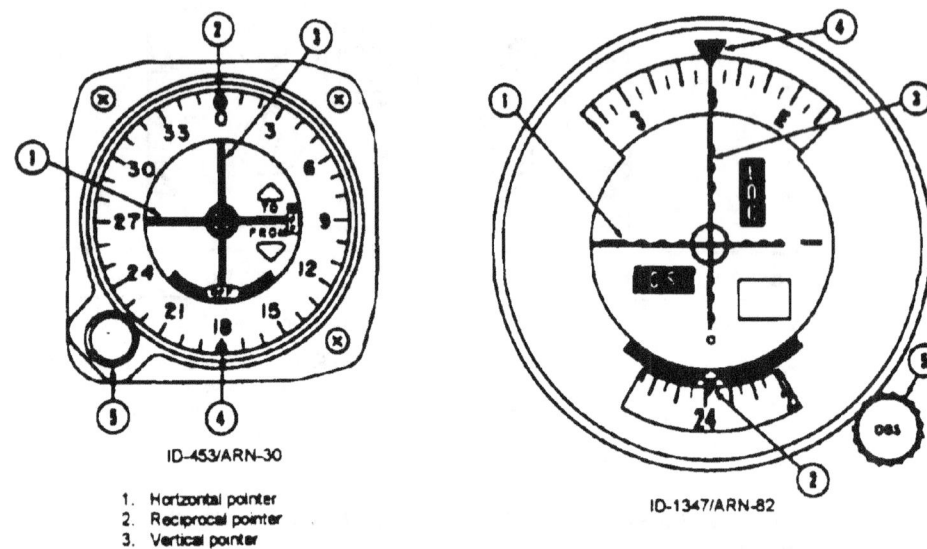

1. Horizontal pointer
2. Reciprocal pointer
3. Vertical pointer
4. Course pointer
5. Course selector knob

INDICATOR		FUNCTION
	OFF vertical	Disappears when FM homing circuits are functioning properly. Remains in view when FM homing circuits are not functioning properly.
	OFF horizontal flag	Disappear when homing circuits are functioning properly. Remains in view when FM homing circuits are not functioning properly NOTE: Do not use if either OFF flag is in view.
	Horizontal pointer	Indicates strength of FM homing signal being received. Deflects downward as signal strength decreases.
	Vertical (reciprocal) pointer	Indicates when pointer is centered that helicopter is flying directly toward or away from the station. Deflection of the pointer indicates the direction (right or left) to turn to fly to the station.

Figure 3-20. Course Deviation Indicators ID-453/ARN-30 and ID-1347/ARN-82

3-28 Change 17

Receiver is installed, data is presented by the horizontal pointer and GS warning flag.

b. Controls and Functions. Refer to figure 3-20.

c. Operation. Refer to the applicable VHF Navigation Receiver and/or FM Radio set operating procedures.

3-23. Gyromagnetic Compass Set.

a. Description.

(1) The Gyromagnetlc Compass Set is a direction sensing system which provides a visual indication of the magnetic heading (MAG) of the helicopter. The information which the system supplies may be used for navigation and to control flight path of the helicopter.

(2) A radio magnetic indicator is installed in the pilot instrument panel. A second radio magnetic indicator (not shown) is installed in the copilots instrument panel. The copilot indicator is a repeater type instrument similar to the pilot indicator except that it has no control knobs. The moving compass card on both indicators displays the gyromagnetic compass heading. The number I pointer on the indicators indicate the bearing to the NDB or course to the VOR station. The number 2 pointer indicates the VOR course to station.

(3) The system does not have a fast-slewing' feature. If the compass is 180° off the correct helicopter heading when the system is energized it will take approximately I hour and 30 minutes (2' per minute) for the compass to slave to the correct headings.

b. Controls and Functions. Refer to figure 3-21.

c. Operation.

(1) INV switch - MAIN or STBY.

(2) Radio magnetic indicator (pilot only) - Check power failure indicator is not in view.

(a) Slaved gyro mode.

1. COMPASS switch - MAG or IN.
2. Synchronizing knob - Center (Null) annunciatior.
3. Magnetic heading - Check.

(b) Free gyro mode.

1. COMPASS switch - DG or OUT
2. Synchronizing knob - Set heading.
3. Annunciator - Center position and then does not change (Annunciator is de-energized in the free gyro (DG) mode).

(c) Inflight operation.

1. Set the COMPASS switch to DG, OUT, MAG or IN as desired for magnetically slaved or free gyro mode of operation. Free gyro (DG or OUT) mode is recommended when flying in latitudes higher than 70 degrees.

2. When operated m the slaved (MAG or IN) mode, the system will remain synchronized during normal flight maneuvers. During violent maneuvers the system may become unsynchronized, as indicated by the annunciator moving off center. The system will slowly remove all errors in synchronization however, if fast synchronization is desired turn the synchronizing knob in the direction indicated by the annunciator until the annunciator is centered again.

3. When operating in the free gyro (DG or OUT) mode, periodically update the heading to a known reference by rotating the synchronizing knob.

3-24. Marker Beacon Receiver.

a. Description. The Marker Beacon Receiver set Is a radio aid to navigation. It receives 75 MHz marker beacon signals from a ground transmitter to provide the pilot with aural and visual information. The marker beacon controls and indicator are located on the instrument panel to aid in determining helicopter position for navigation or instrument approach.

b. Controls and Functions. Refer to figure 3-22.

c. Operation.

(1) VOLUME OFF/INCR control-ON.

(2) Receiver NAV switch (MB switch if SB-329/AR panel is used) - On.

(3) Volume - adjust.

(4) SENSING HIGH/LOW switch-As desired.

d. Stopping Procedures. VOLUME OFF/INCR control - OFF.

TM 55-1520-210-10

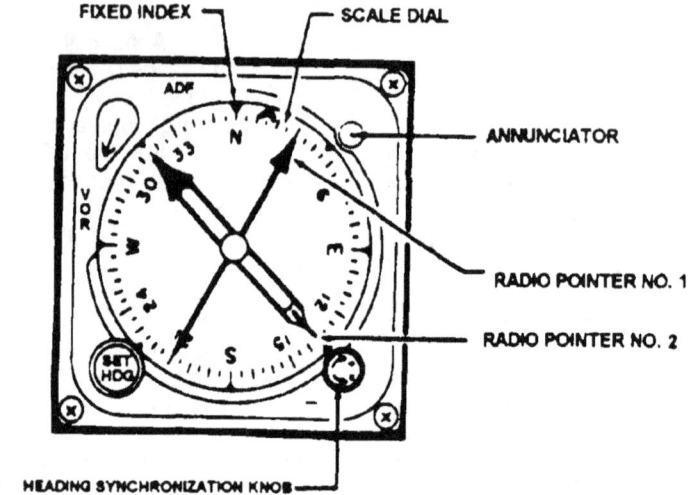

CONTROL/INDICATOR	FUNCTION
Pointer No. 1	Indicates course to ADF or VOR radio station.
Pointer No. 2	Indicates course to VOR station.
Synchronizing control	Is manually rotated to null annunciator and synchronize compass system.
SET HDG control	Moves the heading select cursor to desired heading.
Heading select cursor	Indicates desired heading.
ADF/VOR control	Selects ADF or VOR for pointer No. 1
Fixed index	Provides reference mark for rotating compass card.
Rotating compass card	Rotates under fixed index to indicate helicopter magnetic heading.
Annunciator	Show dot (0) or cross (+) to indicate misalignment (nonsynchronization) of compass system.
Power failure indicator (OFF) (flag)	Shows to indications loss of power to compass system.
Compass switch (located on pilots instrument panel)	MAG or IN position slaved gyro mode DG or OUT position free gyro mode.

Figure 3-21. Gyromagnetic Compass Indicator (RMI)

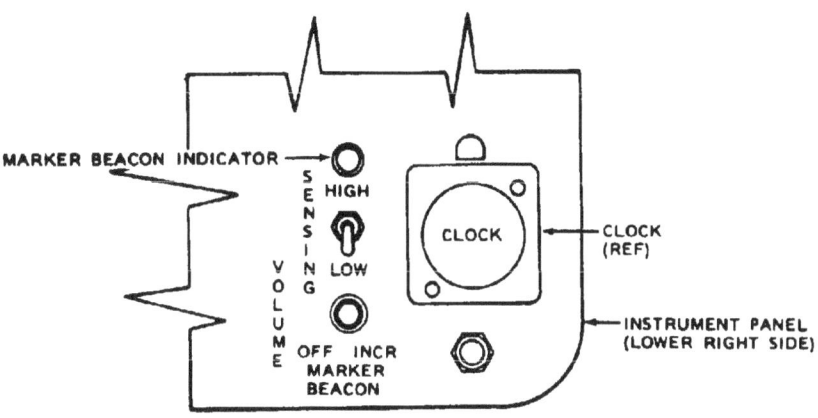

CONTROL/INDICATOR	FUNCTION
VOLUME OFF-INCR control	Turns set ON or OFF and adjusts volume.
SENSING switch	HIGH position — Increases sensitivity.
	LOW position — Decreases sensitivity.
Marker beacon indicator	Flashes when marker beacon receiver is operating and aircraft is passing over the ground transmitter.

Figure 3-22. Marker Beacon Controls

3-24.1 Distance Measuring Equipment (DME) AN/ARN-124.

a. Description.

The AN/ARN-124 DME consists of a receiver-transmitter (interrogator), antenna, indicator and hold light.

The interrogator is installed in the aft left radio-electronics compartment. The indicator and hold light are Installed on the pilot's instrument panel.

The Indicator displays distance In nautical miles from the helicopter to the DME ground station and controls power to the interrogator. The interrogator contains 200 channels covering a frequency range of 962 MHz through 1213 MHz. Signals from the interrogator are responded to by a DME ground station, resulting in a readout on the indicator. DME frequency selection is controlled by the VOR control panel, C-6873B/ARN-82. VOR-DME frequencies are automatically paired. The hold light is controlled by the indicator. Illumination of the hold light indicates a DME frequency is in the hold mode. ILS glideslope indications are not possible with the switch in the hold position. Use of the hold mode permits a change of VOR frequency without changing the DME frequency. DME station identification is accomplished by a continuous 1350 Hz tone In the ICS. Power to operate the DME is from the dc essential bus, through the DME ARN-124 circuit breaker.

b. Controls end Functions. Refer to figure 3-23.

3-24.2 Satellite Signals Navigation Set AN/ASN-175.

a. Description. The AN/ASN-175 is a navigation management system that uses data from the Global Positioning System (GPS) to calculate position, velocity, and time (PVT). It calculates position in three dimensions (3-D): latitude, longitude, and altitude. The AN/ASN-175 utilizes a six channel protective code (P(Y)) continuous tracking, dual frequency (L1/L2) compatible receiver, an omnidirectional flat L1/L2 antenna with an integral preamplifier, and a 3-channel synchro amplifier. The AN/ASN-175 meets the performance standards for instrument flight rules (IFR) for enroute, terminal, and non-precision approach phases of flight.

GPS signals are received by the AN/ASN-175 antenna (hereinafter referred to as the GPS antenna) where it is amplified and sent to the AN/ASN-175 receiver (hereinafter referred to as receiver/display unit) for processing. The receiver/display unit also receives aircraft signals for magnetic compass heading, barometric altitude, and a 26 volt ac reference. Upon processing the input signals, the receiver/display unit provides bearing, course, and distance data which are displayed on existing aircraft navigation equipment when selected. The required amplification for the bearing data from the receiver/display unit is provided by the AN/ASN-175 servo amplifier (hereinafter referred to as the servo amplifier). The receiver/display unit also provides outputs that activate instrument panel mounted annunciators for displaying the operational status of the AN/ASN-175 system. In addition, the receiver/display unit provides a Have-Quick timing signal to any system requiring an accurate time base. For the GPS installation, the Have-Quick timing signal is used by the UHF Receiver/Transmitter in Radio Set AN/ARC-164(V). When operating in the P(Y) mode, the AN/ASN-175 calculates the aircraft's position to within 16 meters. It also provides destination, ground speed, ground track, estimated-time-of-arrival (ETA), and other relevant data to the operator. The AN/ASN-175 uses receiver autonomous integrity monitoring (RAIM) to determine if a set of received GPS signals is sufficient to maintain the required accuracy and alerts the operator if the available GPS signals can not support a 3-D solution. It also can predict RAIM conditions for approach arrival times. When access time to the GPS is less than optimum, the AN/ASN-175 uses the magnetic compass heading and barometric altitude data inputs from the aircraft to validate its calculations and to supplement this data from the GPS. In addition, the AN/ASN-175 protects against deception and denial of the PVT service from the GPS. It does so by providing an anti-jamming capability and by implementing anti-spoofing Y-code functions. Finally, the AN/ASN-175 includes a comprehensive built-in-test (BIT) function that runs when power is applied to the system. BIT monitors the internal operation of the system and

reports detected faults to the operator. Diagnostic routines are also available to the maintainer. Power to operate the AN/ASN-175 is supplied from the 28 vdc essential bus through he GPS ASN-175 circuit breaker on the pilot's overhead circuit breaker panel.
testing

Other components of the GPS installation include a Remote Switch Assembly, a NO. 2 Bearing Pointer switch, a GPS ZEROIZE switch, two Nav select switch-indicator assemblies, two dual display GPS annunciators, and two GPS FILL ports (KYK and DATA). On aircraft equipped with the AN/ARN-124 Distance Measuring Equipment (DME) system, a DME indicator switch is also included to allow the pilot to assign the DME readout to either the GPS or VORTAC navigation system. With the exception of the Remote Switch and Servo Amplifier Assembly, these GPS components are all located on the instrument panel. The operation of all controls and indicators on the receiver/display unit and the GPS controls and indicators on the instrument panel is provided in the controls and functions section that follows:

b. Controls and Functions. Refer to figures 3-22.1 and 3-22.2 and associated tables.

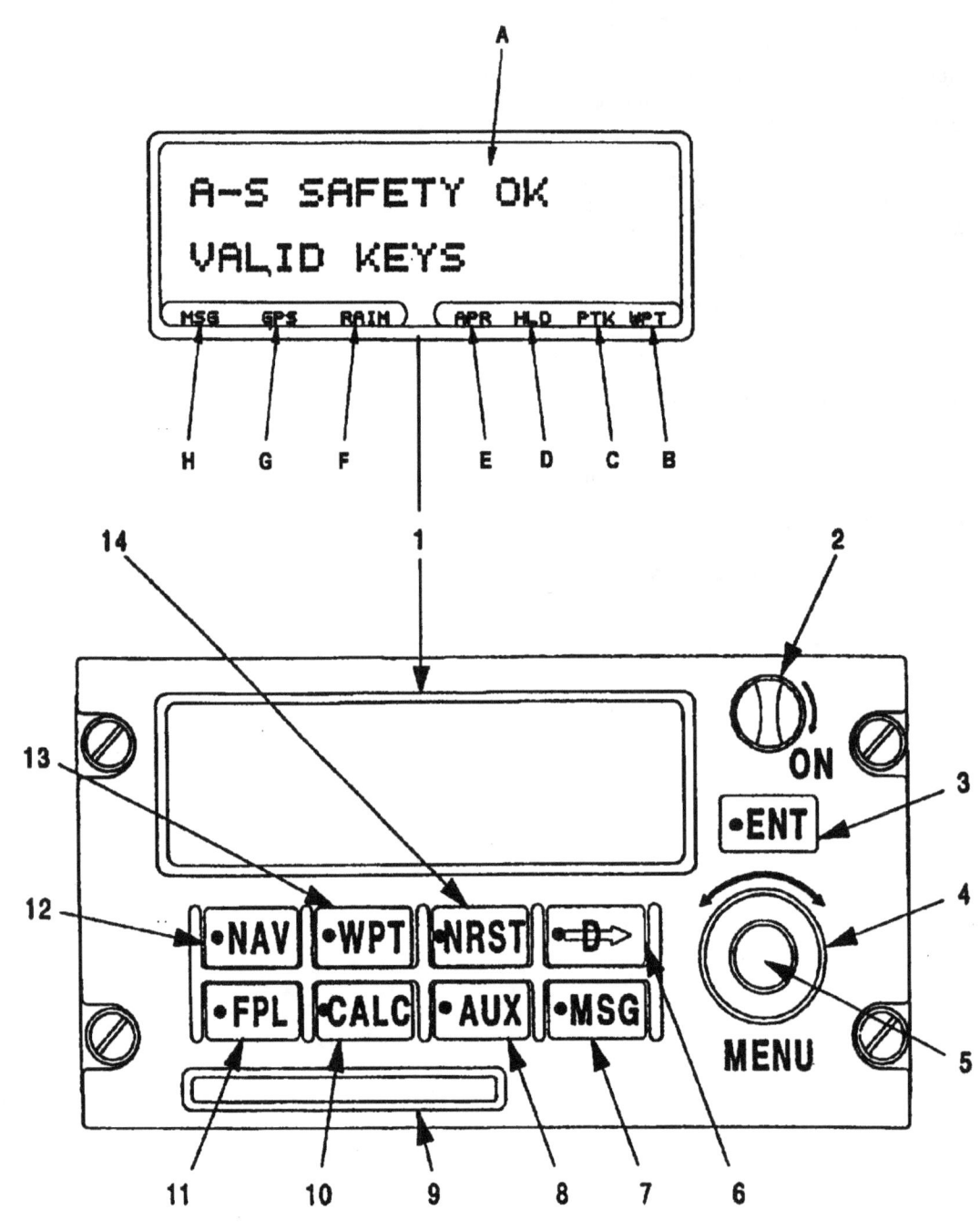

Figure 3-22.1. Receiver/Display Unit

Controls and Functions of Receiver/Display Unit

CONTROL/INDICATOR	FUNCTION
1. Display/Annunciators	Depending on operation, used to display advisory and status information as follows:
A. Display Field	Provides two lines of high intensity light emitting diode (LED) characters with 20 characters per line for displaying information. The information displayed depends on the operational mode and function selection.
B. Waypoint (WPT) Alert Annunciator	Indicates that active waypoint is being approached. The time between illumination of annunciator and arrival at active waypoint may be selected by the operator. The same WPT status information is displayed on the external WPT annunciator.
C. Parallel Track (PTK) Annunciator	Indicates that a track parallel to the direct course has been selected. To display the selected offset, press the MSG key.
D. Hold (HLD) Annunciator	Indicates that active flight plan has been suspended at current active waypoint. The same HLD status information is displayed on the external HLD annunciator.
E. Approach (APR) Annunciator	Indicates that aircraft is at or within two nautical miles of final approach fix and that all approach requirements have been met. The same APR status information is displayed on the external APR annunciator.
F. Receiver Autonomous Integrity Monitoring (RAIM) Annunciator	Indicates that AN/ASN-175 is unable to compute RAIM. When RAIM annunciator is illuminated, the AN/ASN-175 can not enable the approach mode.
G. Sensor Status (GPS) Annunciator	Indicates that AN/ASN-175 is not providing a 3-D solution.
H. Message (MSG) Annunciator	Indicates that one or more of the messages in the queue is unread. When indication is steady, indicates presence of one or more messages in the queue requiring operator action. When indication is not present, indicates that there are no messages in the queue other than CDI scaling message. The same MSG status information is displayed on the external MSG annunciator.
2. Power Switch	Turns power to unit on or off. Power is turned on when switch is rotated to ON (full clockwise) position.

Controls and Functions of Receiver/Display Unit (Cont)

CONTROL/INDICATOR	FUNCTION
3. ENT (Enter) Key	Used in conjunction with MENU controls (inner and outer selector knobs), this key enters, selects, or changes! the information displayed. In general, the first press of key opens an editable field on displayed page and the second press accepts entered data.
4. MENU Control (Outer Selector Knob)	Scrolls through flight plan legs, secondary pages, and bottom lines of displayed mode and moves flashing cursor between editable fields on displayed page.
5. MENU Control (Inner Selector Knob)	Scrolls through primary pages and top lines of displayed mode and changes alphanumeric or available option/function of any editable field.
6. D (Direct To) Key	Changes flight path. Used to fly direct-to any waypoint in database and to activate a procedure or a flight plan. In general, the first press of the pushbutton selects the waypoint, procedure, or flight plan and the second press activates course steering as selected (escape provided by any other key).
7. MSG (Message) Key	Views system messages and displays current course direction indicator (CDI) scaling. The MSG key will flash until all massages have been viewed.

8. AUX (Auxiliary) Key	Accesses a variety of functions to include system information and system status. Also used by maintainer for testing and configuring the AN/ASN-175. Key selection for all displayed functions is as follows:
	
	• <u>Key Selection</u> <u>Displayed Function</u>
	  1st Press System Status
	  2nd Press Sensor Status
	  3rd Press Configure
	  4th Press User Setup
	  5th Press Install Setup
	  6th Press Checklist

9. Navigation Database Card Slot	Accepts Navigation Database Card which contains the database for use with the AN/ASN-175.

TM 55-1520-218-10

Connects and Functions of Reciever/Display Unit (Cont)

CONTROL/INDICATOR	FUNCTION
10. CALC (Calculator) Key	Accesses the capability to perform various computations. Key selection for the displayed computations is as follows: *Key Selection Displayed Computation 1st Press Vertical Navigation Profile 2nd Press flight Plan/Fuel 3rd Press Air Data
11. FPL (Flight Plan) Key	Accesses four modes of flight planning available in the AN/ASN-175. Key selection for the displayed modes is as follows: *Key Selection Displayed Mode 1st Press Active Flight Plan 2nd Press Active Leg, Bearing, Distance, and Estimated Time Enroute 3rd Press Stored Flight Plans 4th Press Stored Leg, Bearing Distance, and Estimated Time Enroute
12. NAV (Navigation) Key	Views navigation and position information along selected route. Key selection for the displayed information is as follows: *Key Selection Displayed Information 1st Press Primary Navigation 2nd Press Waypoint Information
13. WPT (Waypoint) Key	Views and accesses information such as bearing and distance, runway, name, frequencies, and position for waypoints in the database. Key selection for the displayed information is as follows: *Key Selection Displayed Information 1st Press Mark Present Position 2nd Press User 3rd Press Airport 4th Press Approach 5th Press SID 6th Press STAR 7th Press VOR 8th Press NDB 9th Press Intersection

Controls and Functions of Receiver/Display Unit (Cont)

CONTROL/INDICATOR	FUNCTION
14. NRST (Nearest) Key	Views information about the 20 nearest airports, approaches, VHF omnidirectional receivers (VOR) agencies, nondirectional beacons (NDB) intersections, or user waypoints. Key selection for the displayed information is as follows: *Key Selection / Displayed Information 1st Press — Nearest Airport 2nd Press — Nearest Approach 3rd Press — Nearest VOR 4th Press — Nearest Agency 5th Press — Nearest NDB 6th Press — Nearest Intersection 7th Press — Nearest User WPT

* Order of display for indicated key selection is based upon when unit is first turned on.

TM 55-1520-210-10

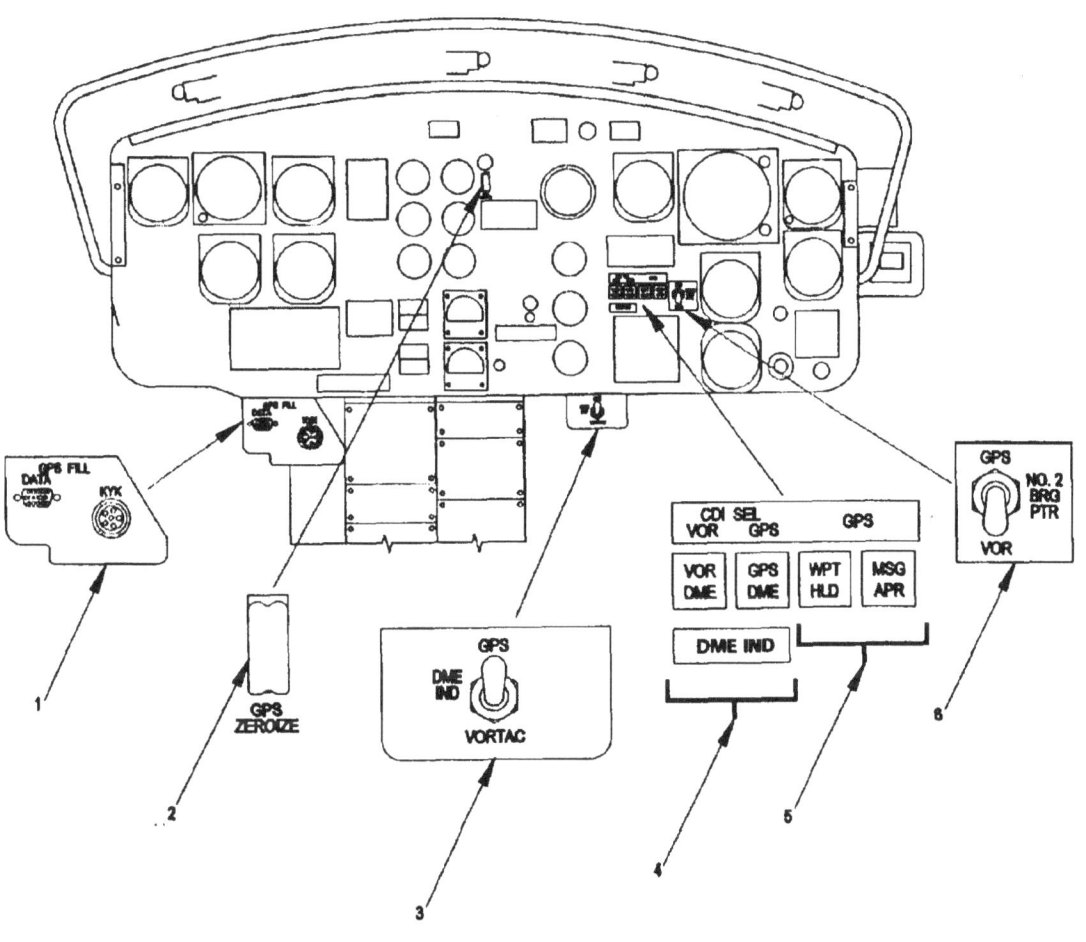

Figure 3-22.2. Instrument Panel - AN/ASN-175 System Components

Change 18 3-32.7

Controls and Functions of Instrument Panel AN/ASN-175 System Components

CONTROL/INDICATOR	FUNCTION
1. GPS FILL Ports	Two independent ports that are used to load data into the AN/ASN-175 system as follows:
DATA Receptacle	Provides connection for Precision Lightweight GPS Receiver (PLGR) AN/PSN-11 to load GPS time and Space Vehicle (SV) data into the AN/ASN-175 system.
KYK Connector	Provides connection for Electronic Transfer Device KYK-13/TSEC to load classified variables (cryptokeys) into the AN/ASN-175 system.
2. GPS ZEROIZE Switch	Enables pilot or copilot to zeroize (erase) all data that has been loaded into the AN/ASN-175 system via the GPS FILL ports (DATA and KYK). Also resets pre-programmed aircraft requirement settings to factory default. It is used only in an emergency situation to prevent potential enemy compromise of classified information. The switch is protected with a guard to prevent inadvertent actuation.
*3. DME IND (Indicator) Switch	Two position toggle switch that selects distance data from either the AN/ARN-124 DME system (VORTAC position) or the AN/ASN-175 system (GPS position) for display on the DME indicator.
4. CDI SEL (Select) VOR/GPS Switches/DME IND Indicators	Two switch-indicator assemblies that provide both DME indications and remote switching control for Course Deviation Indicator (CDI) display as follows:
VOR/DME	When pressed, activates Remote Switch Assembly to select VOR navigation (course deviation) signal for display on the CDI. Also provides DME cue to alert pilot that distance data is supplied from the AN/ARN-124 (VORTAC) Distance Measuring Equipment (DME) system (if installed), as selected by DME IND switch.
GPS/DME	When pressed, activates Remote Switch Assembly to select GPS navigation (course deviation) signal for display on the CDI. Also provides DME cue to alert pilot that distance data is supplied from the AN/ASN-175 (GPS) system, as selected by DME IND switch.

Controls and Functions of Instrument Panel AN/ASN-175 System Components (Cont)

CONTROL/INDICATOR	FUNCTION
5. GPS Annunciators	Two dual annunciator assemblies that display the operational status of the AN/ASN-175 system as follows:
WPT (Waypoint)	Indicates that active waypoint is being approached. The time between illumination of indicator and arrival at active waypoint may be selected by the operator. The same WPT status information is displayed on the WPT annunciator on the receiver/display unit
HLD (Hold)	Indicates that active flight plan has been suspended at current active waypoint. The same HLD status information is displayed on the HLD annunciator on the receiver/display unit.
MSG (Message)	Indicates that one or more of the messages in the queue is unread. When indication is steady, indicates presence of one or more messages in the queue requiring operator action. When indication is not present, indicates that there are no messages in the queue other than CDI scaling message. The same MSG status information is displayed on the MSG annunciator on the receiver/display unit.
APR (Approach)	Indicates that aircraft is at or within two nautical miles of final approach fix and that all approach requirements have been met. The same APR status information is displayed on the APR annunciator on the receiver/display unit.
6. NO. 2 BRG PTR (Bearing Pointer) Switch	Two position toggle switch that selects either GPS bearing (GPS position) or VOR bearing (VOR position) for display by pointer No. 2 on both the pilot's and copilot's Radio Magnetic Indicator (RMI).

* Applicable to aircraft with AN/ARN-124 DME system installed only.

TM 55-1520-210-10

c. *Operation - Satellite Signets Navigation Set AN/ASN-175.*

CAUTION

- The AN/ASN-175 shall not be used as a substitute for the VOR or ADF. When AN/ASN-175 is used for IMC flight, either the VOR or ADF shall be onboard and operational.

- During navigation with the AN/ASN-175 system, avoid operation of the (VHF) Radio on the following frequencies: 121.150 MHz, 121.175 MHZ, 121.200 MHz, 131.250 MHz, 131.275 MHz, and 131.300MHz

- During navigation with the AN/ASN-175 system, avoid operating the AN/ARC-164 radio at 225.100 MHz.

NOTE

The second VOR system (ARN-82) shall not be operated in an aircraft with the AN/ASN-175 installed.

(1) Preoperational and AN/ASN-175 System Instrument Panel Lighting Checks.

(a) GPS ASN-175 circuit breaker - Engaged.

(b) On. .pilot's side of instrument panel, set GPS/DME, controls as follows:

<u>1</u>. NO. 2 BRG PTR switch - GPS.

<u>2</u>. CDI SEL GPS switch/DME indicator assembly - Press. Observe that GPS indicator light in CDI SEL GPS switch/DME indicator assembly comes on.

NOTE

Perform step 3 on aircraft with Distance Measuring Equipment (DME) AN/ARN-124 system installed only.

<u>3</u>. DME IND switch - GPS. Observe that DME indicator light in CDI SEL GPS switch/DME indicator assembly comes on.

(c) Check CDI SEL GPS switch/DME indicator assembly lighting operation with PILOT lighting rheostat on the INST LTS panel located on the overhead console as follows:

<u>1</u>. PILOT lighting rheostat - OFF, Observe that GPS and DME indicator lights are at full brightness level and that pilot's instrument lights are off.

<u>2</u>. PILOT lighting rheostat - Turn clockwise from OFF to on position at minimum setting. Observe that GPS and DME indicator lights and the pilot's instrument lights are at low brightness level.

<u>3</u>. PILOT lighting rheostat - Slowly turn clockwise from minimum to maximum setting. Observe that GPS and DME indicator lights and the pilot's instrument lights change incrementally from low to full brightness.

(d) Adjust instrument lights for best viewing or, if desired, turn them off.

NOTE

The operational procedures that follow in steps (2) through (7) ensure that the AN/ASN-175 system is functional and has the current cryptokeys, valid GPS time and Space Vehicle (SV) data, defined mission duration, and the anti-spoof safety enable required to operate using the P(Y) code. These procedures are then followed by operational procedures RAIM/GPS Status Determination and Preparation for AN/ASN-175 Departure in steps (8) and (9), respectively. Finally, Special Operating Functions and AN/ASN-175 System Shutdown are provided in steps (10) and (11), respectively.

(2) AN/ASN-175 System Power - ON.

NOTE

- Ensure a current Navigation Database Card is installed in GPS Navigation Set Receiver/Display Unit (RDU). Although the following operations can be performed with an expired card, this condition will be reported by the RDU during test.

- When the RDU is turned on, a BIT check is automatically performed in the AN/ASN-175 system. During this time, do not press any of the keys on the RDU until the power on sequence is completed. If any key is pressed during power on sequence, the RDU disregards the key press.

3-32.10   Change 18

(a) Power switch - Turn clockwise to ON position. Several introductory system displays will appear briefly on the RDU and then BIT cycles to a five second lamp self-test.

(b) Observe the five second lamp self-test. All lamps for the annunciators and keys on the RDU and for the GPS annunciators (WPT/HLD indicators and MSG/APR indicators) on the pilot's side of instrument panel come on for approximately five seconds.

(c) Following the lamp self-test, observe BIT result lines that scroll up on display. The following display appears one line at a time on RDU when BIT passes:

```
NAV Computer         OK
AUX IO Computer      -OK
GPS Computer         -OK
GPS Antenna          -OK
Servo Amp            -OK
Memory Battery
Database             -OK
```

NOTE

If BIT fails, the applicable test result line(s) displays a FAIL. If a current Navigation Database Card is not installed or a card is missing, the Database result line displays EXPIRED or N/A, respectively. When a FAIL, EXPIRED, or N/A is displayed, the MSG annunciator on the RDU will flash. This cues the user to press the MSG key on the RDU to display an error message that relates to the failure mode of the AN/ASN-175 system. If more than one failure occurs, as indicated by the flashing MSG annunciator, press MSG key for each error message. Read each error message in turn and take the appropriate action.

(3) Anti-Spoof/Cryptokey Status Determination.

(a) Observe RDU display until ANTI-SPOOF/ CRYPTOKEY status screen appears.

NOTE

In the following display, the second line will scroll across continuously. The full line is NO KEYS NEED INITIALIZE:

```
A-S SAFETY OK
NO KEYS        NEED INITIALIZE
```

NOTE

If display is as shown and GPS time/space vehicle data and cryptokeys are to be loaded into AN/ASN-175 system, proceed to step (4). If display is not as shown and GPS time/space vehicle data and cryptokeys are to be loaded into AN/ASN-175 system, proceed to step (5). If GPS time/space vehicle data and cryptokeys are not going to be loaded into AN/ASN-175 system, proceed as follows:

(b) Observe that ENT key on RDU is flashing.

(c) ENT key - Press. Turn outer selector knob of MENU control counterclockwise until DISABLE

(d) Outer selector knob of MENU control - Turn counterclockwise until DISABLE is displayed and the D in DISABLE is flashing.

(e) ENT key - Press to accept ENABLED setting.

(f) Proceed to step (7).

(4) Cryptokey Loading Initialization For No Keys Display.

(a) Observe that ENT key on RDU is flashing.

(b) ENT key - Press. Observe that A-S SAFETY: ENABLED is displayed and the E in ENABLED is flashing.

(7) Setting Mission Duration.

(a) Outer selector knob of MENU control : Turn until the following display appears:

```
SET MISSION?
                        (ENT)
```

(b) ENT key - Press. Observe that the following START DATE display appears with the first character of date field selected:

```
START DATE: DD-MM-YY
DURATION: 000DAYS
```

(c) inner selector knob of MENU control - Turn until desired character is displayed in that character of date field.

(d) Outer selector knob of MENU control - Turn to select the next character of date field.

(e) Repeat steps (c) and (d) until entire start date has been entered.

(f) Outer selector knob of MENU control - Turn until first digit of mission duration field is selected.

(g) Inner selector knob of MENU control - Turn until desired digit is displayed in that digit of duration field.

(h) Outer selector knob of MENU control - Turn to select next digit of duration field.

(i) Repeat steps (g) and (h) until duration has been completely entered.

(j) ENT key - Press to set mission duration.

(k) After mission duration is set, SETTING MISSION STANDBY will be displayed. wait until display changes to COMMAND COMPLETE and then proceed to step (8).

(8) RAIM/GPS Status Determination.

(a) Observe RAIM annunciator, If RAIM annunciator is illuminated, indicates that AN/ASN-175 cannot provide required integrity for flight and that problem should be referred to AVUM. In the event that this problem occurs during flight, any navigation using the AN/ASN-175 must be crossed checked for position using other approved sources.

(b) Observe GPS annunciator. If GPS annunciator is illuminated, proceed to step (c). if not, proceed to step (d).

(c) The AN/ASN-175 is not providing a 3-D position solution and is not ready for the mission. Wait two minutes and observe GPS annunciator. If GPS annunciator remains illuminated after two minutes, repeat procedures starting from step (5) if operating in a suspected spoofed environment. If GPS annunciator still remains illuminated after repeating procedures, refer problem to AVUM. If operating in a known spoof free environment and GPS annunciator still remains illuminated, refer problem to AVUM for resetting the RDU. When reset, the RDU must be reprogrammed to the required aircraft settings.

(d) The AN/ASN-175 is providing a 3-D position solution and is ready for the mission. To determine the accuracy and Figure of Merit (FOM) of solution, proceed as follows:

NOTE

The AN/ASN-175 is now calculating position and the display will now show the present position.

$\underline{1}$. AUX key - Press and hold for one second until SYSTEM STATUS mode is selected and PRESENT POSITION display appears:

```
POSITION EPE:        XXm
LL XX°XX .xxx  XXXX° xx .xxx x
```

2. AUX key - Press until SENSOR STATUS mode is selected and the GPS STATUS display appears:

```
GPS: 3D/PRS         RAIM
MODE: TERM          1.6
```

NOTE

FOM is an integer between 1 and 9 and is determined from the RDU position error.

3. The FOM values and its meaning as determined from the RDU position error are as follows:

FOM Value	Meaning
1	<25m
2	>25m, <50m
3	>50m, <75m
4	>75m, <100m
5	>100m, <200m
6	>200m, <500m
7	>500m, <1000m
8	>1000m, <5000m
9	>5000m

4. Outer selector knob of MENU control - Turn until the flowing display appears:

```
ESTIMATED ACCURACY:
GPS:  9m   FOM:  1
```

(9) Preparation For AN/ASN-175 Departure.

(a) Flight Plan Loading and Activation.

1. FPL key - Press to select STORED FLIGHT PLANS display.

2. Inner selector knob of MENU control - Turn to select desired flight plan.

3. FPL key - Press. The FPL key will now be flashing.

4. Inner selector knob of MENU control - Turn to select desired leg of flight plan.

5. —D→ key - Press and note leg's course.

6. —D→ key - Press a second time to join leg and activate flight plan.

7. If flight plan includes a Standard Instrument Departure (SID) when ready to depart, depart in accordance with the applicable procedures in step (b) below and then fly the flight plan following the prompts from the AN/ASN-175. If flight plan does not include a SID, depart in accordance with published procedures and then fly the flight plan following the prompts from the AN/ASN-175.

(b) Fly Standard Instrument Departure (SID) Using GPS.

NOTE

Proceed to step 1 to fly direct to the first waypoint in SID and fly the entire procedure, step 6 to join any specific leg in SID and fly the rest of procedure, or step 11 to fly direct to any waypoint In SID and fly the rest of procedure.

1. Select desired SID.

2. -D key- Press

3. Inner selector knob of MENU control - Turn to change course to/from waypoint, if desired.

4. —D→ key - Press a second time to make first waypoint active waypoint and to activate SID.

5. Fly SID following prompts from AN/ASN-175.

6. Select desired SID.

7. Turn outer selector knob of MENU control to select desired leg of SID.

8. Press —D→ key.

9. Press —D→ key a second time to join leg and to activate SID.

TM 55-1520-210-10

10. Fly SID following prompts from AN/ASN-175.

11. Select desired SID.

12. Outer selector knob of MENU control - Turn to select desired leg of SID.

13. —D→ key - Press.

14. Outer selector knob of MENU control - Turn counterclockwise to select first waypoint of leg. Outer selector knob of MENU control - Turn clockwise to select second waypoint of leg.

15. Inner selector knob of MENU control - Turn to change course to/from waypoint, if desired.

16. —D→ - Press key a second time to fly direct to waypoint and to activate SID.

17. Fly SID following prompts from AN/ASN-175.

(c) Fly Direct To A Waypoint.

NOTE

You may fly direct to any waypoint in the database. Select the waypoint from the WPT, NRST, NAV or FPL mode. Flying direct to a waypoint selected from the FPL mode will activate the flight plan starting at the selected waypoint.

1. Select desired waypoint.

2. —D→ key - Press. Observe the following display:

```
FLY COURSE <086°> —D→
           AUSv
```

3. Inner selector knob of MENU control - Turn to change course to/from waypoint, if desired.

4. —D→ key - Press a second time to make waypoint the active waypoint.

5. The AN/ASN-175 automatically switches to NAV mode and displays the PRIMARY NAVIGATION page as follows:

```
ᵀO LAX A 120°  143: 0:34
[i▫i▫| o▫i▫i] ᵀₖ124°  250 ᴷ/ᵀ
```

6. For reference, set Course Deviation (CDI) or Horizontal Situation Indicator (HSI) to displayed course.

7. When ready, depart in accordance with published procedures and follow prompts from AN/ASN-175 to fly to waypoint.

(10) Special Operating Functions.

(a) Zeroizing the Cryptokeys.

NOTE

The procedures that follow provide instructions to zeroize the cryptokeys, if previously loaded, in the RDU. Normally, the cryptokeys should be zeroized after every mission. If the cryptokeys are not zeroized after completion of a mission, it will not be possible to set a new mission duration. The cryptokeys, however, will automatically zeroize when the mission duration expires.

1. AUX key - Press until USER SETUP mode appears on display.

2. Inner selector knob of MENU control - Turn until SECURITY MODULE page appears as follows:

```
A-S SAFETY OK
   VALID KEYS
```

3-32.16 Change 18

3. Outer selector knob of MENU control - Turn until the following display appears:

```
ZEROIZE KEYS?
(ENT)
```

4. ENT key - Press to initiate the keys zeroizing function. Observe that AUX key is flashing and that the following display appears:

```
ZEROIZE KEYS
ARE YOU SURE?  (AUX)
```

NOTE

Press any key other than the AUX key to abort the zeroize keys function.

5. AUX key - Press to complete the zeroize keys function. Observe that display changes to the STANDBY mode as follows:

```
ZEROIZING KEYS
    STANDBY
```

6. After a few seconds, observe that the following display appears:

```
   KEYS ZEROIZED
```

(b) Zeroizing All Variables.

NOTE

The procedures that follow provide instructions to zeroize all mission variables. These variables should be zeroized whenever the RDU is removed for maintenance or for any other purpose.

1. AUX key - Press until USER SETUP mode appears on display.

2. Inner selector knob of MENU control - Turn until SECURITY MODULE page appears as follows:

```
A-S SAFETY OK
VALID KEYS
```

3. Outer selector knob of MENU control - Turn until the following display appears:

```
ZEROIZE ALL?
                (ENT)
```

4. ENT key - Press to initiate the zeroize all function. Observe that AUX key is flashing and that the following display appears:

```
ZEROIZE ALL
ARE YOU SURE?  (AUX)
```

NOTE

Press any key other than the AUX key to abort the zeroize all function.

5. AUX key - Press to complete the zeroize keys function. Observe that the following display appears briefly and then the AN/ASN-175 will reset itself.

```
ZEROIZING ALL
   STANDBY
```

(c) Programming RDU Auxiliary Input/Output Ports.

NOTE

Actuation of the GPS ZEROIZE switch on the instrument panel will erase all variables stored in the RDU and will reset the auxiliary input/output (I/O) ports of the RDU to factory default. As a result, the GPS ZEROIZE switch should be normally used when it is absolutely necessary to verify that it is functional or for emergency situations. In the event that the GPS ZEROIZE switch is actuated, the RDU will have to be reprogrammed to satisfy the aircraft requirements. Instructions for actuating the GPS ZEROIZE switch and reprogramming the RDU are as follows:

1. Locate GPS ZEROIZE switch on center section of instrument panel.

2. GPS ZEROIZE switch - Raise cover and toggle switch to the up position to initiate the zeroize. Observe that RDU resets, displays a ZEROIZE IS SUCCESSFUL message, and then cycles through the power on/BIT checks until the ANTI-SPOOF/CRYPTOKEY status screen appears as follows:

```
A-S   SAFETY   OK
NO KEYS      NEED   INITIALIZE
```

3. ENT key - Observe that it is flashing.

4. ENT key - Press.

5. Outer selector knob of MENU control - Turn counterclockwise until DISABLE is displayed and the D in DISABLE is flashing.

6. ENT key - Press to accept the DISABLE setting.

7. AUX key - Press until INSTALL SETUP mode appears on display.

8. Inner selector knob of MENU control - Turn until AUX I/O SETUP display appears as follows:

```
AUX I/O SETUP
TURN OUTER KNOB
```

TM 55-1520-210-10

Table 3-1. RDU Auxiliary Input/Output Port Settings.

I/O PORT CATEGORY	CHOICE SETTINGS	AIRCRAFT SETTINGS
HEADING INPUT	* None XYZ Magnetic-Synchro XYZ TRUE-Synchro	XYZ Magnetic-Synchro
PRESSURE ALTITUDE INPUT	Serial-RS-422/RS-232 * Parallel	Parallel
OLEO INPUT	* None Air Ground	None
SYNCHRO OUTPUT #1	* Off HDG T HDG DTK TDTK BRG TBRG TKE DA TKE-DA DA-TKE BRG-HDG +0.00 +180 SYNCHRO SIN/COS	** BRG-HDG + 180° SYNCHRO
SYNCHRO OUTPUT #2	Same as SYNCHRO OUTPUT #1	** BRG-HDG + 180° SYNCHRO
SYNCHRO OUTPUT #3	Same as SYNCHRO OUTPUT #1	Off
DIGITAL OUTPUT X3	ARINC 561 *ARINC 568	ARINC 561

*Indicates factory default setting.

**To select BRG-HDG + 180° SYNCHRO setting after obtaining the BRG-HDG +000° SYNCHRO display, proceed as follows:

1. Outer selector knob of MENU control - Turn clockwise one detent position and observe that + sign in BRG-HDG +000° SYNCHRO display flashes.

2. Inner selector knob of MENU control - Turn clockwise one detent position to obtain BRG-HDG + 180° SYNCHRO setting display.

NOTE

There are seven auxiliary I/O port categories (HEADING INPUT, PRESSURE ALTITUDE INPUT, OLEO INPUT, SYNCHRO OUTPUT #1, SYNCHRO OUTPUT #2, SYNCHRO OUTPUT #3, and DIGITAL OUTPUT #3) that must be selected and programmed internally to satisfy the aircraft requirements.

9. Outer selector knob of MENU control - Turn until the first I/O port category (HEADING INPUT) display appears. (Refer to table 3-1.)

10. ENT key - Press to allow configuration of the port.

11. Inner selector knob of MENU control -Turn to select the choice setting (XYZ Magnetic-Synchro) for aircraft.

12. ENT key - Press to save the selection. -

13. Repeat steps 9 through 12 until all I/O port settings are programmed into the aircraft as specified in table 3-1.

(d) Verifying and Programming User Units/Parameters.

NOTE

The following procedures provide instructions for verifying the user unit/parameter settings of the aircraft and, if necessary, reprogramming the RDU to obtain the desired setting(s). The user unit/ parameter settings include: Audio Level, Audio Tone Frequency, CDI Sensitivity, Estimated Time of Arrival (ETA), Position Coordinate System, Position Datum, Distance Units, Speed Units, Elevation Units, Barometric Setting Units, Temperature Units, Fuel Consumption Units, Track Error Graphic, Display Light Intensity for night vision goggles (NVG) and Magnetic Variation (MAGVAR).

Unless otherwise specified, all control settings are performed on the RDU.

1. AUX key - Press until INSTALL SETUP mode is selected.

2. Inner selector knob of MENU control - Turn until SELECT USER UNIT, TURN OUTER KNOB is displayed.

3. Outer selector knob of MENU control - Turn until desired unit/parameter is displayed as follows:.

User Unit/Parameter	Display
ETA	ETA TIME DISPLAY
Distance Units	DISTANCE DISPLAY
Speed Units	SPEED DISPLAY
Barometric Units	SELECT BARO UNITS
Temperature Units	TEMP DISPLAY
Fuel Computation Units	FUEL COMPUTATION

4. ENT key - Press to change setting if displayed setting is incorrect.

5. Inner selector knob of MENU control - Turn to select desired display setting for applicable unit/parameter as follows:

User Unit/Parameter	Display Selection
ETA	LOCAL or ZULU time
Distance Units	Nautical miles, kilometers, or statue miles
Speed Units	Knots, kilometers per hour, or miles per hour
Barometric Units	Inches or millibars
Temperature Units	Centigrade or Fahrenheit
Fuel Computation Units	Gallons, imperial gallons, kilograms (avgas, jet-A or JP-4), liters, or pounds (avgas, jet-A or JP-4)

6. ENT key - Press to save selected settings.

7. Inner selector knob of MENU control - Turn until SET AUDIO LEVEL is displayed.

8. Connect headset to pilot's or copilot's ICS connector.

9. AUX switch on ICS - Set to

10. NAV VOL switch on VOR control unit (AN/ARN-123 system) - Deselect from OFF position.

11. ENT key - Press and observe that the following display appears:

```
VOLUME   : INNER KNOB
FREQUENCY: OUTER KNOB
```

12. Inner selector knob of MENU control - Turn to set comfortable audio level.

13. Outer selector knob of MENU control - Turn to set desired audio tone frequency.

14. ENT key - Press to save setting(s).

15. Inner selector knob of MENU control - Turn until the following display appears:

```
CDI SENSITIVITY
TURN OUTER KNOB
```

16. Outer selector knob of MENU control - Turn until INTERNAL CDI ADJUST display appears.

17. ENT key - Press to change setting if display setting is incorrect.

18. Inner selector knob of MENU control - Turn to select 5.0, 2.5, 1.0, 0.3, or 0.1 nautical miles.

19. ENT key - Press to save the display selection.

20. Outer selector knob of MENU control - Turn-until EXTERNAL CDI ADJUST display appears.

21. ENT key - Press to change setting if display setting is incorrect,.

22. Inner selector knob of MENU control - Turn to select 5.0, 2.5, 1.0, 0.3, or 0.1 nautical miles.

23. ENT key - Press to save the display selection,

24. Inner selector knob of MENU control - Turn until SELECT USER UNITS, TURN LARGE KNOB is displayed.

25. Outer selector knob of MENU control - Turn until POSITION DISPLAY 1 display appears.

26. If display setting is correct, proceed to step 30.

27. ENT key - Press to change coordinate system setting if display setting is incorrect.

NOTE

Coordinate systems available for selection are: latitude/longitude (L/L (DDDMM.MMM)), latitude/ longitude (L/L (DDMMSS.SW, Military Grid Reference System (MGRS), Universal Transverse Mercator/Universal Polar Stereographic (UTM/UPS), British National Grid (BNG), Irish Transverse Mercator (ITM), and User Definable Coordinate (UDC).

28. inner selector knob of MENU control - Turn to select desired coordinate system.

29. ENT key - Press to save position display 1 coordinate system selection.

30. Outer selector knob of MENU control - Turn until POSITION DISPLAY 2 display appears.

NOTE

The POSITION DISPLAY 2 selects a secondary coordinate system that may be displayed. If NONE is selected for POSITION DISPLAY 2, then there will be no secondary coordinate system available for display.

31. ENT key - Press to change setting if display setting Is incorrect.

32. Inner selector knob of MENU control - Turn to select NONE or the desired coordinate system.

33. ENT key - Press to save position display 2 coordinate system selection.

34. Inner selector knob of MENU control - Turn until SELECT USER UNITS, TURN LARGE KNOB is displayed.

35. Outer selector knob of MENU control - Turn until POSITION DATUM display appears.

NOTE

Default datum is world datum WGS-84. If another datum Is selected, POSITION DATUM message appears for approximately 5 seconds during system power on sequence.

36. ENT key - Press to change setting if display setting is Incorrect.

37. Outer selector knob of MENU control - Turn to select datum symbol field or the datum name field.

38. Inner selector knob of MENU control - Turn to select desired datum.

39. ENT key - Press to save position datum selection.

40. Inner selector knob of MENU control - Turn until SELECT USER UNITS, TURN LARGE KNOB is displayed.

41. Outer selector knob of MENU control - Turn until ELEVATION display appears as follows:

```
ELEVATION: FEET
REFERENCE: MN SEA LV
```

42. ENT key - Press to change setting if display setting is incorrect.

43. Outer selector knob of MENU control - Turn to select ELEVATION field.

44. Inner selector knob of MENU control - Turn to select feet or meters.

45. Outer selector knob of MENU control - Turn to select REFERENCE field.

46. Inner selector knob of MENU control - Turn to select MN SEA LV (mean sea level) or GEOD HT (geodetic height).

47. ENT key - Press to save elevation units selection.

48. Inner selector knob of MENU control - Turn until TRACK ERROR GRAPHIC display appears:

```
TRACK ERROR GRAPHIC
COMBINE  TKE/CDI YES
```

49. ENT key - Press to change selection if incorrect.

50. Inner selector knob of MENU control - Turn to select YES or NO.

51. ENT key - Press to save selection.

52. Inner selector knob of MENU control - Turn until SET DISPLAY INTENSITY LEVEL display appears.

NOTE

Pressing ENT key will cause display to go to previously stored or lowest intensity settings for NVG ENABLED intensity settings.

53. ENT key - Press and observe that display changes as follows:

```
BACKLIGHT: INNER KNOB
NIGHT LEVEL: OUT KNOB
```

54. Inner selector knob of MENU control - Turn counterclockwise until intensity of key back-lighting is at a minimum.

55. Outer selector knob of MENU control - Turn counterclockwise until intensity of display is at a minimum.

56. Inner and outer selector knobs of MENU control Turn to adjust key backlighting and display Intensity for optimum NVG levels.

57. ENT key - Press to save selection.

58. Inner selector knob of MENU control - Turn until MAGVAR display appears.

59. ENT key - Press to change selection if display is incorrect.

60. Inner selector knob of MENU control - Turn to select AUTO, DEGREES, or DEG + MIN.

NOTE

When the AN/ASN-175 is set to MAGVAR: AUTO, it will automatically enter the estimated magnetic variation.

61. Outer and inner selector knobs of MENU control - Turn to enter desired values if DEGREES or DEG + MIN is selected.

62. ELT key - Press to save selection.

(11) AN/ASN-175 System Shutdown.

NOTE

The AN/ASN-175 system may be shutdown at any time without any risk of damage.

(12) RDU power switch - Turn full counterclockwise to off position.

Section IV. TRANSPONDER AND RADAR

3-25. Transponder Set AN/APX-72.

a. Description. The AN/APX-72 provides radar identification capability. Five independent coding modes are available. The first three modes may be used independently or in combination. Mode 1 provides 32 possible code combinations, any one of which may be selected in flight. Mode 2 provides 4,096 possible code combinations but only one is available since the selection dial is not available in flight and must be preset before flight. Mode 3/A provides 4,096 possible codes, any of which may be selected In flight. Mode C is used with the AAU-32/A Encoding Altimeter (AIMS). Mode 4, which 6 connected to an external computer, can be programmed prior to flight to display any one of many classified operational codes for security identification. The effective range depends on the capability of interrogation radar and line of sight. The transponder control set is mounted on the center pedestal. The IFF CODE HOLD switch on the instrument panel interfaces with MODE 4 (fig 2-4). This allows the crew to hold the classified operational code that has been programmed.

b. *Controls and Functions.* Refer to figure 3-24.

c. *Operation.*

(1) MASTER control - STBY. Allow approximately 2 minutes for warmup.

(2) MODE and CODE - Select as required.

(3) TEST M-1, 2, 3/A and C as required.

(4) MASTER control - NORM or LOW as required.

(5) IDENT - As required.

(6) STOPPING procedure. MASTER control - OFF.

d. *Emergency Operation.* MASTER control - EMER.

3-26. Transponder Set AN/APX-100.

a. *Description.* The transponder set AN/APX-100 enables the helicopter to identify itself automatically when properly challenged by friendly surface and airborne radar equipment. The control panel enables the set to operate in modes 1, 2, 3A, 4 and test. Mode 4 is operational when computer KIT 1A (-1C)/ TSEC (classified) is installed, properly coded, keyed, and IFF caution advisory light is not on. The range of the receiver-transmitter is limited to line of sight transmission since its frequency of operation is in the UHF band making range dependent on altitude.

b. *Controls and functions* - Transponder Set. Refer to figure 3-25.

c. *Operation - Transponder Set.*

(1) MASTER control - STBY. Allow approximately 2 minutes for warmup.

(2) MODE and CODE - As required.

(3) MASTER control - NORM.

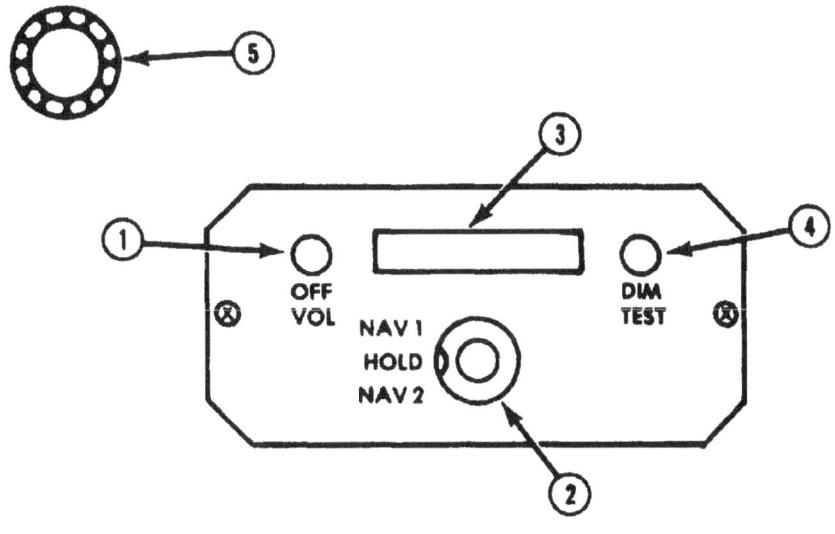

CONTROL	FUNCTION
1. OFF/VOL switch.	Controls powers to indicator and interrogator. Adjusts volume of audio identification (1350 Hz continuous tone).
2. NAV 1/HOLD/NAV 2 switch	
NAV 1	Selects DME frequency controlled by VOR control panel C-6873B/ARN-82.
NAV 2	When two VOR sets are installed, selects DME frequency controlled by No. 2 VOR.
HOLD	Holds DME frequency last selected by VOR control panel. Change of VOR frequency does not change DME frequency.
3. Distance Display	Digital readout indicating distance to DME station in hundreds, tens, units, and tenths of nautical miles.
4. DIM/TEST switch	
DIM	Controls brightness of display lighting.
TEST	Push test function provides digital readout of 0.0 or 0.1 in display window.
5. Hold light.	Lamp illumination indicates a DME frequency is in the hold mode.

Figure 3-23. DME Indicator ID-2192/ARN-124

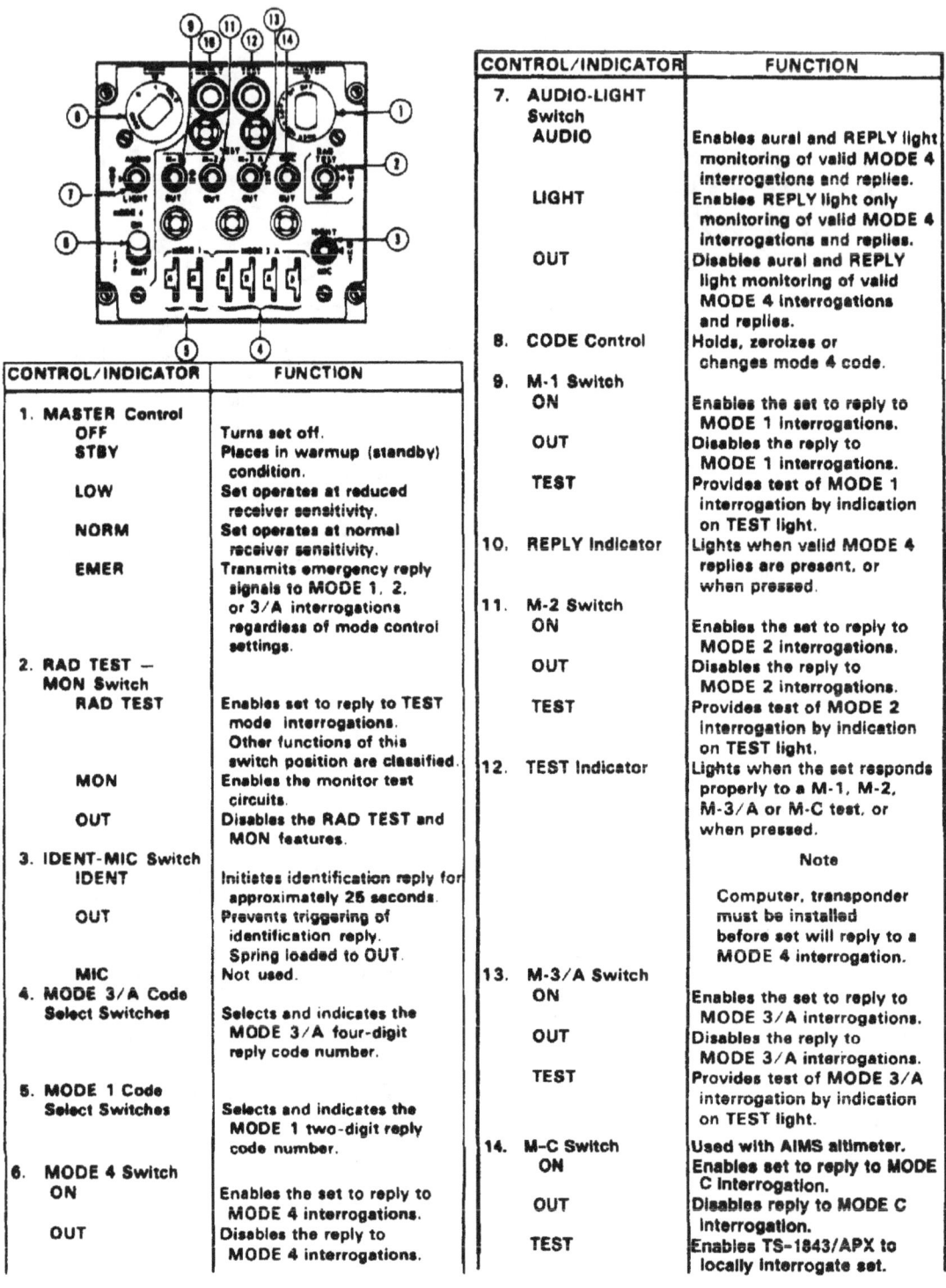

CONTROL/INDICATOR	FUNCTION
1. MASTER Control	
OFF	Turns set off.
STBY	Places in warmup (standby) condition.
LOW	Set operates at reduced receiver sensitivity.
NORM	Set operates at normal receiver sensitivity.
EMER	Transmits emergency reply signals to MODE 1, 2, or 3/A interrogations regardless of mode control settings.
2. RAD TEST – MON Switch	
RAD TEST	Enables set to reply to TEST mode interrogations. Other functions of this switch position are classified.
MON	Enables the monitor test circuits.
OUT	Disables the RAD TEST and MON features.
3. IDENT-MIC Switch	
IDENT	Initiates identification reply for approximately 25 seconds.
OUT	Prevents triggering of identification reply. Spring loaded to OUT.
MIC	Not used.
4. MODE 3/A Code Select Switches	Selects and indicates the MODE 3/A four-digit reply code number.
5. MODE 1 Code Select Switches	Selects and indicates the MODE 1 two-digit reply code number.
6. MODE 4 Switch	
ON	Enables the set to reply to MODE 4 interrogations.
OUT	Disables the reply to MODE 4 interrogations.

CONTROL/INDICATOR	FUNCTION
7. AUDIO-LIGHT Switch	
AUDIO	Enables aural and REPLY light monitoring of valid MODE 4 interrogations and replies.
LIGHT	Enables REPLY light only monitoring of valid MODE 4 interrogations and replies.
OUT	Disables aural and REPLY light monitoring of valid MODE 4 interrogations and replies.
8. CODE Control	Holds, zeroizes or changes mode 4 code.
9. M-1 Switch	
ON	Enables the set to reply to MODE 1 interrogations.
OUT	Disables the reply to MODE 1 interrogations.
TEST	Provides test of MODE 1 interrogation by indication on TEST light.
10. REPLY Indicator	Lights when valid MODE 4 replies are present, or when pressed.
11. M-2 Switch	
ON	Enables the set to reply to MODE 2 interrogations.
OUT	Disables the reply to MODE 2 interrogations.
TEST	Provides test of MODE 2 interrogation by indication on TEST light.
12. TEST Indicator	Lights when the set responds properly to a M-1, M-2, M-3/A or M-C test, or when pressed.
	Note
	Computer, transponder must be installed before set will reply to a MODE 4 interrogation.
13. M-3/A Switch	
ON	Enables the set to reply to MODE 3/A interrogations.
OUT	Disables the reply to MODE 3/A interrogations.
TEST	Provides test of MODE 3/A interrogation by indication on TEST light.
14. M-C Switch	Used with AIMS altimeter.
ON	Enables set to reply to MODE C interrogation.
OUT	Disables reply to MODE C interrogation.
TEST	Enables TS-1843/APX to locally interrogate set.

Figure 3-24. Transponder Set AN/APX-72

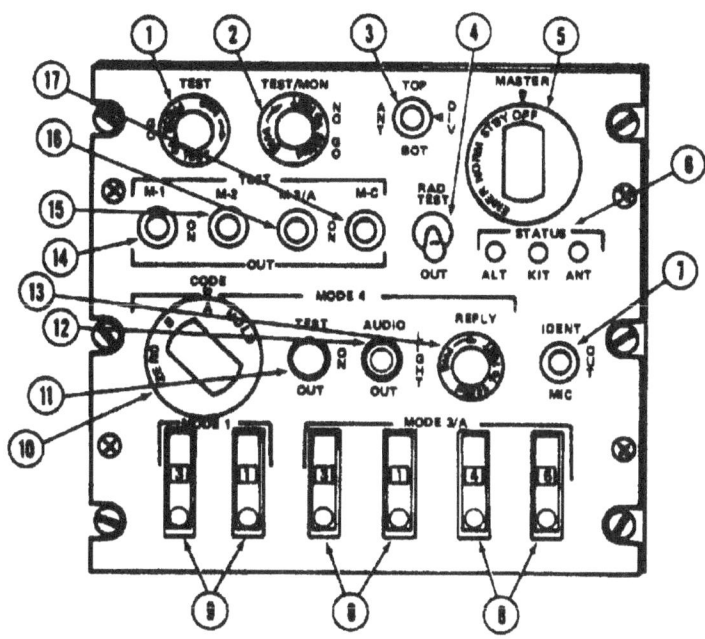

CONTROL/INDICATOR	FUNCTION
1. TEST GO	Indicates successful built in test (BIT).
2. TEST/MON NO GO	Indicates unit malfunction.
3. ANT TOP BOT DIV	 Selects antenna located on top of helicopter. Selects antenna located on bottom of helicopter. Monitor received signals from both antennas and allows transmission via antenna receiving the strongest signal.
4. RAD TEST switch RAD TEST OUT	 Enables set to reply to TEST mode interrogations. Disables to RAD TEST features.
5. MASTER control OFF STBY NORM EMER	 Turns set off. Places in warmup (standby) condition. Set operates at normal receiver sensitivity. Transmits emergency replay signal to MODE 1, 2, or 3/A interrogations regardless of mode control settings.
6. STATUS indicators ANT KIT ALT	 Indicates that built in test (BIT) or monitor (MON) failure is due to high voltage standing wave ratio (VSWR) in antenna. Indicates that built in test (BIT) or monitor (MON) failure is due to external computer. Indicates that built in test (BIT) or monitor (MON) failure is due to altitude digitizer.

Figure 3-25. Transponder Set (AN/APX-100) Control Panel (Sheet 1 of 2)

TM 55-1520-210-10

CONTROL/INDICATOR	FUNCTION

7. IDENT-MIC switch
    IDENT
    OUT
 	
    MIC
	Initiates identification reply for approximately 25 seconds.
	Prevents triggering of identification reply. Spring loaded to OUT.
	Not used.

8. MODE 3/A code select switches	Selects and indicates the MODE 3/A four-digit reply code number.
9. MODE 1 code select switches	Selects and indicates the MODE 1 two-digit reply code number.
10. MODE 4/CODE control HOLD/A/B/ZERO	Selects condition of code changer in remote computer

11. MODE 4 TEST switch
    TEST
    ON
    OUT
	Selects MODE 4 BIT operation.
	Selects MODE 4 ON operation.
	Disables MODE 4 operation.

12. MODE 4 AUDIO/LIGHT control
    AUDIO
    LIGHT
    OUT
	MODE 4 is monitored by audio.
	MODE 4 is monitored by a light.
	MODE 4 not monitored.

13. MODE 4/REPLY	Indicates that a MODE 4 reply is generated.
14. TEST/M-1 TEST/ON/OUT	Selects ON, OFF or BIT of MODE 1 operation.
15. TEST/M-2 TEST/ON/OUT	Selects ON, OFF, or BIT of MODE 2 operation.
16. TEST/M-3/A TEST/ON/OUT	Selects ON, OFF, or BIT of MODE 3/A operation.
17. TEST/M-C TEST/ON/OUT	Selects ON, OFF, or BIT of MODE C operation.

Figure 3-25. Transponder Set (AN/APX-100) Control Panel (Sheet 2 of 2)

(4) TEST - As required.
(5) ANT - As desired.
(6) IDENT - As required.
(7) Stopping procedure. MASTER control - OFF.

d. Emergency Operation - Transponder Set MASTER control - EMERG.

3-27. Mode 4 Operation (APX-72 and APX-100).
 a. Before Exterior Check
 (1) IFF CODE HOLD switch (on the instrument panel) - HOLD and check that the IFF CODE HOLD indicator lamp is on.

NOTE
If the IFF CODE HOLD switch is OFF and the MASTER switch is in any position other than OFF, MODE 4 codes will zeroize when the battery switch is turned off during the BEFORE EXTERIOR check.

 *b. Aircraft Runup - Test: (APX-100 only)
 (1) MASTER switch - STBY FOR 2 minutes.
 (2) CODE switch - A.
 (3) Mode 4 or MODE 4 TEST switch ON.
 (4) MODE 4 AUDIO/LIGHT/OUT switch - AUDIO.
 (5) MODE 4 TEST/ON/OUT switch (APX- 100) TEST momentarily.
 c. AP,Y-72 --Test Response.
 (1) REPLY light should go on.
 (2) Audio tone should be heard.
 (3) If the above indications do not occur, select the opposite code (A or B) and repeat the check.
 d. APX-100 - Test response
 (1) REPLY light should go on.

 (2) If the REPLY light does not Illuminate and/or the audio tone is heard, select the opposite code (A or B) and repeat check.

NOTE
Further testing to check for correct coding responses is done with ground test equipment by moving the MASTER switch to NORMAL. either transponder does not respond to ground test interrogation the IFF caution light should illuminate.

 e. *Zeroizing MODE 4* codes may be accomplished in any one of the following methods:
 (1) CODE switch - ZERO.
 (2) MASTER switch - OFF.

NOTE
If the switch is returned to NORMAL within 5 seconds, zeroizing may not occur.

 (3) Aircraft electrical power - OFF.

NOTE
If the IFF CODE HOLD switch (on the instrument panel) is at HOLD and the CODE switch has been moved to HOLD prior to removing electrical power, zeroizing will not occur.

 (4) Deleted.
 f MODE 4 codes retained after engine shutdown.
 (1) IFF CODE HOLD switch - ON and IFF code HOLD indicator lamp is on.
 (2) CODE switch - HOLD momentarily and then release.
 (3) MASTER switch - OFF.

TM 55-1520-210-10

3-28. Altitude Encoder/Pneumatic Altimeter AAU-32/A.

a. Description The AAU-32/A pneumatic counter-drum-pointer altimeter is a self-contained unit which consists of a precision pressure altimeter combined with an altitude encoder (fig 3-26). The display indicates and the encoder transmits. simultaneously, pressure altitude reporting Altitude is displayed on the altimeter by a 10.000 foot counter, a 1,000 foot counter and a 100 foot drum. A single pointer indicates hundreds of feet on a circular scale, with 50 foot center markings. Below an altitude of 10,000 foot a diagonal warning system will appear on the 10.000 foot counter. A barometric pressure setting knob Is provided to insert the desired altimeter setting In inches of Hg. A dc powered vibrator operates inside the altimeter whenever the aircraft power is on. If dc power to the altitude encoder is lost, a warning flag placarded CODE OFF will appear in the upper left portion of the instrument face indicating that the altitude encoder is inoperative and that the system is not reporting altitude to ground stations. The CODE OFF flag monitors only the encoder function of the altimeter. It does not indicate transponder condition. The AIMS altitude reporting function may be inoperative without the AAU-32/A CODE OFF flag showing, In case of transponder failure or improper control settings It is also possible to get a 'good' MODE C test on the transponder control with the CODE OFF flag showing. Display of the CODE OFF flag only indicates an encoder power failure or a CODE OFF flag failure. In this event. check that dc power Is available and that the circuit breakers are in. If the flag is still visible, radio contact should be made with a ground radar site to determine whether the AIMS altitude reporting function is operative, and the remainder of the flight should be conducted accordingly.

b. *Operation.*

(1) Normal Operation. The AIMS altimeter circuit breaker should be closed prior to flight, the Mode C switch (M-C) on the transponder control should be switched to ON for altitude reporting during flight. The AAU-32.'A altimeter indicates pneumatic altitude reference to the barometric pressure level as selected by the pilot. At ambient pressure, altimeters should agree with ±70 feet of the field elevation when the proper barometric pressure setting is set in the altimeter. A red flag marked CODE OFF is located in the upper left portion of the altimeters face In order to supply Mode C information to the IFF transponder, the CODE OFF flag must not be visible. A vibrator, powered by the dc essential bus, is contained In the altimeter and requires a minimum of one minute warmup prior to checking or setting the altimeter

(2) Abnormal Operation.

(a) If the altimeters internal vibrator becomes inoperative due to internal failure or dc power failure, the pointer and drum may momentarily hang up when passing from 9 through 0 (climbing) or from 0 thorough 9 (descending). This hang-up will cause lag, the magnitude of which will depend on the vertical velocity of the aircraft and the friction in the altimeter. Pilots should be especially watchful for this type failure when the minimum approach altitude lies within the 8-1 part of the scale (800 to 1100, 1800 to 2100, etc).

(b) If the CODE OFF flag is visible, the dc power is not available, the circuit breaker is not in, or there is an internal altimeter encoder failure.

(c) It the altimeter indicator does not correspond within 70 feet of the field elevation (with proper local barometric setting) the altimeter needs rezeroing or there has been an internal failure.

(d) If the baroset knob binds or sticks. abnormal force should not be used to make the setting as this may cause internal gear failure resulting in altitude errors. Settings can sometimes be made by backing off and turning at a slower rate.

3-29.   Proximity Warning System YG-1054.

a. Description The proximity warning transponder, control panel located at the forward left side of the pedestal, operates at frequency 5.08 GHz. The system provides audio and visual intruder indications of similarly equipped aircraft within 5,000 feet laterally and 300 feet vertically. Vertical operation is influenced by barometric pressure from the helicopters pitot static tube.

b. Controls and Functions. Refer to figure 3-28.
c. Operation.
   (1) POWER switch - ON
   (2) Test - CONFIDENCE TEST.
   (3) RANGE SELECT - As desired.
   (4) LIGHT INTENSITY - As desired.
   (5) AUDIO Adjust.
   (6) POWER - OFF

Figure 3-26. AAU-32/A Altitude Encode/Pneumatic Altimeter

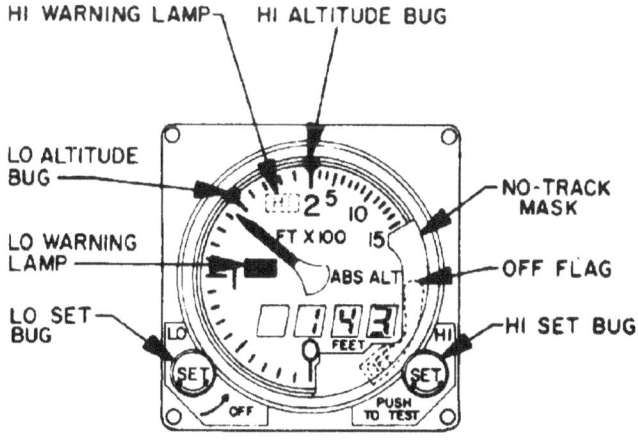

Figure 3-27. AN/APN-209 Radar Altimeter (V)

TM 55-1520-210-10

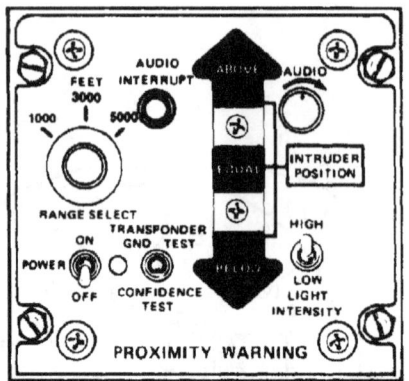

CONTROL/INDICATOR	FUNCTION
POWER ON/OFF switch	Controls 28Vdc power to system
POWER lamp	Indicates when 28Vdc power is applied to system
RANGE SELECT switch	Sets range gate circuitry to accept a reply signal within selected distances
AUDIO INTERRUPT push button switch	Silences audio alarm signal for approximately one minute
INTRUDER POSITION indicator lamps	Flash singly or in combination to indicate position of intruder as follows:
	FLASHING LAMP(S) — RELATIVE INTRUDER POSITION
	ABOVE — Between 110 and 300 feet above
	ABOVE and EQUAL — Between 80 and 110 feet above
	EQUAL — Between 80 feet above and 80 feet below
	EQUAL and BELOW — Between 80 and 110 feet below
	BELOW — Between 110 and 300 feet below
AUDIO control	Varies the volume of the audio tone
LIGHT INTENSITY switch	Switches INTRUDER POSITION and POWER indicator lamps to LOW or HIGH intensity
TRANSPONDER TEST switch	In TRANSPONDER GND TEST position, permits unit to accept signals from ground transponder. In CONFIDENCE TEST position, switch initiates confidence test

Figure 3-28. Proximity Warning Panel

3-30. Radar Warning Set.

a Description The radar warning set AN/APR-39 provides the pilot with visual and audible warning when a hostile fire-control threat is encountered. The equipment responds to hostile fire-control radars but nonthreat radars are generally excluded. The equipment also receives missile guidance radar signals and, when the signals are time-coincident with a radar tracking signal, the equipment identifies the combination as an activated hostile surface to air (SAM) radar system. The visual and aural displays warn the pilot of potential threat so that evasive maneuvers can be initiated.

CAUTION

To prevent damage to the receiver detector crystals, assure that the AN/APR-39V-1 antennas are at least 60 meters from active ground radar antennas or 6 meters from active airborne radar antennas. Allow an extra margin for new, unusual or high power emitters.

1. PWR switch - ON, allow I-minute for warmup.
2. BRIL and filter controls - Adjust as desired.
3. AUDIO control - Adjust volume as desired.
4. DSCRM switch - Set for mission requirement.
5. Stopping Procedure - PWR switch - OFF.

3-31. V Radar Altimeter - AN/APN-209.

a. Description. The radar altimeter set is a high resolution pulse radar that provides an medication of absolute clearance over all types of terrain. The set consists of the following: a panel mounted height indicator receiver transmitter (located on copilot instrument panel); a panel mounted remote height indicator (located on pilot instrument panel), and two flush mounted antennas on the underside of the helicopter. The controls and displays of the height indicator receive-transmitter (IRT) and the remote height indicator (RI) are identical (see Figure 3-27). Absolute altitude is displayed by a pointer and a digital readout. The pointer operates against a fixed dial and indicates tens of feet between 0 to 200 feet, and hundreds of feet between 200 to 1500 feet. Above 1500 feet the pointer is driven behind a mask. The digital display has a four digit readout. The readout is displayed in one foot increments up to 255 feet. At 256 feet the display is rounded up to 260 feet. Between 260 and 1500 feet the readout is displayed in tens of feet. The LO SET control knob functions as the on-off switch and is the low altitude trip point adjustment. Clockwise rotation turns the set on. Continuing a clockwise rotation provides for the setting of the low altitude bug. The HI SET control knob provides for the setting of the high altitude bug. Depressing the HI SET control knob places the altimeter set m the self-test mode. The IRT sends a simulated signal of 1000 feet to both mediators. The indicators display the information via the pointer and digital readout. Whenever the indicated altitude drops below the low altitude bug setting the LO altitude warning lamp is activated. Whenever the indicated altitude goes above the high altitude bug setting, the HI altitude warning lamp is activated. When the LO SET control knob is turned to OFF, or during periods of unreliable operation, the OFF flag comes into view.

b. Operation The following procedures apply to both indicators (IRT on copilot instrument panel, and RI on pilot instrument panel). Accomplish procedures using controls on each indicator.

(1) Initial Operation Turn the IRT and RI on by Turing the LO SET control knob clockwise. Set the low altitude warning bug to 80 feet by turning LO SET control knob clockwise. Set the high altitude warning bug to 800 feet by turning the HI SET control knob clockwise. The indicators should display a track condition within two minutes from the time indicator was turned on. The OFF flag should disappear from view; the pointer read 0 to 3 feet; the digital display -0 to +3 feet; and the LO warning lamp illuminate. Press and hold the HI SET control knob (push to test operation). The indicator pointer and digital display should read 1000 +100 feet; the LO warning lamp should be off and the HI warning lamp on.

NOTE
When using an unmodified indicator during NVG flight, turn the HI/LO and DIGITAL switch to OFF. Use the height needle lite by the eyebrow light The modified indicator will work as advertised.

(2) Normal Operation Adjust LO SET control knob to desired setting for low altitude warning bug. The LO warning lamp will illuminate when indicated altitude drops below this setting. Adjust HI SET control knob to desired setting for high altitude warning bug. The HI warning lamp will illuminate when indicated altitude goes above the high altitude warning bug setting. For daylight operations, set the pilot instrument lighting control (overhead console) to OFF. This setting provides lighting at full brightness to the warning lamps and digital displays on both indicators. Turning the instrument lighting controls (pilot and copilot) controls clockwise dims the indicator lighting. In the event of loss of track due to helicopter attitude (30 degrees pitch or 45 roll) or to operation beyond the range of the altimeter, the altitude pointer swings behind the no-track mask and the digital readout is totally blanked. In addition, the OFF flag comes into view.

(3) Stopping Procedure Turn LO SET control knob (on each indicator) fully counterclockwise.

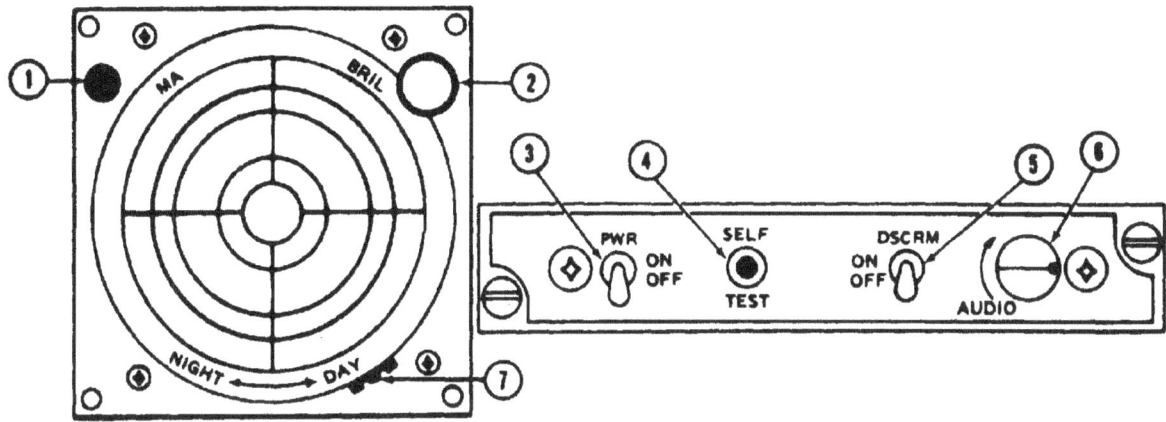

CONTROL/INDICATOR	FUNCTION
1. MA Indicator	Flashing indicates high radar missile threat with DSCRM switch in ON.
2. BRIL Control	Adjusts indicator illumination.
3. PWR Switch:	
ON	Applies power to radar set.
OFF	De-energizes radar set.
4. SELF-TEST Switch:	
With DSCRM Switch OFF	Fore and Aft strobes appear simultaneously and the primary (normal) audio tone is heard. After a short delay, the MA light will start flashing and the audio warning (wailing) tone is heard.
With DSCRM Switch ON	One strobe appears at the top or bottom and primary (normal) audio tone is heard. After short delay, a second strobe will appear 180 degrees from the initial strobe. After another short delay, MA light will start flashing and audio warning (wailing) tone is heard.
5. DSCRM Switch:	
OFF	Without missile activity — Provides strobe lines for ground radar and normal audio indications.
	With missile activity — Provides strobe lines for ground radar, flashing strobe line(s) for missile activity, and flashing MA (missile alert) light.
ON	Without missile activity — No indications.
	With missile activity — Flashing strobe lines for missile activity (no strobe lines for ground radar), flashing MA light, and audio warning (wailing) tone.
6. AUDIO Control	Adjusts radar warning audio volume.
7. NIGHT-DAY Control	Adjust indicator intensity.

Figure 3-29. Radar Warning System

3-32. Receiver-Transmitter Radio, RT-1167/ARC-164(V).

Receiver-Transmitter Radio RT-1167/ARC-164(V) (figure 3-3.1) is an airborne, ultra-high frequency (UHF), amplitude-modulated (AM), radio transmitting-receiving (transceiver) set. It contains a multichannel, electronically-tunable transceiver and a fixed-tuned guard receiver. The transceiver operates on any one of 7,000 channels spaced in 0.025 MHz units in the 225.000 to 399.750 MHz UHF military band. The guard receiver is tunable in the 238.000 to 248.000 MHz frequency range with crystal replacement and realignment (usually 243.000 MHz). The radio set primarily is used for voice communication. An additional radio set capability, although not functional is ADF. Power to operate the ARC-164(V) radio is from the 28 vdc emergency bus through a circuit breaker marked UHF-AM on the pilot overhead circuit breaker panel.

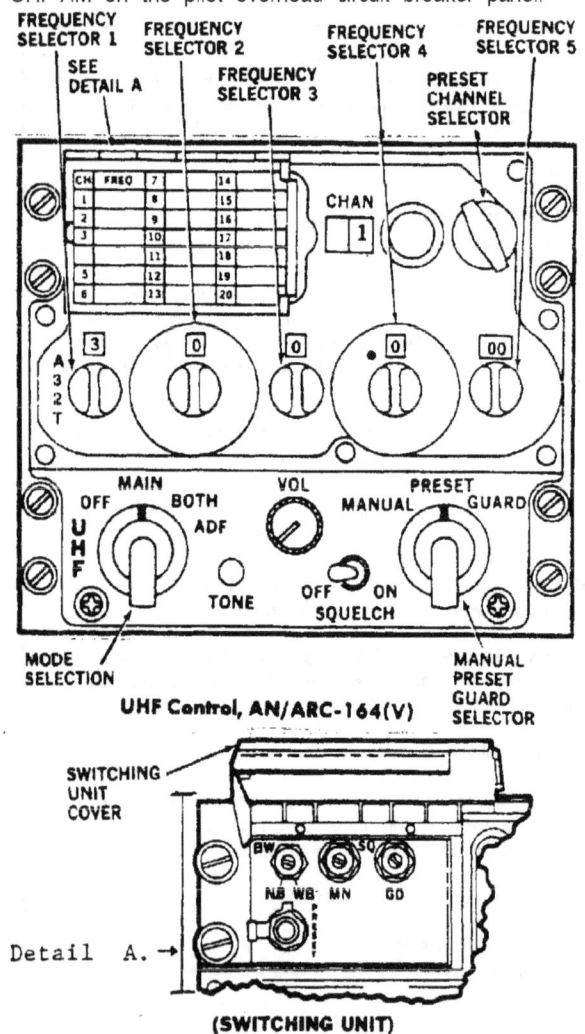

Figure 3-29.1. Receiver-Transmitter Radio, RT-1167/ARC-164(V)

3-33. Receiver-Transmitter Radio, RT-1167C/ARC-164(V).

Receiver-Transmitter Radio RT-1167C/ARC-164(V) has the same functions and capabilities as the RT-1167/ARC-164(V) plus a HAVE QUICK mode of operation. HAVE QUICK is an antijamming mode which uses a frequency hopping scheme to change channels many times per second. Because the HAVE QUICK mode depends on a precise time of day, both HAVE QUICK radios must have synchronized clocks.

A-3-2-T Knob (HAVE QUICK ONLY)

* A- Selects AJ mode.
* 3- Allows manual selection of frequencies.
* 2- Allows manual selection of frequencies.
* T - Momentary position which enables the radio to accept a new TOD for up to 60 seconds after selection. Also used in conjunction with the emergency startup of the TOD clock when TOD is not available from a external source.

TONE Button (Have Quick) - Depressing the TONE button in normal or AJ modes interrupts reception and transmits a tone signal and TOD on the selected frequency. Simultaneously pressing the TONE button in conjunction with the A-3-2-T knob in the T position starts the emergency startup of the TOD clock.

HAVE QUICK System - The HAVE QUICK (HQ) system provides a jam resistant capability through a frequency hopping technique. Frequency hopping is a technique in which the frequency being used for a given channel is automatically changed at some rate common to the transmitter and receiver. The jam resistance of the system is due to the automatic frequency changing and the pseudorandom pattern of frequencies used. In order to defeat this communications system, the jammer must find the frequency being used, jam it and then predictor find the next frequency. The HAVE QUICK modification adds the frequency hopping capability, yet it does not remove any of the previous capabilities of the radio. The HAVE QUICK modified radios retain the standard, single frequency UHF voice mode of operations. This is referred to as the normal mode, while frequency hopping operation is called the anti-jam (AJ) mode. Several ingredients are necessary for successful system operations. These are:

1. Common frequency
2. Time synchronization.
3. Common hopping pattern and rate.
4. Common net number.

The common frequencies have been programmed into all HAVE QUICK radios. Time synchronization is provided via UHF radio and/or hardware by external time distribution system. A time-of-day (TOD) signal must be received from the time distribution system for each time the radio is turned on. The hopping pattern and hopping rate are determined by the operator inserted word-ofday (WOD). The WOD is a multi-digit code, common worldwide to all HAVE QUICK users. In the AJ mode, a communications channel is defined by a net number instead of a signal frequency as in the normal mode. Before operating in the AJ mode, the radio must be primed. This consists of setting the WOD, TOD, and net number. The AJ mode is then selected by placing the A-3-2-T knob to A.

WORD OF DAY (WOD) – The WOD entry is normally entered before flight, but it is possible to enter it in flight. WOD is entered by using one or more of the six preset channels which are 20-15. For a new WOD entry, start at channel 20 use the same method as in entering preset frequencies in the normal mode with the frequency knobs and the PRESENT button. After each entry, a single beep is heard until channel 15 entry; a double bee is heard indicating that the radio has accepted all six WOD entries.

WOD TRANSFER – Select the preset mode and, starting with present channel 20, rotate the preset knob CCW. At channel 20, a single beep is heard. A single beep indicates that channel 20 data has been transferred and accepted. After the single beep is heard, select remaining channels (19-15) in the same manner until a double beep is heard indicating the WOD transfer is complete.

TIME-OF-DAY (TOD) – Transmission - The TOD entry is normally entered before flight, but it is possible to enter it in flight. It is possible to transmit timing information in both normal and AJ modes by momentarily pressing the TONE button. In the normal mode, a complete TOD message is transmitted, while in the AJ mode, only an abbreviated time update is transmitted. A mode time transmission allows a time update if one radio has drifted out of synchronization.

TIME-OF-DAY Reception – Reception is possible in both normal and AJ modes. The radio automatically accepts the first TOD message after the radio is turned on and WOD transferred. Subsequent messages are ignored unless the T position is selected with the A-3-2-T knob. The radio then accepts the next TOD update in either normal or AJ mode, provided the TOD update arrives within 60 seconds of the time the T position has been selected. To receive time in the normal mode, rotate the A-3-2-T knob to the T position and return to a normal channel in either the manual or preset mode. To receive a time update in AJ mode, rotate the A-3-2-T knob to the T position and then back to the A position. A TOD update (time tick) can be received on the selected AJ net.

Net Numbers – After WOD and TOD are entered, any valid AJ net number can be selected by using the manual frequency knob.

Anti-Jamming Mode Operation - A tone is heard in the headset if an invalid AJ net is selected, it TOD was not initially received, or if WOD was not entered. If the function knob is set to both and the AJ mode is selected, any transmission on the guard channel takes precedence over the AJ mode.

Operational Procedures - Radio Set AN/ARC-164(V)

1. Transfer WOD IAW "WOD TRANSFER" paragraph.
2. Setup RT to receive TOD:
   a. With external TOD equipment:
      (1) Select manual mode on MODE switch.
      (2) Set TOD frequency in manual frequency windows.
      (3) Set A-3-2-T to A, after TOD beep is heard. If tone is heard with the A-3-2-T in the A position, reinitialize radio IAW steps in "TOD TRANSMISSION" paragraph.
   b. Without external TOD equipment: Emergency start-up of TOD clock:
      (1) Set and hold A-3-2-T switch to T.
      (2) Press the TONE button.

NOTE

When using this method, the flight commander or lead aircraft should emergency-start his TOD clock. Lead aircraft would then transfer TOD to other aircraft in flight. Aircraft using this method will not be able to communicate with valid TOD signal in the AF mode. A valid TOD signal must be transferred to all aircraft that have invalid TOD time before effective AJ communications can be achieved.

HAVE QUICK Checklist ARC-164. Loading Word-of-Day (WOD).

1. "T, 2,3, A" switch – Not in A position.
2. Functional selector switch - Both.
3. Manual, preset, guard switch – Preset.
4. Manual frequency display - Set WOD 15.
5. Preset channel select- Set to 15.
6. Preset button (under frequency cover) - Press
7. Manual frequency display – Set WOD 16.

8. Preset channel select-Set to 16.
9. Preset button - Press.
10. Repeat steps 7 thru 9 to store WOD 17, 18, 19.
11. Manual frequency display - Set 300.050.
12. Preset channel select - Set to 20.
13. Preset button - Press.
14. Rotate preset select down 19, 18, 17, 16, 15, (hear 1 beep 20-16, 2 beeps on 15).

Receiving Time from Net Control Aircraft.
1. Manual, preset, guard switch - Manual.
2. Set to internal frequency to receive the time.
3. Hear net control aircraft state: "Standby for time."
4. Rotate "T, 2,3, A" switch to "T" and return to established manual frequency, hear.
5. Hear net control aircraft state: "Go active 0 point one."
6. Set A00.100 in manual window and complete commo check; if loud tone is heard, repeat timing.

Sending Time (Net Control Aircraft)
1. Manual, preset, guard switch - Manual.
2. Set to internal frequency.
3. Rotate "T, 2,3, A" switch to "T" and hold.
4. Press tone button and hold (hear no tone).
5. "T, 2,3, A" to internal frequency (.25 second beep, then tone).
6. Call other aircraft to send time.
7. Press tone button to send time.

NOTE

Recall today's WOD by reselecting presets 20 down thru 15, and hear beeps.

3-34. Antenna.

The UHF-AM antenna (figure 3-1) is located on the bottom center fuselage area and is mounted directly aft of the doppler fairing.

3-35. Controls and Functions (RT-1167).

Controls for the ARC-164(V) are on the front panel of the unit (figure 3-29.1). The function of each control is as follows:

CONTROL	FUNCTION
Frequency selector switch 1	Selects 100's digit of frequency (either 2 or 3) in MHz.
Frequency selector switch 2	Selects 10's digit of frequency (0 through 9) in MHz.
Frequency selector switch 3	Selects units digit of frequency (0 through 9) in MHz.
Frequency selector switch 4	Selects tenths digit of frequency (0 through 9) in MHz.
Frequency selector switch 5	Select hundredths and thousandths digits of frequency (00,25,50, or 75) in MHz.
Preset channel selector switch	Selects one of 20 preset channels.
MANUAL-PRESET-GUARD selector	Selects method of frequency selection.
MANUAL	Any of 7,000 frequencies is manually selected using the five frequency selector switches.
PRESET	A frequency is selected using the preset channel selector switch for selecting any one of 20 preset channels as indicated on the CHAN indicator.
GUARD	The main receiver and transmitter are automatically tuned to the guard frequency. Blocks out any frequency set either manually or preset.
SQUELCH ON-OFF switch	Turns squelch of main receiver on or off.
VOL control	Adjusts volume.
TONE switch	Enables transmission and headset monitoring of a 1.020-Hz tone on selected frequency for maintenance check only.

CONTROL	FUNCTION
Mode selector switch	Selects operating mode:
OFF	Turns power off.
MAIN	Enables the transceiver.
BOTH	Enables transceiver and guard receiver.
ADF	Not operational.

3-36. Controls and Functions (RT-1167C).

The controls and functions of the RT-1167C/ARC-164(V) are identical to the RT-1167/ARC-164(V) with the exception of the following:

CONTROL	FUNCTION
Frequency selector switch 1 (T-2-3-A)	Selects 100's digit of frequency (either 2 or 3) in MHz. The A position selects the HAVE QUICK mode. The T position (spring-loaded) allows the radio to receive a new time of day.

3-37. Modes of Operation.

Depending on the settings of the operating controls, the radio set can be used for these modes of operation:

a. Control (Mode) Settings.

(1) MAN mode: two-way voice communications.

(2) BOTH mode: utilizing the transceiver constant monitoring of guard receiver without losing the use of the transceiver.

(3) Transmission of 1,020 Hz TONE signal.

b. Transmit/Receive (MAIN) mode.

(1) Set OFF-MAIN-BOTH-ADF selector switch to MAIN.

(2) Set MANUAL-PRESET-GUARD selector switch to MANUAL for manual frequency selection or to PRESET for preset channel selection.

(3) To manually select a frequency, rotate the five MHz selector switches until desired frequency is displayed in indicator window.

NOTE

Clockwise rotation of the MHz selector switches increases frequency.

(4) To select a preset channel, rotate preset channel selector switch until desired channel is displayed in preset CHAN indicator window.

NOTE

Clockwise rotation of preset channel selector switch will increase the desired channel number (1 to 20).

c. Transmit/Receive/Guard Monitor (BOTH) Mode.

(1) Set OFF-MAIN-BOTH-ADF selector switch to BOTH.

NOTE

The BOTH position turns on the transceiver and the guard receiver. The guard receiver will remain turned to 243 MHz regardless of manual or preset frequencies selected.

(2) Select desired manual frequency or preset channel (paragraph 3-37b (3) and (4)).

NOTE

If reception on the selected frequency interferes with guard reception; detune the set by selecting an open frequency or place MANUAL-PRESET-GUARD selector switch to GUARD.

d. 1020 Hz TONE Signal Transmission (MAIN) mode.

(1) Set OFF-MAIN-BOTH-ADF selector switch to MAIN.

(2) Select a desired frequency for TONE transmission. Refer to steps 3-37b (3) and (4).

(3) Push the TONE switch to transmit the 1020 Hz signal.

NOTE

Tone-modulated signal may be used to check out the radio set and isolate faulty microphone circuitry.

e. *HAVE QUICK mode (RT-1167C only).*

The HAVE QUICK mode can be activated in one of two ways:

(1) Set MANUAL-PRESET-GUARD switch to MANUAL and set frequency selector switch 1 to A.

(2) Set MANUAL-PRESET-GUARD switch to PRESET and set preset channel selector switch to channel 20.

3-38. Operational Procedures Radio Set AN/ARC-164.

a. *Guard (Emergency) Operation.*

(1) Set MANUAL-PRESET-GUARD selector switch to GUARD.

NOTE

Transmission on guard frequency will also occur with transceiver manual frequency or preset channel tuned to the guard frequency.

b. *Loading Preset Channels.*

(1) Use the manual frequency selector switches to select the frequency to be placed into memory.

(2) Set MANUAL-PRESET-GUARD selector switch to PRESET.

(3) Turn preset channel selector switch to the desired channel number.

(4) Raise switching unit cover.

(5) Press and release PRESET switch. Preset frequency is now loaded into memory.

3-39. VOICE SECURITY SYSTEM TSEC/KY-58.

The TSEC KY-58 provides secure voice (ciphony) on the pilot's VHF FM radio. The pilot uses the KY-58 remote control unit (RCU) located in his right-hand console to operate the TSEC/KY-58, which in turn controls the AN/ARC-186(V) (FM No.1) radio set (also located in the right-hand console). Power to operate the TSEC/KY-58 comes from the 28-vdc emergency bus through a circuit breaker labeled KY-58 on the pilot overhead circuit breaker panel. Two operating modes are available: PLAIN mode for in-the-clear voice transmission or reception, and C/RAD 1 (cipher mode for secure radio transmission or reception.

NOTE

The TSEC/KY-58 POWER switch must be set to ON and the KY-58 circuit breaker must be closed before VHF No. 1 radio communication (plain or ciphered) is possible.

3-40. Controls and Functions.

Voice security system controls that require adjustment by the pilot include those on Z-AHQ Power Interface Adapter (located in the aft avionics bay), the Z-AHP KY-58 Remote Control Unit (located in the pilot's right-hand console), and the TSEC/KY-58 (also located in the pilot's right-hand console). Each of these devices is shown in figure 3-14. The function of each control and indicator is as follows:

Z-AHQ POWER INTERFACE ADAPTER

CONTROL OR INDICATOR	FUNCTION
BBV, DPV, BBN, DPN 4-position switch	Set according to type of radio being secured. Set to BBV for pilot's VHF FM radio.
PTT button (push-to-talk)	Clears crypto alarm that occurs upon power up. Alarm can also be cleared by pressing any push-to-talk switch in the pilot compartment.

TM 55-1520-210-10

Z-AHQ POWER INTERFACE ADAPTER (cont)

CONTROL OR INDICATOR	FUNCTION
FILTER IN/OUT Selector	Prevents adjacent channel interference when using radios with channel spacing of 25 kHz. Must be set to IN for pilot's AN/ARC-186(V) VHF-FM radio.

Z-AHP REMOTE CONTROL UNIT

CONTROL OR INDICATOR	FUNCTION
REM/LOC Switch	Sets the Z-AHQ to the local mode. Switch returns to REM (remote) position upon release, but equipment remains in local mode until any PTT is keyed.
ZEROIZE switch (two-position toggle switch housed under a spring-loaded cover)	Use in an emergency to delete all crypto-net variables (CNVs) from KY-58 registers. Renders KY-58 unusable until new variables are loaded.
DELAY Switch	Introduces time delay that is necessary when secure signal from pilot's VHF-FM radio is to be retransmitted by receiving station. Switch is normally in the down (off) position.
C/RAD 1/PLAIN switch	Set switch to C/RAD 1 (cipher radio 1) to use secure voice. Set switch to PLAIN when operating radio in the clear.
Switch guard	Rotate to the left to prevent C/RAD 1/PLAIN switch from accidentally being set to PLAIN.

Z-AHP REMOTE CONTROL UNIT

CONTROL OR INDICATOR	FUNCTION
MODE Switch	Set to OP (operate) to use pilot's VHF radio in either the Ciphered or Plain mode. Set to LD (load) when installing crypto-net variables (CNV) in the TSEC/KY-58 (TM 11-5810-262-12&P). Set to RV (receive variable) during manual remote keying (TM 11-5810-262-12&P).
POWER	Turns KY-58 on and off. Switch must be on (up) for operation in either plain or cipher mode.
FILL switch	Selects desired crypto-net variable (CNV).

TSEC/KY-58

CONTROL OR INDICATOR	FUNCTION
VOLUME control	Sets audio level of pilot's VHF-FM radio.
MODE switch	Set to P (Plain) to operate pilot's VHF-FM radio in the clear. Set to C (Cipher) to operate pilot's VHF-FM radio in the ciphered (secure speech) mode. Set to LD (load) when installing crypto-net variables (CNV) in the TSEC/KY-58 (TM 11-5810-262-12&P). Set to RV (receive variable) during manual remote keying (TM 11-5810-262-12&P).
FILL connector	Used to load crypto-net variables (CNV'S) into the TSEC/KY-58 registers (TM 11-5810-262-12&P).

Change 7 3-49

TSEC/KY-58 (cont)

CONTROL OR INDICATOR	FUNCTION
FILL switch	Pull knob and set to Z1-5 to zeroize (delete) crypto-net variables (CNV's) in TSEC/KY-58 registers 1-5. Set to 1, 2, 3, 4 or 5 to select desired CNV. Pull knob and set to Z-ALL to zeroize (delete) crypto-net variables (CNV's) in all TSEC/KY-58 registers. Zeroizing all registers renders TSEC/KY-58 unusable.
Power switch	Set to OFF to turn off both the TSEC/KY-58 and the pilot's VHF-FM radio. Set to ON to operate the TSEC/KY-58 and pilot's VHF-FM radio. Set to TD (time delay) when secure voice from pilot's VHF-FM radio is to be retransmitted.

3-41. Operation.

  a. *Preliminary Operation.*

NOTE

Before the pilot's VHF-FM radio may be operated in ciphered (secured voice) mode, it must be loaded with one or more crypto-net variables (CNV's). Refer to TM 11-5810-262-12&P for complete details on loading these variables.

(1) Set the TSEC/KY-58 Power switch to ON.

(2) Set the TSEC/KY-58 MODE switch to C (cipher).

(3) Set the TSEC/KY-58 VOLUME control to a comfortable listening level.

(4) Set the TSEC/KY-58 FILL switch to any one of the numbered storage register positions (1-6).

(5) Set the Z-AHQ Power Interface Adapter 4-position switch to BBV.

(6) Set the Z-AHQ Power Interface Adapter FILTER selector to IN.

(7) Place the DELAY switch on the Z-AHP Remote Control Unit (RCU) in the down (off) position.

(8) Set the C/RAD 1 -PLAIN switch on the Z-AHP Remote Control Unit (RCU) to the C/RAD 1 position.

(9) Set the MODE switch on the Z-AHP Remote Control Unit (RCU) to the OP position.

(10) Set the FILL switch on the Z-AHP Remote Control Unit (RCU) to the proper crypto-net variable (CNV).

(11) Set the POWER switch on the Z-AHP Remote Control Unit (RCU) to the ON position.

NOTE

At this time you should hear and intermittent tone and background noise. The background noise is normal. The tone is a crypto alarm that must be cleared before the radio can be used. If step 12 does not clear the intermittent tone, double check steps 1 through 11. If necessary, refer to TM 11-5810-262-OP.

(12) Press and release the ICS switch on the pilot cyclic stick or the pilot's push-to-talk floor switch. This should clear the crypto alarm.

  b. *Cipher Mode.*

(1) After steps 1 through 12 (above) are complete, the radio is ready to transmit and receive secure speech in ciphered mode.

(2) To transmit, press any push-to-talk switch. You may begin speaking following the beep.

  c. *Plain Mode.*

(1) To transmit and receive in the clear, set the C/RAD 1/PLAIN switch on the Z-AHP Remote Control Unit to PLAIN.

(2) To transmit, press any push-to-talk switch. You may begin speaking immediately.

d. Automatic Remote Keying (AK).

NOTE

Automatic Remote Keying (AK) causes an old crypto-net variable in one of the TSEC/KY-58 registers to be replaced by a new one, or an empty register to be filled. Your net controller simply transmits the new CNV to your TSEC/KY-58

(1) Your net controller will contact you by using a secure voice channel, and tell you to wait for an AK transmission. You must not transmit during this peroid.

(2) You will hear one or two beeps in your headset when the AK occurs.

e. Manual Remote Keying (MK).

NOTE

Manual Remote Keying (MK) requires you to use the Z-AHP Remote Control Unit to change crypto-net variables (CNV's).

(1) The net controller will contact you by using a secure voice channel. He will tell you to stand by for a new or replacement CNV and that you will use an MK action.

(2) Set the Z-AHP RCU FILL switch to position 6. Notify the net controller by radio when you have done this and stand by.

(3) The net controller will tell you to set the Z-AHP RCU MODE switch by RV (receive variable). Notify the net controller when you have done this and stand by.

(4) When notified by the net controller, set the Z-AHP RCU FILL switch to the storage position selected to receive the CNV. Notify the net controller when you have done this, and stand by.

(5) The net controller will ask you to listen for a beep, wait two seconds, and set the Z-AHP RCU MODE switch to OP (operate).

(6) If the MK operation was successful, the net controller will contact you via the new CNV. If the MK operation was not successful, the net controller will contact you by a clear voice (plain) transmission, tell you to set your RCU FILL switch to position 6, and stand by while the MK operation is repeated.

3-42. Voice security System TSEC/KY-28.

Not installed.

3-43. #2 VHF-FM-COMM AN/ARC-201.

a. Description. The #2 VHF-FM Comm AN/ARC-201 provides VHF-FM radio communications of voice data, secure or plain text, in single channel (25 KHz) and the SINOGARS ECCM mode of operation. The frequency range is 30 to 87.975 MHz channelized in tuning increments of 25 KHz.

(1) In addition, a frequency offset tuning capability of -10 KHz, -5 KHz +5 KHz and +10 KHz is provided in both receive and transmit mode. This capability is not used in the ECCM mode. Ninety-nine percent of the emitted spectrum of analog and digitized voice (16 Kbs;) and data is contained within a 25 Khz channel.

(2) The #2 VHF-FM Comm AN/ARC-201 will provide independent FM Communications only. It will be interfaced with #1 VHF-FM Comm/Homing AN/ARC-201 for operation in the retransmit mode.

(3) The #2 VHF-FM Comm AN/ARC-201 consists of a Receiver-Transmitter Radio, Panel Mounted (RT-1476).

3-44. HF-SSB RADIO SET AN/ARC-199.

a. Description. The AN/ARC-199 is a high frequency, single-side band radio set. It operates in 2.0 to 29.999 MHz frequency range using 280,000 channels separated by 100 Hz steps. The AN/ARC-199 is capable of for retransmission of data or voice. The system is capable of scanning any or all channels once they have been programmed on the scanned list.

b. Display Fields, Control Knobs and Functions. Refer to Figure 3-29.2.

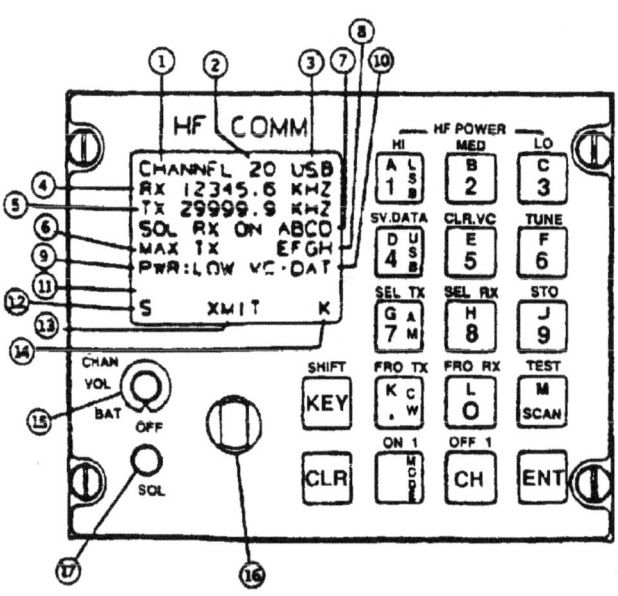

Figure 3-29.2 Control-Display Panel Layout

TM 55-1520-210-10

Field/Functioning of Control-Display Panel

CONTROL/ INDICATOR	FUNCTION
1.	Channel - This field appears in inverse video to indicate that current channel information has not been stored.
2.	Active channel number: 0-20.
3.	Modulation Mode: USB, LSB, AM, CW. CW represents MCW and may be used in conjunction with the mic key to transmit code.
4.	Receive frequency in kilohertz.
5.	Transmit frequency in kilohertz.
6.	Squelch Level - Display MIN, 1,2,3 .... 13, 14, MAX in conjunction with squelch knob in control panel.
7.	Receive Selective Address.
8.	Transmit Selective Address. In the sample display shown above, ON indicates that SELADR mode is operational for RX. If SELADR is operational for TX, ON is annunciated on the line with TX.
9.	Transmitter Output Power – LOW, MED, or HI.
10.	Modulation Source: The displays are: DATA Indicates 600 ohm data input. CIPHER Indicates input form KY 75 input. CLR-VC Indicates non-encrypted KY 75 input.
11.	Fault Field: Display fault messages, NOT TUNED, DATA NOT SAVED, and AUDIO VOLUME LEVEL: VOL MIN 1,2,3....14, MAX.
12.	S: Indicates that the currently displayed channel is on the scan list.
13.	Indicates are: XMIT, TEST, SCAN, TUNE. XMIT - transmitter is keyed & channel is tuned. TEST - Built-in-test mode is active. SCAN – Scan mode is active. TUNE - Tuning for one or all channels - blank if not one of the above.

Change 7   3-53

Field/Functioning of Control-Display Panel (Cont)

CONTROL/ INDICATOR	FUNCTION
14.	K- Indicates KEY has been pressed, and the functions above the keys are active. M - Indicates MODE has been pressed, and USB, LSB, AM, or CW should be selected next. Indicates slewing may be used, or scan flag may be set or cleared.
	CONTROL PANEL KNOBS
15.	Function Select – Power ON/OFF, CRT brightness, audio volume and channel number selection.
16.	Function – Control - Single-step, detent-type switch, with continuous rotation in either direction. Clockwise rotation increases, and counterclockwise rotation decreases the CRT brightness, audio volume, or channel number. In cases of CRT brightness and audio volume, knob has no effect once limit of that particular function has been reached. In channel select mode, function control knob is continuously active. That is, channel 20 is always one position counterclockwise from channel 0.
17.	Squelch Control - Continuous rotation in either direction; squelch level is annunciated in field #6. Once upper or lower limit of squelch has been reached, further rotation of knob in same direction has no effort.

c. Operating Modes/Functions.

(1) Power ON/OFF. On function Select Knob (Reference no. 15 on control panel layout).

(2) Ready indication. When the radio is initially powered on, a system ready message will be displayed for a few seconds. The channel 0 information will then be displayed.

(3) CRT brightness. Set Function Select Knob to BRT. Rotate the Function Control Knob in the desired direction to increase or decrease brightness.

(4) Audio Volume. Set Function Select Knob to VOL, rotate the function Control Knob in the desired direction to increase or decrease audio volume. Audio volume is not a stored parameter. Audio volume level is annunciated briefly in the fault area of the display when the level is being changed. The display levels are: MIN, 1, 2, 3 . . ...14. MAX. A secondary HF audio volume control is located in the lower left console. See figure 3-11.2. This is provided for audio level compatibility with the KY-75. Preset the CDU VOL level to the max. position and adjust the secondary volume control for the desired level.

(5) Channel Number. Channel number may be changed using the Function Select and Function Control Knobs or by using a combination of keystrokes.

(6) Modulation Mode. Four modes are available: USB, LSB, AM (AME), and CW (MCW). To change from one mode to another, press MODE + desed mode key + ENT.

(7) Receive Frequency. 2.0 - 29.9999 MHz, programmable in 100 Hz steps. To change frequencies press KEY + FRQ RX+ desired frequency + ENT.

(8) Transmit Frequency. 2.0 - 29.9999 MHz, programmable in 100 Hz steps. To change frequencies press KEY + FRQ TX + desired frequency + ENT.

(9) Squelch Level. Single step, detent-type control; squelch level is annunciated on the display and varies from MIN, 1, 2, 3 . . . . 14, MAX. The squelch level is not a stored parameter.

(10) Transmit Selective Address. A 4-letter code programmed by pressing .HE KEY + SEL TX + a 4-letter code + ENT. Transmit selective address mode is activated with key sequence, KEY + SEL RX + ON + ENT, or by activating SELADR RX and keying the mic.

(11) Receiver Selective Address. A 4-letter code programmed by pressing KEY + SEL RX + 4-letter code + ENT. Receive selective address mode is activated by using key sequence: KEY+ SEL RX + ON + ENT.

(12) Output Power Level. Three output power levels are selectable from the keyboard; LO, MED, or HI. The key sequence used in KEY+ LO, MED, or HI + ENT.

Figure 3-29.3 HF Volume Control

(13) Modulation Source. Audio sources available are CLR-VC (clear voice), DATA, or encrypted audio when used with voice security equipment. CIPHER is displayed when the KY 75 is in the secure voice mode. DATA and CLR-VC modes are selectable from control panel, when KY 75 is in non-secure mode, using key sequence: KEY + (SV-DATA or CLR-VC) + ENT. The modulation source is not a stored parameter.

(14) Tune. By using appropriate key sequence, either currently displayed channel or all 20 channels may be turned to the antenna. The tuning information is stored for future use with no tuning necessary. Current channel may be tuned by pressing KEY + TUNE + ENT. All 20 channels may be tuned by pressing KEY + TUNE + SCAN + ENT.

(15) TEST. Built-in-Test (BITE) feature allows operator to test both receiving and transmitting capabilities at several frequencies. Any failure to meet predetermined performance levels results in a failure message being displayed. This identifies the faulty unit and provides a maintenance code. The test is initiated by pressing KEY + TEST + ENT.

(16) STORE. ENT key, used to terminate mode changes, does not automatically store channel information; therefore, a store sequence is provided. The key sequence is: KEY + STO + ENT.

(17) SCAN. Displayed channels may be placed on scan list by pressing SCAN + ON + ENT. It can be removed from scan list by pressing SCAN + OFF + ENT. To automatically scan those channels which have been placed on scan list, press the SCAN key, the ENT key.

(18) CW Keying. To utilize the CW keying function, first place the radio in CW mode. This is accomplished by pressing the following key sequence: MODE + CW + ENT. Now either the KEY key on the control panel, or any external key switch (a mic key) may be used to transmit CW.

(18) CW Keying. To utilize the CW keying function, first place the radio in CW mode. This is accomplished by pressing the following key sequence: MODE + CW + ENT. Now either the KEY key on the control panel, or any external key switch (a mic key) may be used to transmit CW.

d. Detailed operation.

(1) Channel Selection. Any one of 3 procedures may be used to select a channel.

(a) Using Function Control Knob.

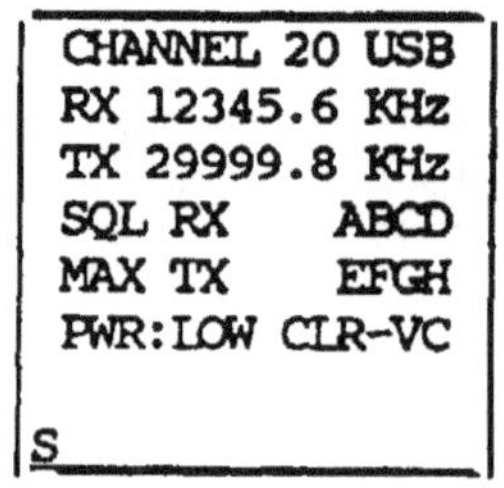

```
CHANNEL 20 USB
RX 12345.6 KHz
TX 29999.8 KHz
SQL RX      ABCD
MAX TX      EFGH
PWR:LOW CLR-VC

S
```

Figure 3-29.4 Channel Selection

1. Set Function Select Knob to CHAN; rotate Function Control Knob to increment channel number, or CCW to decrement channel number. If channels are changed quickly, (approximately 2 channels per second or faster), only word CHANNEL, and an inverse video channel number will be displayed on screen until desired channel is reached.

(b) Channel Slewing.

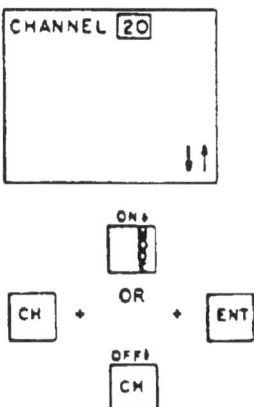

Figure 3-29.5. Channel Slewing

1. Begin by pressing CH key, and note that up and down arrows appear in the lower right corner, (field 14). The up-arrow key increments the channel number by one for each keystroke. The down-arrow key decrements the channel number by one for each keystroke. When the first keystroke using an arrow is made, display will be blanked except for arrows, inverse video channel number, and the work CHANNEL. Once desired channel has been selected, press ENT, and desired channel information will be displayed (See the following Notes).

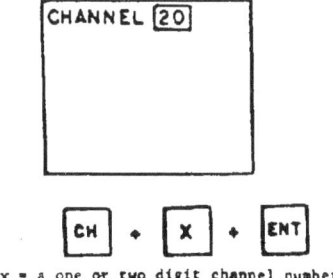

x = a one or two digit channel number

Figure 3-29.6. Numbered Keys

(c) Using Numbered Keys.

1. Begin by pressing CH, but rather than using arrow keys, use the numbered keys to directly enter desired channel number. After first digit is pressed, display will be blanked except for the word CHANNEL, and inverse video channel number. Press ENT to display the information associated with the newly selected channel.

NOTE

In procedures (b) and (c), if CLR is pressed before ENT, the information displayed will be that which was displayed prior to initiation of channel charge.

NOTE

Procedures (b) and (c) provide a convenient method of selecting channels, should the function control knob be damaged or otherwise become inoperable.

(2) Frequency Select.

(a) Frequency Select (RX or TX).

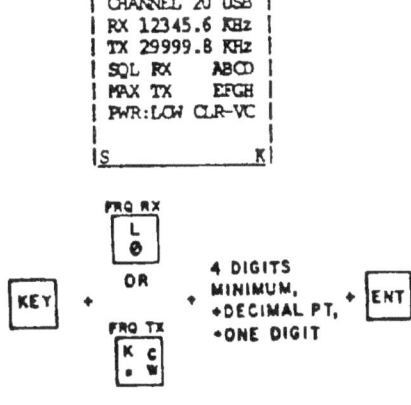

Figure 3-29.7. Frequency Select

1. To initially program, or change, the receive frequency for displayed channel, begin by pressing first KEY and FRQ RX keys. Next, enter desired operating frequency with the decimal point; for example, 12345.0. When new frequency has been correctly entered, press ENT key, and new receive frequency becomes operational.

2. Several changes occur on the display during frequency change and these are as follows. A "K" is annunciated in lower right corner when KEY is pressed (see Notes). The "K" is replaced by arrows when FRQ RX is pressed, and receive frequency digits field goes to inverse video mode. When the first new frequency digit is entered, the previous receive frequency is cleared. After the complete new frequency has been entered and ENT key is pressed, the display returns to normal.

3. When entering the frequency, a minimum of 4 digits must be entered before the decimal point is entered. Otherwise an entry error will result and an ENTRY ERROR message will be annunciated in the fault field. The operator must then press the CLR key and reenter an allowed frequency.

4. The transmit frequency is changed in the same manner, but with the FRQ RX key replaced by FRQ TX. The transmit frequency field (#5) will go to inverse video.

(b) Frequency Slewing (RX only).

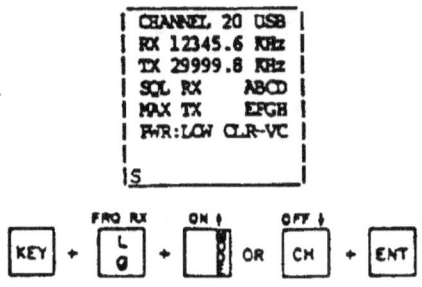

Figure 3-29.8. Frequency Slewing (RX only)

1. Frequency slewing is in 100 Hz increments and is accomplished using the up or down arrow keys. Each keystroke of an arrow key changes the frequency by 100 Hz in the direction indicated by the arrow. To use the frequency slewing feature, first KEY, then FRQ RX is pressed. Then either the up or down arrows, and finally ENT when the desired frequency has been reached. After FRQ RX is pressed, arrows will be annunciated in the lower right corner, (field #14). This cues the operator that slewing mode is available, and the frequency digits field will be in inverse video. When ENT is pressed the display will return to normal.

2. Slewing of the transmit frequency is not allowed. Any attempt to do so will result in an error message being annunciated in the fault field.

(3) Power Level Select.

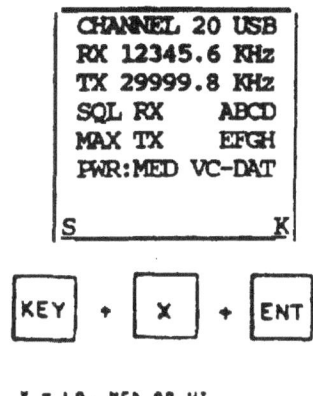

X = LO, MED OR HI

Figure 3-29.9. Power Level Select

(a) If high power lock is in effect, and HI is selected, MED will be displayed.

(b) Display field 9 goes to inverse video when X is pressed and until ENT is pressed. "K" is cleared once "ENT' is pressed.

NOTE

There is a switch on the front of the AM-7201/U which can inhibit the high output power mode.

(4) Modulation Source Selection.

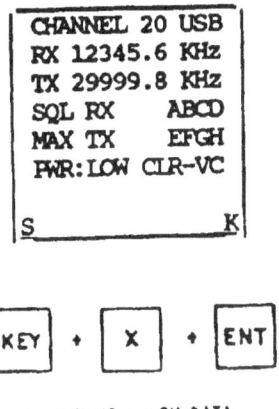

X = CLR-VC or SV-DATA

Figure 3-29.10 Modulation Mode Source

(a) The key sequence shown above can select the 600 ohm data input to the radio using the SV-DATA key. Or it can select 150 ohm compressed audio input, using the CLR-VC key. Display field #10 appears in inverse video when CLR-VC and SV-DATA is pressed. It returns to normal when ENT is pressed.

(b) If voice security equipment indicates that its output is encrypted, CIPHER will be annunciated on the display. Otherwise, pressing CLR-VC displays CLR-VC, and pressing SV-DATA displays DATA.

(5) Modulation Mode.

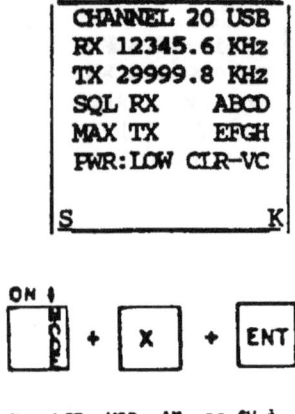

Figure 3-29.11. Modulation Mode

(a) Field 3 appears in inverse video after X is pressed and until ENT is pressed. "M" appears in field 14 to indicate mode is being changed. "M" is cleared once ENT is pressed.

(6) Store.

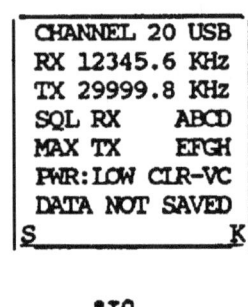

Figure 3-29.12. Store

(a) If new channel data is entered and not subsequently saved, "DATA NOT SAVED" will be annunciated in the fault field. The word CHANNEL will appear in inverse video. Fault messages would have priority over the message. The key sequence above may be used to save new channel information. The "K" will be cleared from field 14 once ENT is pressed.

(7) Selective Address

(a) Selective Receive Address.

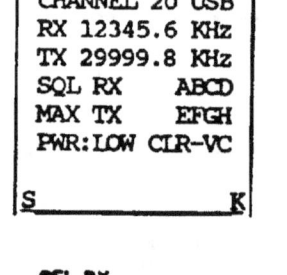

Figure 3-29.13. Selective Receive Address

1. Selective receive address is entered by pressing KEY, SEL RX, then the 4 different letters of the address, and finally ENT.

2. When SEL RX is pressed, the receive address field (#7) goes to inverse video. After the address has been entered and ENT has been pressed, the display returns to normal.

(b) Selective Transmit Address.

(8) SELADR ON/OFF.

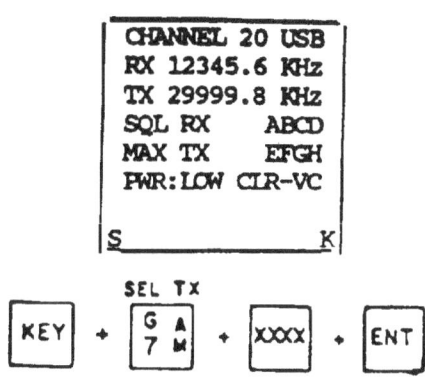

Figure 3-29.14. Selective Transmit Address

1. Selective transmit address is entered by pressing KEY, the SEL TX, then 4-letter address, and finally ENT.

2. When SEL TX is pressed, the transmit address field (#8) goes to inverse video. After the address has been entered and ENT has been pressed, the display returns to normal.

NOTE

Four different letters must be used in the code, and the arrangement of letters is irrelevant. The code ABCD is identical to the code BADC, and the letters will be displayed in alphabetical order.

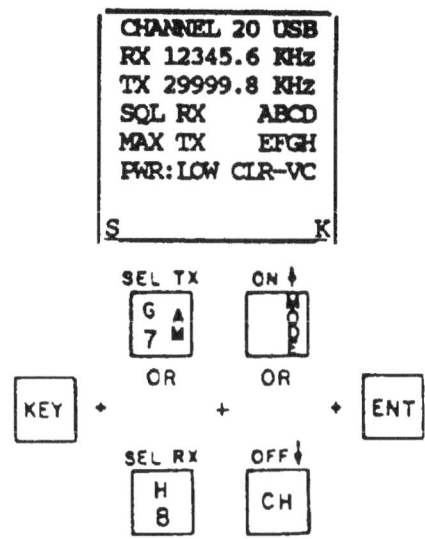

Figure 3-29.15. Seladr On/Off

(a) Seladr RX. To enable Seladr RX, use the key sequence KEY + SEL RX + ON + ENT. With Seladr enabled, receiver is fully squelched until correct Seladr tones are received, and Seladr squelch overrides squelch control. To receive Seladr tones, radio must be tuned to frequency on which Seladr tones, radio must be turned to frequency on which Seladr tones are to be transmitted, or be scanning for that frequency. Reception of a matching, 4 tone Seladr code causes the following events to occur. Seladr RX will be deactivated. An audio tone will alert the operator that he is being called. If the unit was previously scanning, scanning will cease. Squelch will automatically be set to minimum.

NOTE

The operator can take the radio out of the Seladr RX mode either by using the key sequence shown above, or by keying the mic.

TM 55-1520-210-10

(b) Seldar TX. Seladr TX may be activated with either the key sequence shown above, or, when Seladr RX is active, with the mic key. When the keyboard is used, ON is annunciated in the Seladr TX field. XMIT appears in display field 13, and the 4-letter code is automatically transmitted for a predetermined length of time. When mic keying is used, code will be transmitted for predetermined time period. Or it can be as long as mic is keyed, which ever is longer. Seladr TX is deactivated by any keystroke, however, it is recommended that the CLR key be used.

(9) Test Mode Display.

(a) Test Mode.

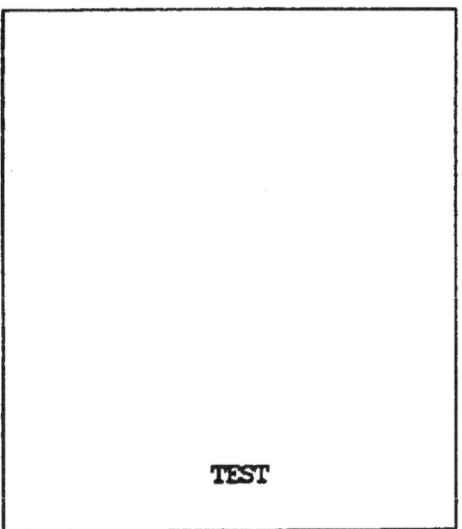

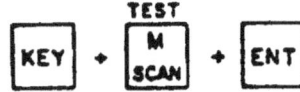

Figure 3-29.16. Test Mode Display

1. Upon initiation of Built-In-Test (BITE) sequence using keystrokes shown, CRT will first display a checkerboard pattern for a few seconds. Then, an inverse checkerboard pattern to test the individual character spaces on the CRT. TEST will be displayed in field 13 with the rest of CRT blank for remainder of test.

2. If BITE must be haulted prior to completion, any keystroke will abort the test. However, for consistency, it is recommended that CLR be used as the terminating keystroke.

3. Once BITE is completed and failed/passed display is annunciated, CLR must be used to return to normal operating conditions.

(b) Failed Test Display.

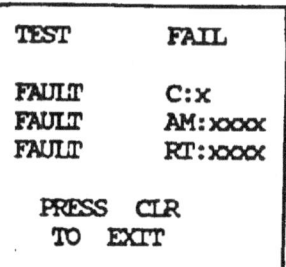

Figure 3-29.17. Failed Test Display

1. First Row: Test Fail Message.

2. Third, fourth & fifth Rows: Unit(s) which failed and failure code(s) for maintenance.

3. Seventh & eighth Rows: Test exit instruction.

3-62 Change 7

(c) Passed Test Display.

(b) All Channels.

Figure 3-29.18. Passed Test Display

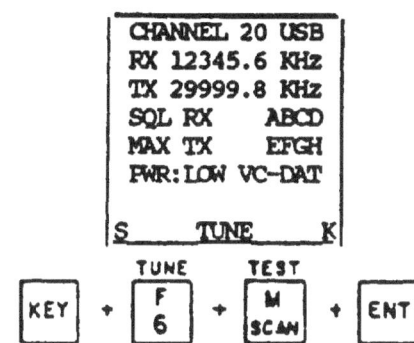

Figure 3-29.20. Tune Mode-All Channels

(10) Tune Mode.

(a) Single Channel.

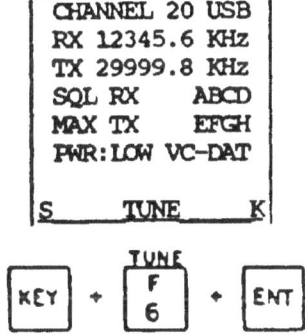

Figure 3-29.19. Tune Mode-Single Channel

1. This sequence will tune only the channel currently displayed. Tune indicator appears in field 13 when TUNE is pressed and until tuning is complete. The "K"s cleared once ENT is pressed.

1. This sequence will tune all channels which have been programmed with frequency information. Any keystroke will be capable of ending either of the tune operations. It is recommended that CLR be used. The "K" cleared once ENT is pressed. TUNE indicator appears in field 13 when the TUNE key is pressed and until tuning is complete.

2. If the mic is keyed, and a channel needs tuning, "NOT TUNED" will be displayed in the fault field.

(11) Scan Mode.

(a) Programming Scan.

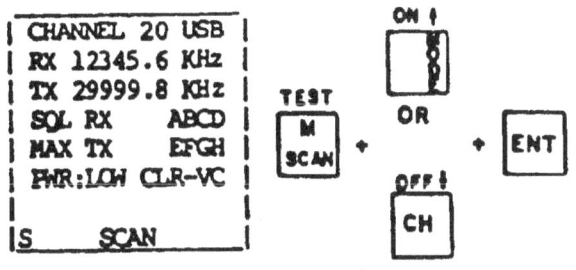

Figure 3-29.21. Scan Mode

Change 7   3-63

1. To place a channel on, or remove a channel from scan list, begin by pressing SCAN key. At this point SCAN will be annunciated in field 13. Arrows will be annunciated in field 14. The up-arrow key sets the scan flag for the displayed channel. The down-arrow key clears the scan flag for the displayed channel.

2. Once the flag has been set or cleared, press ENT The arrows and SCAN will be cleared from the display. If the scan flag was set, and "S will be annunciated in the lower left corner of the display. This indicates that the dislayed channel is on the scan list.

NOTE

The scan flag must be stored after being entered in order for the channel to be placed on the scan list.

(b) Executing Scan.

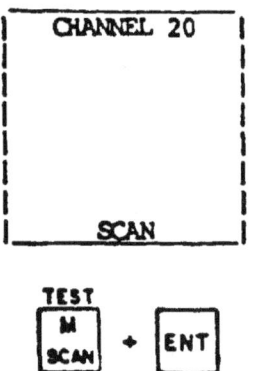

Figure 3-29.22. Executing Scan

1. To scan channels which have been stored onto scan list, press SCAN key and ENT key. When ENT is pressed, the display, except for the channel number, the word CHANNEL, and SCAN in field 13, will be blanked. The channel number will change as scanning takes place.

2. To terminate scanning, it is recommended that the CLR key be used, although any keystroke is capable of ending scanning. Normal radio operation will be restored for that channel which was being scanned when scanning was terminated.

e. *Example Programming One or More Channels.* The following procedure may be used to initially program a single channel with all the necessary operating parameters. To program additional channels, simply change the active channel number and duplicate the procedure. Insert the operating information for the channel.

(1) Power on. Turn the Function Select Knob clockwise one position to BRT. When the radio has warmed up, a "system ready" message will be displayed for a few seconds. The channel 0 information previously stored will be displayed.

(2) Set CRT Brightness. Adjust the Function Control Knob until the display has the desired brightness.

(3) Set Audio Volume. Set the function select knob to the VOL position. Set the CDU VOL knob to the max. position. Adjust the HF volume control to the desired volume.

(4) Set Squelch. With no reception of RF, use the Squelch Knob to adjust the audio to the point where background noise is muted.

(5) Channel Select. Turn Function Select Knob to CHAN and adjust the Function Control Knob to the desired channel.

(6) Operating Parameters. Use procedures in Detailed Operation to select modulation mode, receive and transmit frequencies, receive and transmit selective address, power level and modulation source. Place the channel on the scan list if desired. Place in retransmission mode if desired.

(7) Store. The information that has just been programmed is now operational but is not yet permanently stored. If desired to permanently Store this information for the displayed channel, use the store procedure.

NOTE

The store function stores only the currently displayed channel information. Therefore, the store function must be implemented for each individual channel before selecting a new channel.

(8) Tune. After all the desired channels have been programmed, initiate the tune sequence for all channels.

(9) Test. If a test of the AN/ARC-199 system is desired, initiate the test sequence. The system may be performed at any time after the system is powered on. The radio is now ready to receive or transmit on frequencies being displayed.

Figure 3-29.23. HF Volume Control

3-45. DIRECTION FINDER SET AN/ARN-89.

a. Description. This low frequency automatic direction finder radio (ADF) set provides either automatic or manual compass bearing on any radio signal between 100 and 3,000 KHz. The ADF can identify keyed or continuous wave (CW) stations. If there is no HSI control installed, the ADF displays the bearing of the helicopter relative to a selected radio transmission on the horizontal situation indicator No. 2 bearing pointer (Figure 3-29.29).

(1) If there is an HSI control installed the ADF can display the bearing on either the No. 1 or No. 2 pointer. This is dependent upon the position of the HSI control Mode Select Switch. This unit will also function as AM or CW communication receiver.

b. Controls and Functions. Refer to Figure 3-29.24.

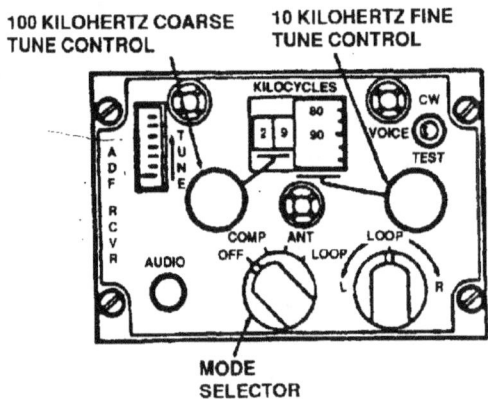

Figure 3-29.24 LF/ADF Control Panel C-7932/ARN-89

Controls and Functions of LF/ADF Control Panel C-7932/ARN-89

CONTROL	FUNCTION
Mode selector switch	Audible tone for tuning to CW station, SS
OFF	Turns power off.
COMP	Provides operation as an ADF.
ATN	Provides for operation as an AM receiver using sense antenna
LOOP	Provides for receiver operation as a manual direction finder using loop only.
LOOP L-R control	Provides manual left and right control of loop when operating mode selector in LOOP position. It is spring loaded to return to center.
AUDIO	Adjusts volume.
100 Kilohertz coarse-tune control knob	Tunes receiver in 100-KHz steps as indicated by first two digits of KILOCYCLES indicator.
CW (COMP mode)	Enables tone oscillator to provide audible tone for tuning to CW station, when mode function switch is at COMP,.
CW (ANT or LOOP mode)	Enables beat frequency oscillator to permit tuning to CW station, when mode function switch is at ANT or LOOP.
VOICE	Permits low frequency receiver to operate as a receiver with mode switch in any position.
TEST (COMP mode)	Provides slewing of loop through 180° to check operation of receiver in COMP mode. (Switch position is inoperative in LOOP and ANT modes.)
TUNE Meter	Indicates relative signal strength while tuning receiver to a specific radio signal.
KILOCYCLES	Indicates operating frequency to which receiver is tuned.

Change 7 3-67

TM 55-1520-210-10

c. Operation

(1) Starting Procedure.

(a) ICS NAV receiver selector - ON.

(b) Mode selector - COMP, ANT, or LOOP.

(c) Frequency - Select.

(d) CW, VOICE, TEST switch - CW or VOICE as al propiate.

(e) ICS NAV switch - ON.

(f) Fine tune control - adjust for maximum upward ir diction on TUNE meter.

(g) AUDIO control - adjust as desired.

(2) ANT Mode Operation.

(a) Mode selector - ANT.

   (b) ICS NAV switch - ON.

   (c) Monitor receiver by listening.

(3) COMP Mode Operation.

(a) Mode selector - COMP.

(b) HSVVSI MODE SEL BRG 2 switch - ADF.

(c) The horizontal situation indicator No. 1 bearing pointer displays the magnetic bearing to the ground station from the helicopter. It is read against the compass card when ADF is selected on the MODE SEL BRG I switch.

(d) ICS NAV switch - ON

(e) To test the ADF, when required.

1. CW, VOICE, TEST switch - Test to see that No

1 bearing pointer changes about.

2. CW, VOICE, TEST switch - release.

   (4) LOOP Mode Operation Manual direction finding uses the LOOP mode.

   (a) Mode selector switch - LOOP

   (b) ICS NAV switch - ON.

   (c) Turn LOOP L-R switch to L (left) (right) to obtain an audio null and a tune In null. Watch HSI No. 1 bearing pointer for a display of magnetic bearing to or from ground station against the compass card. In this mode of operation two null positions 1800 apart as possible

d. *Stopping Procedure.* Mode selector - OFF.

3-45.1. DIRECTION FINDER SET AN/ARN-149 (MWO 1-1520-210-50-30 Installed).

a. Description. This low frequency automatic direction finder (AD F) radio set provides either automatic or manual compass bearing on any radio signal between 100 and 2199.5 kHz. This frequency range includes both commercial broadcast stations and nondirectional beacons (NDB). If there is no Horizontal Situation Indicator (HSI) control installed, the ADF dismays the helicopter relative bearing to a selected radio transmission on the horizontal situation indicator NO. 2 bearing pointer (Figure 3-29.29 if HSI) (Ref Fig 3-21 if RMI).

(1) If there is a HSI control installed, the ADF can display the bearing on either NO. 1 or NO. 2 pointer. This is dependent upon the position of the HSI control Mode Select Switch.

(2) If there is a RMI installed, the ADF will display on NO 1 pointer when ADF is selected

b Controls and Functions. Ref to Figure 3-29.24.1.

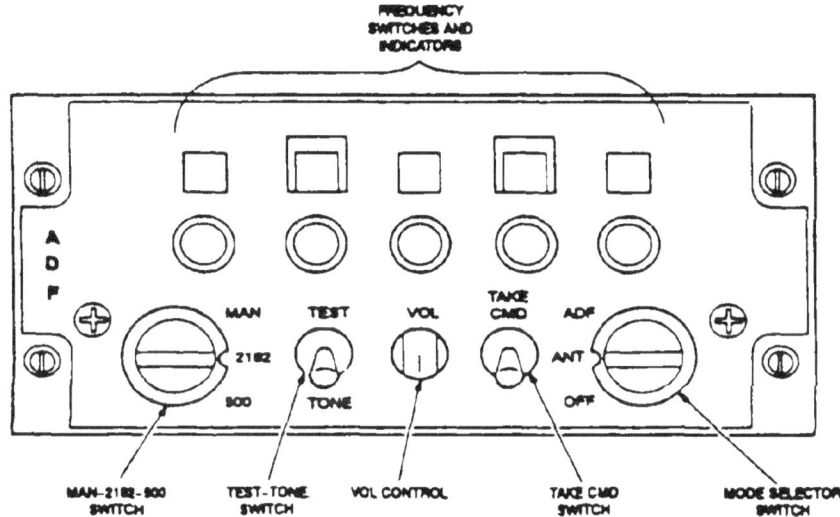

Figure 3-29.24.1 ADF Control Panel C-12192/ARN-149(V)

TM 55-1520-210-10

Controls and Functions of ADF Control Panel C-12192/ARN-149(V)

CONTROL	FUNCTION
Mode Select Switch	
OFF	Turns system power off.
ANT	System functions as an aural receiver providing only aural output of the received signal
ADF	Provides operation as an ADF using the AN/ARN-149 antenna as a signal source, and the aural functions are enabled.
TEST	Test mode causing the RMI pointer to shift 90 degrees as a self test.
TONE	Test mode causing the normal audio to be replaced by a 1000 hertz tone for continuous wave (CW) operation.
TAKE CMD	This switch Is used In a dual control system. Placing the switch In the TAKE CMD position allows control of the receiver. (Not applicable for the UH-1 aircraft.)
VOL control	Controls the volume In 12 discrete steps.
MAN	Enables the frequency controls and indicators.
2182	Selects 2182 kHz as the operating frequency.
500	Selects 500 kHz as the operating frequency.
Frequency switches and indicators	Allows frequency (kHz) selection in manual mode.

c. Operation.

(1) Normal ADF Operation

(a) ICS NAV receiver selector - ON.

(b) Mode selector switch - ADF.

(c) Frequency - Select.

(d) MAN/2182/500 switch - MAN.

(e) HS/VSI MODE SEL BRG 2 switch - ADF.

(f) VOL control - as desired.

(g) TEST/TONE control - TEST. Verify the RMI pointer No. 2 rotates 90 degrees from present bearing Release test switch.

(2) ANT Mode Operation (Optional).

(a) Mode selector switch - ANT. Monitor receiver by listening.

(b) ICS NAV switch - ON.

d. Stopping Procedures. Mode selector switch OFF.

3-46. RADIO RECEIVING SET AN/ARN-123(V) (VOR/ILS/MB).

a. Description. Radio set AN/ARN-123 (V) (Figure 3-29.5) Is a very high frequency receiver that operates from 108 00 to 117 95 MHz. Course information is presented by the HSI course deviation pointer and the selectable No. 2 bearing pointer on the horizontal situation indicator. The combination of the glide slope capability and the localizer capability makes up the instrument landing system (ILS).

(1) The marker beacon portion of the receiver visually indicates to the right of either the ID-2103 or ID-988 a MB advisory light. A Tone can be heard In the head-phones of passage of the helicopter over a marker beacon transmitter

(2) The receiving set may be used as a VCR receiver, or ILS receive. The desired type of operation is selected by tuning the receiving set to the frequency corresponding to that operation. ILS operation is selected by tuning to the odd tenth MHz frequencies between 108.0 and 112.0 MHz. VOR operation is selected by tuning in .050 MHz units to the frequencies between 108.0 and 117.95 MHz. However, the odd tenth MHz between 108.0 and 112.0 MHz are reserved for ILS operation.

(3) The three receiver sections do the intended functions independent of each other. Performance degradation within any one of the major sections will not affect the performance of the others. Power for the AN/ARN-123 is provided from the dc essential bus through a circuit breaker, marked VOR/ILS.

NOTE

Tuning to a localizer frequency will automatically tune to a glide slope frequency, when available.

b. Controls and Functions. Refer to Figure 3-29.25.

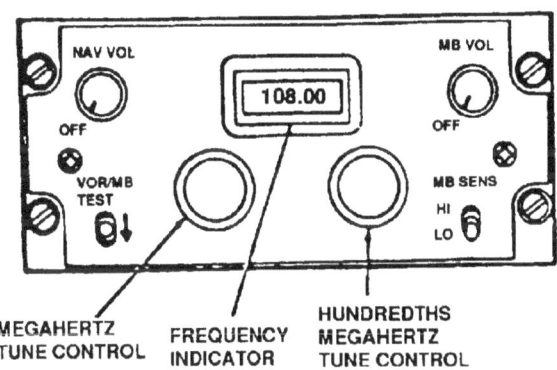

Figure 3-29.25 Radio Receiving Set AN/ARN-123 (V).

Controls and Functions for VOR/ILS/MB Receivers

CONTROL	FUNCTION
NAV VOL-OFF control	Turns VOR/ILS receiver on and off, adjusts volume.
MB VOL-OFF control	Turns marker beacon receiver on and off; adjusts volume.
Megahertz tune control	Tunes VOR/ILS receiver in MHz as indicated on frequency indicator.
Hundredths megahertz tune control	Tunes VOR/ILS receiver in hundredths MHz as indicated on frequency indicator.
VOR/MB TEST control	Activates VOR test circuit and MB receiver lamp self-test circuits.
MB SENS HI-LO control	For controlling MB sensitivity.
LO	Decreases receiver sensitivity: Results in shortening time transmitted signal will be received.
HI	Increases receiver sensitivity: Results in lengthening time transmitted signal will be received.

c. Operation.

(1) Starting Procedure.

(a) ICS AUX selector - ON.

(b) NAV VOL OFF control - ON.

(c) Frequency - Select.

(d) MODE SEL BRG 2 switch - VOR.

(e) MODE SEL VOR/ILS switch - ON.

(2) VOR/Marker Beacon Test.

(a) HSI CRS set -315 on COURSE set display.

(b) VOR/MB TEST switch - down and hold. The MB light on the VSI should go on.

(c) HSI VOR/LOC course bar - centered ±1 dot.

(d) No. 2 bearing pointer - Should go to 310°.

(e) VOR/MB TEST switch - Release.

(3) Communications Test.

(a) ICS AUX receiver selector- ON.

(b) NAV VOL control - Adjust to midrange.

(c) VOR/MB TEST switch - Down and hold. Noise should be heard in headphones.

(d) VOR/MB TEST switch - Release. Noise should not be heard in headphones, indicating that squelch is operation properly.

(4) VOR Operation.

Course - Set.

(5) ILS (LOC/GS) operation.

ILS operation frequency - Set.

(6) Marker Beacon (MB) Operation.

(a) MB VOL OFF switch - ON.

(b) MB SENS switch -as desired.

(7) VOR communications. Receiving Operation.

Frequency - Set.

(8) Stopping Procedure.

NAV VOL OFF switch - OFF.

3-47. DOPPLER NAVIGATION SET AN/ASN-128.

a. Description. The doppler navigation set, AN/ASN-128, in conjunction with the helicopter's heading and vertical reference systems, provides helicopter velocity position. It also provides steering information from ground level to 10,000 feet. The doppler navigation system is a completely self-contained navigation system and does not require any ground-based aids.

(1) The system provides world-wide navigation, with position readout available in both Universal Transverse Mercator (UTM), and Latitude and Longitude (LAT/LONG). Navigation and steering is done using LAT/LONG coordinates, and a bilateral UTM-LAT/LONG conversion routine is provided for UTM operation. Up to ten destinations may be entered in either format and not necessarily the same format. Preset position data entry format is also optional and independent of destination format.

(2) The AN/ASN-128 operates in conjunction with the Horizontal Situation Indicator (HSI) and a Horizontal Situation Indicator Control (HSI Control). A Compass Control C-8021/ASN-75 is also included to synchronize Gyromagnetic Compass Set AN/ASN-43 to correct magnetic heading. This is accomplished when in the SLAVED mode of operation.

b. Controls, Displays, and Function. The controls and displays for the doppler are on the front panel (Figure 3-29.26).

TM 55-1520-210-10

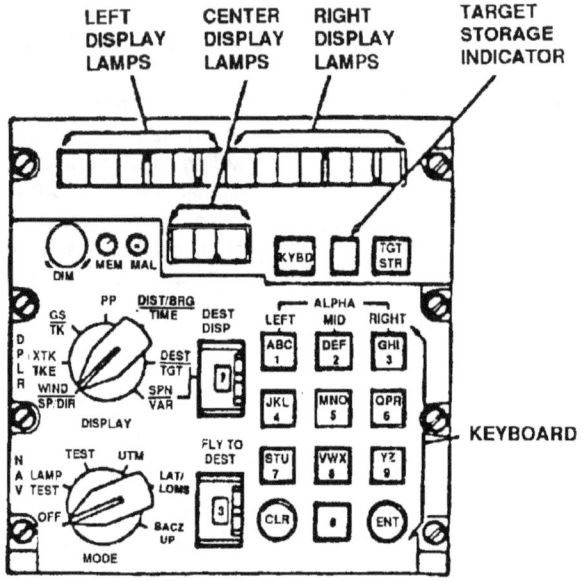

Figure 3-29.26. Doppler Navigation Set AN/ASN-128.

Controls and Functions of Doppler Navigation Set.

CONTROL/INDICATOR	FUNCTION
Mode Selector	Selects Doppler Navigation of operation.
OFF	Turns navigation set off.
LAMP TEST	Checks operation of all lamps.
TEST	Initiates built-in-test exercises for navigation set.
UTM	Selects Universal Transverse Mercator (UTM) navigational mode of operation
LAT/LONG	Select latitude/longitude navigational mode of operation.
BACKUP	Places navigation set in estimated mode of operation or estimated velocity mode of operation.
DISPLAY Selector	Selects navigation data for display.
WIND SP/DIR	Not applicable.
XTK-TKE (Left Display) (Right Display)	Distance crosstrack (XTK) of initial course to destination in km and tenths of a km. Track angle error (TKE) in degrees displayed as right or left of bearing to destination.
GS-TK (Left Display)	Ground speed (GS) in (Left Display) km/hr.

3-72 Change 7

Controls and Functions of Doppler Nav. Set ASN-128 - CONT.

CONTROL/INDICATOR	FUNCTION
(Right Display)	Track angle (TK) in degrees
PP with switch set to UTM (Center Display)	Present position UTM zone.
(Left Display)	Present position UTM area square designator and casting in km to nearest ten meters.
(Right Display)	Present position UTM area northing in km to nearest ten meters.
PP with MODE switch set to LAT/LONG (Left Display)	Present position latitude in degrees, minutes and tenths of minutes.
(Right Display)	Present position longitude in degrees, minutes and tenths of minutes.
DIST/BRG-TIME (Center Display)	Time to destination selected by FLY TO DEST (in minutes and tenth of minutes).
(Left Display)	Distance to destination selected by FLY TO DEST (in KM and tenths of a km).
(Right Display)	Bearing to destination selected by FLY TO DEST (in degrees).
DEST-TGT (Mode switch set to UTM) (Center Display)	UTM zone of destination selected by DEST DISP thumbwheel.
(Left Display)	UTM area and casting of destination set on DEST DISP thumbwheel.
(Right Display)	Northing of destination set on DEST DISP thumbwheel.
DEST-TGT (Mode switch set to LAT/LONG (Left Display)	Longitude of destination set on DEST DISP thumbwheel.
(Right Display)	Latitude (N 84° or S 80° max.) of destination set on DEST DISP thumbwheel.
SPH-VAR (Left Display)	Spheriod code of destination set on DES DISP thumbwheel.
(Right Display)	Magnetic variation (in degrees and tenths of degrees) of destination set on DEST DISP thumbwheel.

Change 7 3-73

Controls and Functions of Doppler Navigation Set - CONT.

CONTROL/INDICATOR	FUNCTION
MEM Indicator Lamp	Lights when radar portion of navigation set is in non-track condition.
MAL Indicator Lamp	Lights when navigation set malfunction is detected by built in self-test.
DIM Control	Controls light intensity of display characters.
Left, Right, and Center Display Lamps	Lights to provide data in alphanumeric and numeric characters, as determined by setting of DISPLAY switch, MODE switch, and operation of keyboard.
Target Storage indicator	Displays destination number (memory location) in which present position will be stored when TGT STR pushbutton is pressed.
TGT STR Pushbutton KYBD Pushbutton	Stores present position data when pressed. Used in conjunction with the keyboard to allow data to be displayed and subsequently entered into the computer when the ENT key is pressed.
DEST DISP Thumbwheel switch	Destination display thumbwheel switch is used along with DEST-TGT and SPH-VAR position of DISPLAY switch. Used to select destination whose coordinates or magnetic variation are to be displayed, or to be entered. Destinations are 0 through 9, P (Present Position) and H (Home).
Keyboard	Used to setup data for entry into memory. When the DISPLAY switch is turned to the position in which new data is required, the KYBD pushbutton is pressed. Data maybe displayed on the appropriate left, right and center display. To display a number, press corresponding key or keys (1 through 0). To display a letter, first depress key corresponding to desired letter. Then depress a key in left, middle, or right column, corresponding to position of the letter on the key. Example: To enter an L, first depress L, then 3,6, or 9 in the

TM 55-1520-210-10

Controls and Functions of Doppler Navigation Set - CONT.

CONTROL/INDICATOR	FUNCTION
FLY-TO-DEST Thumbwheel switch	Selects the destination for XTK/TKE and DIST/BRG/TIME. They are displayed when DISPLAY switch is turned to either of these positions which steering information is desired. Destinations are 0 through 9, P (Present Position) and H (Home).
ENT Key	Enters data set upon keyboard into memory when pressed.
CLR Key	Clears last entered character when pressed once. When pressed twice, clears entire display panel under keyboard control.

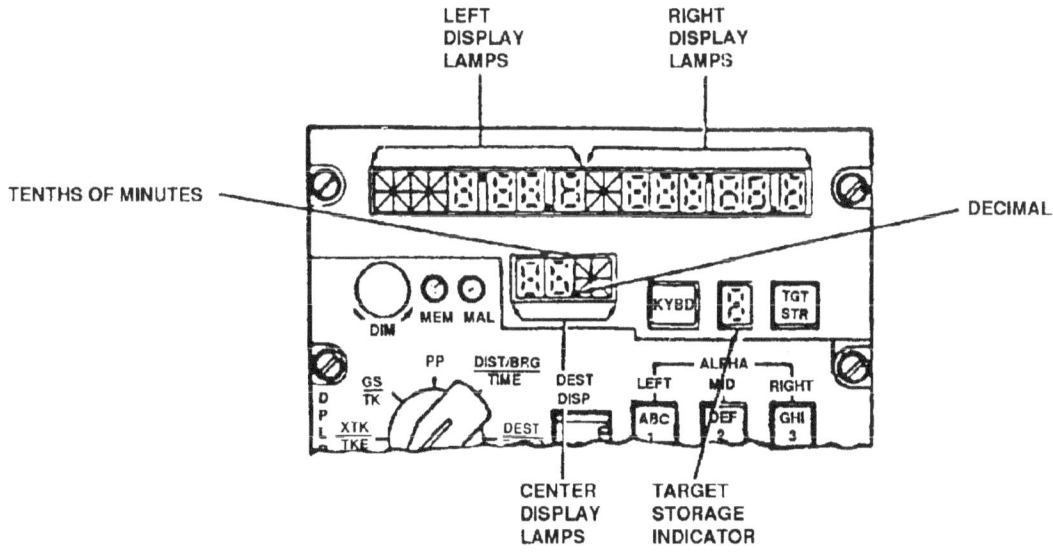

Figure 3-29.27 Doppler Lamp Test Mode Display

c. *Modes of Operation.* The three basic modes of operation are: Navigate, test, and backup.

(1) Test Mode. The TEST mode contains two functions: LAMP TEST mode, in which all display segments are lit, and TEST mode, in which system operation is verified. In LAMP TEST mode, system operation is identical to that of navigate mode. With exception that all lamp segments and MEM and MAL indicator lamps are lighted to verify their operation (see Figure 3-27.2).

(a) The TEST mode, the system antenna no longer transmits or receives electromagnetic energy. Instead, self generated test signals are inserted into the electronics to verify operation. System operation automatically reverts into the backup mode during test mode. Self-test of the doppler set is done using built-in-test equipment (BITE), and all units connected and energized for normal operation.

(b) Self-test isolates failures to one of the three units. The computer-display unit (except for the keyboard and display) is on a continuous basis. Any failure is displayed by turn-on of the MAL indicator lamp on computer-display unit. The signal data converter and receiver-transmitter-antenna are tested by turning MODE switch to TEST. Failure of those components is displayed on computer-display unit by turn-on of the MAL indicator lamp. Identification of the failed unit is indicated by a code on the display panel of the computer-display unit.

(c) Continuous monitoring of the signal data converter and receiver-transmitter-antenna is provided by the MEM indicator lamp. The MEM indicator lamp will light in normal operation when flying over smooth water. However, if lamp remains on for over 10 minutes, over land or rough water, there is a malfunction in the doppler set. Then the operator should turn the MODE switch to TEST, to determine the nature of the malfunction. Keyboard operation is verified by observing the alphanumeric readout as the keyboard is used.

(2) Navigate Mode. In navigate mode (UTM or LAT/LONG position of the MODE selector), power is applied to all system components. All required outputs and functions are provided. Changes in present position are computed and added to initial position to determine the instantaneous latitude/longitude of the helicopter. Destination and present position coordinates can be entered and displayed in UTM and latitude/longitude. At the same time, distance, bearing and time-to-go to any one of ten preset destinations are computed. They are displayed as selected by the FLY-TO-DEST thumbwheel.

(3) Backup Mode. In this mode, remembered velocity data are used for navigation. The operator can insert ground speed and track angle with the keyboard and the display in GS-TK position. This remembered velocity data can be manually updated through use of the keyboard and CDU DISPLAY switch in the GS-TK position. When GS-TK values are inserted under these conditions, navigation continues using only these values.

d. *Operation.*

(1) Window Display and Keyboard Operation. In all data display except UTM coordinates, the two fields are the left and right display windows. In UTM coordinates displays, the first field of control is the center window. The second field is the combination of the left and right displays. When pressing the KYBD pushbutton, one or other of the fields described above is under control.

(a) If it is not desired to change display under control, the pilot can advance to next field of display panel. This is done by pressing the KYBD pushbutton again. The last character entered may be cleared by pressing the CLR key. That character may be a symbol or an alphanumeric character. However, if CLR key is pressed twice in succession, all characters in the field under control will be cleared. That field will still remain under control.

(2) Data Entry. To enter a number, press the corresponding key. To enter a letter, press the key corresponding to the desired letter. Then press a key in left, middle, or right column corresponding to position of letter on pushbutton. Example: To enter an L, first press L, then either 3, 6, or 9 in the right column. The computer program is designed to reject unacceptable data (for example, a UTM area of WI does not exist, and will be rejected). If the operator attempts to insert unacceptable data, the display will be blank after ENT is pressed.

(3) Start Procedure.

(a) MODE selector - LAMP TEST. All lights should be lit.

1. Left, right, Center and Target storage indicator - Lit (Figure 3-29..27). All other lights should be on.

2. Turn DIM control fully clockwise, then fully counterclockwise, and return to full clockwise. All segments of the display should alternately glow brightly, go off, and then glow brightly.

(b) MODE selector - TEST. After about 15 seconds left display should display GO. Ignore the random display of alpha and numeric characters which occurs during the first 15 seconds. Also ignore test velocity and angle data displayed after the display has frozen. After about 15 seconds, one of the following five displays will be observed in the first two character positions in the left display.

NOTE

If the MAL lamp lights during any mode except LAMP TEST, the computer-display unit MODE switch turn to OFF. The turn to TEST, to verify the failure. If the MAL LAMP remains on after recycling to TEST, notify organizational maintenance personnel.

Test Mode Display and Remarks

DISPLAY		REMARKS
LEFT	RIGHT	
GO	No display Display Blanks (normal).	If right display is blank, system is operating satisfactorily.
GO	P	If right display is P, then pitch or roll data is missing, or pitch exceeds 90°. In this case, pitch and roll in the computer are both set to zero and navigation continues in a degraded operation. Problem may be in the vertical gyroscope or helicopter cabling.
		NOTE If TEST mode display is BU, MN or NG, MODE switch should be recycled through OFF. This verifies that failure is not a momentary one. If the TEST mode display is BU or MN, the data entry may be made in the UTM or LAT/LONG mode. However, any navigation must be carried on with the system in the BACKUP mode.
BU	C, R, S, or H followed by a numeric code	A failure has occurred and the system has automatically switched to a BACKUP mode of operation as follows: 1. The operator has the option of turning the MODE switch to BACKUP and entering the best estimate of ground speed and track angle. 2. The operator has the option of turning the MODE switch to BACKUP. He enters his best estimate of wind speed, direction, ground speed and track angle. Update present position as soon as possible, because the significant navigation errors may have accumulated.

Test Mode Display and Remarks - CONT.

DISPLAY		REMARKS
LEFT	RIGHT	
MN	C, R, S, or H followed by a numeric code	A failure has occurred and the BACKUP mode used for manual navigation (MN), is the only means of valid navigation. The operator may use the computer as a dead reckoning device by entering ground speed and track data. The operator should update present position as soon as possible, because it is possible significant navigation errors may have accumulated.
NG	C, R, S, or H followed by a numeric code	A failure has occurred in the system and the operator should not use the system.
EN		The 9V battery has failed. All stored data must be reentered.
		NOTE
		If the TEST mode display is BU, MN or NG, the MODE switch should be recycled through OFF. This verifies that the failure is not a momentary one. If the TEST mode display is BU or MN, the data entry may be made in the UTM or LAT/LONG mode. However, any navigation must be carried on with the system in the BACKUP mode.

(4) Entering UTM Data. This initial data is inserted before navigating with the doppler.

(a) Spheroid of operation, when using UTM coordinates.

(b) UTM coordinates of present position - zone, area, easting (four significant digits) and northing (four significant digits; latitude/longitude coordinates may be used).

(c) Variation of present position to the nearest one-tenth of a degree.

(d) Coordinates of desired destination -0 through 5 and H; (6 through 9 are normally used for target store locations but may also be used for destinations). It is not necessary to enter all destinations in the same coordinate system.

NOTE

It is not necessary to enter destinations. Unless steering information, updating present position, or a present position variation computation is desired. If a present position variation running update is desired, destination must be entered. The operator may enter one or more destinations to effect the variation update. If is not necessary for all destinations to have associated variations entered.

(e) Variations of destinations to be to nearest one-tenth of a degree.

(5) Entering Spheroid and/or Variation.

(a) MODE selector - UTM, LAT/LONG or BACK-UP.

(b) DISPLAY selector - SPH-VAR.

(c) DEST DISP thumbwheel - P, numeral, or H as desired.

(d) KYBD pushbutton - Press. Observe display freezes and TGT STR indicator blanks. Press KYBD pushbutton again and observe left display blinks. If no spheroid data is to be entered, KYBD pushbutton - Press again, go to Step g.

(e) Spheroid data - Entry. (Example: INO). Press keys 3 (left window blanks), 3, 5, 5 and 0. Left display should indicate INO.

(f) ENT pushbutton - Press if no variation data is to be entered.

(g) KYBD pushbutton - Press, if variation data is to be entered, and note right display blanks. (If no variation data is to be entered, ENT key - Press.)

(h) Variation data - Enter. (Example: E001.2, press keyboard keys 2 (right window blanks), 2, 0, 0, 1 and 2. Press ENT key, the entire display will blank and TGT STR number will reappear, display should indicate INO E001 .2).

(6) Entering Present Position or Destination in UTM.

(a) MODE selector - UTM.

(b) DISPLAY selector - DEST-TGT.

(c) DEST DISP thumbwheel - P, numerical, or H as desired.

(d) Present position and destination - Enter. (Example: Entry of zone 31 T, area CF, casting 0958 and northing 3849.)

1. KYBD pushbutton - Press. Observe that display freezes and TGT STR indicator blanks.

2. KYBD button - Press. Observe that center display blanks.

3. Key 3, 1,7 and 8- Press.

4. KYBD button - Press. Observe left and right displays blank.

5. Key 1, 0, 9, 5, 8, 3, 8, 4, 9- Press.

6. ENT pushbutton - Press. Left, right, and center displays will momentarily blank and TGT STR number will appear. Displays should indicate 31T CF 09583849.

(7) Entering Present Position or Destination Variation in LAT/LONG. The variation of a destination must be entered after the associated destination coordinates are entered. As each time a destination is entered its associated variation is deleted. The order of entry for present position is irrelevant.

NOTE

IF operation is to occur in a region with relatively constant variation, the operator enters variation only for present position. The computer will use this value throughout the flight.

(a) MODE selector - LAT/LONG.

(b) DISPLAY selector - DEST-TGT.

(c) DEST DISP thumbwheel - P, numerical or H as desired.

(d) Present position of destination - Enter. (Example: Entry of N 41° 10.1 minutes and E 035° 50.2 minutes.) Press KYBD pushbutton. Observe that display freezes and TGT STR indicator blanks. Press KYBD pushbutton again and observe left display blanks. Press keys 5, 5, 4, 1, 1, 0 and 1. Press KYBD pushbutton (right display should clear), and keys 2, 2, 0, 3, 5, 5, 0 and 2.

(e) ENT pushbutton - Press. Entire display will blank and TGT STR number will reappear. Display should indicate N41° 10.1 E 035° 50.2

(8) Ground Speed and Track.

(a) MODE selector - BACKUP.

(b) DISPLAY selector - GS-TK.

(c) Ground speed and track - Enter. (Example: Enter 131 km/h and 024°. Press KYBD pushbutton, observe that left display freezes and TGT STR indicator blanks. Press keys 3 and 1. Left display indicates 131. Press KYBD pushbutton, control shifts to right display, and right display blanks. Press keys 0, 2 and 4.

(d) ENT pushbutton - Press. The entire display will blank, and TGT STR number will reappear. Display should indicate 131 024°.

(9) Initial Data Entry. Initial data entry variation coordinates are normally done prior to takeoff. To make the initial data entry, do the following:

(a) Present position - variation - Enter Paragraph 5.

(b) DISPLAY selector - DEST-TGT.

(c) DEST DISP thumbwheel - P. Do not press ENT key now.

(d) ENT pushbutton - Press as helicopter is sitting over or overflies initial fix position.

(e) FLY-TO DEST thumbwheel - Desired destination location.

(10) Update of Present. Position From Stored Destination. The helicopter is flying to a destination set by the FLY-TO DEST thumbwheel. When the helicopter is over the destination, the computer updates the present position when the KYBD pushbutton is pressed. Use stored destination coordinates for destination number shown in FLY-TO DEST window. Add the distance traveled between the time KYBD pushbutton was pressed and ENT key was pressed.

(a) DISPLAY selector - DIST/BRG TIME.

(b) KYBD pushbutton - Press, when helicopter is over the destination. Display freezes.

NOTE

If a present position update is not desired, set the DISPLAY selector to some other position. This aborts the update mode.

(c) ENT key - Press.

(11) Update of Present Position from Landmark. There are two methods for updating present position from a landmark. Method 1 is useful if the landmark comes up unexpectedly and the operator needs time to determine the coordinates. Method 2 is used when a landmark update is anticipated.

(a) Method 1.

1. DISPLAY selector - PP.

2. KYBD pushbutton - Press as landmark is overflown. Present position display will freeze.

3. Compare landmark coordinates with those on display.

4. Landmark coordinates - Enter. If difference warrants an update.

5. ENT key - Press is update is required.

6. DISPLAY selector - Set to some other position to abort update.

(b) Method 2.

1. DISPLAY selector - DEST/TGT.

2. DEST DISP thumbwheel - P. Present position coordinates should be displayed.

3. KYBD pushbutton - Press, observe that display freezes.

4. Landmark coordinates - Manually enter via keyboard.

5. ENT key - Press when overflying landmark.

6. DISPLAY selector - Set to some other position to abort update.

(12) Left-Right Steering Signals. Flying shortest distance to destination from present position.

(a) DISPLAY selector - XTK-TKE.

(b) MODE SEL - DPLR.

(c) Fly helicopter in direction of lateral deviation pointer or vertical situation indicator. Center the pointer or course deviation baron HSI.

(13) Target Store (TGT STR) operation. Two methods may be used for target store operation. Method 1 is normally used when time is not available for preplanning a target store operation. Method 2 is used when it is desired to store a target in a specific DEST DISP position.

(a) Method 1.

1. TGT STR pushbutton - Press when flying over target.

2. Present position is automatically stored. The destination location is that which was displayed in target store indicator (position 6, 7, 8 or 9) immediately before pressing TGT STR pushbutton.

(b) Method 2.

1. MODE selector - UTM or LAT/LONG, depending on coordinate format desired.

2. DISPLAY selector - DEST-TGT.

3. DEST DISP thumbwheel - P.

4. KYBD pushbutton - Press when over flying potential target. Display should freeze.

NOTE

Do not press ENT key while DEST DISP thumbwheel is at P.

5. If it is not desired to store the target, turn DEST DISP thumbwheel to destination location desired and press ENT key.

6. If, it is not desired to store the target, place DISPLAY selector momentarily to another position.

(14) Transferring Stored Target Coordinates From One Location to Another. The following procedure allows the operator to transfer stored target coordinates from one thumbwheel location to another. For example, it is assumed that the pilot wants to put the coordinates of stored target 7 into location of destination.

NOTE

Range, time-to-go, bearing and left/right steering data are computed and displayed for destination selected via FLY-TO DEST thumbwheel.

(a) DISPLAY selector -DEST-TGT.

(b) DEST DISP thumbwheel -7.

(c) KYBD pushbutton - Press.

(d) DEST DISP thumbwheel -2.

(e) ENT key - Press.

(14) Transferring Variation From One Location to Another. To transfer variation data to same location where associated stored target coordinates has been transferred is the same as in Stored Target Coordinates From One Location To Another, except that the DISPLAY selector is placed at SPH-VAR.

(15) Dead Reckoning Navigation. As an alternate BACKUP mode, dead reckoning navigation can be done using ground speed and track angle estimates.

(a) MODE selector - BACKUP.

(b) DISPLAY selector - GS-TK.

(c) Best estimate of ground speed and track angle - Enter via keyboard.

(d) Set MODE selector to any other position to abort procedure.

(16) Operation During and After Power Interruption. During a dc power interruption or when power is removed, random access memory (RAM) (stored destination and present position) data is retained.

(a) It is retained by power from an 8.4 volt dc dry cell battery. This makes it unnecessary to reenter any navigational data when power returns or before each flight.

(b) If battery does not stored destination data, the display will indicate on EN when power returns. This indicates to the pilot that previously stored data has been lost. Present position, spheroid/variation, and destinations must be entered.

(c) The computer, upon return of power, resets presents position variation to E OOO.O°. Resets destination and associated variations to a non-entered state, remembers wind to zero and spheroid to CL6.

(d) The following data must be entered following battery failure:

1. Enter spheroid.

2. Enter present position variation.

3. Enter present position.

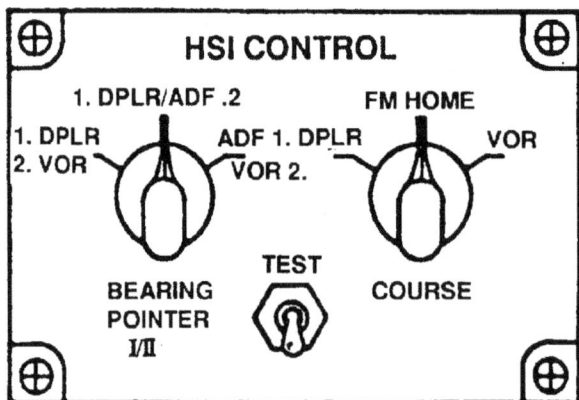

Figure 3-29.28. Horizontal Situation indicator Control (C-11740/A)

4. Enter each destination and its associated variation.

e. *Stopping Procedure.*

Mode selector - OFF.

f. *HSI Control.*

(1) BEARING POINTER NO. I & II Control Switch (Figure 3-29.28) selects either ADF/VOR, DPLR/ADF or DPLR/ADF bearing information to be displayed on the No. I & II BEARING POINTERS on the horizontal situation indicator (HSI).

(2) The CRS DEVN Control Switch (Course Deviation) selects DPLR, FM, HOME or VOR functions to be displayed on the HSI vertical needle. The ID - 250 RM indicator only displays ADF on the No. 1 pointer and VOR on the No. 2 pointer.

g. *Horizontal Situation Indicator.*

Controls and Indicators. Refer to Figure 3-29.29.

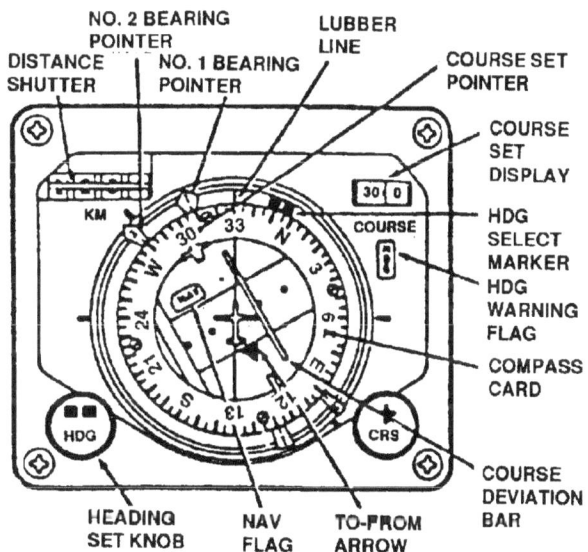

Figure 3-29.29 Horizontal Situation Indicator (ID-2103/A)

Controls/Functions of Horizontal Situation Indicator

CONTROL	FUNCTION
Compass card	The compass is a 360° scale that turns to display heading data obtained from the compass control. The helicopter headings are read at the upper lubber line.
Bearing pointer No. 1	The pointer operates in conjuction with Doppler. Indicates relative bearing to doppler destination set on FLY-TO-DEST thumbwheel.
Bearing pointer No. 2	The pointer operates in conjunction with selected VOR or ADF receiver. The pointer is read against the compass card and indicates the magnetic bearing of the VOR or ADF station.
Course deviation bar	This bar indicates lateral deviation from a selected course. When the helicopter is flying the selected course, the course bar will be aligned with the course set pointer. It will be centered on the fixed aircraft symbol.
CRS knob	Course set (CRS) knob and the course set counter operate in conjunction with the course pointer. Allows the pilot to select any of 360° courses. Once set, the course pointer will turn with the compass card. It will be centered on the upper lubber line when the helicopter is flying the selected course.
KM indicator	Digital distance display in kilometers (KM) to destination set on doppler DEST DISP.
HDG knob	Heading set (HDG) knob operates in conjunction with the heading select marker. Allows the pilot to select any one of 360° headings. Seven full turns to the knob produces a 360° turn to the marker.
TO-FROM arrow	To-from arrow indicates that the helicopter is flying to or away from a selected VOR.
NAV flag	The NAV flag at the top of the to indicator, turns with the compass card. The flag will retract from view when a reliable navigation signal is being applied to the instrument.

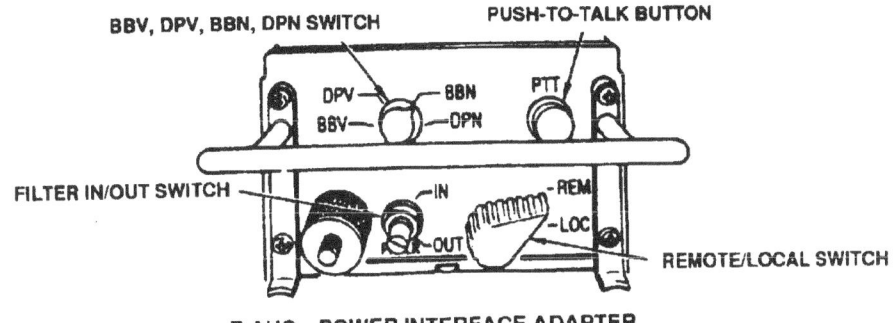

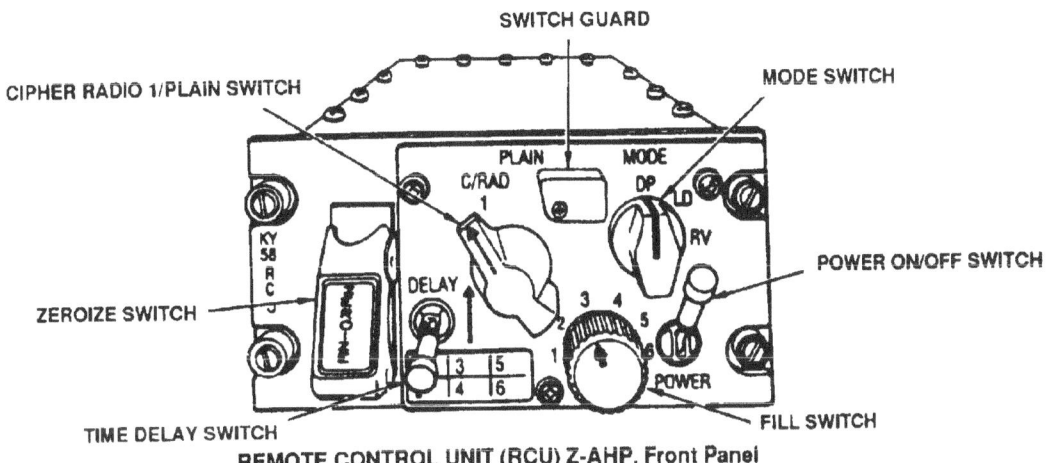

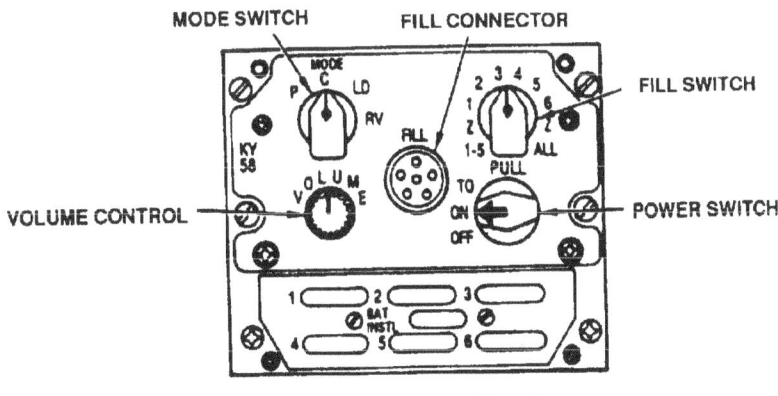

Figure 3-29.30. Voice Security System Equipment

TM 55-1520-210-10

Nomenclature	Common Name	Use	Range	V1	V2	V3	V4
Control Intercommunications Set C-1611/AIC	ICS Box	Integrate Interphone and all communications equipment	Stations within helicopter	X	X	X	X
Receiver-Transmitter, Radio RT-823/ARC-131	FM Radio	Two-way voice communications	Line of sight	X	X	X	X
TSEC/KY-28	Voice Security Equipment	Secure two-way voice communications	N/A	X	X		
Receiver-Transmitter, Radio RT-742/ARC-51BX	UHF Radio set	Two-way voice communications	Line of Sight		X		X
Receiver-Transmitter, Radio RT-1167/ARC-164	UHF Radio set	Two-way voice communications	Line of Sight		X		X
TSEC/KY-58, Z-AHP Control Indicator and Z-AHQ Adapter	Voice Security Equipment	Secure two-way voice communications	N/A			X	X
HYL-3/TSEC Regenerative Repeater	HYL-3/TSEC	Used to increase link reliability	N/A	X	X		
MX-9331A/URC Regenerative Repeater	Repeater	Used to increase link reliability	N/A			X	X
Receiver-Transmitter RT-1343/TSQ-129 Basic User Unit (BUU)	PLRS	Position Locating Reporting System Message Processor	N/A			X	X

Figure 3-30. AN/ASC-15A(V) 1,2,3, and 4 Equipment Configuration (Sheet 1 of 3)

TM 55-1520-210-10

Nomenclature	Common Name	Use	Range	V1	V2	V3	V4
C-10830-/PSQ-4 Control-Readout Unit	URO	Enter and display message	N/A			X	X
CN-1547/ASQ-177, SM-D-911821 Power Adapter	Voltage Regulator	Provide power for the BUU	N/A			X	X
MX-9545/VR Vehicle Adapter	Voltage Regulator	Provide power for the Repeater	N/A			X	X
C-8157/ARC Control Indicator	Control	Control for the ARC-131	N/A	X	X	X	X
VHF-AM Comm ARC/186	VHF-FM Command Set	Two-way voice Communications	Line of Sight				
#1 VHF-FM Comm/Homing ARC/201	VHF-FM Comm/Homing	Two-way voice Communications	Line of Sight				
#2 VHF-FM Comm ARC/201	VHF-FM Comm Set	Two-way voice Communications	Line of Sight				
HF-AM Communications System ARC/199	HF Radio Set	Two-way voice Communications	Long Range				
HF Comm Sec. TSEC/KY-75	COMSEC	Secure Voice HF ARC-199	N/A				

Figure 3-30. AN/ASC-15A(V) 1,2,3, and 4 Equipment Configuration (Sheet 2 of 3)

3-89 Change 7

Nomenclature	Common Name	Use	Range	V1	V2	V3	V4
Direction Finder Set ARN/89	Direction Finder Set	Radio Range Navigation	150 to 200 Mi				
Radio Navigation System ARN/123	VHF Navigation Set	VHF Navigational and VHF Audio	Line of Sight				
Doppler Navigation Set ASN/128	Doppler Navigation Set	Navigational system	Long Range				
Gyromagnetic Compass Set ASN/43	Gyromagnetic Compass	Navigational Aid	N/A				
IFF Transponder AN/APX-100	Transponder Set	Navigational Aid	Line of Sight				

Figure 3-30. AN/ASC-15A(V) 1,2,3, and 4 Equipment Configuration (Sheet 3 of 3)

Chapter 4

Mission Equipment

Section 1. ARMAMENT

4-1. Armament Subsystem M23 The armament subsystem M23 is attached to external stores hard point fittings on both sides of the helicopter. The two flexible 7.62 millimeter machine guns M60D are free pointing but limited in traverse, elevation, and depression by cam surfaces and stops on pointless and pintle post assemblies of the two mount assemblies on which the M60D machine guns are mounted. An ejection control bag is latched to the right side of each M60D machine gun to hold the spent cases, unfired rounds and links. Cartridges travel from ammunition box and cover assemblies to M60D machine gun through flexible chute and brace assemblies. The following paragraphs describe machine gun M60D components.

  a. *Cover Latch.* The cover latch is located at the right rear of the cover assembly. In the vertical position it secures cover assembly in closed position. Turning to horizontal position unlocks cover assembly.

  b. *Barrel Lock Lever.* The barrel lock lever, located at right front of receiver, is secured to barrel locking shaft and rotates shaft to lock or unlock barrel assembly.

WARNING

Cocking handle assembly shall be returned to the forward or locked position before firing to prevent injury to personnel.

  c. *Cocking Handle Assemb/y.* The cocking handle assembly, at right f rent of receiver, is used for manually charging the weapon.

  d. *Safety.* The safety, located at lower front of receiver, consists of a cylindrical pin with a sear clearance cut which slides across receiver to block the sear and prevent accidental firing. Ends of pin are marked for pushing to "S" safe and "F" firing positions.

WARNING

Pressing the trigger to release the bolt assembly also accomplishes feeding and releases the firing mechanism, Weapon shall be cleared of cartridges before pressing trigger assembly, unless firing is intended.

  e. *Grip and Trigger Assembly.* The grip and trigger assembly includes the spade grips and is located at rear of receiver. The U-shaped design permits firing of weapon by index finger of either hand.

Caution

When ammunition is not present in machine gun M60D, retard forward force of released bolt assembly by manually restraining forward movement of cocking handle assembly to prevent damage to cartridge tray.

  f. *Magazine Release Latch.* The magazine release latch, located on left side of receiver, locks adapter of the ammunition chute when it is seated in magazine bracket.

  g, *Ammunition Chute Adapter,* The ammunition chute adapter is required for flexible chute installation.

4-2. Preflight Procedures—Machine Gun M60D

  1. Gun—Secure—Stowed position.

  2. Barrel—Free of obstruction.

  3. Gas cylinder—Plug tight, safety-wired.

  4. Cover—Free movement, latch secure.

  5. Ejection control bag—Latched.

  6. Ammunition box—Latches and cover—Secure. Check cartridges for proper position in links.

7. Chute and brace—Secure.

8. Safety—Safe.

9. Mount—Check free pintle movement.

10. Ammunition boxes—Stowed.

4-3. Before Takeoff/Before Landing Procedure—Machine Gun M60D

1. Bolt—Retract, push handle forward.

2. Safety—Check safe.

3. Cover—Open.

4. Ammunition—Load.

5. Cover—Close, latch secure.

WARNING

Safety harness shall be worn by gunner and attached to helicopter during flight operations.

4-4. Before Leaving Helicopter Procedures—Machine Gun M60D Remove gun. Refer to TM 9-1005-224-10.

4-5. Emergency Procedures-Machine Gun M60D

WARNING

If a stoppage occurs, never retract bolt assembly and allow it to go forward again without inspecting chamber to see it is clear. Such an action strips another cartridge from the belt. if an unfired cartridge remains in the chamber, a second cartridge can fire the first and cause injury to personnel and/or weapon damage. One hundred fifty cartridges fired in a 2 minute period will make a barrel hot enough to produce a cookoff.

a. Misfire. A misfire is a complete failure to fire. It must be treated as a hangfire until possibility of a hangfire is eliminated.

b. Hangfire. A hangfire is a delay in functioning of the propelling charge. If a stoppage occurs, wait five seconds. Pull handle assembly to rear, ensuring operating rod assembly is held back.

c. Double Feeding. When a stoppage occurs with bolt assembly in forward position, assume there is an unfired cartridge in the chamber. Treat this as a hangfire.

d. Runaway Gun. if gun continues to fire after trigger has been released, open cover and permit bolt to go underneath cartridge and stop in the forward position.

e. Cookoff. A cookoff is a functioning of any or all of the explosive components of a cartridge chambered in a very hot machine gun. If the primer or propelling charge should cookoff, the projectile may be propelled from the machine gun with normal velocity, even though no attempt was made to fire the primer, by actuating firing mechanism. In such a case, although there may be uncertainty as to whether or when the cartridge will fire, the precautions to be observed are the same as those prescribed for a "hangfire". To prevent a cookoff, a cartridge, which has been loaded into a very hot machine gun, should be fired immediately or removed within 5 seconds to 10 seconds.

4-6. Armament Subsystem M56 and M132 Mine Dispersing

a. The M56 mine dispersing subsystem is attached to external stores hardpoint fittings on both sides of the helicopter and is electrically or manually jettisonable in an emergency. The mine dispenser is designed to provide release of mines from the 40 canisters with application of current through the intervalometer, which is part of the disperser electrical circuit. Total release of mines in all canisters is accomplished within a variable time span between each canister release, which is set by the pilot. A quick-release safe pin with an attached REMOVE BEFORE FLIGHT red flag is installed in the intervalometer to prevent accidental activation of the intervalometer before flight. A quick-release safe pin with an attached REMOVE BEFORE FLIGHT red flag is also installed in the pylon ejector rack to prevent the accidental dropping of the mines from the pylon. The subsystem consists of a bomb (mine) dispenser SUU-13D/A loaded with 40 mine canisters, each of which contains two anti-tank/anti-vehicle (AT/AV) mines and one mine ejection charge MI 98. The subsystem is used in conjunction with a dispenser control panel and a helicopter cable (harness) assembly (fig 4-1). A pallet, which is used for safety and handling purposes, attaches to the underside of the subsystem. The dispenser control panel allows the pilot to initiate mine dispersing, stop mine dispersing, control quantity of mines dispersed, set the time interval between the ejection of mines, and electrically jettison the subsystems in an emergency. The dispenser is fired by pressing the FIRE button of the DISP control. The firing sequence will continue until the quantity of mines selected have been ejected from the dispenser. Anytime after FIRE button is pressed, the firing sequence may be terminated by resetting the SAFE-ARM switch to the center STBY (standby) position. When the switch is again set in the ARM position and the FIRE button is again pressed, a new firing sequence is initiated. The helicopter cable (harness) assembly provides connection of the dispenser control panel to the heated blanket receptacle and to the subsystem firing and jettison circuitry.

b, The subsystem M132 is used by helicopter crews for gaining experience in dispersing mines which simulate those in the M56 subsystem. The M132 consists of a dispenser SUU-13D/A containing three practice mine canisters. Dispenser loading for a practice mining mission consists of three practice mine canisters loaded into each dispenser in firing locations 1, 20, and 40. The remaining 37 positions will be left empty. With the dispenser control panel mode selector switch set to PAIRS and the QUANTITY selector switch set to ALL, the dummy mines will be dispersed to land at the beginning, in the middle and at the end of the target area.

4-7. Preflight Procedures—M56 and M132 Mine Dispersing Subsystem

1. Pylons and supports—Secure.
2. Sway braces—Secure to disperser pads.
3. Electrical connectors—Secure.
4. Wiring harness—Taped to pylon support.
5. Pallet—In place.

Caution

Connector marked with a plus (+) sign must be placed in the heater blanket receptacle properly.

6. Wiring harness—Connected to heater blanket receptacle.
7. HEATED BLANKET circuit breakers—in.
8. Wiring harness—Secure to cabin deck.
9. Press to test lights—Check.
10. HEATED BLANKET circuit breakers—Out.

4-8. Before Takeoff Procedures—M56 and M132 Mine Dispersing Subsystem

1. SAFE/STBY/ARM switch—SAFE.
2. Safety pallets—Remove.
3. Intervalometer safety pins—Remove.
4. Pylon safety pins—Remove.

4-9. Inflight Procedures—M56 and M132 Mine Dispersing Subsystem

1. HEATED BLANKET circuit breakers—in.
2. SAFE-STBY-ARM switch—STBY.
3. Mode selector switch—As desired.
4. QUANTITY selector switch—As desired.
5. INTERVAL selector switch—As desired. Switch shall be position 1 through 10.
6. SAFE-STBY-ARM switch—ARM.
7. FIRE button—Press.

4-10. Before Landing Procedures—M56 and M132 Mine Dispersing Subsystem

1. SAFE-STBY-ARM switch—SAFE.
2. HEATED BLANKET circuit breakers—Out.

4-11. Before Leaving Helicopter Procedures—M56 and M132 Mine Dispersing Subsystem

1. Subsystem—Check for unfired canisters.
2. Maintenance checks—Refer to TM 9-1345-201-12.

4-12. Emergency Procedures—Electrical—M56 and M132 Mine Dispersing Subsystem

1. HEATED BLANKET circuit breakers—Check in.
2. NON-ESS BUS switch—MANUAL ON.
3. FIRE button—Press.

TM 55-1520-210-10

4-13. Emergency Procedures–Fire–M56 and M132 Mine Dispersing Subsystem

1. JETTISON switch cover–Up.

2. JETTISON switch–Up.

4-14. Safety–M56 and M132 Mine Dispersing Subsystem

WARNING

Unfired canisters and mines accidentally released from subsystem will not be handled or moved.

1. Failure to fire–After completion of mission and a check of the subsystem reveals unfired canisters, install safety pallets and notify explosive ordnance disposal or other authorized personnel.

2. If dangerous explosive item is encountered, all operation in the immediate vicinity will be shut down, personnel evacuated to a safe location (800 foot radius) and explosive ordnance disposal or other authorized personnel notified to render assistance in elimination of the hazard.

3. Refer to TM 9-1345-201-12 for minimum safety standards and requirements.

4-15. M52 Smoke Generator Subsystem

WARNING

Never operate the smoke generating subsystem when the helicopter is on the ground and engine is operating.

The smoke generating subsystem basically consists of the oil tank assembly, pump and motor assembly, nozzle ring assembly, operating switch and fog oil level gage. The smoke generating subsystem discharges atomized fog oil into the hot exhaust gases of a helicopter jet engine. A dense white smoke is formed which settles rapidly to the ground when fog oil is released at altitudes less than 50 feet and airspeeds less than 90 knots. The tank capacity is 50 gallons (approximately) and provide approximately three minutes of smoke generator operation. The length of time the smoke screen will obscure enemy vision depends on wind conditions and the altitude at which the smoke is released. The operating switch is a hand-held push button switch, attached to the end of a six foot cable, suspended from the cabin roof and held by a clip near the center line of the roof structure. Its location is accessible to the pilot, copilot, or crewmembers. The tank level fog oil circuit breaker is located in the overhead panel. The circuit breaker protects the pump and motor assembly. An oil level gage is mounted on the center post in the cockpit. The gage is marked from E (empty) to F (full) in \1/4\ tank increments, to indicate the quantity of oil remaining in the oil tank. The prescribed fog oil is type SFG2 (Military Specification MIL-F-12070).

WARNING

Alternate fluids shall not be used in the oil tank.

Caution

Do not operate the smoke generating subsystem when there is no fog oil in the oil tank.

4-16. Preflight Procedures–M52 Smoke Generator Subsystem

1. Fluid–Check.

2. Pump and motor–Secure.

3. Hoses and connections–Leaks–Security.

4. Exhaust ring–Secure.

5. Electrical connections–Secure.

4-17. Before Takeoff–M52 Smoke Generator Subsystem

1. SMOKE GENERATOR circuit breaker–OUT.

2. The circuit breaker must be in to provide operating power to the pump and motor when the operating switch is activated.

4-18. Inflight Procedures–M52 Smoke Generator Subsystem

1. SMOKE GENERATOR circuit breaker–in.

2. Operating switch–Push–As desired. Smoke can be generated either continuously or in short bursts. Smoke generation will stop when the operating switch push button is released.

4-19. Before Landing–M52 Smoke Generator Subsystem SMOKE GENERATOR circuit breaker–out.

TM 55-1520-210-10

4-20. Before Leaving Helicopter-M52 Smoke Generator Subsystem.

1. System - check for leaks.

2. Ring - Condition and security.

Section II MISSION AVIONICS

4-20.1. Communications Command Console AN/ASC-15A(V) 1, 2, 3, 4 (if installed).

a The communications command console provides tactical commands with air-to-ground command and control communications in a battlefield environment. The console provides ground-air ground automatic secure transmission from an airborne platform and a Position Locating Reporting System (PLRS).

b. Use:

(1) When installed in the UH-IH helicopter, AN/ASC-15A(V)3, 4, configured m the command post mode, can be used as a forward area airborne command and observation post. This mode provides six separate intercommunication stations. Three of the six stations have control of three separate very high frequency, frequency-modulated (VHF-FM) radio communicator links (V3) or two VHF-FM links (V4), and one ultra high frequency, amplitude-modulated (UHF-AM) link.

(2) The PLRS system provides timely and accurate positioning information in support of tactical commander.

(3) The VHF-FM links have voice encryption capabilities if the TSEC/KY-28 or TSEC/KY-58 security equipment Is employed. The UHF-AM link cannot be voice encrypted.

(4) The intercommunicatlon control set provides intercommunication circuit for two-way voice communications between the operator; pilot, copilot, communications officer or observer.

(5) The regenerative repeater is used with two FM receiver-transmitter units to automatically retransmit plain or secure voice message from two other receiver-transmitter units which are too far apart to communicate with each other using normal communications.

c. AN/ASC-15A(V) 1, 2, 3, and 4 equipment configuration. Refer to Figure 3-30.

Section III. CARGO HANDLING

Paragraphs 4-21. through 4-26. and table 4-1 have been deleted. This Includes all data from pages 4-5 through 4-8.

Change 17 4-5/(4-6 blank)

NOTE

During hoist operation overtravel of the cable assembly may occur in the extended mode of operation after stopping hoist operation in MID-TRAVEL. Cable over-travel should not exceed 10 feet. If cable overtravel is observed, refer hoist to maintenance for repair.

4-27. High Performance Hoist. Provisions have been made for the installation of an internal rescue hoist (Figure 4-2). The hoist may be installed in any one of our positions in the helicopter cabin. The hoist installation consists of a vertical column extending from the floor structure to the cabin roof, a boom with an electrically powered traction sheave, and an electrically operated winch. Two electrical control stations for the operation of the rescue hoist are provided, one for the pilot, and one for the hoist operator. A control switch is located on the cyclic control stick and provides up and down operation of the hoist as well as positioning the boom (Figure 2-5). A pendant control is provided for the hoist operator and contains a boom positioning switch and a toggle switch for hoist operation (Figure 4-6). The pilot control will override the hoist operators control. A pressure cartridge cable cutter is provided with two guarded cable cutter switches. The pilot cable cutter switch is mounted on the pedestal and the hoist operators cable cutter switch is mounted on the back of the hoist control box (Figure 4-4 and Figure 4-5). The high performance hoist is an electronically speed controlled unit. Speed varies from 125 fpm at 600 pounds to 250 fpm at 300 pounds. The winch has four positive action switches. Number One is an all-stop switch that opens when three wraps of cable remain on drum. Number Two is a deceleration switch that opens when five wraps of cable remain on drum. Number Three switch has two functions, operates caution indicator light on control pendant (when caution light is on, a cable deceleration should occur) and limits cable speed when hook is 8 to 10 feet from up-stow position. Number Four switch further limits cable speed when hook is 12 to 18 inches from the up-stow position. The first and last 20 feet of the cable are painted red. An elapsed time meter and power-on indicator are located on the control panel. A pistol grip control (Figure 4-6) is provided for the hoist operator and contains a boom in/out switch, a variable speed control, cable limit and overtemperature indicator (when hoist operating temperature limit has been exceeded the over temp light will come on). (Secure hoist as soon as operations permit), and an intercommunication switch. The hoist has 250 feet of usable cable. Power is provided by the essential bus. Circuit protection is provided by the RESCUE HOIST POWER, RESCUE HOIST CONT, and RESCUE HOIST CABLE CUTTER circuit breakers. RESCUE HOIST CABLE CUTTER circuit breaker controls only the pilot's cable cutter switch.

4-28. Preflight Procedures.

> **WARNING**
> If hoist is installed check for installation of safety clip.

1. Check that vertical shaft for ceiling attaching point is raised vertically to prevent the ceiling attaching device from disconnecting.

2. Oil level Check in hoist and boom head.

3. RESCUE HOIST CONT, RESCUE HOIST POWER AND RESCUE HOIST CABLE CUTTER circuit breakers Check out.

4. CABLE CUT switches (pilot and hoist operator) guard Down and safetied.

5. Deleted.

6. Boom sheave Check that no foreign matter is entrapped at sheave.

7. GPU Connect to helicopter.

8. RESCUE HOIST CONT and RESCUE HOIST POWER circuit breakers In. Blue POWER ON light and yellow CAUTION light should be on and fan should be operating.

9. BOOM switch (Pendant) Rotate boom out and in, check hoist switch (pilot) override during operation.

10. HOIST switch (pilot) Rotate boom out.

> **WARNING**
> The cable should be reeled out and in within 30 degrees of vertical during these checks. Care should be taken to avoid twisting the cable which will cause it to kink.

NOTE
Observe the condition of the hoisting cable to assure that there are no broken wires or kinks.

11. SPEED MODE switch High.

12. HOIST switch (pilot) Down. Reel cable out until caution light is out on pendant (approximately 10 feet).

13. HOIST control switch (pilot) Reel m cable and observe that cable speed slows when caution light comes ON (approximately 10 feet).

14. Boom up limit switch actuator arm-Push up on arm during reeling in to check that hoist stops running when up limit switches are actuated. Observe that cable speed slows when hook is 12 to 18 inches from the full up position when cable is reeled in with no load on hook.

15. Repeat steps 12 through 14 using the boom switch (pendant). Check that cable speed can be regulated by the control from 0 to 250 foot per minute when cable is reeled out beyond the 10 feet caution light. (Caution light is out). Check pilots override during reeling out and in.

16. SPEED MODE switch LOW SPEED and repeat steps 12 through 15.

17. Hoist switch (pilots) Rotate boom in the stowed position.

18. RESCUE HOIST CONT, RESCUE HOIST POWER and RESCUE HOIST CABLE CUTTER circuit breakers Out upon completion of preflight check.

4-29. Operating Procedures.

1. RESCUE HOIST CONT, RESCUE HOIST POWER and CABLE CUTTER breakers In.

2. Blue POWER ON and yellow CAUTION indicator lights should be on.

> **WARNING**
> Hands must be kept off hoist boom during operation to prevent hand entrapment and injury.

3. BOOM switch Rotate boom out.

4. SPEED MODE switch As required.

TM 55-1520-210-10

5. HOIST switch DOWN. Adjust cable reel-out speed as required. CAUTION light should be out when 8 to 10 feet of cable is reeled out

6. HOIST control switch UP and adjust cable reeling speed as required. CAUTION light should be ON when rescue hook is 8 to 10 feet from up stow position. Reel cable completely up.

CAUTION
When hoist is installed in positions 1 or 4, the boom head assembly and hook assembly could bump the pilot/copilot helmets if stowed behind seat back.

7. BOOM OUT/IN switch Rotate boom in.

8. RESCUE HOIST POWER, RESCUE CONT and CABLE CUTTER circuit breakers Out.

4-30. Before Takeoff RESCUE HOIST CABLE CUTTER, RESCUE HOIST CONT and RESCUE HOIST POWER circuit breakers Out.

4-31. Inflight Procedures.

WARNING
Operations during gusty or turbulent wind conditions may result in contracting the lateral cyclic control stops. During hoisting operations the helicopter should be positioned to maximize the control margins.

1. Hover over pick-up location.

2. Use operating procedures as required. Pilot should lift load off ground by increasing collective to ensure helicopter control with the load.

WARNING
When a load is attached on the hoist hook (and if conditions permit), it is advisable not to make abrupt changes in helicopter attitude until load is aboard or raised as dose as possible. G-forces on hoist could become excessive if hoist load is being raised during abrupt movements of helicopter. These G-forces could result in the yield or failure of the hoist cable.

4-32. Inflight Procedures Hoist Operator.
Refer to FM 8-10-6 for litter missions.

WARNING
When any crewmember is not in his seat and is in the vicinity of open cargo door, he shall be secured with a gunner harness. All hoist operations will be coordinated with the pilot. Continuous status reports required.

1. Doors Open as required.

2. Hoist operator ICS panel HOT MIC/PRIVATE.

WARNING
Attempt to discharge electrostatic charge on hook before letting it touch person to be hoisted. With personnel suspended on the hoist cable, adjust cable sway and speed as needed in order to avoid catching personnel under the aircraft or bumping personnel against the aircraft.

3. When helicopter is hovered over pickup location use operational procedures as required.

4. Pull out RESCUE HOIST CONT, RESCUE HOIST POWER and RESCUE HOIST CABLE CUTTER circuit breakers upon completion of hoist operations.

4-33. Engine Shutdown Procedures

1. RESCUE HOIST CONT circuit breaker–in.

2. Hoist–Stowed position.

3. RESCUE HOIST CONT circuit breaker–Out.

4. Enter the length of cable and number of lifts used in the remarks section of DA Form 2408-13.

4-34. Cargo Hook

Caution

Helicopters equipped with a nonrotating cargo suspension unit, which maintains the hook in a fixed position (facing forward), should be used only with a cargo sling having a swivel attachment ring. A device which may be used for this application is: Sling, Endless, Nylon Webbing, Type 1, 10 inch, NSN 3940-00-675-5001.

a. *Description.* External cargo can be carried by means of a short single cable suspension unit, secured to the primary structure and located at the approximate center of gravity. This method of attachment and location has proved to be the most satisfactory for carrying external cargo. Pitching and rolling due to cargo swinging is minimized, and good stability and control characteristics are maintained under -load. A MANUAL CARGO RELEASE PUSH pedal is located between the pilot tail rotor control pedals, and an electrical release pushbutton switch is on the cyclic control stick, Before the electrical release switch on the cyclic control stick can be actuated, the CARGO RELEASE switch on the overhead panel must be positioned to ARM MISC. When not in use, the cargo suspension unit need not be removed, nor does it require stowing. Three cable and spring attachments keep the unit centralized, and the hook protrudes only slightly below the lower surface of the helicopter. A rear view mirror enables the pilot to visually check operation of the external cargo suspension hook.

b. *Preflight Procedure.*

1. Hook assembly–Check as follows:

(a) Condition and installation.

(b) Freedom of movement: fore, aft, and lateral.

(c) Centering springs (3)–Check for centering of the hook.

(d) Shear pin installation–The hook should not rotate.

(e) Electrical wiring–Condition and installation.

(f) Manual release cable–Condition and installation.

(g) Cargo hook–Closed.

2. Hook operation–Check as follows:

(a) BAT switch–ON.

(b) CARGO RELEASE switch–ARM. The CARGO RELEASE light should illuminate.

(c) Pilot electrical release switch–Press and hold. The cargo hook should open with slight pressure applied to the hook.

(d) Cargo hook–Close. Release the pilot electrical release switch.

(e) Copilot electrical release switch–Press and hold. The cargo hook should open with slight pressure applied to the hook.

(f) Cargo hook–Close. Release the copilot electrical release switch.

(g) Manual release–Press. The cargo hook should open with 20 to 30 pounds pressure applied to the hook.

(h) Cargo hook–Close.

(i) CARGO RELEASE switch–OFF The CARGO RELEASE light should go off.

(j) Apply approximately 20 to 30 pounds pressure to the hook–The cargo hook should not open.

(k) Pilot and copilot electrical release switches–Press. The cargo hook should not open. Release the switches.

(l) BAT switch–OFF.

c. Deleted.

d. Deleted.

4-35. Parachute Operations

a. Crewmembers must become familiar with procedures outlines in TM 57-220 prior to parachute operations.

Caution

At no time during flight will the static line, snap hook or safety pins be disconnected from the aircraft static line anchor cable.

b. After the last chutist has exited the aircraft, the crew chief will pull in the static lines and will hold them secured until the aircraft has landed.

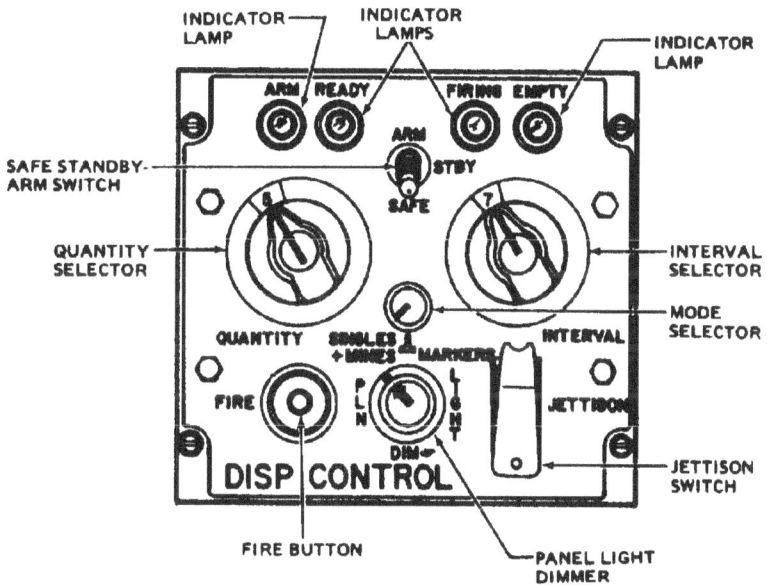

Figure 4-1. Mine Dispenser Control Panel—Typical

TM 55-1520-210-10

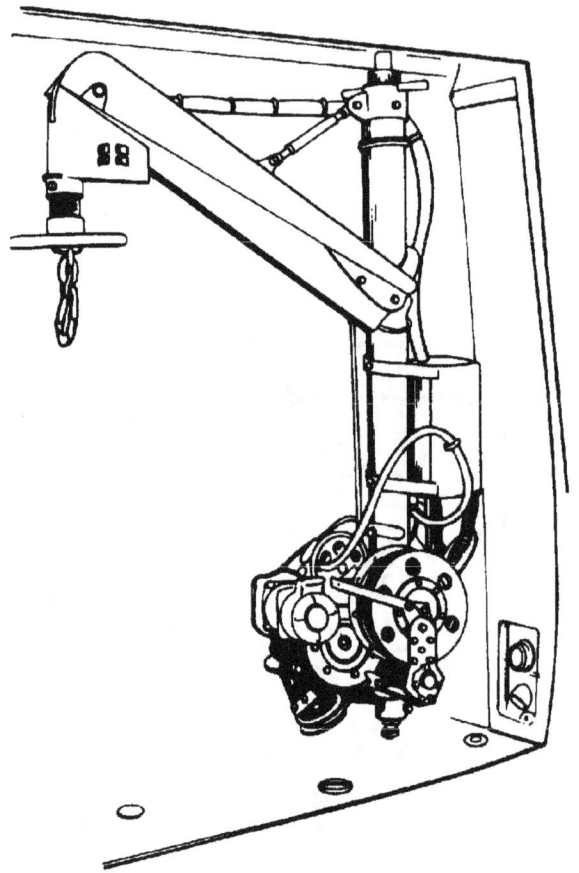

Figure 4-2. Hoist Installation—Typical

Figure 4-3, 4-4 and 4-5 has been deleted.

TM 55-1520-210-10

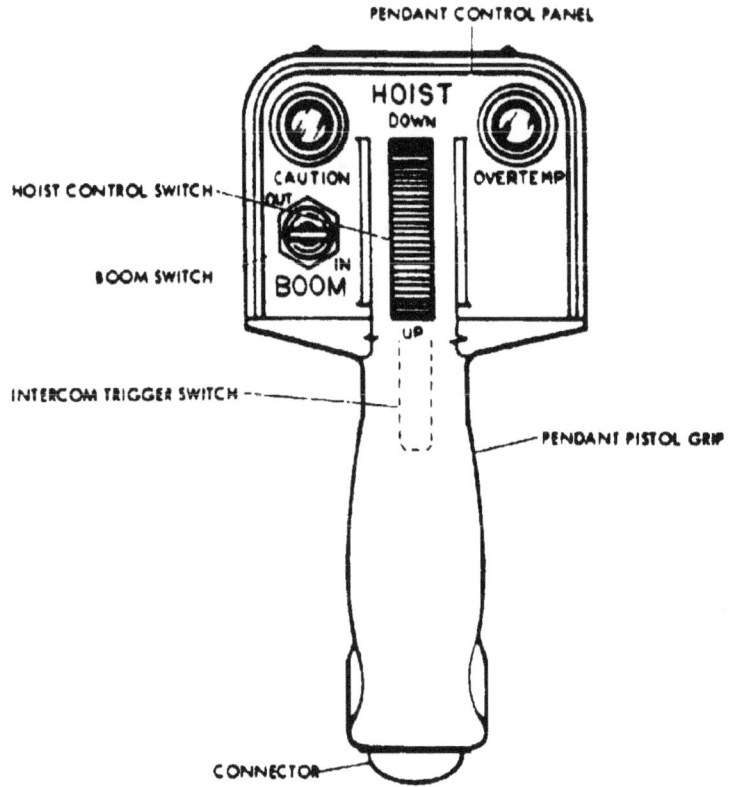

Figure 4-6. Control Pendant Assembly, High Performance Hoist

Chapter 5
Operating Limits and Restrictions

Section I. GENERAL

5-1. Purpose. This chapter identifies or refers to all important operating limits and restrictions that shall be observed during ground and flight operations.

5-2. General. The operating limitations set forth in this chapter are the direct results of design analysis, tests, and operating experiences. Compliance with these limits will allow the pilot to safely perform the assigned missions and to derive maximum utility from the helicopter.

5-3. Exceeding Operational Limits. Anytime an operational limit is exceeded an appropriate entry shall be made on DA Form 2408-13. Entry shall state what limit or limits were exceeded, range, time beyond Limits, and any additional data that would aid maintenance personnel in the maintenance action that may be required.

5-4. Minimum Crew Requirements. The minimum crew required to fly the helicopter is one pilot whose station is in the right seat. Additional crewmembers as required will be added at the discretion of the commander, in accordance with pertinent Department of the Army regulations.

Section II. SYSTEM LIMITS

5-5. Instrument Markings (Figure 5-1).

a Instrument Marking Color Codes.. Operating limits and ranges color markings which appear on the dial faces of engine, flight, and utility system instruments are illustrated with the following symbols:

R-Red, G-Green, Y-Yellow

RED markings on the dial faces of these instruments indicate the limit above or below which continued operation is likely to cause damage or shorten life. The GREEN markings on instruments indicate the safe or normal range of operation. The YELLOW markings on instruments indicate the range when special attention should be given to the operation covered by the instrument.

b. Instrument Glass Alignment Mark. Limitation markings consist of strips of semitransparent color tape which adhere to the glass outside of an indicator dial. Each tape strip aligns to increment marks on the dial face so correct operating limits are portrayed. The pilot should occasionally verify alignment of the glass to the dial face. For this purpose, all instruments that have range markings have short, vertical white alignment marks extending from the dial glass onto the fixed base of the indicator. These slippage marks appear as a single vertical line when limitation markings on the glass properly align with reading increments on the dial face. However, the slippage marks appear as separate radial lines when a dial glass has rotated.

5-6. Rotor Limitations.

a. Refer to Figure 5-1.

b. When metal main rotor blades are installed, restrict rotor speed to 319 to 324 RPM (6500 to 6600 Engine RPM) during cruise flight This restriction does not apply when composite main rotor blades (CB) are installed.

Section II. POWER LIMITS

5-7. Engine Limitations.

a. Refer to Figure 5-1.

b. Maximum starter energize time is 40 seconds with a three-minute cooling time between start attempts with three attempts in any one hour.

c. Health Indicator Test When a difference between a recorded EGT and the baseline EGT is plus or minus 20° C or greater, make an entry on DA Form 2408-13-1; if +/-30° C or greater, make an entry on DA Form 240813-1 and do not fly the aircraft.

Section IV. LOADING LIMITS

5-8. Center of Gravity Limitations.

a. Center of gravity limits for the helicopter to which this manual applies and instructions for computation of the center of gravity are contained in Chapter 6.

b. Do not carry external loads if the cg is aft of station 142 prior to lifting external load.

c. When flying at an aft cg (station 140 to 144) terminate an approach at a minimum of five-foot hover prior to landing to prevent striking the tail on the ground. Practice touchdown autorotations shall not be attempted with the cg aft of 140 because termination at 5 feet is not possible.

5-9. Weight Limitations.

a. Maximum Gross Weight. The maximum gross weight for the helicopter is 9500 pounds. The maximum gross weights for varying conditions of temperature, altitude, wind velocity, and skid height are shown in Chapter 7 or Chapter 7.1.

b. Maximum Gross Weight for Towing. The maximum gross weight for towing is 9500 pounds.

c. Cargo Hook Weight Limitations. Maximum allowable weight for the cargo hook is 4000 pounds.

d. Weight Distribution Limitations. Cargo distribution over the cargo floor area shall not exceed 100 pounds per square foot. For information pertaining to weight distribution, refer to Chapter 6.

5-10. Turbulence Limitations.

a. Intentional flight into severe or extreme turbulence is prohibited.

b. Intentional flight into moderate turbulence is not recommended when the report or forecast is based on aircraft above 12,500 pounds gross weight.

c. Intentional flight into thunderstorms is prohibited.

Section V. AIRSPEED LIMITS

5-11. Airspeed Limitations.

a. Refer to Figure 5-2 **MB** or Figure 5-2.1 **CB** for forward airspeed limits.

b. Sideward flight limits are 30 knots.

c. Rearward flight limit is 30 knots.

d. The helicopter can be flown up to VNE with the cabin doors locked in either the closed position or the fully open position. Flight above 50 KIAS with the cabin doors in the unlocked position is prohibited

e. The helicopter can be flown up to an IAS of 50 knots with one door open and one door closed. This will allow for missions such as rappelling, paradrop, and use of rescue hoist If a door comes open or unlocked from the fully open position, speed should be reduced to 50 KIAS or below until the door is secured. Crewmembers should ensure that they are fastened to the helicopter by seat belts or other safety devices while securing the cabin doors inflight.

f. Flight above 60 KIAS with roof mounted pilot tube or 50 KIAS with nose mounted pilot tube with one M56 mine disperser installed and the other disperser subsystem removed is prohibited.

g. Mine Disperser Jettisoning Limits. Except in an emergency, the mine dispersing subsystem M56 shall not be jettisoned above 60 KIAS with roof mounted pilot tube or 50 KIAS with nose mounted pilot tube.

Section VI. MANEUVERING LIMITS

5-12. Prohibited Maneuvers.

a. Abrupt inputs of flight controls cause excessive main rotor flapping, which may result in mast bumping and must be avoided.

b. Intentional maneuvers beyond attitudes of +/- 30 degrees in pitch or +/- 60 degrees m roll are prohibited.

c. Intentional flight below +0.5 G is prohibited. Refer to low G maneuvers, paragraph 8-53.

d. The speed for any and all maneuvers shall not exceed the level flight velocities as stated on the airspeed operating limits chart (Figure 5-2).

TM 55-1520-210-10

Section VII ENVIRONMENTAL RESTRICTIONS

5-13. Environmental Restrictions.

a This helicopter is qualified for flight under instrument meteorological conditions.

b. Intentional flight into known icing conditions with the rotor blade erosion protection coating and polyurethane tape installed is prohibited. Icing conditions include 7RACE', 'LIGHT, 'MODERATE' and 'HEAVY'. This helicopter may be flown in light or trace icing conditions when the rotor blade erosion protection coating and polyurethane tape are no installed.

c. Wind Limitation.

(1) Maximum cross wind for hover is 30 knots

(2) Maximum tail wind for hover Is 30 knots.

d. Wind Limitation for Starting. Helicopter can be started in a maximum wind velocity of 30 knots or a maximum gust spread of 15 knots. Gust spreads are not normally reported. To obtain spread, compare minimum and maximum wind velocity.

e Temperature Limitation (Hub Spring Aircraft Only). Remove elastomeric springs prior to operating aircraft when OAT is below -20° C (-5°F) or If this temperature is anticipated to occur during flight. If, however, sub -20°C temperatures are encountered during flight change altitude in an attempt to find warmer air Elastomeric springs shall be reinstalled when the OAT is expected to stay above -20°C or the threat of sub 20°'C temperatures no longer exists.

Section III HEIGHT VELOCITY

5-14. Height Velocity. The Height Velocity diagram (fig 9-3) Is based on an extrapolation of test data. The chart is applicable for all gross weights up to and including 9500 pounds.

Section IX INTERNAL RESCUE HOIST (BREEZE ONLY)

WARNING

Use of a Breeze BL 8300 series Internal Rescue Hoist is prohibited.

5-15. Deleted.

Section X OTHER LIMITATIONS

5-16. Towing. The helicopter should not be towed for 25 minutes after the battery and inverter switches have been turned off to prevent damage to attitude and directional gyros. If the helicopter must be towed prior to the 25 minute limit, the battery and inverter switches shall be turned on. Wait five minutes after the switches are on before moving the helicopter.

Caution is to be exercised for slopes greater than 5 degrees, since rigging, loading, and wind conditions may result in contacting the control stops.

5-17. Slope Landing Limitations. Analysis indicates the following maximum slope landing capability under nominal conditions.

1. Cross slope or nose-up slope 10 degrees.

2. Nose down slope 7 degrees.

COLOR MARKING CODES
R - Red
G - Green

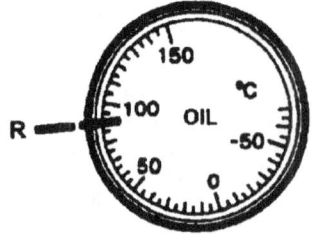

ENGINE OIL PRESSURE

- R — 25 PSI Minimum – Engine Idle
- G — 80 to 100 PSI Continuous
- R — 100 PSI Maximum

ENGINE OIL TEMPERATURE

- R — 93° C Maximum Below 30° C FAT
  100° C Maximum At 30° C FAT and Above
  (Write Up Required Anytime 93°C Exceeded.)

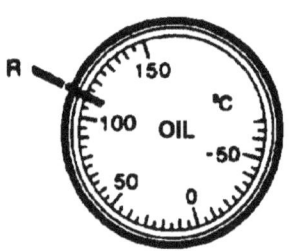

TRANSMISSION OIL TEMPERATURE

- R — 110°C Maximum

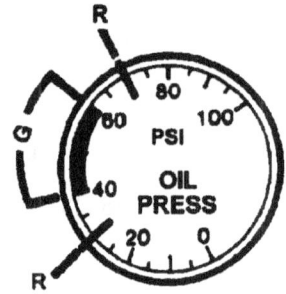

TRANSMISSION OIL PRESSURE

- R — 30 PSI Minimum
- G — 40 to 60 PSI Continuous
- R — 70 PSI Maximum

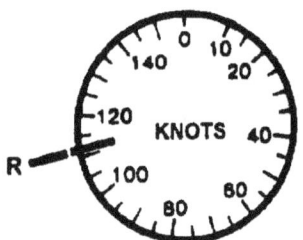

**AIRSPEED
NOSE MOUNTED PITOT TUBE**

- R — 112 Knots Maximum
  Refer to Figure 6-2, Airspeed Operating
  Limits for Additional Limitations.

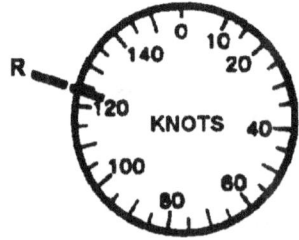

**AIRSPEED
ROOF MOUNTED PITOT TUBE**

- R — 124 Knots Maximum
  Refer to Figure 5-2, Airspeed Operating
  Limits for Additional Limitations.

Figure 5-1. Instrument Markings (Sheet 1 of 3)

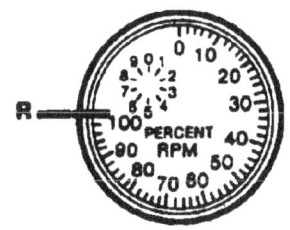

GAS PRODUCER TACHOMETER (N1)

R ▬ 101.5 Percent Maximum

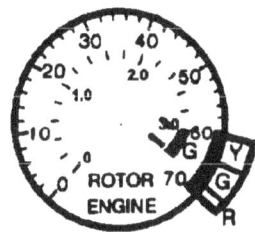

ROTOR TACHOMETER

G ▬ 294 TO 324 RPM Continuous

    319 TO 324 RPM Continuous
                     MB Cruise

R ▬ 339 RPM Maximum

ENGINE TACHOMETER (N2)

NOTE

Due to above rotor limits, engine operation will be limited to:

G ▬ 6400 TO 6600 RPM Continuous

    6500 TO 6600 RPM Continuous
                       MB Cruise

Actual engine limits are shown below:

Y ▬ 6000 to 6400 RPM Transient

R ▬ 6700 RPM Maximum Continuous above 15 PSI Torque

    6900 RPM Maximum Continuous at 15 PSI Torque or less

    6900 RPM Maximum Transient (3 sec) above 15 PSI Torque

R ▬ 6900 RPM Maximum

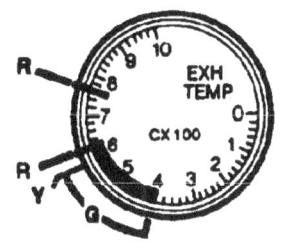

EXHAUST TEMPERATURE

G ▬ 400°C to 610°C Continuous

Y ▬ 610°C to 625°C 30 Minutes

R ▬ 625°C maximum 30 Minutes

    625°C to 675°C 10 Second Limit for Starting and Acceleration

    675°C to 760°C 5 Second Limit for Starting and Acceleration

R ▬ 760°C Maximum

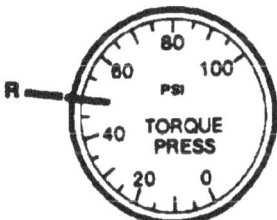

TORQUE PRESSURE

Meter is marked with the maximum torque limit for each engine as reflected by the individual engine Data Plate Torque. Refer to Torque Available Chart, Chapter 7.

NOTE

Line at 50 PSI shown on dial face is for illustration only. Actual location will vary.

Figure 5-1. Instrumental Markings (Sheet 2 of 3)

TM 55-1520-210-10

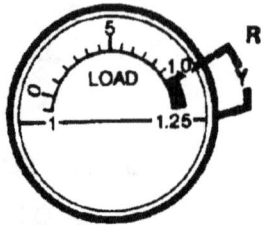

LOADMETER MAIN GENERATOR

Y ■ 1.0 to 1.25 Transient

STANDBY GENERATOR

R ■ 1.0 Maximum

FUEL PRESSURE

G ■ 5 to 35 PSI Continuous

Figure 5-1. Instrument Marking (Sheet 3 of 3)

AIRSPEED OPERATING LIMITS

EXAMPLE

WANTED

INDICATED AIRSPEED
AND DENSITY ALTITUDE

KNOWN

GROSS WEIGHT = 8500 LB
PRESSURE ALTITUDE = 7500 FEET
FAT = -20°C
ROOF MOUNTED SYSTEM

METHOD

ENTER PRESSURE ALTITUDE
MOVE RIGHT TO FAT
MOVE DOWN TO GROSS WEIGHT
MOVE LEFT, READ INDICATED
AIRSPEED = 110 KNOTS
REENTER PRESSURE ALTITUDE
MOVE RIGHT TO FAT
MOVE DOWN, READ DENSITY
ALTITUDE = 5000 FEET

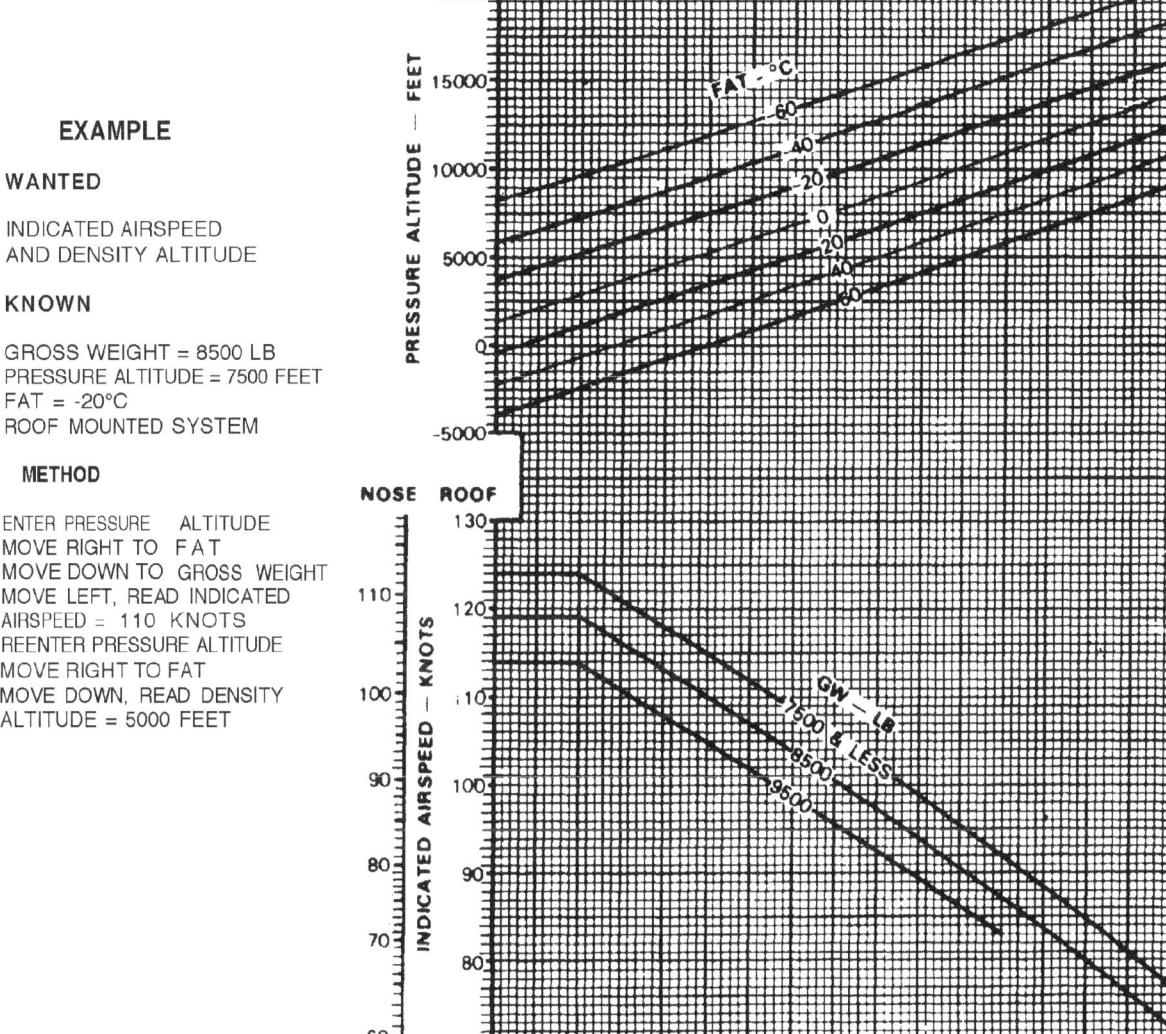

DATA BASIS: DERIVED FROM FLIGHT TEST

Figure 5-2. Airspeed operating limits chart

AIRSPEED OPERATING LIMITS

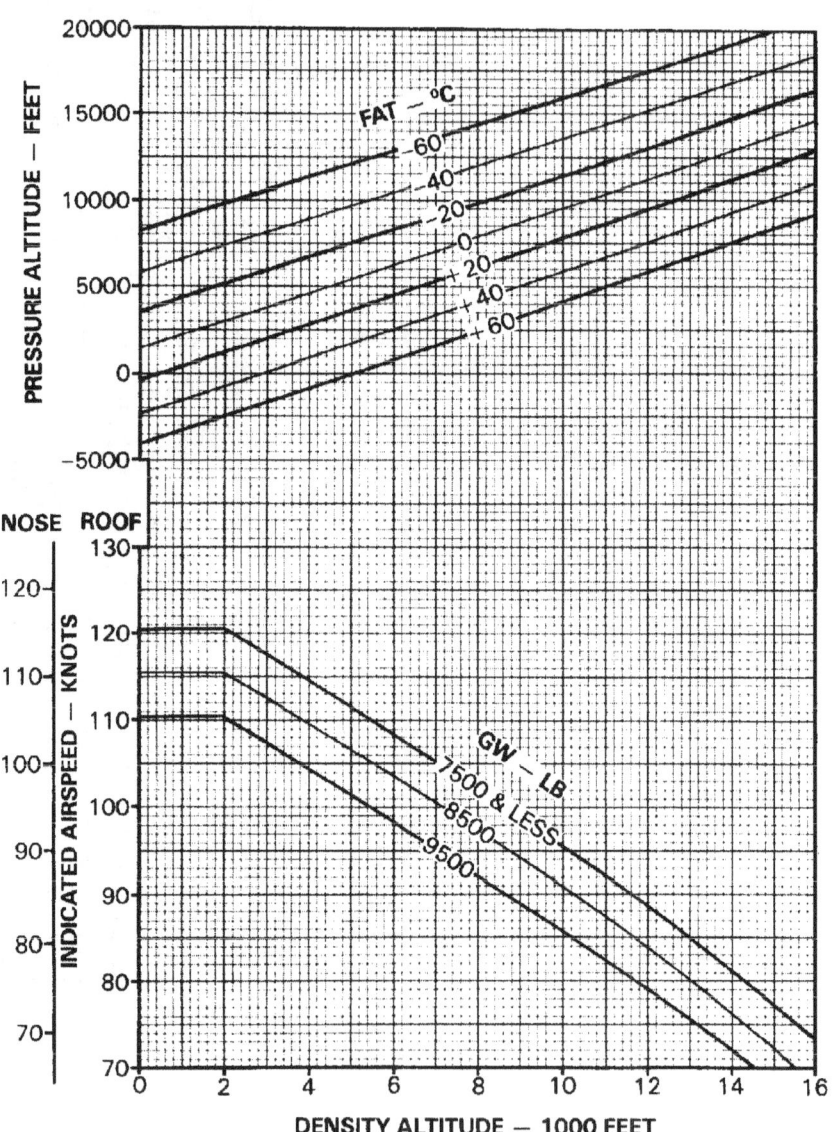

Figure 5-2.1 Airspeed operating limits chart

Chapter 6

Weight/Balance and Loading

Section I GENERAL

6-1. General. Chapter 6 contains sufficient instructions and data so that an aviator knowing the basic weight and moment of the helicopter can compute any combination of weight and balance.

6-2. Classification of Helicopter. Army UH-IH/V helicopters are in class 2. Additional directives governing weight and balance of class 2 aircraft forms and records are contained in AR 95-1, TM 55-1500-342-23, and DA PAM 738-751.

6-3. Helicopter Station Diagram. Figure 6-1 show the helicopter reference datum lines, fuselage stations, butt lines, water lines and jack pad locations. The primary purposes of the figure is to aid personnel m the computation of helicopter weight/balance and loading.

Section II WEIGHT AND BALANCE

64. Loading Charts.

  a Information The loading data contained in this chapter is intended to provide information necessary to work a loading problem for the helicopters to which this manual is applicable.

  b. Use. From the figures contained in this chapter weight and moment are obtained for all variable load items and are added to the current basic weight and moment (DD Form 365-4) to obtain the gross weight and moment.

    (1) The gross weight and moment are checked on DD Form 365-3 to determine the approximate center of gravity (cg).

    (2) The effect on cg by the expenditures in flight of such items as fuel, ammunition etc., may be checked by subtracting the weights and moments of such items from the takeoff weight and moments and checking the new weight and moment on the CG limits Chart.

6-5. DD Form 365-1-Basic Weight Checklist The form is initially prepared by the manufacturer before the helicopter is delivered. The form is a tabulation of equipment that is, or may be, installed and for which provision for fixed stowage has been made in a definite location. The form gives the weight, arm and moment/100 of individual Items for use in correcting the basic weight and moment on DD Form 365-3 as changes are made m this equipment.

6-6. DD Form 365-3-Basic Weight and Balance Records. The form is initially prepared by the manufacturer at time of delivery of the helicopter. The form is a continuous history of the basic weight and moment resulting from structural and equipment changes. At all times the last entry is considered current weight and balance status of the basic helicopter.

6-7. DD Form 365Weight and Balance Clearance Form F.

  a General. The form is a summary of actual disposition of the load in the helicopter It records the balance status of the helicopter, step-by-step. It serves as a worksheet on which to record weight and balance calculations, and any corrections that must be made to ensure that the helicopter will be within weight and cg limits.

  b. Form Preparation. Specific instructions for filling out the form are given in TM 55-1500-342-23

NOTE
Allowable gross weight for take off and landing is 9500 pounds.

Section III. FUEL/OIL

6-8. Fuel. Refer to Figure 6-2.

a. For a given weight of fuel n the crashworthy system tanks, there is a very small variation m fuel moment with change in fuel specific weight. Fuel moments should be determined from Figure 6-2 (Sheet 1 of 2) which is based on a specific weight of 6 5 lb/gal. Additional correction for fuel specific weight is not required. For the auxiliary fuel tank the fuel arms are constant. Thus, for a given weight of fuel there is no variation m fuel moment with change in fuel specific weight.

b The fuel tank usable fuel weight will vary depending upon fuel specific weight. The aircraft fuel gage system was designed for use with JP-4, but does tend to compensate for other fuels and provide acceptable readings. When possible the weight of fuel onboard should be determined by direct reference to the aircraft fuel gages. The following information is provided to show the general range of fuel specific weights to be expected.

c. The following information is provided to show the general range of fuel specific weights to be expected. Specific weight of fuel will vary depending on fuel temperature. Specific weight will decrease as fuel temperature increases and increase as fuel temperature decreases at the rate of approximately 0.1 lb/gal for each 15° C change. Specific weight may also vary between lots of the same type fuel at the same temperature by as much as 0.5 lb/gal. The following approximate fuel specific weights at 15° C may be used for most mission planning.

FUEL TYPE	SPECIFIC WEIGHT
JP-4	6 5 lb/gal
JP-5	6.8 lb/gal
JP-8	6 7 lb/gal

6-9. Oil. For weight and balance purposes, engine oil is a part of basic weight.

Section IV. PERSONNEL

6-10. Personnel Compartment and Litter Provisions.

a The personnel compartment provides seating for eleven combat equipped troops (Figure 6-3). Seat belts are provided for restraint.

b. Provisions and hardware are provided for up to six patients. Refer to Figure 6-3.

6-11. Personnel Loading and Unloading. When helicopter is operated at critical gross weights, the exact weight of each individual occupant plus equipment should be used. If weighing facilities are not available, or if the tactical situation dictates otherwise loads shall be computed as follows:

a. Combat equipped soldiers: 240 pounds per individual.

b. Combat equipped paratroopers: 260 pounds per individual.

c. Crew and passengers with no equipment compute weight according to each individual's estimate.

d. Litter Weight and Balance Data Refer to Figure 6-3. Litter loads shall be computed at 265 pounds (litter and patient's weight combined).

6-12. Personnel Moments. Refer to Figure 6-3.

Section V. MISSION EQUIPMENT

6-13. Weight and Balance Loading Data

a. System Weight and Balance Data. Refer to Figure 6-6.

b. Hoist-Loading Data. Use Hoist Loading Limitations charts for hoist in forward right or forward left positions only (Figures 6-4 and 6-5).

WARNING

Longitudinal or lateral cg limits may not permit maximum hoist loading capability. The lesser of the two loads derived from lateral and longitudinal charts shall be used.

NOTE
If additional internal load is carried during hoisting operations this load should be positioned on opposite side from hoist.

c. Positions Hoist May Occupy in Cabin. Refer to Figure 6-7.

Section VI. CARGO LOADING

6-14. Cargo Loading. The large cargo doors, open loading area and low floor level preclude the need for special loading aids. Through loading may be accomplished by securing cargo doors m the fully open position. Cargo tiedown fittings (Figures 6-8 and 6-9) are located on cabin floor for securing cargo to prevent cargo shift during flight.

6-15. Preparation of General Cargo.

a. The loading crew shall assemble the cargo and baggage to be transported. At time of assembly and prior to loading, the loading crew shall compile data covering weight, dimensions, center of gravity (c.g.) location and contact areas for each item.

b. Heavier packages to be loaded shall be loaded first and placed in the aft section against the bulkhead for c.g. range purposes.

c. Calculation of the allowable load and loading distribution shall be accomplished by determining the final c. . location and remain within the allowable limits for safe operating conditions.

6-16. Cargo Center of Gravity (cg.) Planning.

a. *Planning.* The items to be transported should be assembled for loading after the weight and dimensions have been recorded.

(1) Loading tune will be gained if the packages are positioned as they are to be located in the helicopter.

(2) To assist m determining the locations of the various items, the individual weights and total weight must be known.

(3) When these factors are known the cargo loading charts (Figures 6-10 and 6-11) can be used as a guide to determine the helicopter station at which the package c.g. shall be located and the moment for each item.

(4) Aircraft c.g. will be affected by fuel quantity. Variation in fuel loadings from that on board at takeoff to empty must be considered during data computation.

(5) Final analysis of helicopter c.g. location for loading shall be computed from the data presented in this chapter.

b. *Computation of Cargo Center of Gravity.*

(1) The loading data in this chapter will provide information to work a loading problem. From the loading Charts, weight and moment/100 are obtained for all variable load items and are added mathematically to the current basic weight and moment/100 obtained from chart C to arrive at the gross weight and moment.

(2) The c.g. of the loaded helicopter can be determined from the gross weight and moment using the c.g. limits chart (Figure 6-12). This figure may also be used to determine if the helicopter is loaded within the gross weight and c.g. limits

(3) The effect on c.g. of the expenditure inflight of such items as fuel and cargo should be checked by subtracting the weight and moment of such items from the takeoff gross weight and moment and checking the resulting weight and moment with the c.g limits chart (Figure 6-12).

(4) This check will be made to determine whether the c.g. will remain within limits during the entire flight.

6-17. Loading Procedures. The helicopter requires no special loading preparation.

a. The loading procedure consists of locating the load items in a manner which will maintain the c.g. within limits. In general, the heaviest items should be placed in the aft section near or against the aft bulkhead. Such placement locates the cargo near the helicopter c g. and allows maximum cargo load to be transported, as well as maintaining the helicopter within safe operating c g. limits for flight.

b. The mission to be performed should be known to determine the weight and moment of cargo, troop transport, or litter patients to be carried on the return trip

c. If troops or litter patients are to be carried, troop seats and litter racks shall be loaded aboard and stowed.

d. Deleted.

6-18. Loading and Unloading of Other Than General Cargo.

WARNING
Before transporting nuclear weapons, the pilot shall be familiar with AR 95-27, AR 504 and AR 50-5.

The helicopter is capable of transporting nuclear weapons, if required.

6-19. Tiedown Devices. Refer to Figures 6-8 and 6-9.

TM 55-1520-210-10

Section VII. CENTER OF GRAVITY LIMITS

6-20. Center of Gravity Limits. Refer to figure 6-12 for longitudinal limits. The lateral c.g. limits are 5 inches (5 inches to the right and left of the helicopter centerline). The lateral c.g. limits will not be exceeded if external store loadings, are symmetrical, the hoist loading limits (fig 6-4 and fig 6-5) are observed, and a reasonable effort is made to evenly distribute internal loads from left to right.

6-21. Restraint Criteria The amount of restraint that must be used to keep the cargo from moving in any direction is called the "Restraint Criteria' and is usually expressed in units of the force of gravity, of G's. Following are the units of the force of gravity or G's needed to restrain cargo in four directions:

DIRECTION	RESTRAINT CRITERIA
Forward	8.0 G's
Aft	4.0 G's
Lateral	8.0 G's
Vertical	4.0 G's (UP)

Change 17 6-4

HELICOPTER DIAGRAM

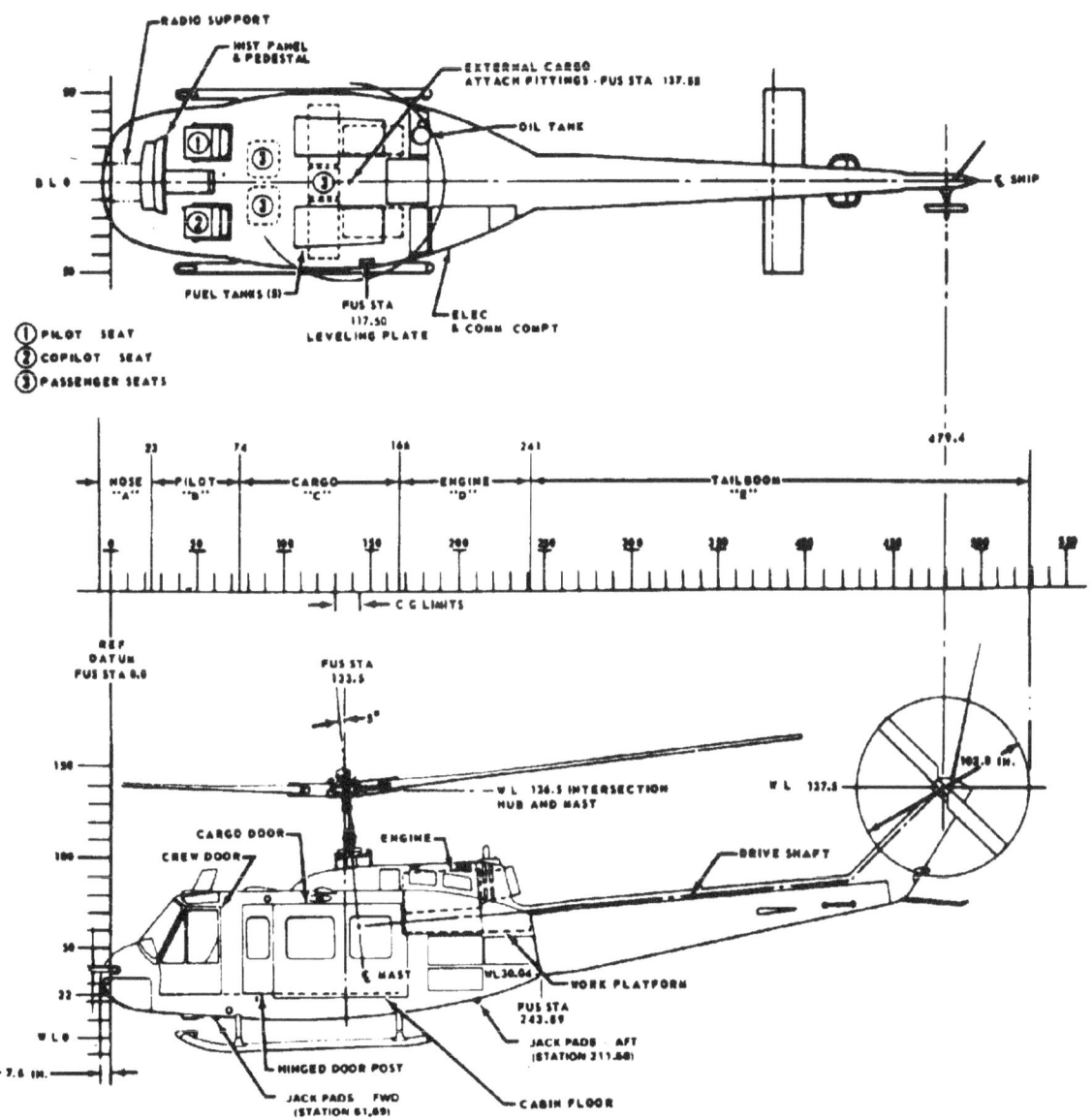

Figure 6-1. Helicopter Station Diagram

TM 55-1520-210-10

FUEL LOADING

CRASHWORTHY SYSTEM TANKS

FUEL MOMENT

EXAMPLE

WANTED
WEIGHT AND MOMENT FOR A GIVEN QUANTITY OF USABLE FUEL IN CRASHWORTHY FUEL SYSTEM.

KNOWN
U.S. GALLONS OF JP-4 FUEL.

METHOD
ENTER AT GALLONS ON JP-4 SCALE. MOVE RIGHT TO READ WEIGHT CONTINUE RIGHT TO INTERSECT DIAGONAL LINE, THEN PROJECT DOWN TO READ MOMENT/100 SCALE.

NOTE

THIS CHART PRESENTS FUEL MOMENT AS A FUNCTION OF WEIGHT, UTILIZING A SINGLE CURVE FOR ALL FUEL TYPES. GALLON EQUIVALENT SCALES ARE BASED ON NOMINAL DENSITIES AT 15°C

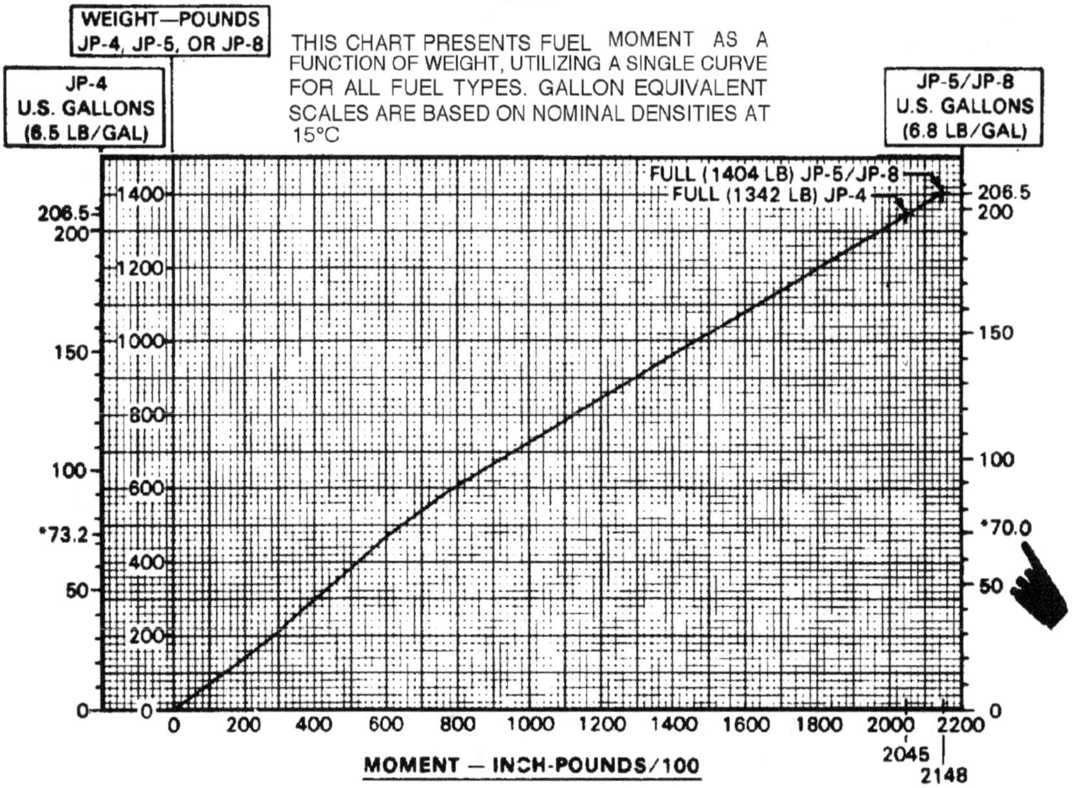

WEIGHT—POUNDS JP-4, JP-5, OR JP-8

JP-4 U.S. GALLONS (6.5 LB/GAL)

JP-5/JP-8 U.S. GALLONS (6.8 LB/GAL)

*MOST FORWARD FUEL CG

Figure 6-2. Fuel Loading (Sheet 1 of 2)

6-6 Change 5

FUEL LOADING

AUXILIARY FUEL
300 GALLONS INTERNAL
(F.S. 151.0)

FUEL MOMENT

EXAMPLE

WANTED
WEIGHT AND MOMENT FOR A GIVEN QUANTITY OF FUEL IN AUXILIARY FUEL TANKS.

KNOWN
300 U.S. GALLONS OF JP-4 FUEL (IN AUXILIARY TANKS ONLY).

METHOD
ENTER AT GALLONS ON JP-4 SCALE.
MOVE RIGHT TO READ WEIGHT.
CONTINUE RIGHT TO INTERSECT DIAGONAL LINE, THEN PROJECT DOWN TO READ MOMENT/100 SCALE.

NOTE

THIS CHART PRESENTS FUEL MOMENT AS A FUNCTION OF WEIGHT, UTILIZING A SINGLE CURVE FOR ALL FUEL TYPES. GALLON EQUIVALENT SCALES ARE BASED ON NOMINAL DENSITIES AT 15°C.

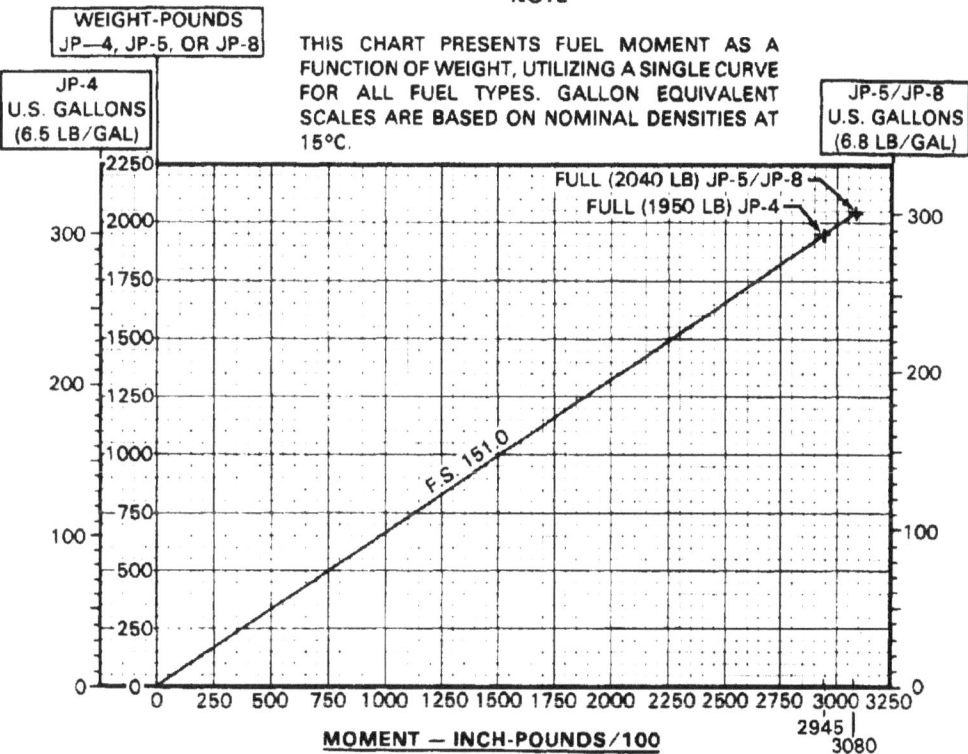

Figure 6-2. Fuel Loading (Sheet 2 of 2)

TM 55-1520-210-10

PERSONNEL LOADING CHART

MOMENT FOR PERSONNEL

EXAMPLE

WANTED

PERSONNEL MOMENT FOR A GIVEN WEIGHT AND LOCATION

KNOWN

PERSONNEL WEIGHT OF 200 POUNDS AT F.S. 117.0 (Row 4)

METHOD

MOVE RIGHT FROM 200 LBS TO THE LINE CONNECTING WITH SEAT ROW 4.
PROJECT DOWN TO READ 234 ON THE MOMENT/100 SCALE.

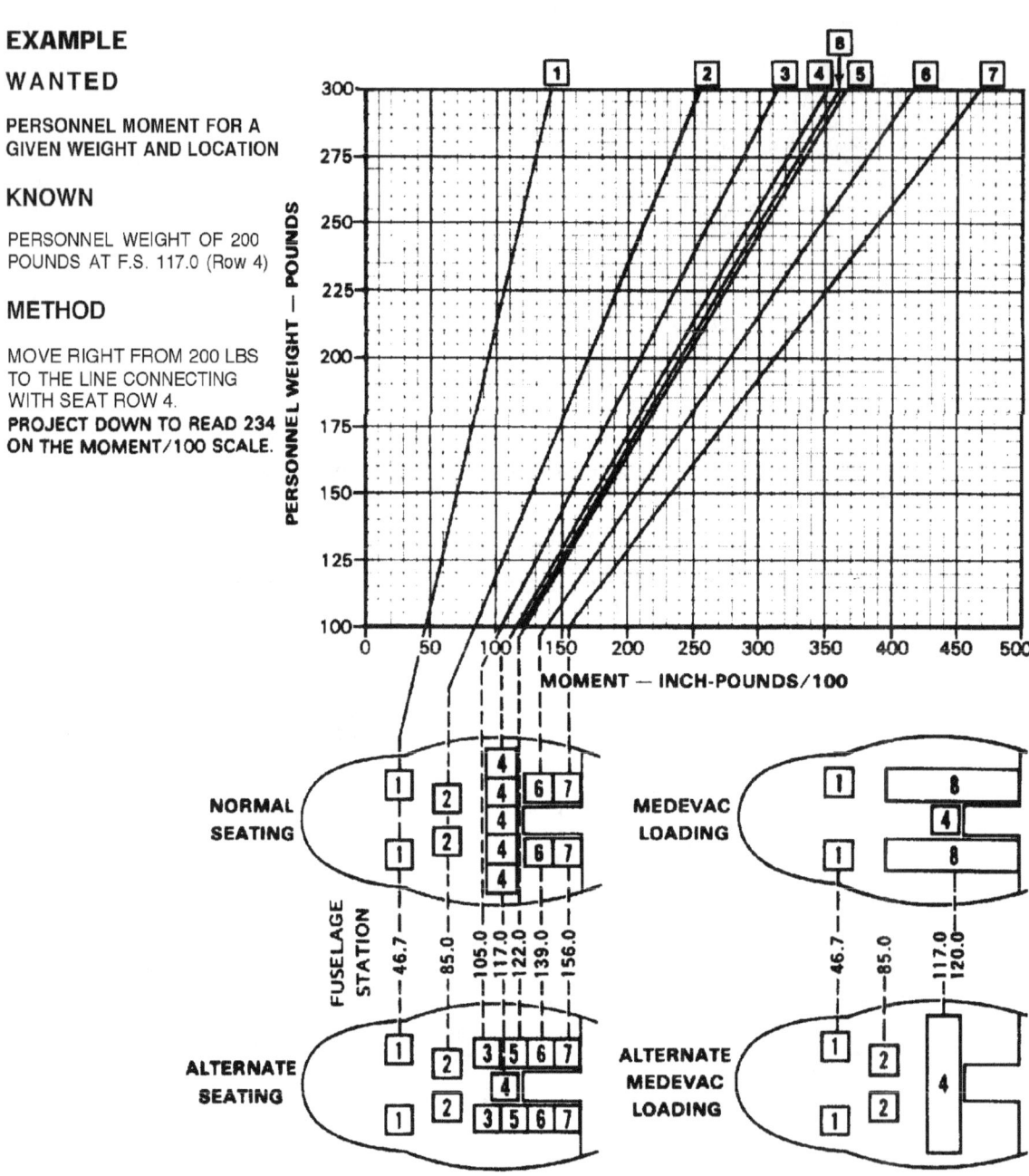

Figure 6-3. Personnel Loading

6-8

HOIST LOADING LIMITATIONS
DUE TO LATERAL C.G. LIMITS

HOIST IN FORWARD RIGHT POSITION

EXAMPLE

WANTED

MAXIMUM ALLOWABLE
HOIST LOAD

KNOWN

GROSS WEIGHT 8600 LBS
LONGITUDINAL C. G. 133.5,
CREW – PILOT & HOIST OPERATOR.

METHOD

ENTER GROSS WEIGHT
MOVE RIGHT TO INTERSECT
PILOT & HOIST OPERATOR CURVE.
MOVE DOWN TO READ
ALLOWABLE HOIST LOAD 550 LBS

NOTE

THE LESSER OF THE TWO WEIGHTS DERIVED FROM LATERAL AND LONGITUDINAL CHARTS SHALL BE USED (EXAMPLE 335 POUNDS).

GROSS WEIGHT TO BE THE LIGHTEST WEIGHT OF THE HELICOPTER DURING HOISTING OPERATIONS, BUT NOT INCLUDING THE WEIGHT OF THE HOIST LOAD. FUEL BURNED PRIOR TO HOISTING OPERATION MUST BE DEDUCTED FROM TAKEOFF GROSS WEIGHT BEFORE COMPUTING ALLOWABLE HOIST LOAD.

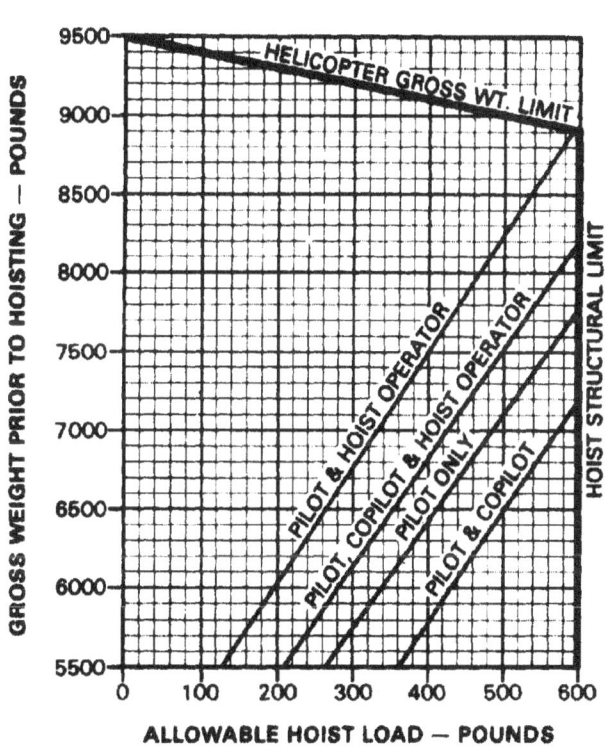

Figure 6-4. Hoist Loading Limitations (Lateral CG)

HOIST LOADING LIMITATIONS
DUE TO LONGITUDINAL C.G. LIMITS

HOIST IN FORWARD RIGHT OR FORWARD LEFT POSITION

EXAMPLE

WANTED

MAXIMUM ALLOWABLE
HOIST LOAD

GROSS WEIGHT 8600 LBS
LONGITUDINAL C.G. 133.5
PRIOR TO HOISTING.

METHOD

ENTER GROSS WT.
MOVE RIGHT TO C.G.
MOVE DOWN TO READ
ALLOWABLE HOIST LOAD 335 LBS

*GROSS WEIGHT AND C.G.
DO NOT INCLUDE HOIST LOAD

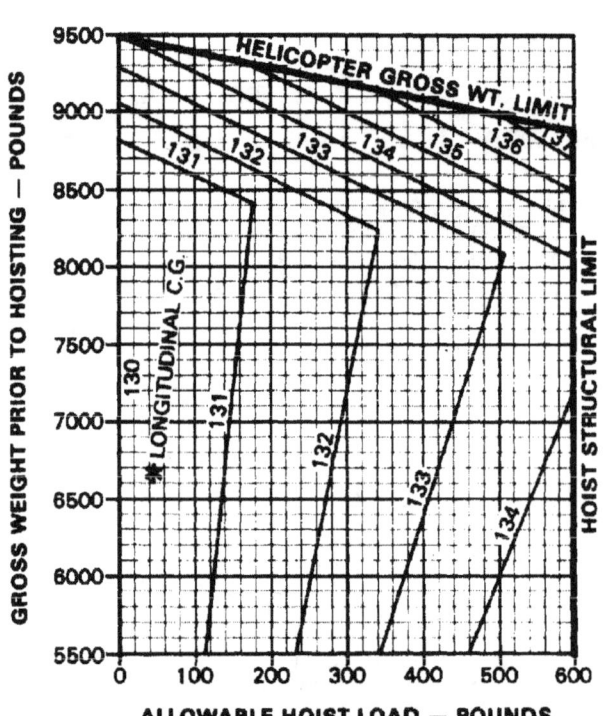

Figure 6-5. Hoist Loading Limitations (Longitudinal CG)

TM 55-1520-210-10

100,000 BTU HEATER

WINTERIZATION KIT

ITEM	WEIGHT	ARM	MOMENT/100
Complete Heater Instl. (205-706-001)	73.2	197.0	144.2
Winterization Kit (Muff Heater)	61.0	212.0	129.3

AFT BATTERY INSTALLATION

ITEM	WEIGHT	ARM	MOMENT/100
Battery (Fwd)	80.0	5.0	4.0
Battery (Aft)	80.0	233.0	186.4
Aft Battery Provisions (205-1682-1)	15.0	224.8	33.8

300 GALLON INTERNAL AUXILIARY FUEL TANK

ITEM	WEIGHT	ARM	MOMENT/100
Deleted			
Deleted			
Tank, LH, Crashworthy	(*)	151.3	(**)
Tank, RH, Crashworthy	(*)	151.3	(**)

* Tank weight varies; use weight stamped on tank (use fuel loading chart for fuel weight).
**Depends on tank weight.

GLASS WINDSHIELD INSTALLATION

ITEM	WEIGHT	ARM	MOMENT/100
Glass Windshield-Pilot Copilot (Both)	30.0	27.0	8.1
Glass Windshield-Pilot Only or Copilot Only	15.0	27.0	4.1

Figure 6-6. System Weight and Balance Data Sheet (Sheet 1 of 3)

RESCUE HOIST (HIGH PERFORMANCE)

ITEM	WEIGHT	ARM	MOMENT/100
Hoist-Forward RH Position (Arm Stowed Forward)	180¹	80.0	144.0
Hoist-Forward RH Position (Arm Stowed Aft)	180¹	84.0	151.2
Hoist-Forward LH Position (Arm Stowed Forward)	180¹	82.0	147.6
Hoist-Forward LH Position (Arm Stowed Aft)	180¹	84.0	151.2

¹Weight after servicing with cable installed

M-23 DOOR MOUNTED M-60

ITEM	WEIGHT	ARM	MOMENT/100
Armament Subsystem W/O Ammunition	128.0	142.6	182.5
Ammunition 7.62 MM (1200 Rounds)	78.0	142.6	111.2
Total Armament Subsystem W/Ammunition (1200 Rounds)	206.0	142.6	293.8
Ammunition Box (2 each) W/Cover Assembly	8.5	142.6	12.1
Machine Guns W/Ejection Control Bags (2 each) and Chute Assembly (2 each)	66.5	142.0	94.4
Mount Assembly (2 each) W/Hardware	53.0	142.6	75.6

EXTERNAL STORES SUPPORT

ITEM	WEIGHT	ARM	MOMENT/100
Stores Rack			
Cross Beam Assys.	29.5	142.5	42.1
Fwd. Beam Assys.	11.5	129.0	14.8
Aft Beam Assys.	11.9	155.1	18.4
Fwd. Sway Brace Assys.	1.1	135.3	1.5
Aft Sway Brace Assys.	1.2	149.7	1.9
Hardware	3.1	142.9	4.4
Total Aft Stores Instl.	58.3	142.5	83.1
Stores Rack (205-707-013-11)			
Cross Beam Assys.	13.1	73.9	23.0
Fwd. Beam Assys.	11.7	63.0	
Aft Beam Assys.	13.6	84.5	11.5
Fwd. Sway Brace Assys.	1.9	68.4	1.3
Aft Sway Brace Assys.	1.5	79.7	1.2
Hardware	3.2	74.0	2.4
Total Fwd. Stores Instl.	63.0	74.2	46.8

Figure 6-6. System Weight and Balance Data Sheet (Sheet 2 of 3)

M52 SMOKE GENERATOR SUBSYSTEM

ITEM	WEIGHT	ARM	MOMENT/100
A Kit	16.7	161.67	27.0
B Kit	39.64	120.08	47.6
	-20.62	122.21	-25.2
C Kit Without Oil in Tank	117.5	127.57	149.9
C Kit With Oil in Tank (50 Gal)	492.5	121.81	599.9

MULTIARMAMENT STRUCTURAL SUPPORT KIT

ITEM	WEIGHT	ARM	MOMENT/100
A Kit (Roof Hardpoints)	5.83	146.71	8.6
B Kit	205.87	141.87	292.1

M56 MINE DISPENSER (SUN-13D/A)

ITEM	WEIGHT	ARM	MOMENT/100
Each Dispenser Empty, Without Pallet	117	145.83	170.6
Each Dispenser with Canisters Only	188	145.83	274.2
Each Dispenser-Loaded as Flown	640	143.79	920.3

AUXILIARY SUPPRESSOR KIT, EXHAUST SUPPRESSOR

ITEM	WEIGHT	ARM	MOMENT/100
A Kit	4.0	228.0	9.1
B Kit	47	230.2	108.2

Figure 6-6. System Weight and Balance Data Sheet (Sheet 3 of 3)

TM 55-1520-210-10

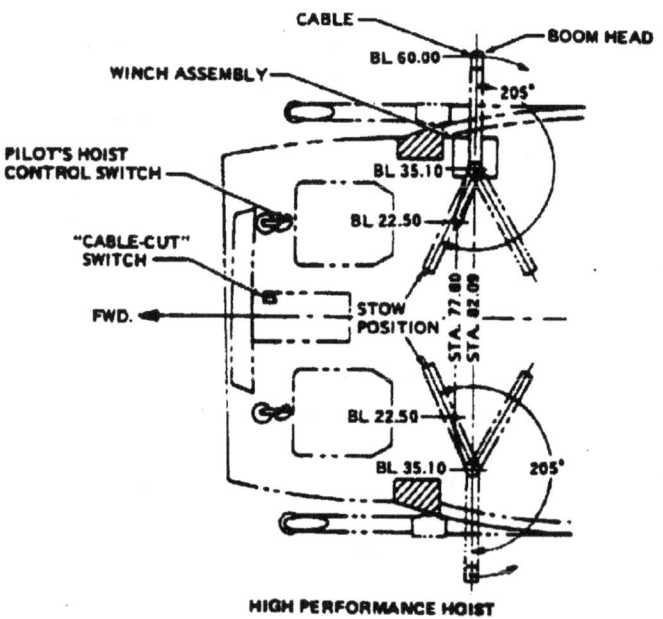

Figure 6-7. Hoist Installation Positions

TM 55-1520-210-10

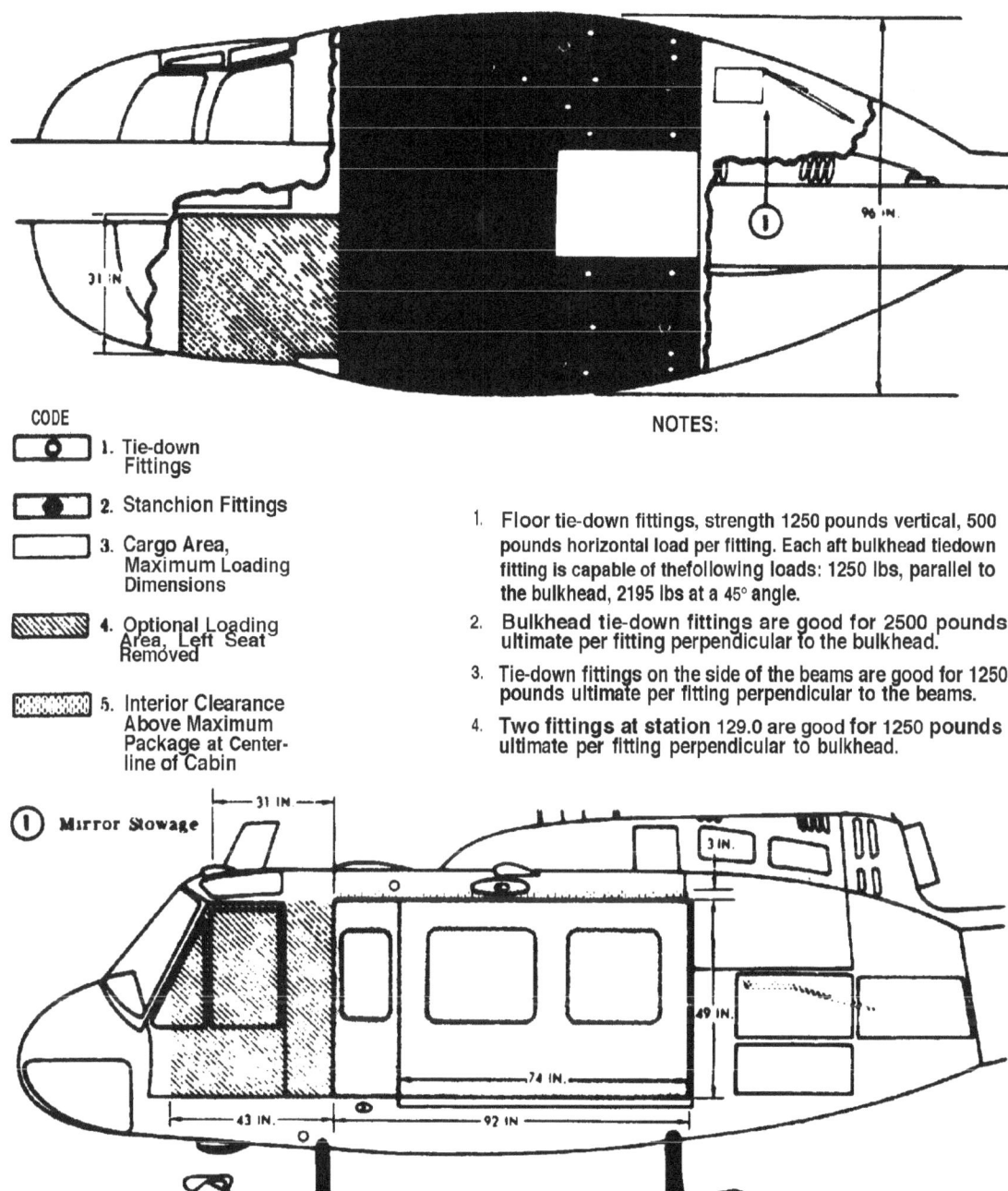

CODE
1. Tie-down Fittings
2. Stanchion Fittings
3. Cargo Area, Maximum Loading Dimensions
4. Optional Loading Area, Left Seat Removed
5. Interior Clearance Above Maximum Package at Centerline of Cabin

① Mirror Stowage

NOTES:

1. Floor tie-down fittings, strength 1250 pounds vertical, 500 pounds horizontal load per fitting. Each aft bulkhead tiedown fitting is capable of the following loads: 1250 lbs, parallel to the bulkhead, 2195 lbs at a 45° angle.
2. Bulkhead tie-down fittings are good for 2500 pounds ultimate per fitting perpendicular to the bulkhead.
3. Tie-down fittings on the side of the beams are good for 1250 pounds ultimate per fitting perpendicular to the beams.
4. Two fittings at station 129.0 are good for 1250 pounds ultimate per fitting perpendicular to bulkhead.

Figure 6-8. Cargo Compartment

6-15

CARGO TIE DOWN FITTING DATA

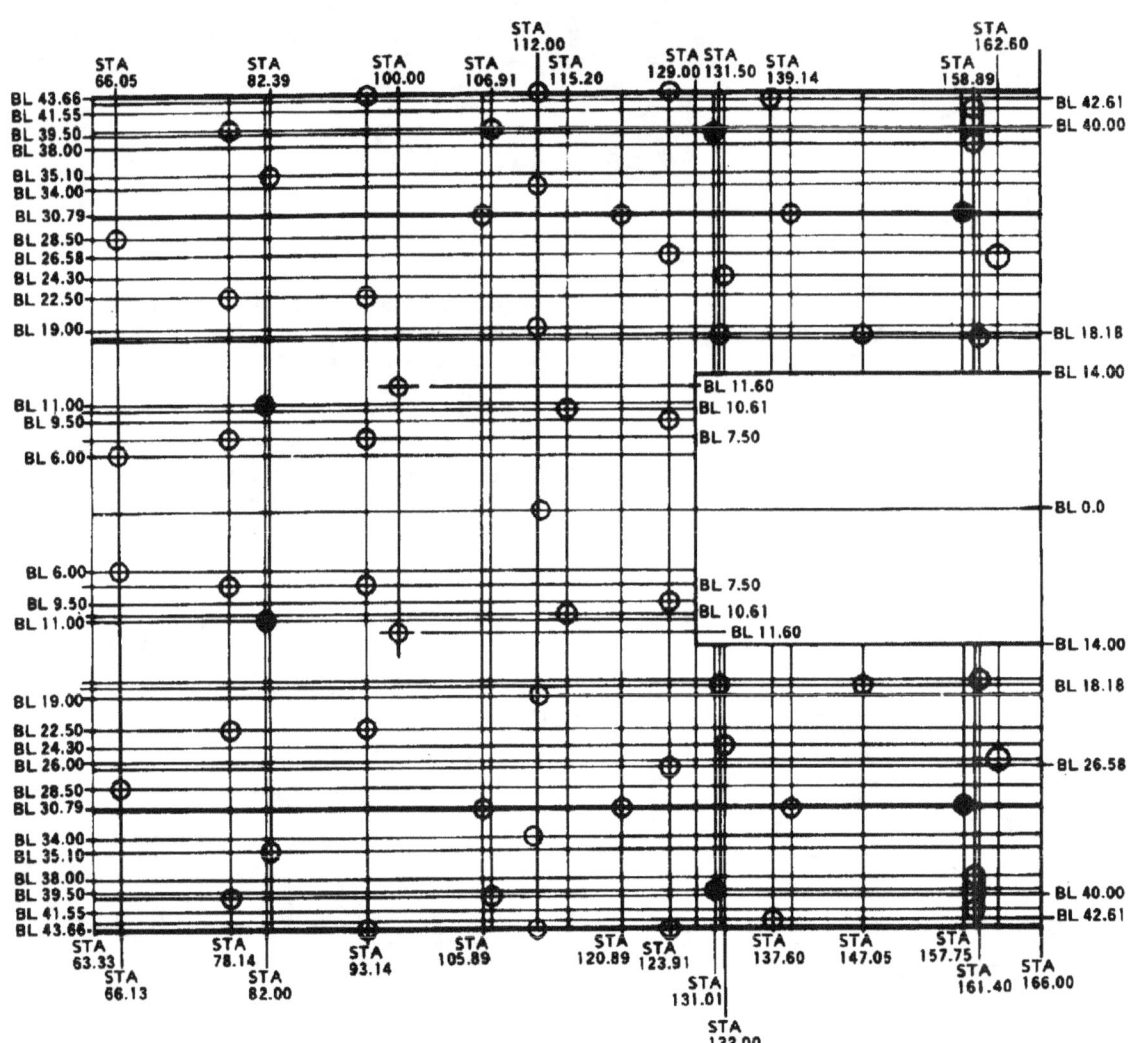

Figure 6-9. Cargo Tiedown Fitting Data

INTERNAL CARGO WEIGHT AND MOMENT

EXAMPLE

WANTED

CARGO MOMENT FOR A GIVEN CARGO WEIGHT AND FUSELAGE STATION

KNOWN

CARGO WEIGHT 1000 LBS
LOCATION FS105

METHOD

ENTER INTERNAL CARGO WEIGHT
MOVE RIGHT TO FS105
MOVE DOWN TO BASE-LINE AND READ
1050 INCH POUNDS/100

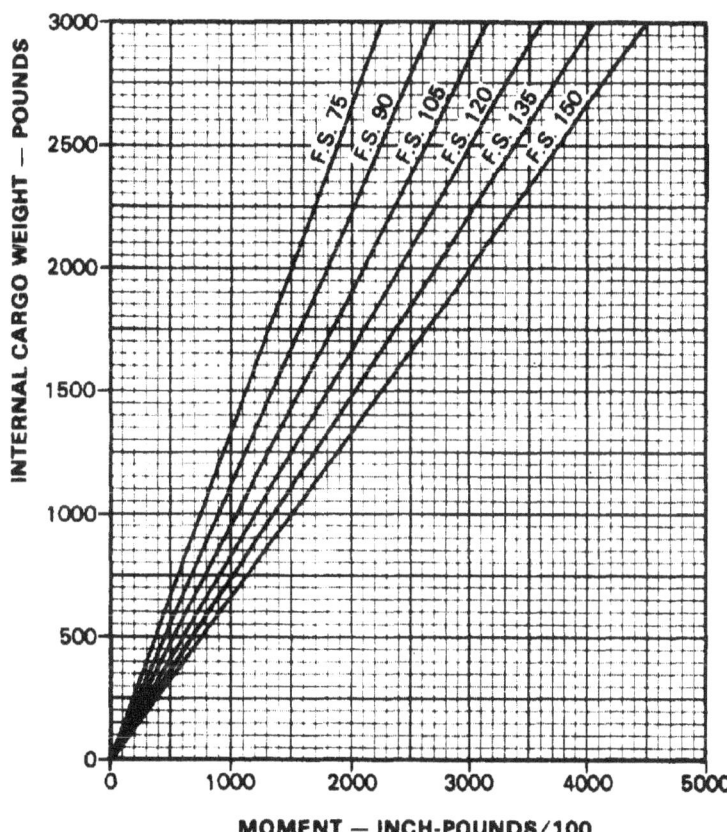

Figure 6-10. Internal Cargo Weight and Moment

EXTERNAL CARGO WEIGHT AND MOMENT
F.S. 137.55

EXAMPLE

WANTED

CARGO MOMENT/100 FOR A GIVEN CARGO WEIGHT.

KNOWN

CARGO WEIGHT 3000 LBS

METHOD

ENTER EXTERNAL CARGO WEIGHT MOVE RIGHT TO DIAGONAL LINE MOVE DOWN TO BASELINE AND READ 4127 ON MOMENT/100 SCALE.

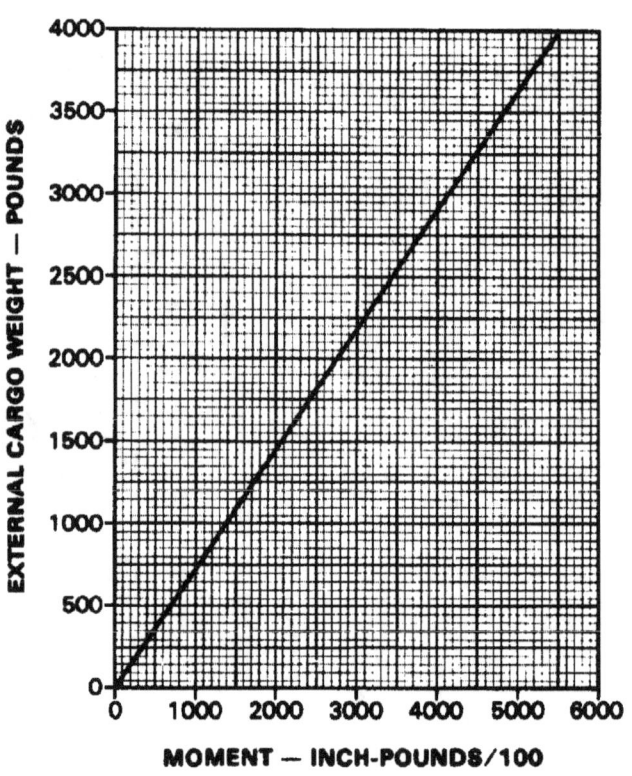

FIGURE 6-11. External Cargo Weight and Moment

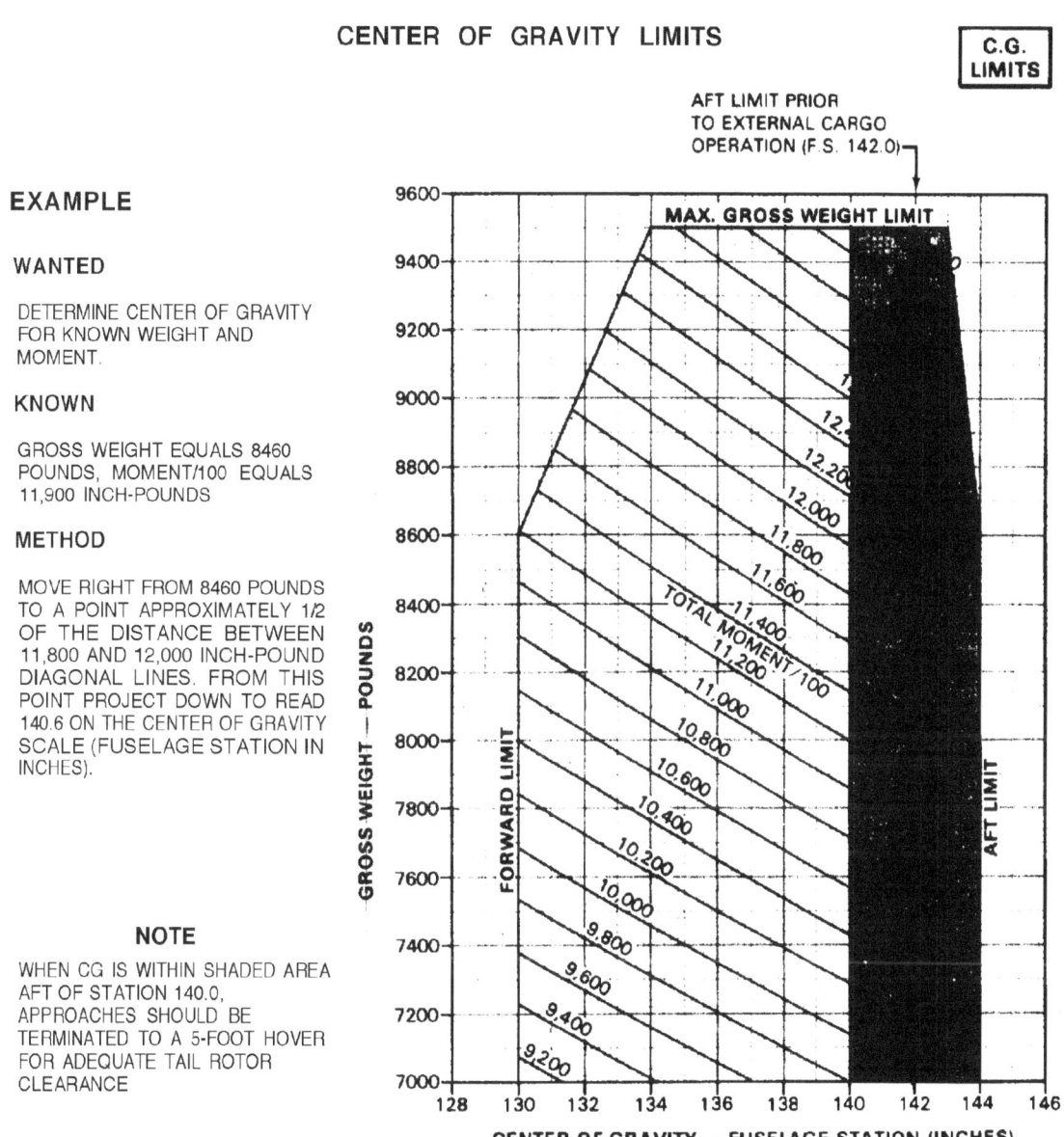

Figure 6-12. Center of Gravity Limits (Sheet 1 of 2)

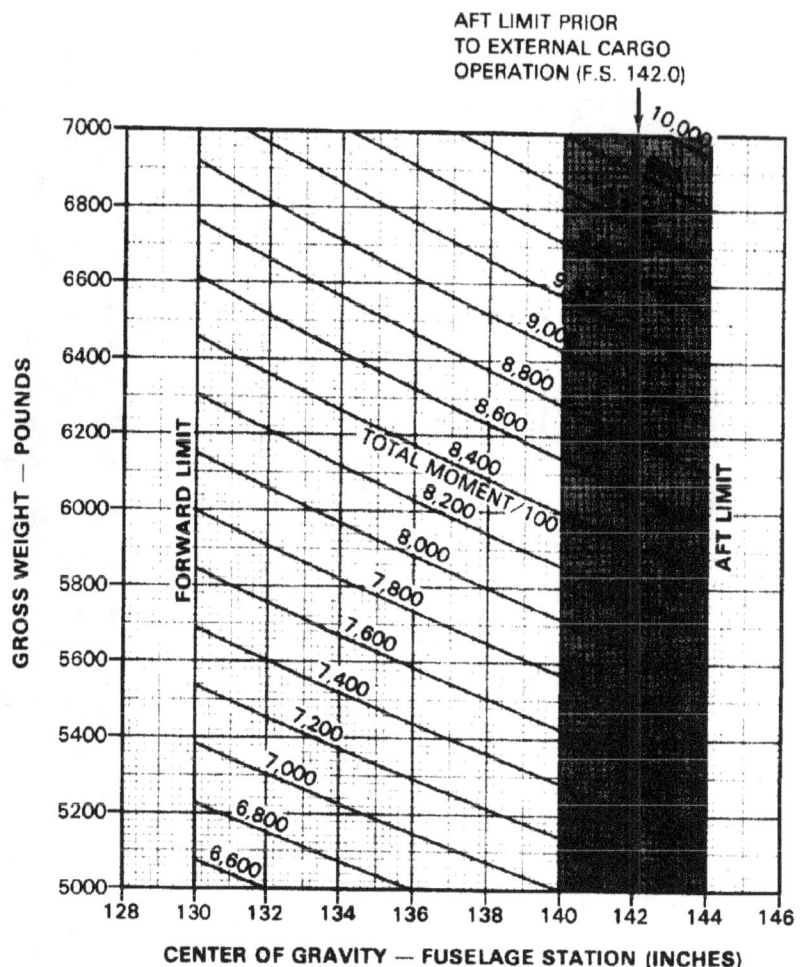

Figure 6-12. Center of Gravity Limits (Sheet 2 of 2)

TM 55-1520-210=10

Chapter 7

MB Performance Data

Section I. INTRODUCTION

7-1. Purpose The purpose of this chapter is to provide performance data. Regular use of this information will enable you to receive maximum safe utilization from the helicopter. Although maximum performance is not always required, regular use of this chapter is recommended for the following reasons:

a. Knowledge of your performance margin will allow you to make better decisions when unexpected conditions or alternate missions are encountered.

b. Situations requiring maximum performance will be more readily recognized.

c. Familiarity with the data will allow performance to be computed more easily and quickly.

d. Experience will be gained in accurately estimating the effects of variables for which data are not presented.

NOTE

Chapter 7 provides information for the UH-1H equipped with metal main rotor blades and chapter 7.1 provides data for the UH-1H equipped with CMRB. The information provided in this chapter is primarily intended for mission planning and is most useful when planning operations in unfamiliar areas or at extreme conditions. The data may also be used to revise mission planning in flight, to establish unit or area standing operating procedures, and to inform ground commanders of performance/risk tradeoffs.

7-2. Chapter 7 Index Deleted.

NOTE

Tabular hover performance and power available data is presented in Appendix C. The data in Appendix C may be used in lieu of Figures 7-2 and 7-3 MB or Figure 7.1-2 and 7.1-3 CB to obtain maximum hover weight, torque required to hover, and maximum calibrated torque available. The data for operation with CMRB presented in chapter 7.1 reflects an update in torque available and airspeed calibration. That update is based on more recent test data than the basis used in this chapter for operation with metal rotor blades. Thus some of the difference between the performance values shown in these two chapters is due to the difference in data basis. Update of the data for metal rotor blades to the more recent test data basis will be provided in an upcoming change.

Change 8 7-1

7-3. General The data presented covers the maximum range of conditions and performance that can reasonably be expected. In each area of performance, the effects of altitude, temperature, gross weight, and other parameters relating to that phase of flight are presented. In addition to the presented data, your judgment and experience will be necessary to accurately obtain performance under a given set of circumstances. The conditions for the data are listed under the title of each chart. The effects of different conditions are discussed in the text. Where practical, data are presented at conservative conditions, However NO GENERAL CONSERVATISM HAS BEEN APPLIED. All performance data presented are within the applicable limits of the helicopter.

7-4. Limits Applicable limits are shown on the charts. Performance generally deteriorates rapidly beyond limits. If limits are exceeded, minimize the amount and time. Enter the maximum value and time above limits on DA Form 2408-13 so proper maintenance action can be taken.

7-5. Use of Charts

a. Chart Explanation. The first page of each section describes the chart (s) and explains its uses.

b. Shading. Shaded areas on charts indicate precautionarry or time limited operation.

c. Reading the Charts. The primary use of each chart is given in an example to help you follow the route through the chart. The use of a straight edge (ruler or page edge) and a hard fine point pencil is recommended to avoid cumulative errors. The majority of the charts provide a standard pattern for use as follows: enter first variable on top left scale, move right to the second variable, reflect down at right angles to the third variable, reflects left at right angles to the fourth variable, reflect down, etc. until the final variable is read out at the final scale.

NOTE

An example of an auxiliary use of the charts referenced above is as follows: Although the hover chart is primarily arranged to find torque required to hover, by entering torque available as required, maximum skid height for hover can also be found, In general, any single variable can be found if all others are known. Also, the tradeoffs between two variables can be found. For example, at a given pressure altitude, you can find the maximum gross weight capability as free air temperature changes.

d. Dashed Line Data. Data beyond conditions for which tests were conducted are shown as dashed lines.

7-6 Data Basis The type of data used is indicated at the bottom of each performance chart under DATA BASIS. The applicable report and date are also given. The data provided generally is based on one of four categories:

a. Flight Test Data. Data obtained by flight test of the aircraft by experienced flight test personnel at precise conditions using sensitive calibrated instruments.

b. Derived From Flight Test. Flight test data obtained on a similar rather than the same aircraft and series. Generally small corrections will have been made.

c. Calculated Data. Data based on tests, but not on flight test of the complete aircraft.

d. Estimated Data. Data based on estimates using aerodynamic theory or other means but not verified by flight test.

7-7. Specific Conditions The data presented are accurate only for specific conditions listed under the title of each chart. Variables for which data are not presented, but which may affect that phase of performance, are discussed in the text. Where data are available or reasonable estimates can be made, the amount that each variable affects performance will be given.

Chapter 7.1

CB Performance Data

Section I. INTRODUCTION

7.1-1. Purpose The purpose of this chapter is to provide performance data for those helicopters equipped with composite main rotor blades. Regular use of this information will enable you to receive maximum safe utilization from the helicopter. Although maximum performance is not always required, regular use of this chapter is recommended for the following reasons:

   a. Knowledge of your performance margin will allow you to make better decisions when unexpected conditions or alternate missions are encountered.

   b. Situations requiring maximum performance will be more readily recognized.

   c. Familiarity with the data will allow performance to be computed more easily and quickly.

   d. Experience will be gained in accurately estimating the effects of variables for which data are not presented.

> **NOTE**
>
> Chapter 7 provides information for the UH-1H equipped with metal main rotor blades and chapter 7.1 provides data for the UH-1H equipped with CMRB. The information provided in this chapter is primarily intended for mission planning and is most useful when planning operations in unfamiliar areas or at extreme conditions. The data may also be used to revise mission planning in flight, to establish unit or area standing operating procedures, and to inform ground commanders of performance/risk tradeoffs.

7.1-2. Chapter 7.1 Index Deleted.

7.1-3. General The data presented covers the maximum range of conditions and performance that can reasonably be expected. In each area of performance, the effects of altitude, temperature, gross weight, and other parameters relating to that phase of flight are presented. In addition to the presented data, your judgment and experience will be necessary to accurately obtain performance under a given set of circumstances. The conditions for the data are listed under the title of each chart. The effects of different conditions are discussed in the text. Where practical, data are presented at conservative conditions. However, NO GENERAL CONSERVATISM HAS BEEN APPLIED. All performance data presented are within the applicable limits of the helicopter.

7.1-4. Limits Applicable limits are shown on the charts. Performance generally deteriorates rapidly beyond limits. If limits are exceeded, minimize the amount and time. Enter the maximum value and time above limits on DA Form 2408-13 so proper maintenance action can be taken.

7.1-5. Use of Charts

a. Chart Explanation An explanation for the usage of each chart is provided.

b. Shading. Shaded areas on charts indicate precautionary or time-limited operation.

c. Reading the Charts. The primary use of each chart is given in an example to help you follow the route through the chart. The use of a straight edge (ruler or page edge) and a hard, fine point pencil is recommended to avoid cumulative errors. The majority of the charts provide a standard pattern for use as follows: enter first variable on top left scale, move right to the second variable, reflect down at right angles to the third variable, reflect left at right angles to the fourth variable, reflect down, etc. until the final variable is read out at the final scale.

7.1-6. Data Basis The type of data used is indicated at the bottom of each performance chart under DATA BASIS. The applicable report and date are also given. The data provided generally is based on one of four categories:

a. *Flight Test Data.* Data obtained by flight test of the aircraft by experienced flight test personnel at precise conditions using sensitive calibrated instruments.

b. Derived From Flight Test. Flight test data obtained on a similar rather than the same aircraft and series. Generally small corrections will have been made.

c. *Calculated Data* Data based on tests, but not on flight test of the complete aircraft.

d. *Estimated Data* Data based on estimates using aerodynamic theory or other means but not verified by flight test.

7.1-7. Specific Conditions The data presented are accurate only for specific conditions listed under the title of each chart. Variables for which data are not presented, but which may affect that phase of performance, are discussed in the text. Where data are variable or reasonable estimates can be made, the amount that each variable affects performance will be given.

7.1-8. General Conditions In addition to the specific conditions, the following general conditions are applicable to the performance data.

a. *Rigging.* All airframe and engine controls are assumed to be rigged within allowable tolerances.

b. Pilot Technique. Normal pilot technique is assumed. Control movements should be smooth and continuous.

NOTE

An example of an auxiliary use of the charts referenced above is as follow Although the hover chart is primarily arranged to find torque required to hover, by entering torque available as required, maximum skid height for hover can also be found. In general, any single variable can be found if all others are known. Also, the tradeoffs between two variables can be found. For example, at a given pressure altitude, you can find the maximum gross weight capability as free air temperature changes.

---

d. Dashed Line Data Data beyond conditions for which tests were conducted are shown as dashed lines.

c. *Helicopter Variations.* Variations in performance between individual helicopters are known to exist; however, they are considered to be small and cannot be individually accounted for.

d. *Instrument Variation.* The data shown in the performance charts do not account for instrument inaccuracies or malfunctions.

e. *Types of Fuel.* All flight performance data is based on JP-4 fuel. The change in fuel flow and torque available, when using IP-5, IP-8, aviation gasoline or any other approved fuels, is insignificant

7.1-9. Performance Discrepancies. Regular use of this chapter will allow you to monitor instruments and other helicopter systems for malfunction, by comparing actual performance with planned performance. Knowledge will also be gained concerning the effects of variables for which data are not provided, thereby increasing the accuracy of performance predictions.

7.1-10. Definitions of Abbreviations.

a. Unless otherwise indicated, abbreviations and symbols used in this manual conform to those established in Military Standard MILSTD-12, which is periodically revised to reflect current changes in abbreviations usage.

b. Capitalization and punctuation of abbreviations varies depending upon the content In which they are used. In general, lower case abbreviations are used in text material, whereas abbreviations used in charts and illustrations appears in full capital letters. Periods do not usually follow abbreviations; however, periods are used with abbreviations that could be mistaken for whole words if the period were omitted.

7.1-11. Temperature Conversion. The temperature conversion chart (Figure 7.1-1) is arranged so that degrees Celsius can be converted quickly and easily by reading Celsius and looking directly across the charts for the Fahrenheit equivalent and vice versa.

Section II. TORQUE AVAILABLE

7.1-12. Description. The torque available charts (Figure 7.1-2) show the effects of altitude and temperature on engine torque

7.1-13. Chart Differences. Both pressure altitude and FAT affect engine power production. Figure 7.1-2 shows power available data at 30-mmnunute power ratings in terms of calibrated and indicated torque. Note that the power output capability of the T53-L-13 engine can exceed the transmission structural limit (50 psi calibrated torque under certain conditions.

a. Figure 7.1-2 (sheet 1) is applicable for maximum power, 30-minute operation at 324 rotor/6600 engine rpm with particle separator installed.

b. Figure 7.1-2 (sheet 2) is applicable for maximum power, 30-minute operation at 314 rotor/6600 engine rpm with particle separator installed.

c. Prolonged IGE hover may increase engine inlet temperature as much as 10° C, therefore a 10° higher FAT must be used to correct for this condition

d. If the IR Scoup Suppressor is installed on the aircraft, subtract one psi for the torque values obtained from Figure 7.1-2, sheets 1 and 2.

7.1-14. Use of Charts. The primary use of the torque available charts is illustrated by the examples m general, to determine the maximum power available, it is necessary to know the pressure altitude and temperature. The calibration factor (Data Plate Torque), obtained from the engine data plate or from the engine acceptance records, is the indicated torque pressure at 1125 ft-lbs actual output shaft torque, and is used to correct the error of individual engine torque indicating system.

NOTE
Torque available values determined are not limits. Any torque which can be achieved, without exceeding engine, transmission, or other limits, may be used.

7.1-15. Conditions. The torque available charts (Figure 7.1-2) are based upon speeds of 324 rotor/6600 engine rpm, 314 rotor/6400 engine rpm and grade JP-4 fuel The use of aviation gasoline will not influence engine power. Fuel grade of JP-5 will yield the same nautical miles per pound of fuel and, being 6.8 pounds per gallon, will only result in increased fuel weight. All torque available data are presented for bleed air heater and device off. Decrease torque available 1.4 psi for heater on and 2.1 for device on; decrease torque available 3.5 psi if both bleed air heater and device are operating.

Section I. HOVER

7.1-16. Description. The hover charts (Figure 7.1-3, Sheets 1 and 2) show the hover ceiling and the torque required to hover at various pressure altitudes, ambient temperatures, gross weights, and skid heights. Maximum skid height for hover can also be obtained by using the torque available from Figure 7.1-2. The hover capabilities (Table 7.1-1, Sheets 1 and 2) present OGE gross weight in pounds, OGE and IGE (5 ft. skid height) hover torque required in calibrated PSI, for temperature of 40°C to +45° C in 5°C increments and pressure altitudes from-sea level to 16,000 feet in 500 foot increments.

7.1-17. Use of Charts. The primary use of the hover charts is Illustrated by examples. In general, to determine the hover ceiling or the torque required to hover, it is necessary to know the pressure altitude, temperature, gross weight and the desired skid height. In addition to the primary use, the hover charts can also be used to determine the predicted maximum hover height, which is needed for use of the takeoff chart (Figure 7.1-5). The hover capability table (Table 7.1-1, Sheets 1 and 2) is limited by either maximum OGE gross weight or maximum torque available.

7.1-18. Control Margin Charts.

a. Sheet I of the control margin chart (Figure 7.1-4) shows the maximum right crosswind in which directional control can be maintained as a function of pressure altitude, temperature, and gross weight. Sheet 2 of the control margin chart, (Figure 7.1-4) shows the combinations of relative wind velocity and azimuth which may result in marginal directional or longitudinal control.

b. Use of the control margin chart is illustrated by the I example on Sheet 1. Ten percent pedal margin (full right to full left) is considered adequate for directional control when hovering. The shaded area on Sheet I indicates conditions where the directional control margin may be less than ten percent m zero wind hover. The shaded area on Sheet 2 labeled DRECTIONAL, indicates conditions where the directional control margin may be less than ten percent for crosswind components in excess of those determined from Sheet 1. The shaded area on Sheet 2 labeled LONGITUDINAL indicates wind conditions where longitudinal cyclic control margin may be less than 10 percent. These charts are based on control margins only.

1-19. Conditions.

a. The hover charts are based upon calm wind conditions, a level ground surface, and the use of 324 rotor rpm.

b. Use of control margin charts is to determine if adequate control margin will be available for IGE and OGE hover m winds or low speed translation.

c. The hover charts do not account for the effect of an IR suppressor device. The hover ceiling chart (Figure 7.1-3, Sheet 2) is not usable if a suppressor device is installed. The IR Scoup Suppressor creates a download of approximately 140 pounds.

d. For the IR Scoup Suppressor

(1) To determine hover torque required,-enter the hover power required chart (Figure 7.1-3, Sheet 1) at a gross weight of 140 pounds heavier than the actual gross weight.

(2) To determine predicted maximum hover height, first subtract one psi from power available (Figure 7.1-2); then increase the hover gross weight by 140 pounds. Use this power available and gross weight m the hover power required chart (Figure 7.1-3, Sheet 1).

(3) To determine maximum gross weight, first subtract one psi from power available (Figure 7.1-2); then decrease the hover gross weight determined from the hover power required chart (Figure 7.1-3, Sheet 1) by 140 pounds.

e. With the rotor blade erosion protection coating and polyurethane tape installed, it will be necessary to make the following corrections. Add I psi to the hover torque required, for OGE and IGE, as determined from Figure 7-3 (Sheet 2). In Figure 7-3 (Sheet 1), subtract 100 pounds from the maximum gross weight to hover. When determining maximum hover wheel height, enter the chart at the gross weight plus 100 pounds.

Section IV. TAKEOFF

7.1-20. Description. The takeoff charts (Figure 7.1-5) show the distances to clear various obstacle heights based upon several hover height capabilities. The upper chart grid presents data for climbout at a constant INDICATED airspeed. The two lower grids present data for climbouts at various TRUE airspeeds. Figure 7.1-5, Sheet 1 is based upon level acceleration technique; Sheet 2 is based upon a climb and acceleration from a 3-foot skid height; and Sheet 3 is based upon a level acceleration from a 15-foot skid height.

NOTE
The hover heights shown on the charts are only a measure of the aircraft's climb capability and do not imply that a higher than normal hover height should be used during the actual takeoff.

7.1-21. Use of Charts. The primary use of takeoff charts is illustrated by examples. The main consideration for takeoff performance is the hover skid height capability, which includes the effects of pressure altitude, free air temperature, gross weight, and torque. Hover height capability is determined by use of the hover charts (Figure 7.1-3). A hover check can be made to verify the hover capability. If winds are present, the hover check may disclose that the helicopter can actually hover at a greater skid height than the calculated value, since the hover charts are based upon calm wind conditions.

7.1-22. Conditions.

a. Wind. The takeoff charts are based upon calm wind conditions. Since surface wind velocity and direction cannot be accurately predicted, all takeoff planning should be based upon calm wind conditions. Takeoff into any prevailing wind will improve the takeoff performance.

WARNING
A tailwind during takeoff and climbout will Increase the obstacle clearance distance and could prevent a successful takeoff.

b. Power Settings. All takeoff performance data are based upon the torque used in determining the hover capabilities in Figure 7.1-3.

Section V. CRUISE

7.1-23. Description. The cruise charts (Figure 7.1-6, sheets I through 24) are based upon operation with a clean configuration. They show the torque pressure and engine rpm required for level flight at various pressure altitudes, airspeeds, gross weights, and fuel flows.

> **NOTE**
> Each chart has a dashed line that represents a 10 square-foot equivalent flat plate drag area This allows quick determination of delta PSI for other than clean configurations.

7.1-24. Use of Charts. The primary use of the cruise charts is illustrated by the examples provided in Figure 7.1-6. The first step for chart use is to select the proper chart, based upon the pressure altitude and anticipated free air temperature. (Refer to Chapter 7.1 index, paragraph 7.1-2. Normally sufficient accuracy can be obtained by selecting the chart nearest to the planed cruising altitude and FAT, or the next higher altitude and FAT. If greater accuracy is required, interpolation between altitudes and/or temperatures will be required. You may enter the charts on any side (TAS, IAS, torque pressure, or fuel flow) then move vertically or horizontally to the gross weight, and then to the other three parameters. Determine maximum performance conditions by entering the chart where the maximum range or maximum endurance and rate of climb lines intersect the appropriate gross weight, then read airspeed, fuel flow and PSI torque pressure For conservatism, use the gross weight at the beginning of cruise flight. For greater accuracy on long flights it is preferable to determine cruise information for several flight segments m order to allow for decreasing fuel weights reduced gross weight). Estimated performance data is presented for hover (KTAS= 0) in Figure 7.1-6; however, the hover performance data presented in Figure 7.1-3 is more accurate and should be used in planning critical hover performance. The following parameters contained in each chart are further explained as follows:

a. Airspeed. True and indicated airspeeds are presented at opposite sides of each chart. On any chart, indicated airspeed can be converted to true airspeed (or vice versa) by reading directly across the chart without regard for other chart information. Maximum permissible airspeed (V_{NE}) limits appear on some charts. If no line appears, V_{NE}, is above the limits of the chart.

b. Torque Pressure (PSI). Since pressure altitude and temperature are fixed for each chart, torque pressures vary according to gross weight, airspeed and bleed air operation. See paragraph 7.1-15. for effect of bleed air heater and device.

> **NOTE**
> Torque available values determined are not limits. Any torque which can be achieved, without exceeding engine, transmission, or other limits, may be used.

c. Fuel Flow. Fuel flow scales are provided opposite the torque pressure scales. On any chart, torque pressure may be converted directly to fuel flow without regard for other chart information. All fuel flows are presented for bleed air heater and device off. Add 2 percent fuel flow (about 14 lbs) for heater on and increase fuel flow 3 percent (approximately 21 lb/hr) for device on. If both are operating, add 5 percent fuel flow (about 35 lb/hr) to chart values.

d. Maximum Range. The maximum range lines indicate the combinations of weight and airspeed that will produce the greatest flight range per gallon of fuel under zero wind conditions. When a maximum range condition does not appear on a chart it is because the maximum range speed is beyond the maximum permissible V_{NE} In such cases, use V_{NE} cruising speed to obtain-maximum range.

e. Maximum Endurance and Rate of Climb. The maximum endurance and rate of climb lines indicate the airspeed for minimum torque pressure required to maintain level flight for each gross weight, FAT and pressure altitude. Since minimum torque pressure will provide minimum fuel flow, maximum flight endurance will be obtained at the airspeeds indicated.

7.1-25. Conditions. The cruise charts are based upon operations at 324 rotor/6600 engine rpm below 40 KTAS and 314 rotor/6400 engine rpm for true airspeeds above 40 knots. With the rotor blade erosion protection coating and polyurethane tape installed, add I psi to the torque required obtained from Figure 7.1-6 for true airspeeds less than 100 KTAS.

TM 55-1520-210-10

Section VI. DRAG

7.1-26. Description. The drag chart (Figure 7.1-7, sheet 1 of 2) shows the equivalent flat plate drag area changes for additional authorized configurations. There is no increase in drag with cargo doors fully open. The upper left portion of Figure 7.1-7, sheet 2 of 2, presents drag areas of typical external loads as a function of the load frontal area. The balance of the chart shows the additional torque required m level flight due to the increase in drag caused by external loads or aircraft modifications. The IR Scoop Suppressor has a drag of two square feet.

7.1-27. Use of Chart. The primary use of the drag chart is Illustrated by the example. To determine the change in torque, it is necessary to know the drag area change, the true airspeed, the pressure altitude and the free air temperature. Enter at the known drag area change, move right to TAS, move down to pressure altitude, move left to FAT, then move down and read change in torque. In addition, by entering the chart in the opposite direction, C drag area change may be found from 2 known torque change. This chart is used to adjust cruise chart torque and fuel flow due to equivalent flat plate drag area change (^F). For frontal areas exceeding values shown on Figure 7.1-7 (sheet 2 of 2) use a smaller value and multiply, e.g. 36 sq. ft. 12 sq. ft. X 3.

7.1-28. Conditions. The drag chart is based upon 314 rotor/6400 engine rpm.

Section VII. CLIMB

7.1-29. Description. The climb performance chart (Figure 7.1-8, sheet 1) represents a synthesis of the cruise charts to ease estimation of the climb portion of the flight plan. The chart shows the time, distance, and fuel required to climb from an initial altitude to a final altitude. The chart provides for variation in gross weight and ambient temperature and may be used for minor configuration deviations.

7.1-30. Use of Chart. Enter at the known gross weight, move up to the initial altitude and standard day free air temperature. Calculate delta FAT between the actual FAT and the standard day FAT. Move right from the initial altitude and interpolate for the delta FAT point; drop down and read the time and distance scale. Continue down to the appropriate delta FAT curve, move left to the fuel scale, and read fuel in pounds. Repeat above procedure for final altitude values. Use the previous delta FAT and the final altitude to determine the new values. Subtract initial altitude values from the final altitude values to obtain the actual time, distance and fuel.

7.1-31. Conditions. The climb-performance chart represents climb at optimum conditions, that is, at best rate-of-climb airspeed and at maximum power available 0-minute operation). Climb is assumed to be at 55 indicated airspeed as this is near the airspeed for rate of climb at most atmospheric conditions.

d taxi fuel are not included in fuel calculations. Climb performance is calculated for 314 rotor/ 6400 engine rpm. The charts are based upon a no-wind condition; therefore, distance traveled will not be valid when winds are present.

7.1-32. Description. The climb-descent chart (Figure C 7.1-8, sheet 2), shows the change in torque (above or below torque required for level flight under the same gross weight and atmospheric conditions) to obtain a given rate of climb or descent.

7.1-33. Use of Chart The primary uses of the climb-descent chart are Illustrated by the chart examples

  a. The torque change obtained from the grid scale must be added to (for climb) or subtracted from (for descent) the torque required for level flight to obtain a total climb or descent torque. (Torque required for level flight is obtained from the appropriate cruise chart.)

  b. By entering the bottom of the grid with a known torque change, moving upward to the gross weight, then left, the corresponding rate of climb or descent may also be obtained.

7.1-34. Conditions. The climb-descent chart is based on the use of constant rotor or engine rpm. A decrease in rpm could decrease the rate of climb or increase the rate of descent shown.

Change 17 7.

Section VIII. FUEL FLOW

7.1-35. Description.

a. The flat pitch fuel flow chart (Fig. 7.1-9, sheet 1) shows the fuel flow at engine flat pitch.

b. The fuel flow vs torque chart (Fig. 7.1-9, sheet 2) shows fuel flow at 314 rotor/6,400 engine RPM in pounds-per-hour versus torquemeter psi for pressure altitudes from sea level to 14,000 feet and for 0° C free air temperature.

7.1-36. Use of Chart.

a. The primary use of the flat pitch fuel flow chart is illustrated by the example. To determine the flat pitch fuel flow, it is necessary to know the pressure altitude and free air temperature. Enter the pressure altitude, move right to FAT in appropriate grid, then move down and read fuel flow on the bottom scale.

b. The primary use of the fuel flow vs torque chart is illustrated by the example. To determine fuel flow, it is necessary to know the torquemeter pressure (psi) and the FAT as well as the pressure altitude. Fuel flow will increase about 2 percent with the bleed air heater on and 3 percent with deice on. When both systems are on, fuel flow will increase 5 percent. Also, a range or endurance penalty should be accounted for when working cruise chart data. A fairly accurate rule of thumb to correct fuel flow for temperatures other than 0° C FAT is to increase/decrease fuel flow 1 percent for each 10° C increase/decrease in FAT.

7.1-37. Conditions. The fuel flow charts are based upon the use of JP-4 fuel. The change in fuel flow when using other jet fuels is insignificant.

TEMPERATURE CONVERSION CHART

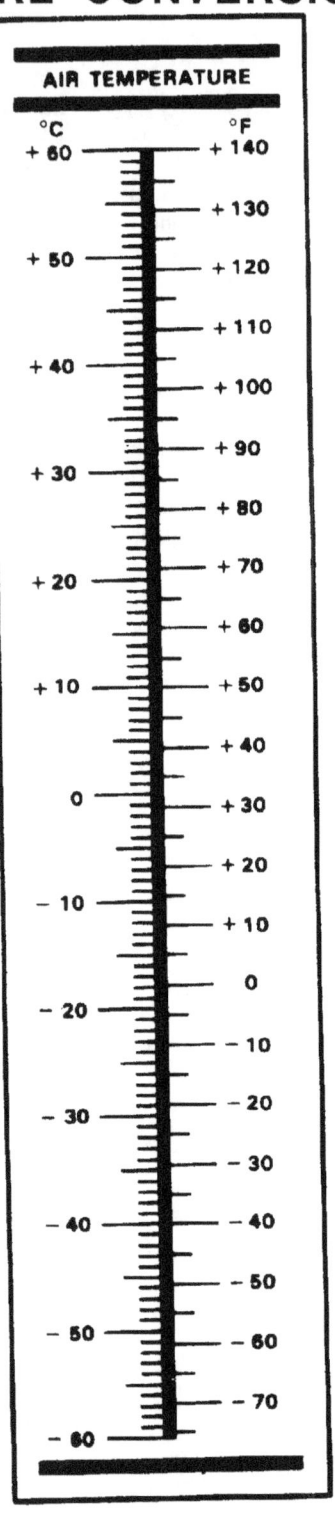

Figure 7.1-1. Temperature conversion chart

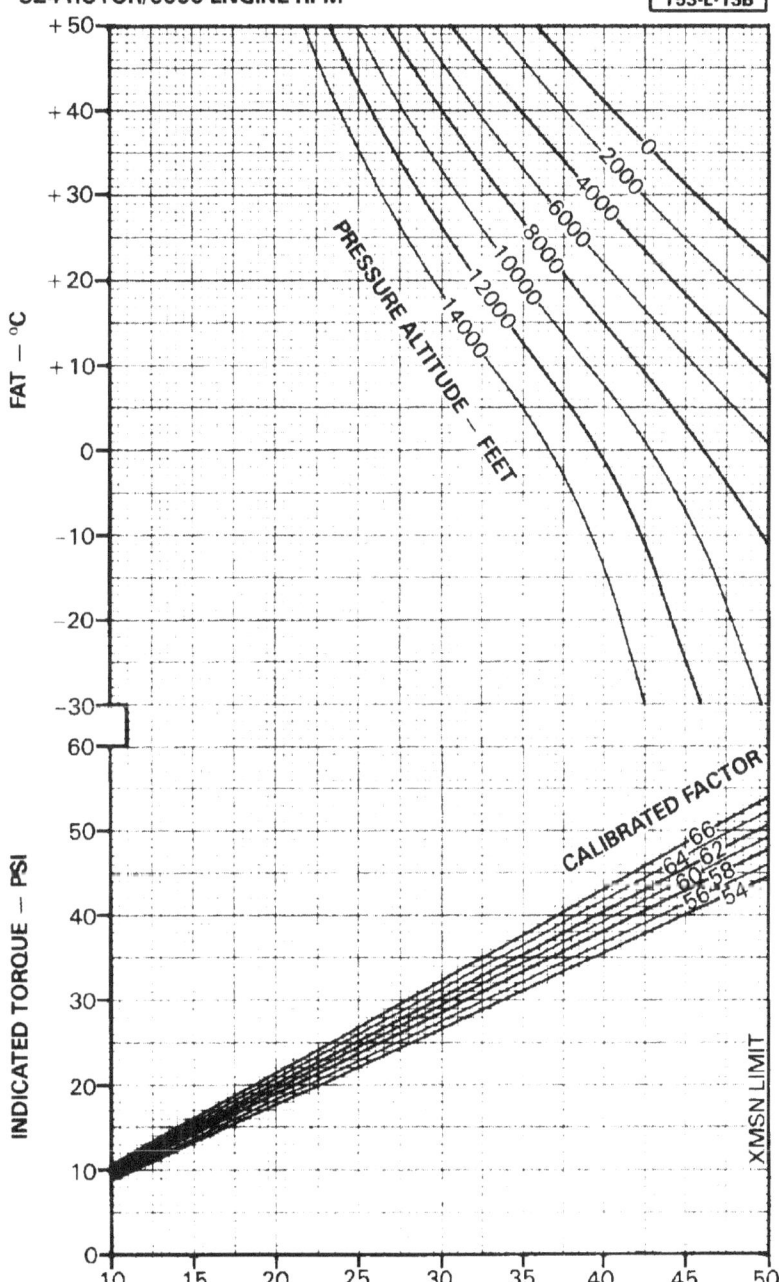

Figure 7.1-2. Maximum torque (30 minute operation) chart (Sheet 1 of 2)

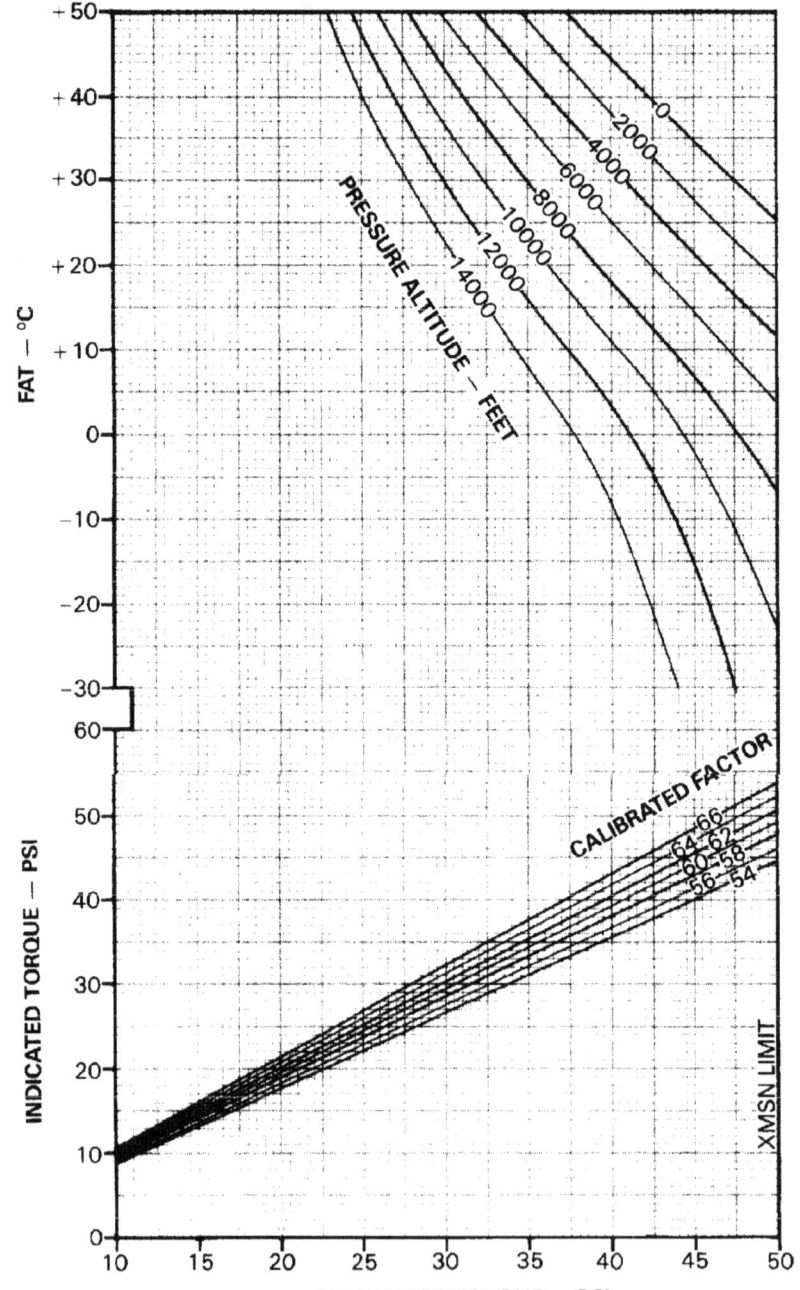

Figure 7.1-2. Maximum torque (30 minute operation) chart (Sheet 2 of 2)

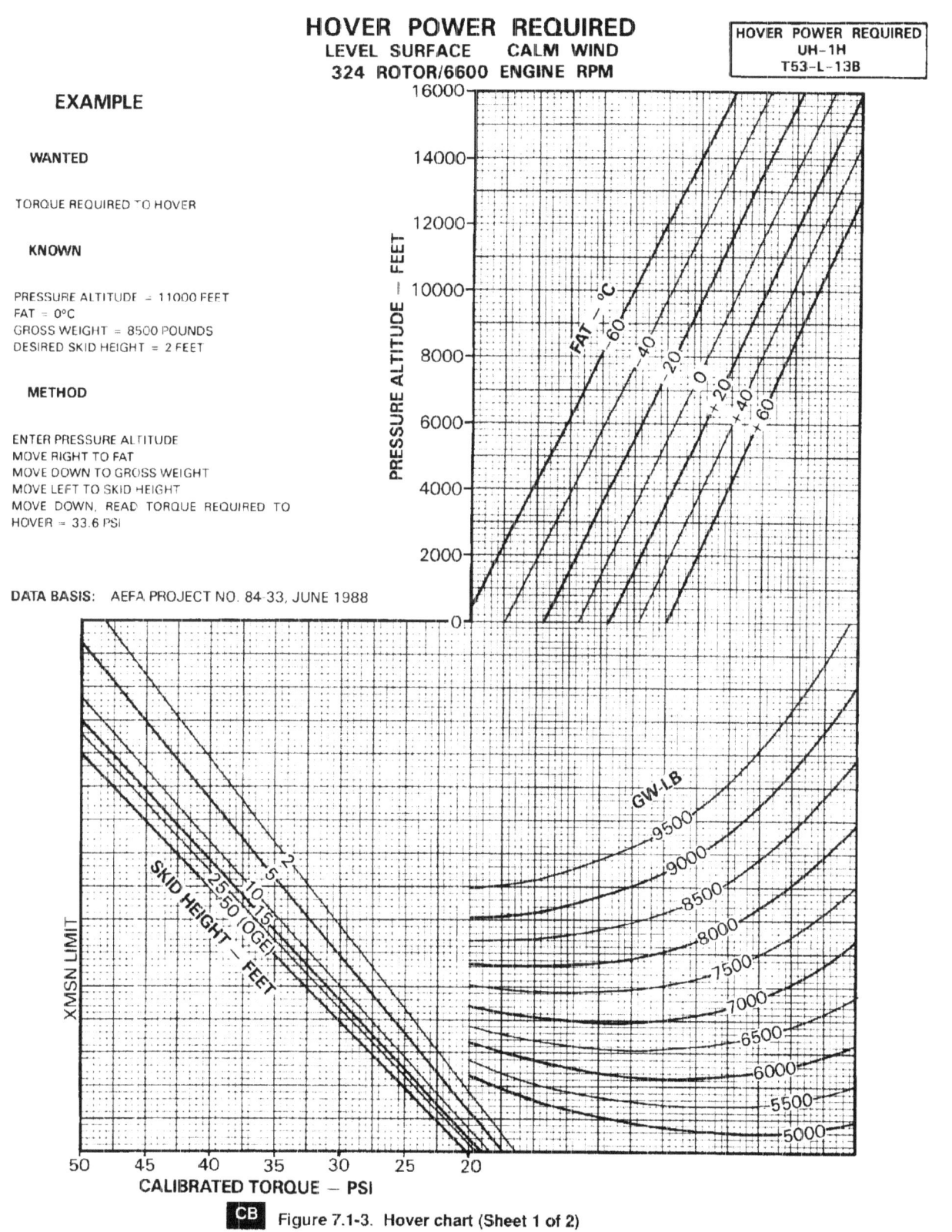

Figure 7.1-3. Hover chart (Sheet 1 of 2)

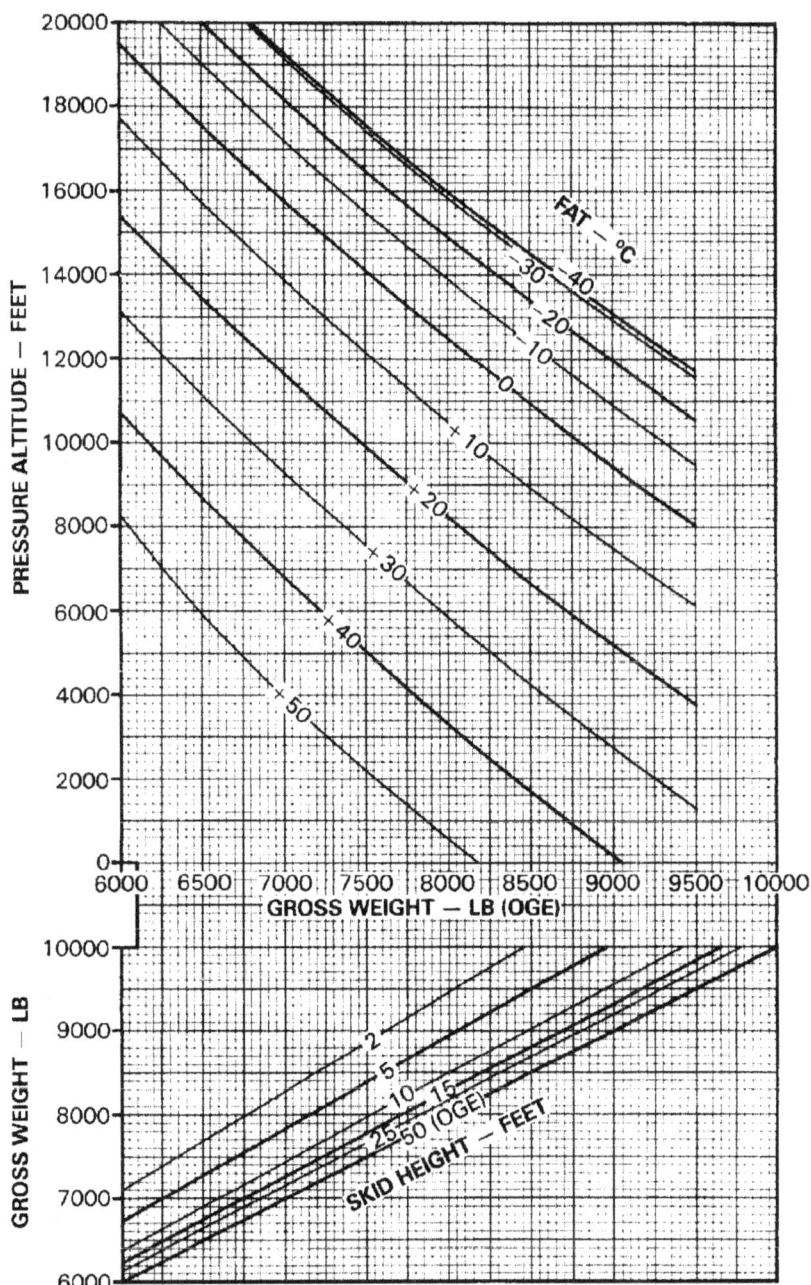

Figure 7.1-3. Hover chart (Sheet 2 of 2)

TM 55-1520-210-10

Table 7.1-1 CB Hover Capability (Sheet 1 of 2)
Multiply all Gross Weights by 10

OAT DEGREES CELCIUS	GW, LB REQD, PSI IGE 5 FT	PRESSURE ALTITUDE IN FEET CALIBRATED TORQUE REQUIRED TO HOVER @ 324 ROTOR/6600 ENGINE, PSI																
		0	500	1000	1500	2000	2500	3000	3500	4000	4500	5000	5500	6000	6500	7000	7500	8000
-40	OGE GW	950	950	950	950	950	950	950	950	950	950	950	950	950	950	950	950	950
	OGE	40.7	40.7	40.8	40.9	40.9	41.1	41.2	41.3	41.5	41.6	41.8	42.0	42.2	42.4	42.7	43.0	43.3
	IGE	36.6	36.5	36.5	36.5	36.5	36.5	36.5	36.6	36.6	36.7	36.7	36.8	36.9	37.0	37.1	37.2	37.4
-35	OGE GW	950	950	950	950	950	950	950	950	950	950	950	950	950	950	950	950	950
	OGE	40.7	40.8	40.9	41.0	41.1	41.2	41.3	41.5	41.6	41.8	42.0	42.2	42.5	42.7	43.0	43.3	43.6
	IGE	36.5	36.5	36.5	36.5	36.5	36.5	36.6	36.6	36.7	36.7	36.8	36.9	37.0	37.1	37.3	37.4	37.6
-30	OGE GW	950	950	950	950	950	950	950	950	950	950	950	950	950	950	950	950	950
	OGE	40.8	40.9	41.0	41.1	41.2	41.3	41.5	41.7	41.9	42.1	42.3	42.5	42.8	43.0	43.3	43.6	43.9
	IGE	36.5	36.5	36.5	36.5	36.5	36.6	36.6	36.7	36.7	36.8	36.9	37.0	37.1	37.3	37.4	37.6	37.7
-25	OGE GW	950	950	950	950	950	950	950	950	950	950	950	950	950	950	950	950	950
	OGE	40.9	41.0	41.1	41.2	41.4	41.5	41.7	41.9	42.1	42.3	42.5	42.8	43.0	43.3	43.6	44.0	44.3
	IGE	36.5	36.5	36.5	36.5	36.6	36.6	36.7	36.7	36.8	36.9	37.0	37.1	37.3	37.4	37.6	37.8	37.9
-20	OGE GW	950	950	950	950	950	950	950	950	950	950	950	950	950	950	950	950	950
	OGE	41.0	41.1	41.2	41.4	41.5	41.7	41.9	42.1	42.3	42.5	42.8	43.1	43.3	43.7	44.0	44.3	44.7
	IGE	36.5	36.5	36.5	36.6	36.6	36.7	36.8	36.8	36.9	37.0	37.2	37.3	37.4	37.6	37.8	38.0	38.2
-15	OGE GW	950	950	950	950	950	950	950	950	950	950	950	950	950	950	950	950	950
	OGE	41.1	41.2	41.4	41.5	41.7	41.9	42.1	42.3	42.6	42.8	43.1	43.4	43.7	44.0	44.3	44.7	45.1
	IGE	36.5	36.5	36.6	36.6	36.7	36.8	36.8	36.9	37.0	37.2	37.3	37.4	37.6	37.8	38.0	38.2	38.4
-10	OGE GW	950	950	950	950	950	950	950	950	950	950	950	950	950	950	950	950	950
	OGE	41.3	41.4	41.6	41.7	41.9	42.1	42.3	42.6	42.8	43.1	43.4	43.7	44.0	44.3	44.7	45.1	45.5
	IGE	36.5	36.6	36.6	36.7	36.8	36.8	36.9	37.0	37.2	37.3	37.4	37.6	37.8	38.0	38.2	38.4	38.6
-5	OGE GW	950	950	950	950	950	950	950	950	950	950	950	950	950	950	950	950	950
	OGE	41.4	41.6	41.7	41.9	42.1	42.3	42.6	42.8	43.1	43.4	43.7	44.0	44.3	44.7	45.1	45.5	45.9
	IGE	36.6	36.6	36.7	36.8	36.8	36.9	37.0	37.2	37.3	37.4	37.6	37.8	38.0	38.2	38.4	38.6	38.9
0	OGE GW	950	950	950	950	950	950	950	950	950	950	950	950	950	950	950	950	950
	OGE	41.6	41.7	41.9	42.1	42.3	42.6	42.8	43.1	43.4	43.7	44.0	44.3	44.7	45.1	45.5	45.9	46.4
	IGE	36.6	36.7	36.8	36.8	36.9	37.0	37.2	37.3	37.4	37.6	37.8	38.0	38.2	38.4	38.6	38.8	39.1
+5	OGE GW	950	950	950	950	950	950	950	950	950	950	950	950	950	950	950	935	917
	OGE	41.7	41.9	42.1	42.3	42.6	42.8	43.1	43.4	43.7	44.0	44.3	44.7	45.1	45.5	45.9	45.2	44.3
	IGE	36.7	36.8	36.8	36.9	37.0	37.2	37.3	37.4	37.6	37.8	38.0	38.1	38.4	38.6	38.8	38.2	37.4
+10	OGE GW	950	950	950	950	950	950	950	950	950	950	950	950	950	935	917	900	882
	OGE	41.9	42.1	42.3	42.6	42.8	43.1	43.3	43.6	44.0	44.3	44.7	45.0	45.4	44.8	43.9	43.1	42.2
	IGE	36.8	36.8	36.9	37.0	37.2	37.3	37.4	37.6	37.8	37.9	38.1	38.4	38.6	37.9	37.1	36.4	35.7
+15	OGE GW	950	950	950	950	950	950	950	950	950	950	948	930	913	895	878	861	845
	OGE	42.1	42.3	42.5	42.8	43.1	43.3	43.6	44.0	44.3	44.6	44.9	44.0	43.2	42.3	41.5	40.7	39.9
	IGE	36.8	36.9	37.0	37.2	37.3	37.4	37.6	37.7	37.9	38.1	38.2	37.4	36.7	36.0	35.3	34.6	33.9
+20	OGE GW	950	950	950	950	950	950	950	950	941	923	906	889	872	855	839	823	807
	OGE	42.3	42.5	42.8	43.0	43.3	43.6	43.9	44.3	44.0	43.1	42.3	41.5	40.7	39.9	39.2	38.4	37.7
	IGE	36.9	37.0	37.1	37.3	37.4	37.6	37.7	37.9	37.4	36.6	36.0	35.3	34.6	33.9	33.3	32.6	32.0
+25	OGE GW	950	950	950	950	950	950	934	917	900	883	866	850	834	818	802	787	772
	OGE	42.5	42.8	43.0	43.3	43.6	43.9	42.4	41.6	40.8	40.0	39.2	38.5	37.8	37.0	36.3	35.6	
	IGE	37.0	37.1	37.3	37.4	37.6	37.7	36.9	36.0	35.4	34.7	34.0	33.3	32.7	32.1	31.5	30.9	30.2
+30	OGE GW	950	950	950	942	924	907	891	874	858	842	826	810	795	780	765	750	736
	OGE	42.7	43.0	43.3	43.0	42.2	41.4	40.7	39.9	39.2	38.4	37.7	37.0	36.3	35.6	34.9	34.2	33.6
	IGE	37.1	37.3	37.4	36.9	36.1	35.4	34.7	34.0	33.4	32.7	32.1	31.5	30.9	30.3	29.7	29.1	28.6
+35	OGE GW	950	933	916	899	882	866	850	834	819	803	788	773	759	744	730	716	702
	OGE	43.0	42.2	41.4	40.6	39.9	39.1	38.4	37.7	37.0	36.3	35.6	34.9	34.3	33.6	33.0	32.3	31.7
	IGE	37.2	36.5	35.8	35.0	34.5	33.7	33.1	32.5	31.9	31.3	30.6	30.0	29.4	28.8	28.2	27.8	27.1
+40	OGE GW	905	888	872	855	840	824	809	794	779	764	750	736	722	708	694	681	668
	OGE	40.5	39.7	39.0	38.3	37.5	36.9	36.2	35.5	34.8	34.2	33.5	32.9	32.3	31.6	31.0	30.4	29.8
	IGE	35.0	34.3	33.7	33.0	32.5	31.7	31.1	30.5	29.8	29.3	28.7	28.2	27.6	26.9	26.5	25.9	25.4
+45	OGE GW	856	844	829	813	798	783	768	753	739	725	711	698	685	673	661	649	637
	OGE	38.0	37.4	36.7	36.0	35.3	34.7	34.0	33.3	32.7	32.1	31.5	30.9	30.3	29.8	29.2	28.7	28.2
	IGE	32.8	32.3	31.7	31.0	30.4	29.9	29.3	28.6	28.1	27.6	27.1	26.5	26.0	25.5	24.9	24.5	24.1

Change 8   7.1-13

TM 55-1520-210-10

Table 7.1-1 CB Hover Capability (Sheet 2 of 2)
Multiply all Gross Weights by 10

CALIBRATED TORQUE REQUIRED TO HOVER @ 324 ROTOR/6600 ENGINE, PSI

OAT DEGREES CELSIUS	GW, LB REQD, PSI IGE 5 FT	PRESSURE ALTITUDE IN FEET																
		8000	8500	9000	9500	10000	10500	11000	11500	12000	12500	13000	13500	14000	14500	15000	15500	16000
-40	OGE GW	950	950	950	950	950	950	950	950	937	919	901	884	866	849	833	816	800
	OGE	43.3	43.6	43.9	44.2	44.6	45.0	45.4	45.8	45.3	44.5	43.6	42.8	41.9	41.1	40.3	39.5	38.7
	IGE	37.4	37.5	37.7	37.9	38.1	38.3	38.6	38.8	38.1	37.5	36.7	35.9	35.2	34.5	33.8	33.1	32.5
-35	OGE GW	950	950	950	950	950	950	950	950	936	917	900	882	865	848	831	815	799
	OGE	43.6	43.9	44.3	44.6	45.0	45.4	45.9	46.3	45.7	44.8	44.0	43.1	42.3	41.5	40.6	39.8	39.1
	IGE	37.6	37.7	37.9	38.1	38.3	38.6	38.8	39.1	38.6	37.7	37.0	36.2	35.5	34.7	33.9	33.2	32.7
-30	OGE GW	950	950	950	950	950	950	950	950	934	916	898	880	863	846	830	813	797
	OGE	43.9	44.3	44.7	45.1	45.5	45.9	46.4	46.8	46.1	45.2	44.3	43.5	42.6	41.8	41.0	40.2	39.4
	IGE	37.7	37.9	38.1	38.4	38.6	38.8	39.1	39.4	38.8	38.0	37.1	36.5	35.7	34.9	34.2	33.6	32.9
-25	OGE GW	950	950	950	950	950	950	950	933	915	897	880	862	846	829	813	797	781
	OGE	44.3	44.7	45.1	45.5	45.9	46.4	46.9	46.0	45.1	44.3	43.4	42.6	41.8	40.9	40.1	39.4	38.6
	IGE	37.9	38.1	38.4	38.6	38.8	39.1	39.4	38.6	37.9	37.2	36.2	35.6	34.9	34.2	33.3	32.7	32.0
-20	OGE GW	950	950	950	950	950	950	950	932	914	896	879	862	845	828	812	796	780	765
	OGE	44.7	45.1	45.5	45.9	46.4	46.9	46.0	45.1	44.2	43.4	42.5	41.7	40.9	40.1	39.3	38.5	37.8
	IGE	38.2	38.4	38.6	38.9	39.1	39.4	38.6	37.9	37.1	36.5	35.7	35.0	34.4	33.7	33.0	32.3	31.8
-15	OGE GW	950	950	950	950	950	931	914	896	879	862	845	828	812	796	781	765	750
	OGE	45.1	45.5	45.9	46.4	46.8	45.9	44.1	44.2	43.3	42.5	41.7	40.9	40.1	39.3	38.5	37.8	37.0
	IGE	38.4	38.6	38.9	39.1	39.3	38.6	37.0	37.1	36.4	35.7	35.0	34.4	33.7	33.0	32.3	31.8	31.1
-10	OGE GW	950	950	950	949	931	913	896	878	862	845	828	812	797	781	766	750	735
	OGE	45.5	45.9	46.4	46.8	45.9	45.0	44.2	43.3	42.5	41.7	40.9	40.1	39.3	38.5	37.8	37.0	36.3
	IGE	38.6	38.9	39.1	39.3	38.6	37.8	37.1	36.4	35.7	35.0	34.4	33.7	33.0	32.3	31.8	31.1	30.5
-5	OGE GW	950	950	941	923	906	888	871	854	837	821	805	789	773	758	743	728	713
	OGE	45.9	46.4	46.2	45.3	44.3	43.6	42.7	41.9	41.1	40.3	39.5	38.7	37.9	37.2	36.4	35.7	35.0
	IGE	38.9	39.1	38.8	38.1	37.2	36.6	35.9	35.2	34.5	33.9	33.2	32.5	31.8	31.2	30.6	30.0	29.4
0	OGE GW	950	933	915	898	880	863	846	830	813	797	781	766	750	735	720	706	691
	OGE	46.4	45.6	44.7	43.8	43.0	42.1	41.3	40.5	39.7	38.9	38.1	37.3	36.6	35.8	35.1	34.4	33.7
	IGE	39.1	38.3	37.5	36.8	36.1	35.4	34.7	34.0	33.3	32.7	32.0	31.3	30.7	30.1	29.5	28.9	28.3
+5	OGE GW	917	900	882	865	848	832	816	800	784	768	753	738	723	709	694	680	666
	OGE	44.3	43.5	42.6	41.8	41.0	40.2	39.4	38.6	37.9	37.1	36.4	35.6	34.9	34.2	33.5	32.8	32.2
	IGE	37.4	36.5	35.8	35.1	34.4	33.8	33.1	32.4	31.8	31.2	30.6	29.9	29.3	28.7	28.1	27.6	27.0
+10	OGE GW	882	866	849	832	816	800	785	769	754	739	724	710	696	682	668	655	641
	OGE	42.2	41.4	40.6	39.8	39.0	38.3	37.5	36.8	36.0	35.3	34.6	33.9	33.2	32.6	31.9	31.3	30.6
	IGE	35.7	34.8	34.1	33.4	32.8	32.2	31.5	30.9	30.2	29.7	29.1	28.5	27.9	27.4	26.8	26.3	25.7
+15	OGE GW	845	829	813	797	781	766	751	736	722	707	693	680	666	653	639	627	614
	OGE	39.9	39.2	38.4	37.7	36.9	36.2	35.5	34.8	34.1	33.4	32.7	32.1	31.4	30.8	30.2	29.6	29.0
	IGE	33.9	32.9	32.3	31.7	31.0	30.4	29.8	29.2	28.6	28.1	27.5	27.0	26.4	25.9	25.4	24.9	24.4
+20	OGE GW	807	791	776	761	746	731	717	703	689	675	662	649	636	623	610	598	586
	OGE	37.7	36.9	36.2	35.5	34.8	34.1	33.4	32.8	32.1	31.5	30.9	30.2	29.6	29.0	28.4	27.9	27.3
	IGE	32.0	31.0	30.4	29.8	29.2	28.6	28.1	27.6	27.0	26.5	26.0	25.4	24.9	24.4	23.9	23.4	22.9
+25	OGE GW	772	757	742	728	713	700	686	672	659	646	633	620	607	595	583	570	558
	OGE	35.6	34.9	34.2	33.6	32.9	32.3	31.6	31.0	30.4	29.8	29.2	28.6	28.0	27.5	26.9	26.3	25.7
	IGE	30.2	29.3	28.7	28.2	27.6	27.1	26.5	26.0	25.5	25.0	24.5	24.0	23.5	23.1	22.5	22.1	21.6
+30	OGE GW	736	721	707	694	680	667	654	641	628	616	603	591	578	566	554	542	530
	OGE	33.6	32.9	32.3	31.6	31.0	30.4	29.8	29.2	28.6	28.1	27.5	26.9	26.3	25.8	25.2	24.6	24.1
	IGE	28.6	27.6	27.1	26.5	26.0	25.5	25.0	24.5	24.0	23.6	23.1	22.6	22.1	21.7	21.2	20.7	20.2
+35	OGE GW	702	689	675	662	650	637	625	613	602	591	580	569	558	547	536	524	513
	OGE	31.7	31.1	30.5	29.9	29.3	28.8	28.2	27.7	27.2	26.7	26.2	25.7	25.2	24.7	24.2	23.7	23.2
	IGE	27.1	26.1	25.6	25.1	24.6	24.2	23.7	23.3	22.8	22.4	22.0	21.6	21.2	20.7	20.3	19.9	19.5
+40	OGE GW	668	655	642	630	618	607	596	585	575	565	555	546	537	527	517	507	495
	OGE	29.8	29.3	28.7	28.1	27.6	27.1	26.6	26.2	25.7	25.3	24.9	24.5	24.1	23.7	23.2	22.8	22.2
	IGE	25.4	24.6	24.1	23.6	23.2	22.8	22.3	22.0	21.6	21.3	20.9	20.6	20.2	19.9	19.5	19.2	18.6
+45	OGE GW	637	626	615	604	593	582	572	562	552	543	533	524	515	506	497	488	479
	OGE	28.2	27.7	27.2	26.8	26.3	25.8	25.4	25.0	24.5	24.1	23.7	23.3	22.9	22.6	22.2	21.8	21.4
	IGE	24.1	23.3	22.8	22.5	22.1	21.7	21.3	21.0	20.6	20.2	19.9	19.6	19.2	19.0	18.6	18.3	18.0

7.1-14 Change 8

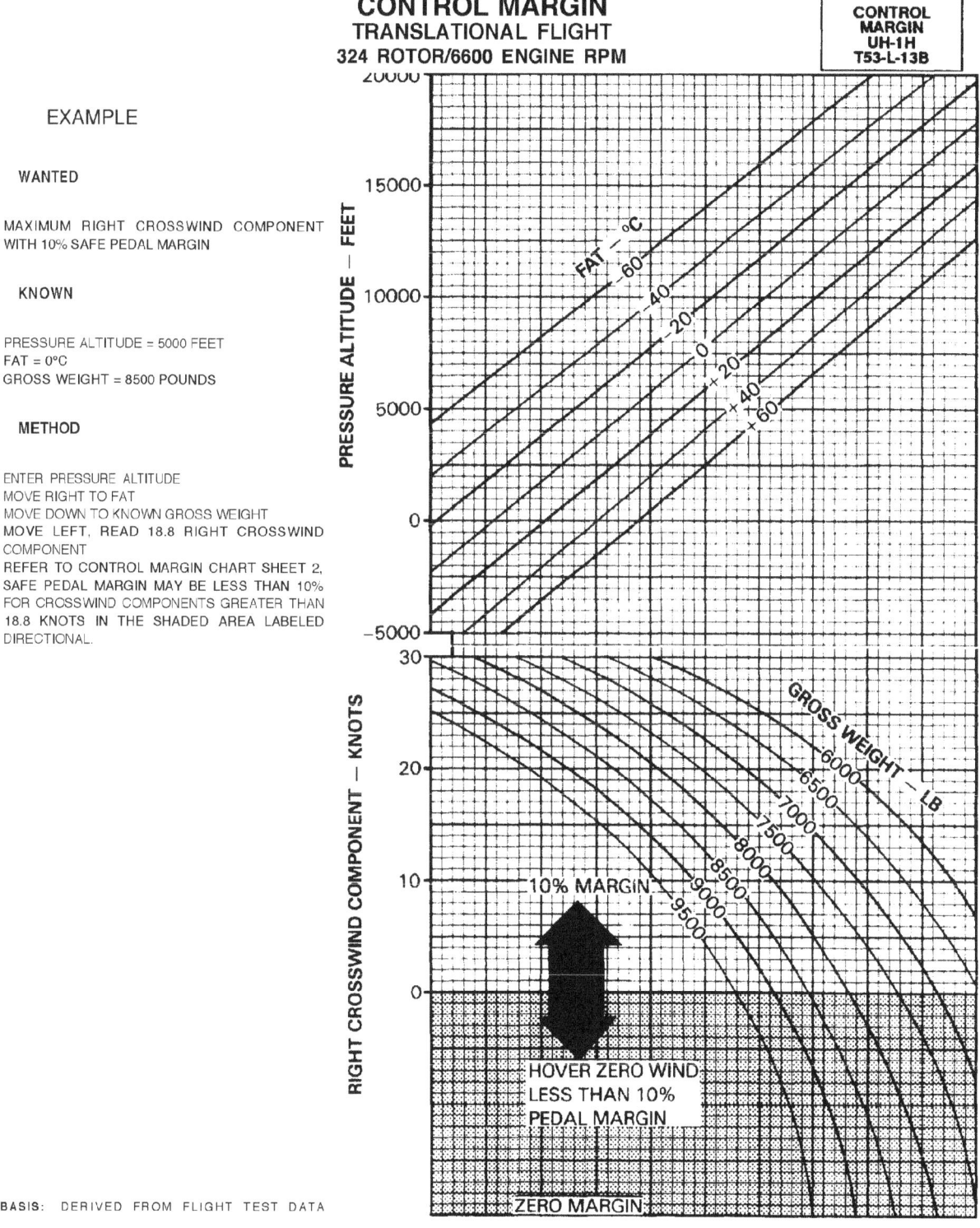

Figure 7.1-4. Control margin chart (Sheet 1 of 2)

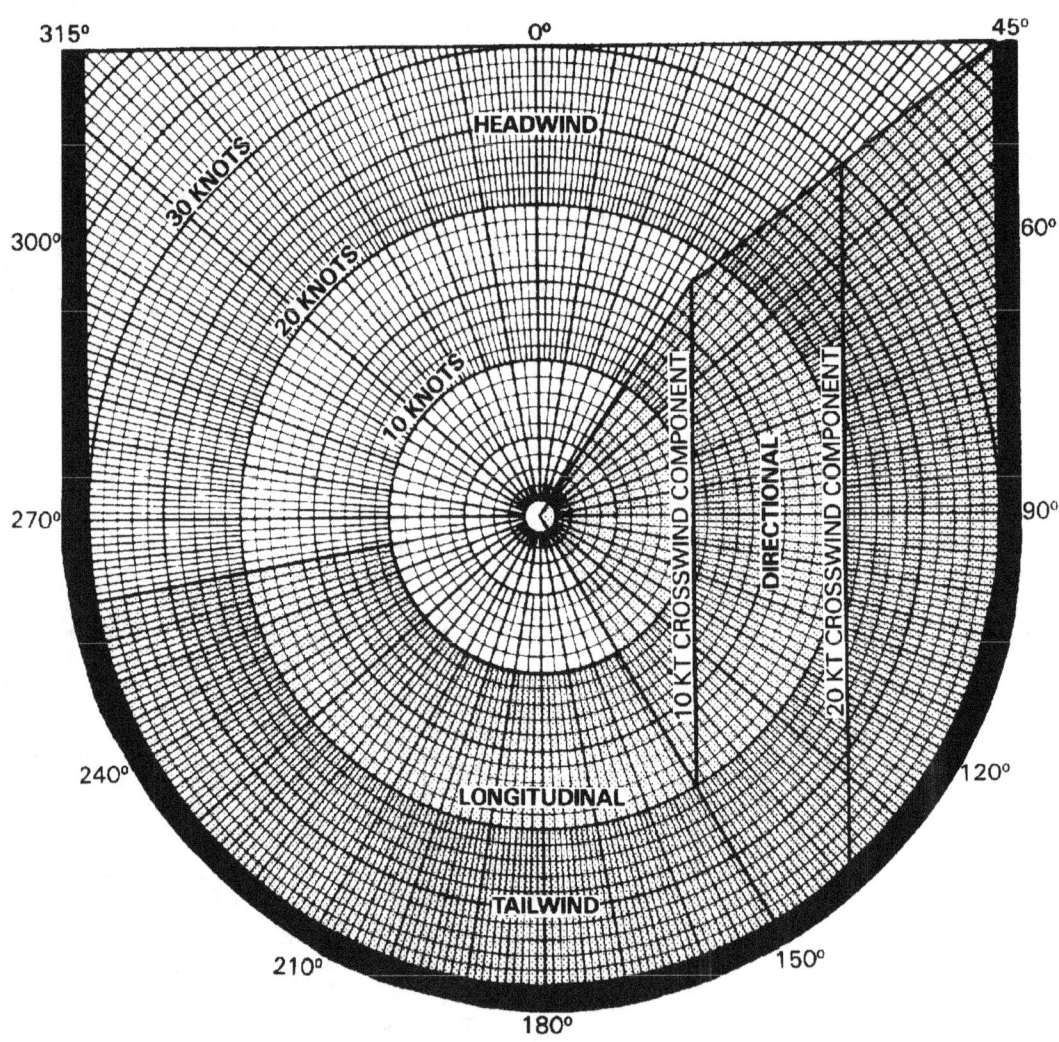

Figure 7.1-4. Control margin chart (Sheet 2 of 2)

TM 55-1520-210-10

TAKEOFF
LEVEL ACCELERATION, 3 FT SKID HEIGHT
324 ROTOR/6600 ENGINE RPM   MAXIMUM TORQUE AVAILABLE
CALM WIND LEVEL SURFACE ALL CONFIGURATIONS

EXAMPLE A

WANTED

DISTANCE TO CLEAR OBSTACLE

KNOWN

MAXIMUM HOVER HEIGHT = 10 FEET
OBSTACLE HEIGHT = 50 FEET

METHOD

ENTER MAXIMUM HOVER HEIGHT
MOVE RIGHT TO OBSTACLE HEIGHT
MOVE DOWN, READ DISTANCE TO CLEAR 50 FOOT
OBSTACLE = 700 FEET

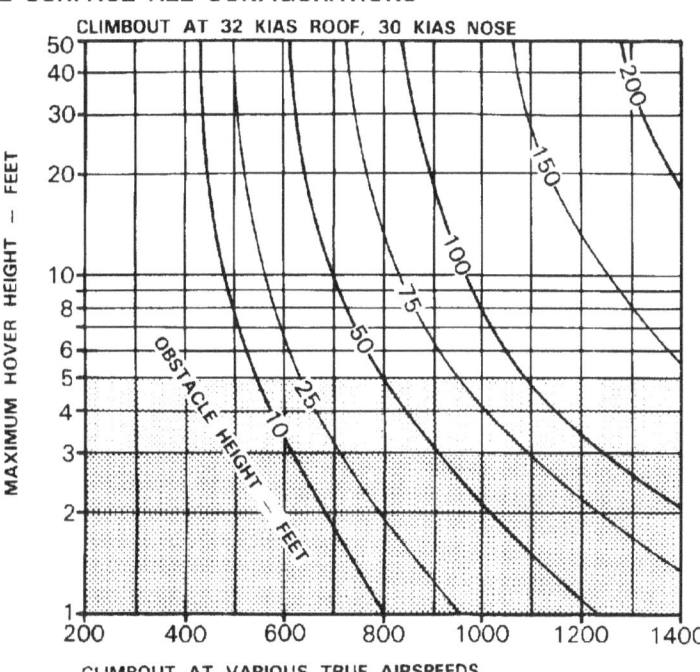

EXAMPLE B

WANTED

DISTANCE TO CLEAR OBSTACLE

KNOWN

MAXIMUM HOVER HEIGHT = 8 FEET
OBSTACLE HEIGHT = 50 FEET
CLIMBOUT AIRSPEED = 40 KNOTS

METHOD

ENTER MAXIMUM HOVER HEIGHT
MOVE RIGHT TO CLIMBOUT TRUE AIRSPEED
MOVE DOWN TO OBSTACLE HEIGHT
MOVE LEFT, READ DISTANCE TO CLEAR 50 FOOT
OBSTACLE = 630 FEET

DATA BASIS: DERIVED FROM FLIGHT TEST DATA OF SIMILAR AIRCRAFT, DECEMBER 1984.

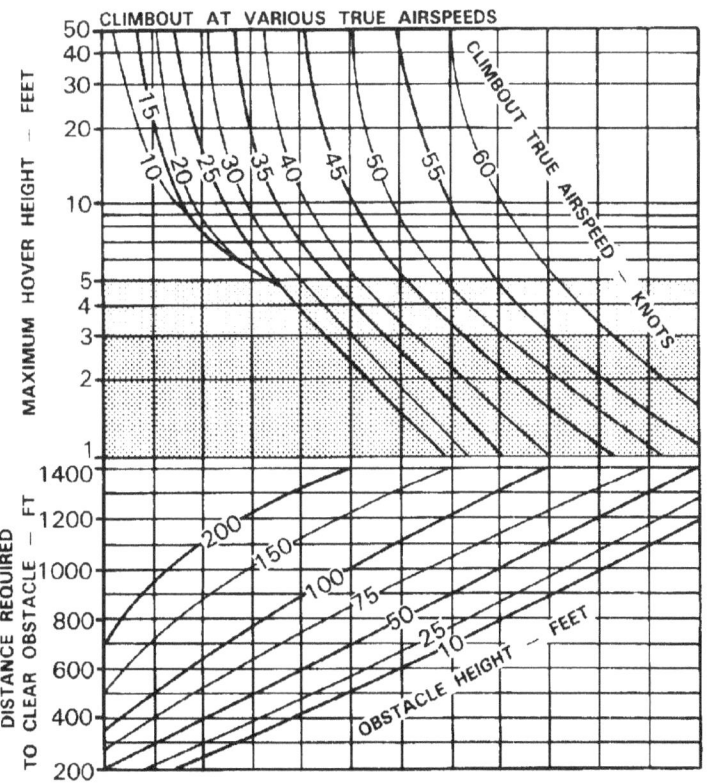

CB Figure 7.1-5. Takeoff chart (Sheet 1 of 3)

Change 8   7.1-17

TAKEOFF
CLIMB AND ACCELERATION, 3 FT SKID HEIGHT
324 ROTOR/6600 ENGINE RPM MAXIMUM TORQUE AVAILABLE
CALM WIND LEVEL SURFACE ALL CONFIGURATIONS

TAKEOFF
UH-1H
T53-L-13B

EXAMPLE A

WANTED

DISTANCE TO CLEAR OBSTACLE

KNOWN

MAXIMUM HOVER HEIGHT = 17 FEET
OBSTACLE HEIGHT = 120 FEET

METHOD

ENTER MAXIMUM HOVER HEIGHT
MOVE RIGHT TO OBSTACLE HEIGHT
MOVE DOWN, READ DISTANCE TO CLEAR 120
FOOT OBSTACLE = 1420 FEET

EXAMPLE B

WANTED

DISTANCE TO CLEAR OBSTACLE

MAXIMUM HOVER HEIGHT = 17 FEET
OBSTACLE HEIGHT = 120 FEET
CLIMBOUT AIRSPEED = 50 KNOTS

METHOD

ENTER MAXIMUM HOVER HEIGHT
MOVE RIGHT TO CLIMBOUT AIRSPEED
MOVE DOWN TO OBSTACLE HEIGHT
MOVE LEFT, READ DISTANCE TO CLEAR 120 FOOT
OBSTACLE = 1610 FEET

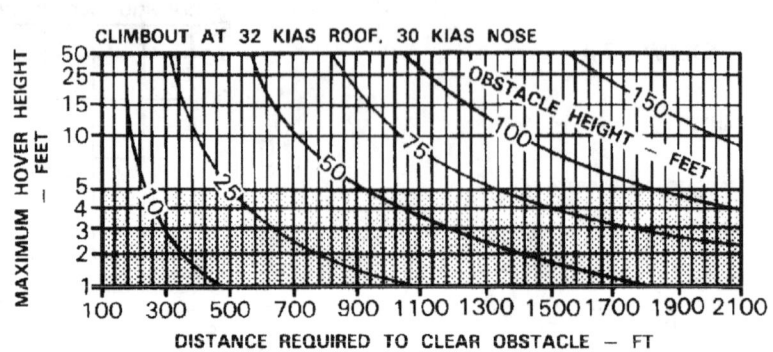

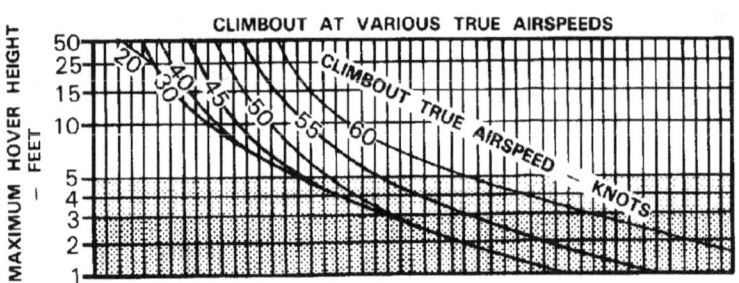

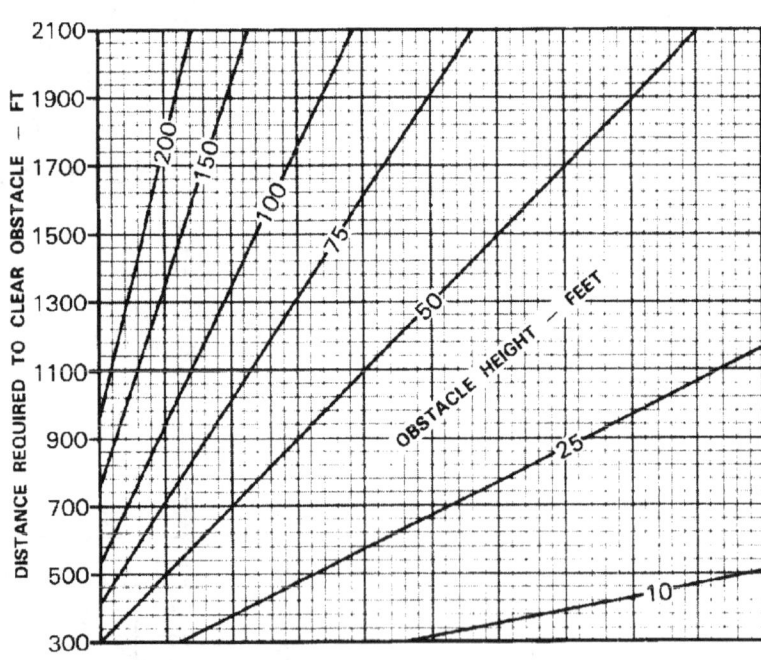

DATA BASIS: DERIVED FROM FLIGHT TEST DATA OF SIMILAR AIRCRAFT, DECEMBER 1984.

CB Figure 7.1-5. Takeoff chart (Sheet 2 of 3)

TAKEOFF
LEVEL ACCELERATION, 15 FT SKID HEIGHT
324 ROTOR/6600 ENGINE RPM MAXIMUM TORQUE AVAILABLE
CALM WIND LEVEL SURFACE ALL CONFIGURATIONS

EXAMPLE A

WANTED

DISTANCE TO CLEAR OBSTACLE

KNOWN

MAXIMUM HOVER HEIGHT 17 FEET
OBSTACLE HEIGHT = 120 FEET

METHOD

ENTER MAXIMUM HOVER HEIGHT
MOVE RIGHT TO OBSTACLE HEIGHT
MOVE DOWN, READ DISTANCE TO CLEAR 120
FOOT OBSTACLE = 1125 FEET

EXAMPLE B

WANTED

DISTANCE TO CLEAR OBSTACLE

KNOWN

MAXIMUM HOVER HEIGHT = 17 FEET
OBSTACLE HEIGHT = 120 FEET
CLIMBOUT AIRSPEED = 40 KNOTS

METHOD

ENTER MAXIMUM HOVER HEIGHT
MOVE RIGHT TO CLIMBOUT TRUE AIRSPEED
MOVE DOWN TO OBSTACLE HEIGHT
MOVE LEFT, READ DISTANCE TO CLEAR 120 FOOT
OBSTACLE = 1000 FEET

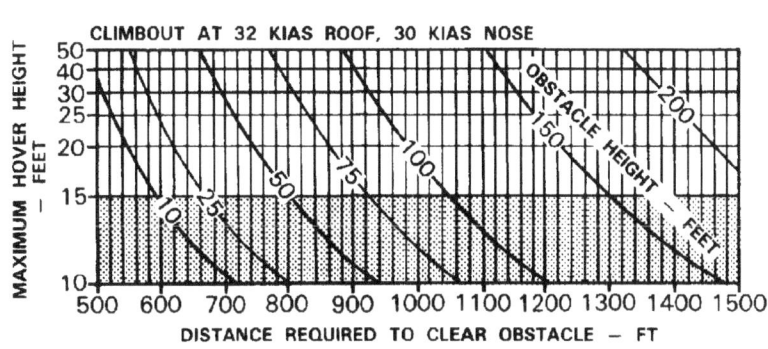
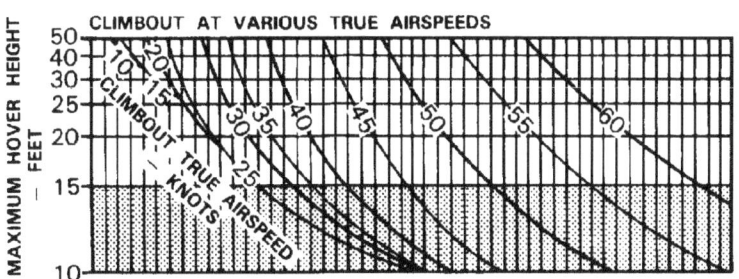
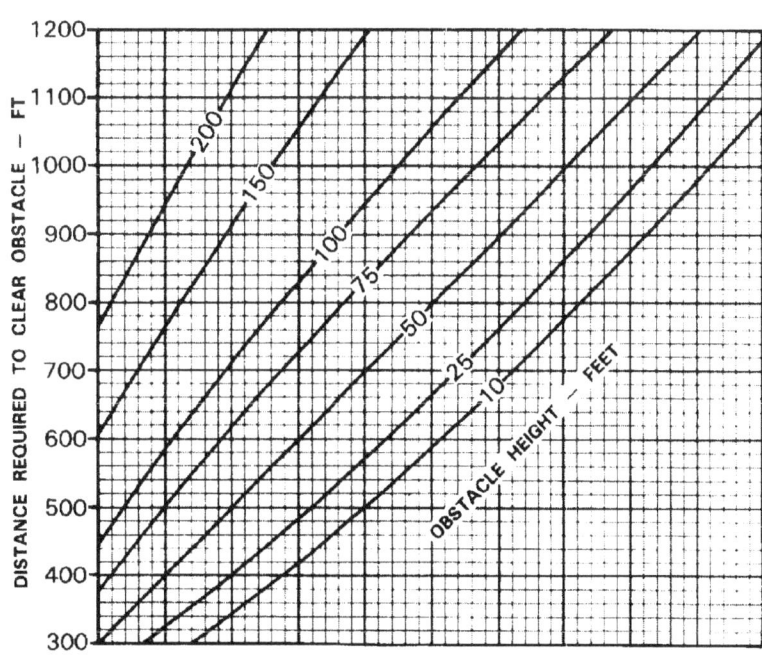

DATA BASIS: DERIVED FROM FLIGHT TEST DATA OF SIMILAR AIRCRAFT, DECEMBER 1984.

Figure 7.1-5. Takeoff chart (Sheet 3 of 3)

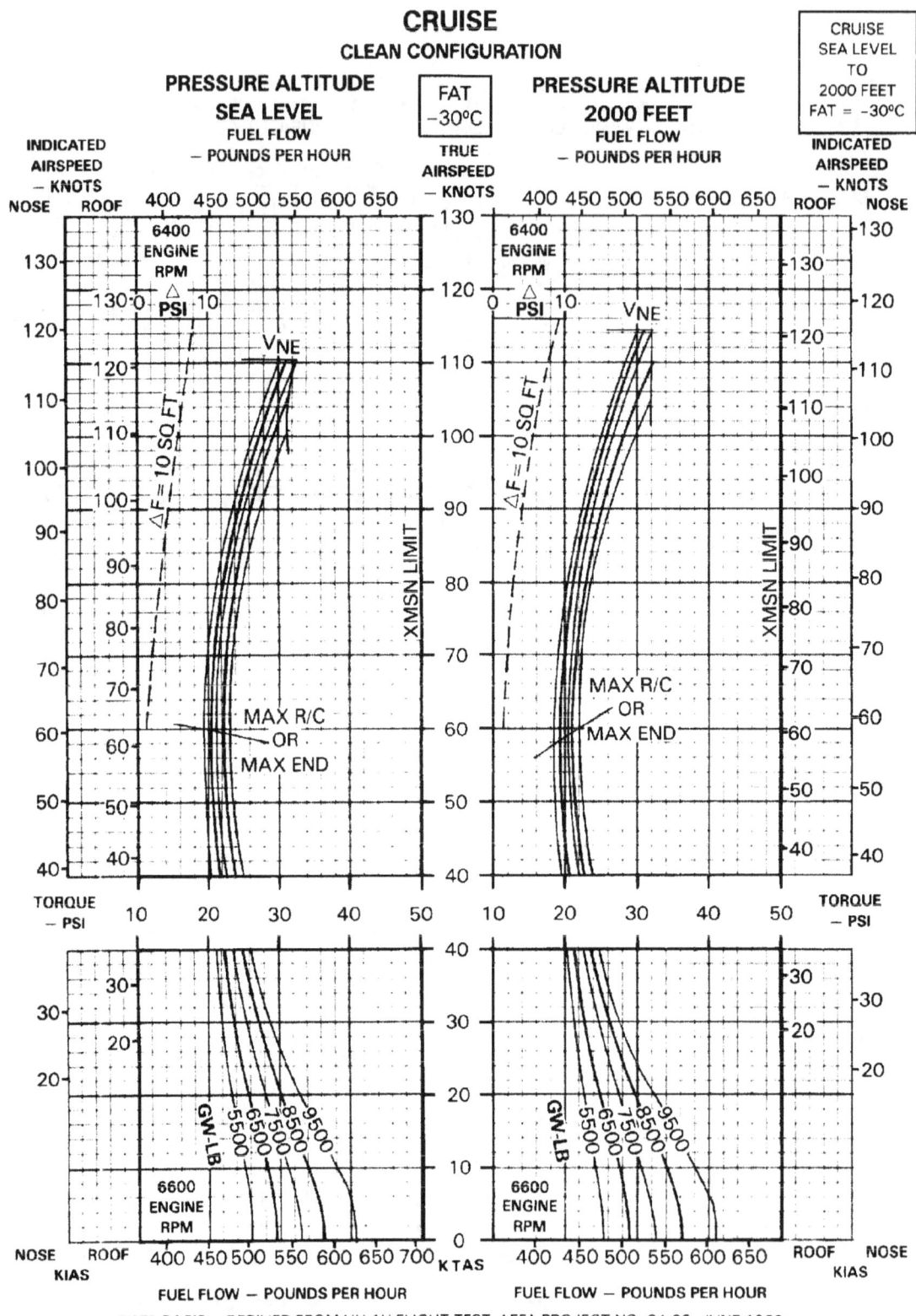

Figure 7.1-6. Cruise chart (Sheet 1 of 23)

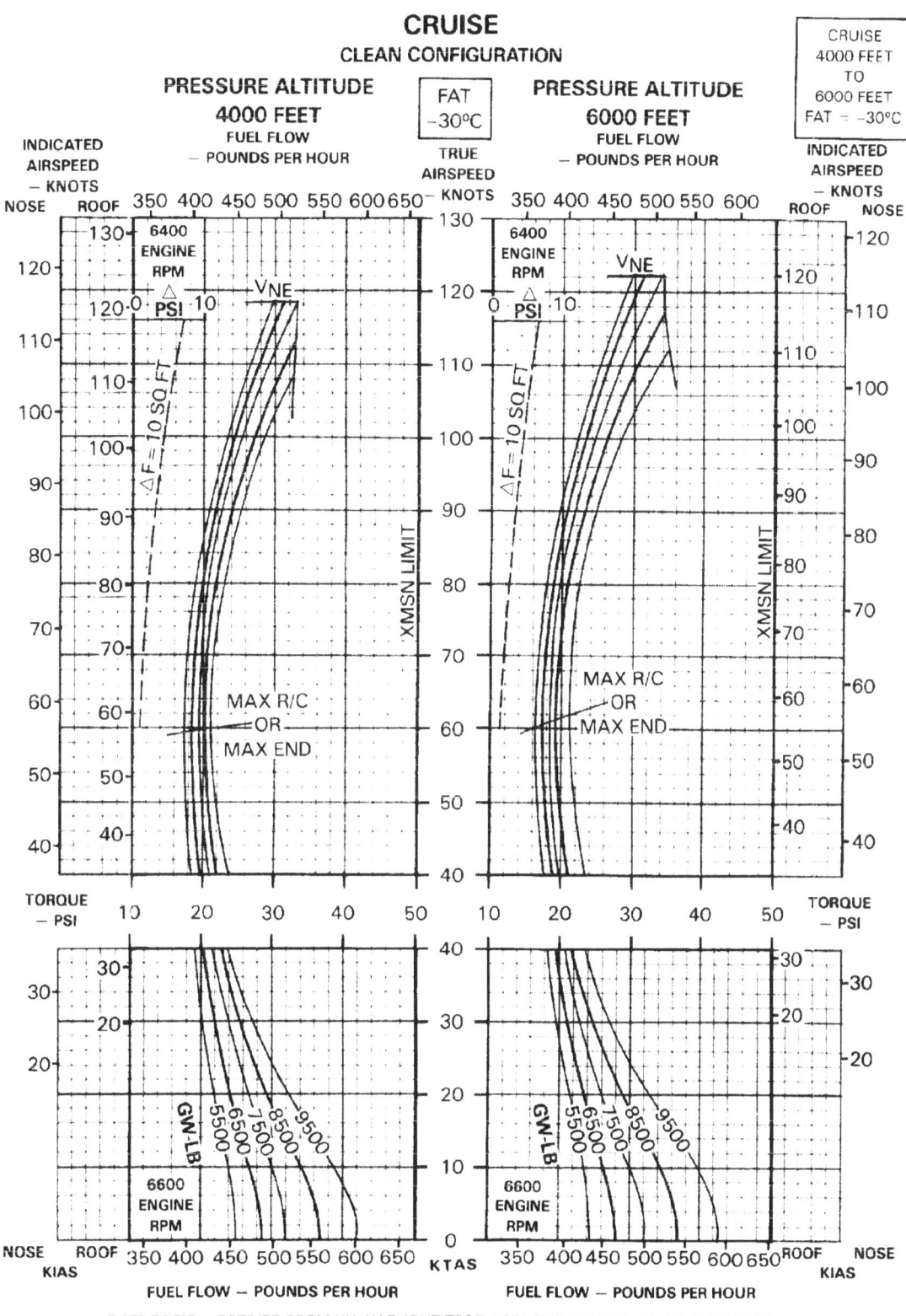

Figure 7.1-6. Cruise chart (Sheet 2 of 23)

EXAMPLE

WANTED

CALIBRATED TORQUE REQUIRED FOR LEVEL FLIGHT, FUEL FLOW, INDICATED AIRSPEED

KNOWN

CLEAN CONFIGURATION
GROSS WEIGHT = 9500 POUNDS
PRESSURE ALTITUDE = 5000 FEET
FAT = - 30°C
DESIRED TRUE AIRSPEED = 100 KNOTS
ROOF MOUNTED PITOT TUBE SYSTEM

METHOD

LOCATE CHARTS FOR ALTITUDE AND/OR FREE AIR TEMPERATURES ABOVE AND BELOW KNOWN CONDITIONS. ENTER EACH CHART AT 100 KNOTS TRUE AIRSPEED AND READ INDICATED AIRSPEED. MOVE LATERALLY BACK TO INTERSECT 9500 POUNDS GROSS WEIGHT CURVE, THEN PROJECT VERTICALLY TO READ CALIBRATED TORQUE AND FUEL FLOW ON EACH CHART. INTERPOLATE BETWEEN RESULTS DERIVED FROM CHARTS TO OBTAIN VALUES FOR KNOWN CONDITIONS AS FOLLOWS:

ALTITUDE	4000 FEET	6000 FEET	5000 FEET
FAT, °C	-30	-30	-30
CALIBRATED TORQUE, PSI	28.8	28.2	28.6
FUEL FLOW, POUNDS/HOUR	480	460	470
INDICATED AIRSPEED, KNOTS	102	98	100

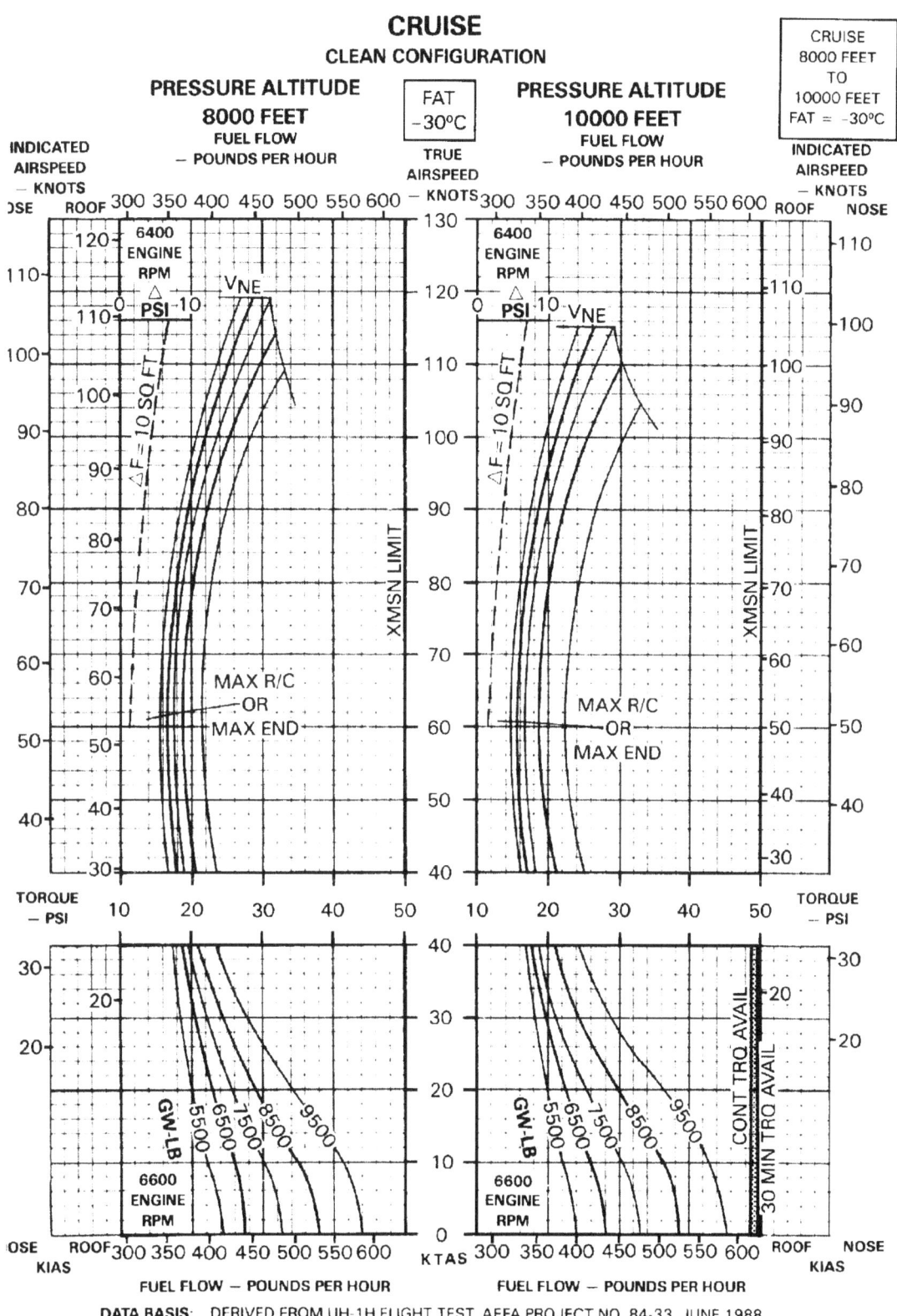

Figure 7.1-6. Cruise chart (Sheet 3 of 23)

EXAMPLE

WANTED

SPEED FOR MAXIMUM RANGE, CALIBRATED TORQUE REQUIRED AND FUEL FLOW AT MAXIMUM RANGE SPEED, AND SPEED FOR MAXIMUM ENDURANCE

KNOWN

CLEAN CONFIGURATION
FAT = -30°C
PRESSURE ALTITUDE = 8000 FEET
GROSS WEIGHT = 7500 POUNDS
ROOF MOUNTED PITOT TUBE SYSTEM

METHOD

LOCATE APPROPRIATE CHART
FIND INTERSECTION OF 7500 POUND GROSS WEIGHT LINE WITH THE MAXIMUM RANGE LINE (DETERMINE THAT MAXIMUM RANGE IS LIMITED BY V_{NE}). FROM THIS INTERSECTION DETERMINE THE FOLLOWING:
TO READ SPEED FOR MAXIMUM RANGE:
  MOVE RIGHT, READ TRUE AIRSPEED = 120.8 KNOTS
  MOVE LEFT, READ INDICATED AIRSPEED = 114.0 KNOTS
TO READ FUEL FLOW REQUIRED FOR MAXIMUM RANGE:
  MOVE UP, READ FUEL FLOW = 475 POUNDS PER HOUR
TO READ CALIBRATED TORQUE REQUIRED FOR MAXIMUM RANGE:
  MOVE DOWN, READ CALIBRATED TORQUE REQUIRED = 32.0 PSI

FIND THE INTERSECTION OF 7500 POUNDS GROSS WEIGHT LINE WITH THE MAXIMUM ENDURANCE LINE FROM THIS INTERSECTION DETERMINE THE FOLLOWING:
TO READ SPEED FOR MAXIMUM ENDURANCE:
  MOVE RIGHT, READ TRUE AIRSPEED = 61.8 KNOTS
  MOVE LEFT, READ INDICATED AIRSPEED = 54.2 KNOTS

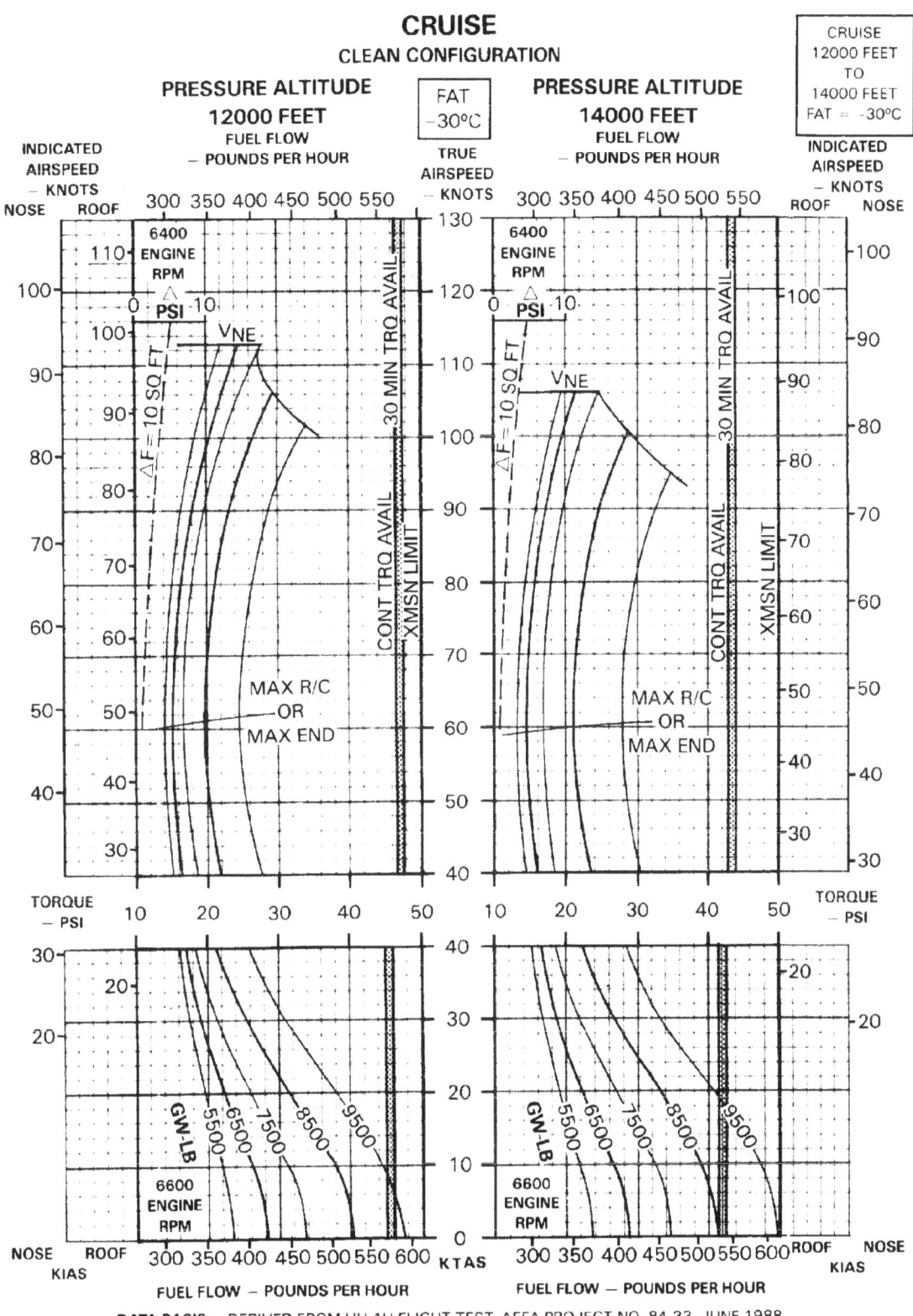

Figure 7.1-6. Cruise chart (Sheet 4 of 23)

EXAMPLE

WANTED

ADDITIONAL CALIBRATED TORQUE REQUIRED AND FUEL FLOW FOR EXTERNAL CONFIGURATION

KNOWN

Δ F FOR EXTERNAL DRAG CONFIGURATION = 4 SQUARE FEET
GROSS WEIGHT = 8500 POUNDS
FAT = - 30°C
PRESSURE ALTITUDE = 12000 FEET
TRUE AIRSPEED = 105 KNOTS

METHOD

ENTER TRUE AIRSPEED AT 105 KNOTS
MOVE LEFT TO 8500 POUNDS GROSS WEIGHT LINE AND FROM THIS INTERSECTION:
  MOVE UP TO FUEL FLOW SCALE AND READ 420 POUNDS PER HOUR
  MOVE DOWN, READ CALIBRATED TORQUE = 28.8 PSI
  MOVE LEFT TO 10 SQ. FT. Δ F LINE
    MOVE UP, READ 4.0 Δ PSI
DIVIDE 4 SQ. FT. BY 10 SQ. FT. TO OBTAIN A PERCENTAGE = 40%.
MULTIPLY 4 SQ. FT. BY 40% TO OBTAIN 1.6 Δ PSI
ADD 1.6 Δ PSI TO 28.8 PSI TO OBTAIN A TOTAL OF 30.4 PSI FOR EXTERNAL DRAG CONFIGURATION
FROM THIS POINT ON THE TORQUE SCALE, MOVE VERTICALLY TO THE FUEL FLOW SCALE AND READ 432 POUNDS PER HOUR.

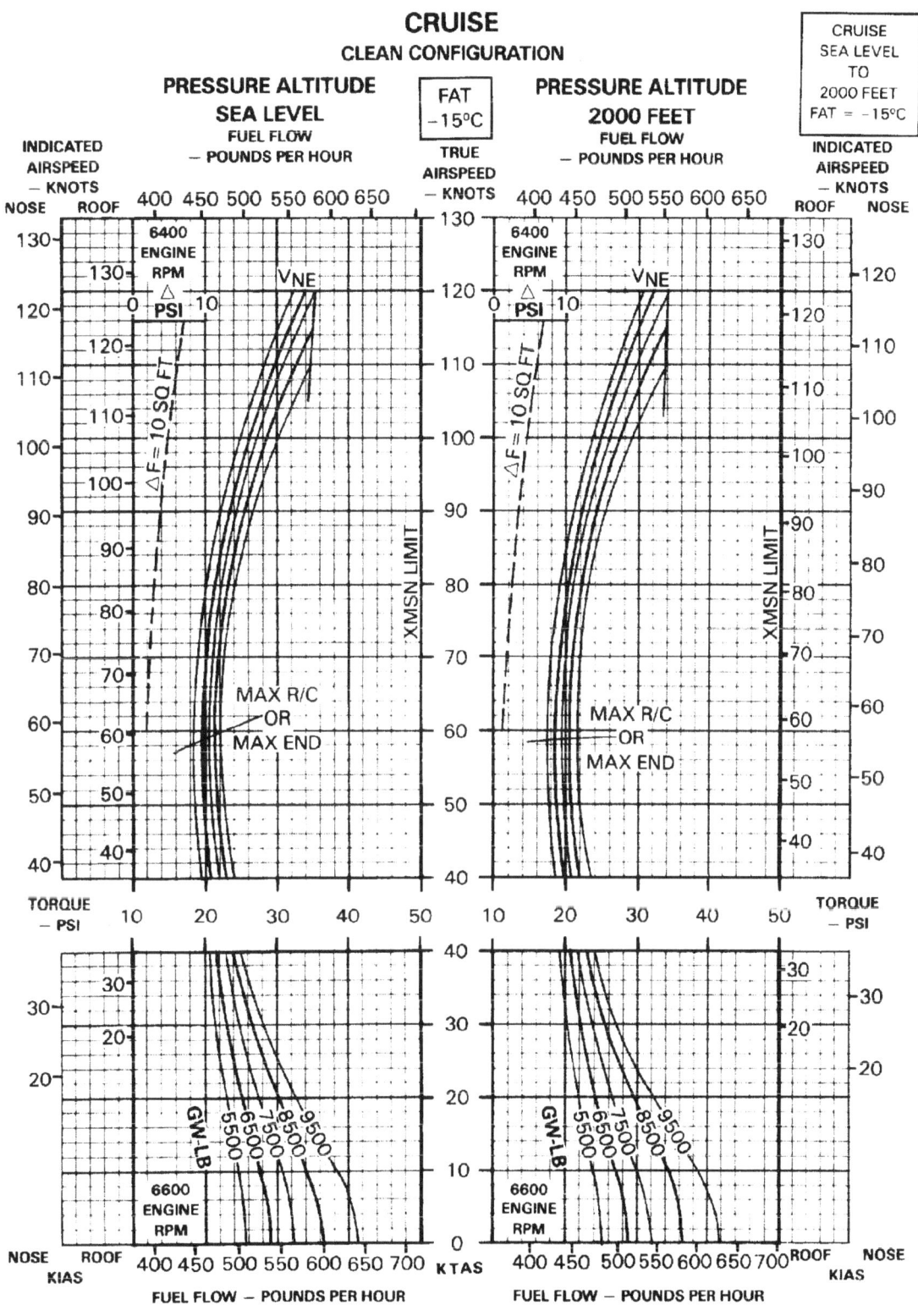

Figure 7.1-6. Cruise chart (Sheet 5 of 23)

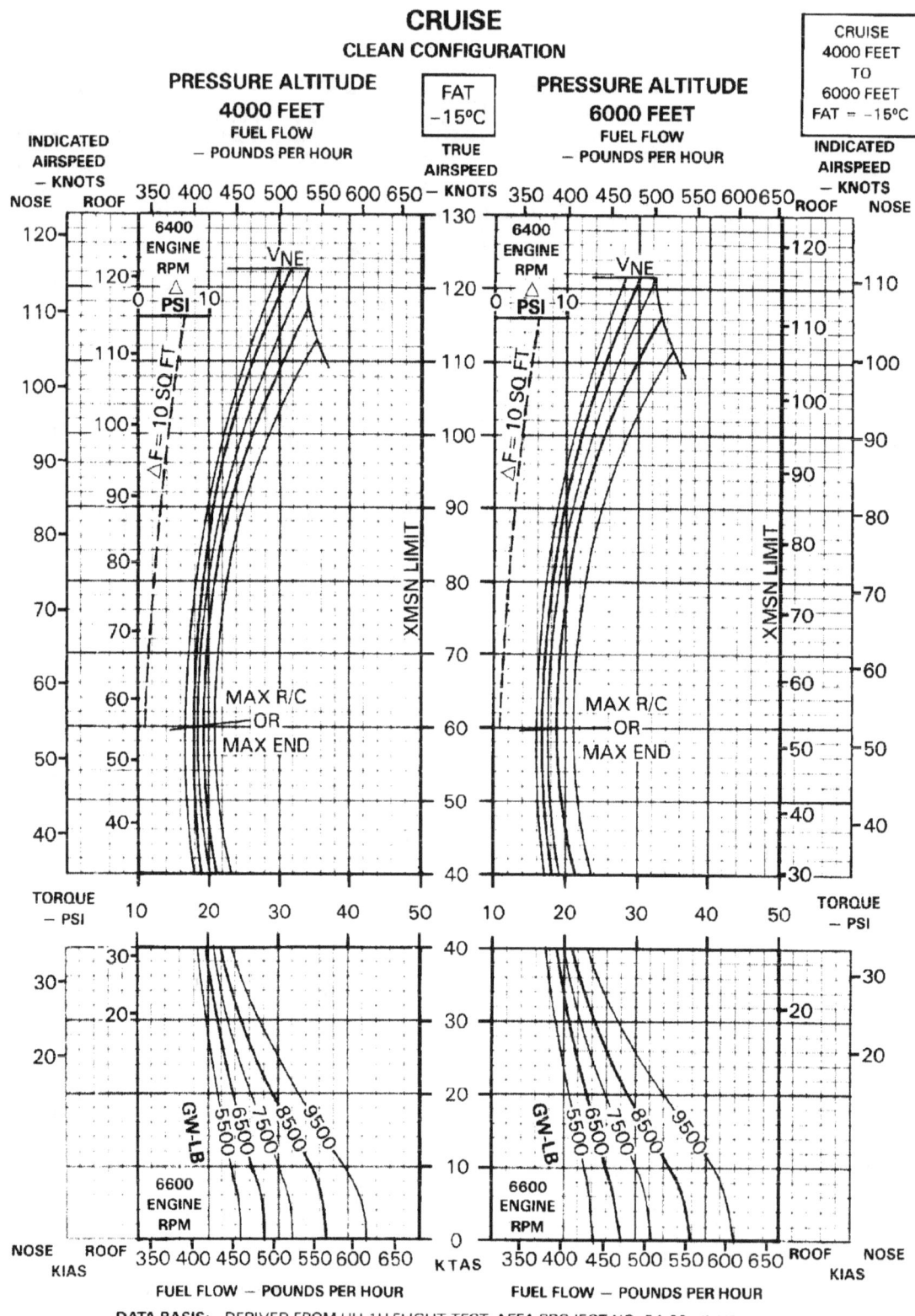

Figure 7.1-6. Cruise chart (Sheet 6 of 23)

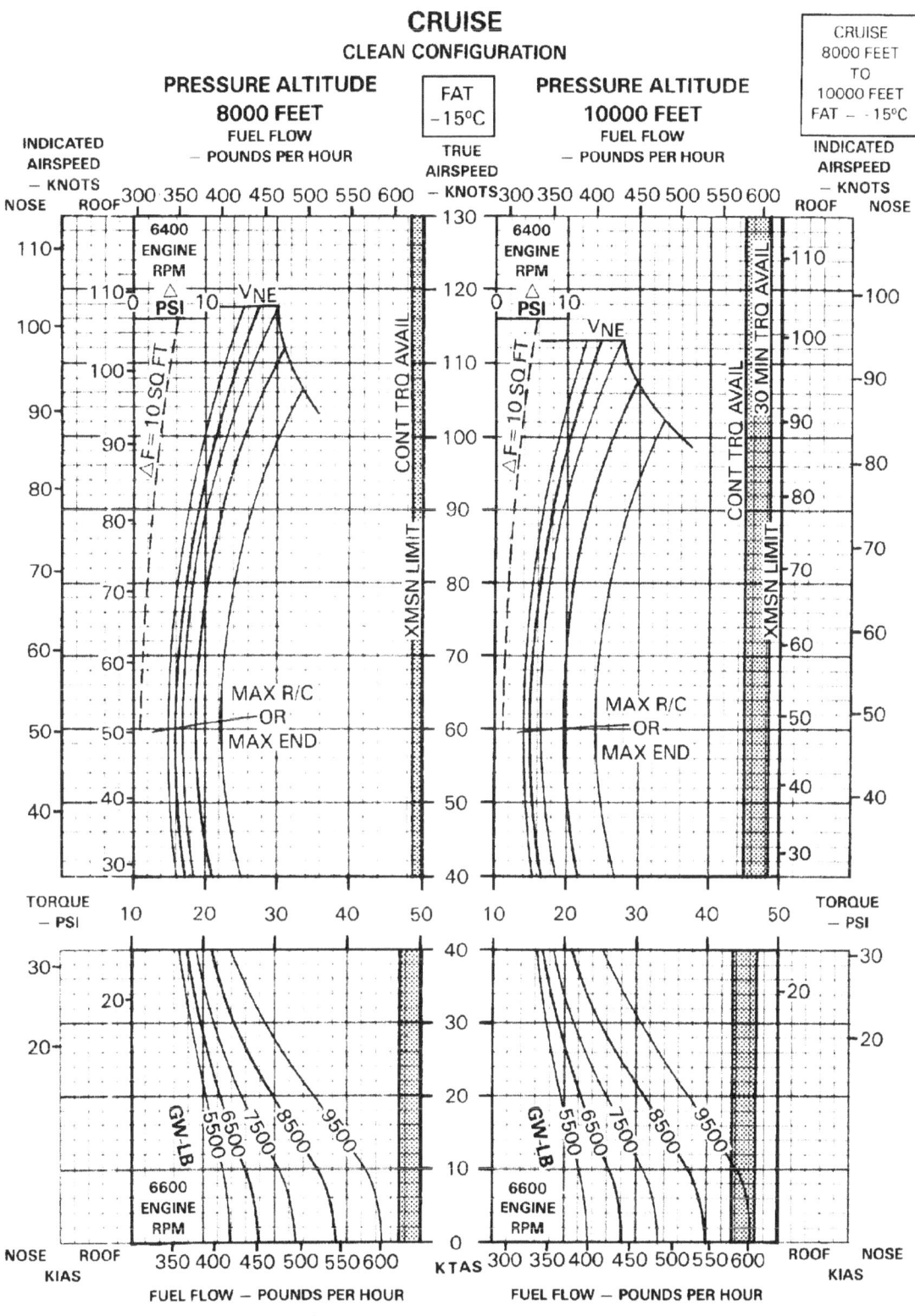

Figure 7.1-6. Cruise chart (Sheet 7 of 23)

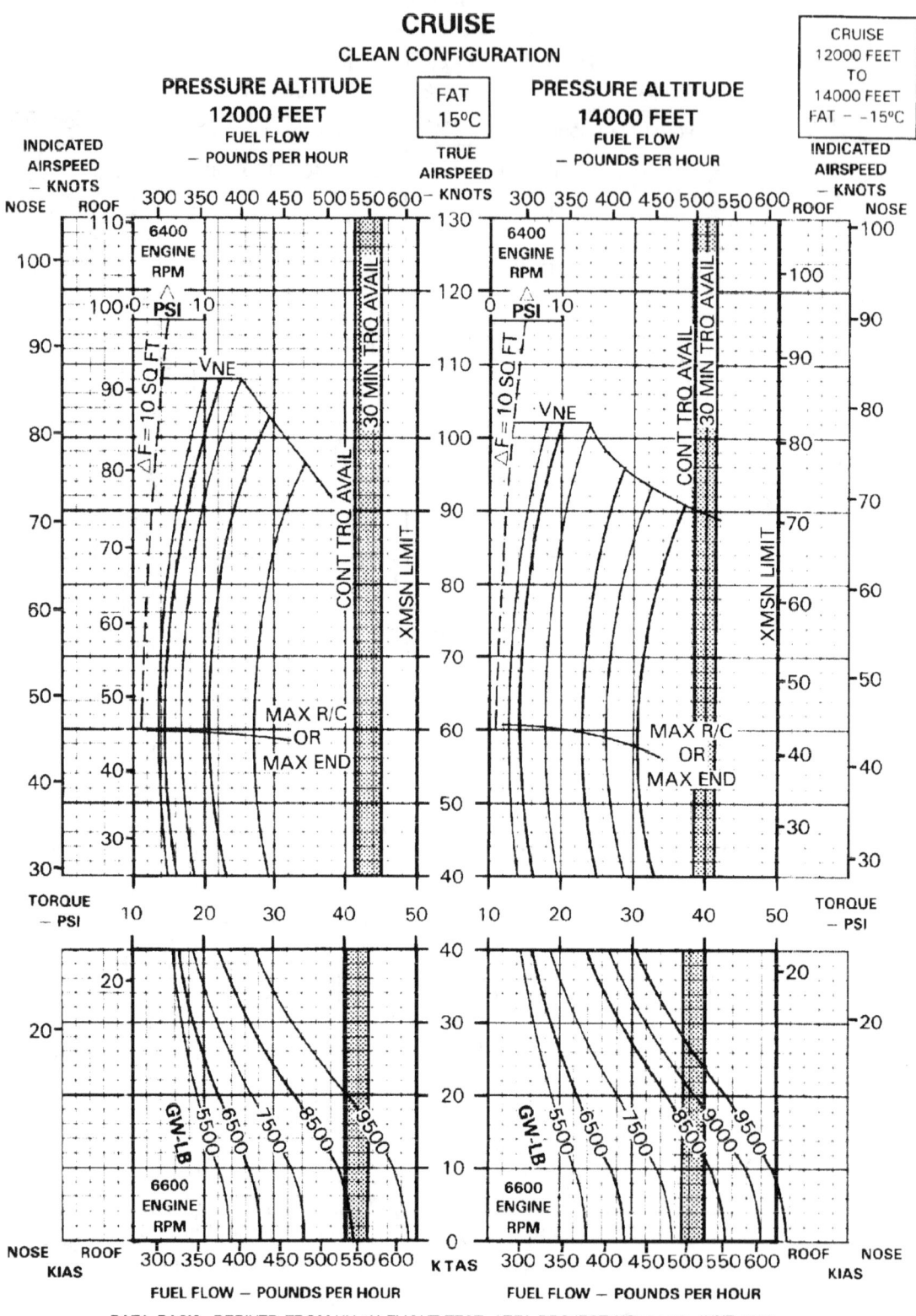

Figure 7.1-6. Cruise chart (Sheet 8 of 23)

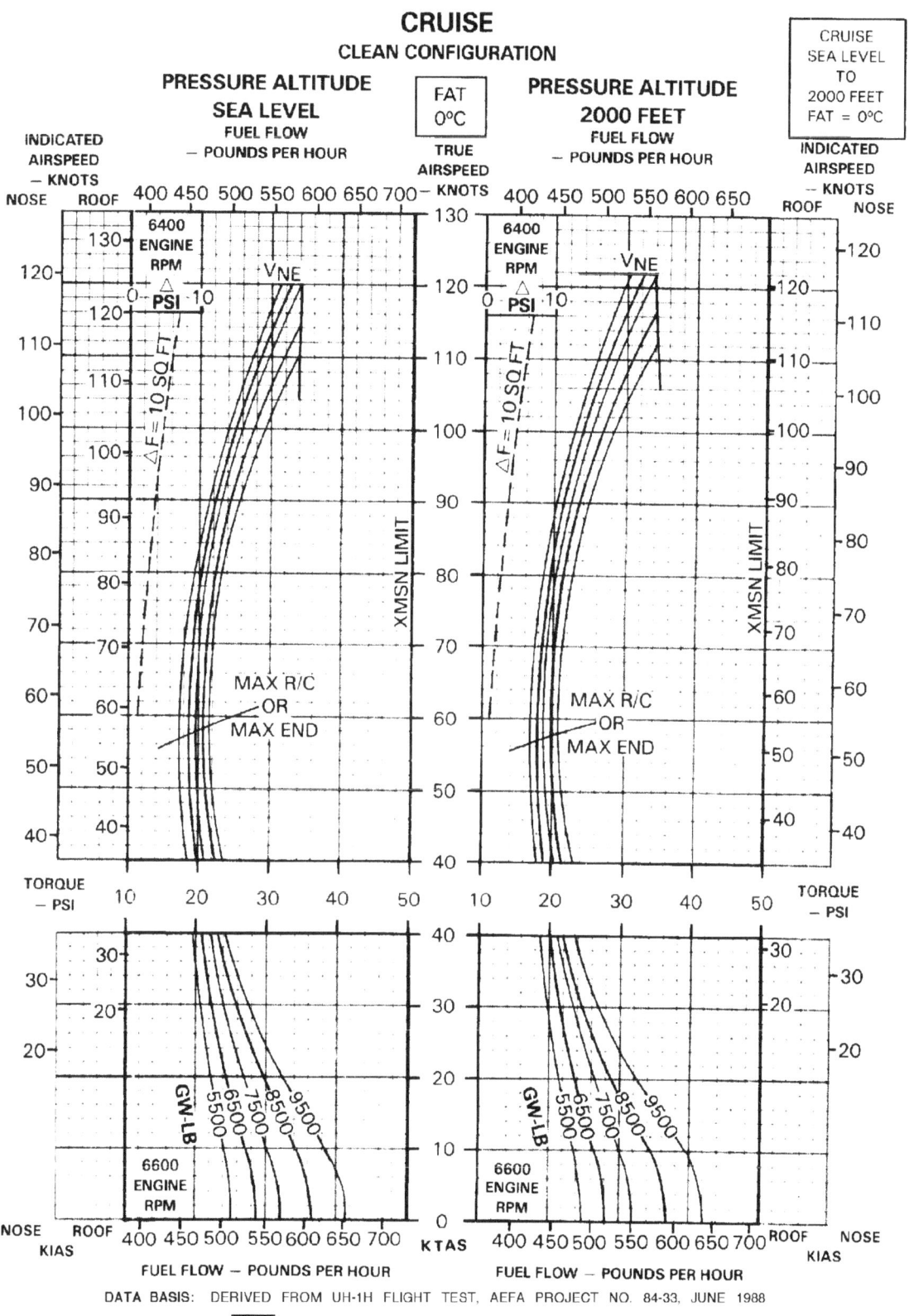

Figure 7.1-6. Cruise chart (Sheet 9 of 23)

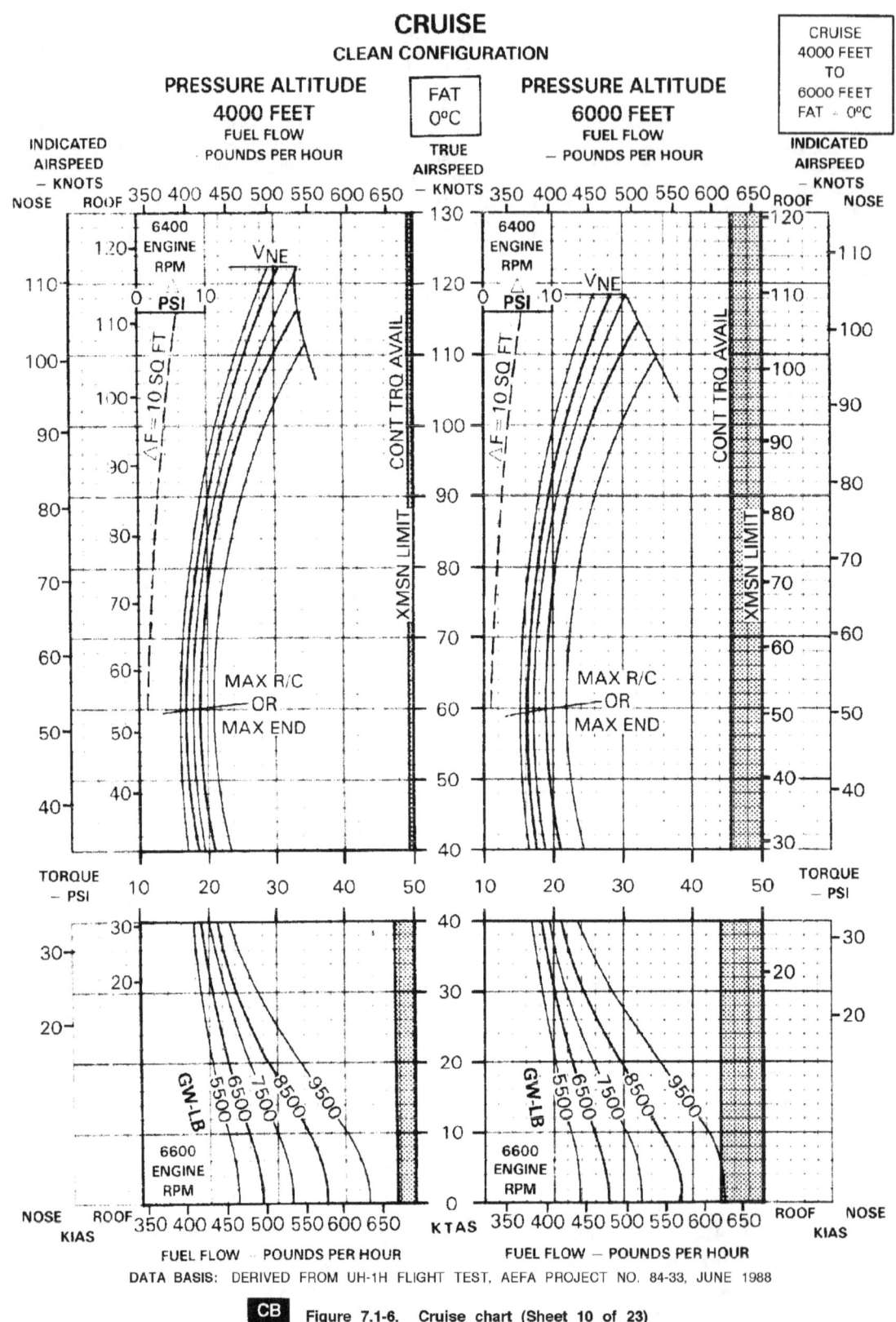

Figure 7.1-6. Cruise chart (Sheet 10 of 23)

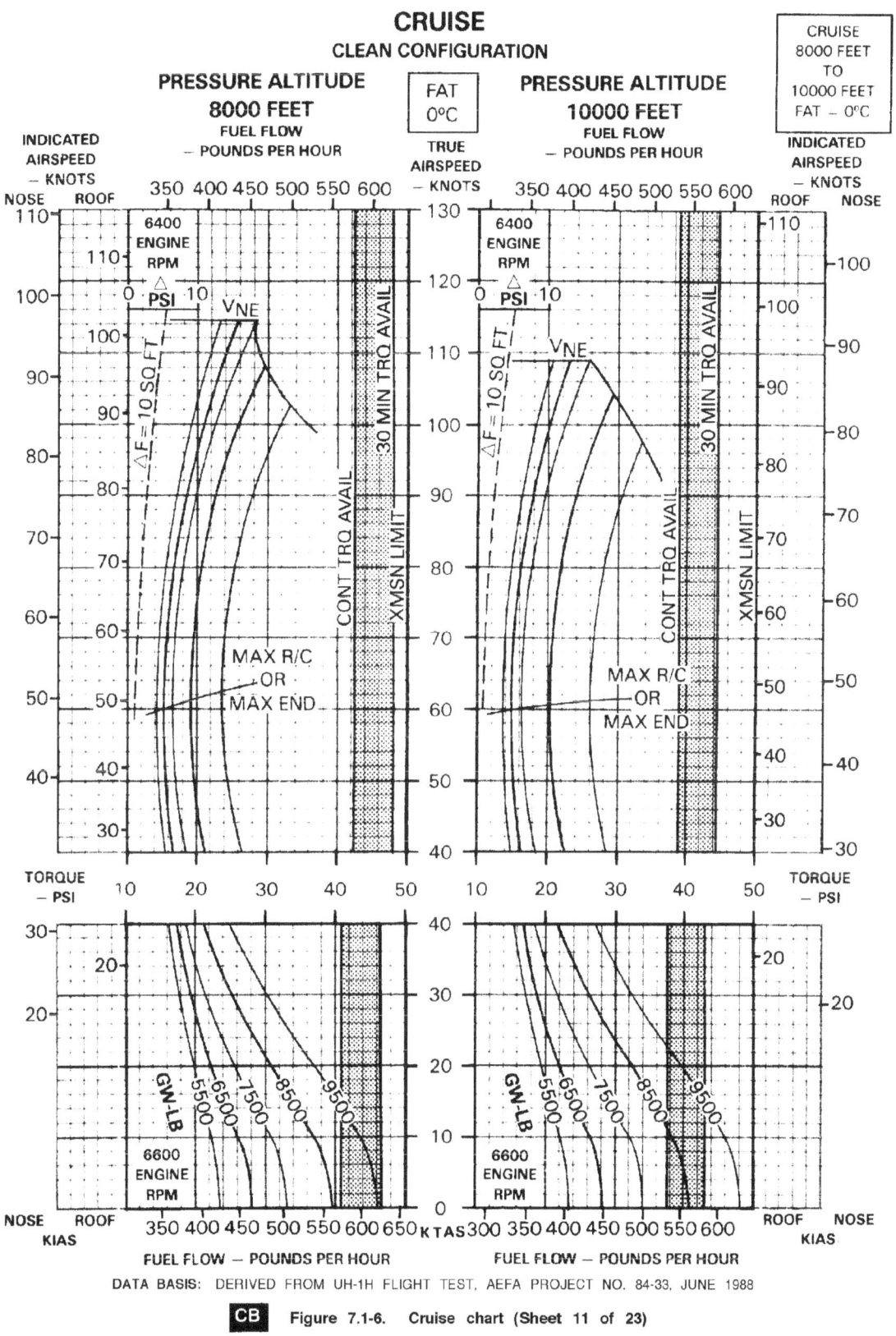

Figure 7.1-6. Cruise chart (Sheet 11 of 23)

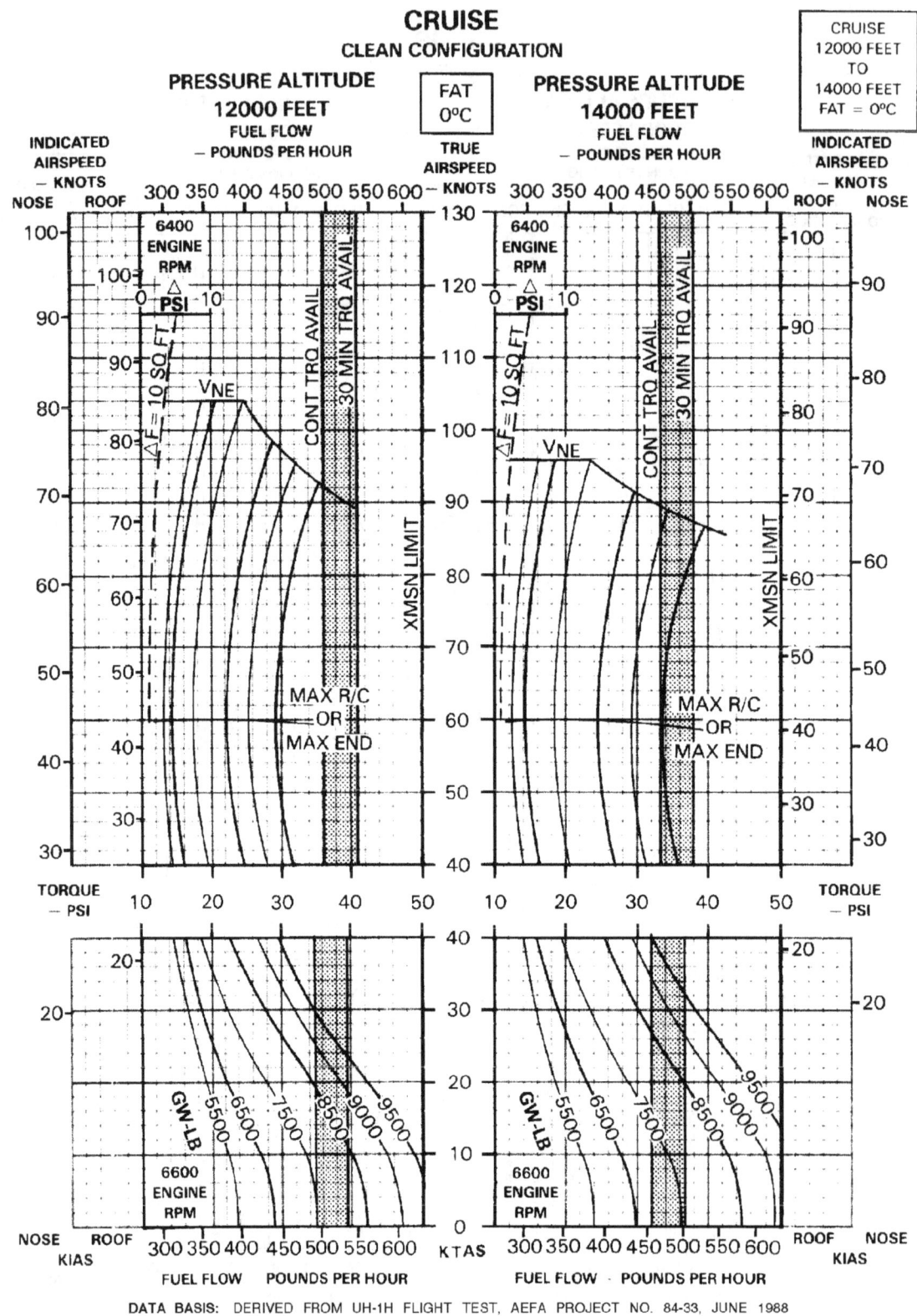

Figure 7.1-6. Cruise chart (Sheet 12 of 23)

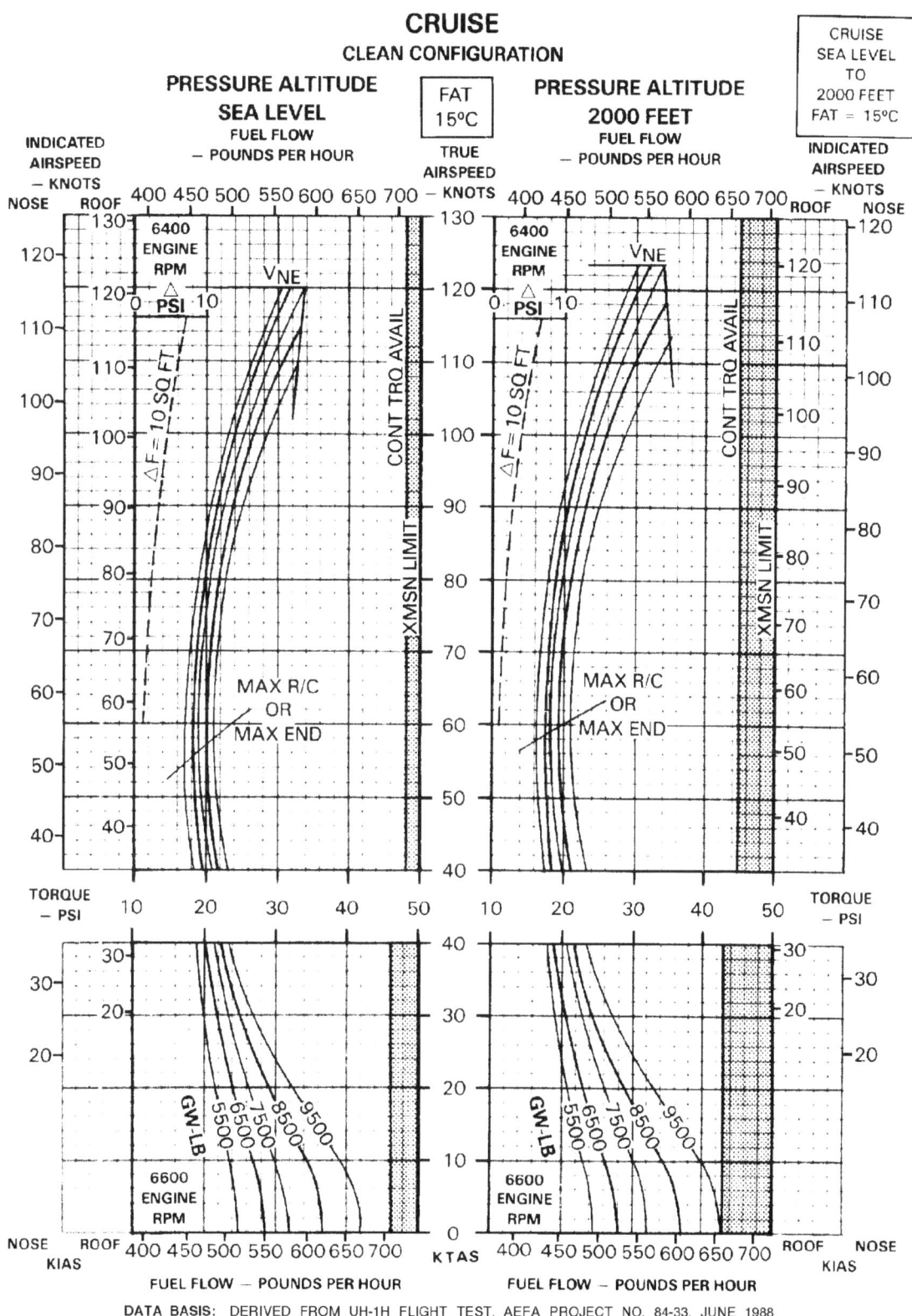

Figure 7.1-6. Cruise chart (Sheet 13 of 23)

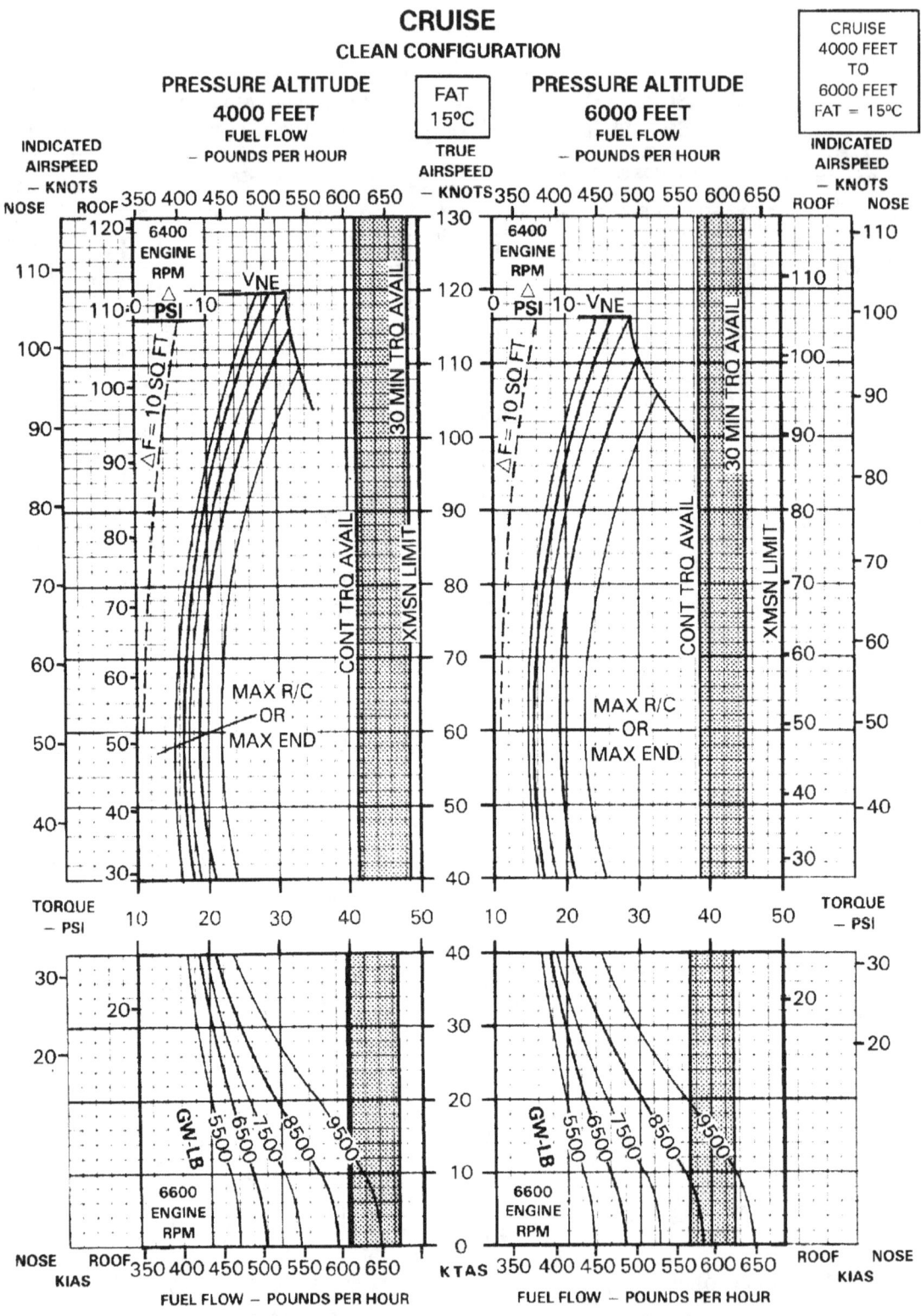

Figure 7.1-6. Cruise chart (Sheet 14 of 23)

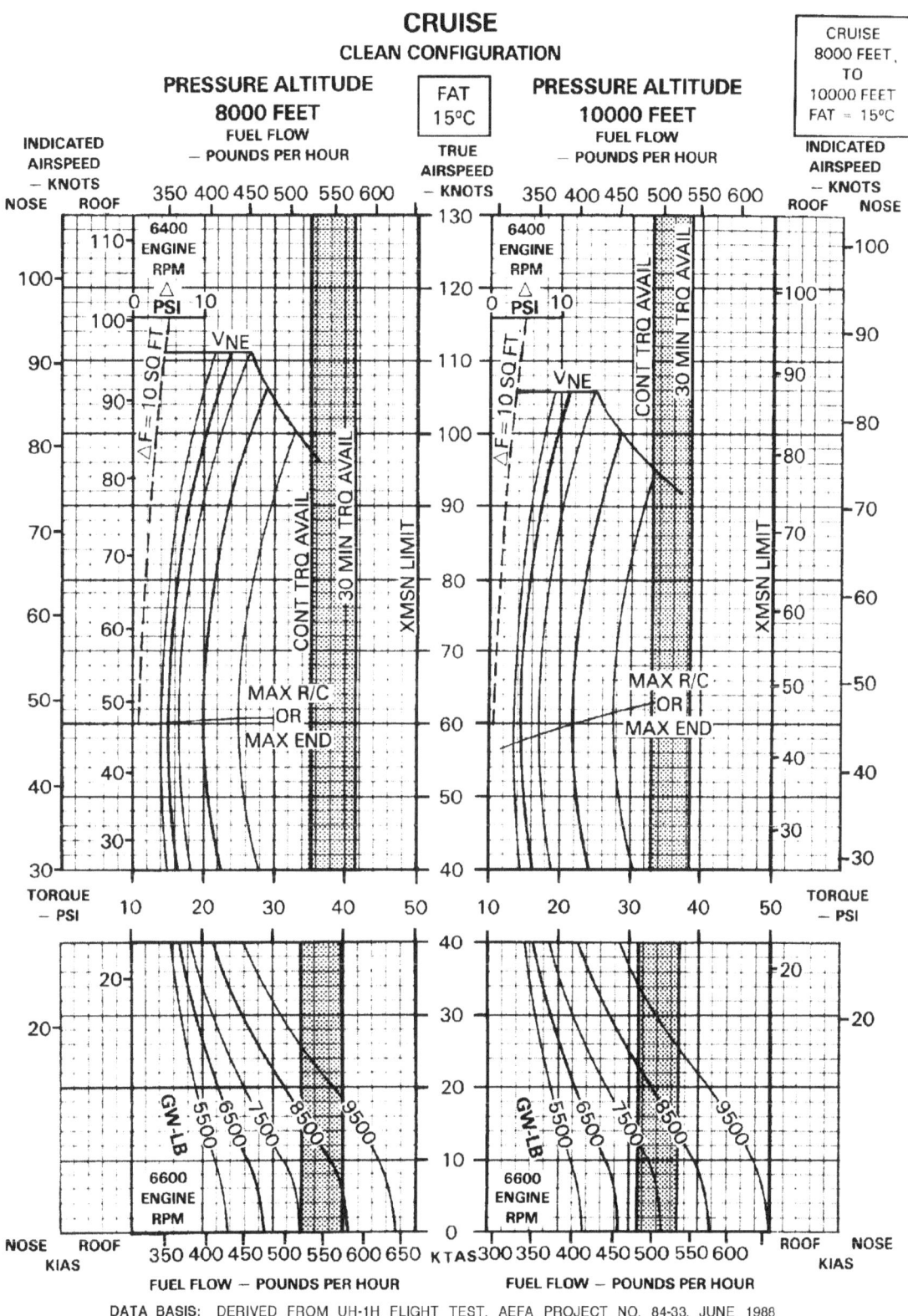

Figure 7.1-6. Cruise chart (Sheet 15 of 23)

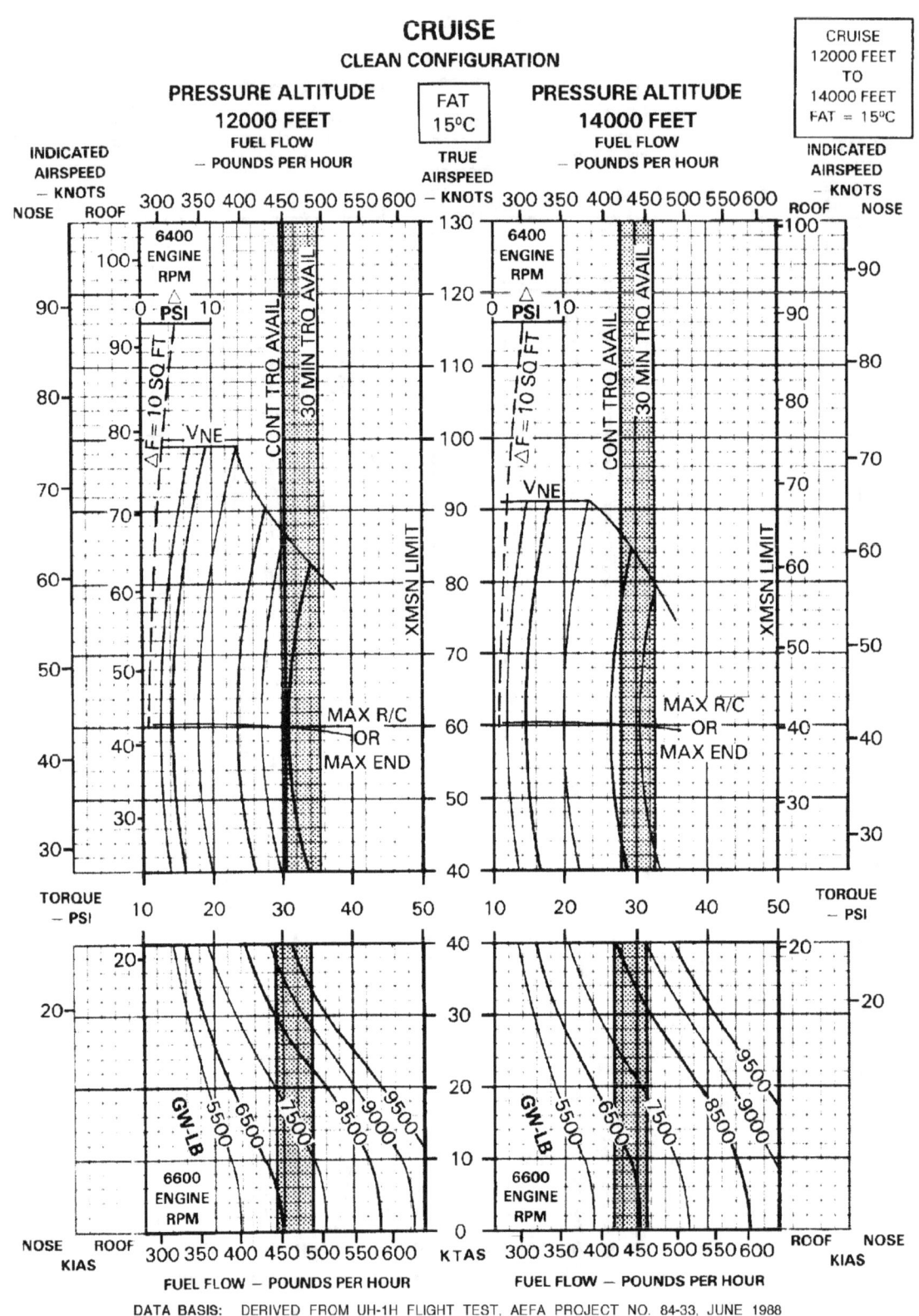

Figure 7.1-6. Cruise chart (Sheet 16 of 23)

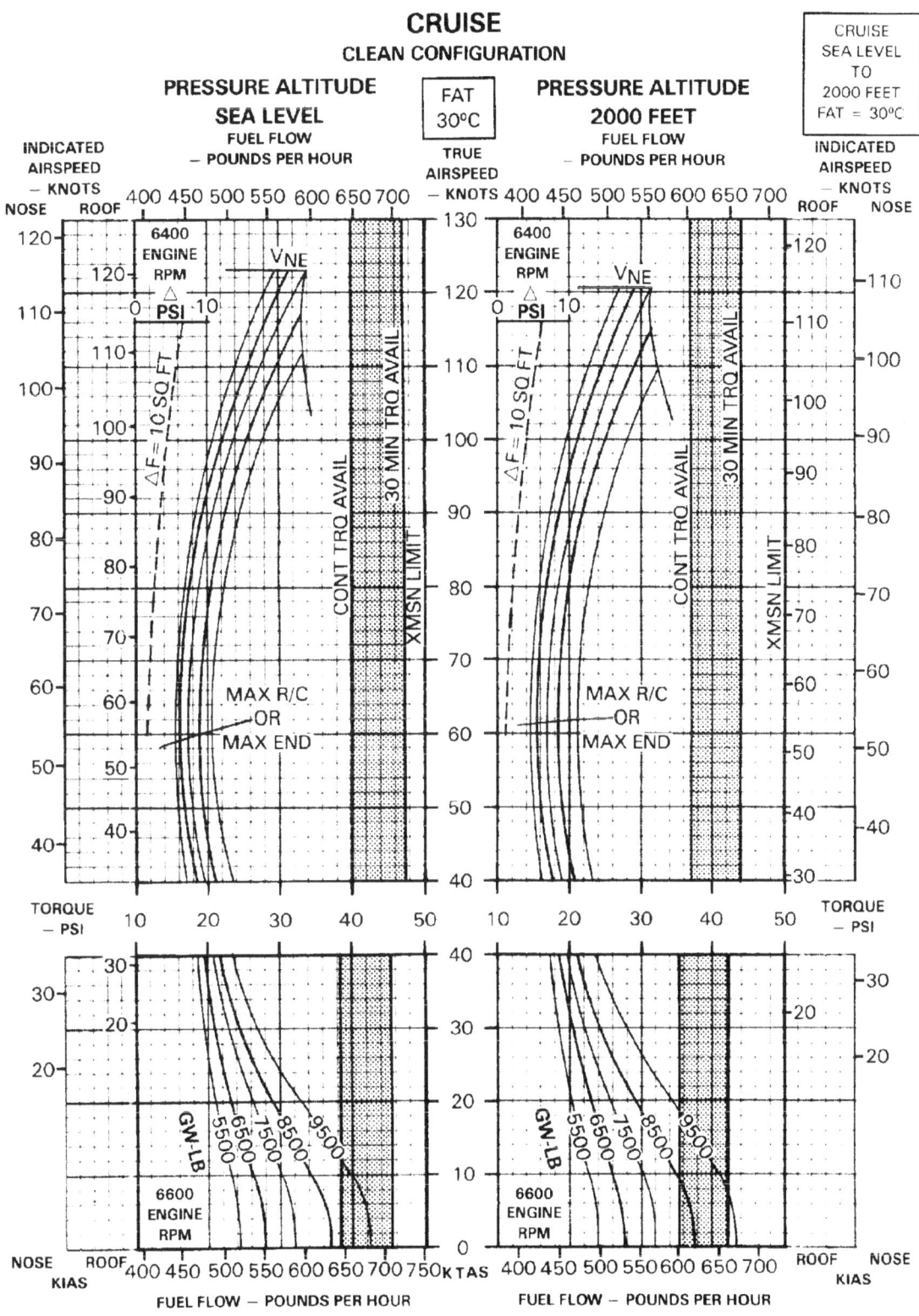

Figure 7.1-6. Cruise chart (Sheet 17 of 23)

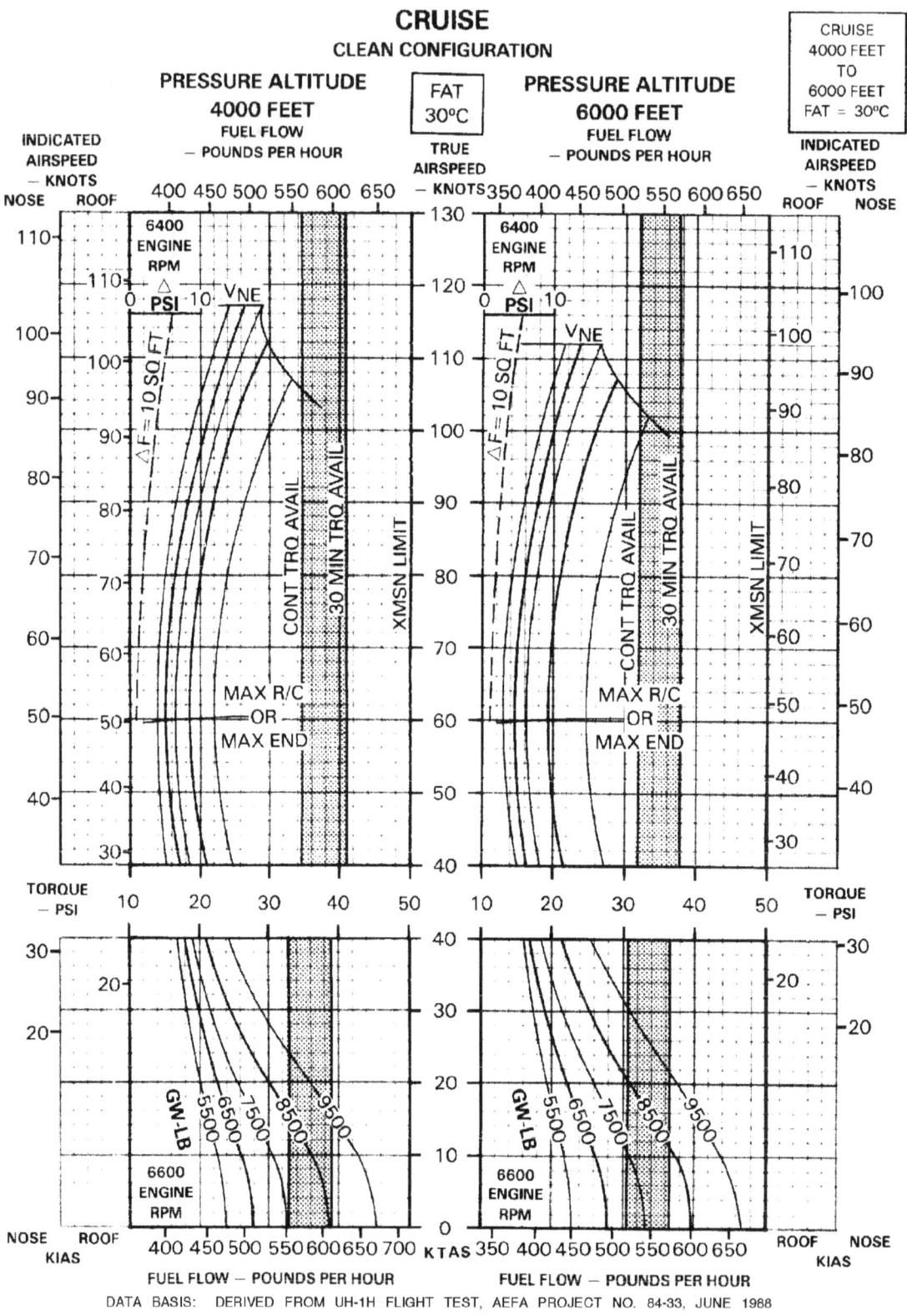

Figure 7.1-6. Cruise chart (Sheet 18 of 23)

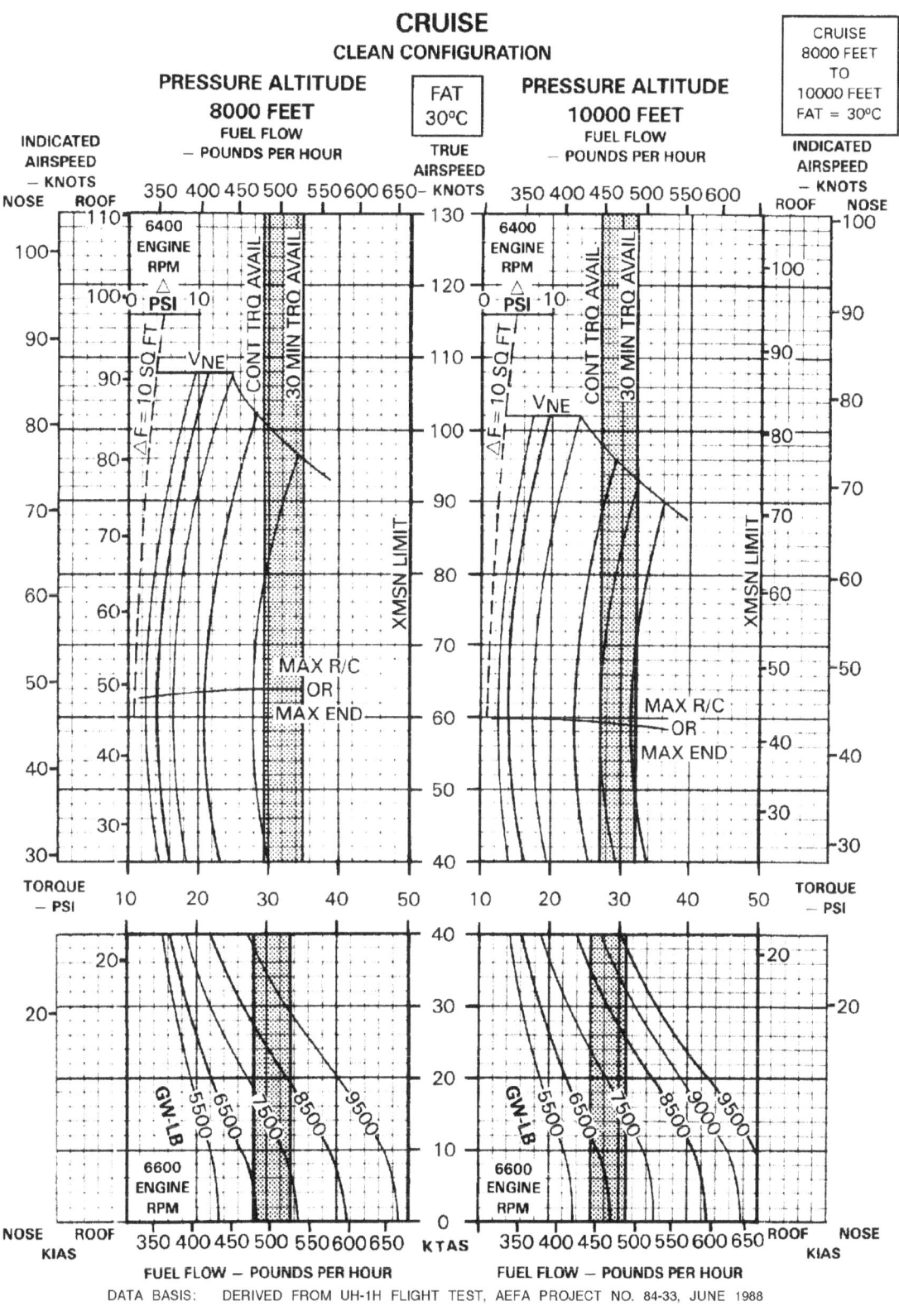

Figure 7.1-6. Cruise chart (Sheet 19 of 23)

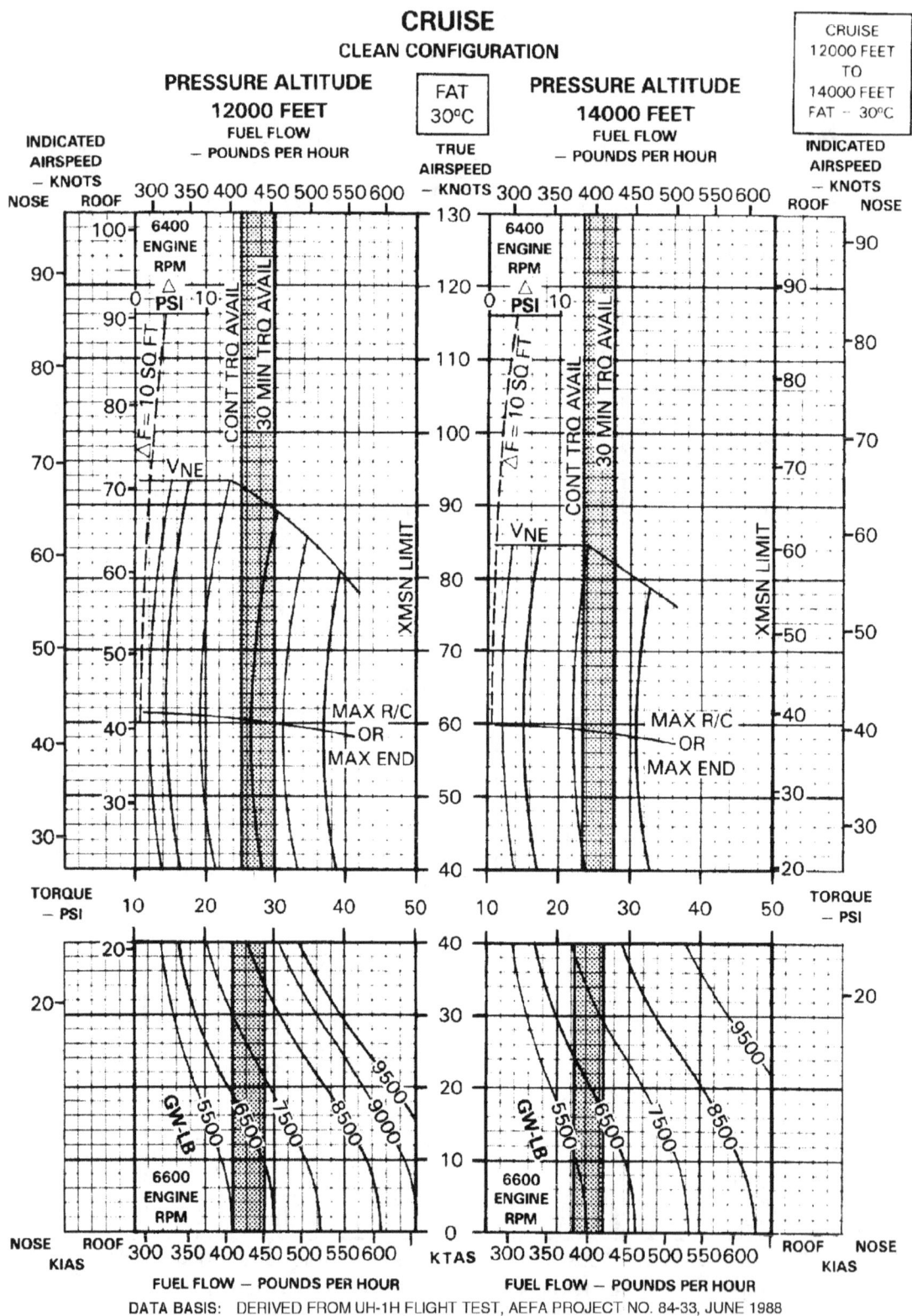

Figure 7.1-6. Cruise chart (Sheet 20 of 23)

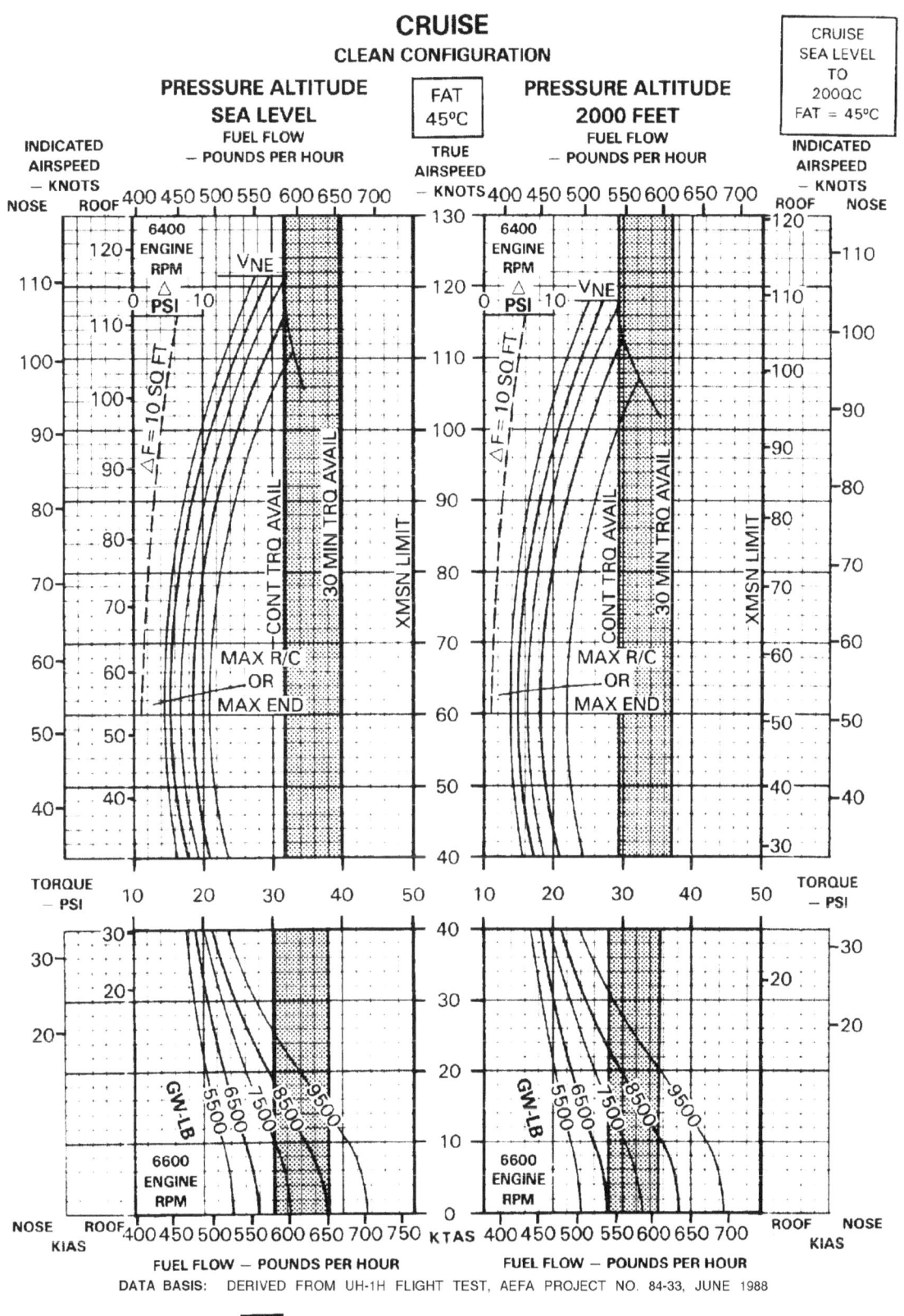

Figure 7.1-6. Cruise chart (Sheet 21 of 23)

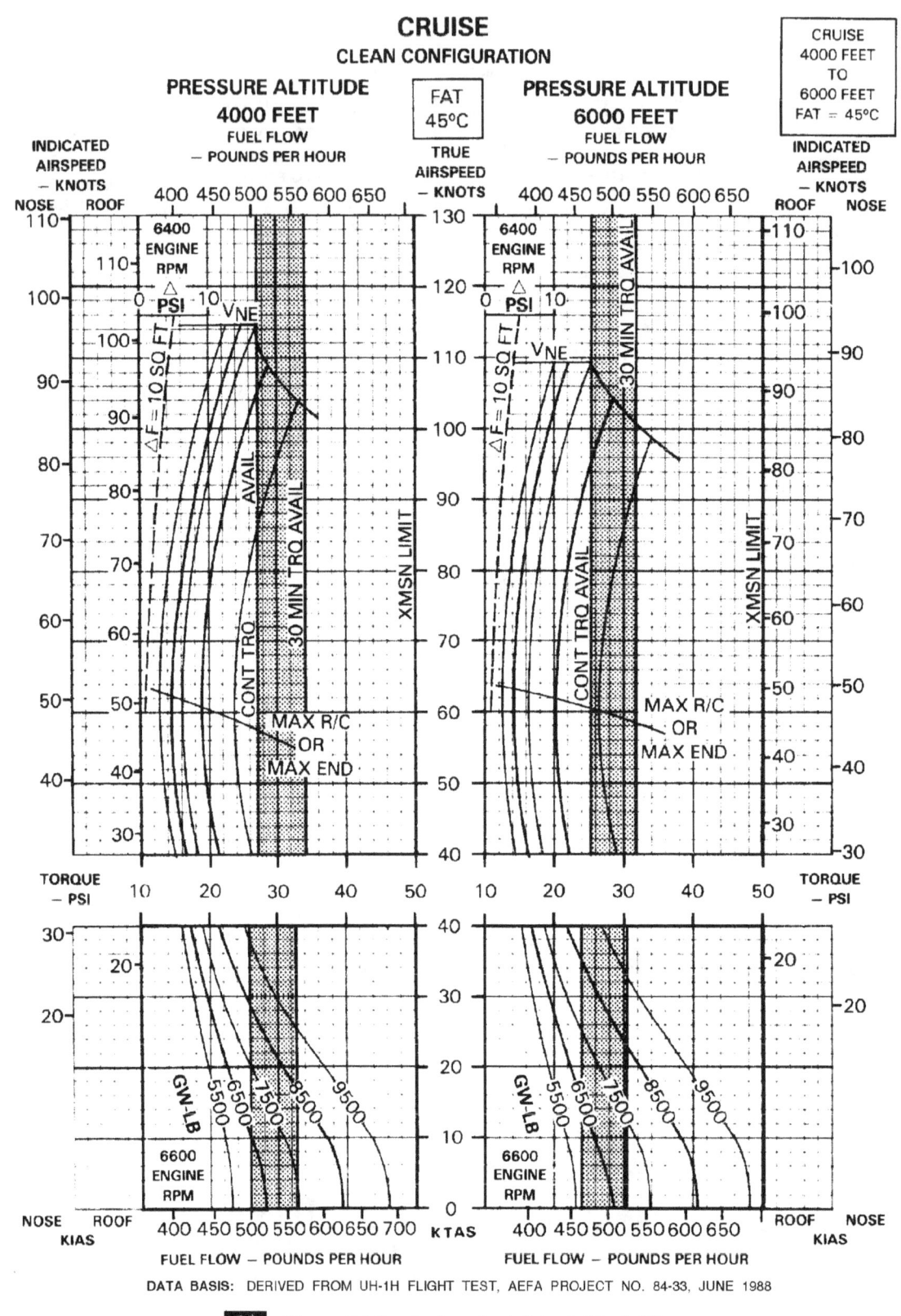

Figure 7.1-6. Cruise chart (Sheet 22 of 23)

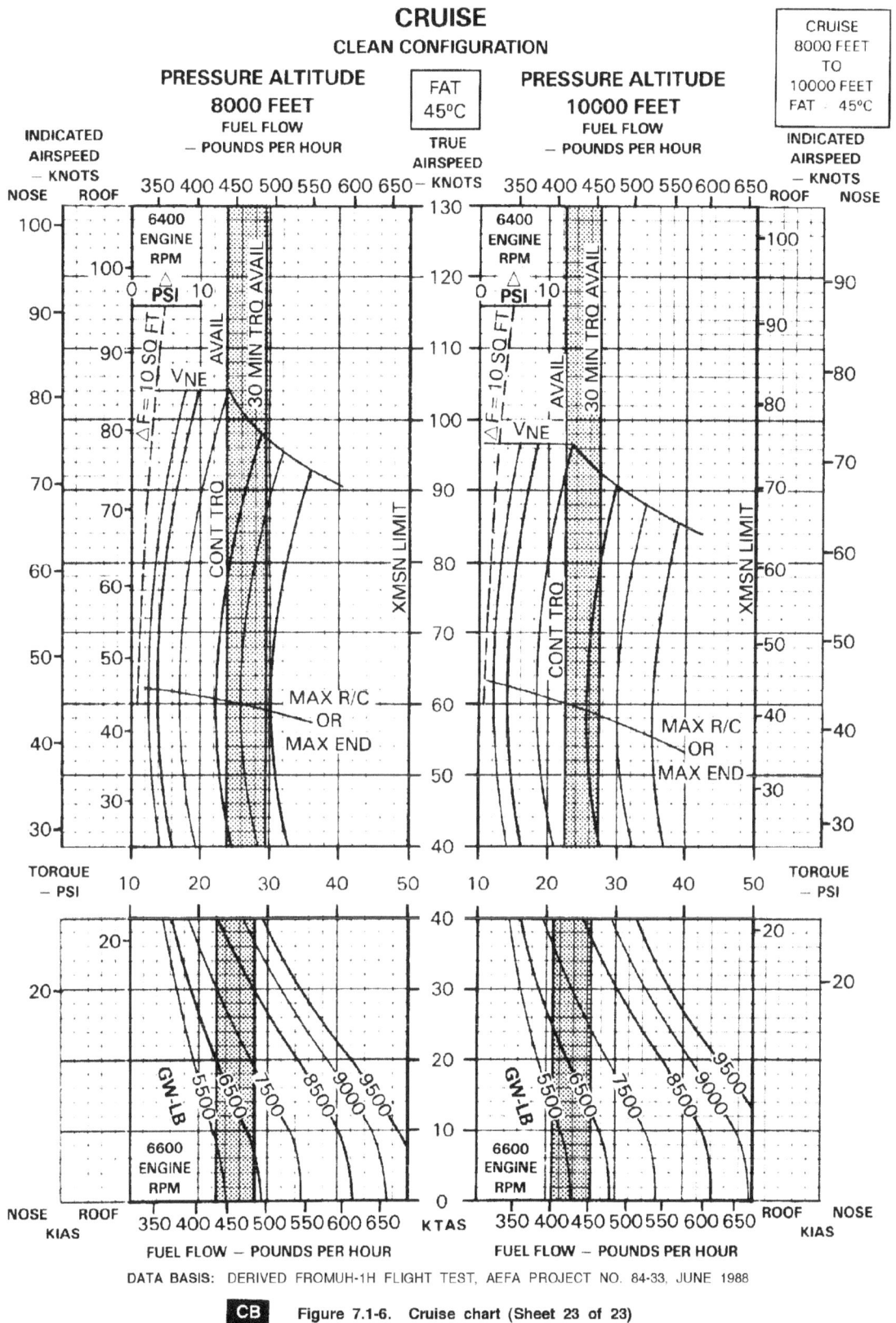

Figure 7.1-6. Cruise chart (Sheet 23 of 23)

TM 55-1520-210-10

DRAG

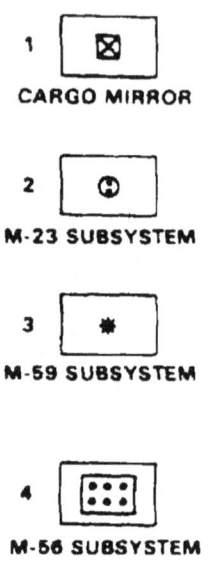

NOTE

The IR Scoup Suppressor has a drag of two square feet.

Figure 7.1-7. Drag Chart (Sheet 1 of 2)

EXAMPLE A

WANTED

CHANGE IN TORQUE REQUIRED DUE TO EQUIVALENT FLAT PLATE DRAG AREA CHANGE (ΔF) FROM CLEAN (BASELINE) CONFIGURATION TO AN M-56 SUBSYSTEM CONFIGURATION

KNOWN

ΔF DRAG AREA CHANGE
TRUE AIRSPEED = 120 KNOTS
PRESSURE ALTITUDE = SEA LEVEL
FAT = 0°C

METHOD

ENTER DRAG AREA CHANGE
MOVE RIGHT TO TRUE AIRSPEED
MOVE DOWN TO PRESSURE ALTITUDE
MOVE LEFT TO FREE AIR TEMPERATURE
MOVE DOWN, READ CHANGE IN TORQUE = 12.3 PSI

EXAMPLE B

WANTED

INCREASE IN DRAG AREA DUE TO EXTERNAL CARGO

KNOWN

SHAPE OF EXTERNAL LOAD IS A CYLINDER WITH A FRONTAL AREA OF 6.8 SQ. FT. ΔF

METHOD

ENTER CHART AT SYMBOL FOR CYLINDER
MOVE DOWN TO 6.8 SQ. FT.
MOVE RIGHT, READ INCREASED DRAG AREA = 4 SQ. FT.

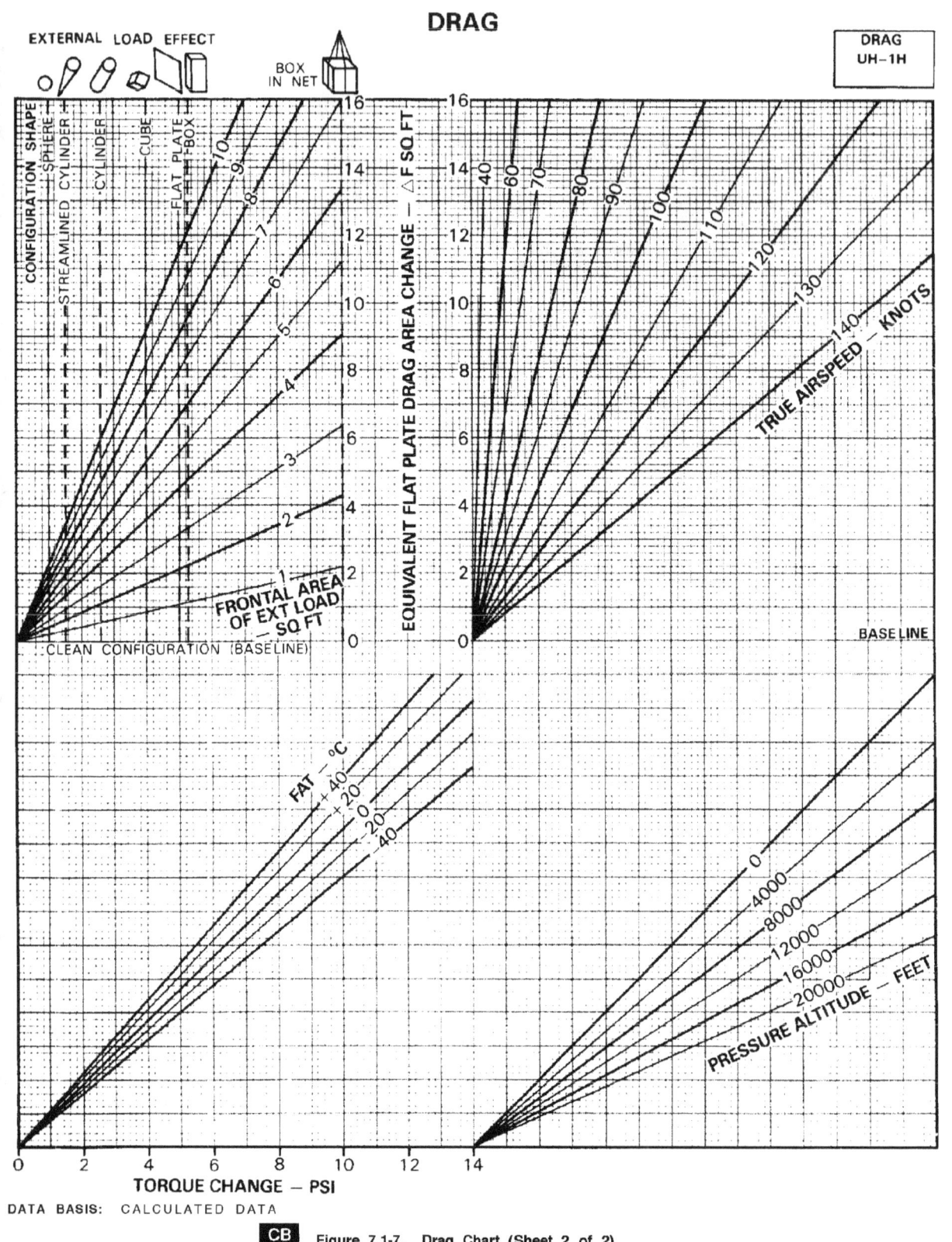

Figure 7.1-7. Drag Chart (Sheet 2 of 2)

EXAMPLE

WANTED

TIME DISTANCE AND FUEL

KNOWN

GROSS WEIGHT = 9000 POUNDS
INITIAL PRESSURE ALTITUDE = 4000 FEET
FINAL PRESSURE ALTITUDE = 10000 FEET
FAT = 17°C

METHOD

ENTER GROSS WEIGHT
MOVE UP TO INITIAL PRESSURE ALTITUDE
DETERMINE INITIAL FAT = 7 ° C
CALCULATE Δ FAT FROM STANDARD DAY FREE AIR TEMPERATURE
  (ACTUAL FAT MINUS STANDARD DAY FAT) = Δ FAT
  (17°C - 7°C) = 10°C
MOVE RIGHT TO ISA + 10 ° C LINE
DROP VERTICALLY, READ
  DISTANCE = 2.0 NAUTICAL MILES
  TIME = 2.0 MINUTES
CONTINUE DOWN TO ISA + 10 ° C FUEL LINE
MOVE LEFT, READ FUEL = 23 POUNDS

REENTER GROSS WEIGHT
MOVE UP TO FINAL PRESSURE ALTITUDE
MOVE RIGHT TO ISA + 10 ° C LINE
DROP VERTICALLY, READ
  DISTANCE = 5.5 NAUTICAL MILES
  TIME = 5.5 MINUTES
CONTINUE DOWN TO ISA + 10 ° C FUEL LINE
MOVE LEFT, READ FUEL = 63 POUNDS

FINAL TIME = (5.5 - 2.0) = 3.5 MINUTES
FINAL DISTANCE = (5.5 - 2.0) = 3.5 NAUTICAL MILES
FINAL FUEL = (63 - 23) = 40 POUNDS

TM 55-1520-210-10

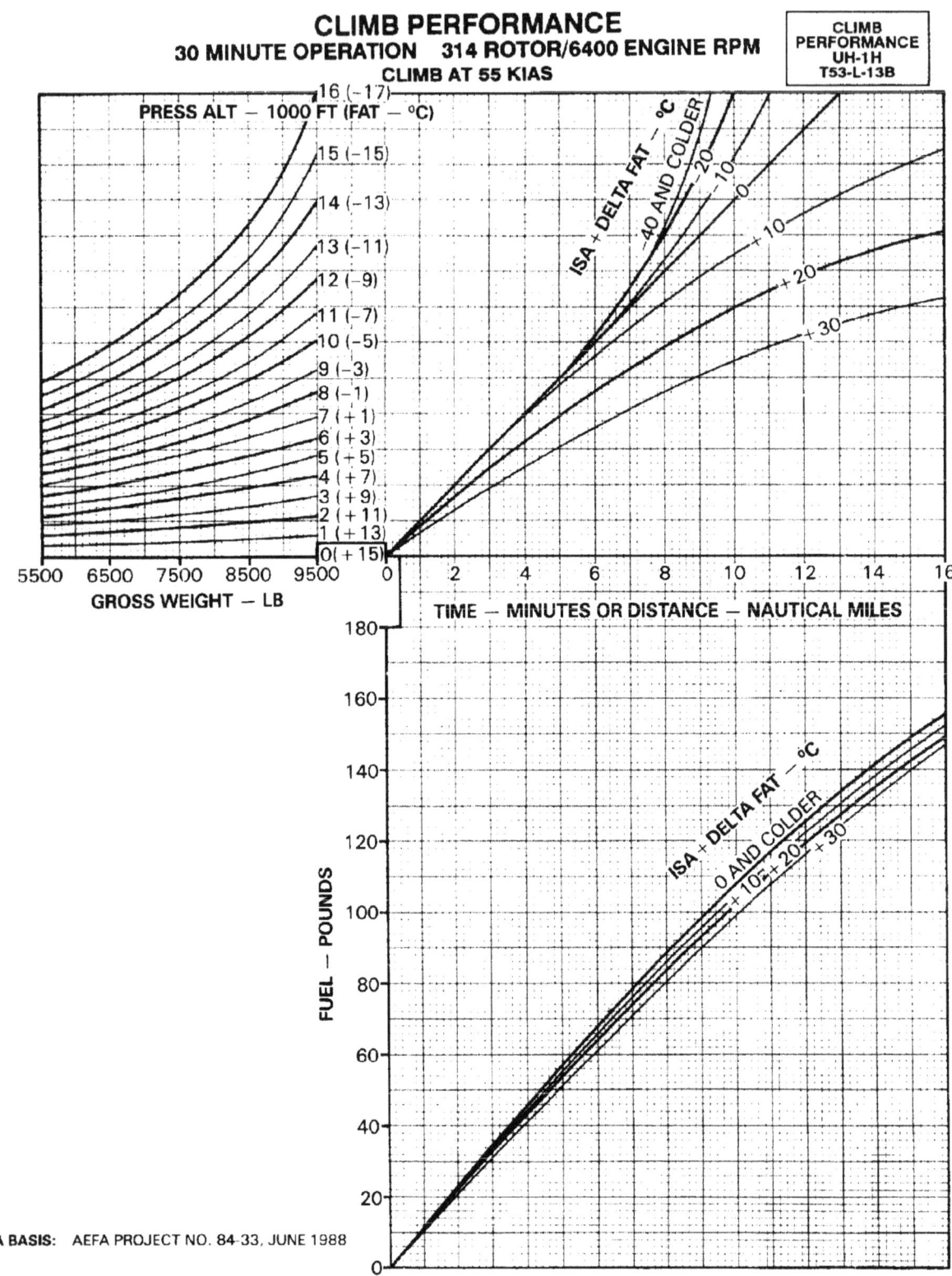

Figure 7.1-8. Climb chart (Sheet 1 of 2)

CLIMB – DESCENT

314 ROTOR/6400 ENGINE RPM

CLIMB – DESCENT
UH-1H
T53-L-13B

EXAMPLE

WANTED

CALIBRATED TORQUE CHANGE FOR DESIRED RATE OF CLIMB OR DESCENT

KNOWN

GROSS WEIGHT = 6000 POUNDS
DESIRED RATE OF CLIMB = 1200 FEET PER MINUTE

METHOD

ENTER RATE OF CLIMB
MOVE RIGHT TO GROSS WEIGHT
MOVE DOWN, READ CALIBRATED TORQUE CHANGE
= 12.5 PSI

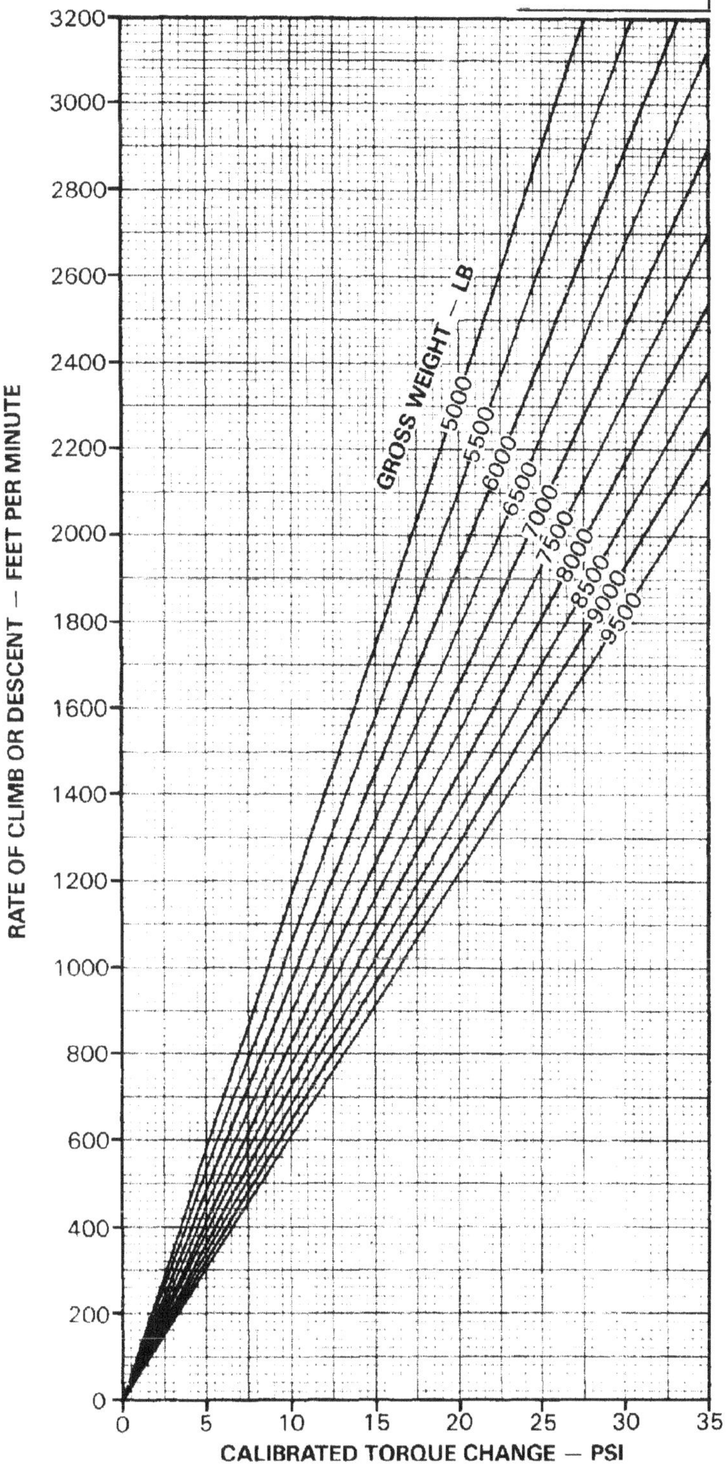

DATA BASIS: CALCULATED DATA, DECEMBER 1989

Figure 7.1-8. Climb chart (Sheet 2 of 2)

FLAT PITCH FUEL FLOW
JP-4 FUEL

FLAT PITCH
FUEL FLOW
UH-1H
T53-L-13B

EXAMPLE

WANTED

FUEL FLOW AT FLAT PITCH

KNOWN

PRESSURE ALTITUDE = 11000 FEET
F A T = 0°C

METHOD

ENTER PRESSURE ALTITUDE
MOVE RIGHT FAT
MOVE DOWN, READ FUEL FLOW = 254
POUNDS PER HOUR

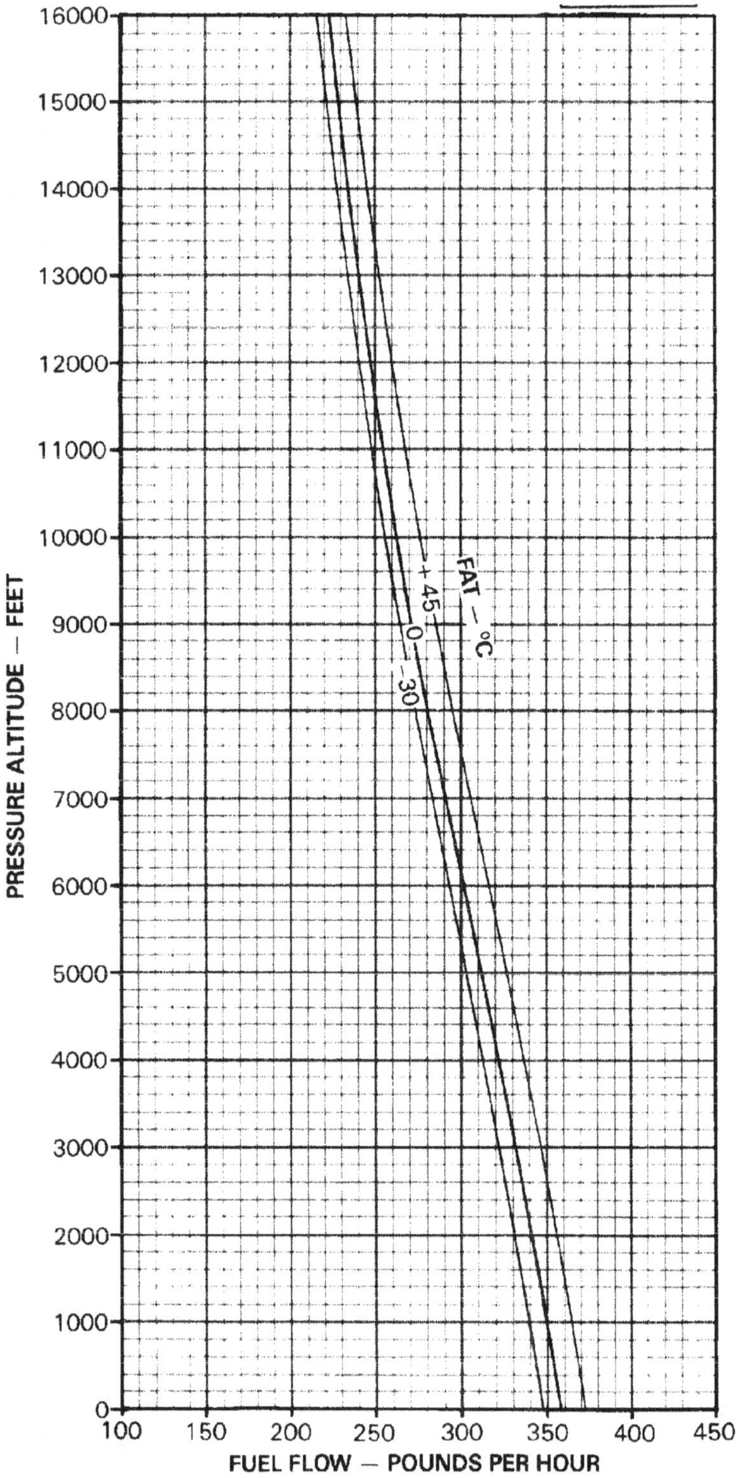

DATA BASIS: CALCULATED FROM AVCO LYCOMING SPEC 19.28.25.03, JULY 1982, CORRECTED FOR INSTALLATION LOSSES BASED ON USAAEFA PROJECT NO. 81-01 LR, SEPT 1982.

Figure 7.1-9. Fuel flow chart (Sheet 1 of 2)

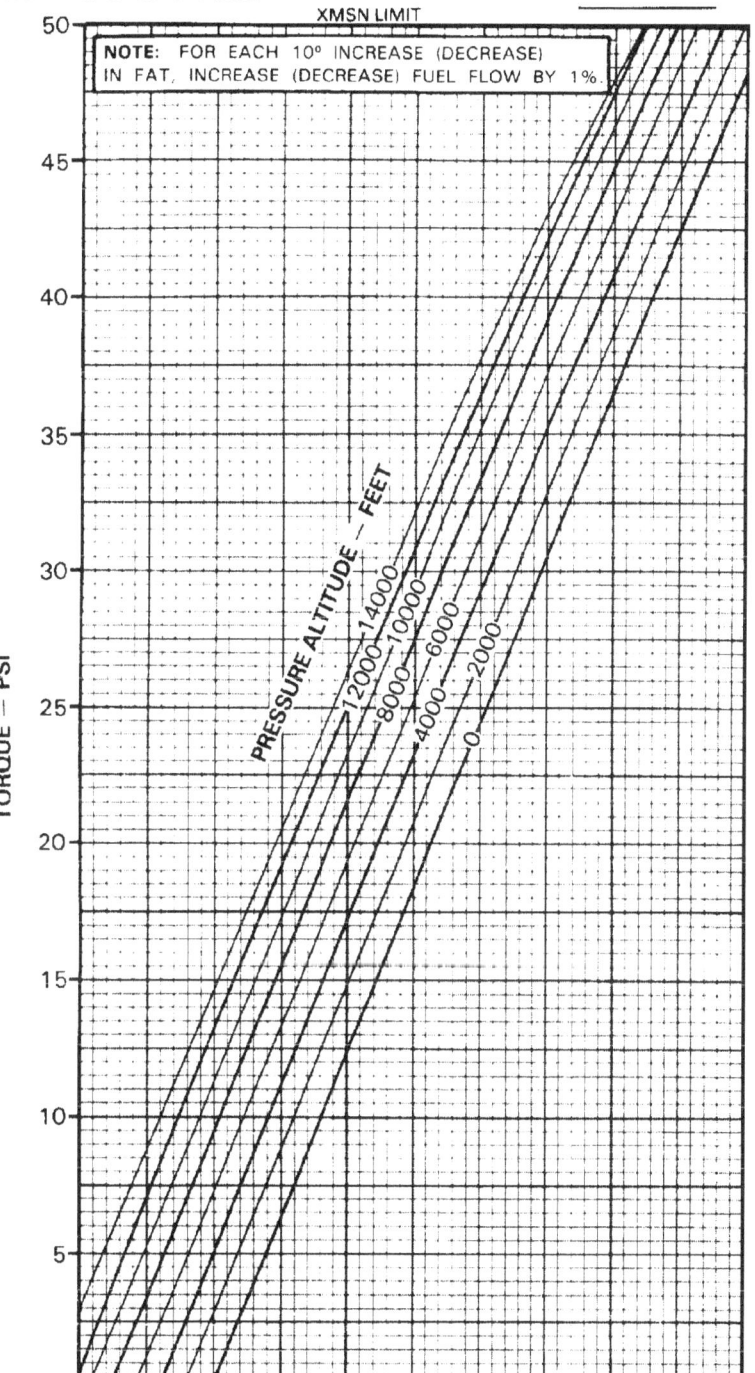

Figure 7.1-9. Fuel flow chart (Sheet 2 of 2)

7-8. General Conditions. In addition to the specific conditions, the following general conditions are applicable to the performance data.

 a. *Rigging.* All airframe and engine controls are assumed to be rigged within allowable tolerances.

 b. *Pilot Technique.* Normal pilot technique is assumed. Control movements should be smooth and continuous.

 c. *Helicopter Variation.* Variation in performance between individual helicopters are known to exist; however, they are considered to be small and cannot be individually accounted for.

 d. *Instrument Variation.* The data shown in the performance charts do not account for instrument inaccuracies or malfunctions.

 e. *Types of Fuel.* All flight performance data is based on IP4 fuel. The change in fuel flow and torque available, when using JP-5, JP-8, aviation gasoline or any other approved fuels, is insignificant.

7-9. Performance Discrepancies. Regular use of this chapter will allow you to monitor instruments and other helicopter systems for malfunction, by comparing actual performance with planned performance. Knowledge will also be gained concerning the effects of variable for which data are not provided, thereby increasing the accuracy of performance predictions.

7-10. Definitions of Abbreviations.

 a Unless otherwise indicated abbreviations and symbols used in this manual conform to those established in Military Standard MIL-ST12, which is periodically revised to reflect current changes in abbreviations usage.

 b. Capitalization and punctuation of abbreviations varies, depending upon the context m which they are used. In general, lower case abbreviations are used in text material, whereas abbreviations used in charts and illustrations appears in full capital letters. Periods do not usually follow abbreviations; however, periods are used with abbreviations that could be mistaken for whole words if the period were omitted.

7-11. Temperature Conversion. The temperature conversion chart Figure 7-1 is arranged so that degrees Celsius can be converted quickly and easily by reading Celsius and looking directly across the charts for Fahrenheit equivalence and vice versa.

Section II TORQUE AVAILABLE

7-12. Description. The torque available charts show the effects of altitude and temperature on engine torque.

7-13. Chart Differences. Both pressure altitude and FAT affect engine power production. Figure 7-2 shows power available data at 30 minute power ratings in terms of the allowable torque as recorded by the torquemeter (psi). Note that the power output capability of the T53-L-13 engine can exceed the transmission structural limit (50 psi calibrated) under certain conditions.

 a. Figure 7-2 is applicable for maximum power, 30 minute operation at 324 rotor/6600 engine rpm.

 b. If the IR Scoup Suppressor is installed, subtract one psi from the torque values obtained from Figure 7-2.

7-14. Use of Chart The primary use of the chart is illustrated by the examples. In general, to determine the maximum power available, it is necessary to know the pressure altitude and temperature. The calibration factor (Data Plate Torque), obtained from the engine data plate or from the engine acceptance records, is the indicated torque pressure at 1125 ft-lbs actual output shaft torque, and is used to correct the error of individual engine torque indicating system.

NOTE
Torque available values determined are not limits. Any torque which can be achieved, without exceeding engine, transmission, or other limits, may be used

7-15. Conditions. Chart (Figure 7-2) is based upon speeds of 324 rotor/6600 engine rpm grade J-4 fuel. The use of aviation gasoline will not influence engine power. All torque available are presented for bleed air heater and device off. Decrease power available 1.4 psi for heater on and 2.1 psi for device on; decrease torque available 3.5 psi if both bleed air heater and device are operating.

Change 17 7-3

TM 55-1520-210-10

Section III HOVER

7-16. Description. The hover charts (Figure 7-3, Sheets 1 and 2) shows the hover ceiling and the torque required to hover respectively at various pressure altitudes, ambient temperatures, gross weights, and skid heights. Maximum skid height for hover can also be obtained by using the torque available from Figure 7-2.

7-17. Use of Chart. The primary use of the hover charts is illustrated by the charts examples. In general, to determine the hover ceiling or the torque required to hover, it is necessary to know the pressure altitude, temperature, gross weight and the desired skid height. In addition to Its primary use, the hover chart (Sheet 2) can also be used to determine the predicted maximum hover height, which is needed for use of the takeoff chart (Figure 7-5).

7-18. Control Margin.

a. Sheet 1 of the control margin charts (Figure 7-4) shows the maximum right crosswind which one can achieve and still maintain directional control as a function of pressure altitude, temperature, and gross weight. Sheet 2 of the control margin chart (Figure 7-4) shows the combinations of relative wind velocity and azimuth which may result in marginal directional or longitudinal control.

b. Use of the control margin charts is Illustrated by example on Sheet 1. Ten percent of total control travel (full right to full left) is considered adequate margin when hovering. The shaded area on Sheet 1 indicates conditions where the directional control margin may be less than ten percent m zero wind hover. The shaded area on sheet 2 labeled DIRECTIONAL indicates conditions where the directional control margin may be less than ten percent for crosswind components in excess of those determined from Sheet 1. The shaded area on sheet 2 labeled LONGITUDINAL indicates wind conditions where longitudinal control may be less than 10 percent. These charts are based on control margin only.

7-19. Conditions

a. The hover charts are based upon calm wind conditions, a level ground surface, and the use of 324 rotor rpm.

b. Use of control margin charts Is to determine If adequate control margin will be available for IGE and OGE hover in winds or low speed translation.

c. The hover charts do not account for the effect of an IR suppressor device. The hover ceiling chart (Figure 7-3, Sheet 1) is not usable if a suppressor device is installed. The IR Scoup Suppressor creates a download of approximately 140 pounds.

d. For the IR Scoup Suppressor

(1) To determine hover torque required, enter the hover power required chart (Figure 7-3, Sheet 2) at a gross weight of 140 pounds heavier than the actual gross weight.

(2) To determine predicted maximum hover height, first subtract one psi from power available (Figure 7-2); then increase the hover gross weight by 140 pounds. Use this power available and gross weight m the hover power required chart (Figure 7-3, Sheet 2).

(3) To determine maximum gross weight, first subtract one psi from power available (Figure 7-2), then decrease the hover gross weight determined from the hover power required chart (Figure 7-3, Sheet 2) by 140 pounds.

e. With the rotor blade erosion protection coating and polyurethane tape installed, it will be necessary to make the following corrections. Add 1 psi to the hover torque required, for OGE and IGE, as determined from Figure 7-3 (Sheet 2). In Figure 7-3 (Sheet 1). subtract 100 pounds from the maximum gross weight to hover When determining maximum hover wheel height, enter the chart at the gross weight plus 100 pounds.

Section IV. TAKEOFF

7-20. Description. The takeoff chart (Figure 7-5) shows the distances to clear various obstacle heights, based upon several hover height capabilities. The upper chart grid presents data for climbout at a constant INDICATED airspeed. The two lower grids present data for climbouts at various TRUE airspeeds. Figure 7-5, sheet 1, is based upon level acceleration technique, sheet 2 is based upon a climb and acceleration from a 3 foot skid height and sheet 3 is based upon a level acceleration from a 15 foot skid height.

NOTE
The hover heights shown on the chart are only a measure of the aircraft's climb capability and do not imply that a higher than normal hover height should be used during the actual takeoff.

7-21. Use of Charts. The primary use of these charts is illustrated by the charts examples. The main consideration for takeoff performance is the hovering skid height capability, which includes the effects of pressure altitude, free air temperature, gross weight, and torque. Hover height capability is determined by use of the hover chart, Figure 7-3. A hover check can be made to verify the hover capability. If winds are present, the hover check may disclose that the helicopter can actually hover at a greater skid height than the calculated value, since the hover chart is based upon calm wind conditions.

7-22. Conditions.

  a. Wind. The takeoff chart is based upon calm wind conditions. Since surface wind velocity and direction cannot be accurately predicted, all takeoff planning should be based upon calm wind conditions. Takeoff into any prevailing wind will improve the takeoff performance.

  b. Power Settings. All takeoff performance data are based upon the torque used m determining the hover capabilities in Figure 7-3.

Change 17   7-4.1/(7-4.2 blank)

Section V. CRUISE

7-23. Description. The cruise charts (Figure 7-6 sheets 1 through 24) show the torque pressure and engine rpm required for level flight at various pressure altitudes airspeeds gross weights and fuel flows.

> **NOTE**
> The cruise charts are basically arranged by FAT groupings. Figure 7-6, sheets 1 through 24 are based upon operation with clean configuration. Each chart has a dashed line that represents a ten square foot equivalent flat plate drag area This allows quick determination of Delta PSI for other than clean configurations.

7-24. Use of Charts.

> **CAUTION**
> Cruise flight is restricted to 319 to 324 Cruise flight is restricted to 319 to 324 Rotor RPM (6500 to 6600 Engine RPM.). Cruise at 324 Rotor/6600 Engine RPM is recommended. The cruise chart data for true airspeeds above 40 KTAS is based on 314 Rotor/6400 Engine RPM. Until the cruise charts are revised performance planning shall be accomplished using the procedures and torque corrections from Table 7-1. These restrictions do not apply when composite main rotor blades (CB) are installed.

The primary use of the charts is illustrated by the examples provided in Figure 7-6. The first step for chart use is to select the proper chart, based upon the planned drags configuration, pressure altitude and anticipated free air temperature; refer to Chapter 7 index (paragraph 7-2). Normally, sufficient accuracy can be obtained by selecting the chart nearest to the planned cruising altitude and FAT, or the next higher altitude and FAT. If greater accuracy is required, interpolation between altitudes and/or temperatures will be required. You may enter the charts on any side: TAS, IAS, torque pressure, or fuel flow, and then move vertically or horizontally to the gross weight, then to the other three parameters. Maximum performance conditions are determined by entering the chart where the maximum range or maximum endurance and rate of climb lines intersect the appropriate gross weight; then read airspeed, fuel flow and PSI torque pressure. For conservatism, use the gross weight at the beginning of cruise flight. For greater accuracy on long flights It is preferable to determine cruise information for several flight segments in order to allow for decreasing fuel weights (reduced gross weight). Estimated performance data is presented for hover (KTAS-O) in Figure 7-6, however, the hover performance data presented in figure 7-3 is more accurate and should be used in planning critical hover performance. The following parameters contained in each chart are further explained as follows:

a. Airspeed. True and indicated airspeeds are presented at opposite sides of each chart. On any chart, indicated airspeed can be directly converted to true airspeed (or vice versa) by reading directly across the chart without regard for other chart information. Maximum permissible airspeed (VNE) limits appear on some charts. If no line appears VNE is above the limits of the chart.

b. Torque Pressure (PSI). Since pressure altitude and temperature are fixed for each chart torque pressures vary according to gross weight, airspeed and bleed air on or off. See paragraph 7-15 for effect of bleed air heater and device.

> **NOTE**
> Torque available values determined are not limits. Any torque which can be achieved without exceeding engine transmission or other limits may be used.

c. Fuel Flow. Fuel flow scales are provided opposite the torque pressure scales. On any chart, torque pressure may be converted directly to fuel flow without regard for other chart information. All fuel flows are presented for bleed air heater and device off. Add two percent fuel flow (about 14 lb/hr) for heater on and increase fuel flow three percent (approximately 21 lb/hr) for device on. If both are operating, add five percent fuel flow (about 35 lb/hr) to chart values.

d. Maximum Range. The maximum range lines indicate the combinations of weight and airspeed that will produce the greatest flight range per gallon of fuel under zero wind conditions. When a maximum range condition does not appear on a chart it is because the maximum range speed is beyond the maximum permissible speed (VNE); m such cases, use VNE cruising speed to obtain maximum range.

e. *Maximum Endurance and Rate of Climb.* The maximum endurance and rate of climb lines indicate the airspeed for minimum torque pressure required to maintain level flight for each gross weight FAT and pressure altitude. Since minimum torque pressure will provide minimum fuel flow maximum flight endurance will be obtained at the airspeeds indicated.

7-25. Conditions. The cruise charts are based upon operations at 324 rotor / 6600 engine rpm below 40 KTAS and 314 rotor/6400 engine rpm for true airspeeds above 40 knots. With the rotor blade erosion protection coating and polyurethane tape installed, add 2 psi to the torque required obtained from Figure 7-6.

Section VI. DRAG

7-26. Description. The drag chart (Figure 7-7, Sheet 1 of 2) shows the authorized configuration or the equivalent flat plate drag area changes for additional aircraft modifications. There is no increase in drag with cargo doors fully open. The upper left portion of Figure 7-7 (Sheet 2 of 2) presents drag areas of typical external loads as a function of the load frontal area. The balance of the charts shows the additional torque required in level flight due to the increase in drag caused by external loads, aircraft modifications or authorized configurations. The IR Scoup Suppressor has a drag of two square feet.

7-27. Use of Chart. The primary use of the chart is illustrated by the example. To determine the change in torque it is necessary to know the drag area change the true airspeed the pressure altitude and the free air temperature. Enter at the known drag area change, move right to TAS move down to pressure altitude move left to FAT then move down and read change in torque. In addition, by entering the chart in the opposite direction, drag area change may be found from a known torque change. This chart is used to adjust cruise charts for appropriate torque and fuel flow due to equivalent flat plate drag area change (AF). For frontal areas exceeding values shown on Figure 7-7 (Sheet 2 of 2) use a smaller value and multiply (e.g 36 sq. ft. 9 sq ft. x 4).

7-28. Conditions. The drag chart is based upon 314 rotor/6400 engine rpm.

Section VII. CLMB-DESCENT

7-29. Description.

The climb descent chart (Figure 7-8) shows the change in torque (above or below torque required for level flight under the same gross weight and atmospheric conditions) to obtain a given rate of climb or descent.

7-30. Use of Chart.

Climb-Descent The primary uses of the chart are illustrated by the chart examples.

a. The torque change obtained from the grid scale must be added to the torque required for level flight (for climb) or subtracted from the torque required for level flight (for descent)-obtained from the appropriate cruise chart in order to obtain a total climb or descent torque.

b. By entering the bottom of the grid with a known torque change, moving upward to the gross weight, and left to the corresponding rate of climb or descent may also be obtained.

7-31. Conditions.

Climb-Descent The climb-descent chart is based on the use of constant rotor or engine rpm. The rate of climb (descent) presented is for steady state conditions and rpm bleed could increase (decrease) the rate of climb (descent) shown.

Section VIII. FUEL FLOW

7-32. Description

a. The fuel flow chart (fig 7-9) shows the fuel flow at engine idle and 324 rotor/6600 engine rpm with flat pitch.

b. Fuel flow vs torque, shows fuel flow in pound-per-hour versus torquemeter psi for pressure altitudes from sea level to 14000 feet and for 0°C free air temperature.

7-33. Use of Chart

a. The primary use of the idle fuel flow chart is illustrated by the example. To determine the idle fuel flow, it is necessary to know the idle condition, pressure altitude, and free air temperature. Enter at the pressure altitude, move right to FAT in appropriate grid, then move down and read fuel flow on the scale corresponding to the condition. Refer to the cruise charts to obtain fuel flow for cruise power conditions.

b. Fuel flow will increase about two percent with the bleed air heater on and three percent with deice on. When both systems are on, increase fuel flow five percent. Also a range or endurance penalty should be accounted for when working cruise chart data. A fairly accurate rule-of-thumb to correct fuel flow for temperatures other than 0°C FAT is to increase (decrease) fuel flow 1 percent for each 10°C increase (decrease) in FAT.

7-34. Conditions

These charts are based upon the use of JP-4 fuel. The change in fuel flow when using other jet fuels is insignificant.

TM 55-1520-210-10

Table 7-1 Torque Correction (Sheet 1 of 4)

To determine cruise performance data for 324 Rotor/6600 Engine RPM at speeds above 40 KTAS, follow the instructions in paragraph 7-24 except:

    a. Add appropriate torque correction from this table to the calibrated torque required values determined from the intersection of the airspeed and gross weight lines on the upper (6400 Engine RPM) portion of the cruise chart.

    b. Determine fuel flow corresponding to the corrected torque required from the lower (6600 Engine RPM) portion of the cruise chart.

    c. Determine continuous torque available (CONT TRQ AVAIL) and 30 minute torque available (30 MIN TRQ AVAIL) from the lower (6600 Engine RPM) portion of the cruise chart.

EXAMPLE

WANTED

Speed for Maximum Range
Calibrate Torque Required and Fuel Flow at Maximum Range

KNOWN

324 Rotor/6600 Engine RPM
Clean Configuration
FAT = -30°C
Pressure Altitude = 8000 feet
Gross Weight = 8500 pounds
Roof Mounted System

METHOD

Locate (-30°C FAT, 8000 Feet) Chart (figure 7-6 Sheet 3 of 24)
Find Intersection of 8500 LB Gr Wt Line With the Max Range Line
To Read Speed for Maximum Range:
   Move Right, Read TAS = 105.3 Knot
   Move Left, Read IAS = 102.3
To Read Calibrated Torque Required @ 314 Rotor/6400 Engine RPM
   Move Down, Read Torque = 41.2 PSI
To Correct Torque Required for 6600 Engine RPM
   From Table for Sheet 3 (8000 Ft -30°C) @ 8500 Lb Gross Weight
     For 90 KTAS, Torque Correction = 3.5 PSI
     For 110 KTAS, Torque Correction = 5.7 PSI
   Interpolate for 105.3 KTAS   Torque Correction = 5.2 PSI
   Corrected Torque Required = 41.2 PSI + 5.2 PSI = 46.4 PSI
To Determine Fuel Flow
   Enter Figure 7-6, Sheet 3 of 24 At 46.4 PSI Torque:
   Move Down Read Fuel Flow = 614 Lb/Hr

TABLE 7-1 TORQUE CORRECTION (Sheet 2 of 4)

TORQUE CORRECTION - PSI

(-30°C FAT)		SHEET 1		SHEET 2		SHEET 3		SHEET 4	
GW-LB	KTAS	SL	2000	4000	6000	8000	10000	12000	14000
5500	50	NA	NA	NA	2.4	2.2	2.1	1.9	1.8
	70	NA	NA	NA	2.8	2.6	2.4	2.2	2.2
	90	NA	NA	NA	3.5	3.4	3.2	3.0	2.9
	110	NA	NA	NA	5.9	5.5	5.2	4.9	4.5
6500	50	3.0	2.8	2.6	2.4	2.2	2.2	2.1	1.9
	70	3.3	3.2	3.1	2.9	2.6	2.5	2.4	2.3
	90	4.3	4.1	3.9	3.7	3.5	3.4	2.9	2.9
	110	7.3	6.9	6.4	6.1	5.6	5.3	4.5	4.6
7500	50	3.1	2.9	2.6	2.5	2.3	2.3	1.7	1.4
	70	3.5	3.3	3.0	3.0	2.8	2.7	2.2	2.2
	90	4.5	4.3	4.1	3.9	3.4	3.3	2.9	2.7
	110	7.4	7.0	6.5	6.2	5.3	5.3	4.7	4.7
8500	50	3.0	2.9	2.7	2.6	2.3	1.8	1.1	0.8
	70	3.5	3.4	3.3	3.1	2.8	2.6	1.8	1.1
	90	4.6	4.4	4.0	3.7	3.5	3.2	1.9	0.8
	110	7.5	7.1	6.4	6.0	5.7	5.5	2.6	0.6
9500	50	3.1	3.0	2.9	2.1	1.7	1.1	0.1	-1.8
	70	3.8	3.5	3.4	2.8	2.8	1.9	-0.6	-2.3
	90	4.9	4.2	4.2	3.5	3.5	2.0	-2.4	-1.5
	110	7.7	6.6	6.7	6.0	5.9	2.5	-4.8	1.4
[-15°C FAT]		SHEET 5		SHEET 6		SHEET 7		SHEET 8	
GW-LB	KTAS	SL	2000	4000	6000	8000	10000	12000	14000
5500	50	NA	NA	1.3	1.2	1.1	1.0	1.0	1.0
	70	NA	NA	1.9	1.7	1.7	1.5	1.5	1.3
	90	NA	NA	2.6	2.5	2.3	2.2	2.1	1.9
	110	NA	NA	3.0	2.9	2.6	2.4	2.3	2.0
6500	50	1.5	1.4	1.3	1.2	1.1	1.1	1.0	0.5
	70	2.2	2.1	1.9	1.7	1.7	1.6	1.5	1.3
	90	3.0	2.9	2.7	2.5	2.4	2.2	2.1	1.8
	110	3.5	3.3	3.1	2.8	2.7	2.3	2.2	1.8
7500	50	1.6	1.4	1.3	1.3	1.2	0.7	0.7	0.3
	70	2.2	2.0	2.0	1.9	1.8	1.6	1.6	0.6
	90	3.2	2.9	2.8	2.6	2.4	2.1	2.0	0.9
	110	3.6	3.3	3.2	2.7	2.5	2.2	2.1	-0.5
8500	50	1.6	1.5	1.4	1.1	0.7	0.5	0.5	-0.9
	70	2.3	2.2	2.1	1.9	1.7	1.2	0.8	-1.4
	90	3.3	3.1	2.8	2.6	2.2	1.6	1.3	-3.2
	110	3.6	3.3	2.8	2.7	2.3	0.8	-0.2	-7.5
9500	50	1.6	1.4	0.8	0.9	0.4	-0.1	-0.8	-7.5
	70	2.3	2.3	2.0	2.0	0.8	-0.2	-1.2	-6.6
	90	3.2	3.1	2.6	2.6	1.2	-0.8	-2.9	-6.8
	110	3.2	3.1	2.7	2.7	-0.7	-3.8	-7.2	-6.9

TABLE 7-1 TORQUE CORRECTION   (Sheet 3 of 4)

TORQUE CORRECTION - PSI

[0°C FAT]		SHEET 9		SHEET 10		SHEET 11		SHEET 12	
GW-LB	KTAS	SL	2000	4000	6000	8000	10000	12000	14000
5500	50	NA	NA	1.1	1.1	1.0	0.9	0.9	0.8
	70	NA	NA	1.2	1.1	1.1	1.0	0.9	0.8
	90	NA	NA	1.4	1.3	1.2	1.1	1.1	1.0
	110	NA	NA	2.5	2.3	2.1	2.0	1.9	1.6
6500	50	1.4	1.3	1.1	1.2	1.1	0.9	0.7	0.6
	70	1.4	1.3	1.2	1.2	1.1	0.9	0.8	0.8
	90	1.6	1.5	1.4	1.4	1.2	1.2	0.9	0.9
	110	2.9	2.7	2.5	2.4	2.1	2.0	1.8	1.6
7500	50	1.3	1.3	1.2	1.1	0.9	0.7	0.4	0.4
	70	1.4	1.4	1.3	1.1	1.0	0.8	0.2	0.0
	90	1.6	1.6	1.4	1.3	1.2	0.9	0.3	0.0
	110	3.0	2.7	2.5	2.3	2.1	1.9	0.5	-0.1
8500	50	1.4	1.3	1.1	0.7	0.7	0.4	-0.5	-3.0
	70	1.5	1.3	1.2	0.9	0.8	0.1	-1.5	-3.8
	90	1.7	1.5	1.5	1.0	0.8	0.1	-3.8	-5.9
	110	3.0	2.5	2.5	2.1	1.8	0.0	-4.9	-8.8
9500	50	1.3	1.0	0.8	0.5	0.4	-0.8	-6.9	NA
	70	1.4	1.2	1.1	0.3	0.0	-2.0	-7.3	NA
	90	1.6	1.3	1.2	0.3	-0.3	-5.3	-8.5	NA
	110	2.8	2.6	2.4	0.4	-0.4	-6.3	-15.4	NA

(15°C FAT)		SHEET 13		SHEET 14		SHEET 15		SHEET 16	
GW-LB	KTAS	SL	2000	4000	6000	8000	10000	12000	14000
5500	50	NA	0.7	0.7	0.6	0.6	0.7	0.6	0.5
	70	NA	0.9	0.9	0.8	0.7	0.7	0.6	0.5
	90	NA	1.0	1.1	0.9	0.9	0.8	0.8	0.7
	110	NA	0.9	0.9	0.9	0.8	0.8	0.8	0.8
6500	50	0.8	0.7	0.7	0.8	0.7	0.6	0.4	0.2
	70	1.0	1.0	0.9	0.9	0.6	0.5	0.4	0.1
	90	1.2	1.1	1.0	0.9	0.9	0.8	0.6	0.3
	110	1.1	1.0	1.0	0.9	0.8	0.8	0.6	-0.3
7500	50	0.9	0.9	0.8	0.7	0.4	0.4	0.1	-1.0
	70	1.1	1.0	0.7	0.7	0.5	0.2	-0.2	-1.7
	90	1.2	1.1	1.0	1.0	0.6	0.5	-0.1	-4.2
	110	1.1	1.0	0.9	1.1	0.7	0.1	-1.2	-6.7
8500	50	0.9	0.8	0.6	0.5	0.0	-0.5	-1.3	-7.3
	70	0.9	0.8	0.6	0.5	-0.3	-0.9	-2.0	-7.1
	90	1.1	1.2	0.8	0.8	-0.1	-2.0	-5.0	-7.9
	110	1.0	1.1	0.8	0.8	-1.5	-4.0	-8.2	-19.6
9500	50	0.8	0.6	0.4	0.0	-1.4	-4.9	NA	NA
	70	0.7	0.6	0.2	-0.2	-2.2	-5.2	NA	NA
	90	1.2	0.8	0.4	0.0	-5.4	-7.3	NA	NA
	110	1.2	0.9	-0.2	-1.5	-8.7	-15.2	NA	NA

TABLE 7-1 TORQUE CORRECTION (Sheet 4 of 4)

TORQUE CORRECTION - PSI

[30°C FAT]		SHEET 17		SHEET 18		SHEET 19		SHEET 20	
GW-LB	KTAS	SL	2000	4000	6000	8000	10000	12000	14000
5500	50	0.5	0.5	0.5	0.5	0.6	0.5	0.5	0.3
	70	0.8	0.7	0.7	0.6	0.6	0.5	0.3	0.3
	90	0.5	0.5	0.4	0.3	0.3	0.2	0.3	0.1
	110	0.8	0.8	0.8	0.7	0.7	0.7	0.7	0.6
6500	50	0.6	0.6	0.7	0.5	0.5	0.3	0.4	0.0
	70	0.7	0.7	0.6	0.5	0.4	0.4	0.3	-0.2
	90	0.6	0.4	0.3	0.3	0.4	0.1	0.1	-0.6
	110	1.0	0.9	0.8	0.8	1.0	0.6	0.5	-0.9
7500	50	0.9	0.7	0.6	0.5	0.4	-0.1	-0.6	-1.6
	70	0.8	0.5	0.5	0.4	0.3	-0.3	-0.9	-2.0
	90	0.3	0.3	0.4	0.1	0.2	-0.7	-2.7	-5.1
	110	0.9	1.0	1.0	0.8	0.7	-1.1	-2.8	-7.4
8500	50	0.7	0.6	0.5	0.1	0.0	-1.6	-6.3	NA
	70	0.5	0.4	0.4	0.0	-0.1	-2.1	-6.0	NA
	90	0.4	0.3	0.2	-0.4	-0.7	-5.7	-7.9	NA
	110	1.2	1.0	0.7	-0.6	-1.1	-8.0	-16.3	NA
9500	50	0.5	0.5	-0.1	-1.0	-2.2	-8.3	NA	NA
	70	0.4	0.5	-0.3	-1.3	-2.7	-7.7	NA	NA
	90	0.1	0.2	-0.8	-3.9	-6.6	-9.3	NA	NA
	110	0.8	0.8	-1.3	-5.4	-9.7	-21.5	NA	NA
[45°C FAT]		SHEET 21		SHEET 22		SHEET 23		SHEET 24	
GW-LB	KTAS	SL	2000	4000	6000	8000	10000	12000	14000
5500	50	0.5	0.5	0.5	0.6	0.5	0.4	0.3	0.2
	70	0.4	0.5	0.4	0.3	0.3	0.1	0.2	0.1
	90	0.5	0.5	0.3	0.2	0.2	0.3	0.3	0.1
	110	0.3	0.3	0.3	0.3	0.4	0.4	0.3	0.0
6500	50	0.6	0.6	0.5	0.4	0.3	0.2	-0.1	-0.3
	70	0.5	0.4	0.3	0.2	0.2	0.1	-0.3	-0.6
	90	0.3	0.2	0.2	0.4	0.3	0.1	-0.4	-1.3
	110	0.3	0.4	0.4	0.4	0.3	0.0	-1.1	-2.5
7500	50	0.6	0.4	0.4	0.3	0.0	-0.1	-1.5	-5.9
	70	0.3	0.2	0.3	0.2	-0.2	-0.2	-2.1	-5.7
	90	0.3	0.4	0.4	0.1	-0.4	-0.6	-5.0	-6.9
	110	0.4	0.5	0.3	0.0	-0.9	-1.5	-7.9	-14.7
8500	50	0.5	0.3	0.2	-0.2	-1.4	-3.6	7.2	NA
	70	0.3	0.2	0.1	-0.3	-1.9	-3.9	8.0	NA
	90	0.5	0.1	0.0	-0.8	-4.4	-6.4	11.0	NA
	110	0.6	0.0	-0.3	-1.8	-7.2	-11.7	NA	NA
9500	50	0.4	-0.1	-0.4	-1.9	-7.7	NA	NA	NA
	70	0.2	-0.4	-0.6	-2.6	-7.5	NA	NA	NA
	90	0.3	-0.7	-1.4	-6.3	-8.8	NA	NA	NA
	110	0.1	-1.6	-2.8	-10.0	-18.8	NA	NA	NA

TEMPERATURE CONVERSION CHART

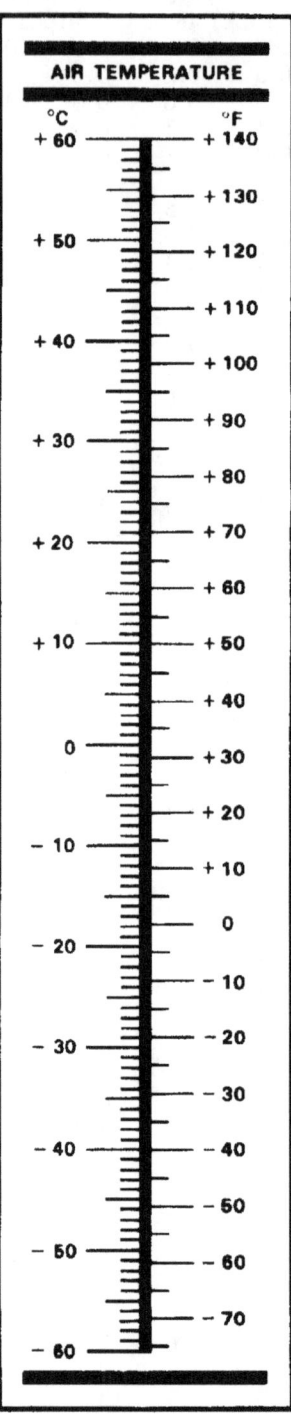

Figure 7-1. Temperature Conversion Chart

TM 55-1520-210-10

MAXIMUM TORQUE AVAILABLE (30 MINUTE OPERATION)
ANTI-ICE OFF BLEED AIR HEATER OFF
324 ROTOR/6600 ENGINE RPM

EXAMPLE

WANTED

INDICATED TORQUE
CALIBRATED TORQUE

KNOWN

PRESSURE ALTITUDE = 10,000 FT.
OAT = 15°C
CALIBRATION FACTOR = 66.0

METHOD

ENTER FAT
MOVE RIGHT TO PRESSURE ALTITUDE
MOVE DOWN TO CALIBRATION FACTOR
MOVE LEFT, READ INDICATED TORQUE = 39 PSI
FOR CALIBRATED TORQUE CONTINUE DOWN THRU CALIBRATION FACTOR, READ CALIBRATED TORQUE = 36.0 PSI

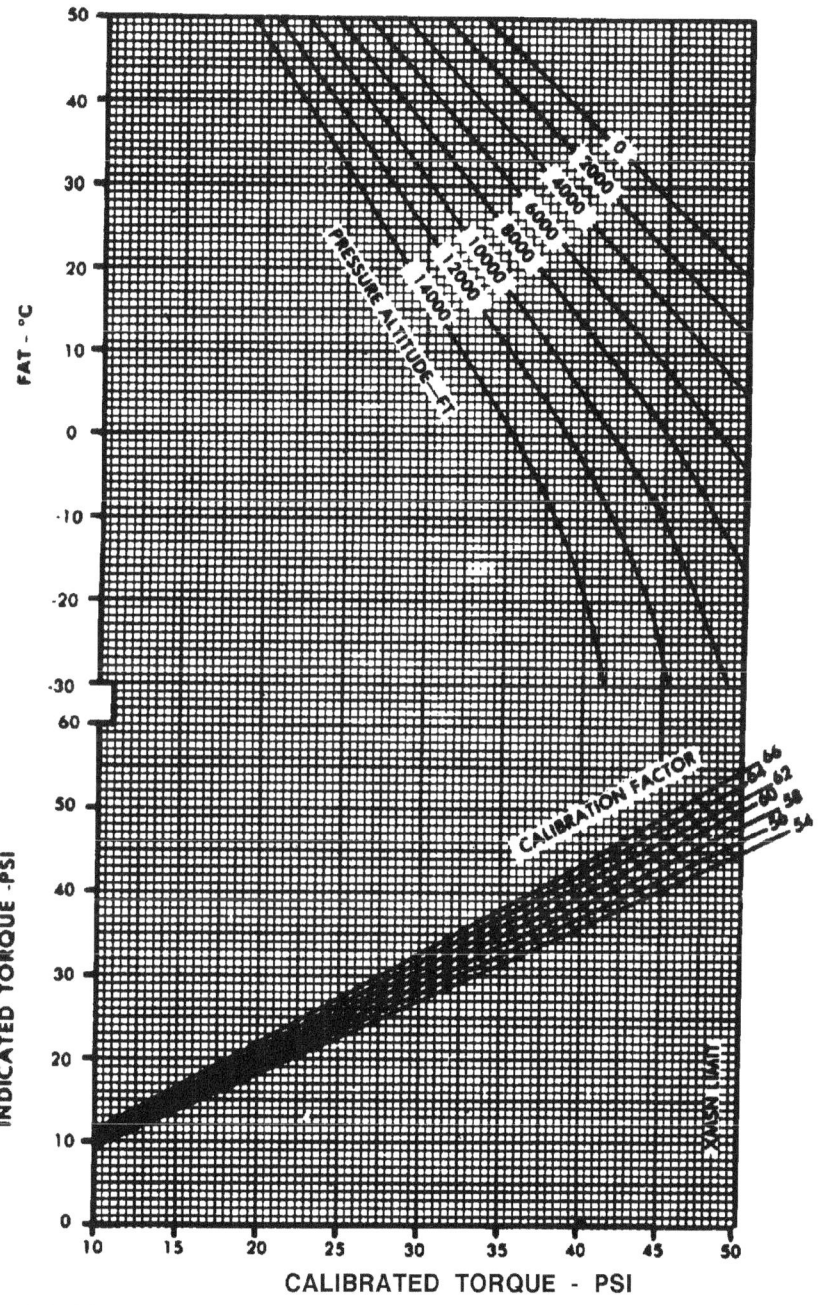

DATA BASIS: CALCULATED FROM T53-L-13B ENGINE PROGRAM 19.28.25.03 CORRECTED FOR INSTALLATION LOSSES BASED ON FLIGHT TEST, ASTA 66-04, NOVEMBER 1970, AND LOSS DUE TO PARTICLE SEPARATOR

Figure 7-2. Maximum Torque Available (30 Minute Operation) Chart

TM 55-1520-210-10

HOVER CEILING
MAXIMUM TORQUE AVAILABLE (30 MINUTE OPERATION)
324 ROTOR/6600 ENGINE RPM

EXAMPLE

WANTED

GROSS WEIGHT TO HOVER

KNOWN

PRESSURE ALTITUDE = 10600 FEET
FAT = 10°C
SKID HEIGHT = 2 FEET

METHOD

ENTER PRESSURE ALTITUDE
MOVE RIGHT TO FAT
MOVE DOWN TO SKID HEIGHT
MOVE LEFT, READ GROSS WEIGHT
TO HOVER = 8500 POUNDS

CORRECTION TABLE

FAT	TORQUE CORRECTION PSI *			
	CALIBRATED TORQUE-PSI			
	20	30	40	50
0°C	.2	.3	.4	.5
-20°C	.4	.6	.8	1.0
-40°C	1.4	2.1	2.8	3.5
-50°C	2.4	3.6	4.8	6.0
-60°C	4.0	6.0	8.0	10.0

*When operating at or below 0°C increase the calibrated torque determined from sheet 2 by the amount shown in the table to determine torque required. See example on sheet 2.

DATA BASIS: DERIVED FROM YUH-1H FLIGHT TEST, ASTA-TDR 66-04 NOVEMBER 1970

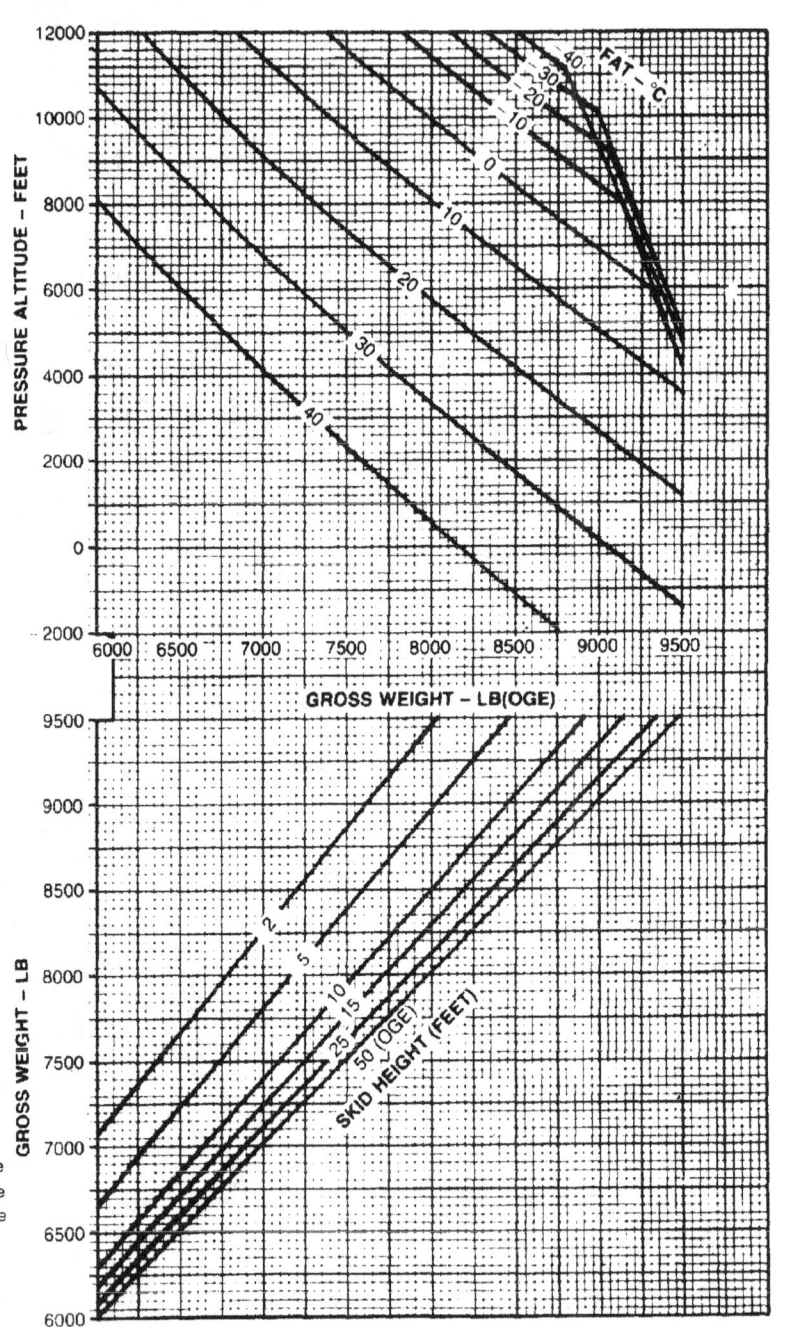

Figure 7-3. Hover (Ceiling) Chart (Sheet 1 of 2)

HOVER POWER REQUIRED
LEVEL SURFACE CALM WIND
324 ROTOR/6600 ENGINE RPM

EXAMPLE

WANTED

TORQUE REQUIRED TO HOVER

KNOWN

PRESSURE ALTITUDE = 2000 FEET
FAT = -40°C
GROSS WEIGHT = 8500 LB
DESIRED SKID HEIGHT = 2 FEET

METHOD

ENTER PRESSURE ALTITUDE
MOVE RIGHT TO FAT
MOVE DOWN TO GROSS WEIGHT
MOVE LEFT TO SKID HEIGHT
MOVE DOWN, READ CALIBRATED
TORQUE = 31.5 PSI
FROM THE TABLE FOR FAT
 = -40°C AND 31.5 PSI TORQUE
DETERMINE TORQUE CORRECTION OF
 2.2 PSI
TORQUE REQUIRED TO HOVER IS
 31.5 + 2.2 = 33.7 PSI

DATA BASIS: DERIVED FROM YUH-1H FLIGHT TEST, ASTA-TDR 66-04, NOVEMBER 1970

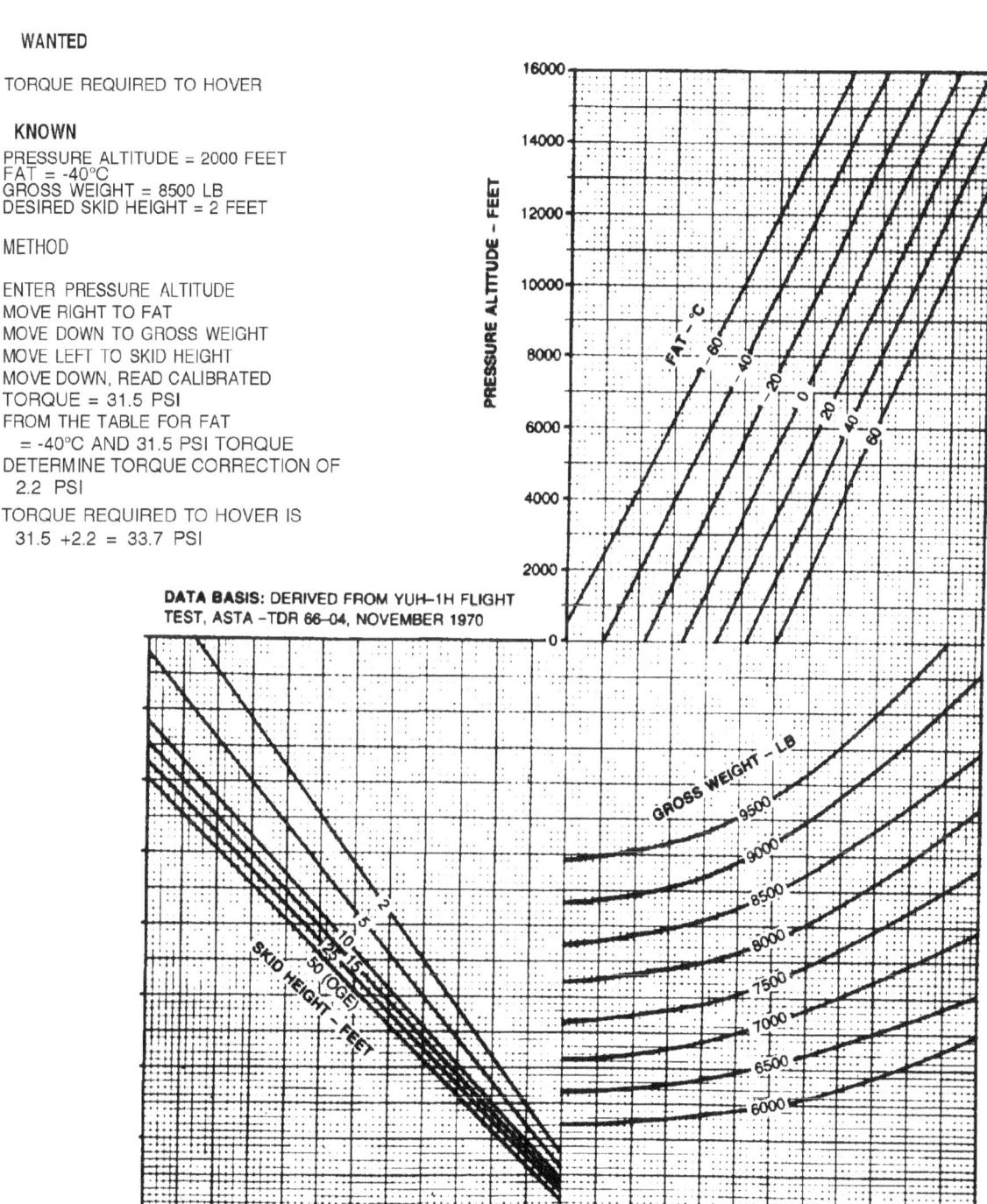

Figure 7-3. Hover (Power Required) Chart (Sheet 2 of 2)

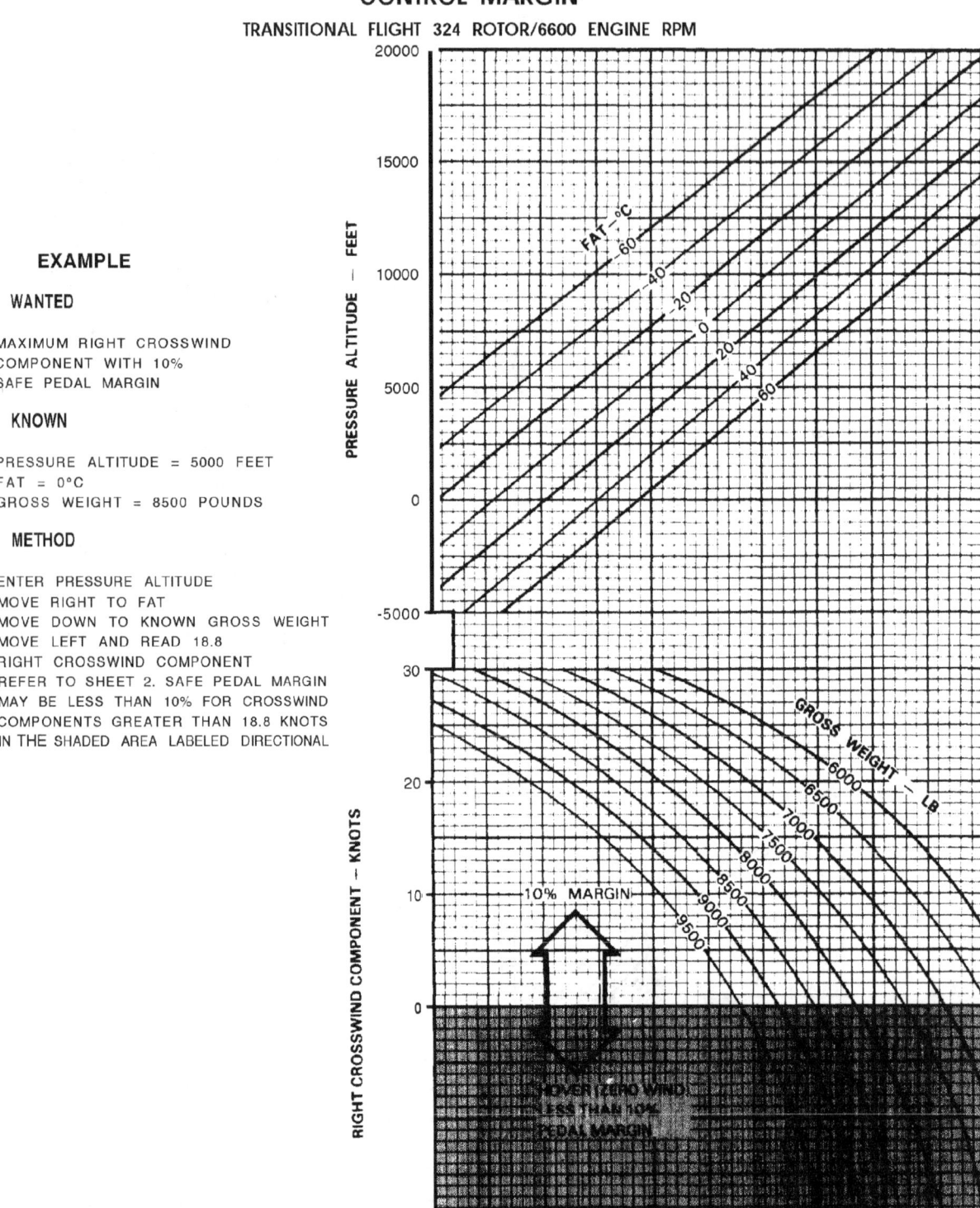

Figure 7-4. Control margin (Sheet 1 of 2)

CONTROL MARGIN
TRANSLATIONAL FLIGHT 324 ROTOR/6600 ENGINE RPM

CONDITIONS WHERE THE CONTROL MARGIN MAY BE LESS THAN 10% ARE SHOWN IN SHADED AREA

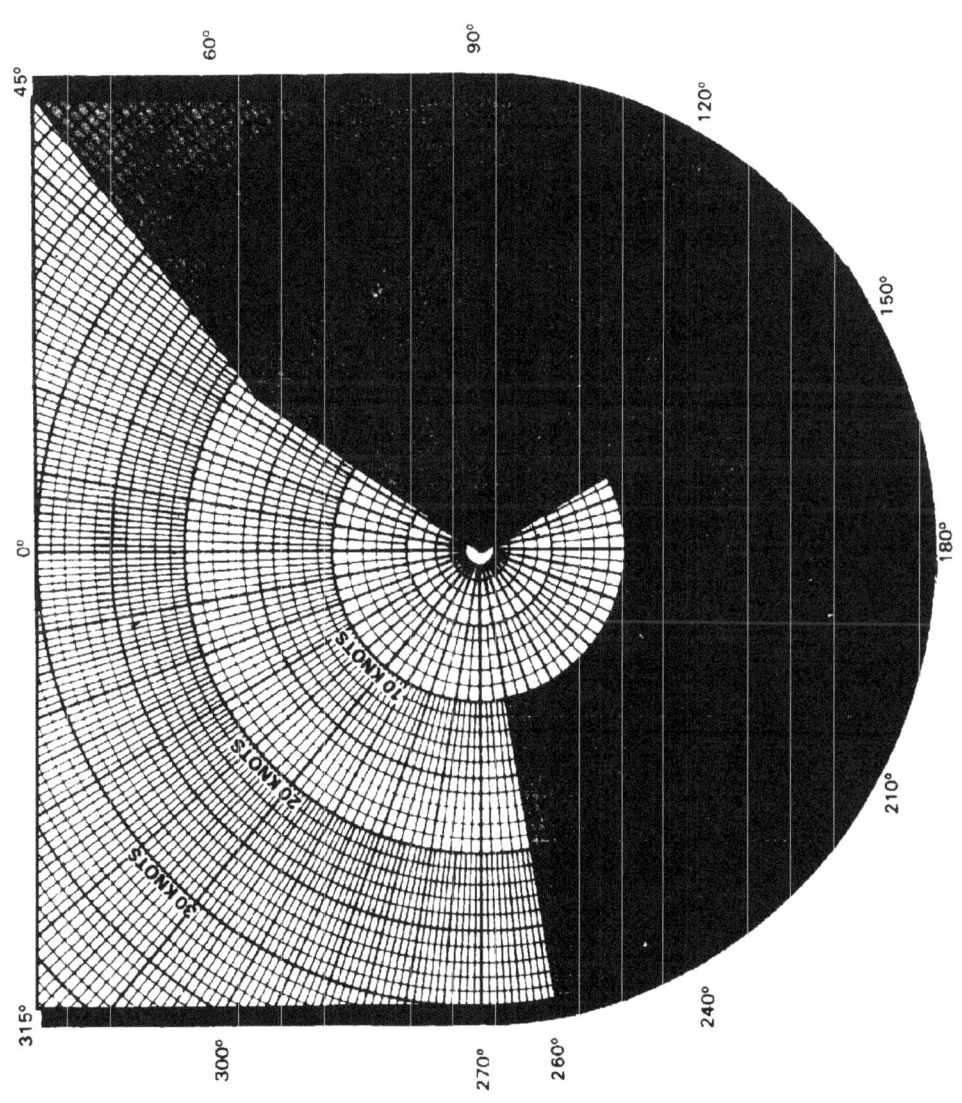

TM 55-1520-210-10

TAKEOFF
LEVEL ACCELERATION, 3 FT SKID HEIGHT
324 ROTOR/6600 ENGINE RPM   MAXIMUM TORQUE AVAILABLE
CALM WIND LEVEL SURFACE ALL CONFIGURATIONS

EXAMPLE A

WANTED

DISTANCE TO CLEAR OBSTACLE

KNOWN

MAXIMUM HOVER HEIGHT = 10 FEET
OBSTACLE HEIGHT = 50 FEET

METHOD

ENTER MAX HOVER HEIGHT
MOVE RIGHT TO OBSTACLE HEIGHT
MOVE DOWN, READ DISTANCE
TO CLEAR OBSTACLE = 700 FEET

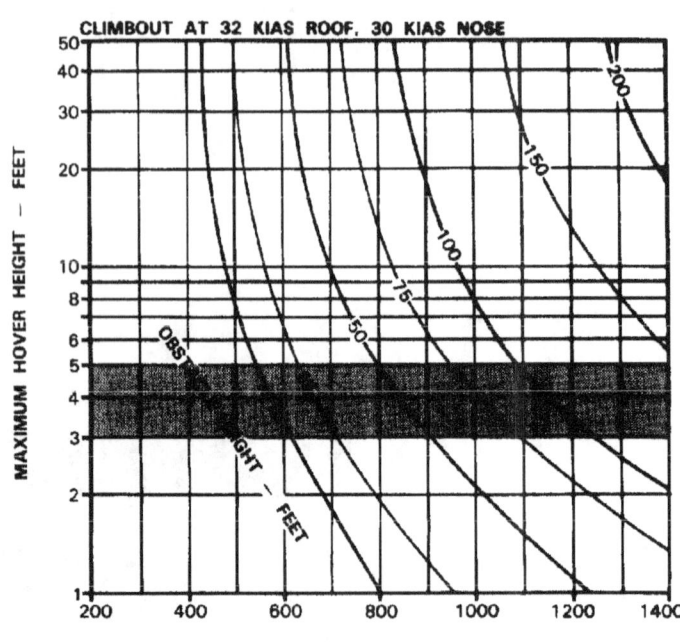

EXAMPLE B

WANTED

DISTANCE TO CLEAR OBSTACLE

KNOWN

MAX HOVER HEIGHT = 8 FEET
OBSTACLE HEIGHT = 50 FEET
CLIMBOUT AIRSPEED = 40 KNOTS

METHOD

ENTER MAX HOVER HEIGHT
MOVE RIGHT TO CLIMBOUT TRUE AIRSPEED
MOVE DOWN TO OBSTACLE HEIGHT
MOVE LEFT READ DISTANCE
TO CLEAR OBSTACLE = 630 FEET

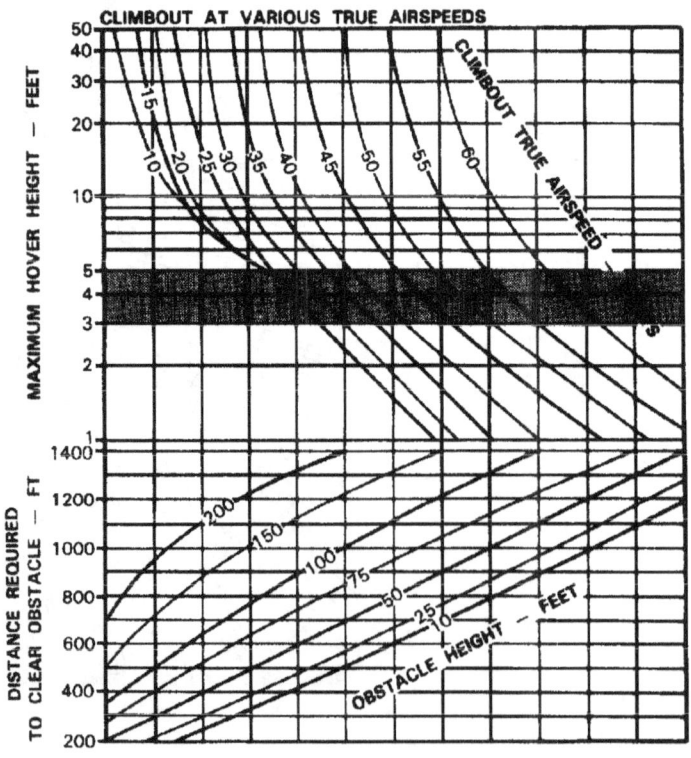

DATA BASIS: DERIVED FROM FLIGHT TEST FTC-TDR 64-27, NOVEMBER 1964

Figure 7-5. Takeoff chart (Sheet 1 of 3)

TAKEOFF
CLIMB AND ACCELERATION, 3 FT SKID HEIGHT
324 ROTOR/6600 ENGINE RPM MAXIMUM TORQUE AVAILABLE
CALM WIND LEVEL SURFACE ALL CONFIGURATIONS

EXAMPLE A

WANTED

DISTANCE TO CLEAR OBSTACLE

KNOWN

MAX HOVER HEIGHT = 17 FEET
OBSTACLE HEIGHT = 120 FEET

METHOD

ENTER MAX HOVER HEIGHT
MOVE RIGHT TO OBSTACLE HEIGHT
MOVE DOWN, READ DISTANCE
TO CLEAR OBSTACLE = 1420 FEET

EXAMPLE B

WANTED

DISTANCE TO CLEAR OBSTACLE

KNOWN

MAX HOVER HEIGHT = 17 FEET
OBSTACLE HEIGHT = 120 FEET
CLIMBOUT AIRSPEED = 50 KTAS

METHOD

ENTER MAX HOVER HEIGHT
MORE RIGHT TO AIRSPEED
MOVE DOWN TO OBSTACLE HEIGHT
MOVE LEFT, READ DISTANCE
TO CLEAR OBSTACLE = 1610 FEET

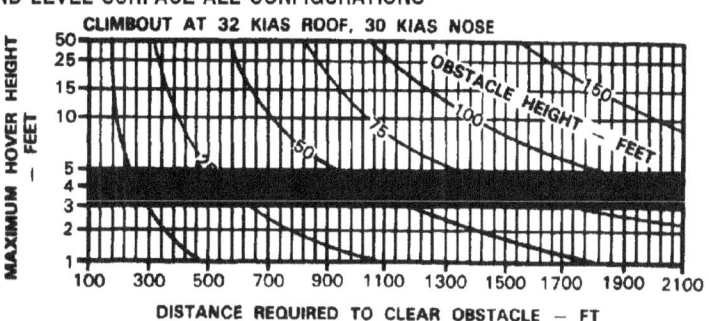
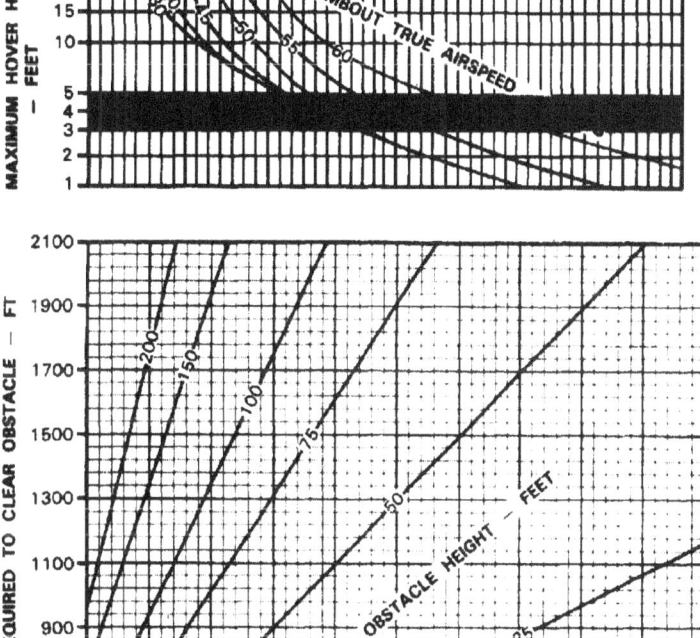

DATA BASIS: DERIVED FROM YUH-1H FLIGHT TEST, ASTA-TDR 66-04, NOVEMBER 1970

Figure 7-5. Takeoff Chart (Sheet 2 of 3)

TAKEOFF

LEVEL ACCELERATION, 15 FT SKID HEIGHT
324 ROTOR/6600 ENGINE RPM MAXIMUM TORQUE AVAILABLE
CALM WIND LEVEL SURFACE ALL CONFIGURATIONS

EXAMPLE A

WANTED

DISTANCE TO CLEAR OBSTACLE

KNOWN

MAX HOVER HEIGHT = 17 FEET
OBSTACLE HEIGHT = 120 FEET

METHOD

ENTER MAX HOVER HEIGHT
MOVE RIGHT TO OBSTACLE HEIGHT
MOVE DOWN, READ DISTANCE
TO CLEAR OBSTACLE

EXAMPLE B

WANTED

DISTANCE TO CLEAR OBSTACLE

KNOWN

MAX HOVER HEIGHT = 17 FEET
OBSTACLE HEIGHT = 120 FEET
CLIMBOUT AIRSPEED = 40 KTAS

METHOD

ENTER MAX HOVER HEIGHT
MOVE RIGHT TO CLIMBOUT
TRUE AIRSPEED
MOVE DOWN TO OBSTACLE HEIGHT
MOVE LEFT, READ DISTANCE
TO CLEAR OBSTACLE = 1000 FEET

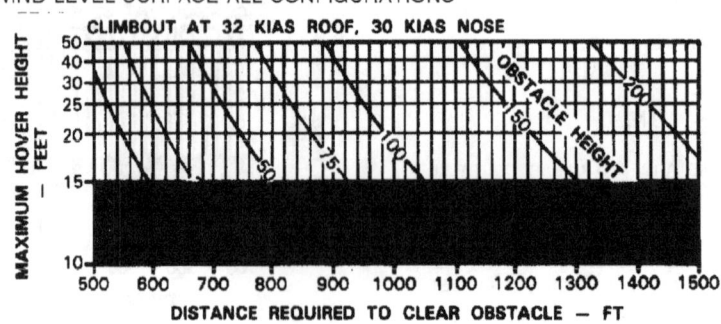
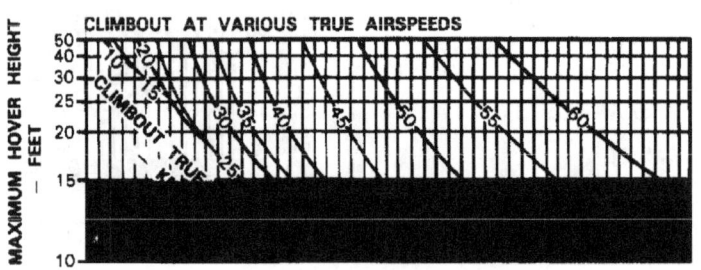
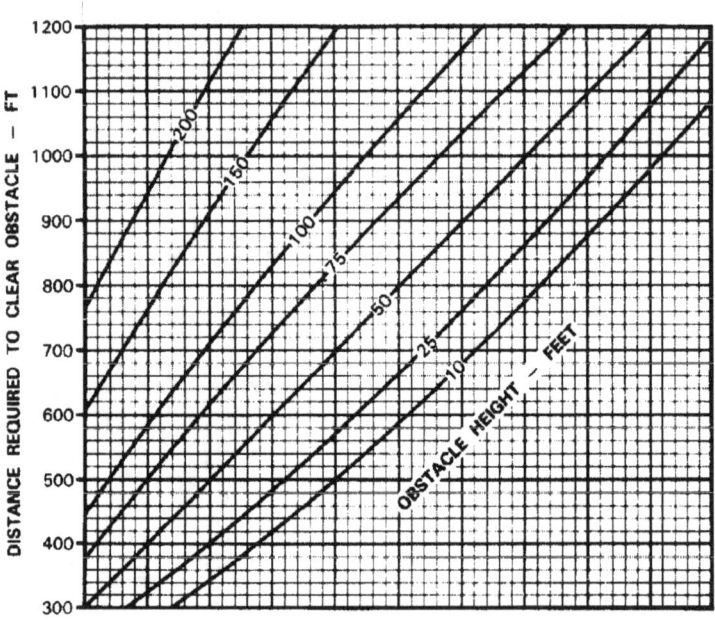

DATA BASIS: DERIVED FROM YUH-1H FLIGHT TEST, ASTA-TDR 66-04, NOVEMBER 1970

Figure 7-5. Takeoff Chart (Sheet 3 of 3)

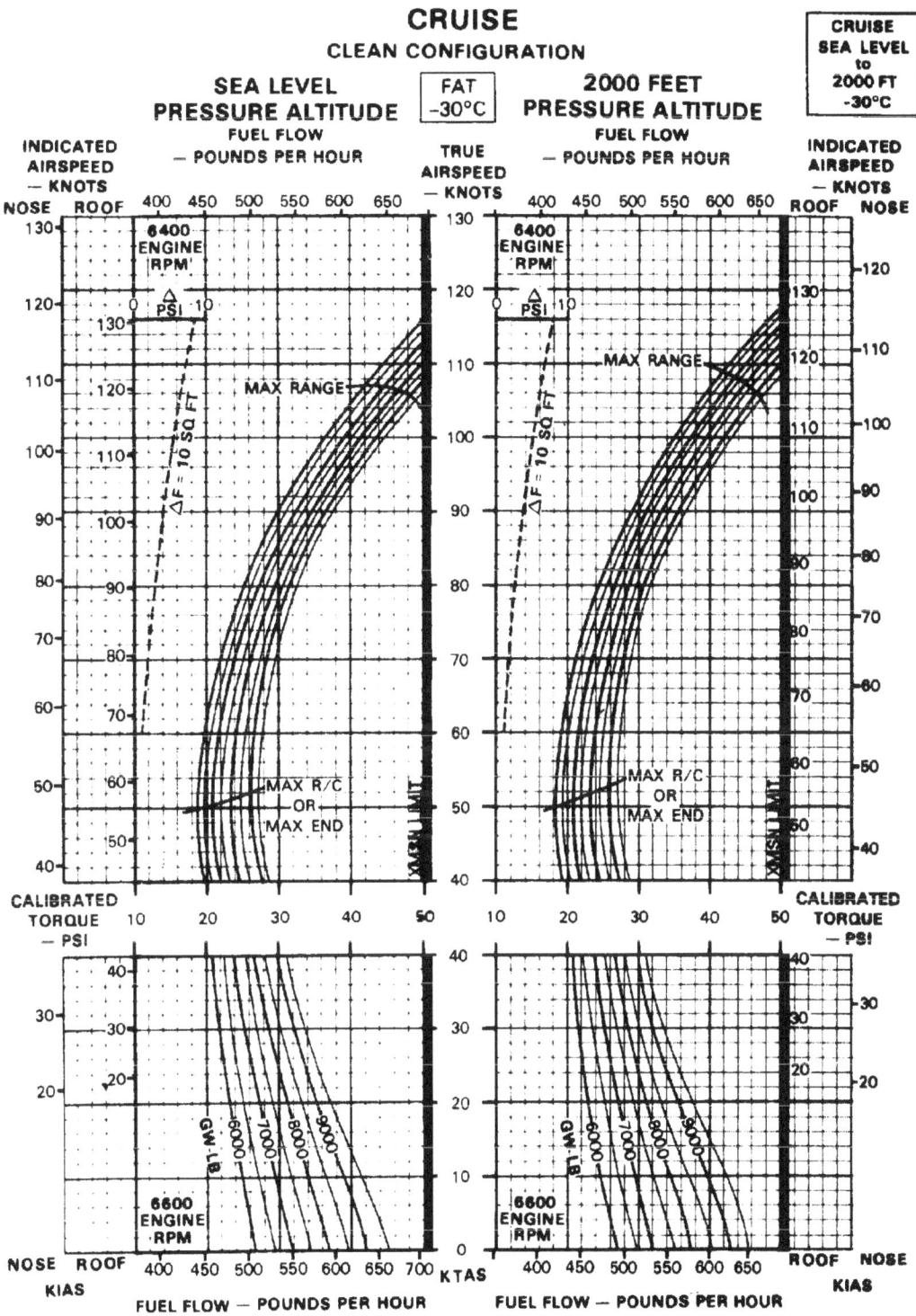

Figure 7-6. Cruise Chart (Sheet 1 of 24)

EXAMPLE

WANTED

CALIBRATED TORQUE REQUIRED FOR LEVEL FLIGHT, FUEL FLOW, INDICATED AIRSPEED

KNOWN

CLEAN CONFIGURATION
GROSS WEIGHT = 9000 LB
PRESSURE ALTITUDE = 5000 FEET
FAT = -30°C
DESIRED TRUE AIRSPEED = 100 KNOTS ROOF MOUNTED SYSTEM

METHOD (INTERPOLATE)

ENTER TRUE AIRSPEED
READ CALIBRATED TORQUE, FUEL FLOW, AND IAS ON EACH ADJACENT ALTITUDE AND/OR FAT, THEN INTERPOLATE BETWEEN ALTITUDE AND/OR FAT.

ALTITUDE, FEET	4000 FT	6000 FEET	5000 FEET
FAT, C	-30	-30	-30
CALIBRATED TORQUE, PSI	41.2	40.2	40.7
FUEL FLOW, LB/HR	582	558	570
IAS, KNOTS	104.5	100.7	102.6

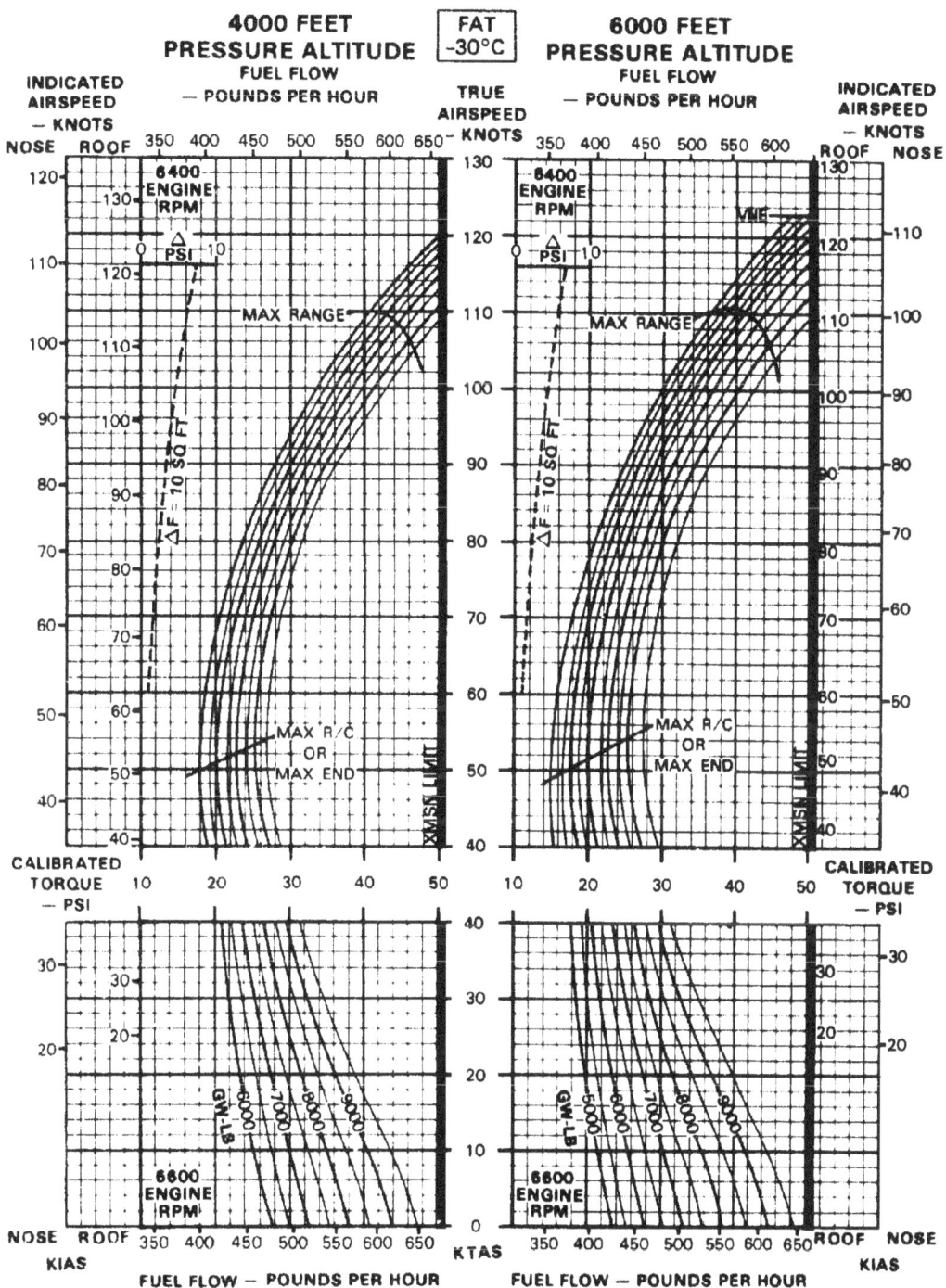

Figure 7-6. Cruise Chart (2 of 24)

EXAMPLE

WANTED

SPEED FOR MAXIMUM RANGE
CALIBRATE TORQUE REQUIRED AND FUEL FLOW AT MAXIMUM RANGE
SPEED FOR MAXIMUM ENDURANCE

KNOWN

CLEAN CONFIGURATION, FAT = -30°C
PRESSURE ALTITUDE = 8000 FEET,
AND GROSS WEIGHT = 8500 POUNDS
ROOF MOUNTED SYSTEM

METHOD

LOCATE (-30°C FAT, 8000 FEET) CHART
FIND INTERSECTION OF 8500 GROSS WEIGHT LINE
WITH THE MAXIMUM RANGE LINE
TO READ SPEED FOR MAXIMUM RANGE:
    MOVE RIGHT, READ TAS = 105.3 KNOT AND MOVE LEFT,
    READ IAS = 102.3
TO READ FUEL FLOW REQUIRED:
    MOVE UP, READ FUEL FLOW = 554 LB/HR
TO READ CALIBRATED TORQUE REQUIRED:
    MOVE DOWN, READ TORQUE = 41.2 PSI
FIND INTERSECTION OF 8500 LB GROSS WEIGHT LINE
WITH THE MAXIMUM ENDURANCE LINE
TO READ SPEED FOR MAXIMUM ENDURANCE
    MOVE RIGHT, READ TAS = 53.9 KNOTS AND MOVE LEFT,
    READ IAS = 50.5 KNOTS

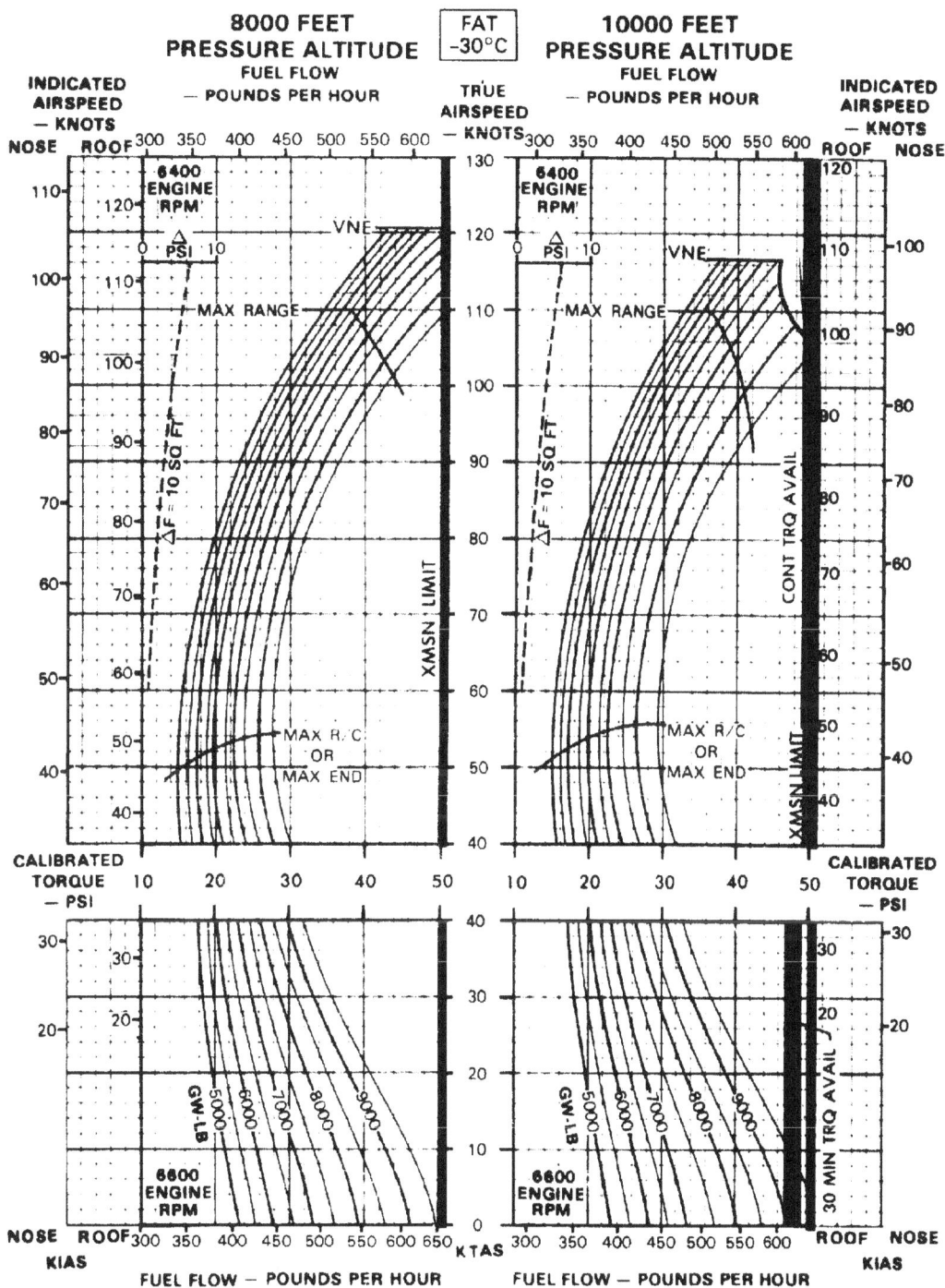

Figure 7-6. Cruise Chart (Sheet 3 of 24)

EXAMPLE

WANTED

ADDITIONAL CALIBRATED TORQUE REQUIRED AND FUEL FLOW FOR EXTERNAL DRAG CONFIGURATION

KNOWN

DF FOR EXTERNAL DRAG CONFIGURATION (FROM FIGURE 7-7, EXAMPLE B) = 4 SQUARE FEET
GROSS WEIGHT = 8000 POUNDS
FAT = -30°C
PRESSURE ALTITUDE = 12000 FEET
TRUE AIRSPEED = 105 KNOTS

METHOD

ENTER TRUE AIRSPEED AT 105 KNOTS AND MOVE LEFT TO 8000 POUND GROSS WEIGHT LINE. MOVE UP TO FUEL FLOW SCALE AND READ 510 LB/HR. MOVE DOWN TO CALIBRATED TORQUE SCALE AND READ 39.0 PSI. MOVE LEFT (AT 105 KNOTS) TO 10 SQ FEET OF LINE, MOVE UP AND READ 4.0 DPSI. DIVIDE 4 SQ FEET BY 10 SQ FEET = 40%. 40% OF 4.0 DPSI = 1.6 DPSI. ADD 1.6 AND 39.0 = 40.6 PSI. MOVE UP FROM TORQUE SCALE AT THIS POINT TO FUEL FLOW SCALE AND READ 537 LB/HR.

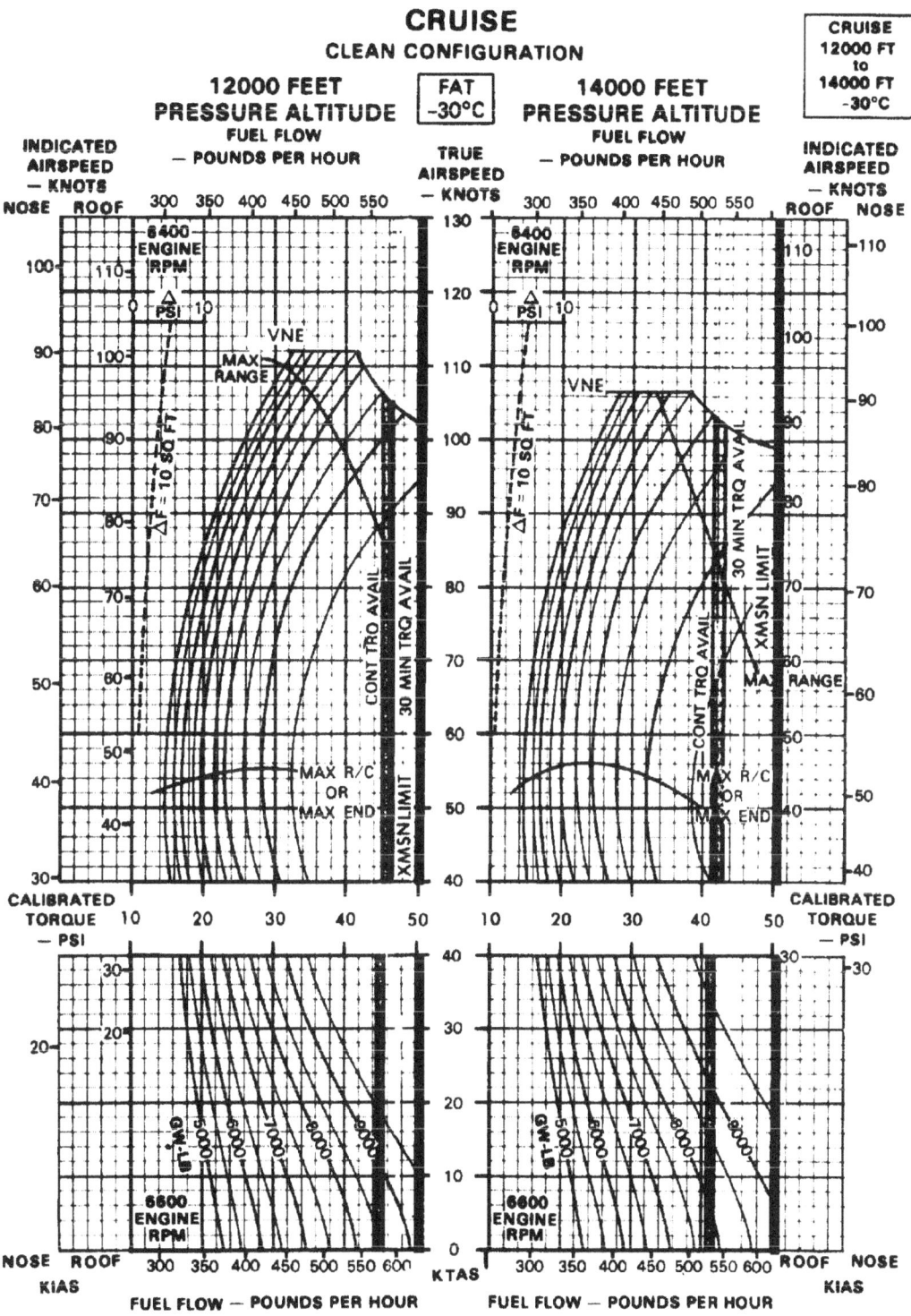

Figure 7-6. Cruise Chart (Sheet 4 of 24)

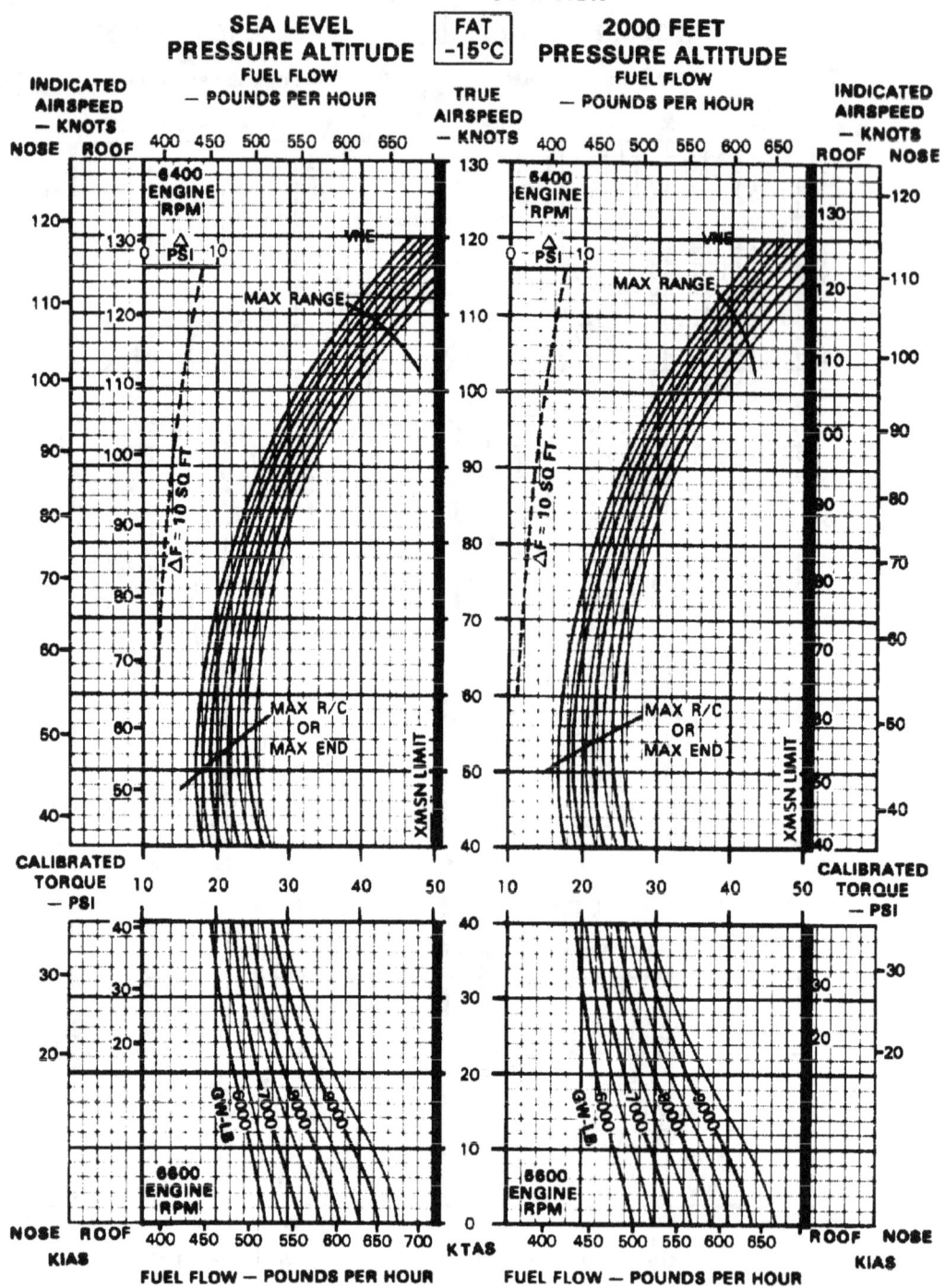

Figure 7-6. Cruise Chart (Sheet 5 of 24)

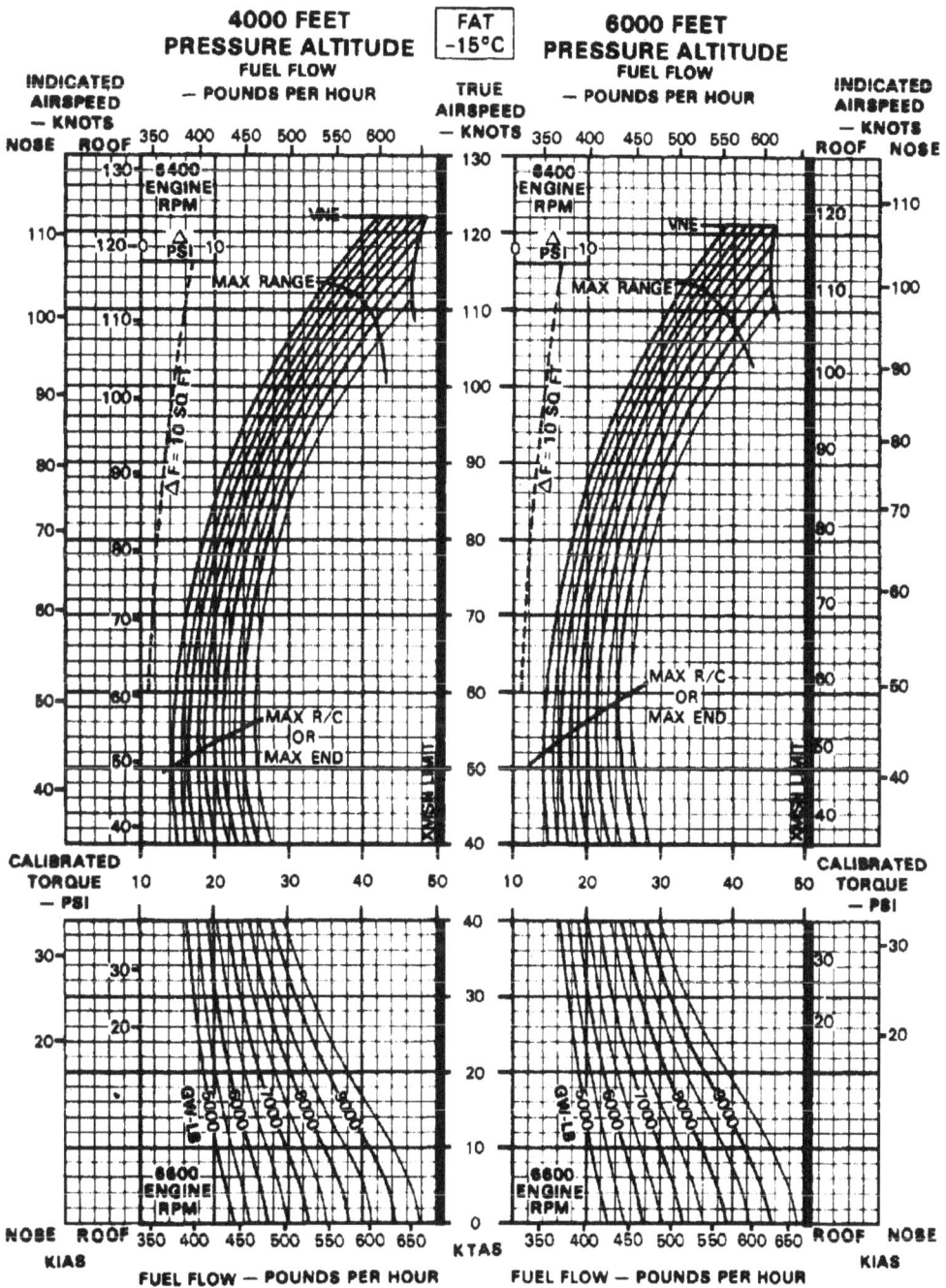

Figure 7-6. Cruise Chart (Sheet 6 of 24)

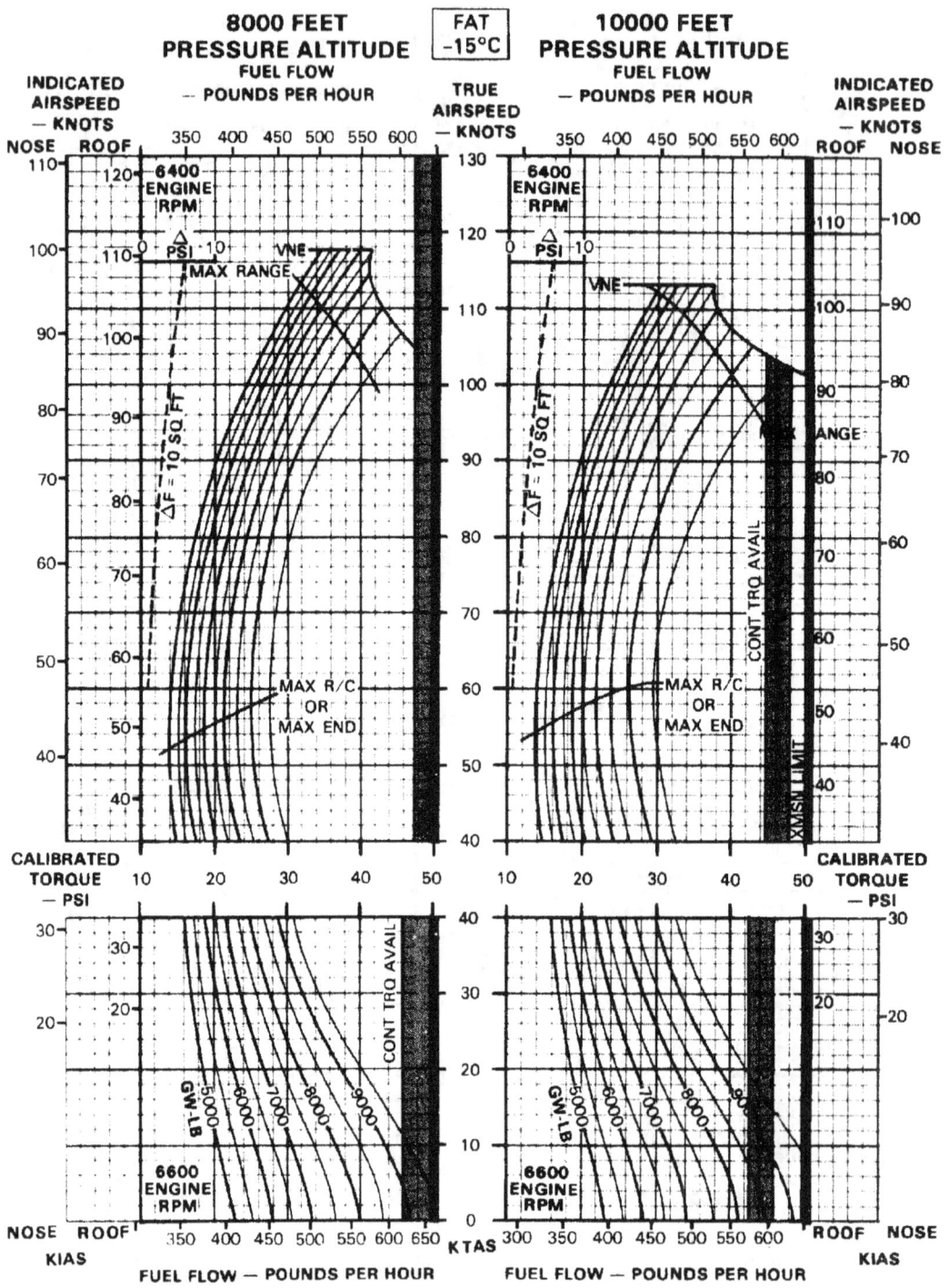

Figure 7-6. Cruise chart (Sheet 7 of 24)

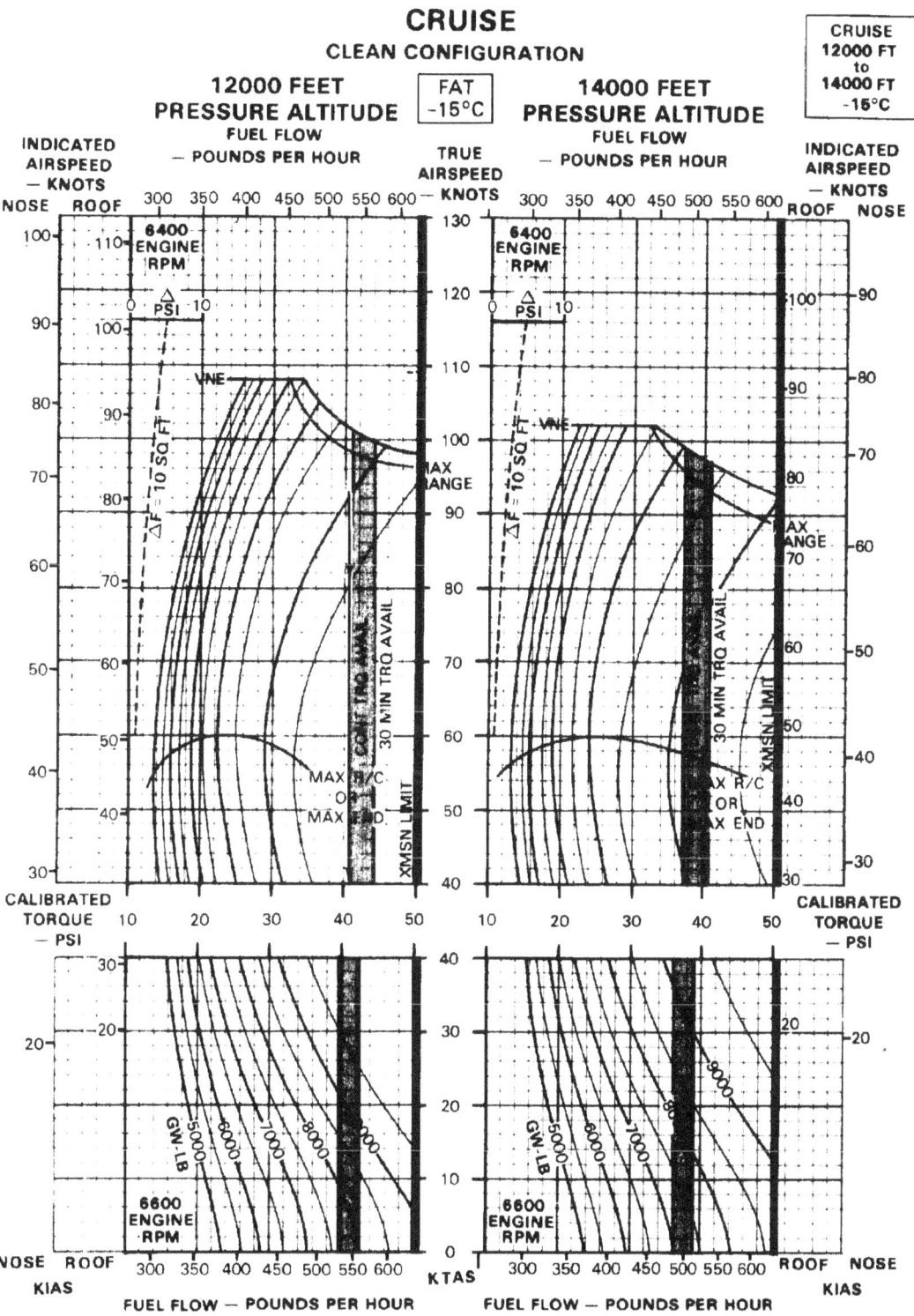

Figure 7-6. Cruise chart (Sheet 8 of 24)

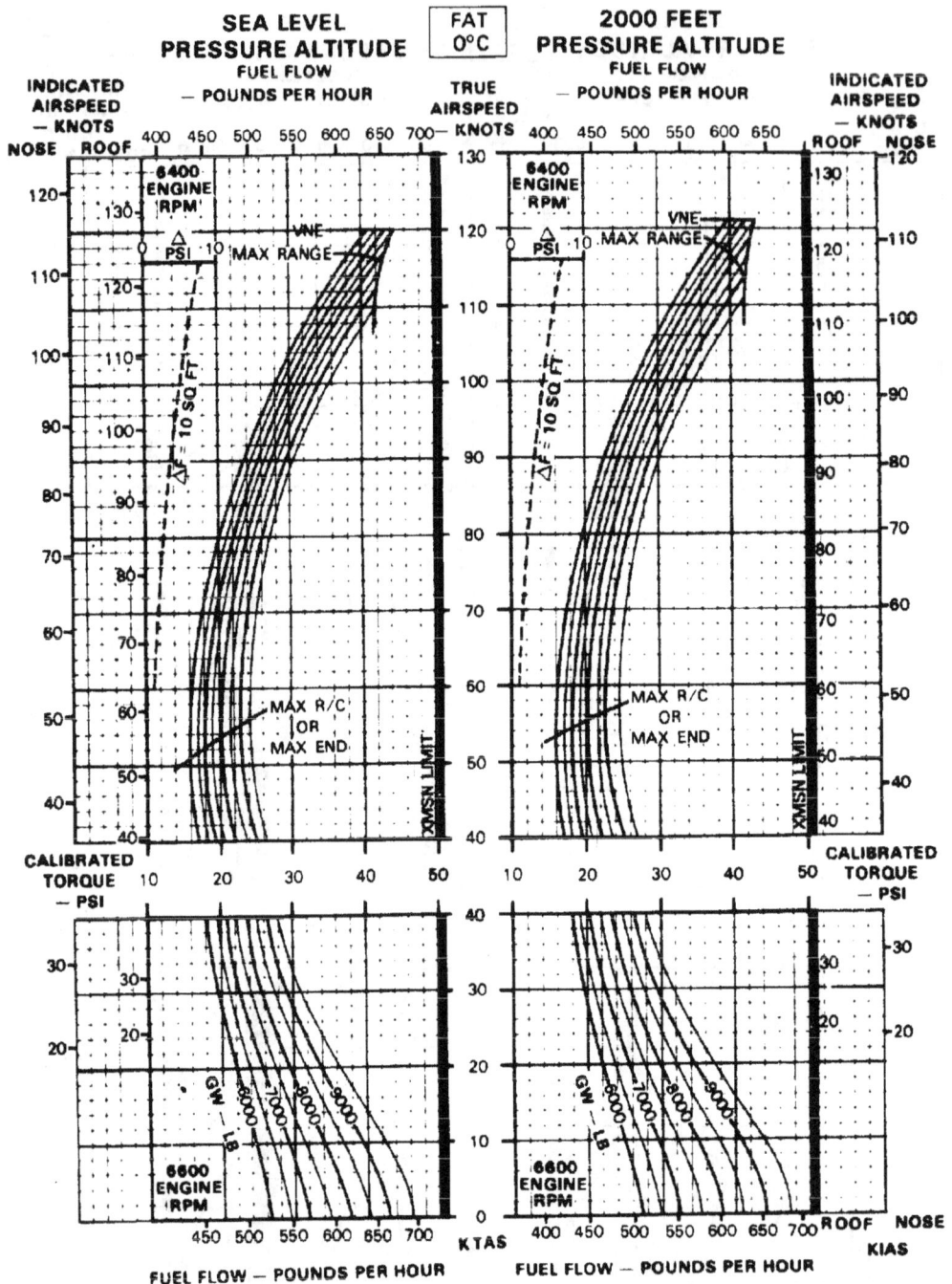

Figure 7-6. Cruise Chart (Sheet 9 of 24)

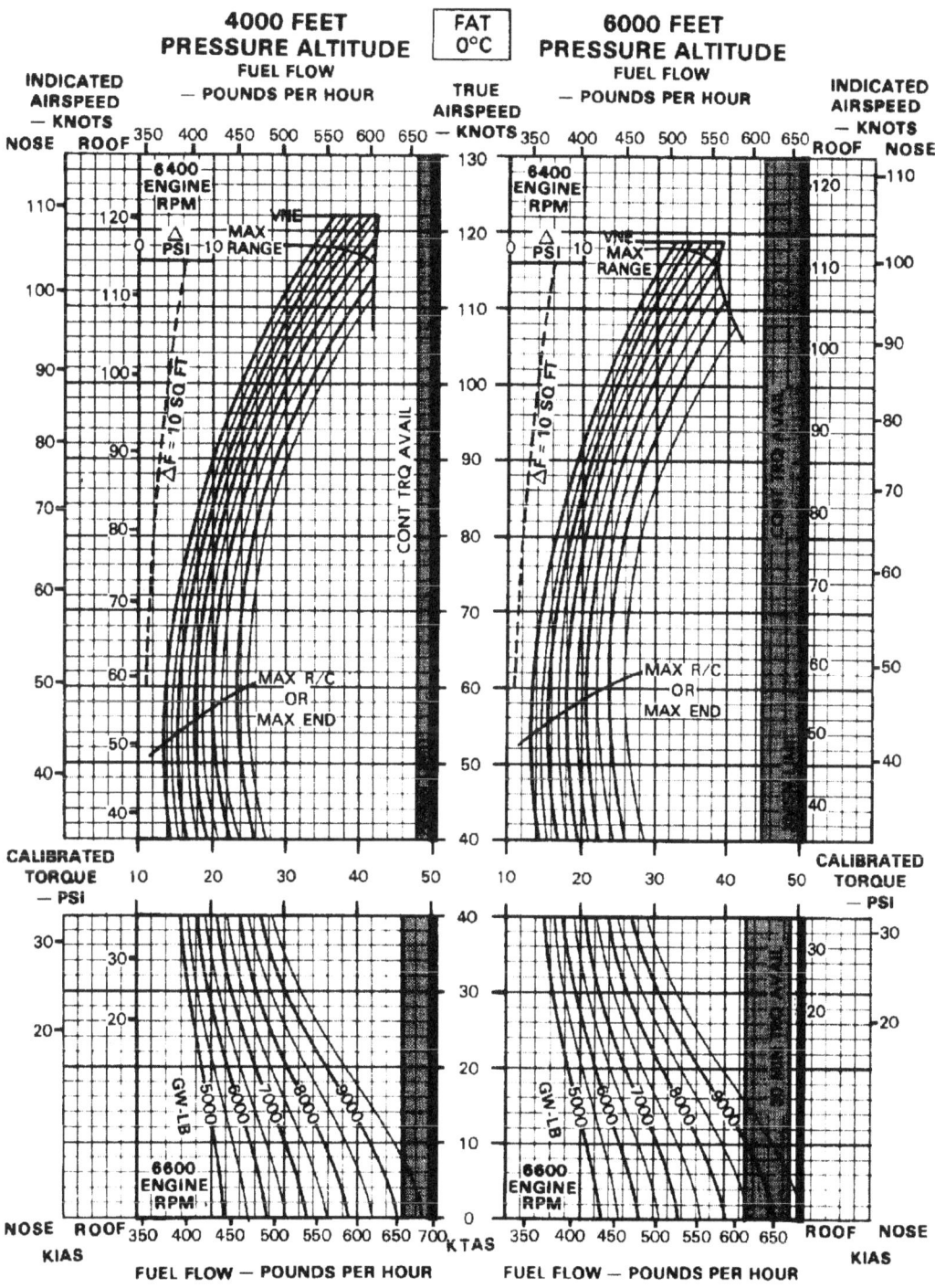

Figure 7-6. Cruise chart (Sheet 10 of 24)

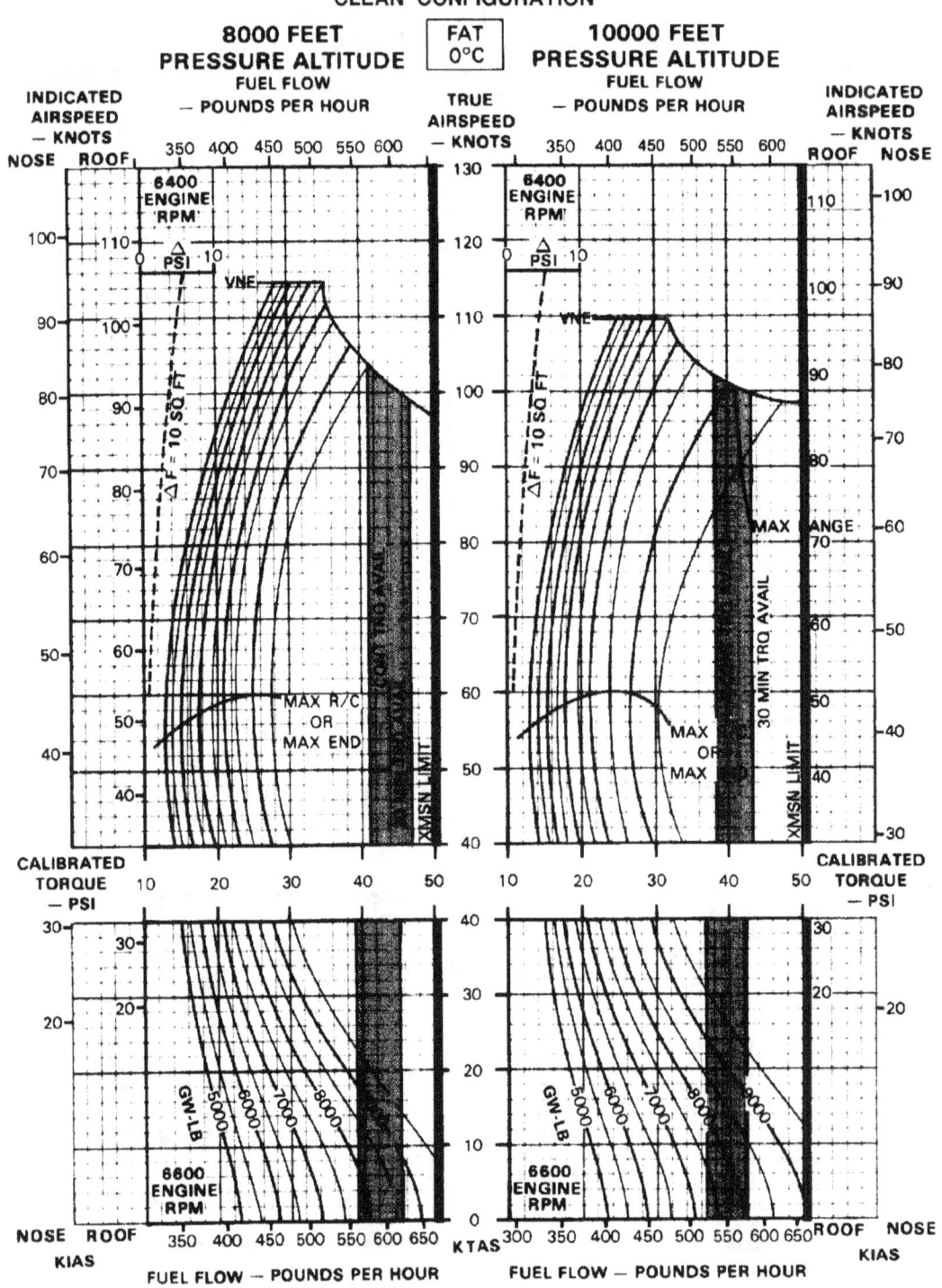

Figure 7-6. Cruise chart (Sheet 11 of 24)

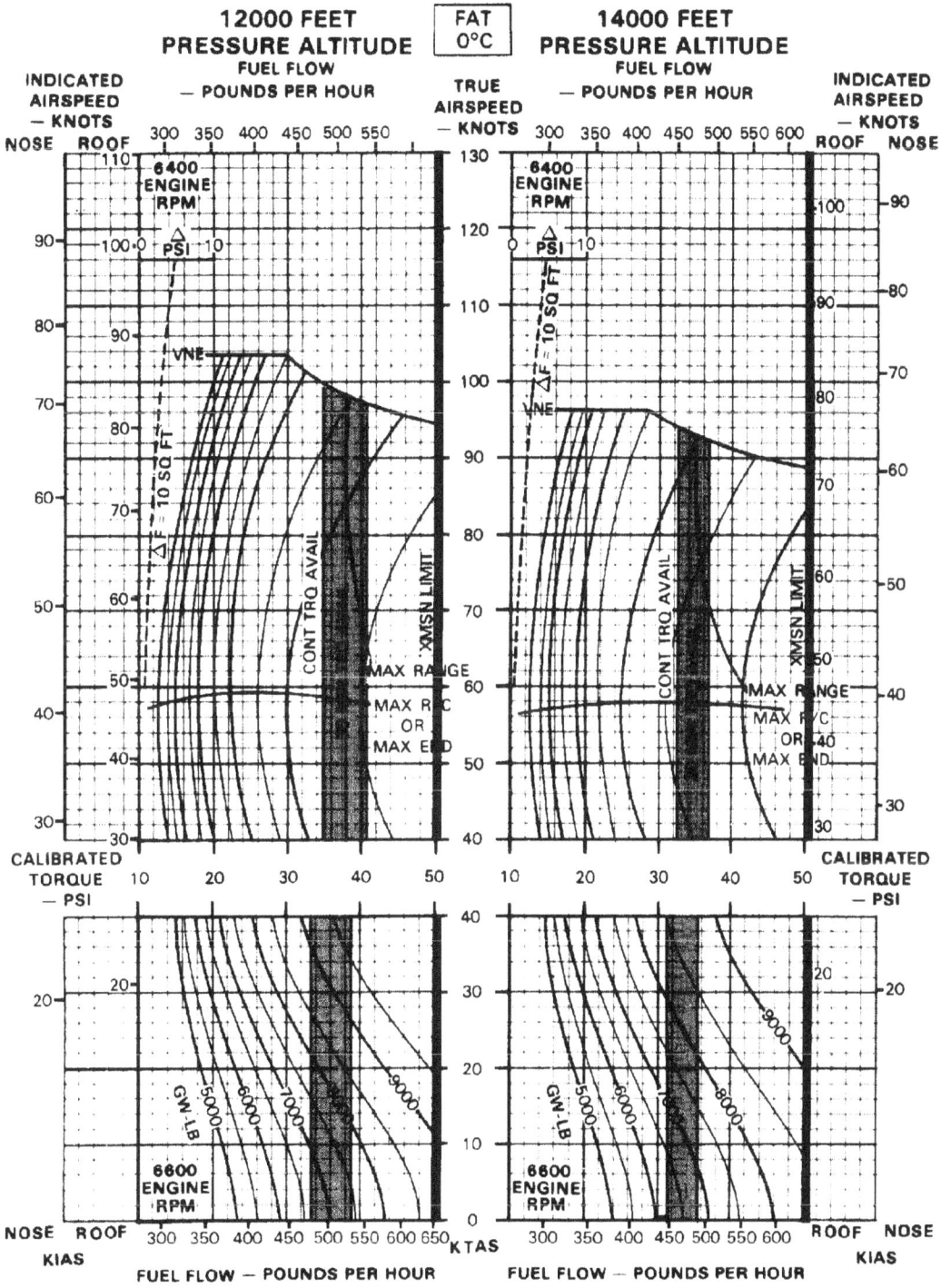

Figure 7-6. Cruise chart (Sheet 12 of 24)

TM 55-1520-210-10

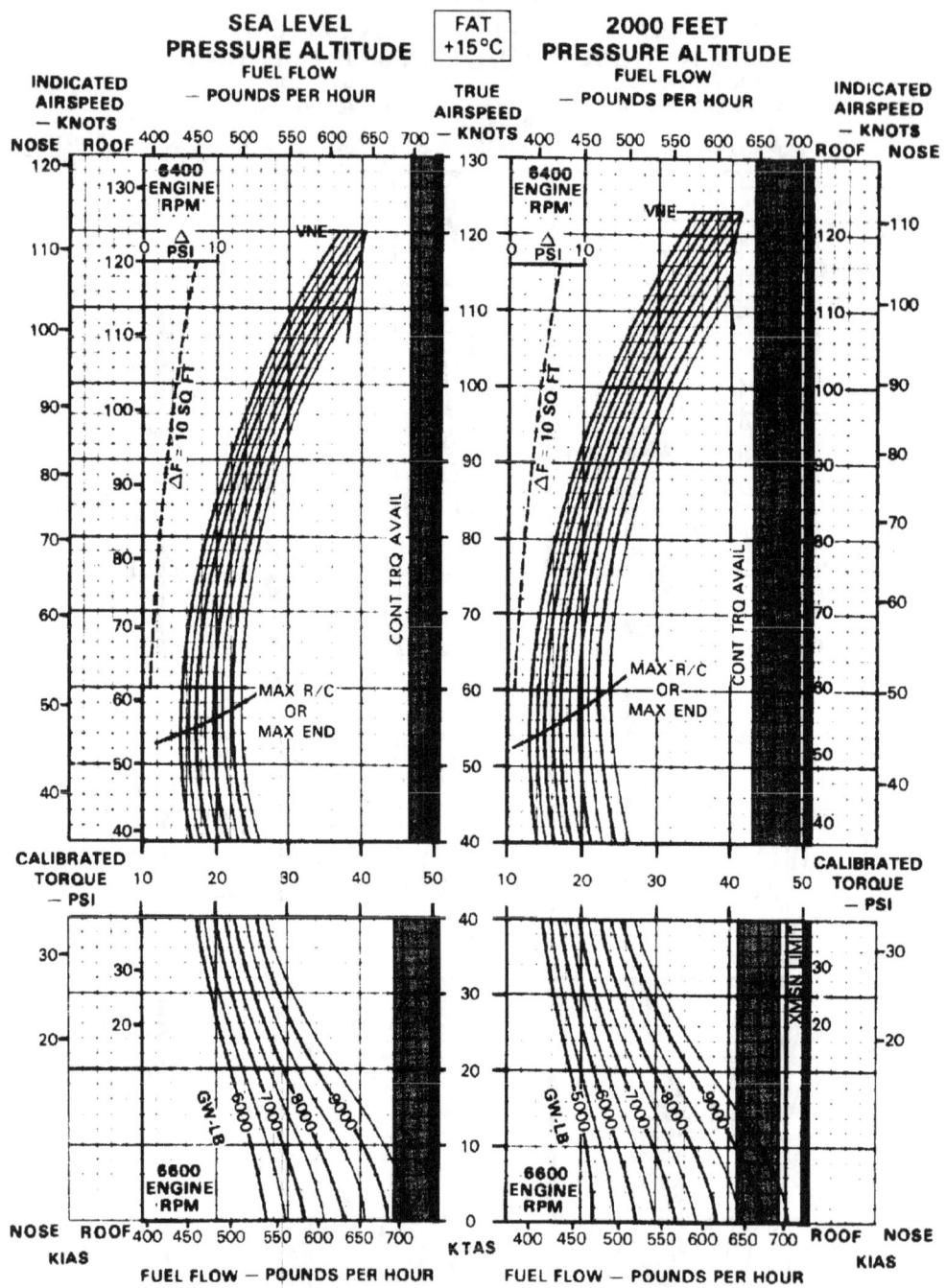

DATA BASIS: DERIVED FROM YUH-1 FLIGHT TEST, ASTA-TDR 66-04, NOVEMBER 1970

Figure 7-6. Cruise Chart (Sheet 13 of 24)

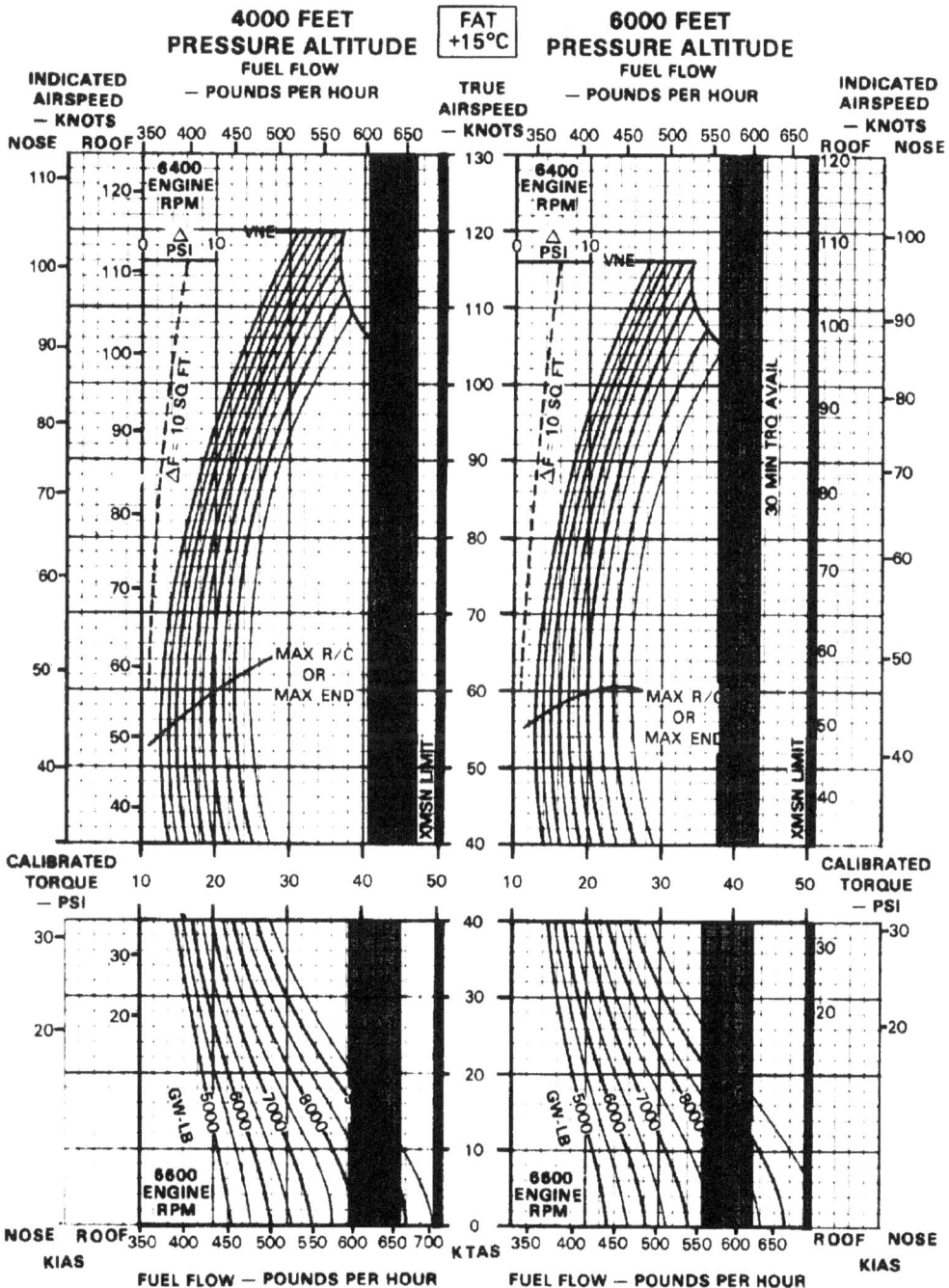

Figure 7-6. Cruise Chart (Sheet 14 of 24)

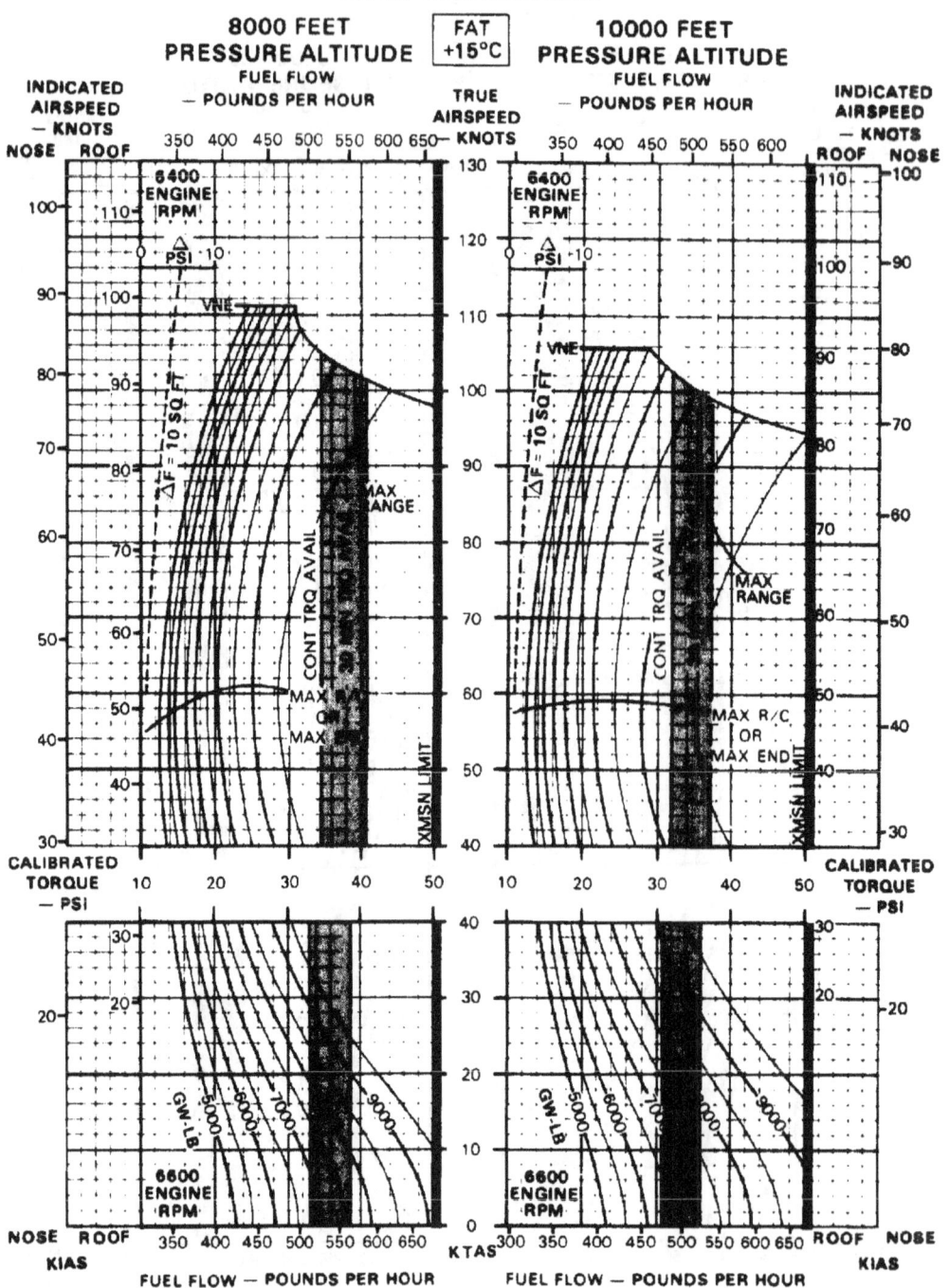

Figure 7-6. Cruise Chart (Sheet 15 of 24)

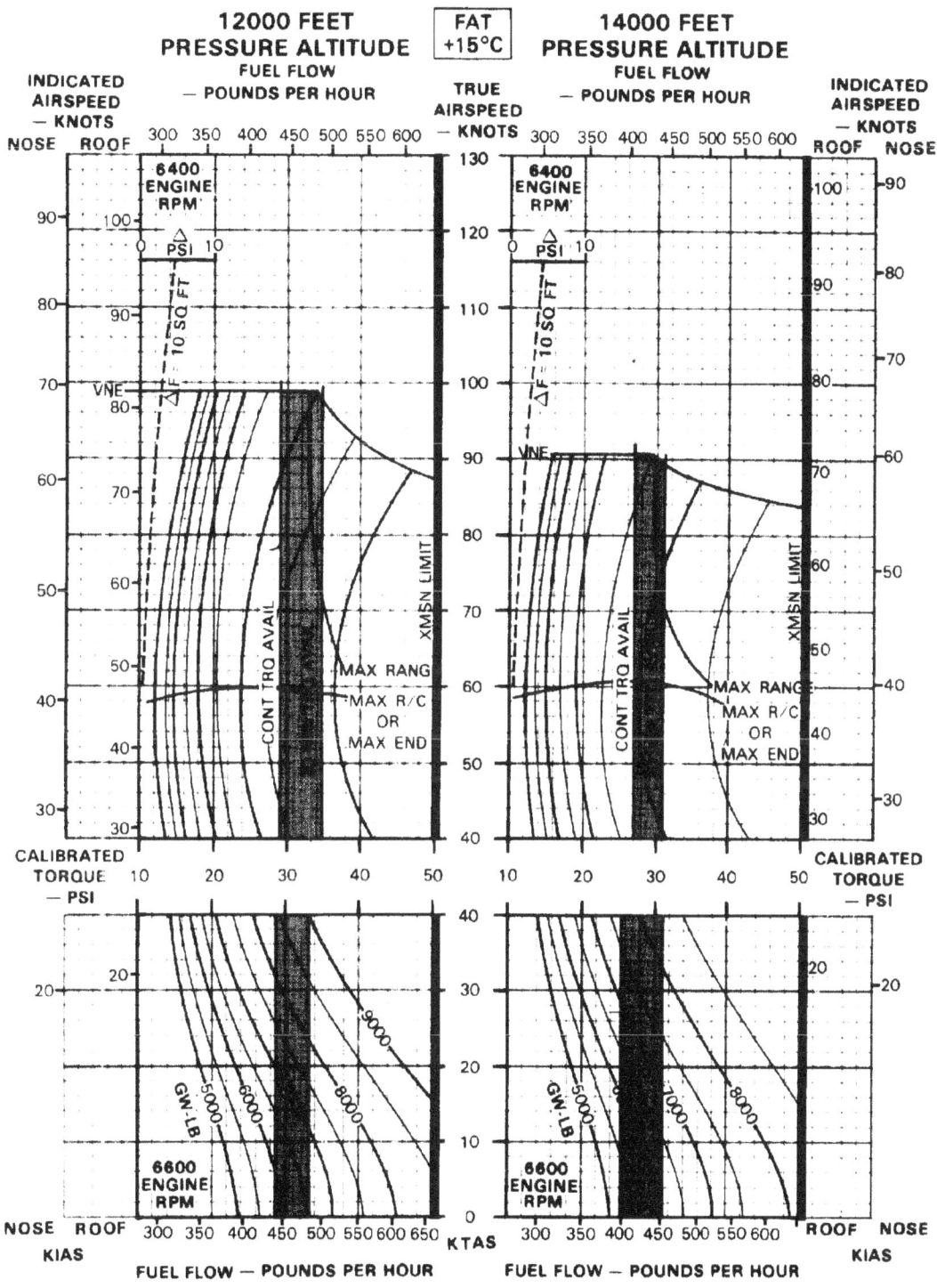

Figure 7-6. Cruise chart (Sheet 16 of 24)

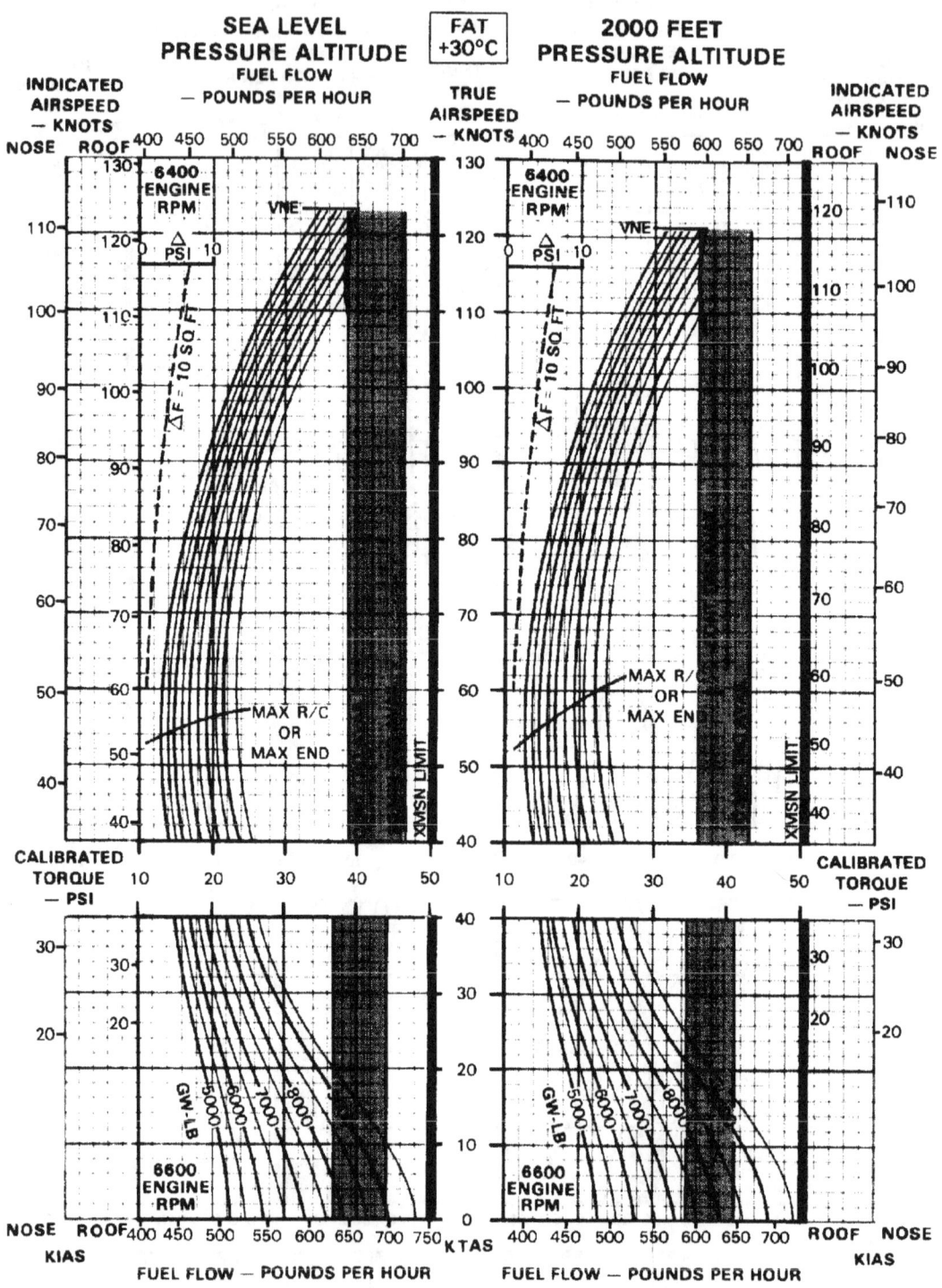

Figure 7-6. Cruise chart (Sheet 17 of 24)

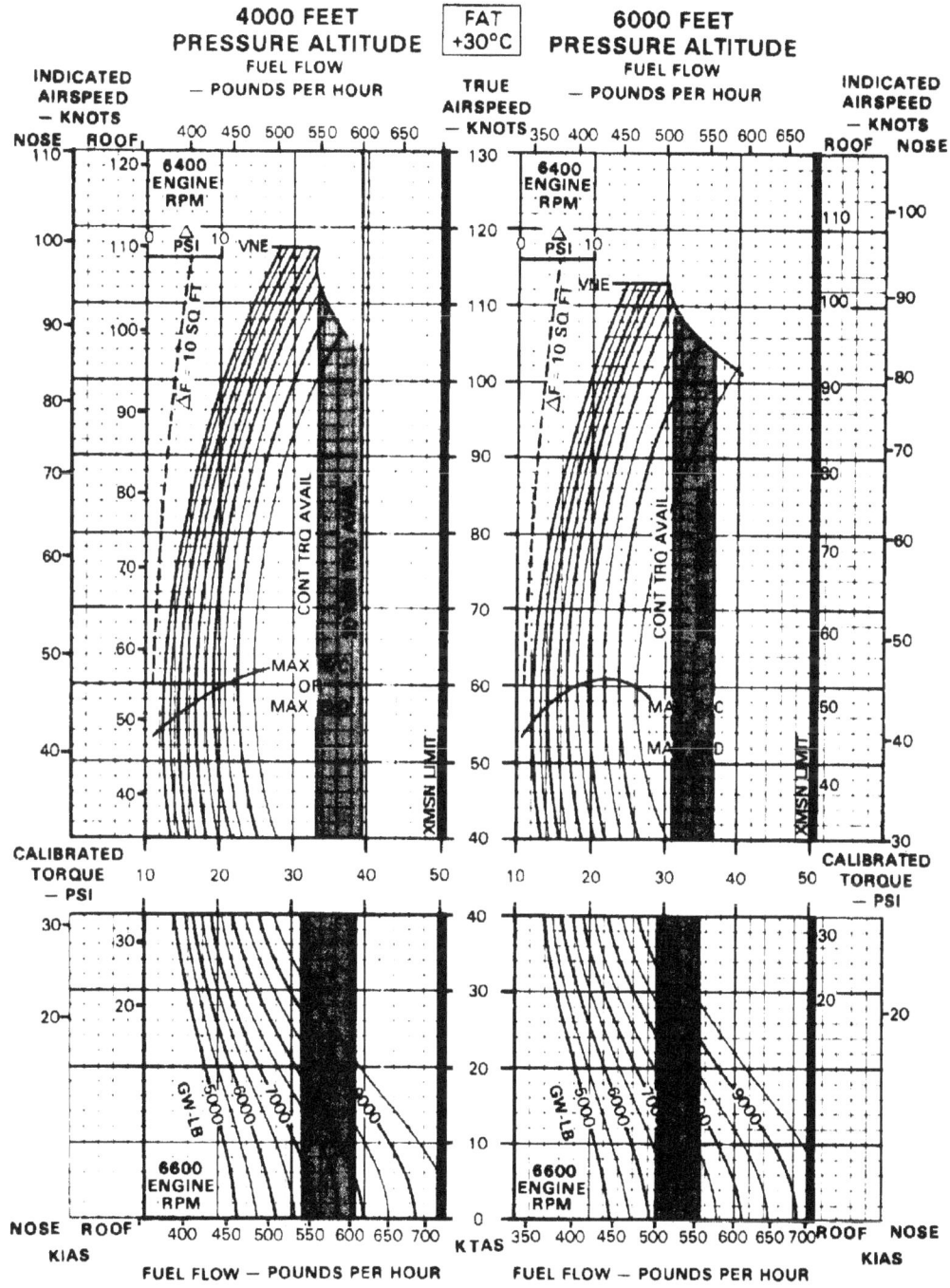

DATA BASIS: DERIVED FROM YUH1-1H FLIGHT TEST, ASTA-TDR 66-04, NOVEMBER 1970

Figure 7-6. Cruise Chart (Sheet 18 of 24)

TM 55-1520-210-10

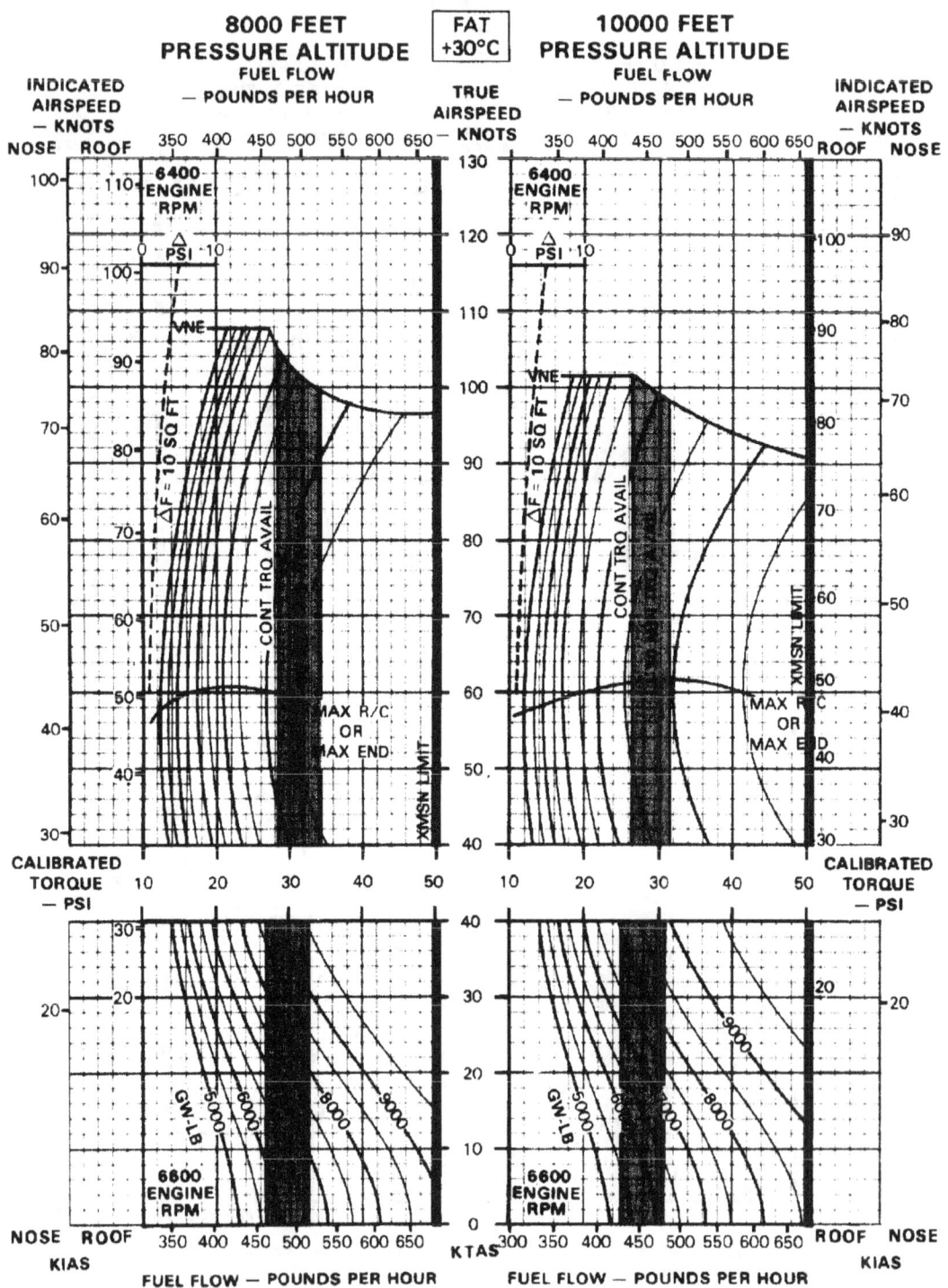

Figure 7-6. Cruise chart (Sheet 19 of 24)

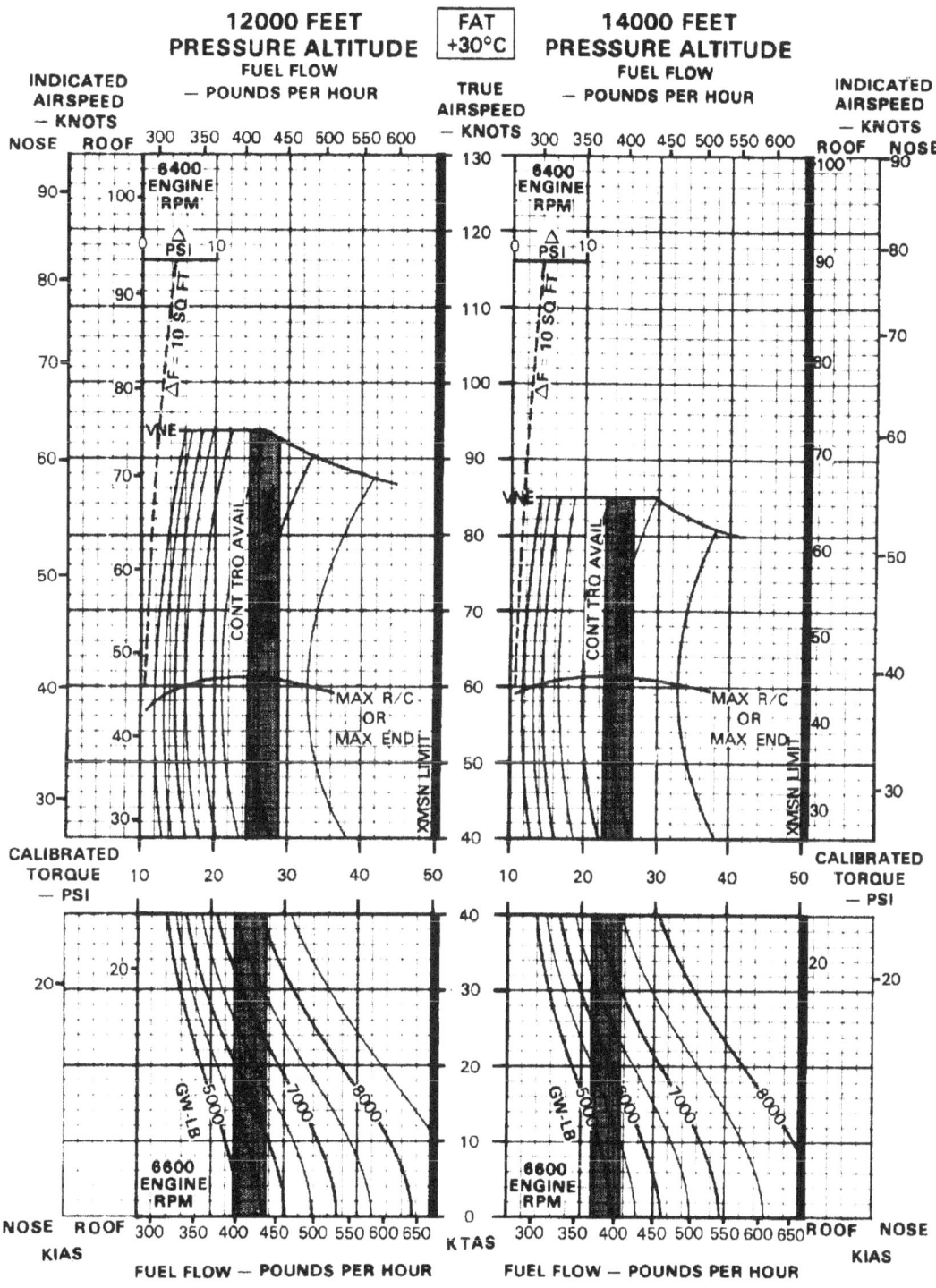

Figure 7-6. Cruise chart (Sheet 20 of 24)

TM 55-1520-210-10

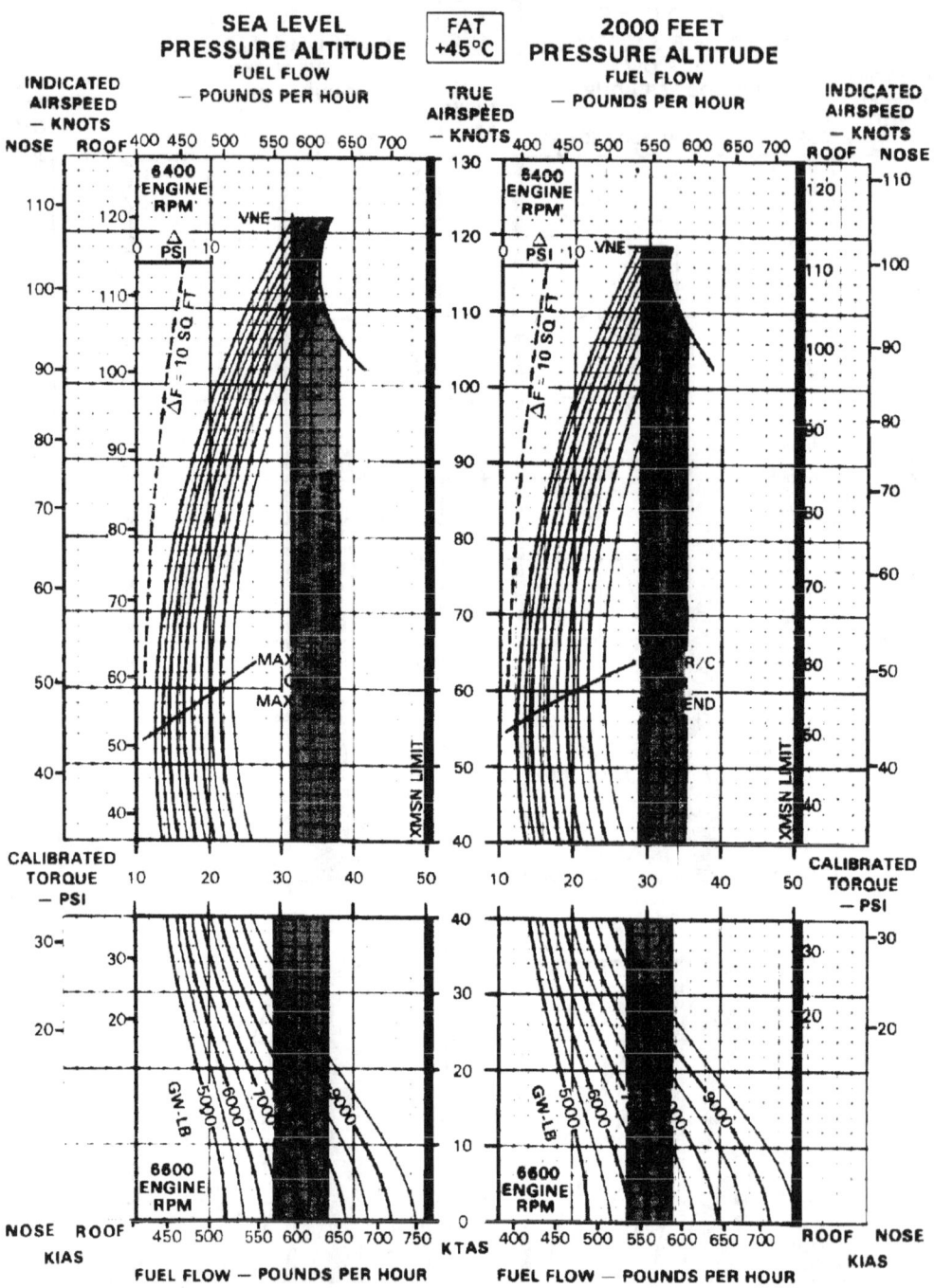

DATA BASIS: DERIVED FROM YUH-1 FLIGHT TEST, ASTS-TDR 66-04, NOVEMBER 1970

Figure 7-6. Cruise Chart (Sheet 21 of 24)

7-44

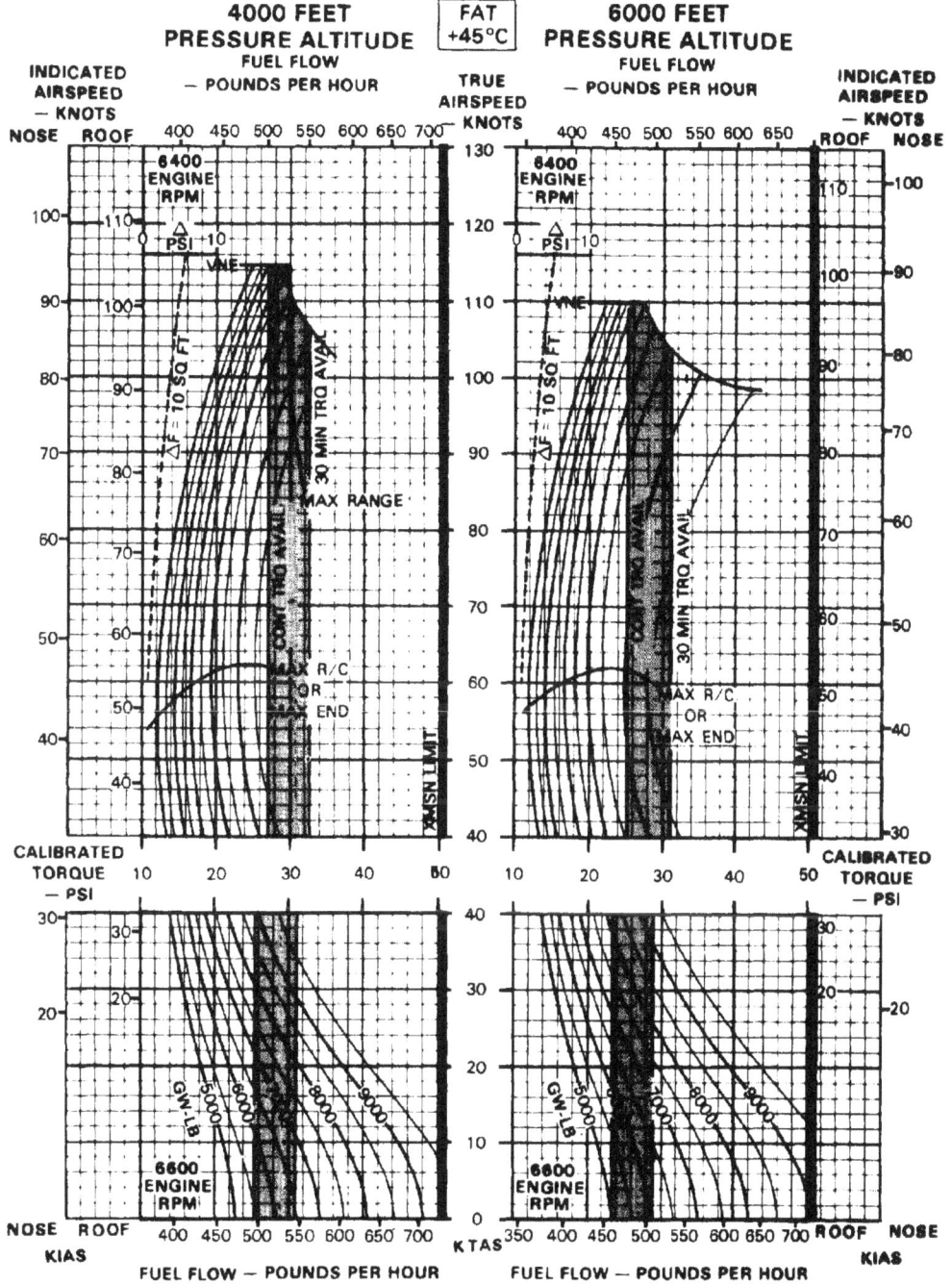

Figure 7-6. Cruise Chart (Sheet 22 of 24)

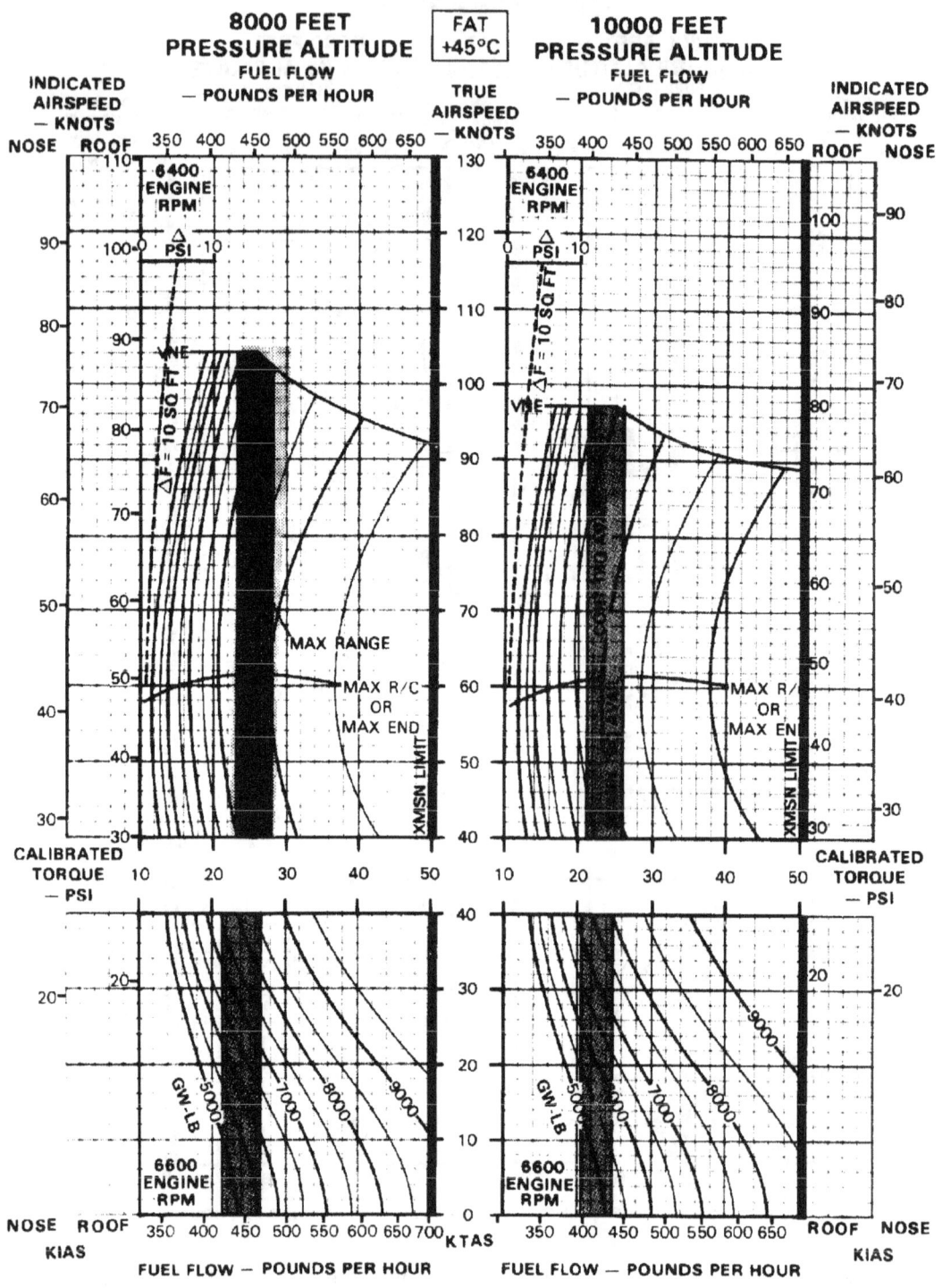

Figure 7-6. Cruise chart (Sheet 23 of 24)

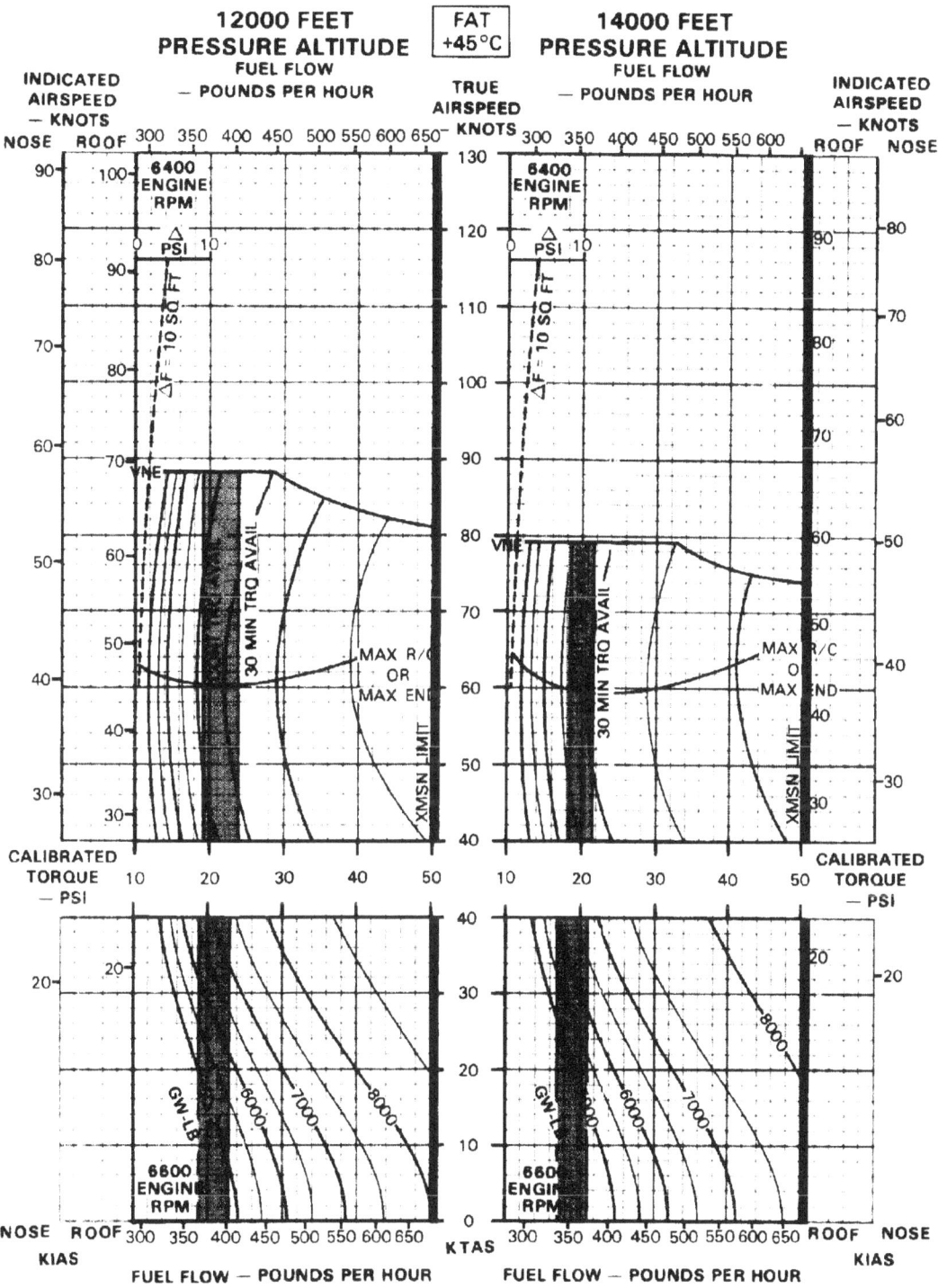

Figure 7-6. Cruise chart (Sheet 24 of 24)

DRAG

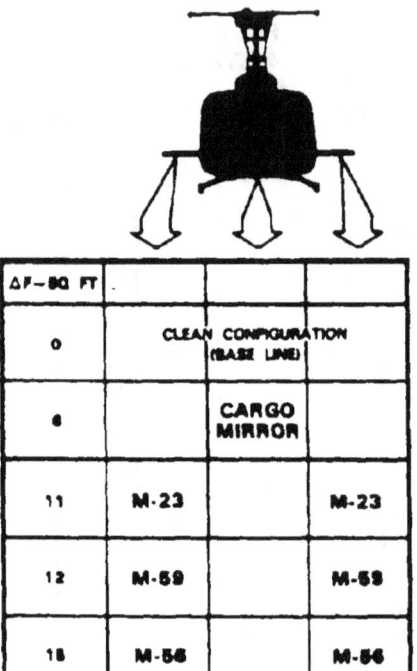

NOTE

The IR Scoup Suppressor has a drag of two square feet

EXAMPLE A

WANTED

CHANGE IN TORQUE REQUIRED DUE TO EQUIVALENT FLAT PLATE DRAG AREA CHANGE (AF) FROM CLEAN (BASELINE) CONFIGURATION TO AN M-56 SUBSYSTEM CONFIGURATION

AF DRAG AREA CHANGE - 15 SQ. FT.
TRUE AIRSPEED - 120 KNOTS
PRESSURE ALITITUDE - SEA LEVEL
FAT - 0 °C

METHOD

ENTER DRAG AREA CHANGE
MOVE RIGHT TO TRUE AIRSPEED
MOVE DOWN TO PRESSURE ALTITUDE
MOVE LEFT TO FREE AIR TEMPERATURE
MOVE DOWN. READ CHANGE IN
TORQUE - 122 PSI

EXAMPLE B

WANTED

INCREASE IN DRAG AREA DUE TO EXTERNAL CARGO

KNOWN

SHAPE OF EXTERNAL LOAD - CYLINDER
FRONTAL AREA OF EXTERNAL LOAD - 6.8 SQ. FT.

METHOD

ENTER CHART AT SYMBOL FOR CYLINDER
MOVE DOWN TO 6.8 SQ. FT.
MOVE RIGHT AND READ INCREASED DRAG AREA - 4.0 SQ. FT.

Figure 7-7. Drag Chart (Sheet 1 of 2)

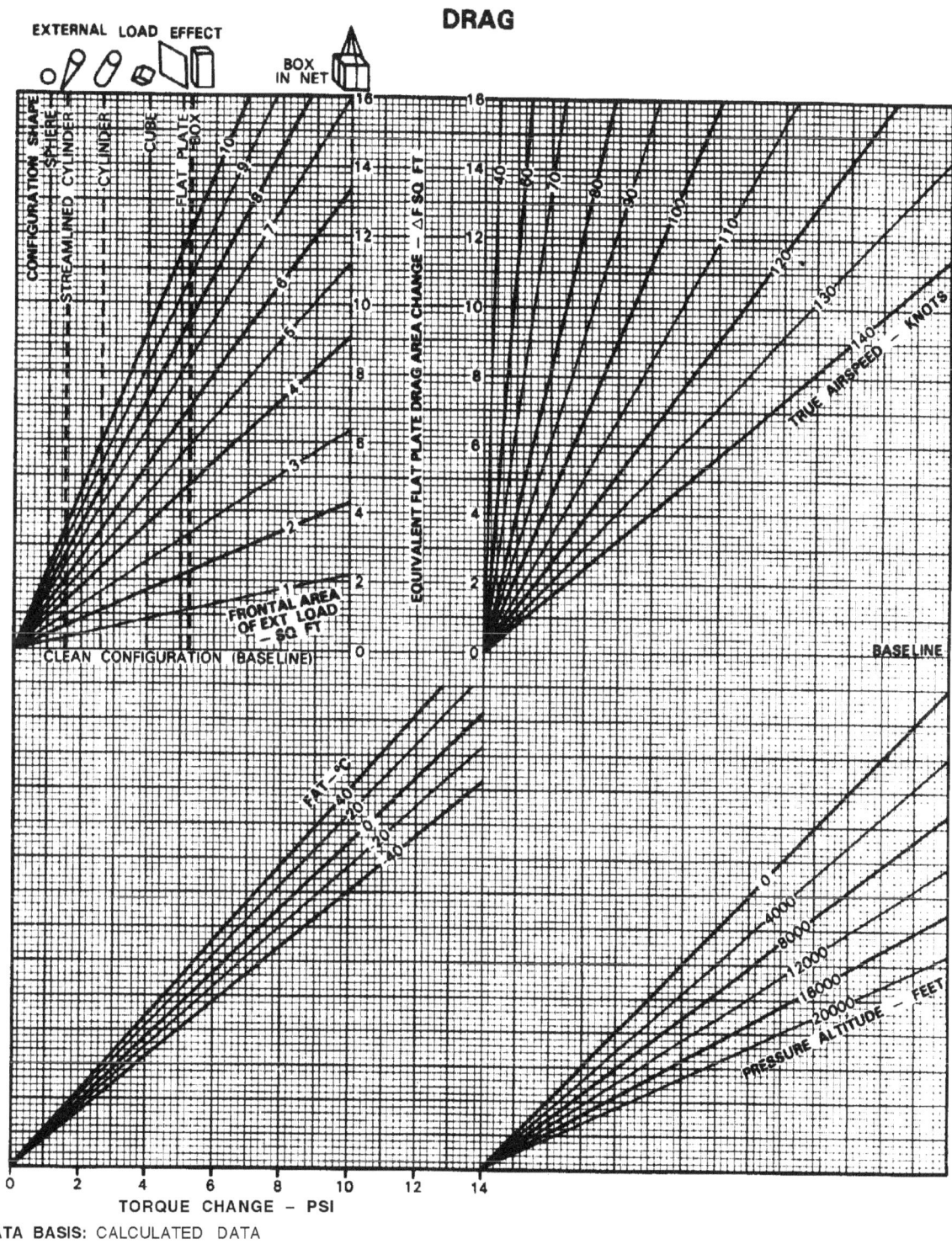

Figure 7-7. Drag Chart (Sheet 2 of 2)

CLIMB−DESCENT
314 ROTOR/6400 ENGINE RPM

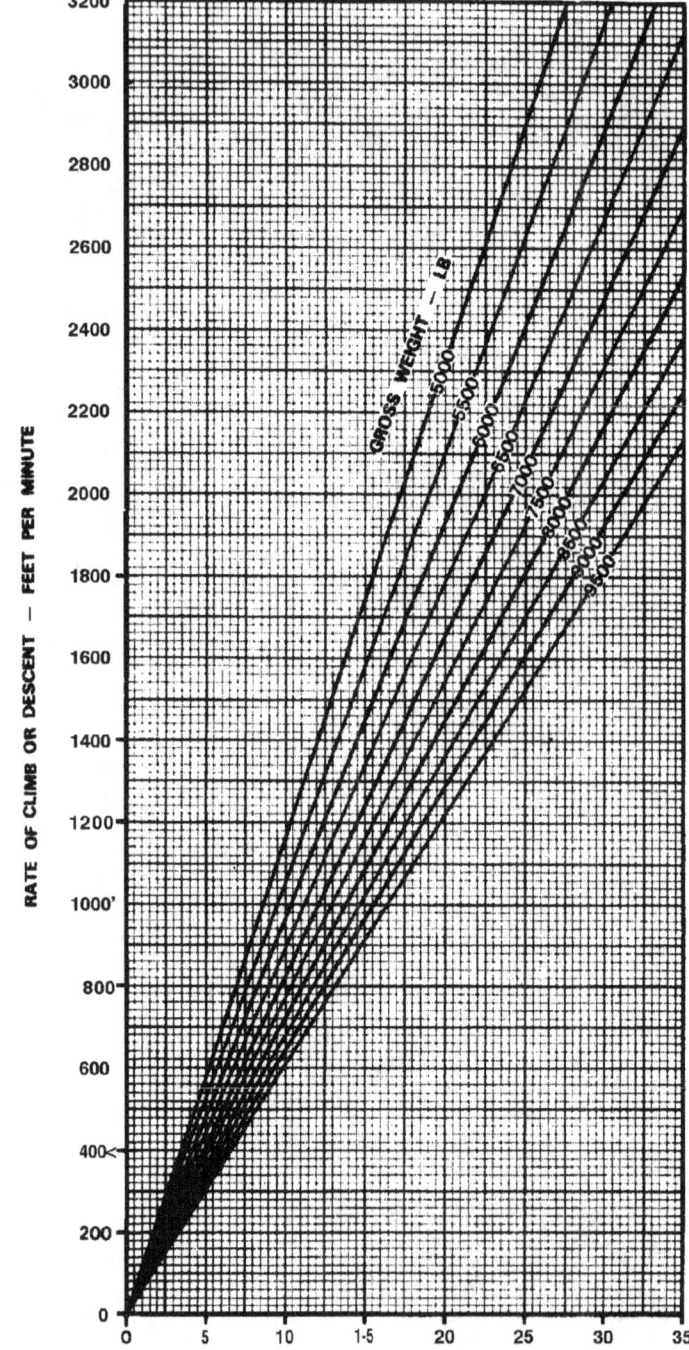

EXAMPLE

WANTED

CALIBRATED TORQUE CHANGE FOR DESIRED R/C OR R/D

KNOWN

GROSS WEIGHT = 6000 LB
DESIRED R/C = 1200 FT/MIN

METHOD

ENTER R/C
MOVE RIGHT TO GROSS WEIGHT
MOVE DOWN, READ CALIBRATED
TORQUE CHANGE = 12.5 PSI

DATA BASIS: DERIVED FROM FLIGHT TEST FTC-TDR 62-21, DECEMBER 1962, AND CALCULATED DATA.

Figure 7-8 Climb-Descent Chart

TM 55-1520-210-10

FUEL FLOW
JP-4 FUEL

EXAMPLE B

WANTED

FUEL FLOW AT ENGINE IDLE AND AT 324 ROTOR/6600 ENGINE RPM WITH FLAT PITCH

KNOWN

PRESSURE ALTITUDE = 11000 FEET, FAT = 0°

METHOD

ENTER PRESSURE ALTITUDE
MOVE RIGHT TO (ENGINE IDLE) FAT
MOVE DOWN, READ ENGINE IDLE
FUEL FLOW = 223 LB/HR
REENTER PRESSURE ALTITUDE
MOVE RIGHT TO (FLAT PITCH) FAT
MOVE DOWN, READ FLAT PITCH
FUEL FLOW = 265 LB/HR

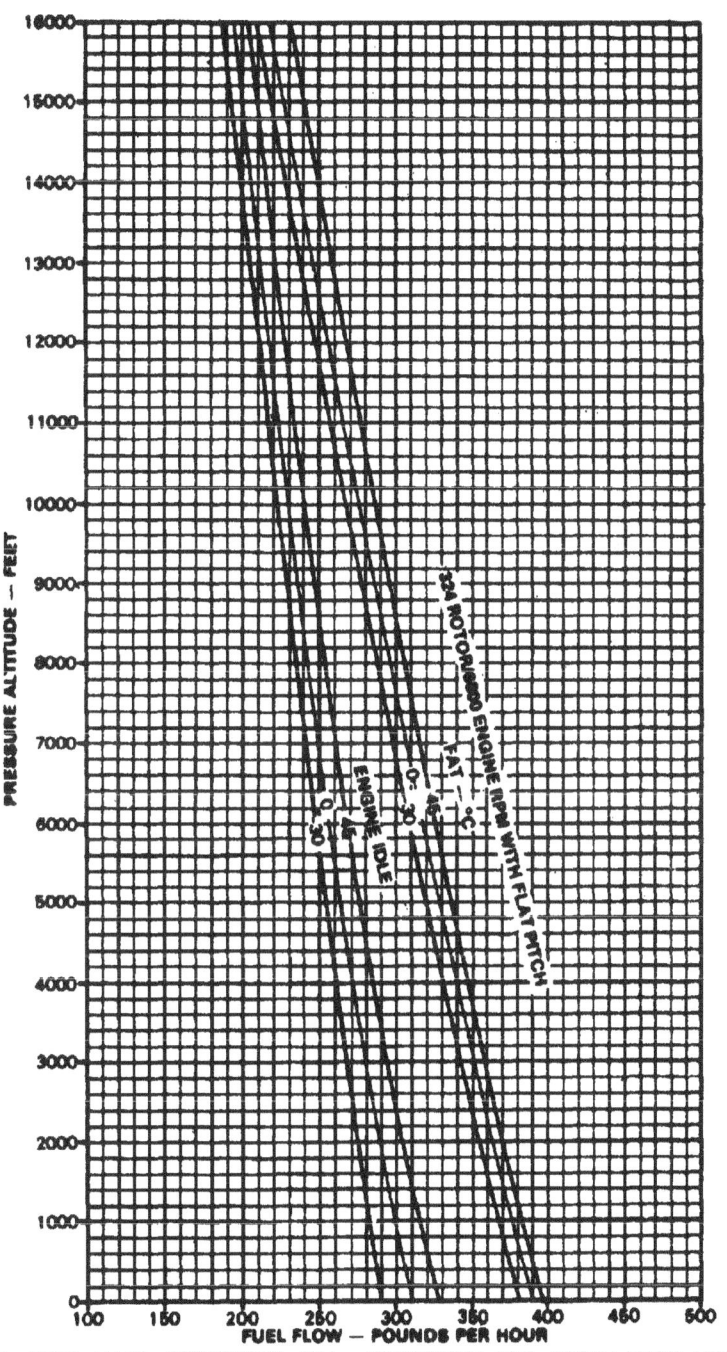

DATA BASIS: CALCULATED FROM MODEL SPEC 104.33, SEPTEMBER 1964; CORRECTED FOR INSTALLATION LOSSES BASED ON FLIGHT TEST FTC-TDR 64-27, NOVEMBER 1964

Figure 7-9. Idle Fuel Flow Chart

ALL DATA ON PAGE 7-52 INCLUDING FIGURE 7-9 (SHEET 2) DELETED.

Change 2   7-51/(7-52 blank)

TM 55-1520-210-10

Chapter 8
Normal Procedures

Section 1. MISSION PLANNING

8-1. Mission Planning. Mission planning begins when the mission is assigned and extends to the preflight check of the helicopter. It includes but is not limited to checks of operating limits and restrictions; weight balance and loading; performance; publication; flight plan and crew and passenger briefings. The pilot in command shall ensure compliance with the contents of this manual that are applicable to the mission.

8-2. Operating Limits and Restrictions. The minimum maximum normal and cautionary operational ranges represent careful aerodynamic and structural calculation substantiated by flight test data. These limitations shall be adhered to during all phases of the mission. Refer to chapter 5 OPERATING LIMITS AND RESTRICTIONS for detailed information.

8-3. Weight Balance and Loading. The helicopter shall be loaded cargo and passengers secured and weight and balance verified in accordance with chapter 6 WEIGHT BALANCE AND LOADING. This helicopter requires a weight and balance clearance in accordance with AR 95-1. The helicopter weight and center-of-gravity conditions shall be within the limits prescribed in Chapter 5 OPERATING LIMITS AND RESTRICTIONS.

8-4. Performance. Refer to chapter 7 or 7.1 PERFORMANCE DATA to determine the capability of the helicopter for the entire mission. Consideration shall be given to changes in performance resulting from variation in loads temperatures and pressure altitudes. Record the data on the Performance Planning Card for use in completing the flight plan and for reference throughout the mission.

8-5. Crew and Passenger Briefings. A crew briefing shall be conducted to ensure a thorough understanding of individual and team responsibilities. The briefing should include but not be limited to copilot crew chief mission equipment operator, and ground crew responsibilities and the coordination necessary to complete the mission In the most efficient manner. A review of visual signals Is desirable when ground guides do not have direct voice communications link with the crew.

Section 11. CREW DUTIES

86. Crew Duties.

 a. Responsibilities. The minimum crew required to fly the helicopter is a pilot. Additional crewmembers as required may be added at the discretion of the commander. The manner in which each crewmember performs his related duties is the responsibility of the pilot in command.

 b. Pilot. The pilot in command is responsible for all aspects of mission planning preflight and operation of the helicopter. He will assign duties and functions to all other crewmembers as required. Prior to or during preflight the pilot will brief the crew on the mission performance data procedures taxi and load operations.

 c. Copilot (when assigned). The copilot must be familiar with the pilots duties and the duties of the other crew positions. The copilot will assist the pilot as directed.

 d. Crew Chief (when assigned). The crew chief will perform all duties as assigned by the pilot.

 e. Passenger Briefing. The following is an outline that should be used in accomplishing required passenger briefings. Items that do not pertain to a specific mission may be omitted.

    (1) Crew Introduction.

    (2) Equipment.

        (a) Personal to include ID tags.

        (b) Professional.

        (c) Survival.

    (3) Flight Data.

        (a) Route.

TM 55-1520-210-10

    (b) Altitude.

    (c) Time enroute.

    (d) Weather.

(4) Normal Procedures.

    (a) Entry and exit of helicopter.

    (b) Seating.

    (c) Seat belts.

    (d) Movement m helicopter.

    (e) Internal communications.

    (f) Security of equipment.

    (g) Smoking.

    (h) Oxygen.

    (i) Refueling.

    (j) Weapons.

    (k) Protective masks.

    (l) Parachutes.

    (m) Ear protection.

    (n) ALSE.

(5) Emergency procedures.

    (a) Emergency exits.

    (b) Emergency equipment.

    (c) Emergency landing/ditching procedures.

8-7. Danger Areas. Refer to Figure -1.

Section III. OPERATING PREDURES AND MANEUVERS

8-8. Operating Procedures and Maneuvers. This section deals with normal procedures and includes all steps necessary to ensure safe and efficient operating of the helicopter from the time a preflight begins until the flight is completed and the helicopter is parked and secured. Unique feel, characteristics and reaction of the helicopter during various phases of operation and the techniques and procedures used for taxiing, takeoff, climb, etc., are described including precautions to be observed. Your flying experience is recognized; therefore basic flight principles are avoided. Only the duties of the minimum crew necessary for the actual operation of the helicopter are included

8-9. Additional Crew. Additional crew duties are covered as necessary in Section II, CREW DUTIES. Mission equipment checks are contained in Chapter 4, MISSION EQUIPMENT. Procedures specifically related to instrument flight that are different from normal procedures are covered in this section following normal procedures. Descriptions of functions operations and effects of controls are covered in Section V, FLIGHT CHARACTERISTICS and a repeated in this section only when required for emphasis. Checks that must be performed under adverse environmental conditions such as desert and cold weather operations supplement normal procedure checks in this section and are covered in Section VI, ADVERSE ENVIRONMENTAL CONDITIONS.

8-10. Checklist. Normal procedures are given primarily in checklist form and amplified as necessary in accompanying paragraph form when a detailed description of a procedure or maneuver is required. A condensed version of the amplified checklist omitting all explanatory text is contained in the Operator's Checklist TM 55-1520210-CL. To provide for easier cross-referencing the procedural steps in CL are numbered to coincide with the corresponding numbered steps in this manual.

8-11. Checks. The checklist may include items for day, night, and instrument flight with annotative indicators immediately preceding the check to which they are pertinent; N for night operation only; I for instrument operations only; and 0 to indicate a requirement if the equipment is installed When a helicopter is flown on a mission requiring intermediate stops it is not necessary to perform all of the normal checks. The steps that are C essential for safe helicopter operations on intermediate stops are designated as "thru-flight" checks. An asterisk (*) indicates that performance of steps is mandatory for all "thru-flights". The asterisk (-) applies only to checks performed prior to takeoff..

> **WARNING**
>
> Do not preflight until armament systems are safe.

812. Before Exterior Checks.

* 1. Covers, locking devices, tiedowns, and cables Removed, except aft main rotor tiedown.

2. Publications - Check in accordance with DA PAM 738-751 and locally required forms and publications.

3. AC circuit breakers - IN.

4. BAT switch ON. Check battery voltage. A minimum of 24 volts should be indicated on the DC voltmeter for a battery start.

5. Lights--ON. Check landing, search, anti-collision, position, interior lights and NVG lighting as required for condition and operation as required; position landing and search lights as desired; then OFF.

* 6. Fuel - Check quantity. Caps secure.

7. Fuel sample Check for contamination before first flight of the day. If the fuel sumps, and filter have not been drained by maintenance personnel, dram a sample as follows:

    a. Sumps - Drain sample and check.
    b. MAIN FUEL switch - ON.
    c. Filter - Dram sample and check.
O   d. Auxiliary fuel tanks - Drain sample and check
    e. MAIN FUEL switch - OFF.

O 8. Cargo hook Check as required, if use is anticipated, refer to Chapter 4, MISSION EQUIPMENT, for checks of the system.

9. BAT switch - OFF.

10. Flight Controls - Check freedom of movement of cyclic and collective; center cyclic, collective down.

8-13. Exterior Check. (Fig 8-2).

8-14. Area 1.

* 1. Main rotor blade - Check condition.

2. Fuselage - Check as follows:

    a. Cabin top - Check windshields, wipers, FAT probe, WSPS, for condition.

    b. Radio compartment - Check security of all equipment. Check battery, If installed. Secure door.

    c. Antennas - Check condition and security.

O   d. Pitot tube - Check security and unobstructed.

    e. Cabin lower area - Check condition of windshield, antennas, WSPS and fuselage. Check for loose objects inside winch might Jam controls.

O   f. Cargo suspension mirror - Check security and cover installed. Uncover and adjust if cargo operations are anticipated.

8-15. Area 2.

1. Fuselage - Check as follows:
O   a. Static port - Check unobstructed.

    b. Copilot seat, seat belt and shoulder harness - Check condition and security; secure belt and harness if seat is not used during flight.

    c. Copilot door - Check condition and security.

    d. Cabin doors - Check condition and security.

    c. Landing gear - Check condition and security; ground handling wheels removed.

    f. Radio and electrical compartments - Check condition, circuit breakers m and components secure. Secure access doors.

O* g. Armament systems -Check weapon(s) safe. Check condition and security. Refer to Chapter 4, MISSION EQUIPMENT, for checks of the system.

2. Engine compartment - Check fluid lines and connections for condition and security. Check general condition. Cowling secure

816. Area 3.

1. Tailboom - Check as follows:
    a Skin - Check condition.
    b. Driveshaft cover - Check secure.
    c. Synchronized elevator - Check condition and security.
    d. Antennas - Check condition and security.
    e. Tail skid - Check condition and security.

TM 55-1520-210-10

* 2. Tail rotor Check condition and free movement on flapping axis. The tail rotor blades should be checked as the main rotor blade is rotated. Visually check all components for security.

* 3. Main rotor blade - Check condition, rotate in normal direction 90 degrees to fuselage, tiedown removed.

8-17. Area 4.

* 1. Tail rotor gearboxes (90 and 42 degrees) - Check general condition, oil levels, filler caps secure.

2. Tailboom - Check as follows;

 a. Skin - Check condition.
 b. Antennas - Check condition and security.
 c. Synchronized elevator - Check condition and security

3. Engine exhaust/smoke generator - Check condition. Refer to Chapter 4, MISSION EQUIPMENT, for systems check.

4. Oil cooling fan and heater compartments - Check condition of fan, flight control and cables, tail rotor servo for leaks and security and battery if installed; check for installation of structural support; check tailboom attachment bolts; check heater for condition and security if installed; check area clear of obstructions; secure doors.

8-18. Area 5.

* 1. Engine compartment - Check fluid lines and connections for condition and security. Check fluid levels and general condition; cowling secure.

2. Hydraulic fluid sight gage - Check.

3. Fuselage - Check as follows:

O* a. Armament systems - Check weapon(s) safe. Check condition and security. Refer to Chapter-4, MISSION EQUIPMENT, for systems check.
 b. Cabin doors - Check condition and security.
 c. Landing gear - Check condition and security; ground handling wheels removed.
O d. Static port -Check unobstructed.
 e. Pilot door -Check condition and security.
 f. Pilot seat, seat belt and shoulder harness - Check condition and security.

O g. Fire extinguisher - Check secure.

8-19. Area 6.

* l. Man rotor system - Check condition and security; check level of fluid in dampers, blade grips, and pillow blocks.

2. Transmission area - Check as follows:

 a. Transmission and hydraulic filler caps - Secure.
 b. Main driveshaft - Check condition and security.
 c. Engme air intake - Check unobstructed.
 d. Engine and transmission cowling - Check condition and security.
 e. Antennas - Check condition and security.

0 f. Pitot static tube - Check security and unobstructed.

8-2t Interior Check - Cabin.

* 1. Transmission oil level - Check.

* 2. Cabin area - Check as follows:

O a Cargo - Check as required for proper loading and security.

 b. Loose equipment - Stow rotor blade tiedown, pitot tube cover, tailpipe cover and other equipment.

O c. Mission equipment - Check condition and security. Refer to Chapter 4, MISSION EQUIPMENT, for equipment checks.

 d. Passenger seats and belts - Check condition and security.

 e. First aid kits - Check secure.

O f. Fire extinguisher - Check secure.

* 3. Crew and passenger briefing - Complete as required

8-21. Before Starting Engine.

1. Overhead switches and circuit breakers - Set as follows:

0 a. Smoke generator operating switch - Check condition and security. Refer to Chapter 4, MISSION EQUIPMENT, for systems check.

b. DC circuit breakers—in, except for armament and special equipment.

O c. DOME LT switch—As required.

d. PITOT HTR switch—OFF.

*e. EXT LTS switches—Set as follows:

(1) ANTI COLL switch—ON.

(2) POSITION lights switches—As required: STEADY or FLASH for night; OFF for day.

f. MISC switches—Set as follows:

(1) CARGO REL switch—OFF.

(2) WIPERS switch—OFF.

g. CABIN HEATING switches—OFF.

h. INST LTG switches—As required.

I. AC POWER switches—Set as follows:

(1) PHASE switch—AC.

(2) INVTR switch—OFF.

j. DC POWER switches—Set as follows:

(1) MAIN GEN switch—ON and cover down.

(2) VM selector—ESS BUS.

(3) NON-ESS BUS switch—As required.

(4) STARTER GEN switch—START.

*(5) BAT switch—ON.

*2. Ground power unit—Connect for GPU start.

O 3. Smoke gage—Check.

4. FIRE warning indicator light—Test.

5. Press to test caution/warning lights—Check as required.

6. Systems instruments—Check engine and transmission systems for static indications, slippage marks, and ranges.

7. Center pedestal switches—Set as follows:

a. Avionics equipment—Off; set as desired.

b. External stores jettison handle—Check safetied.

O c. DISP CONTROL panel—Check ARM/STBY/SAFE switch is SAFE; check that JETTISON switch is down and covered.

d. GOV switch—AUTO.

e. DE-ICE switch—OFF.

*f. FUEL switches—Set as follows:

(1) MAIN FUEL switch—ON.

O (2) START FUEL switch—ON.

(3) All other switches—OFF.

g. CAUTION panel lights—TEST and RESET.

h. HYD CONT switch—ON.

i. FORCE TRIM switch—ON.

j. CHIP DET switch—BOTH.

8. Flight controls—Check freedom of movement through full travel: center cyclic and pedals; collective pitch full down.

9. Altimeters—Set to field elevation.

*8-22. Starting Engine

1. Fireguard—Posted if avaliable.

2. Rotor blades—Check clear and untied.

3. Ignition key lock switch—On.

4. Throttle—Set for start. Position the throttle as near as possible (on decrease side) to the engine idle stop.

5. Engine—Start as follows:

a. Start switch—Press and hold; start time. Note DC voltmeter indication. Battery starts can be made when voltages less than 24 volts are indicated, provided the voltage is not below 14 volts when cranking through 10 percent N1 speed.

b. Main rotor—Check that the main rotor is turning as N1 reaches 15 percent. If the rotor is not turning, abort the start.

O c. START FUEL switch—OFF at 40 percent N1.

d. Start switch—Release at 40 percent N1 or after 40 seconds, whichever occurs first. Refer to chapter 5 for starter limitations.

e. Throttle—Slowly advance past the engine idle stop to the engine idle position. Manually check the engine idle stop by attempting to close the throttle.

TM 55-1520-210-10

f. N1 68 to 72 percent. Hold a very slight pressure against the engine idle stop during the check. A slight rise in N1 may be anticipated after releasing pressure on throttle.

CAUTION

The copilot attitude indicator should be caged and held momentarily as inverter power is applied.

6. INVTR switch - MAIN ON.

7. Engine and transmission oil pressures - Check.

8. GPU - Disconnect.

8-23. Engine Runup.

* 1. Avionics - On.

* 2. STARTER GEN switch- STBY GEN.

* 3. Systems - Check as follows:

   a. FUEL.

   b. Engine.

   c. Transmission.

   d. Electrical.

      (1) AC - 112 to 118 volts.

      (2) DC - 27 volts at 26°C and above. 28 volts from 0°C to 26°C. 28.5 volts below 0°C.

* 4. RPM--6600. As throttle is increased, the low rpm audio and warning light should be off at 6100 to 6300 rpm.

* 5. Deleted.

* 6. Avionics and flight instruments Check and set as required.

NOTE

HIT Checks while operating in adverse conditions (e.g., dust, desert, coastal beach area, dry riverbeds) may be deferred (maximum of 5 flight hours) at the discretion of the pilot in command until a suitable location is reached.

7. Health Indicator Test (HIT) Check Perform as required. Refer to HIT/EGT Log in helicopter log book. Normal HIT Check not required if utilizing in-flight HIT checks unless engine maintenance has taken place since last return flight.

8-24. Deleted.

8-25. Deleted.

8-26. Deleted.

8-27. Deleted.

8-28. Hover/Taxi Check. Perform the following checks at a hover:

* 1. Engine and transmission instruments - Check.

* 2. Flight Instruments - Check as required.

   a. VSI and altimeter Check for indication of climb and descent.

   b. Slip Indicator Check ball free in race.

   c. Turn needle heading indicator and magnetic compass Check for turn indication left and right.

   d. Attitude Indicator Check for indication of nose high and low and banks left and right.

   e. Airspeed Indictor Check airspeed.

3. Power Check as required. The power check is performed by comparing the indicated torque required to hover with the predicted values from performance charts.

8-29. Deleted.

* 8-30. **Before Take-off.** Immediately prior to take-or the following checks shall be accomplished.

1. RPM - 6600.

2. Systems - Check engine, transmission, electrical and fuel systems indications.

3. Avionics - As required.

4. Crew passengers and mission equipment -- Check

8-31. Take-off.

CAUTION

During take-off and at any time the helicopter skids are close to the ground, negative pitch attitudes (nose low) of 10' or more can result in ground contact of the WSPS lower cutter the forward cg. high gross weight, high density altitude, transitional lift setting, and a tail wind increases the probability of ground contact.

8-32. Deleted.

8-33. Maximum Performance. A take-off that demands maximum performance from the helicopter necessary because of various combinations of hear helicopter loads limited power and restricted performance due to high density altitudes barriers that must be clean and other terrain features. The decision to use either of the following take-off techniques must be based on evaluation of the conditions and helicopter performance The copilot (when available) can assist the pilot maintaining proper rpm by calling out rpm and torque power changes are made thereby allowing the pilot more attention outside the cockpit.

a. Coordinated Climb. Align the helicopter with the desired take-off course at a stabilized hover approximately three feet (skid height). Apply forward cyclic pressure smoothly and gradually which simultaneously increasing collective pitch to begin coordinated acceleration and climb. Adjust pedal pressure as necessary to maintain the desired heading. Maximum torque available should be applied (without exceeding helicopter limits) as the helicopter attitude is establish that will permit safe obstacle clearance. The climb out continued at that attitude and power setting until t obstacle is cleared. After the obstacle is cleared adjust helicopter attitude and collective pitch as required to establish a climb at the desired rate and airspeed. Continuous coordinated application of control pressures is necessary to maintain trim heading flight path airspeed and rate of climb. This technique is desirable when OGE hover capability exists. Take-off may be made from the ground by positioning the cyclic control slightly forward of neutral prior to increasing collective pitch.

b. Level Acceleration Align the helicopter with the desired take-off course at a stabilized hover of approximately three feet (skid height). Apply forward cyclic pressure smoothly and gradually while simultaneously increasing collective pitch to begin an acceleration at approximately 3 to 5 feet skid height. Adjust pedal pressure as necessary to maintain the desired heading. Maximum torque available should be applied (without exceeding helicopter limits) prior to accelerating through effective transitional lift. Additional forward cyclic pressure will be necessary to allow for level acceleration to the desired climb airspeed. Approximately five knots prior to reaching the desired climb airspeed gradually release forward cyclic pressure and allow the helicopter to begin a constant airspeed climb to clear the obstacle. Care must be taken not to decrease airspeed during the climb out since this may result m the helicopter descending. After the obstacle is cleared adjust helicopter attitude and collective pitch as required to establish a climb at the desired rate and airspeed. Continuous coordinated application of control pressures is necessary to maintain trim heading flight path airspeed and rate of climb. Take-off may be made from the ground by positioning the cyclic control slightly forward of neutral prior to increasing collective pitch.

c Deleted.

d Comparison of Techniques. Refer to Chapter 7, Performance Data for a comparison of take-off distances. Where the two techniques yield the same distance over a fifty-foot obstacle the coordinated climb technique will give a shorter distance over lower obstacles and the level acceleration technique will give a shorter distance over obstacles higher than fifty feet. The two techniques give approximately the same distance over a fifty-foot obstacle when the helicopter can barely hover OGE. As hover capability is decreased the level acceleration technique gives increasingly shorter distances than the coordinated climb technique. In addition to the distance comparison the main advantages of the level acceleration technique are: (1) It requires less or no time in the avoid area of the height velocity diagram; (2) performance is more repeatable since reference to attitude which changes with loading and airspeed is not required; (3) at the higher climb out airspeeds (30 knots or greater) reliable indicate airspeeds are available for accurate airspeed reference from the beginning of the climb out therefore minimizing the possibility of descent. The main advantage of the coordinated climb technique is that the climb angle is established early in the take-off and more distance and time are available to abort the take-off if the obstacle cannot be cleared Additionally large attitude changes are not required to establish climb airspeed.

8-34. Slingload. The slingload take-off requiring the maximum performance (when OGB hover is not possible) is similar to the level acceleration technique except the take-off is begun and the acceleration made above 15 feet. Obstacle heights include the additional height necessary for a 15-foot sling load.

8-35. Climb. After take-off select the speed necessary to clear obstacles. When obstacles are cleared adjust the airspeed as desired at or above the maximum rate of climb airspeed. Refer to Chapter 7 for recommended airspeeds.

8-36. Cruise. When the desired cruise altitude is reached adjust power as necessary to maintain the required airspeed. Refer to Chapter 7 for recommended airspeeds power settings and fuel flow.

8-37. Descent. Adjust power and attitude as necessary to attain and maintain the desired speed and rate during descent. Refer to Chapter 7 for power requirements at selected airspeeds and rates of descent All checks of mission equipment that must be made in preparation for landing should be accomplished during descent.

8-38. Before landing. Prior to landing the following checks shall be accomplished:

1. RPM 6600.

2. Crew passengers and mission equipment--Check.

8-39. Landing.

a. Approach Refer to the Height Velocity Diagram. Figure 9-3 for avoid area during the approach.

b. Run-on Landing. A run-on landing may be used during emergency conditions of hydraulic power failure and some flight control malfunctions, and environmental conditions. The approach is shallow and flown at-an airspeed that provides safe helicopter control. Airspeed is maintained as for normal approach except that touchdown is mode at an airspeed above effective transitional lift After ground contact is made, slowly decrease collective pitch to minimize forward speed. If braking action is necessary, the collective pitch may be lowered as required for quicker stopping.

c. Landing from a Hover. Refer to FM 1-203 Fundamentals of Flight 840. Engine Shutdown.

CAUTION

If throttle is inadvertently rolled to the OFF position do not attempt to roll it back on.

1. Throttle Engine idle for two minutes.

2. FORCE TRIM switch ON.

NOTE

Steps 3 through 8 are to be completed after the last flight of the day if the system operation was not verified during the mission.

3. PITOT HTR Check. Place the PTOT HTR switch in the ON position. Note loadmeter increase then OFF.

4. INVTR switch OFF. Check for INST INVERTER caution light illumination. Switch to SPARE check caution light OFF.

5. AC voltmeter Check 112 to 118 volts.

6. MAIN GEN switch OFF. The DC GENERATOR caution light should illuminate and the standby generator loadmeter should indicate a load

7. Deleted

8. MAIN GEN SWITCH ON and guard closed The DC GENERATOR caution light should be out and the main generator loadmeter should indicate a load

9. STARTER GEN switch START.

10. Throttle - Off.

11. Center Pedestal switches Off.

   a. FUEL.

   b. Avionics.

12. Overhead switches Off.

   a. INVTR.

   b. PITOT HTR.

   c. LTS.

   d. MISC.

   e. CABIN HEATING.

   f. INST LTG.

   g. BAT.

13. Ignition keylock switch Remove key as required.

8-41. Before Leaving The Helicopter.

1. Walk-around-complete, checking for damage, fluid leaks and levels.

2. Mission equipment Secure.

3. Complete DA Forms 240812 and 13. An entry in DA Form 240813 is required if any of the following conditions were experienced:

   a. Flown in a loose grass environment.

   b. Operated in a salt4aden environment.

   c. Exposed to radioactivity.

   d. Operated in rain, ice, or show.

   e. Operated in a volcanic ash environment.

4. Secure helicopter.

Section IV. INSTRUMENT FLIGHT

8-42 Instrument Flight - General. The helicopter is qualified for operation in instrument meteorological conditions. Flight handling qualities, stability characteristics, and range are the same for instrument flight as for visual flight Navigation and communication equipment are adequate for instrument flight Refer to FM 1240, Instrument Flying and Navigation for Army Aviators.

Section V. FLIGHT CHARACTERISTICS

8-43. Flight Characteristics.

8-44. Operating Characteristics. The flight characteristics of this helicopter in general are similar to other single rotor helicopters.

8-45. Mast Bumping.

> **WARNING**
>
> Abrupt inputs of fight controls cause excessive main rotor flapping, which may result in mast bumpin and must be avoided.

Mast bumping (flapping-stop contact) is the main yoke contacting the mast It may occur during slope landings, rotor startup/coastdown, or when the flight envelope is exceeded. If mast bumping is encountered in flight land as soon as possible. At moderate to high airspeeds it becomes increasingly easy to approach less than +0.5G by abrupt forward cyclic inputs or rapid collective reduction. Variance, in such things as sideslip, airspeed, gross weight, density altitude, center of gravity and rotor speed, may increase main rotor flapping and increase the probability of mast bumping. Rotor flapping is a normal part of maneuvering and while excessive flapping can occur during flight of one G or greater, flapping becomes more excessive for any given maneuver at progressively lower load factors.

   a. If bumping occurs during a slope landing, reposition the cyclic to stop the bumping and reestablish a hover.

   b. If bumping occurs during startup or shutdown, move cydic to minimize or eliminate bumping.

   c. As collective pitch is reduced after engine failure or loss of tail rotor thrust cyclic must be position to maintain positive "G forces during autorotation. Touchdown should be accomplished prior to excessive rotor rpm decay.

8-45.1. Hub Spring Contact.

   a. With the addition of the Hub Spring the likelihood that mast bumping will occur is reduced. A 2 per rev. vibration will be noticed when the hub spring makes contact with the plate assembly on the hub. With the hub spring modification, contact is made at rotor flapping angles greater than 4 degrees and becomes more pronounced as the angle increases. Without the Hub Spring, contact is made at 11 degrees (contact between yolk and mast i.e., mast bumping).

b. Due to the difference In contact limitations (4 degrees compared to 11 degrees) it is likely that this vibration (2 per rev) will be felt while flying within the flight envelope Gusting winds, landings with slope angles, greater than 4 degrees and hoisting operations are several situations that increase main rotor flapping angles, thus increasing the possibility of hub spring contact While the hub spring will not prohibit mast bumping, it will aid In controlling rotor flapping angles, and provide an extra margin of safety. Installation of the hub spring does not change In any way the approved fight envelope. Should hub spnng contact occur during normal operations, no special inspections or maintenance actions are required Anytime operating limitations or the flight envelope is exceeded and hub spnng contact is encountered, a mast bump inspection will be performed

8-46. Collective Bounce. Collective bounce is a pilot Induced vertical oscillation of the collective control system when an absolute friction (either pilot applied or control rigged) is less than seven pounds It may be encountered in any flight condition by a rapid buildup of vertical bounce at approximately three cycles per second. The seventy of the oscillation is such that effective control of the helicopter may become difficult to maintain The pilot should apply and maintain adequate collective friction In all flight conditions

8-47. Blade Stall. Refer to FM 1-203, Fundamentals of Flight
8-48. Setting with Power. Refer to FM 1-203, Fundamentals of Flight
8-49. Maneuvering Flight. Acton and response of the controls during maneuvering flight are normal at all times when the helicopter is operated within the limitations set forth In this manual
8-50. Hovering Capabilities. Refer to Chapter 7
8-51. Flight With External Loads. The airspeed with external cargo is limited by controllability
8-52. Types of vibration.

a. The source of vibration of various frequencies are the rotating and moving components on the helicopter, other components vibrate in response to an existing vibration.

b. Rotor vibrations felt during in-flight or ground operations are divided In general frequencies as follows.

(1) Extreme low frequency - Less than one per revolution (pylon rock).
(2) Low frequency - One or two per revolution
(3) Medium frequency - Generally, four, five, or six per revolution
(4) High frequency - Tall rotor frequency or higher

c. Most vibrations are always present at low magnitudes The main problem is deciding when a vibration level has reached the point of being excessive.

d. Extreme low, and most medium frequency vibrations are caused by the rotor or dynamic controls Various malfunctions In stationary components can affect the absorption or damping of the existing vibrations and Increase the overall level

e. A number of vibration are present which are considered a normal characteristic Two per revolution is the next most prominent of these, with four or six per revolution the next most prominent There Is always a small amount of high-frequency vibration present that may be detectable. Expedience Is necessary to learn the normal vibration levels. Sometimes the mistake is made of concentrating on feeling one specific vibration and concluding that the level is higher than normal.

8-53. Low G Maneuvers.

| WARNING |

Intentional flight below +0.SG is prohibited.

| WARNING |

Abrupt inputs of flight controls cause excessive main rotor flapping, which may result in mast bumping and must be avoided.

a. Because of mission requirements, it may be necessary to rapidly lower the nose of the helicopter. At moderate to high airspeeds, It becomes increasingly easier to approach zero or negative load factors by abrupt forward cyclic inputs. The helicopter may exhibit a tendency to roll to the right-simultaneously with the forward cyclic Input.

b. Such things as sideslip, weight and location of external stores and airspeed will affect the seventy of the right roll. Variances In gross weight longitudinal cg, and rotor rpm may affect the roll characteristics The right roll occurs throughout the normal operating airspeed range and becomes more violent at progressively lower load factors. When it is necessary in rapidly lower the nose of the helicopter, it is essential that the pilot monitor changes In roll attitude as the cyclic is moved forward.

c. If the flight envelope is inadvertently exceeded, causing a low "G" condition and right roll, move cyclic aft to return rotor to positive thrust condition, then roll level, continuing flight if mast bumping has not occurred.

S-54. Rollover Characteristics. Refer to FM 1-203, Fundamentals of Flight

8-54.1 CB Operation Differences With Composite Main Rotor Blade.

> **WARNING**
>
> Abrupt rolling maneuvers coupled with aft cyclic inputs which induce a high pitch rate must not be continued beyond the point of significantly increased one per/rev vibration onset. If notably increased one per/rev vibrations occur during maneuvering flight, the severity of the maneuver must be reduced or control feedback and loss of aircraft control may result.

a. *Guidance for Maneuvering Flight.* Increasing bank angle up to the limit will Induce correspondingly increasing vibration levels of the one and two per/rev type due to hub spnng contacts. As the bank angle limit of the aircraft is approached, the two per/rev vibration increase will be the first and most notable vibration As the bank angle Is further increased, a sudden increase In the one per/rev vibration will occur The one per/rev vibration will have a pounding characteristic A slight increase in bank angle beyond this point could result In control feed back and exceeding the flight envelope Aircraft damage and loss of aircraft control may result if bank angle is further Increased The aircraft bank angle limit can be reached, at the lighter gross weights before encountering the one per/rev vertical vibration, however, as gross weight Is increased, the above condition (one per/rev pounding and feedback) will occur at reduced bank angles.

b. *Guidance for Autorotational Flight.* In aircraft equipped with CMRB, additional collective pitch application may be required to maintain rpm dunng autorotatonal maneuvering flight Collective must be increased simultaneously or slightly before increasing the bank angle and/or pitch rate Rotor speed will tend to overspeed more rapidly and with less warning than Is charactenstc of metal main rotor blades. Additionally, more collective application is required to control and/or stop the rotor speed increase

c. Guidance for Cyclic Flares Current advanced airfoils, as used on the CMRB, can cause a more raid rotor rpm build up dunng cyclic flare A larger collective input is necessary to maintain rpm within limits for this rotor than for the metal blade rotor

d. Run-up and Shutdown Characteristics On some UH-1H helicopters with CMRBs, on rotor run-up and/or shutdown an audible, nonmetallic thump is heard This Is normal and not a cause for any maintenance action or inspection. The noise is coming from the main bolt hole area and is caused by the combination of tolerance and torque on the joint The CMRB has an ant-fretting pad protecting the main bolt hole area The ant-fretting pad acts like a lubricant (like Teflon) and allows the joint to relieve itself as the centrifugal force is reduced with rpm, thus the noise The metal blade does the same thing except It does not have the ant-fretting pad Therefore, the high function In the joint allows the joint to relieve Itself very slowly, and no audible noise is heard This noise has also been heard when the UH-1H is on ground handling wheels (rotors not turning) and the helicopter Is subject to an Impact loading when the aircraft is be towed over a sharp bump or hanger sill This noise Is also normal

Section VI. ADVERSE ENVIRONMENTAL CONDITIONS

8-55. General. This section provides information relative to operation under adverse environmental conditions (snow Ice and rain turbulent air extreme cold and hot weather desert operations mountainous and altitude operation) at maximum gross weight. Section H check list provides for operational requirements of this section.

> **CAUTION**
>
> Extreme care should be exercised under adverse environmental conditions when using NVG. Such conditions deflect light and could significantly decrease or destroy the effectiveness of NVG to the extent of creating unsafe flight conditions. Use of NVG should be discontinued under such conditions and assure that the NVG searchlight and/or landing light and NVG position lights may be extinguished.

8-56. Cold Weather Operations. Operation of the helicopter in cold weather or an arctic environment presents no unusual problems if the operators are aware of those changes that do take place and conditions that may exist because of the lower temperatures and freezing moisture.

   a. *Inspection.* The pilot must be more thorough in the preflight check when temperatures have been at or below 0'C (32'F). Water and snow may have entered many parts during operations or in periods when the helicopter was parked unsheltered. This moisture often remains to form ice which will immobilize moving parts or damage structure by expansion and will occasionally foul electric circuitry. Protective covers afford protection against ram, freezing ram., sleet, and snow when installed on a dry helicopter pnor to the precipitation. Since it is not practicable to completely cover an unsheltered helicopter those parts not protected by covers and those adjacent to cover overlap and joints require closer attention especially after blowing snow or freezing rain. Remove accumulation of snow and ice pnor to flight. Failure to do so can result m hazardous flight due to aerodynamic and center of gravity disturbances as well as the introduction of snow water and ice into internal moving parts and electrical systems. The pilot should be particularly attentive to the main and tail rotor systems and their exposed control linkages.

> **CAUTION**
>
> At temperatures of -35'C (-31'F) and lower, the grease in the spherical couplings of the main transmission driveshaft may congeal to a point that the couplings cannot operate properly.

   b. *Transmission.* Check for proper operation by turning the main rotor opposite to the direction of rotation while observer watches the driveshaft to see there is no tendency for the transmission to wobble while the driveshaft is turning. If found frozen apply heat (do not use open flame, avoid overheating boot) to thaw the spherical couplings before attempting to start engine.

> **CAUTION**
>
> Prior to starting engine, on aircraft with Improved particle separators and parked without covers installed, the upper half of separator should be removed and inspected by maintenance personnel for ice and/or snow. Any accumulation of these elements should be removed to prevent damage to engine.

   c. *Check.*

   (1) Before exterior check 0'C (32'F) and lower. Perform check as specified m Section III.

   (2) Exterior check 0'C (32'F) to -54'C (-65'F). Perform the following checks. Check that all surfaces and controls are free of Ice and snow Contraction of the fluids in the helicopter system at extreme low temperatures causes indication of low levels. A check made Just after the previous shutdown and carried forward to the walk around check is satisfactory If no leaks are m evidence. Filling when the system is cold-soaked will reveal an over-full condition immediately after flight with the possibility of forced leaks at seals.

   (a) Main rotor - Check free of Ice frost and snow.

   (b) Main driveshaft - Check for freedom of movement.

   (c) Engine air inlet and screens - Remove all loose snow that could be pulled into and block the engine intake during starting.

   (d) Oil cooling fan compartment - Check oil cooling fan blades for Ice.

   (3) Interior check - All flights 0'C (32'F) to -54'C (-65'F). Perform check as specified m Section III.

(4) Engine starting check 0°C (32°F) to -54°C (-65°F). As the engine cools to an ambient temperature below 0°C (32°F) after engine shutdown condensed moisture may freeze engine seals. Ducting hot air from an external source through the air inlet housing will free a frozen rotor. If temperature is 44°C (-47°F) or below the pilot must be particularly careful to monitor engine and transmission instruments for high oil pressure. During cold weather starting the engine oil pressure gage will indicate maximum (100 psi). The engine should be warmed up at engine idle until the engine oil pressure indication is below 100 psi. The time required for warmup is entirely dependent on the starting temperature of the engine and lubrication system.

(5) Engine runup check - Perform the check as outlined in section III.

WARNING

Control system checks should be performed with extreme caution when helicopter is parked on snow and ice. There is reduction in ground friction holding the helicopter * stationary. Controls are sensitive and response is immediate.

d. *Engine Starting Without External Power Supply.* If a battery start must be attempted when the helicopter and battery have been cold-soaked, preheat the engine and battery if equipment is available and time permits. Preheating will result in a faster starter cranking speed which tends to reduce the hot start hazard by assisting the engine to reach a self-sustaining speed (40 percent NI) m the least possible time. Electrical load may be reduced by leaving inverter lights and other electrical equipment off during start.

8-57. Before Leaving the Helicopter. Open vents to permit free circulation of air install protective covers as required.

8-58. Snow. Refer to FM 1-202 Environmental Flight.

8-59. Desert and Hot Weather Operations. Refer to FM 1-202 Environmental Flight.

8-60. Turbulence and Thunderstorms.

8-61. Turbulence.
a. In turbulence check that all occupants are seated with seat belts and harnesses tightened.
b. Helicopter controllability is the primary consideration; therefore if control becomes marginal exit the turbulence as soon as possible.

c. To minimize the effects of turbulence encountered in flight the helicopter should be flown at an airspeed corresponding to maximum endurance airspeed. There will be a corresponding increase in control movements at the reduced airspeed

8-62. Thunderstorms.

a. To minimize the effects of thunderstorms encountered in flight perform the following:

(1) Adjust torque to maintain maximum endurance airspeed.
(2) Check that all occupants are seated with seat belts and harnesses tightened.
(3) PITOT HTR switch - ON.
(4) Avionics - Reduce volume on any equipment affected by static
(5) Interior lights - Adjust to full bright at night to minimize blinding effect of lightning.

b. In the Storm.

(1) Maintain a level attitude and constant power setting. Airspeed fluctuations should be expected and disregarded
(2) Maintain original heading turning only when necessary.
(3) The altimeter is unreliable due to differential barometric pressures within the storm. An indicated gain or loss of several hundred feet is not uncommon-and should be allowed for in determining minimum safe altitude.

8-63. Lightning Strikes.

a. Although the possibility of a lighting strike is remote, with increasing use of all-weather capabilities the helicopter could inadvertently be exposed to lightning damage. Therefore static tests have been conducted to determine lightning strike effects on rotors

b. Simulated lightning tests indicate that lighting strikes may damage helicopter rotors. The degree of damage will depend on the magnitude of the charge and the point of contact. Catastrophic structural failure is not anticipated. However, lightning damage to hub bearing, blade aft section, trim tabs, and blade tips was demonstrated. Also, adhesive bond separations occurred between the blade spar and aft section between the spar and leading edge abrasion strip. Some portions of blade aft sections deformed to the extent that partial or complete separation of the damaged section could be expected. Such damage can aerodynamically produce severe structural vibration and serious control problems which, If prolonged, could endanger the helicopter and crew.

> **WARNING**
>
> Avoid flight in or near thunderstorms especially in areas of observed or anticipated lightning discharges.

c. If lightning damage occurs, indications such as control problems or vibration changes, especially abnormal noise may or may not be evident.

NOTE
Abnormal operating noises almost always accompany rotor damage, but loudness or pitch are not valid indications of the degree of damage sustained.

d. If lightning strike occurs or is suspected, the following precautions are recommended to minimize further risk.

(l) Reduce airspeed as much as practical to maintain safe flight.

(2) Avoid abrupt control inputs.

8-64. Ice and Rain.

a. In heavy rain, a properly adjusted wiper can be expected to clear the windshield adequately throughout the entire speed range. However, when poor visibility is encountered while cruising in rain, it is recommended that the pilot fly by reference to the flight instruments and the copilot attempt to maintain visual reference. Rain has no noticeable effect on handling or performance of the helicopter. Maintenance personnel are required to perform a special inspection after the helicopter has been operated in ram.

NOTE
If the windshield wiper does not start in LOW or MED position, turn the control to HIGH. After the wiper starts, the control may be set at the desired position.

b. Continuous flight in light icing conditions is not recommended because the ice shedding induces rotor blade vibrations, adding greatly to the pilots work load If icing conditions are encountered during flight every effort should be made to vacate the icing environment On aircraft modified with the improved particle separator, the upper step screen may be removed prior to flight if icing conditions are probable.

When operating at outside air temperatures of 40'F (5'C) or below icing of the engine air inlet screens can be expected. Ice accumulation on inlet screens can be detected on non-purging and some selfpurging particle separator systems by illumination of the ENGINE INLET AIR cateye on the instrument panel or the ENGINE INLET AIR caution panel segment light. Continued accumulation of ice will result in partial or complete power loss. It should be noted that illumination of the ENGINE INLET AIR caution light indicates blockage at the inlet screen only and does not reveal icing conditions in the particle separator or on the FOD screen.

To preclude the possibility of icing on aircraft equipped with non-purging or selfpurging particle separators, it is recommended that the right and left engine air inlet filters be removed from the cowling when it is anticipated that the helicopter will be flown under atmospheric conditions conductive to icing. (Do not remove the top filter.)

NOTE
The use of engine de-ice on aircraft modified with the improved particle separator swirl tubes) should be limited to environmental conditions in which OAT is 4'C or below.

c. If icing conditions become unavoidable the pilot should actuate the pitot heat, windshield defroster and de-ice switches.

d. Flight tests in closely controlled icing conditions have indicated that the pilot can expect one or all of the following to occur.

(1) Obscured forward field of view due to ice accumulation on the windscreens and chin bubbles. If the windshield defrosters fail to keep the windshield clear of ice, the side windows may be used for visual reference during landing.

(2) One-per-rotor-revolution vibrations ranging from mild to severe caused by asymmetrical ice shedding from the main rotor system. The seventy of the vibration will depend upon the temperatures and the amount of ice

accumulation on the blades when the ice shed occurs. Flight test experience has shown that the possibility of an asymmetric ice shed occurring increases as the outside air temperature decreases.

(3) An increase m torque required to maintain a constant airspeed and altitude due to ice accumulation on the rotor system.

(4) Possible degradation of the ability to maintain auto-rotational rotor speed within operating limits.

e. Severe vibrations may occur as a result of main rotor asymmetrical ice shedding. If icing conditions are encountered while in flight, land as soon as practical_ All ice should be removed from the rotor system before attempting further flight.

f. Control activity cannot be depended upon to remove ice from the main rotor system. Vigorous control move-ments should not be made in an attempt to reduce low frequency vibrations caused by asymmetrical shedding of ice from the main rotor blades. These movements may induce a more asymmetrical shedding of Ice, further aggravating helicopter vibration levels.

g. If a 5 psi (or greater) torque pressure increases is

required above the cruise torque setting used prior to entering icing conditions it may not be possible to (maintain autorotational rotor speed within operational limits, should an engine failure occur.

H. Ice shed from the rotor blades and/or other rotating components presents a hazard to personnel during landing and shutdown. Ground personnel should remain well clear of the helicopter during landing and shutdown, and passengers and crewmembers should not exit the helicopter until the rotor has stopped turning.

8-65. High or Gusty Wind.

a. High or gusty wind operations require no special procedures or techniques while m flight however, special parking precautions are necessary to ensure that the main rotor blades do not flex downward contacting the tail rotor driveshaft during rotor coast down.

b. To reduce the possibility of main rotor/tailboom contact during engine shutdown, land the helicopter on an upwind heading. During engine shutdown, displace cyclic into the wind, adding cyclic as necessary as rotor rpm decreases.

TM 55-1520-210

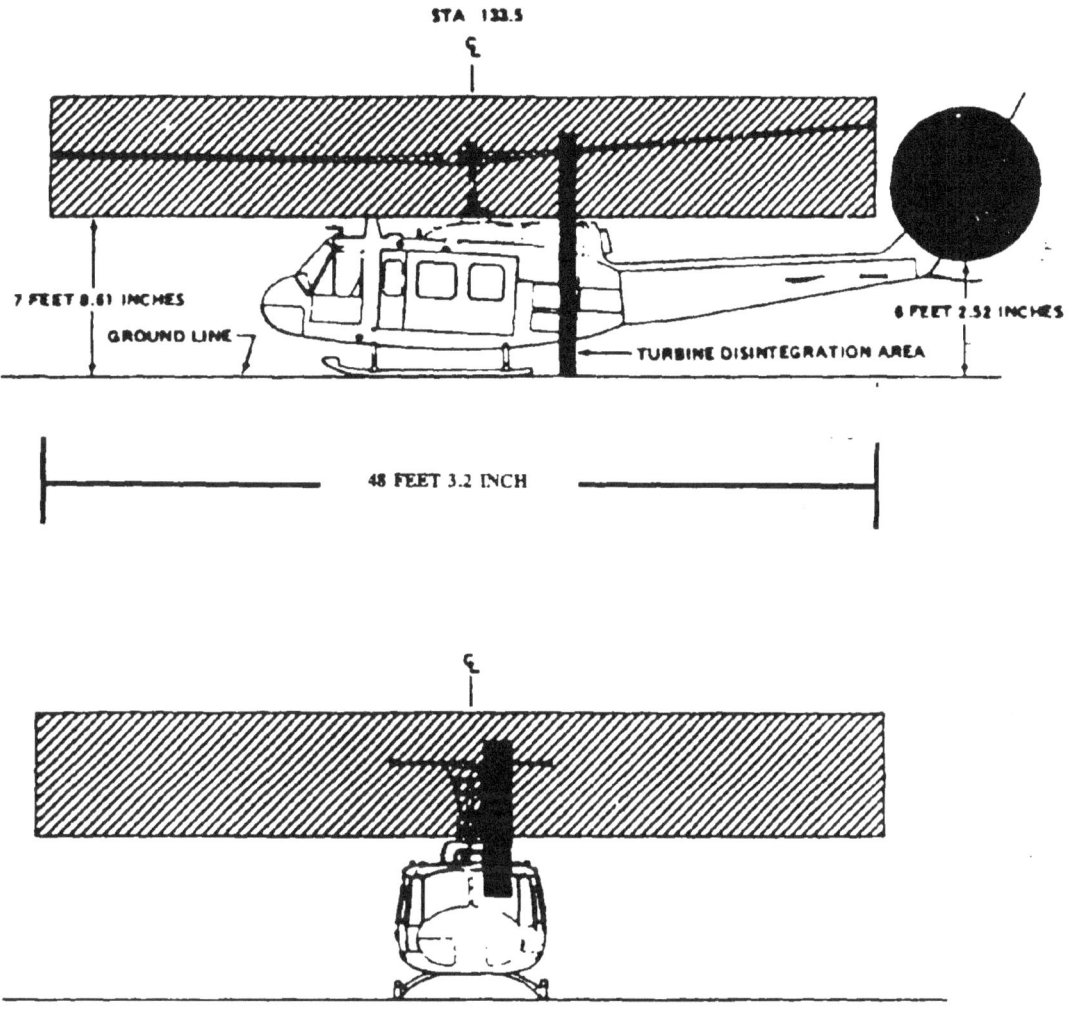

DANGER AREA

Figure 8-1. Danger Area

Change 17

TM 55-1520-210-10

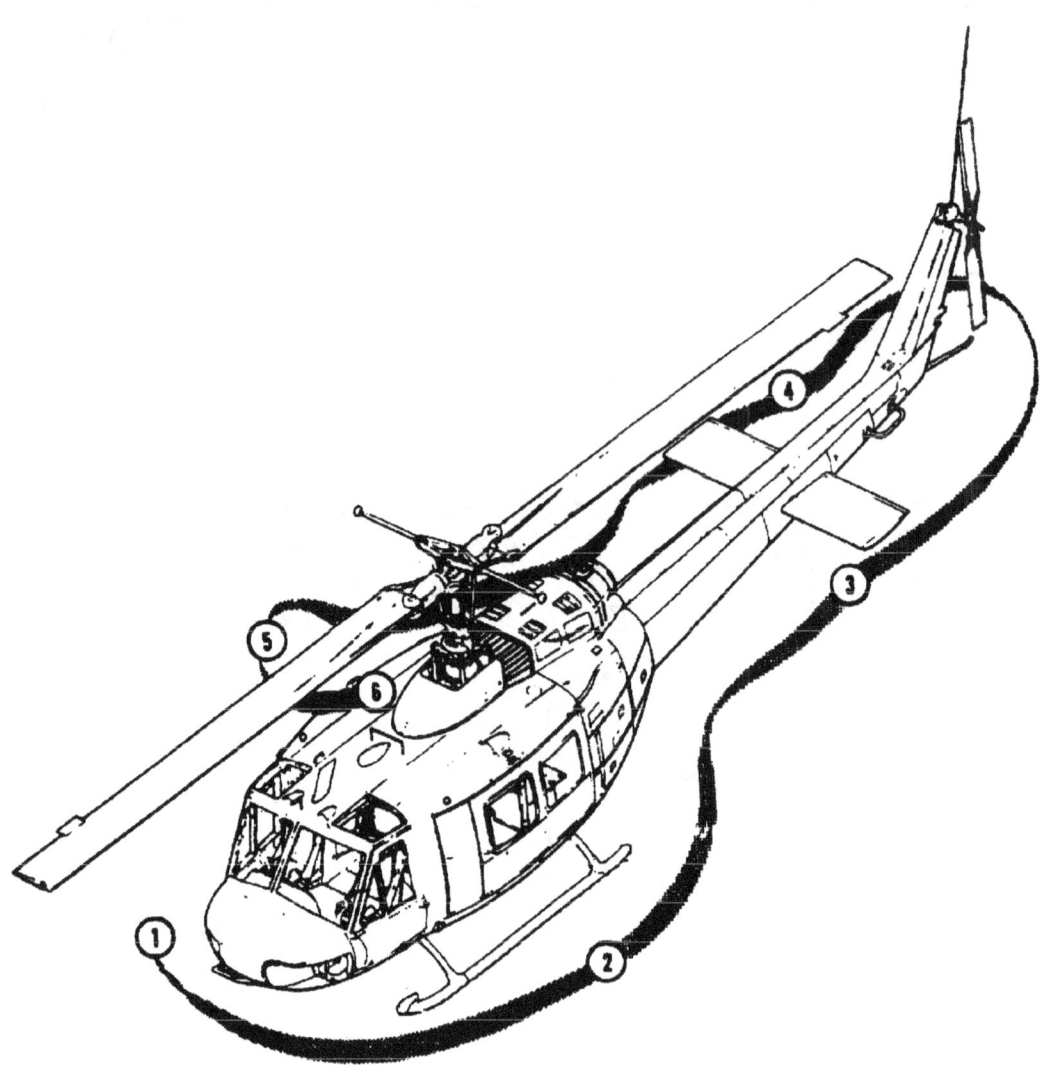

Figure 8-2. Exterior Check Diagram

8-16

TM 55-1520-210-10

Chapter 9

Emergency Procedures

Section I. HELICOPTER SYSTEMS

9-1. Helicopter Systems. This section describes the helicopter systems emergencies that may reasonably be expected to occur and presents the procedures to be followed. Emergency operation of mission equipment is contained in this chapter insofar as its use affects safety of flight. Emergency procedures are given in checklist form when applicable. A condensed version of these procedures is contained in the condensed checklist TM 55-1520-210 CL.

9-2. Immediate Action Emergency Steps. Those steps that must be performed immediately in an emergency situation are underlined. These steps must be performed without reference to the checklist. When the situation permits, non-underlined steps will be accomplished with use of the checklist.

NOTE

The urgency of certain emergencies requires immediate and instinctive action by the pilot. The most important single consideration is aircraft control. All procedures are subordinate to this requirement.

9-3. Definition Of Emergency Terms. For the purpose of standardization the following definitions shall apply:

   a. The term LAND AS SOON AS POSSIBLE is defined as executing a landing to the nearest suitable landing area without delay. The primary consideration is to assure the survival of occupants.

   b. The term LAND AS SOON AS PRACTICABLE is defined as executing a landing to a suitable airfield, heliport, or other landing area as the situation dictates.

   c. The term AUTOROTATE is defined as adjusting the flight controls as necessary to establish an autorotational descent. See figure 9-2 and FM 1-203.

   1. COLLECTIVE ADJUST as required to maintain rotor RPM.

   2. PEDALS ADJUST as required.

   3. THROTTLE ADJUST as required.

   4. AIRSPEED ADJUST as required.

   d. The term EMER SHUTDOWN is defined as engine stoppage without delay.

   1. THROTTLE - OFF.

   2. FUEL switches - OFF.

   3. BAT switch - OFF.

CAUTION

The maximum engine torque available for any ambient condition will be reduced by 6 to 8 PSI when the GOV AUTO/EMER switch is placed in the EMER position.

   e. The term EMER GOV OPNS is defined as manual control of the engine RPM with the GOV AUTO/EMER switch in the EMER position. Because automatic acceleration, deceleration, and overspeed control are not provided with the GOV switch in the EMER position, throttle and collective coordinated control movements must be smooth to prevent compressor stall, overspeed, overtemperature, or engine failure.

   1. GOV - switch - EMER.

   2. Throttle - adjust as necessary to control RPM.

   3. Land as soon as possible.

9-4. Emergency Exits. Emergency exits are shown in figure 9-1. Emergency exit release handles are yellow and black striped.

   a. Cockpit Doors.

   (1) Pull handle.

   (2) Push door out.

   b. Cabin Door Windows.

   (1) Pull handle.

   (2) Lift window inward.

Change 15   9-1

TM 55-1520-210-10

9-5. Emergency Equipment.

WARNING

Toxic fumes of the extinguishing agent may cause injury, and liquid agent may cause frost bite or low-temperature burns.

Refer to figure 9-1 for fire extinguisher and first aid kit locations.

9-6. Minimum Rate of Descent. See figure 9-2.

9-7. Maximum Glide Distance. See figure 9-2.

9-8. Engine Oil Temperature High. If the engine oil temperature exceeds operating limits as specified in Chapter 5, land as soon as possible.

9-9. Engine Malfunction-Partial or Complete Power Loss.

a. The indications of an engine malfunction, either a partial or a complete power loss are left yaw, drop in engine rpm, drop in rotor rpm, low rpm audio alarm, illumination of the rpm warning light, change in engine noise.

b. Flight characteristics:

(1) Control response with an engine inoperable is similar to a descent with power.

(2) Airspeed above the minimum rate of descent values (figures 9-2) will result in greater rates of descent and should only be used as necessary to extend glide distance.

(3) Airspeeds below minimum rate of descent airspeeds will increase rate of descent and decrease glide distance.

(4) Should the engine malfunction during a left bank maneuver, right cyclic input to level the aircraft must be made simultaneously with collective pitch adjustment. If the collective pitch is decreased without a corresponding right cyclic input, the helicopter will pitch down and the roll rate will increase rapidly, resulting in a significant loss of altitude.

WARNING

Do not close the throttle. Do not respond to the rpm audio and/or warning light illumination without first confirming engine malfunction by one or more of the other indications. Normal indications signify the engine is functioning properly and that there is a tachometer generator failure or an open circuit to the warning system, rather than an actual engine malfunction.

c. Partial power condition:

Under partial power conditions, the engine may operate relatively smoothly at reduced power or it may operate erratically with intermittent surges of power. In instances where a power loss is experienced without accompanying power surging, the helicopter may sometimes be flown at reduced power to a favorable landing area. Under these conditions, the pilot should always be prepared for a complete power loss. In the event a partial power condition is accompanied by erratic engine operation or power surging, and flight is to be continued, the GOV switch may be moved to the EMER position and throttle adjusted in an attempt to correct the surging condition. If flight is not possible, close the throttle completely and complete an autorotational landing.

d. Complete power loss:

(1) Under a complete power loss condition, delay in recognition of the malfunction, improper technique or excessive maneuvering to reach a suitable landing area reduces the probability of a safe autorotational landing. Flight conducted within the caution area of the height-velocity chart (fig 9-3) or (fig 9-3.1) exposes the helicopter to a high probability of damage despite the best efforts of the pilot.

(2) From conditions of low airspeed and low altitude, the deceleration capability is limited, and caution should be used to avoid striking the ground with the tail rotor. Initial collective reduction will vary after an engine malfunction dependent upon the altitude and airspeed at the time of the occurrence. For example, collective pitch must not be decreased when an engine failure occurs at a hover in ground effect; whereas, during cruise flight conditions, altitude and airspeed are sufficient for a significant reduction in collective pitch, thereby, allowing rotor rpm to be maintained in the safe operating range during autorotational descent. At high gross weights, the rotor may tend to overspeed and require collective pitch application to maintain the rpm below the upper limit. Collective pitch should never be applied to reduce rpm below normal limits for extending glide distance because of the reduction in rpm available for use during autorotational landing.

NOTE

If time permits, during the autorotative descent, transmit a "May Day" call, set transponder to emergency, jettison external stores, and lock shoulder harness.

9-10. Deleted.

9-11. **Engine Malfunction — Hover.**

Autorotate.

9-12. **Engine Malfunction — Low Altitude/Low Airspeed or Cruise.**

1. Autorotate.

2. EMER GOV OPNS.

9-13. **Engine Restart — During Flight.** After an engine failure in flight, resulting from a malfunction of fuel control unit, an engine start may be attempted. Because the exact cause of engine failure cannot be determined in flight, the decision to attempt the start will depend on the altitude and time available, rate of descent, potential landing areas, and crew assistance available. Under ideal conditions approximately one minute is required to regain powered flight from time the attempt start is begun. If the decision is made to attempt an in-night start:

1. Throttle - Off.

2. STARTER GEN switch - START.

3. FUEL switches - ON.

4. GOV switch - EMER.

5. Attempt start

    a. Starter switch - Press.

    b. Throttle - Open slowly to 6400 to 6600 rpm as N1 passes through 8 percent Control rate of throttle application se necessary to prevent exceeding EGT limits.

    c. Starter Switch-Release as N1 passes through 40 percent After the engine is started and powered flight is reestablished, continue with manual control. Turn the START FUEL switch OFF and return the STARTER GEN switch to STANDBY.

6. Land as soon as possible.

9-14. **Droop Compensator Failure.** Droop compensator failure will be indicated when engine rpm fluctuates excessively during application of collective pitch.

The engine will tend to overspeed as collective pitch is decreased and will underspeed as collective pitch is increased. If the droop compensator fails, make minimum collective movements and execute a shallow approach to the landing area. If unable to maintain the operating rpm within limits:

EMER GOV OPNS.

9-15. **Engine Compressor Stall.** Engine compressor stall (surge) is characterized by a sharp rumble or loud sharp reports, severe engine vibration and a rapid rise in exhaust gas temperature (EGT) depending on the severity of the surge. Maneuvers requiring rapid or maximum power applications should be avoided. Should this occur.

1. Collective - Reduce.

2. DE-ICE and BLEED AIR switches - OFF.

3. Land as soon as possible.

9-16. **Inlet Guide Vane Actuator Failure — Closed or Open.**

a. Closed. If the guide vanes fail in the closed position, a maximum of **20 to 25** psi of torque will be available although N1 may indicate normal. Power applications above **20 to 25** psi will result in deterioration of N2 and rotor rpm while increasing N1. Placing the GOV switch in the EMER position will not provide any increase power capability and increases the possibility of an N1 overspeed and an engine over-temperature. Should a failure occur, accomplish an approach and landing to the ground with torque not exceeding the maximum available. If possible, a running landing is recommended.

b. Open. If the inlet guide vanes fail in the open position during normal flight, it is likely that no indications will be evidenced. In this situation, increased acceleration times will be experienced. As power applications are made from increasingly lower N1 settings, acceleration times will correspondingly increase.

9-17. **Engine Overspeed.** Engine overspeed will be indicated by a right yaw, rapid increase in both rotor and engine rpm, rpm warning light illuminated, and an increase in engine noise. An engine overspeed may be caused by a malfunctioning N2 governor or fuel control. Although the initial indications of high N2 rpm and rotor rpm are the same in each case, actions that must be taken to control rpm are distinctly different. If the N2 governor malfunctions, throttle reduction will result in a corresponding decrease in N2 rpm. In the event of a fuel control malfunction, throttle reduction will have no effect on N2 rpm. If an overspeed is experienced:

1. **Collective-Increase** to load the rotor in an attempt to maintain rpm below the maximum operating limit.

2. Throttle-Reduce until normal operating rpm is attained. Continue with manual throttle control. If reduction of throttle does not reduce rpm as required:

> **WARNING**
>
> **Land even if manual throttle corrects the overspeed since there is a chance of an Impending engine failure due to the debris generated by the Initial N2 failure.**

3. **FMFRGOV OPNS**.

9-18. Transmissions and Drive Systems.

9-19. Transmission Oil-Hot or Low Pressure. If the transmission oil temperature XMSN OIL Hot caution light illuminates, limits on the transmission oil temperature gage are exceeded; XMSN OIL PRESS caution light illuminates, or limits on the transmission oil pressure gage are exceeded (low or high)-

1. **Land as soon as possible.**

2. **FMFR SHUTDOWN - After landing.**

> **WARNING**
>
> **Do not close throttle during this emergency procedure. Descent and landing must be made with normal engine operating RPM.**

Should transmission oil pressure drop to zero psi, a valid cross reference cannot be made with the oil temperature indicators. The oil temperature gage and transmission oil hot warning lights are dependent on fluid for valid indications.

9-20. Tall Rotor Malfunctions. Because the many different malfunctions that can occur, it is not possible to provide a solution for every emergency. The success in coping with the emergency depends on quick analysis of the condition.

9-21. Complete Loss of Tall Rotor Thrust This situation involves a break in the drive system, such as a severed driveshaft, wherein the tail rotor stops turning or tail rotor controls fail with zero thrust a Indications.
  (1) In-Flight.

(a) Pedal input has no effect on helicopter trim.
(b) Nose of the helicopter turns to the right (left sideslip).
(c) Roll of fuselage along the longitudinal axis.
(d) Nose down tucking will also be present.

> **WARNING**
>
> **At airspeeds below 30 to 40 knots, the sideslip may become uncontrollable, and the helicopter will begin to revolve on the vertical axis (right or left depending on power, gross weight, etc.).**

(2) Hover.
Helicopter heading cannot be controlled with pedals.
  b. Procedures.
    (1) In- Right.
      (a) if safe landing area is not immediately available and powered flight is possible, continue flight to a suitable landing area at above minimum rate of descent airspeed. Degree of roll and sideslip may be varied by varying throttle and/or collective.
      (b) When landing area is reached, AUTORO TATE using an airspeed above minimum rate of descent

> **CAUTION**
>
> **The flare and the abrupt use of collective will cause the nose to rotate left, but do not correct with throttle. Although application of throttle will result In rotation to the right, addition of power is a very strong response measure and is too sensitive for the pilot to manage property at this time. DO NOT ADD POWER AT THIS TIME. Slight rotation at time of impact at zero ground speed should not cause any real problem.**

      (c) If landing area is suitable, touchdown at a ground speed above effective transitional lift utilizing throttle as necessary to maintain directional control.
      (d) If landing area is not suitable for a run-on lancing a minimum ground run autorotation must be performed, enter autorotation descent (throttle off) start to decelerate at about 75 feet altitude so that forward ground speed is at a minimum when the helicopter reaches 10 to 20 feet, execute the touchdown with a rapid collective pull just prior to touchdown in a level altitude with minimum ground speed.

(2) Hover.

AUTOROTATE.

9-22. Fixed Pitch Settings. This is a malfunction involving a loss of control resulting in a fixed-pitch setting. Whether the nose of the helicopter yaws left or right is dependent upon the amount of pedal applied at the time of the malfunction, a varying amount of tail rotor thrust will be delivered at all times during flight.

a. Reduced power (low torque).

(1) Indications: The nose of the helicopter will turn right when power is applied.

(2) Procedure: Reduced power situations:

(a) If helicopter control can be maintained in powered flight, the best solution is to maintain control with power and accomplish a run-on landing as soon as practicable.

(b) If helicopter control cannot be maintained, close the throttle immediately and accomplish an autorotational landing.

b. Increased power (high torque).

(1) Indications: The nose of the helicopter will turn left when power is reduced.

(2) Procedure.
(a) Maintain control with power and airspeed between 40 and 70 knots.
(b) If needed, reduce rpm (not below 6000) to control sideslip.
(c) Continue powered flight to a suitable landing area where a run-on landing can be accomplished.
(d) On final, reduce rpm to 6000 and accomplish a run-on landing.

c. Hover.

(1) Indication. Helicopter heading cannot be controlled with pedals.

(2) Procedure.

(a) Fixed Pedal-Land.

(b) Delete.

9-23. Loss of Tail Rotor Components. The seventy of this situation is dependent upon the amount of weight lost. Any loss of this nature will result m a forward center of gravity shift, requiring aft cyclic.

a. Indications:

(1) Varying degrees of right yaw depending on power applied and airspeed at time of failure.

(2) Forward CG shift.

(3) Abnormal vibrations.

b. Procedures:

(1) Enter authoritative descent (power off).

(2) Maintain airspeed above minimum rate of descent airspeed.

(3) If run-on landing is possible, complete autorotation with a touchdown airspeed as required for directional control.

(4) If run-on landing is not- possible, start to decelerate from about 75 feet altitude, so that forward groundspeed is at a minimum when the helicopter reaches 10 to 20 feet; execute the termination with a rapid collective pull just prior to touchdown in a level attitude
with minimum ground speed.

9-24. Loss of Tail Rotor Effectiveness. This is a situation involving a loss of effective tail rotor thrust without a break in the drive system. The condition is most likely to occur at a hover or low airspeed as a result of one or more of the following.

a. Out-of-ground effect hover.
b. High pressure altitude/high temperature.
c. Adverse wind conditions.
d. Engine/rotor rpm below 6600/324.
c. Improperly rigged tail rotor.
f. High gross weight.

(1) Indications: The first indication of this condition will be a slow starting right turn of the nose of the helicopter which cannot be stopped with full left pedal application. This turn rate will gradually increase until It becomes uncontrollable or, depending upon conditions, the aircraft aligns itself with the wind.

(2) Procedures: Lower collective to regain control and as recovery is effected adjust controls for normal flight.

9-25. Main Driveshaft Failure. A failure of the main driveshaft will be indicated by a left yaw (this is caused by the drop in torque applied to the main rotor), increase in engine rpm, decrease m rotor rpm, low rpm audio alarm (unmodified system), and illumination of the rpm warning light. This condition will result m complete loss of power to the rotor and a possible engine overspeed. If a failure occurs:

1. Autorotate.

2. EMER SHUTDOWN.

9-26. Clutch Fails to Disengage. A clutch failing to disengage in flight will be indicated by the rotor rpm decaying with engine rpm as the throttle is reduced to the engine idle position when entering autorotational descent. This condition results in total loss of autorotational capability. If a failure occurs, do the following:

1. Throttle - On.

2. Land as soon as possible.

9-27. Clutch Fails to Re-engage. During recovery from autorotational descent clutch malfunction may occur and will be indicated by a reverse needle split (engine rpm higher than rotor rpm):

1. Autorotate.
2. EMER SHUTDOWN.

9-28. Collective Bounce. If collective bounce occurs.

1. Relax pressure on collective. (Do not 'stiff arm' the collective.)
2. Male a significant collective application either up or down.
3. Increase collective friction.

9-29. Fire. The safety of helicopter occupants is the primary consideration when a fire occurs; therefore, it is imperative that every effort be made by the flight crew to put the fire out. On the ground it is essential that the engine be shut down, crew and passengers evacuated and fire fighting begun immediately. If time permits, a 'May Day' radio call should be made before the electrical power is OFF to expedite assistance from fire fighting equipment and personnel. If the helicopter s airborne when a fire occurs, the most important single action that can be taken by the pilot is to land the helicopter. Consideration must be given to jettison external stores pnor to landing.

9-30. Fire-Engine Start. The following procedure is applicable during engine start, if EGT limits are exceeded, or if it becomes apparent that they will be exceeded. Flames emitting from the tailpipe are acceptable if the EGT limits are not exceeded.

1. Start switch - Press. The starter switch must be held until EGT is in the normal operating range.

2. Throttle - Off. The throttle must be closed immediately as the starter switch is pressed.

3. FUEL switches - OFF.

9-31. Fire-Ground.

EMER SHUTDOWN

9-32. Fire-Flight. If the fire light illuminates and/or fire is observed during flight, prevailing circumstances (such as VFR, IMC, night, altitude, and landing areas available), must be considered in order to determine whether to execute a power-on, or a power-off landing.

a. Power-On.

1. Land as soon as possible.

2. EMER SHUTDOWN after landing.

b. Power-Off.

1. Autorotate.

2. EMER SHUTDOWN.

9-33. Electrical Fire-Flight. Prior to shutting off all electrical power, the pilot must consider the equipment that is essential to a particular flight environment that will be encountered, e.g., flight instruments, and fuel boost pumps. In the event of electrical fire or suspected electrical fire in flight:

1. BAT, STBY. and MAIN GEN switches - OFF

2. Land as soon as possible.

If landing cannot be made soon as possible and flight must be continued, the defective circuits may be identified and isolated as follows:

3. Circuit breakers - Out. As each of the following steps is accomplished, check for indications of the source of the fire.

4. MAIN GEN switch - ON.

5. STARTER GEN switch - STBY GEN.

6. BAT switch - ON.

7. Circuit breakers - In. One at a time in the priority required, GEN BUS RESET first. When malfunctioning circuit is identified, pull the applicable circuit breaker out.

9-34. Overheated Battery.

> **WARNING**
>
> Do not open battery compartment or attempt to disconnect or remove overheated battery. Battery * fluid will cause burns and overheated battery may cause thermal burns and may explode. If an overheated battery is suspected or detected.

1. BAT switch - OFF.

2. Land ac soon as possible.

3. EMFR SHUTDOWN after landing.

9-35. Smoke and Fume Elimination. Smoke and/or toxic fumes entering the cockpit and cabin can be exhausted as follows:

Doors. windows. and vents - Open

> **CAUTION**
>
> Do not jettison doors in flight

9-36. Hydraulic.

> **WARNING**
>
> During actual or simulated hydraulic failure, do not pull or push circuit breakers or move the HYD CONT switch during takeoff, map of the earth flying, approach and landing or while the aircraft is not in level flight. This prevents any possibility of a surge in hydraulic pressure and the resulting loss of control.

P37. Hydraulic Power Failure. Hydraulic power failure will be evident when the force required for control movement increases; a moderate feedback m the controls when moved is felt, and/or the HYD PRESSURE caution light illuminates. Control movements will result m normal helicopter response. In the event of hydraulic power failure:

1. Airspeed - Adjust as necessary to attain the most comfortable level of control movements.
2. HYD CONT circuit breaker - Out. If hydraulic power is not restored:
3. HYD CONT circuit breaker - In.
4. HYD CONT switch - OFF.
5. Land as soon as practicable at an area that will permit a run-on landing with power. Maintain airspeed at or above effective transitional lift until touchdown.

9-38. Control Stiffness. A failure within the irreversible valve may cause extreme stiffness in the collective or two of the four cyclic control quadrants. If the failure is in one of the two cyclic irreversible valves, caution is necessary to avoid over controlling between the failed and operational quadrants.

1. HYD CONT switch - OFF then ON.

Check for restoration of normal flight control movements.
Repeat as necessary.
If control response is not restored:

2. HYD CONT switch - OFF.
If normal operation is not restore!

3. Land as soon as practicable at an area that will permit a run-on landing with power. Maintain airspeed at or above effective transitional lift until touchdown.

9-39. Flight Control Servo Hardover.

a. Cyclic hardover is caused by a sequencing valve failure within the Irreversible valve on either or both cyclic servos. Cyclic servo hardover will cause the cyclic to move full night forward, full left rear, full left forward, or full right rear.

b. Collective hardover is caused by a sequencing valve failure within the Irreversible valve on the collective servo. The collective will move to the full up or full down position.

c. A failure of any flight control servo may render the helicopter uncontrollable unless the following action is taken.

    1. <u>HYD CONT select - Select opposite position.</u>

    2. <u>LAND AS SOON AS POSSIBLE</u> at an area that will permit a run-on landing with power. Maintain airspeed at or above effective translational lift at touchdown.

9-40. Flight Control/Main Rotor System Malfunctions.

a. Failure of components within the flight control system may be indicated through varying degrees of feedback, binding, resistance, or sloppiness. These malfunctions are normally in isolated controls, i.e. cyclic, cyclic/collective, or anti-torque. These conditions should not be mistaken for hydraulic power failure.

b. Imminent failure of main rotor components may be indicated by a sudden increase in main rotor vibration and/or unusual noise. Severe changes in lilt characteristics and/or balance condition can occur due to blade strikes, skin separation, shift or loss of balance weights or other material. Malfunctions may result in severe main rotor flapping. In the event of a main rotor system malfunction, proceed as follows:

WARNING

Danger exists that the main rotor system could collapse or separate from the aircraft after landing. A decision must be made whether occupant egress occurs before or after the rotor has stopped.

    1. <u>Land as soon as possible.</u>

    2. <u>EMER SHUTDOWN after landing.</u>

9-41. Mast Bumping.

If mast bumping occurs:

    1. Reduce severity of maneuver.
    2. Land as soon as possible.

9-42. Fuel System.

9-43. Fuel Boost Pump Failure.

If both FUEL BOOST caution lights come on:

    1. Check fuel pressure.

If fuel pressure is zero:

    2. Descend to a pressure altitude of 4600 feet or less if possible.

    3. Land as soon as practicable. No attempt should be made to troubleshoot the system while in flight.

9-44. Electrical System

9-45. Main Generator Malfunction. A malfunction of the main generator will be indicated by zero indication of the Main Generator Loadmeter and DC GENERATOR caution light illumination. An attempt may be made to put the generator back on line as follows:

    1. GEN and BUS RESET circuit breaker - In.

    2. MAIN GEN switch - RESET then ON. Do not hold the switch in the RESET POSITION. If the main generator is not restored or If it goes off again:

    3. MAIN GEN switch - OFF.

NOTE

Check that the standby generator loadmeter is indicating a load Flight may be continued using the standby generator.

9-46. Landing and Ditching.

9-47. Landing In Trees. A landing in trees should be made when no other landing area is available. Select a landing area containing the least number of trees of minimum height Decelerate to a zero ground speed at tree-top level and descend into the trees vertically, applying collective pitch as necessary for minimum rate of descent. Prior to the main rotor blades entering the trees, ensure throttle is OFF and apply all of the remaining collective pitch.

9-48. Ditching-Power on. If it becomes necessary to ditch the helicopter, accomplish an approach to an approximate 3-foot hover above the water and proceed as follows:

1. Cockpit doors - Jettison at a hover.

2. Cabin doors - Open.

3. Crew (except pilot) and passengers - Exit.

4. Hover a safe distance away from personnel.

5. Throttle-Off and autorotate. Apply full collective pitch prior to the main rotor blades entering the water. Maintain a level attitude as the helicopter sinks and until it begins to roll, then apply cyclic in direction of the roll.

6. Pilot-Exit when the main rotor is stopped.

9-49. Ditching-Power Off. If ditching is imminent, accomplish engine malfunction emergency procedures. Decelerate to zero forward speed as the helicopter nears the water. Apply all of the collective pitch as the helicopter enters the water. Maintain a level attitude as the helicopter sinks and until it begins to roll, then apply cyclic m the direction of the roll. Exit when the main rotor is stopped.

1. <u>Cockpit doors--Jettison</u>

2. <u>Cabin Doors - open.</u>

3. <u>Exit when main rotor has stopped</u>

TM 55-1520-210-10

Table 9-1 Emergency Procedures for Caution Segments

Light	Corrective Action
MASTER CAUTION	Check the CAUTION panel for the condition. If master caution only (no segment light), land as soon as possible.
AUX FUEL LOW	INT AUX FUEL transfer switches-OFF.
DC GENERATOR	Check GEN AND BUS RESET circuit breaker in MAIN GEN switch RESET then ON. Switch to STBY GEN.
INST INVERTER	Switch to other inverter.
EXTERNAL POWER	Close door.
XMSM OIL PRESS	Land as soon as possible. (Ref to para 9-19)
XMSM OIL HOT	Land as soon as possible. (Ref to para 9-19)
ENGINE INLET AIR	Land as soon as practicable.
CHIP DETECTOR	Land as soon as possible.
LEFT FUEL BOOST	Land as soon as practicable.
RIGHT FUEL BOOST	Land as soon as practicable.
20 MINUTE FUEL	Land as soon as practicable.
IFF	Information/System Status
ENGINE OIL PRESS	Land as soon as possible.
ENGINE CHIP DET	Land as soon as possible.
GOV EMER	Information/System Status
ENGINE ICE DET	Land as soon as possible.
ENGINE FUEL PUMP	Land as soon as possible.
ENGINE ICING	Land as soon as possible.
FUEL FILTER	Land as soon as practicable.
HYD PRESSURE	Land as soon as practicable.
SPARE	Land as soon as possible.

Change 8 9-9

TM 55-1520-210-10

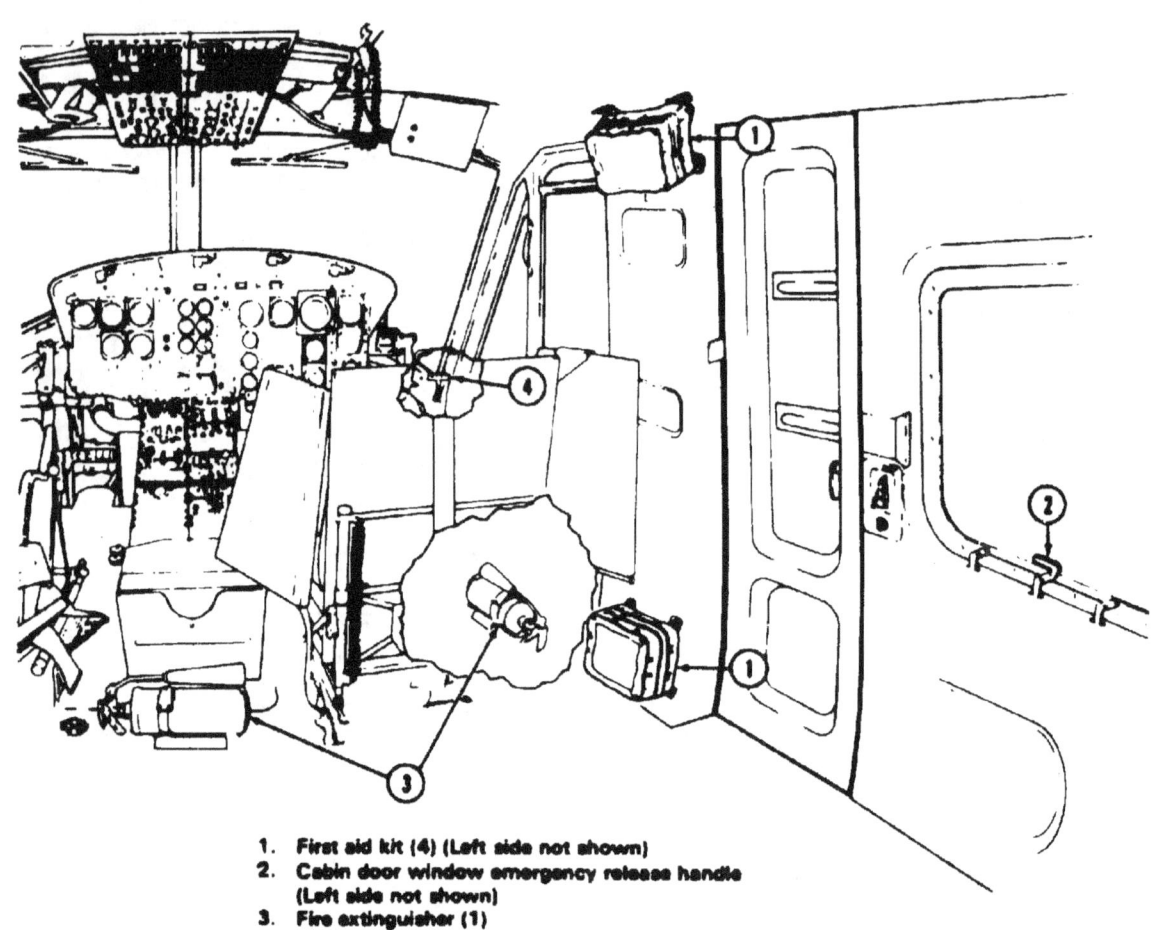

1. First aid kit (4) (Left side not shown)
2. Cabin door window emergency release handle (Left side not shown)
3. Fire extinguisher (1)
4. Crew door jettison handle (Left side not shown)

Figure 9-1. Emergency Exits and Equipment

AUTOROTATIONAL GLIDE CHARACTERISTICS
POWER OFF

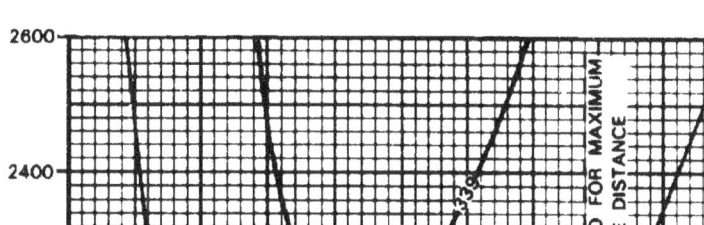

EXAMPLE

WANTED

GLIDE RATIO AND RATE OF DESCENT

KNOWN

AIRSPEED = 80 KIAS ROOF
ROTOR RPM = 314

METHOD

ENTER INDICATED AIRSPEED
MOVE UP TO 314 ROTOR RPM LINE
MOVE LEFT, READ GLIDE RATIO.
CONTINUE UP 80 KIAS TO 314 ROTOR
RPM LINE ON UPPER GRAPH. MOVE
LEFT, READ RATE OF DESCENT.

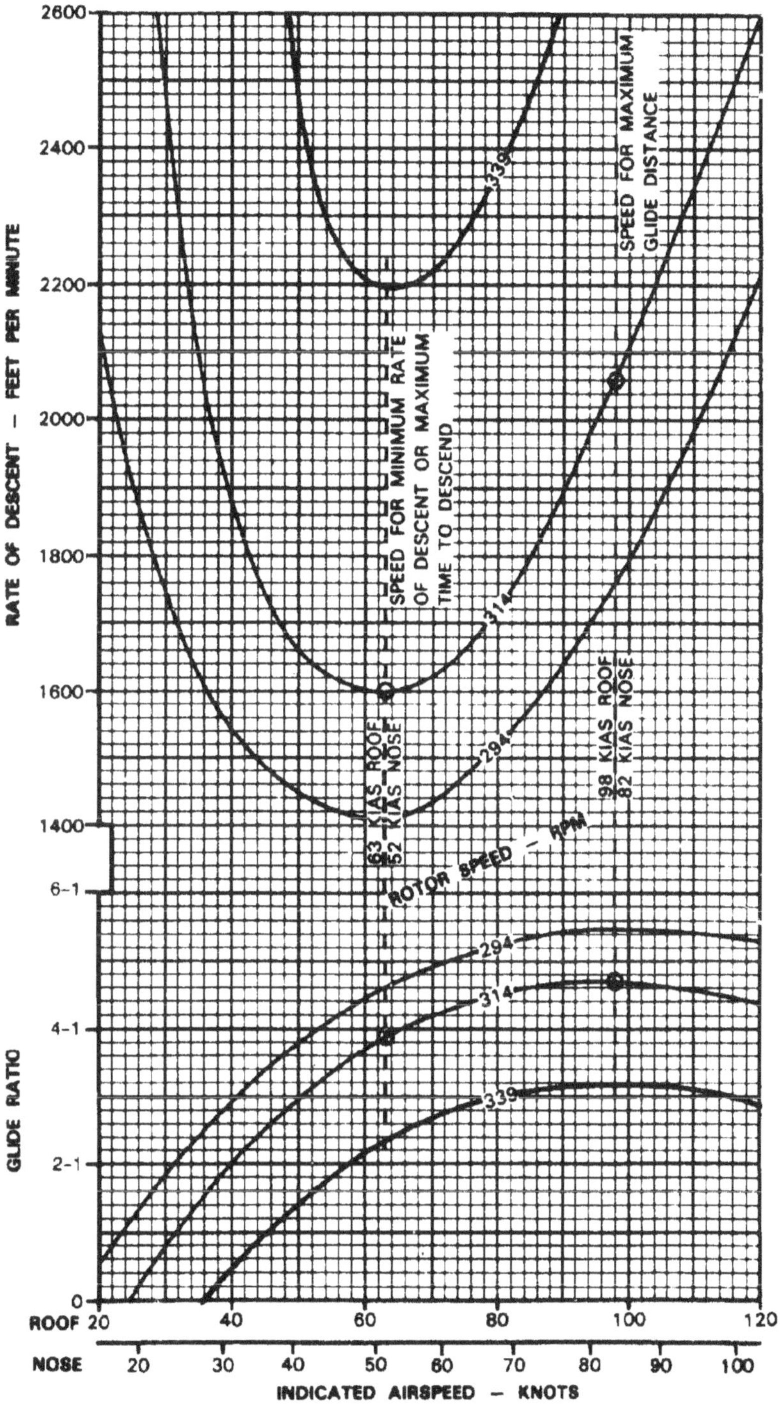

Figure 9-2. Autorotational Glide Characteristics Chart

TM 55-1520-210-10

AUTOROTATIONAL GLIDE CHARACTERISTICS
POWER OFF

AUTOROTATIONAL GLIDE
UH-1H
T53-L-13B

NOTE: AUTOROTATIONAL DESCENT PERFORMANCE IS A FUNCTION OF AIRSPEED AND IS ESSENTIALLY UNAFFECTED BY DENSITY, ALTITUDE, AND GROSS WEIGHT.

EXAMPLE

WANTED

GLIDE RATIO AND RATE OF DESCENT

KNOWN

AIRSPEED = 80 KIAS ROOF
ROTOR RPM 314

METHOD

ENTER INDICATED AIRSPEED HERE MOVE UP TO 314 ROTOR RPM LINE MOVE LEFT, READ GLIDE RATIO = 4.5 CONTINUE UP 80 KIAS TO 314 ROTOR RPM LINE ON UPPER GRAPH MOVE LEFT, READ RATE OF DESCENT = 1725 FPM

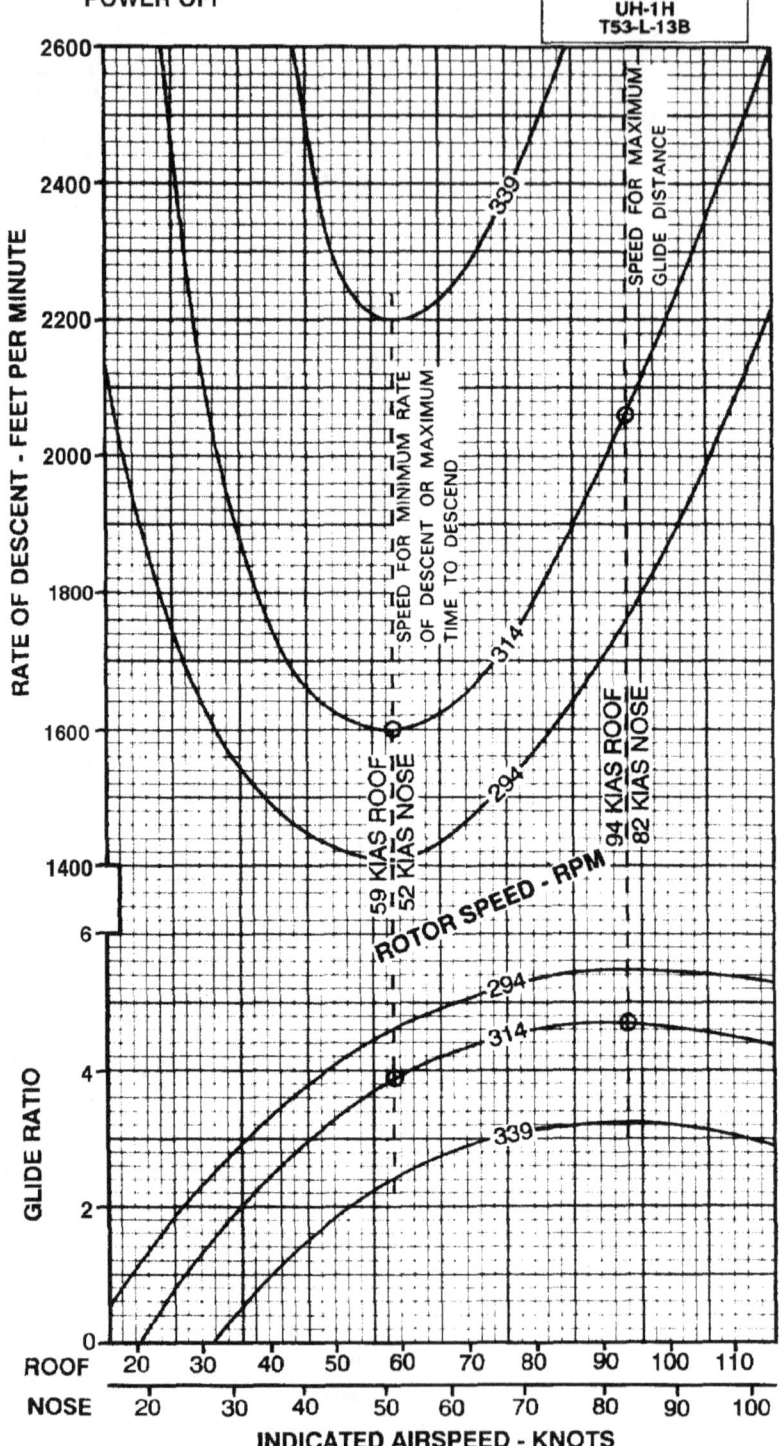

DATA BASIS: DERIVED FROM FLIGHT TEST DATA OF SIMILAR AIRCRAFT

Figure 9-2.1. Autorotational glide characteristics chart

HEIGHT VELOCITY DIAGRAM
324 ROTOR RPM

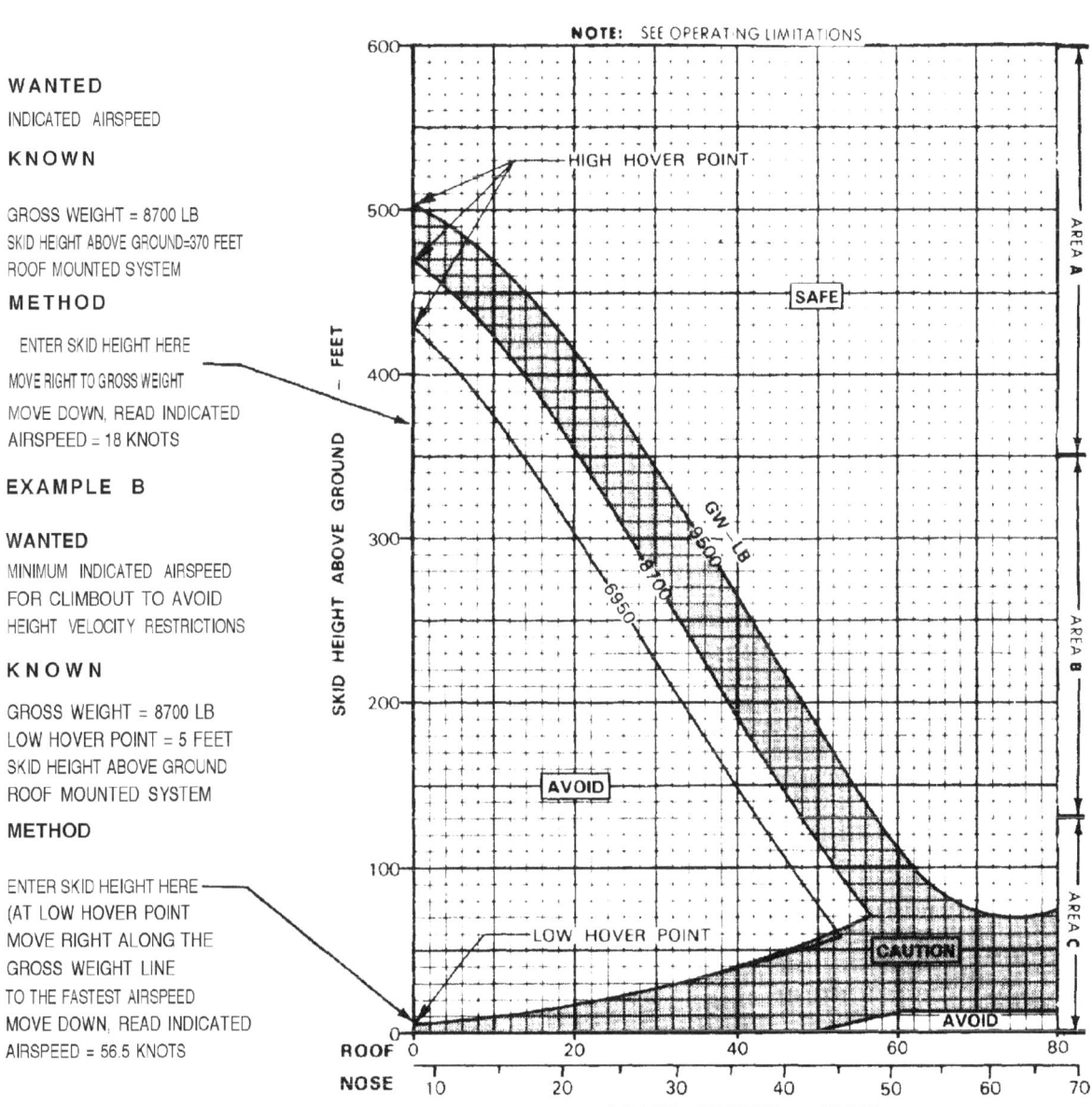

Figure 9-3 Height Velocity Diagram

TM 55-1520-210-10

HEIGHT VELOCITY DIAGRAM
324 ROTOR RPM

HEIGHT VELOCITY DIAGRAM
UH-1H
T53-L-13B

EXAMPLE A

WANTED

INDICATED AIRSPEED

KNOWN

GROSS WEIGHT = 8700 LB
SKID HEIGHT ABOVE GROUND = 370 FEET
ROOF MOUNTED SYSTEM

METHOD

ENTER SKID HEIGHT HERE
MOVE RIGHT TO GROSS WEIGHT
MOVE DOWN, READ INDICATED
AIRSPEED = 14 KNOTS

EXAMPLE B

WANTED

MINIMUM INDICATED AIRSPEED
FOR CLIMBOUT TO AVOID
HEIGHT VELOCITY RESTRICTIONS

KNOWN

GROSS WEIGHT = 8700 LB
LOW HOVER POINT = 5 FEET
SKID HEIGHT ABOVE GROUND
ROOF MOUNTED SYSTEM

METHOD

ENTER SKID HEIGHT HERE
(AT LOW HOVER POINT)
MOVE RIGHT ALONG THE
GROSS WEIGHT LINE
TO THE FASTEST AIRSPEED
MOVE DOWN, READ INDICATED
AIRSPEED = 52.5 KNOTS

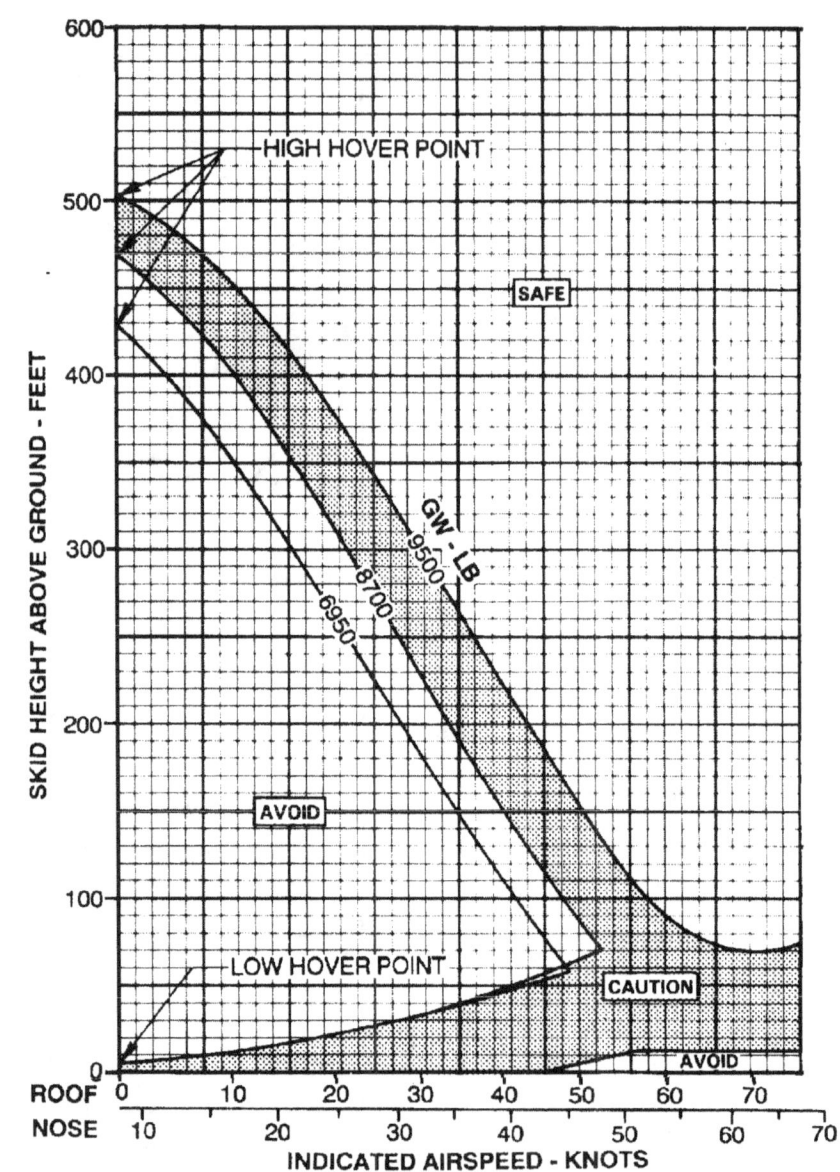

DATA BASIS: DERIVED FROM FLIGHT TEST FTC-TDR 67-27, NOVEMBER 1964

Figure 9-3.1. Height velocity diagram

Appendix A
References

AR 50-4
Safety Studies and Reviews of Nuclear Weapon Systems

AR 50-5
Nuclear Surety

AR 70-50
Designating and Naming Military Aircraft, Rockets, and Guided Missiles

AR 95-1
Army Aviation: Flight Regulations

Deleted

AR 95-27
Operational Procedures for Aircraft Carrying Dangerous Materials

AR 385-40
Accident Reporting and Records

TB 55-9150-200-24
Engine and Transmission Oils, Fuels
and Additives for Army Aircraft

TB MED 501
Noise and Conservation of Hearing

TM 9-1005-224-10
Operators Manual for M60, 7.62-MM Machine Gun (NSN 1005-00-605-7710)

TM 9-1005-224-12
Operator and Organizational Maintenance Manual Including Repair Parts and Special Tool List: Machine Gun 7.62-MM M60, and Mount, Tripod, Machine Gun M122

TM 9-1345-201-12
Operators and Organizational Maintenance Manual: Mine Dispersing Subsystem, Aircraft: M56 and M132

TM 11-5810-262-OP
Loading Procedures, TSEC Equip
TM 11-5810-262-12&P

TM 55-1500-342-23
Army Aviation Maintenance Engineering Manual-Weight and Balance

TM 55-1500-334-25
Conversion of Aircraft to Fire Resistant Hydraulic Fluid

TM 55-1520-210-CL
Operators and Crewmembers Checklist--H-IH/V Helicopters

TM 57-220
Technical Training of Parachutists

TM 750-244-1-5
Procedures for the Destruction of Aircraft and Associated Equipment to Prevent Enemy Use

DA Pam 738751
Functional Users Manual for the Army Maintenance Management System-Aviation (TAMMS-A)

DOD FLIP
DOD Flight Information Publication (Enroute)

FM 1-202
Environmental Flight

FM 1-203
Fundamentals of Flight

FM 1-204
Night Flight Techniques and Procedures

FM 1-240
Instrument Flying and Navigation for Army Aviators

FM 10-68
Aircraft Refueling-

FM 10-1101
Petroleum Handling Equipment and Operation

Appendix B
Abbreviations and Terms

AC
Alternating Current

ADF
Automatic Direction Finder

AGL
Above Ground Level

AI
Attack Imminent

ALT
Alternator

ALT
Altitude/Altimeter

ALTM
Altimeter

AM
Amplitude Modulation

AMP
Ampere

ANT
Antenna

ATTD
Attitude

AUTO
Automatic

AUX
Auxiliary

AVGAS
Aviation Gasoline

BAT
Battery

BDHI
Bearing Distance Heading Indicator

BFO
Beat Frequency Oscillator

BL
Butt Line

BRIL
Brilliance

BRT
Bright

C
Celsius

CARR
Carrier

CAS
Calibrated Airspeed

CCW
Counter Clockwise

CDI
Course Deviation Indicator

CG
Center of Gravity

CL
Centerline

CMPS
Compass

CNVTR
Converter

COLL
Collision

COMM
Communication

COMPT
Compartment

CONT
Control

CONT
Continuous

CONV
Converter

CW
Clockwise

DC
Direct Current

DCP
Dispenser Control Panel

DF
Direction Finding

DECR
Decrease

DELTA A
Incremental Change

DET
Detector

DG
Directional Gyro

DIS
Disable

DISP
Dispense

DSCRM
Discriminator

ECM
Electronic Countermeasures

EGT
Exhaust Gas Temperature

ELEC
Electrical

EMER
Emergency

END
Endurance

ENG
Engine

ESS
Essential

EXH
Exhaust

EXT
Extend

EXT
Exterior

F
Fahrenheit

FAT
Free Air Temperature

FITG
Fitting

FM
Frequency Modulation

FOD
Foreign Object Damage

FPS
Feet Per Second

FREQ
Frequency

FS
Fuselage Station

FT
Foot

FT/MIN
Feet Per Minute

FUS
Fuselage

FWD
Forward

ΔF
Increment of Equivalent Flat Plate Drag Area

G
Gravity

G
Guard

GAL
Gallon

GD
Guard

GEN
Generator

GND
Ground

GOV
Governor

GPU
Ground Power Unit

GRWT
Gross Weight

GW
Gross Weight

HDG
Heading

HF
High Frequency

HIT
Health Indicator Test

HTR
Heater

HYD
Hydraulic

IAS
Indicated Airspeed

ICS
Interphone Control Station

IDENT
Identification

IFF
Identification Friend or Foe

IGE
In Ground Effect

IN
Inch

INCR
Increase

IND
Indication/Indicator

INHG
Inches of Mercury

INOP
Inoperative

INST
Instrument

INT
Internal

INT
Interphone

INV
Inverter

INVTR
Inverter

IR
Infrared

IRT
Indicator Receiver Transmitter

ISA
International Standard Atmosphere

KCAS
Knots Calibrated Airspeed

kHz
Kilohertz

KIAS
Knots Indicated Airspeed

km
Kilometer

KTAS
Knots True Airspeed

KN
Knots

kva
Kilovolt-Ampere

kw
Kilowatt

L
Left

LB
Pounds

LDG
Landing

LH
Left Hand

LSB
Lower Sideband

LT
Lights

LTG
Lighting

LTS
Lights

MAG
Magnetic

MAN
Manual

MAX
Maximum

MED
Medium

MHF
Medium-High Frequency

MHz
Megahertz

MIC
Microphone

MIN
Minimum

MIN
Minute

MISC
Miscellaneous

mm
Millimeter

MON
Monitor

MWO
Modification Work Order

NAV
Navigation

NET
Network

NO
Number

NM
Nautical Mile

NON-ESS
Non-Essential

NON-SEC
Non-Secure

NORM
Normal

NVG
Night Vision Goggles

NR
Gas Turbine Speed

N2
Power Turbine Speed

OGE
Out of Ground Effect

PED
Pedestal

PLT
Pilot

PRESS
Pressure

PRGM
Program

PSI
Pounds Per Square Inch

PVT
Private

PWR
Power

QTY
Quantity

%Q
Percent Torque

R
Right

RCVR
Receiver

R/C
Rate of Climb

R/D
Rate of Descent

RDR
Radar

RDS
Rounds

REL
Release

REM
Remote

RETR
Retract

RETRAN
Retransmission

RF
Radio Frequency

RH
Right Hand

RI
Remote Height Indicator

RPM
Revolutions Per Minute

SAM
Surface to Air Missile

SEC
Secondary

SEC Secure

SEL Select

SENS Sensitivity

SL Searchlight

SOL Solenoid

SQ Squelch

SSB Single Sideband

STA Station

STBY Standby

SQ FT Square Feet

TAS True Airspeed

TEMP Temperature

TGT Turbine Gas Temperature

T/R Transmit-Receive

TRANS Transfer

TRANS Transformer

TRANS Transmitter

TRQ Torque

UHF Ultra-High Frequency

USB Upper Sideband

VAC Volts, Alternating Current

VDC Volts, Direct Current

VHF Very high Frequency

VM Volt Meter

VOL Volume

VOR VHF Omni Directional Range

VNE Velocity, Never Exceed (Airspeed Limitation)

WL Water line

WPN Weapon

XCVR Transceiver

XMIT Transmit

XMTR Transmitter

XMSN Transmission

APPENDIX C
TABULAR PERFORMANCE DATA

Use of the TABULAR CHARTS is illustrated by the following examples:

TABULAR PERFORMANCE DATA (Pages C-2 through C-4)

KNOWN:
Pressure Altitude (PA) = 1000 FEET
Free Air Temperature (FAT) = +25

WANTED:
Maximum GW for Hover OGE.
Torque Required for Hover OGE.
Torque Required for Hover IGE (2 FEET).

METHOD:

1. Enter PA at 1,000 Feet, and Move Right to +25 C.

2. The Top Number (912) is the Maximum GW to Hover OGE. **(= 9,120 POUNDS.)**

3. The Middle Number (45) is the Torque required to Hover OGE at the Maximum GW to Hover OGE (9,120). **(= 45 PSI.)**

4. The Bottom Number (37) is the Torque required at a 2 Foot Hover at the Maximum GW to Hover OGE (9,120). **(- 37 PSI.)**

TABULAR PERFORMANCE DATA (Page C-5)

KNOWN:
Pressure Altitude (PA) = 1000 FEET
Free Air Temperature (FAT) = +25

WANTED:
Maximum Torque available (30 MINUTES).

METHOD:

1. Enter PA at 1,000 Feet, and Move Right to +20 C and +30 C.

2. Interpolate between 48.0 and 42.7 PSI, the Maximum Torque available will be between. (45.4)

3. Torque Values outlined in Tabular Data are Calibrated Values and should be converted to indicated before use in the cockpit.

APPENDIX C
TABULAR PERFORMANCE DATA

TM 55-1520-210-10

MAXIMUM HOVER WEIGHT AND TORQUE REQUIRED
LEVEL SURFACE CALM WIND TEMPERATURE
324 ROTOR / 6600 ENGINE RPM

* GW - 10LB = GW DIVIDED BY 10 LB
Q = TORQUE PSI
IGE = 2 FOOT SKID HEIGHT

PRES ALT FT	*	FREE AIR TEMPERATURE °C																								
		-60	-55	-50	-45	-40	-35	-30	-25	-20	-15	-10	-5	0	5	10	15	20	25	30	35	40	45	50	55
0	GW-10LB	915	942	950	950	950	950	950	950	950	950	950	950	950	950	950	950	950	946	902	859	816	765	715	663
	Q OGE-PSI	50	50	49	48	47	46	46	46	46	46	46	46	46	36	47	47	47	47	44	41	38	35	33	31
	Q IGE-PSI	43	43	42	41	40	39	39	38	38	38	38	38	38	38	38	38	38	38	36	34	32	30	27	26
500	GW-10LB	912	939	950	950	950	950	950	950	950	950	950	950	950	950	950	950	950	929	886	844	801	751	702	651
	Q OGE-PSI	50	50	49	48	47	47	46	46	46	46	46	46	47	47	47	47	47	46	44	41	38	35	33	30
	Q IGE-PSI	43	43	42	41	40	39	39	38	38	38	38	38	38	38	38	38	38	38	36	34	32	29	27	25
1000	GW-10LB	909	936	950	950	950	950	950	950	950	950	950	950	950	950	950	950	950	912	870	826	787	737	689	639
	Q OGE-PSI	50	50	49	48	47	47	47	47	46	46	46	47	47	47	47	47	48	45	43	40	38	35	32	29
	Q IGE-PSI	43	43	42	41	40	39	39	39	38	38	38	38	38	38	38	39	39	37	35	33	31	29	27	25
1500	GW-10LB	906	934	950	950	950	950	950	950	950	950	950	950	950	950	950	950	937	895	854	813	772	724	676	627
	Q OGE-PSI	50	50	50	48	48	47	47	47	47	47	47	47	47	47	48	48	47	44	42	39	37	34	32	29
	Q IGE-PSI	43	43	42	41	40	39	39	39	39	39	38	38	39	39	39	39	38	36	34	32	30	28	26	24
2000	GW-10LB	903	931	950	950	950	950	950	950	950	950	950	950	950	950	950	950	920	879	838	798	758	710	664	615
	Q OGE-PSI	50	50	50	49	48	47	47	47	47	47	47	47	47	48	48	48	46	44	41	39	36	34	31	28
	Q IGE-PSI	43	43	42	41	40	40	39	39	39	39	39	39	39	39	39	39	37	36	34	32	30	28	26	24
2500	GW-10LB	901	928	950	950	950	950	950	950	950	950	950	950	950	950	950	944	903	863	823	783	744	697	651	604
	Q OGE-PSI	50	50	50	49	48	48	47	47	47	47	47	48	48	48	48	48	45	43	40	38	36	33	30	28
	Q IGE-PSI	43	43	42	41	41	40	39	39	39	39	39	39	39	39	39	39	37	35	33	31	29	27	25	23
3000	GW-10LB	899	926	948	950	950	950	950	950	950	950	950	950	950	950	950	927	886	847	807	769	730	684	639	592
	Q OGE-PSI	50	50	50	49	48	48	48	47	47	48	48	48	48	48	49	47	45	42	40	37	35	32	30	27
	Q IGE-PSI	43	43	42	41	40	40	39	39	39	39	39	39	39	39	39	38	36	34	32	31	29	27	25	23
3500	GW-10LB	896	923	944	950	950	950	950	950	950	950	950	950	950	950	950	910	870	831	792	754	716	671	627	581
	Q OGE-PSI	50	50	50	49	49	48	48	48	48	48	48	48	48	49	49	46	44	41	39	37	34	32	29	27
	Q IGE-PSI	43	43	42	42	41	40	40	39	39	39	39	39	39	39	39	37	35	34	32	30	28	26	24	22
4000	GW-10LB	894	920	941	950	950	950	950	950	950	950	950	950	950	950	932	893	853	815	777	740	703	659	615	570
	Q OGE-PSI	50	50	50	50	49	48	48	48	48	48	48	49	49	49	48	45	43	40	38	36	34	31	29	26
	Q IGE-PSI	43	43	42	42	41	40	40	40	39	39	39	39	39	39	39	37	35	33	31	29	28	26	24	22
4500	GW-10LB	892	918	937	950	950	950	950	950	950	950	950	950	950	950	915	876	837	800	763	723	690	646	604	559
	Q OGE-PSI	50	50	50	50	49	49	49	48	49	49	49	49	49	49	47	45	42	40	37	35	33	31	28	26
	Q IGE-PSI	43	43	42	42	41	40	40	40	40	40	40	40	40	40	38	36	34	32	31	29	27	25	23	22

TM 55-1520-210-10

MAXIMUM HOVER WEIGHT AND TORQUE REQUIRED
LEVEL SURFACE CALM WIND TEMPERATURE
324 ROTOR / 6600 ENGINE RPM

* GW - 10LB = GW DIVIDED BY 10 LB
Q = TORQUE PSI
IGE = 2 FOOT SKID HEIGHT

APPENDIX C
TABULAR PERFORMANCE DATA

PRES ALT FT	*	FREE AIR TEMPERATURE °C																								
		-60	-55	-50	-45	-40	-35	-30	-25	-20	-15	-10	-5	0	5	10	15	20	25	30	35	40	45	50	55
5000	GW-10LB	890	915	933	946	950	950	950	950	950	950	950	950	950	935	896	859	822	785	748	712	677	634	592	549
	Q OGE-PSI	50	50	50	50	50	49	49	49	49	49	49	49	50	49	46	44	41	39	37	35	32	30	28	25
	Q IGE-PSI	43	43	42	42	41	41	40	40	40	40	40	40	40	39	37	35	33	32	30	28	27	25	23	21
5500	GW-10LB	888	911	928	942	950	950	950	950	950	950	950	950	950	917	881	843	806	770	734	699	664	622	581	538
	Q OGE-PSI	50	50	50	50	50	49	49	49	49	49	49	50	50	48	45	43	41	38	36	34	32	29	27	25
	Q IGE-PSI	43	43	42	42	41	41	40	40	40	40	40	40	40	38	36	35	33	31	29	28	26	24	23	21
6000	GW-10LB	886	908	924	937	946	950	950	950	950	950	950	950	934	900	864	827	791	755	720	686	651	610	570	528
	Q OGE PSI	50	50	50	50	50	50	50	50	50	50	50	49	47	45	42	40	37	35	33	31	29	27	24
	Q IGE-PSI	43	42	42	42	41	41	41	40	40	40	40	39	38	36	34	32	30	29	27	26	24	22	20
6500	GW-10LB	883	904	919	932	841	947	950	950	949	947	945	942	916	**883**	848	811	776	741	707	673	639	599	559	518
	Q OGE-PSI	50	50	50	50	50	50	50	50	50	50	50	48	46	44	41		39	37	35	33	31	28	26	24
	Q IGE-PSI	43	42	42	42	41	41	41	41	40	40	40	40	39	37	35	33	32	30	28	27	25	23	22	20
7000	GW-10LB	880	899	915	927	936	942	945	945	944	942	940	927	899	866	831	796	761	727	693	660	627	587	549	508
	Q OGE-PSI	50	50	50	50	50	50	50	50	50	50	50	49	47	45	43	40	38	36	34	32	30	28	26	23
	Q IGE-PSI	43	42	42	42	41	41	41	40	40	40	40	39	38	36	34	33	31	29	28	26	25	23	21	20
7500	GW-10LB	877	895	910	922	931	937	940	940	939	937	932	910	882	850	816	781	746	713	680	647	615	576	538	
	Q OGE-PSI	50	50	50	50	50	50	50	50	50	50	50	48	46	44	42	40	37	35	33	31	29	27	25	
	Q IGE-PSI	43	42	42	42	41	41	41	40	40	40	40	39	37	36	34	32	30	29	27	26	24	22	21	
8000	GW-10LB	873	890	905	917	926	932	935	935	933	931	915	892	865	834	800	766	732	699	667	635	603	565	528	
	Q OGE-PSI	50	50	50	50	50	50	50	50	50	50	49	47	46	43	41	39	37	35	33	31	29	27	25	
	Q IGE-PSI	43	42	42	41	41	41	41	40	40	40	39	38	36	35	33	31	30	28	27	25	24	22	20	
8500	GW-10LB	869	885	900	912	921	927	929	929	928	915	897	875	848	818	785	751	718	686	654	623	592	554	518	
	Q OGE-PSI	50	50	50	50	50	50	50	50	50	49	48	46	45	43	40	38	36	34	32	30	28	26	24	
	Q IGE-PSI	43	42	42	41	41	41	40	40	40	39	38	37	36	34	32	31	29	28	26	25	23	22	20	
9000	GW-10LB	864	880	895	907	916	922	924	921	911	898	880	859	832	802	769	736	704	672	641	611	581	544	508	
	Q OGE-PSI	50	50	50	50	50	50	50	50	49	48	47	46	44	42	40	37	35	33	31	30	28	26	24	
	Q IGE-PSI	43	42	42	41	41	41	40	40	39	39	38	36	35	34	32	30	29	27	26	24	23	21	20	
9500	GW-10LB	860	875	890	902	911	917	917	904	894	880	863	842	816	786	755	722	690	659	629	599	569	533		
	Q OGE-PSI	50	50	50	50	50	50	50	49	48	47	46	45	43	41	39	38	35	33	31	29	27	25		
	Q IGE-PSI	43	42	42	41	41	41	40	39	39	38	37	36	34	33	31	30	28	27	25	24	22	21		
10000	GW-10LB	855	870	884	897	906	910	899	886	877	864	747	826	800	771	740	708	677	647	617	588	558	523		
	Q OGE-PSI	50	50	50	50	50	50	49	48	47	46	45	44	42	40	38	36	34	32	30	28	27	25		
	Q IGE-PSI	42	42	42	41	41	40	39	39	38	37	36	35	34	32	31	29	28	26	25	23	22	20		

Change 17   C-3

TM 55-1520-210-10

MAXIMUM HOVER WEIGHT AND TORQUE REQUIRED
LEVEL SURFACE CALM WIND TEMPERATURE
324 ROTOR / 6600 ENGINE RPM

* GW - 10LB = GW DIVIDED BY 10 LB
Q = TORQUE PSI
IGE = 2 FOOT SKID HEIGHT

APPENDIX C
TABULAR PERFORMANCE DATA

PRES ALT FT	*	FREE AIR TEMPERATURE °C																						
		-60	-55	-50	-45	-40	-35	-30	-25	-20	-15	-10	-5	0	5	10	15	20	25	30	35	40	45	50	55
10500	GW-10LB	850	865	879	892	900	893	882	869	860	847	830	810	785	756	725	694	664	634	605	576	548	513		
	Q OGE-PSI	50	50	50	50	50	49	48	47	46	46	44	43	41	39	37	35	33	31	30	28	26	24		
	Q IGE-PSI	43	42	42	41	41	40	39	38	37	36	36	34	33	32	30	28	27	26	24	23	22	20		
11000	GW-10LB	845	860	874	886	883	876	865	853	843	831	814	794	769	741	711	681	651	621	593	565	537	503		
	Q OGE-PSI	50	50	50	50	49	48	47	46	45	45	44	42	40	39	37	35	33	31	29	27	26	24		
	Q IGE-PSI	43	42	41	41	40	39	38	37	36	36	35	34	32	31	29	28	26	25	24	22	21	20		
11500	GW-10LB	839	855	869	870	866	859	849	836	827	814	798	778	754	727	697	667	638	609	581	554	527			
	Q OGE-PSI	50	50	50	49	48	47	46	45	45	44	43	41	40	39	36	34	32	30	28	27	25			
	Q IGE-PSI	42	42	41	40	39	38	37	36	36	35	34	33	32	30	29	27	26	25	23	22	21			
12000	GW-10LB	834	850	853	853	849	842	832	820	811	798	783	763	739	712	683	654	625	597	570	543	516			
	Q OGE-PSI	50	50	49	48	47	46	45	44	44	43	42	41	39	37	35	33	31	30	28	26	25			
	Q IGE-PSI	42	42	41	39	38	37	37	36	35	34	33	32	31	30	28	27	25	24	23	22	20			
12500	GW-10LB	828	833	836	836	833	826	816	804	795	783	767	748	724	698	669	641	612	585	558	532	506			
	Q OGE-PSI	50	49	48	47	46	45	44	43	43	42	41	40	38	36	34	33	31	29	27	26	24			
	Q IGE-PSI	42	41	40	39	38	37	36	35	34	34	33	32	31	29	28	26	25	24	22	21	20			
13000	GW-10LB	812	817	819	820	816	809	800	788	779	767	752	733	710	684	656	628	600	573	547	521				
	Q OGE-PSI	49	48	47	46	45	44	43	43	42	41	40	39	37	36	34	32	30	28	27	25				
	Q IGE-PSI	41	40	39	38	37	36	35	34	34	33	32	31	30	29	27	26	24	23	22	21				
13500	GW-10LB	796	801	803	803	800	793	784	772	763	751	736	718	695	680	642	625	588	561	536	511				
	Q OGE-PSI	48	47	46	45	44	43	43	42	41	40	39	38	36	35	33	31	29	28	26	25				
	Q IGE-PSI	41	40	38	37	36	35	34	34	33	32	31	30	29	28	26	25	24	23	21	20				
14000	GW-10LB	778	782	785	785	781	775	765	753	745	733	718	700	678	653	626	599	573	547	522					
	Q OGE-PSI	47	46	45	44	43	42	42	41	40	39	38	37	36	34	32	30	29	27	26					
	Q IGE-PSI	40	39	38	36	35	34	34	33	32	31	31	30	29	27	26	25	23	22	21					
14500	GW-10LB	761	765	768	768	764	758	748	737	728	717	703	685	663	639	612	586	560	535	510					
	Q OGE-PSI	46	45	44	43	42	41	41	40	39	38	37	36	35	33	31	30	28	26	25					
	Q IGE-PSI	38	38	37	35	35	34	33	32	31	31	30	29	28	27	25	24	23	22	20					
15000	GW-10LB	745	749	751	751	748	741	732	721	712	701	687	669	648	624	598	572	547	523						
	Q OGE-PSI	45	44	43	42	41	41	40	39	38	37	37	35	34	32	31	29	27	26						
	Q IGE-PSI	38	37	36	35	34	33	32	31	31	30	29	28	27	26	25	23	22	21						

MAXIMUM TORQUE AVAILABLE—30 MINUTE LIMIT ANTI-ICE OFF BLEED AIR HEATER OFF
324 ROTOR / 6600 ENGINE RPM

PRES ALT FT	FREE AIR TEMPERATURE C						PRES ALT FT	FREE AIR TEMPERATURE C					
	-50	-40	-30	-20	-10	0.0		0.0	+10	+20	+30	+40	+50
0	50.0	50.0	50.0	50.0	50.0	50.0	0	50.0	50.0	49.8	44.3	39.1	33.4
500	50.0	50.0	50.0	50.0	50.0	50.0	500	50.0	50.0	48.9	43.5	38.4	32.8
1000	50.0	50.0	50.0	50.0	50.0	50.0	1000	50.0	50.0	48.0	42.7	37.7	32.2
1500	50.0	50.0	50.0	50.0	50.0	50.0	1500	50.0	50.0	47.2	41.9	37.0	31.6
2000	50.0	50.0	50.0	50.0	50.0	50.0	2000	50.0	50.0	46.3	41.1	36.3	31.0
2500	50.0	50.0	50.0	50.0	50.0	50.0	2500	50.0	50.0	45.4	40.4	35.6	30.4
3000	50.0	50.0	50.0	50.0	50.0	50.0	3000	50.0	49.9	44.6	39.6	35.0	09.8
3500	50.0	50.0	50.0	50.0	50.0	50.0	3500	50.0	49.0	43.7	38.9	34.3	29.3
4000	50.0	50.0	50.0	50.0	50.0	50.0	4000	50.0	48.0	42.9	38.1	33.7	28.7
4500	50.0	50.0	50.0	50.0	50.0	50.0	4500	50.0	47.1	42.1	37.4	33.0	28.2
5000	50.0	50.0	50.0	50.0	50.0	50.0	5000	50.0	46.2	41.3	36.7	32.4	27.6
5500	50.0	50.0	50.0	50.0	50.0	50.0	5500	50.0	45.4	40.5	36.0	31.8	27.1
6000	50.0	50.0	50.0	50.0	50.0	49.2	6000	49.2	44.5	39.7	35.3	31.2	26.6
6500	50.0	50.0	50.0	50.0	50.0	48.2	6500	48.2	43.7	39.0	34.6	30.6	26.1
7000	50.0	50.0	50.0	50.0	50.0	47.3	7000	47.3	42.8	38.2	34.0	30.0	25.6
7500	50.0	50.0	50.0	50.0	49.9	46.4	7500	46.4	42.0	37.5	33.3	29.4	25.1
8000	50.0	50.0	50.0	50.0	48.9	45.5	8000	45.5	41.2	36.8	32.7	28.9	24.6
8500	50.0	50.0	50.0	50.0	48.0	44.7	8500	44.7	40.4	36.0	32.1	28.3	24.2
9000	50.0	50.0	50.0	49.1	47.1	43.8	9000	43.8	39.6	35.3	31.4	27.8	23.7
9500	50.0	50.0	49.8	48.2	46.2	43.0	9500	43.0	38.8	34.7	30.8	27.3	23.2
10000	50.0	50.0	48.9	47.3	45.3	42.1	10000	42.1	38.1	34.0	30.2	26.7	22.8
10500	50.0	50.0	48.0	46.6	44.4	41.3	10500	41.3	37.3	33.3	29.6	26.2	22.4
11000	50.0	49.0	47.1	45.5	43.5	40.5	11000	40.5	36.6	32.7	29.1	25.7	21.9
11500	50.0	48.1	46.2	44.6	42.7	39.7	11500	39.7	35.9	32.0	28.5	25.2	21.5
12000	49.0	47.1	45.3	43.7	41.8	38.9	12000	38.9	35.1	31.4	27.9	24.7	21.1
12500	48.1	46.2	44.4	42.8	41.0	38.1	12500	38.1	34.4	30.7	27.3	24.2	20.7
13000	47.1	45.3	43.5	42.0	40.2	37.3	13000	37.3	33.7	30.1	26.8	23.7	20.3
13500	46.2	44.4	42.6	41.1	39.3	36.6	13500	36.6	33.0	29.5	26.2	23.2	19.9
14000	45.1	43.3	41.5	40.0	38.3	35.6	14000	35.6	32.1	28.7	25.5	22.6	19.3
14500	44.1	42.3	40.6	39.1	37.4	34.8	14500	34.8	31.4	28.0	24.9	22.1	18.9
15000	43.1	41.4	39.6	38.2	36.5	33.9	15000	33.9	30.6	27.3	24.3	21.6	18.4

Index

This Index is organized alphabetically by paragraph number topics.

AC Circuit Breaker Panel, 2-64
AC Power Indicators and Controls, 2-63
AC Power Supply System, 2-61
Additional Crew, 8-9
ADF Set AN/ARN-59, 3-19
ADF Set AN/ARN-83, 3-18
Air Induction System, 2-18
Airspeed Indicators, 2-76
Airspeed Limitations, 5-11
Altitude Encoder/Pneumatic Altimeter AAU-32/A, 3-28
Anti-Collision Light, 2-66
Appendix A, References, 1-4
Appendix B, Abbreviations and Terms, 1-5
Approved Commercial Fuel, Oils, and Fluids, 2-88
Armament Subsystem M23, 4-1
Armament Subsystem M56 and M132 Mine Dispersing, 4-6
Army Aviation Safety Program, 1-7
Attitude Indicators, 2-80
Auxiliary Fuel System, 2-27
Avionics Equipment Configuration, 3-2

Battery, 2-57
Before—Exterior Checks, 8-12
Before Landing, 838
Before Landing-M52 Smoke Generator Subsystem, 4-19
Before Landing Procedures—M56 and M132 Mine Dispersing Subsystem, 4-10
Before Leaving the Helicopter, 8-41
Before Leaving the Helicopter, 8-57
Before Leaving the Helicopter—M52 Smoke Generator Subsystem, 4-20
Before Leaving Helicopter Procedures—M56 and M132 Mine Dispersing Subsystem, 4-11

Before Leaving Helicopter Procedures—Machine Gun M60D, 4-4
Before Starting Engine, 8-21
Before Takeoff, 8-30
Before Takeoff/Before Landing Procedures—Machine Gun M60D, 4-3
Before Takeoff-M52 Smoke Generator Subsystem, 4-17
Before Takeoff Procedures—M56 and M132 Mine Dispersing Subsystem, 4-8
Before Takeoff, 4-30
Before Takeoff—Rescue Hoist, 4-24
Blackout Curtains, 2-48
Blade Stall, 8-47
Blood Bottle Hangars, 2-49

Cargo Center-of-Gravity Limits 6-20
Cargo Hook, 4-34
Cargo Loading, 6-14
Center-of-Gravity Limitations, 5-8
Center-of-Gravity Limits, 6-20
Checklist, 8-10
Checks, 8-11
Chip Detectors, T9-1
Circuit Breaker Panel, 2-60
Classification of Helicopter, 6-2
Climb, 8-35
Climb-Descent, Conditions, 7-31 **MB** 7.1-31 **CB**
Climb-Descent, Descriptions, 7-29 **MB** 7.1-29 **CB**
Climb-Descent, Use of Chart, 7-30 **MB** 7.1-33 **CB**
Clutch Fails to Disengage, 9-26
Clutch Fails to Re-Engage, 9-27
Cockpit and Cabin Doors, 2-9
Cockpit Map Lights, 2-70
Cold-Weather Operations, 8-56
Collective Bounce, 8-46
Collective Bounce, 9-28
Collective Control System, 2-30

Complete Loss of Tail Rotor—Thrust, 9-21
Controls and Indicators, 2-26
Control Stiffness, 9-38
Control Switch, 2-34
Course Deviations Indicators 1D-453 and ID-1347 1, 3-22
Crew and Passenger Briefings, 8-5
Crew Compartment Diagram, 2-8
Crew Duties, 8-6
Cruise, 8-36
Cruise Conditions, 7-25, **MB** 7.1-25 **CB**
Cruise, Description, 7-23 **MB** 7.1-23 **CB**
Cruise, Use of Charts, 7-24 **MB** 7.1-24 **CB**
Cyclic Control System, 2-29
Cyclic Hardover, 9-39

Danger Areas, 8-7
Data Basis, 7-6 **MB** , 7.1-6 **CB**
Data Case, 2-47
DC and AC Power Distribution, 2-54
DC Power Indicators and Controls, 2-59
DC Power Supply System, 2-55
DD Form 365A—Basic Weight Checklist, 6-5
DD Form 365 C-Basic Weight and Balance Records, 6-6
DD Form 365 F-Weight and Balance Clearance Form F, 6-7
Definitions of Abbreviations, 7-10 **MB** 7.1-10 **CB**
Definitions of Emergency Terms, 9-3
Descent, 8-37
Description, Introductory, 1-3
Desert and Hot-Weather Operations, 8-59
Designator Symbols, 1-10
Destruction of Army Materiel to Prevent Enemy Use, 1-8
Dimensions, 2-3

Change 8   Index 1

Direction Finder Set ARN-89, 3-45
Direction Finder Set ARN-149, 3-45.1
Distance Measuring Equipment (DME) AN/ARN-124, 3-24.1
Ditching-Power Off, 9-49
Ditching-Power On, 9-48
Dome Lights, 2-69
Doppler Navigation Set ASN-128, 3-47
Drag, Conditions, 7-28 MB 7.1-2 CB
Drag, Description, 7-26 MB 7.1-26 CB
Drag, Use of Chart, 7-27 MB 7.1-2 CB
Driveshafts, 2-41
Droop Compensator, 2-23
Droop Compensator Failure, 9-14

Electrical Circuit, 2-38
Electrical Fire Flight, 9-33
Electrical System 9-44
Emergency Equipment 2-13
Emergency Equipment, 9-5
Emergency Exits, 9-4
Emergency Procedures-Electcal-M56 and M 132 Mine Dispersing Subsystem, 4-12

Emergency Procedures-Fire-M56 and M132 Mine Dispersing Subsystem. 4-13
Emergency Procurers-Machine Gun M60D, 4-5
Emer Gov Opns, 9-10
Engine, 2-16
Engine, 9-8
Engine Compartment Cooling, 2-17
Engine Compressor Stall. 9-15
Engine Fuel Control System. 2-19
Engine Fuel Pump Malfunction. T9-1
Engine Inlet Filter Clogged/Engine Inlet Air Caution Light Illumination, T9-1
Engine Instruments and Indicators. 2-24

Engine Limitations, 5-7
Engine Malfunction-Hover, 9-11
Engine Malfunction-Low Altitude/Low Airspeed or Cruse, 9-12
Engine Malfunction-Partial or Complete Power Loss, 9-9
Engine Oil-Hot or Low Pressure T9-1
Engine Oil Supply System, 2-20
Engine Overspeed, 9-17
Engine Restart-During Flight, 9-13
Engine Run-Up, 8-23
Engine Shutdown, 8-40
Engine Shutdown Procedures, 4-33
Environmental Restrictions, 5-13
Exceeding Operational Limits, 5-3
Exterior Check, 8-13
Exterior Check (Area 1), 8-14
Exterior Check (Area 2), 8-15
Exterior Check (Area 3), 8-16
Exterior Check (Area 4), 8-17
Exterior Check (Area 5), 8-18
Exterior Check (Area 6), 8-19
External Cargo Rear-View Mirror, 2-50
External Power Receptacle, 2-56

Fire, 9-29
Fire Detector Warning System, 2-83
Fire-Engine start, 9-30
Fire-Flight, 9-32
Fire-Ground, 9-31
First Aid Kits, 2-15
Fixed-Pitch Settings, 9-22
Flight Characteristics, 8-43
Flight Control/Main Rotor System Malfunctions, 9-40
Flight Control/Main Rotor System Malfunctions, 9-48
Flight Control System, Description, 2-28
Flight With External Loads, 8-51
FM Radio Set, 3-12
FM Radio Set AN/ARC-44, 3-15
FM Radio Set AN/ARC-54, 3-14
FM Radio Set AN/ARC-1 31, 3-13
Force Trim System, 2-32
Forms and Records, 1-9
Free-Air Temperature Indicator (FAT), 2-81
Fuel, 6-8
Fuel Boost Pump Failure, 9-43
Fuel Caution Light, 9-43.1
Fuel Filter Contamination, 9-46. T9-1
Fuel Flow, Conditions, 7-34 MB 7.1-37 CB

Fuel Flow, Description, 7-32 MB 7.1-35 CB
Fuel Flow, Use of Chart 7-33 MB 7.1-36 CB
Fuel Supply System, 2-25
Fuel Supply, 9-42
Fuel System Servicing, 2-87
Fuselage, 2-5

Gearboxes, 2-40
General Arrangement, 2-2
General Avionics, 3-1
General Conditions, 7-8 MB 7.1-8 CB
General Description, 2-1
General Introduction, 1-1
Governor RPM Switch, 2-22
Gyromagnetic Compass Set, 3-23

Heated Blanket Receptacles, 2-46
Heating and Defrosting System, 2-53
Height Velocity, 5-14
Helicopter Station Diagram 6-3
Helicopter Systems, 9-1
High- Performance Hoist, 4-27
HF Radio Set AN/ARC-102, 3-17
HF Radio Set AN/ARC-220, 3-17.1
High or Gusty Wind, 8-65

Hoist Restrictions, 5-15
Hoist Systems, 4-21
Hover Conditions, 7-19
Hover, Control Margin, 7-18 MB 7.1-18 CB
Hovering Capabilities, 8-50
Hover, Description, 7-16 MB **7.1-16** CB
Hover/Taxi, 8-27
Hover/Taxi Check, 8-28
Hover, Use of Chart, 7-17 MB 7.1-17 CB
Hovering Turns, 8-25
Hydraulic, 9-36
Hydraulic Filter, 2-36
Hydraulic Power Failure, 9-37
Hydraulic Pressure Caution Light, 2-37

Hydraulic System, Description, 2-33

Ice and Rain, 8-64
Ignition Starter System, 2-21
Immediate Action Emergency Steps, 9-2

Index, 1-6
Indicators and Caution Lights, 2-42
In-Flight Procedures, 4-31
In-Flight Procedures-Hoist Operator, 4-32
In-Flight Procedures-Hoist Operator-Rescue Hoist, 4-26
In-Flight Procedures-Pilot-Rescue Hoist, 4-25
In-Flight Procedures-M52 Smoke Generator Subsystem, 4-18
In-Flight Procedures-M56 and M132 Mine Dispersing Subsystem, 4-9
Inlet Guide Vane Actuator Failure-Closed or Open, 9-16
Instruments and Controls, 2-12
Instruments Flight-General, 8-42
Instrument Lights, 2-71
Instrument Markings, 5-5
Interior Check-Cabin, 8-20
Inverters, 2-82

Landing, 8-39
Landing and Ditching, 9-48
Landing from a Hover, 8-29
Landing Gear System, 2-7
Landing in Trees, 9-47
Landing Light, 2-67
Lightning Strikes, 8-63
Limits, 7-4
Loading and Unloading of Other Than General Cargo, 6-18
Loading Charts, 6-4
Loading Procedures, 6-17
Loss of Tail Rotor Components, 9-23
Loss of Tail Rotor Effectiveness, 9-24
Low G Maneuvers, 8-53

M52 Smoke Generator Subsystem, 4-15
Main and Standby Starter-Generator, 2-58
Main Driveshaft Failure, 9-25
Main Generator Malfunction, 9-45
Main Rotor, 2-43
Maneuvering Flight, 8-49
Marker Beacon Receiver, 3-24
Mast Bumping, 9-41
Mast Bumping, 8-45
Master Caution System, 2-84
Maximum Glide Distance, 9-7
Maximum Performance, 8-33

Medium-Frequency Vibrations, 8-52
Minimum Crew Requirements, 5-4
Minimum Rate of Descent, 9-6
Mission Planning, 8-1
Mode 4 Operation (APX-72 and APX-100) 3-27

Normal, 8-32

Oil, 6-9
Oil Debris Detection System (ODDS), 2-19
Operating Characteristics, 8-44
Operating Limits and Restrictions, 8-2
Operating Limits and Restrictions, General, 5-2
Operating Limits and Restrictions, Purpose, 5-1
Operating Procedures, 4-29
Operating Procedures and Maneuvers, 8-8
Overheated Battery, 9-34
Overhead Console Panel Lights, 2-72

Parachute Operations, 4-35
Pedestal Lights, 2-73
Performance, 8-4
Performance Data General, 7-3 **M**, 7.1-3 **CB**
Performance Data Purpose, 7-1, **M** 7.1-1 **CB**
Performance Discrepancies, 7-9 **M**, 7.1-9 **CB**
Personnel Compartment and Litter Provision, 6-10
Personnel Loading and Unloading, 6-11
Personnel Moments, 6-12
Personnel Seats, 2-11
Pilot/Copilot Seats, 2-10
Pilot Heater, 2-45
Portable Fire Extinguisher, 2-14
Position Lights, 2-65
Preflight Procedures, 4-28
Preflight Procedures-M56 and M132 Mine Dispersing Subsystem, 4-7
Preflight Procedures-M52 Smoke Generator Subsystem, 4-16
Preflight Procedures-Machine Gun M60D, 4-2

Preflight Procedures-Rescue Hoist, 4-23
Preparation of General Cargo, 6-15
Pressure Altimeter, 2-79
Prohibited Maneuvers, 5-12
Proximity Warning System YG-1054, 3-29

Radar Altimeter-AN/APN-209, 3-31
Radar Warning Set, 3-30
Radio Receiving Set ARN-123(V), 3-46
RDU Auxiliary Input/Output Port Settings, Table 3-1
Receiver Transmitter Radio RT-1167/ARC-164(V), 3-322
Rescue Hoist, 4-22
Reservoir and Sight Glass, 2-35
Rollover Characteristics, 8-54
Rotor Limitations, 5-6
RPM High-Low Limit Warning System, 2-85

Safety-M56 and M132 Mine Dispersing Subsystem, 4-14
Satellite Signals Navigation Set AN/ASN-175, 3-24.2
Searchlight, 2-68
Servicing, 2-86
Settling with Power, 8-48
Sideward and Rearward Hovering Flight, 8-26
Signal Distribution Panel C-1611/A/C, 3-4
Signal Distribution Panel C-6533/ARC, 3-5
Signal Distribution Panel SB-329/AR, 3-3
Slingload, 8-34
Smoke and Fume Elimination, 9-35
Snow, 8-58
Spare Lamp Kit, 2-75
Specific Conditions, 7 **MB** 7.1-7 **CB**
Standby Compass, 2-82
Starting Engine, 8-22

Tailboom, 2-6
Tail Rotor, 2-44
Tail Rotor Control System, 2-31

Change 18 Index 3

Tail Rotor Malfunctions, 9-20
Takeoff, 8-31
Takeoff, Conditions, 7-22 MB 7.1-22
Takeoff Descriptions 7-20 MB 7.1-20 CB
Takeoff to Hover, 8-24
Takeoff, Use of Charts. 7-21, MB 7.1-2 CB
Temperature Conversion, **7-11** MB 7.1-11 CB
Tiedown . . Devices, -6-19
Thunderstorms, 8-82
Torque Available, Chart Differences, 7-13
Torque Available, Conditions, 7-15 MB 7.1-15 CB
Torque Available, Description 7-12 MB 7.1-12 CB
Torque Available, Use of chart MB CB
Towing, 5-15
Transmission, 2-39
Transmission, and Drive Systems Malfunctions', 9-18

Transmission Oil-Hot or Low Pressure, 9-19
Transmission Oil Level Light, 2-74
Transponder Set AN/APX-72, 3-25
Transponder Set AN/APX-100, 3-28
Turn-and-Slip, Indicator, 2-77
Turbulence, 8-61
Turbulence and Thunderstorms, 8-60
Turbulence Limitations, 5-10
Turning Radius, 2-4
Types of Vibration, 8-52

UHF Radio Set AN/ARC-51BX, 3-6
UHF Radio Set AN/ARC-51X, 3-7
UHF Radio Set AN/ARC-55B, 3-8
Use of Charts, 7-5
Use of Fuel, 2-89
Use of Words Shall, Should, May, 1-11

Ventilating System, 2-52
Vertical Velocity Indicator, 2-78
VHF Navigation Set AN/ARN-30E, 3-21
VHF Navigation Set AN/ARN-82, 3-20
VHF Radio Set AN/ARC-73, 3-11
VHF Radio Set AN/ARC-116, 3-9
VHF Radio Set AN/ARC-134, 3-10
Voice Security Equipment TSEC/KY-58, 3-16.1, 3-39
TSEC/KY-100, 3-17.2

Warnings, Cautions, and Notes 1-2
Weight/Balance and Loading, 8-3
Weight/Balance and Loading, Data 6-13
Weight/Balance and Loading, General, 8-1
Weight Limitations, 5-9
Windshield Wiper, 2-51
Wire Strike Protection System (WSPS), 2-12.1

TM 55-1520-210-10

By Order of the Secretary of the Army:

CARL E. VUONO
General, United States Army
Chief of Staff

Official:

R. L. DILWORTH
Brigadier General, United States Army
The Adjutant General

DISTRIBUTION:

To be distributed in accordance with DA Form 12-31, -10 & CL Maintenance requirements for UH-1H Helicopter, Utility and UH-1V Helicopter, Utility.

*U.S. GOVERNMENT PRINTING OFFICE : 1988 0 - 211-919

RECOMMENDED CHANGES TO EQUIPMENT TECHNICAL PUBLICATIONS

SOMETHING WRONG WITH THIS PUBLICATION?

THEN... JOT DOWN THE DOPE ABOUT IT ON THIS FORM. CAREFULLY TEAR IT OUT, FOLD IT AND DROP IT IN THE MAIL!

FROM: (PRINT YOUR UNIT'S COMPLETE ADDRESS)
PFC JOHN DOE
CO A, 3d ENGINEER BN
FT. LEONARDWOOD, MO 63108

DATE SENT

PUBLICATION NUMBER	PUBLICATION DATE	PUBLICATION TITLE

BE EXACT... PIN-POINT WHERE IT IS

PAGE NO	PARA-GRAPH	FIGURE NO	TABLE NO	IN THIS SPACE TELL WHAT IS WRONG AND WHAT SHOULD BE DONE ABOUT IT:
6	2-1a			In line 6 of paragraph 2-1a the manual states the engine has 6 cylinders. The engine on my set only has 4 cylinders. Change the manual to show 4 cylinders.
B1		4-3		Callout 16 on figure 4-3 is pointing at a _bolt_. In key to figure 4-3, item 16 is called a _shim_. Please correct one or the other.
125	line 20			I ordered a gasket, item 19 on figure B-16 by NSN 2910-00-762-3001. I got a gasket but it doesn't fit. Supply says I got what I ordered, so the NSN is wrong. Please give me a good NSN

PRINTED NAME, GRADE OR TITLE, AND TELEPHONE NUMBER
JOHN DOE, PFC (268) 317-7111

SIGN HERE: John Doe
JOHN DOE

DA FORM 2028-2, JUL 79

PREVIOUS EDITIONS ARE OBSOLETE.
DRSTS-M Overprint 1, 1 Nov 80

P.S.--IF YOUR OUTFIT WANTS TO KNOW ABOUT YOUR RECOMMENDATION MAKE A CARBON COPY OF THIS AND GIVE IT TO YOUR HEADQUARTERS.

RECOMMENDED CHANGES TO EQUIPMENT TECHNICAL PUBLICATIONS

SOMETHING WRONG WITH THIS PUBLICATION?

THEN... JOT DOWN THE DOPE ABOUT IT ON THIS FORM, CAREFULLY TEAR IT OUT, FOLD IT AND DROP IT IN THE MAIL!

FROM: (PRINT YOUR UNIT'S COMPLETE ADDRESS)

DATE SENT

PUBLICATION NUMBER	PUBLICATION DATE	PUBLICATION TITLE
TM 55-1520-210-10	15 Feb 88	Operator's Manual UH-1H/V Helicopter

BE EXACT PIN-POINT WHERE IT IS

PAGE NO	PARA-GRAPH	FIGURE NO	TABLE NO	IN THIS SPACE TELL WHAT IS WRONG AND WHAT SHOULD BE DONE ABOUT IT:

PRINTED NAME GRADE OR TITLE AND TELEPHONE NUMBER

SIGN HERE

DA FORM 2028-2 1 JUL 79

PREVIOUS EDITIONS ARE OBSOLETE

P.S.--IF YOUR OUTFIT WANTS TO KNOW ABOUT YOUR RECOMMENDATION MAKE A CARBON COPY OF THIS AND GIVE IT TO YOUR HEADQUARTERS

REVERSE OF DA FORM 2028-2 Reverse of DRSTS-M Overprint 2,
1 Nov 80

FILL IN YOUR UNIT'S ADDRESS

FOLD BACK

DEPARTMENT OF THE ARMY

OFFICIAL BUSINESS

COMMANDER
U S ARMY AVIATION SYSTEMS COMMAND
ATTN: AMSAV-MMD
4300 GOODFELLOW BOULEVARD
ST. LOUIS, MO 63120-1798

TEAR ALONG PERFORATED LINE

The Metric System and Equivalents

Linear Measure

1 centimeter = 10 millimeters = .39 inch
1 decimeter = 10 centimeters = 3.94 inches
1 meter = 10 decimeters = 39.37 inches
1 dekameter = 10 meters = 32.8 feet
1 hectometer = 10 dekameters = 328.08 feet
1 kilometer = 10 hectometers = 3,280.8 feet

Weights

1 centigram = 10 milligrams = .15 grain
1 decigram = 10 centigrams = 1.54 grains
1 gram = 10 decigram = .035 ounce
1 dekagram = 10 grams = .35 ounce
1 hectogram = 10 dekagrams = 3.52 ounces
1 kilogram = 10 hectograms = 2.2 pounds
1 quintal = 100 kilograms = 220.46 pounds
1 metric ton = 10 quintals = 1.1 short tons

Liquid Measure

1 centiliter = 10 milliters = .34 fl. ounce
1 deciliter = 10 centiliters = 3.38 fl. ounces
1 liter = 10 deciliters = 33.81 fl. ounces
1 dekaliter = 10 liters = 2.64 gallons
1 hectoliter = 10 dekaliters = 26.42 gallons
1 kiloliter = 10 hectoliters = 264.18 gallons

Square Measure

1 sq. centimeter = 100 sq. millimeters = .155 sq. inch
1 sq. decimeter = 100 sq. centimeters = 15.5 sq. inches
1 sq. meter (centare) = 100 sq. decimeters = 10.76 sq. feet
1 sq. dekameter (are) = 100 sq. meters = 1,076.4 sq. feet
1 sq. hectometer (hectare) = 100 sq. dekameters = 2.47 acres
1 sq. kilometer = 100 sq. hectometers = .386 sq. mile

Cubic Measure

1 cu. centimeter = 1000 cu. millimeters = .06 cu. inch
1 cu. decimeter = 1000 cu. centimeters = 61.02 cu. inches
1 cu. meter = 1000 cu. decimeters = 35.31 cu. feet

Approximate Conversion Factors

To change	To	Multiply by	To change	To	Multiply by
inches	centimeters	2.540	ounce-inches	newton-meters	.007062
feet	meters	.305	centimeters	inches	.394
yards	meters	.914	meters	feet	3.280
miles	kilometers	1.609	meters	yards	1.094
square inches	square centimeters	6.451	kilometers	miles	.621
square feet	square meters	.093	square centimeters	square inches	.155
square yards	square meters	.836	square meters	square feet	10.764
square miles	square kilometers	2.590	square meters	square yards	1.196
acres	square hectometers	.405	square kilometers	square miles	.386
cubic feet	cubic meters	.028	square hectometers	acres	2.471
cubic yards	cubic meters	.765	cubic meters	cubic feet	35.315
fluid ounces	milliliters	29.573	cubic meters	cubic yards	1.308
pints	liters	.473	milliliters	fluid ounces	.034
quarts	liters	.946	liters	pints	2.113
gallons	liters	3.785	liters	quarts	1.057
ounces	grams	28.349	liters	gallons	.264
pounds	kilograms	.454	grams	ounces	.035
short tons	metric tons	.907	kilograms	pounds	2.205
pound-feet	newton-meters	1.356	metric tons	short tons	1.102
pound-inches	newton-meters	.11296			

Temperature (Exact)

| °F Fahrenheit temperature | 5/9 (after subtracting 32) | Celsius temperature | °C |

Warships DVD Series

Now Available!

WARSHIPS DVD SERIES

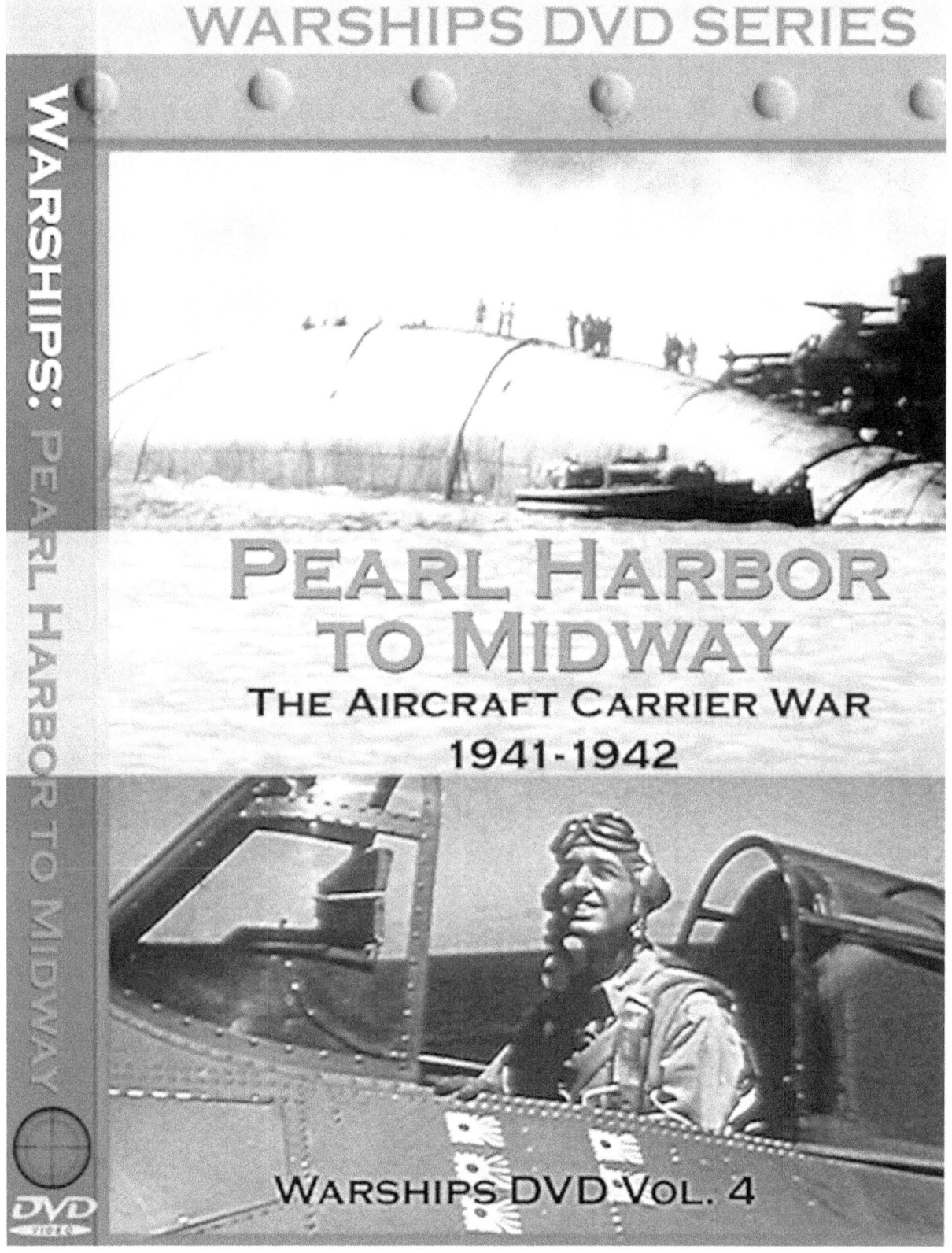

Pearl Harbor to Midway
The Aircraft Carrier War 1941-1942

Warships DVD Vol. 4

HISTORIC U.S. NAVY FILMS ON DVD!

Aircraft At War DVD Series

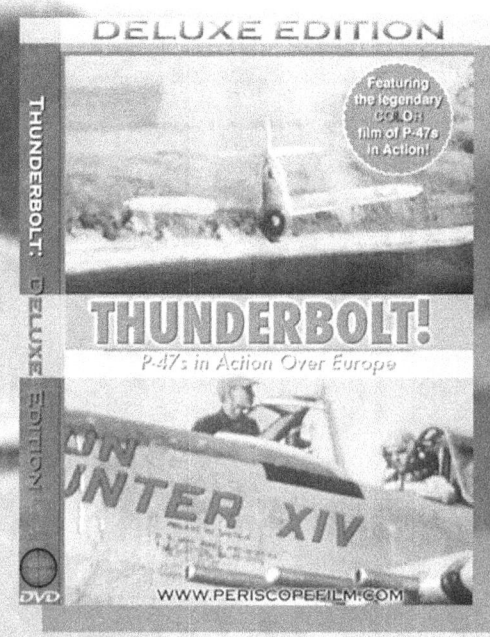
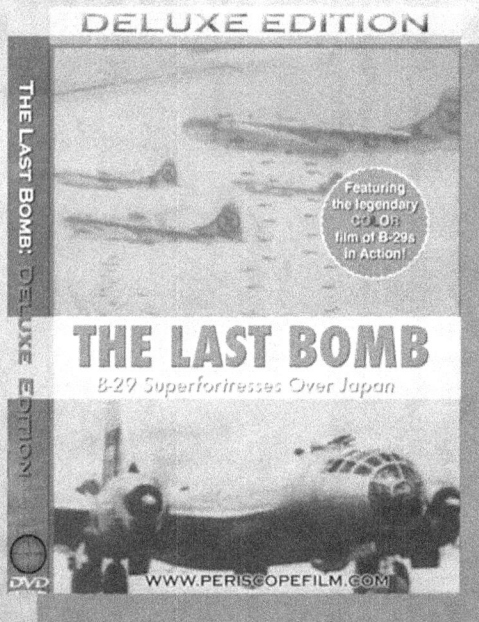
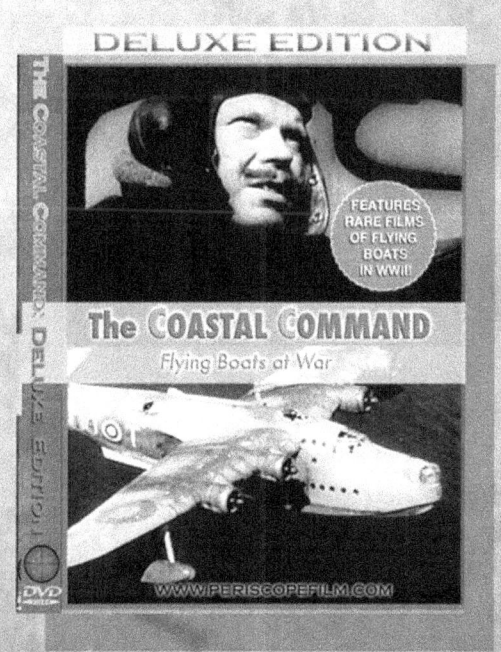

Now Available!

EPIC BATTLES OF WWII

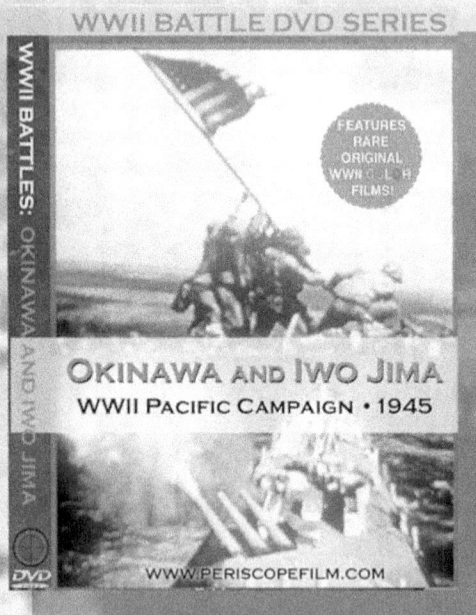

NOW AVAILABLE ON DVD!

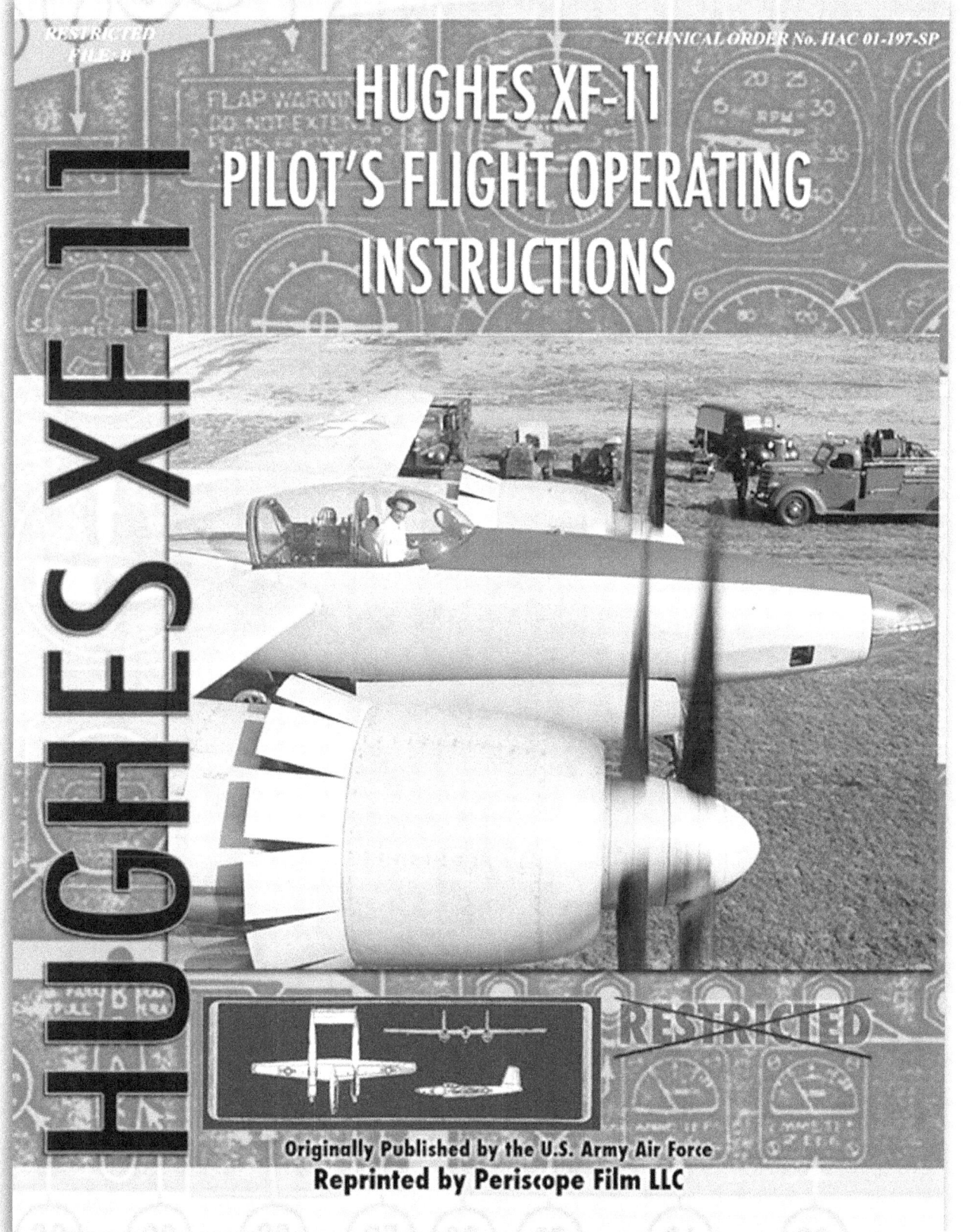

NOW AVAILABLE!

HUGHES FLYING BOAT MANUAL

SPRUCE GOOSE

~~RESTRICTED~~

Originally Published by the War Department
Reprinted by Periscope Film LLC

NOW AVAILABLE!

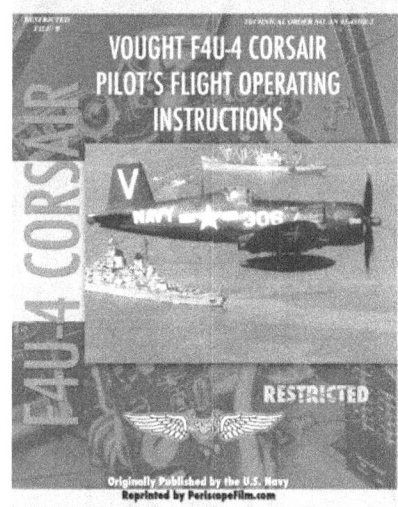
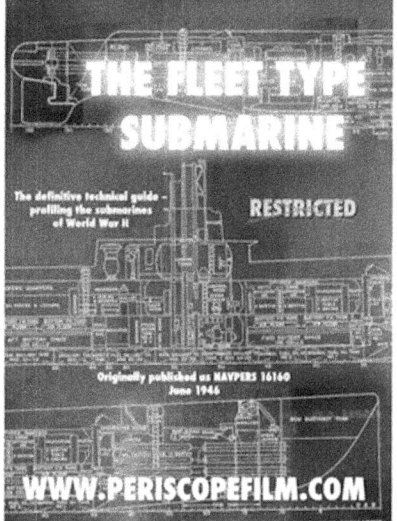

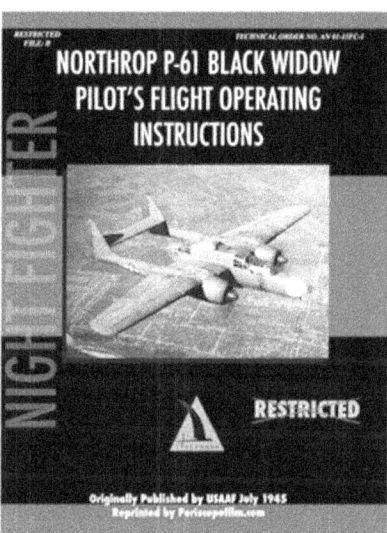

ALSO NOW AVAILABLE
FROM PERISCOPEFILM.COM

©2011 Periscope Film LLC
All Rights Reserved
ISBN #978-1-935700-65-4
www.PeriscopeFilm.com